D1130705

Affect Dysregulation

&

Disorders of the Self

The Norton Series on Interpersonal Neurobiology
Daniel J. Siegel, M.D., Series Editor

The field of mental health is in a tremendously exciting period of growth and conceptual reorganization. Independent findings from a variety of scientific endeavors are converging in an interdisciplinary view of the mind and mental well-being. An "interpersonal neurobiology" of human development enables us to understand that the structure and function of the mind and brain are shaped by experiences, especially those involving emotional relationships.

The Norton Series on Interpersonal Neurobiology will provide cutting-edge, multidisciplinary views that further our understanding of the complex neurobiology of the human mind. By drawing on a wide range of traditionally-independent fields of research — such as neurobiology, genetics, memory, attachment, complex systems, anthropology, and evolutionary psychology — these texts will offer mental health professionals a review and synthesis of scientific findings often inaccessible to clinicians. These books aim to advance our understanding of human experience by finding the unity of knowledge, or "consilience," that emerges with the translation of findings from numerous domains of study into a common language and conceptual framework. The series will integrate the best of modern science with the healing art of psychotherapy.

A NORTON PROFESSIONAL BOOK

Affect Dysregulation & Disorders of the Self

ALLAN N. SCHORE

W.W. Norton & Company
New York • London

Since this page cannot accommodate all the copyright notices, pages 307–312 constitute an extension of the copyright page.

For information about permission to reproduce
selections from this book, write to
Permissions, W. W. Norton & Company, Inc.,
500 Fifth Avenue, New York, NY 10110

Production Manager: Leeann Graham
Manufacturing by Haddon Craftsmen, Inc.

Library of Congress Cataloging-in-Publication Data

Schore, Allan N., 1943–
Affect dysregulation and disorders of the self / Allan N. Schore.
    p.   cm.
  "A Norton professional book."
  Includes bibliographical references and index.
  Contents: v. 1 [no distinct title]–v. 2 Affect regulation and repair of the self.
  ISBN 0-393-70408-4 (set) — **ISBN 0-393-70406-8 (v. 1)** — ISBN 0-393-70407-6 (v. 2)
  1. Affective disorders.   2. Self.   3. Self psychology.   I. Title.

RC537.S3848 2003
616.85′27 — dc21   2002038055

W. W. Norton & Company, Inc., 500 Fifth Avenue, New York, N.Y. 10110
www.wwnorton.com

W. W. Norton & Company Ltd., Castle House, 75/76 Wells St., London W1T 3QT

4   5   6   7   8   9   0

Dedication

To Judith
Wing to wing, oar to oar

We dance round in a ring and suppose,
But the Secret sits in the middle and knows.

Robert Frost, "The Secret Sits"

Contents

Acknowledgments xi

Preface xiii

PART I. DEVELOPMENTAL AFFECTIVE NEUROSCIENCE

1. The Experience-Dependent Maturation of a Regulatory System in the Orbital-Prefrontal Cortex and the Origin of Developmental Psychopathology 5

2. The Experience-Dependent Maturation of an Evaluative System in the Cortex 36

3. Attachment and the Regulation of the Right Brain 54

4. Parent-Infant Communications and the Neurobiology of Emotional Development 71

PART II. DEVELOPMENTAL NEUROPSYCHIATRY

5. Early Organization of the Nonlinear Right Brain and the Development of a Predisposition to Psychiatric Disorders 89

6. The Effects of a Secure Attachment Relationship on Right Brain Development, Affect Regulation, and Infant Mental Health 128

7. The Effects of Relational Trauma on Right Brain Development, Affect Regulation, and Infant Mental Health 178

8. Dysregulation of the Right Brain: A Fundamental Mechanism of Traumatic Attachment and the Psychopathogenesis of Posttraumatic Stress Disorders 234

9. Effect of Early Relational Trauma on Affect Regulation:
    The Development of Borderline and Antisocial Personality
    Disorders and a Predisposition to Violence   266

Permissions   307

References   313

Index   389

Acknowledgments

I N THE COURSE of my lectures and travels since the publication of *Affect Regulation and the Origin of the Self*, I have had the good fortune to enter into an ongoing dialogue with a substantial number of colleagues. Due to the interdisciplinary nature of my work, these scientists and clinicians span a number of different fields, and yet all share a common curiosity and passionate interest in the deeper mechanisms that underlie the human condition. In more cases than I would have thought, many of these individuals have turned out to be not only of like mind, but also of like heart.

I would like to thank but a small number of the people who have enriched my thinking. I have been fortunate to interact with pioneers in their fields: Karl Pribram, Henry Krystal, Jim Masterson, Frank Putnam, Berry Brazelton, Ed Zigler, Lou Sander, Heidelise Als, Alan Sroufe, and Dan Stern. In the neurosciences, I have been enriched by dialogues with Colwyn Trevarthen, Don Tucker, Steve Suomi, Sheila Wang, Bob Scaer, Katharina Braun, Ron Sullivan, Linda Mayes, Mark Solms, Jaak Panksepp, and Ralph Adolphs. In psychiatry, I greatly value my connections with Graeme Taylor, Vadim Rotenberg, Russell Meares, Thomas Verny, Ellert Nijenhuis, Onno van der Hart, Kathy Steele, Paul Valent, and especially Bessel van der Kolk. And in the developmental sciences, I deeply appreciate communications with Ed Tronick, Ruth Feldman, Arieta Slade, Steve Seligman, Susan Coates, Mary Sue Moore, Alan Fogel, Mary Rothbart, Karin Grossmann, Jay Belsky, Robin Karr-Morse, Peter Fonagy, and Beatrice Beebe. I am also most appreciative of the opportunities that have been afforded me by a number of editors — Joy Osofsky, Dante Cicchetti, Sidney Bloch, Marc Lewis, Isabela Granic, Paul Gilbert, Bernice Andrews, Heidi Keller, David Chamberlain, and Howard Steele.

Of equal importance to these exchanges with researchers have been the countless enriching and challenging dialogues I continue to have with numerous clinicians from literally around the world and whose work span the field from infant to adult psychopathologies.

I would like to thank Peter Whybrow for providing me with invaluable computer connections with the UCLA libraries. I am most appreciative of the support of my work shown by Marion Solomon and Robert Neborsky. The many members of and guest visitors to my Study Groups in Developmental Affective Neuroscience and Clinical Practice have inspired me to translate theoretical science into practical clinical applications. Over the years, conversations with Jim Grotstein, John Schumann, and Lou Cozolino have served as sources of both intellectual stimulation and friendship. On this matter, it has been my great fortune to enthusiastically share so many common interests, both academic and personal, with my friend and fellow explorer, Dan Siegel.

To my fellow writers, I enthusiastically recommend W. W. Norton as a publisher that supports not only scholarship but innovative thinking and creative expression. It has been an absolute pleasure working with Andrea Costella and Michael McGandy. But, in particular, I would like to express my deep gratitude to Deborah Malmud, whose vision and guidance are singly responsible for this groundbreaking series on interpersonal neurobiology.

Closer to my heart, the support from my family, my in-laws Mickey and the late Al Rothman, and my parents, George and the late Barbara Schore, has sustained me for the more than two decades that I have devoted to this work, and indeed over the course of my life. I am greatly indebted to my computer experts, Beth and David Schore, for the invaluable help in so many instances of software and hardware peril.

But at the core is my relationship with my wife, Judith. A full expression of my gratitude for her contribution to these books, like so many other areas of my life, is beyond words. The large amount of time that I spend on studying, absorbing the flows of information in various fields, and in writing continues to be supported financially by our clinical incomes. The fact that her total commitment to my work is expressed both pragmatically and emotionally has great meaning to me, and is responsible for the appearance of both of these new volumes. In return, I am delighted to share with her the wonderful places and people in this world to which this work has led us.

Wing to wing, oar to oar.

Preface

I N 1994 I PUBLISHED *Affect Regulation and the Origin of the Self*, and in the very first paragraph I asserted, "The beginnings of living systems set the stage for every aspect of an organism's internal and external functioning throughout the lifespan." In that book I outlined the principles of regulation theory. Using then-current information, I applied the theory to a model of how regulated and dysregulated affective transactions within the infant's attachment relationship with the primary caregiver facilitate or inhibit the experience-dependent maturation of the infant's brain, especially the early developing right brain. I then used the theory to generate a model of normal social-emotional development, of abnormal development and psychopathogeneis, and of the mechanism of developmental change, as expressed in the psychotherapeutic context.

Since 1994, and over the course of "the Decade of the Brain," a vast amount of new information on these matters has appeared. Along the way I incorporated this data from a wide range of the biological, psychological, and social sciences into my research and publications. Due to the interdisciplinary nature of my work, these articles and chapters appear in journals and edited collections in a variety of fields — developmental psychopathology, psychiatry, neuroscience, psychoanalysis, as well as in the emotion, attachment, and trauma literatures.

This volume, *Affect Dysregulation and Disorders of the Self* and its companion, *Affect Regulation and the Repair of the Self*, are sequels to the first book, and represent expansions of my earlier presentation of regulation theory. Each contains a combination of already-published contributions as well as new material. Due to the fact that my writings are distributed over a wide array of disciplines, it has been difficult for a reader in one field to find publications in another. My intention is to provide readers with not only newer findings in a multitude of basic and clinical sciences, but also to offer an overarching perspective on regulation theory as it has expanded in the nine years since my first book. These two volumes thus represent the first comprehensive articulation of regulation theory as it has developed since *Affect Regulation and the Origin of the Self*.

In this volume, in Part 1 I present chapters in developmental affective neuroscience and then, in Part 2, developmental neuropsychiatry. Each chapter rep-

resents a further development of the original model. Because each development occurred at a particular point in time, and was guided by then-current
research, the chapters in both parts are presented in chronological order. Some
of the earlier chapters have been edited, and the more recent ones contain a
good deal of new material that has not been previously published. The citations
in each chapter reflect the incorporation of research that was available at the
time of the original writing. The progression over the chapters reflects not only
the tremendous expansion of relevant developmental and brain studies over
the last decade, but also the dramatic emergence of data from neuroimaging
technologies in this same time period. In essence, each chapter is a revision of
the data and concepts of classical neuroscience — i.e., from the lesion, neuroanatomical, and histological studies of brain preparations of classical nineteenth
century neurology through the end of the twentieth century — upon which *Affect Regulation and the Origin of the Self* was built.

The current explosion of research in the life sciences is commonly attributed
to the remarkable advances in various technologies. Perhaps an even greater
factor has been the significant increase in the amount of interdisciplinary research. In my earlier book I suggested that the frontiers of science are located
in the borderland between the separate fields of science. Since 1994, this relationship between the biological and psychological realms has not only produced an enriched environment for multilevel research, but has also provided
a powerful psychobiological perspective that has generated hypotheses for studies that assess human functions at various levels of analysis.

It is commonly accepted that this interdisciplinary approach is manifest in
the construction of collaborative research teams that bring together scientists
and clinicians from various fields of study. I suggest that progress in scientific
knowledge also relies on interdisciplinary theoretical science — that is, the integration of the findings of interdisciplinary research data into testable and clinically relevant psychobiological models of human function and dysfunction.
This synthesis of theoretical constructs and data is an intellectual enterprise.
My own work in theoretical science is a contribution towards that effort. In this
volume, along with the other two of the *Affect Regulation* triad, I offer regulation theory with that goal in mind.

I use the phrase *regulation theory* in the literal sense. I have placed the
concept of *regulation* at the heart of the theory because it is used as a central
construct in every field of science. In the opening chapter of *Affect Regulation
and the Origin of the Self* I argued that "the concept of regulation is one of the
few theoretical constructs that is now being utilized by literally every developmental discipline. The current focus on adaptive regulatory phenomena, from
the molecular to the social levels, represents a powerful central linking concept that could potentially elucidate the 'hidden' processes in development
and thereby organize what appear to be disparate bodies of developmental
knowledge" (1994, pp. 7–8). Since then a consensus has been established
that development fundamentally represents the emergence of more complex

forms of self-regulation over the stages of the lifespan, and that the attachment relationship is critical because it facilitates the development of the brain's major self-regulatory systems.

The second term, regulation *theory*, denotes that what I am offering in the current 2 volumes is a theory—a systematic exposition of the general principles of a science. Specifically, I offer a formulation of an explanatory conception of the processes of development, which I have asserted is one of the fundamental objectives of science. Basic theory has, of course, played a critical role in the physical sciences, where it has been a rich source of testable hypotheses for experimental research. But in the life sciences there has been almost an aversion to overarching theoretical schemas.

In the area of normal and abnormal development, perhaps the last scientist to offer such a wide-ranging view was John Bowlby, who conceptualized attachment theory, which is now the dominant conception of social and emotional development available to science. In his ground-breaking work Bowlby asserted, "The merits of a scientific theory are to be judged in terms of the range of phenomena it embraces, the internal consistency of its structure, the precision of the predictions it can make and the practicability of testing them" (1969, p. 173). Regulation theory, as outlined in all my published work, is presented to be evaluated against those criteria.

As a clinician-scientist, the practical applications of regulation theory are of great personal interest. In this volume I will cite an extremely large body of interdisciplinary data which suggests that the self-organization of the developing brain occurs in the context of a relationship with another self, another brain. This primordial relational context can be growth-facilitating or growth-inhibiting, and so it imprints into the early developing right brain either a resilience against or a vulnerability to later forming psychiatric disorders. The latter issues are covered in chapters on the psychoneurobiological pathogenesis of postraumatic stress disorders, borderline disorders, and antisocial personality disorders. A predisposition to these severe disorders of the self is associated with early traumatic attachments that are burnt into the right brain, thereby impairing its regulatory capacities to cope with interpersonal stressors throughout the lifespan.

In recent writings Richard Davidson and Heleen Slagter concluded, "we believe that the time is right to increase the utilization of functional neuroimaging, particularly fMRI to probe affective dysfunction in developmental disorders . . . . [W]e can look forward to an increase in the use of those methods to study the devastating and often long-lasting consequences of childhood disorders of emotion. We also believe that the judicious use of these methods may enable us to better predict which children may be particularly at-risk for serious psychopathology, facilitating the earlier introduction of remedial interventions" (2000, p. 169). In my own writings on this subject, I have called for studies that concurrently measure brain, behavioral, and bodily changes in both members of the infant-mother (as well as adult-adult) dyad. Autonomic measures of synchronous changes in the infant's and mother's bodily states need to be included in studies of attachment functions, and the development of coordinated interactions between the maturing central and autonomic nervous systems should be investigated in research on attachment structures.

The following chapters stress the importance of the prenatal and postnatal periods of human life. It is true that some degree of brain plasticity remains at later points in the lifespan, and, because of this, in *Affect Regulation and the Repair of the Self*, I detail the relevance of regulation theory to the process of change as it occurs in the psychotherapeutic context. But, in this volume, I want to emphasize the implications of this work for early prevention. These interventions should represent applications of what developmental science knows about the remarkable plasticity and responsiveness of the developing brain to enriched interpersonal environments.

In my introduction to a special edition of the *Infant Mental Health Journal* (2001h) I described the current debate in American society, channeled through the broadcast and written media, about the importance of the first three years of human life. Neuroscience has been placed at the center of this debate and neuroscientists have become the arbiters. A number of authors are now painting what they see as brain-mind portraits of infants, each highlighting certain very prescribed areas of developmental neurobiology and developmental psychology. The different portraits, in turn, reflect the different images of infancy that are prevalent in current society.

How we, as adults, "see" our infants, how we attempt to understand the baby's structural development and expanding functional capacities and potentialities, is biased by our own individual perceptual lenses as well as by the cultural filters mediating our experience. These unique and shared biases strongly influence the subjective perception of our infants as relatively independent or fundamentally dependent on adult caregivers, as passive or active agents, as open and plastic or closed and fixed systems, as durable or fragile biological organisms, and as cognitive machines or feeling, sensate beings. Perhaps the greatest point of difference in the debate is the question of mind — since infants have no verbal abilities, are they mindless or do they possess a communicating, developing consciousness?

These different images of the earliest stages of humanhood are critical because they contain within them the representations of our possible futures — they model the potential developmental extension of our individual and collective social identities. The ongoing debate among the different theories of brain-mind development is, in turn, tightly coupled to pragmatic questions: When and where shall we place our current resources in order to optimize the future of human societies? And so we turn to science, and particularly to our most recent and powerful brain technologies, to offer us more "objective data" on the matter. The interpretation of this data will have extremely important social, political, and economic implications. How much should we value the very beginnings of human life, in tangible social program dollars?

The vast amounts our society spends on defense budgets and medical research is directed towards allowing each of us to feel secure (in mind and body) in our everyday life. This matter of inner security is clearly a psychological state. Even though an internal sense of security is a desirable, indeed longed-for state, it cannot be imposed upon a passive individual. External and internal conditions must be appraised in order for the self-system to actively create and maintain the internal sense of safety that comes from the implicit knowledge that one can cope with the various stressors that accompany human existence.

It is now clear that the development of the critical capacity to create and maintain an internal sense of emotional security comes from the inner (but not necessarily conscious) knowledge that during times of stress, one can cope. Coping can occur either by autoregulation or by means of going to others for interactive regulation. The findings of developmental psychology and neuroscience are converging on this issue as different strands of research show that this adaptive ability is essentially established in the first three years of human life, and that it is the product of our early attachments. The intense interest in early development in every discipline of mental health strongly suggests that further interdisciplinary research will lead to increasing amounts of information that will be directly translatable into the creation of more effective programs of early prevention and which will have an impact on development over the course of the entire lifespan.

Current developmental conceptions that integrate the psychological and biological realms are bringing us closer to a complex biopsychosocial model that can serve as a source of not only the next level of questions for science, but also for pragmatic applications. These deeper investigations of infant mental health, of the primary forces that impact the development of human nature, can do more than alter the intergenerational transmission of psychopathology. They can also significantly increase the numbers of individuals who possess an intuitive sense of emotional security, and thereby improve the quality of life of the infant, child, and adult members of our societies.

These conclusions are the product of my own appraisals of the recent interdisciplinary developmental literatures — from developmental psychology, through developmental biology, neurobiology and neurochemistry, to developmental psychoanalysis. In all of my writings, I customarily cite a large number of studies, not only to offer readers a representation of the current trends within a number of different fields, but also as a resource for their own research. In presenting a large number of studies in this volume's bibliography, I exhort readers to evaluate for themselves the meaning of the current findings of the developmental sciences for both the individual and for the culture.

Affect Dysregulation

&

Disorders of the Self

PART I

DEVELOPMENTAL AFFECTIVE
NEUROSCIENCE

The Experience-Dependent Maturation of a Regulatory System in the Orbital-Prefrontal Cortex and the Origin of Developmental Psychopathology

T HE ONTOGENESIS OF SELF-REGULATION is an essential organizing principle, if not a fundamental mechanism, of the development of dynamic living systems. The concept of regulation is one of the few theoretical constructs utilized by literally every scientific discipline. The robustness and heuristic nature of this construct are reflected in the fact that regulatory processes can be studied simultaneously along several separate but interrelated dimensions, ranging from the molecular level of organization through the social and cultural levels. In fact, the adoption of this multilevel, multidisciplinary perspective is an absolute necessity for a deeper understanding of ontogeny, since development represents a progression of stages in which emergent adaptive self-regulatory structures and functions enable qualitatively new interactions between the individual and his environment. Since this early dialectic between the changing organism and the changing environment involves dynamic alterations in both structure and function, these "self-regulatory structures" need to be identified in terms of what is currently known about biological structure as it exists in nature. The phenomena of self-regulation thus represents a potential convergence point of psychology and neuroscience.

In discussing the development of self-regulatory structures of the mind, Cicchetti and Tucker (1994) asserted that "the best description of development may come from a careful appreciation of the brain's own self-organizing operations" (p. 544). There is now widespread agreement that the brain is a self-organizing system, but there is perhaps less of an appreciation of the fact that the self-organization of the developing brain occurs in the context of a relationship with another self, another brain. This other self, the primary caregiver, acts as an external psychobiological regulator of the "experience-dependent" growth of the infant's nervous system, whose components are rapidly organizing, disorganizing, and reorganizing in the brain growth spurt of the first two years of life. This "experience" is specifically affective, and the system of reciprocal mutual influences that is created by the caregiver-infant dyad accounts for the central role of affect in the formation of an attachment bond between the pair. These experiences are also shaping the maturation of structural connections within the cortical and subcortical limbic areas that come to mediate socioaffective functions. This interactively regulated affective interchange therefore constitutes a mechanism by which the social environment influences the development of psychobiological systems involved in homeostatic regulation. In optimal growth-facilitating socioemotional environments that provide modulated and varied affective experiences, the structural maturation of the brain in infancy and childhood is expressed in the ontogenetic emergence of more complex autoregulatory functional systems. In contrast, misattuned relational environments that generate high levels of negative affect act as growth-inhibiting environments for developing corticolimbic systems.

In *Affect Regulation and the Origin of the Self* (1994), I integrated current ideas about the origins of social functioning from the developmental sciences, recent data on emotional phenomena from the behavioral sciences, and new research on limbic structures from the brain sciences in order to generate models of the adaptive development of self-regulation as well as the origins of dysregulated systems that characterize both internalizing and externalizing forms of developmental psychopathology. Drawing from and expanding upon that multidisciplinary work, in this work I utilize a multilevel approach to characterize the structure-function relationships that underlie the development of affect regulation in the first and then the second year. I describe how different types of age-appropriate transactions of regulated positive and negative affect between the primary caregiver and the infant act as a growth-facilitating environment for the postnatal maturation of a specific corticolimbic system in the prefrontal cortex that mediates regulatory, homeostatic, and attachment functions. Then, I present evidence to show that deprivations of interactive affective experiences and/or failures of various classes of external affect regulation define growth-inhibiting environments for the development of this same system. In this way, different types of unregulated stresses that occur during the critical period of growth of the orbitofrontal cortex act as a source generator for insecure attachments. Finally, I suggest that such events predispose the vulnerable individual to future psychopathology by permanently altering corticolimbic circuits that are implicated in the regulatory failures that underlie the pathophysiology of psychiatric disorders.

This work is presented as a contribututuon toward the creation of what Hinde (1990) refered to as "an integrated developmental science." I should note that the developmental models that I am presenting are offered not as fixed statements or established principles but as heuristic proposals that can be evaluated by experimental and clinical research. This integrative, multilevel approach does, however, suggest a definite overarching psychoneurobiological perspective with which to view early development, one quite compatible with and supportive of a developmental psychopathological viewpoint that conceptualizes normal and aberrant development in terms of common underlying mechanisms.

AFFECT REGULATION IN THE FIRST YEAR

From the moment of birth, the primary caregiver plays an essential role in regulating her infant's psychobiological states, especially disruptions of ongoing states and transitions between states. Because the infant's organ systems (especially its central and peripheral nervous systems) continue to mature over the course of infancy, her involvement is critical to processes as basic as the infant's fluid balance regulation and temperature regulation, life-sustaining functions that ultimately become autoregulated. These very earliest "psychosocial contacts" that entrain biological rhythms primarily involve olfactory-gustatory and tactile-thermal sensory modalities, but by the second quarter of the first year, with the increasing myelination of the occipital areas of the cerebral cortex, a particular type of visual information which conveys the mother's affective responses to the infant is now capable of triggering synchronous changes in the both the child's and the mother's internal state.

Affective Transmissions in Mutual Gaze Transactions

Over the first year of life visual experiences play a paramount role in social and emotional development. In particular, the mother's emotionally expressive face is, by far, the most potent visual stimulus in the infant's environment, and the child's intense interest in her face, especially in her eyes, leads him to track it in space, and to engage in periods of intense mutual gaze. The infant's gaze, in turn, reliably evokes the mother's gaze, and this dyadic system forms an efficient interpersonal channel for the transmission of reciprocal mutual influences. These mutual gaze interactions represent the most intense form of interpersonal communication, and in order to enter into this affective communication, the mother must be psychobiologically attuned not so much to the child's overt behavior as to the reflections of his internal state. She initially attunes to and resonates with the infant's resting state, but as this state is dynamically activated (or deactivated or hyperactivated) she contingently fine tunes and corrects the intensity and duration of her affective stimulation in order to maintain the child's positive affect state. As a result of this moment-by-moment matching of affective direction, both partners increase together their degree of engagement and facially expressed positive affect. The more the mother tunes her activity level to the infant during periods of social engagement, and the more she allows him to recover quietly in periods of disengagement, the more synchronized their interaction. In this way, not only the tempo of their engagement but also their disengagement are coordinated. By doing so the caregiver facilitates the infant's information processing by adjusting the mode, amount, variability, and timing of stimulation to the infant's actual integrative capacities. Facial mirroring thus illustrates interactions organized by ongoing regulations, and the development of mutually attuned synchronized interactions is fundamental to the ongoing affective development of the infant.

At another level, this overt, behavorial synchronization reflects a transformation of inner events, namely a powerful state transition. In synchronized gaze, the dyad creates a mutual regulatory system of arousal in which both move together from a state of neutral affect and low arousal to one of heightened positive emotion and high, yet modulated, arousal. According to Beebe and Lachmann (1988a), as the mother and infant match each other's temporal and affective patterns, each recreates an inner psychophysiological state similar to the partner's. Dyadically resonating, mirroring gaze transactions thus induce a psychobiologically attuned, affect-generating merger state in which a match occurs between the expression of accelerating, rewarding, positively hedonic internal states in both partners. The child is motivated to enter into a "reciprocal reward system" because "euphoric states are perhaps the most appetitively compelling experiences available to life forms as so far evolved" (Schwartz, 1990, p. 125). The dyadic nature of this system is seen in the fact that the mother's face, the child's "emotional" or "biological" mirror, reflects back her baby's "aliveness" in a "positively amplifying circuit mutually affirming both partners" (Wright, 1991, p. 12). The result is a transformation of state and the production of what Stern (1985) called vitality or crescendo affects. The burgeoning capacity of the infant to experience increasing levels of self-maintaining vitality affects is thus at this stage externally regulated by the psychobiologically attuned mother, and depends upon her capacity to engage in an interactive emotion communicating mechanism that generates these in herself and her child. Fogel (1982) underscored the developmental principle that a major task of the first year is the evolution of affective tolerance for increasingly higher levels of arousal, and that this is facilitated by the mother's modulation of the infant's highly stimulated states.

Indeed, regulatory processes are the precursors of psychological attachment and its associated emotions (Hofer, 1994), and psychobiological attunement is now thought to be the mechanism that mediates attachment bond formation (Field, 1985). These dialogues between mother and child increase over the second and third quarter of the first year, and in them the pair creates a symbiotic "merger" experience that acts as a crucible for the forging of preverbal affective ties, that is, for the generation of a bond between the infant and the attachment object. Infant research now suggests that the baby becomes attached to the modulating caregiver who expands opportunities for positive affect and minimizes negative affect (Demos & Kaplan, 1986). The positive emotions of pleasure and interest are the major indicators of affect attunement (Stern, 1985). In other words, the affective state underlies and motivates attachment, and the central adaptive function of dyadic attachment dynamics is to interactively generate and maintain optimal levels of the pleasurable states of "interest-excitement" and "enjoyment-joy" (Tomkins, 1963).

The Neurobiology and Psychobiology of Dyadically Regulated Positive Affect

According to Bowlby (1969), vision is central to the establishment of a primary attachment to the mother, and imprinting is the learning mechanism that underlies attachment bond formation. Furthermore, attachment is more than overt behavior, it is internal, "being built into the nervous system, in the course and as a result of the infant's experience of his transactions with the mother" (Ainsworth, 1967, p. 429). Imprinting involves a state of mutually entrained central nervous system propensities and a synchrony between sequential infant-maternal stimuli and behavior (Petrovich & Gewirtz, 1985). This points to another level of analysis—the neurobiological level. In this "transfer of affect between mother and infant," how is the infant's growing brain influenced by these events?

Trevarthen's work (1993) on maternal-infant protoconversations bears directly on this problem. A traffic of visual and prosodic auditory signals induce instant emotional effects, namely excitement, and pleasure builds within the dyad. The resonance of the dyad ultimately permits the intercoordination of positive affective brain states. His work underscores the fundamental principles that not only is the baby's brain affected by these transactions, but also that its growth literally requires brain-brain interaction and occurs in the context of a positive affective relationship between mother and infant. Trevarthen concluded that "the affective regulations of brain growth" are embedded in the context of an intimate relationship, and that they promote the development of cerebral circuits. This interactive mechanism requires older brains to engage with mental states of awareness, emotion, and interest in younger brains, and involves a coordination between the motivations of the infant and the feelings of adults.

Even more specifically, what is happening here is that the infant's early maturing right hemisphere, which is dominant for the child's processing of visual emotional information, the infant's recognition of the mother's face, and the perception of arousal-inducing maternal facial expressions, is psychobiologically attuned to the output of the mother's right hemisphere, which is involved in the expression and processing of emotional information and in nonverbal communication. The right cortex is known to be specifically impacted by early social experiences, to be activated in intense states of elation, and to contribute to the development of reciprocal interactions within the mother-infant regulatory system. The child uses the output of the mother's emotion- regulating right cortex as a template for the imprinting, the hard wiring of circuits in his own right cortex that will come to mediate his expanding affective capacities. In this way, the parenting environment influences the developing patterns of neuronal connectivity that underlie behavior (Dawson, 1994).

In fact, the mother's face is triggering high levels of endogenous opiates in the child's growing brain. These endorphins are biochemically responsible for the pleasurable qualities of social interaction, social affect, and attachment, as they act directly on subcortical reward centers of the infant's brain (Bozarth & Wise, 1981). As a consequence of this, the catecholamine dopamine, an essential neuromodulator of reward effects, is released from the anterior regions of the reticular formation in the ventral tegmental area, thereby triggering an elevation of dopaminergic-driven, energy-mobilizing, sympathetic-dominant ergotropic arousal and dopamine-mediated elation. There is now agreement that in postnatal life experience-dependent visual processes rely both upon cortical sensory processing of information from the "outer" world, and upon internally generated signals involving catecholamines from the reticular formation (Singer, 1986). Maternally induced increasing amounts of dopamine and endorphins thereby mediate the experience of enjoyment in the infant. Amplified levels of interest in her face are also accompanied by elevated levels of corticotropin releasing factor (CRF), a neuropeptide produced in hypothalamic centers that regulates the production of endorphins by the pituitary and activates the sympathetic division of the autonomic nervous system (Brown et al., 1982). Heightened activity in the sympathetic nervous system (which is in an active stage of growth at this time) is associated with intense elation, increased arousal, and elevated activity level in infants. The caregiver also modulates nonoptimal high levels of stimulation, thereby down-regulating supra-heightened levels of sympathetic arousal. In this manner, the attachment relationship is essentially a regulator of (ergotropic) arousal (van der Kolk & Fisler, 1994). By promoting a symbiotic entrainment between the mother's mature and the infant's immature nervous systems, the child is stimulated into a similar state of heightened sympathetic activity and resultant positive affect, alert activity, and behavioral activation. It is now well established both that it is the affective state that underlies and motivates attachment behavior and that the combination of joy and interest motivates attachment bond formation.

Furthermore, the mother is not only acting as a modulator of the child's current affective state, she is also regulating the infant's production of neurohormones and hormones which influence the activation of gene-action systems that program the structural growth of brain regions that are essential to the future socioemotional development of the child. Dopamine increases the transcription of the gene that encodes the precursor of endorphin in the pituitary, and circulating endorphins act as a controlling mechanism of postnatal development by influencing DNA synthesis and regulating dendritic growth and spine formation (Bartolome, Lerber, Dileo, & Schonberg, 1991; Hauser, McLaughlin, & Zagon, 1989). These biochemical events may explain the principle that stable attachment bonds that transmit high levels of positive affect are vitally important for the infant's continuing neurobiological development

(Trad, 1986). Such findings have significant implications for an overarching conceptualization of the adaptive function of positive affect in early development. Current developmental psychoanalytic research indicates that "It is the emotional availability of the caregiver in intimacy which seems to be the most central growth-promoting feature of the early rearing experience" (Emde, 1988, p. 32).

Interactive transactions that regulate positive affect, in addition to producing neurobiological, structural consequences, are also generating important events in the infant's bodily state, that is, at the psychobiological level. In describing the mother-infant experience of mutuality, Winnicott (1986, p. 258) proposed that "The main thing is a communication between the baby and mother in terms of the anatomy and physiology of live bodies." Hofer's (1990) developmental psychobiological research revealed that in the "symbiotic" state the adult's and infant's individual homeostatic systems are linked together in a superordinate organization which allows for mutual regulation of vital endocrine, autonomic, and central nervous systems of both mother and infant by elements of their interaction with each other. Furthermore, he stated that "in postnatal life, the neural substrates for simple affective states are likely to be present and that the experiences for the building of specific pleasurable states are likewise built into the symbiotic nature of the earliest mother-infant interaction" (1990, p. 62). Hofer emphasized the importance of "hidden" psychobiological regulatory processes — in these, dyadic symbiotic states are physiologically mediated by the regulation of the infant's "open," immature, developing internal homeostatic systems by the caregiver's more mature and differentiated nervous system. Importantly, a primary function of this symbiotic state is the generation of pleasurable states, that is, states marked by high levels of positive affect. These studies support the earlier work of Mahler, who posited a "symbiotic" stage of development in the second and third quarters of the first year (Mahler, Pine, & Bergman, 1975).

The Attainment of an Early Capacity for the Self-Regulation of Affect at the End of the First Year

In observational research, Mahler, a pioneer of developmental psychoanalysis, proposed that the symbiotic phase is followed by a "practicing" subphase that begins at 10 to 12 months and extends through 16 to 18 months. She further divided this critical period into an early phase at the end of the first year and a late phase which extends into the middle of the second year. The onset of the practicing period is defined by rapid changes in motor behavior, that is, the attainment at the end of the first year of upright posture and locomotion that supports the child's first independent steps. This capacity allows the neo-toddler to separate himself from the mother in order to begin to explore the nonmaternal physical environment, a fundamental event in the development of autonomy. The child is often observed to be relatively emotionally independent from the mother and absorbed in his own narcissistic pleasures, but upon the attainment of mastery of some autonomous ego function (or stressful encounters with the environment), he becomes aware of his need for his mother's acceptance and "renewed participation." This need for "emotional refueling" occurs in "reunion" episodes that occur after periods of separation between the practicing age infant and the primary caregiver. Reunion behavior, a central focus of study of attachment theory, is an even more important indicator of the quality of attachment than the child's protest at the point of separation. What interactive mechanism can account for what Brent and Resch (1987) called "reunions that occur across social space"?

It is known that when the infant locomotes more widely in its environment, vision is the primary mode of connection with the mother (Rosenblum, 1987). The child's sorties into the world occur under "the watchful eye of the caregiver," in which he uses the mother as a "beacon of orientation." But at the point when he returns to the secure base the mother's attention to the child's emotionally expressive face intensifies. With these facial cues the psychobiologically attuned mother is now able to appraise the child's internal state, and on the basis of this she reengages in synchronized patterns of visuoaffective communication. The toddler, in turn, attentively responds to the visual (and prosodic auditory) stimulation emanating from the mother's emotionally expressive face. In this dialectic the mother's communications provide the infant with salient maternal appraisals of interactions and events in order to regulate the child's internal state of arousal that supports his affect and behavior. The "renewed participation" at the reunion is thus an affective re-attunement. These episodes of "microregulation," in which each partner responds to the other in latencies ranging from simultaneous to one-half second, are thus critical moments of reciprocal signaling that mediate emotional reconnection after separations. The dyad thus evolves an operative mechanism for processing high intensity affective transmissions that efficiently reestablishes psychobiological attunement without the need for frequent and prolonged physical contact.

This mutual regulatory system is adaptive in that it allows for the arousal level of the child's developing nervous system to be rapidly recalibrated against the reference standard of the mother's. Since arousal levels are associated with changes in metabolic energy, the primary caregiver is thus modulating shifts in the child's energetic state. Indeed, these interactive refueling reunion transactions involving patterned energy transmissions between caregiver and infant may represent the fundamental mechanism of the attachment dynamic. Field (1985) defined psychobiological attunement in terms of the dyad being "on the same wavelength." This may in fact be more than a metaphor; it may refer to similar brain and thereby bodily states. Furthermore, synchronized bioenergetic transmissions not only sustain the toddler's activity level and emotional state, they also supply the modulated stimulation required to supply the enormously increasing bioenergetic demands of the "experience-dependent" growth of the child's developing brain. Reite and Capitanio (1985) suggested that an essential function of attachment is to promote the synchrony or regulation of biological and behavioral systems on an organismic level.

Bowlby (1988) described how the emotionally responsive mother creates a "secure base" from which the mobile toddler may circle out in order to explore the world and then return. To accomplish this, the child uses the mother's affective expression as a signal, an indicator of her appraisal of safety or danger in a particular environmental circumstance. However, although the phenomenon may be more covert and subtle, the mother's facially expressed affective transmissions also act as an amplifier of positive arousal, a generator of energy required for further physical explorations of the environment by the infant. In social referencing, the infant is guided in exploration by the mother's emotional expression, underscoring the importance for the child to "keep an eye on" what mother is feeling, thereby allowing for rapid mood modification effects via dyadic resonance or contagion of positive affect. Emde (1988) characterized the 12-month-old toddler's "sparkling-eyed pleasure" associated with early mastery experiences, which is amplified under the watchful eye of the approving caregiver. Affect-transmitting, attention-focusing social referencing experiences are mediated by a fast-acting dyadic visuoaffective psychobiological mechanism, and this interactive dynamic that generates and maintains high levels of the positive affects of elation and excitement allows for the appearance of an ontogenetic adaptation, play behavior. Play transforms an environment into one that facilitates the processing of novel information and thereby improves learning capacity. These incipient experiences of separations and reconnections that support play enable the child to be exposed to an "enriched" environment, one that shapes developing brain networks (Tucker, 1992) and increases neural interconnectivity (Fagen, 1977).

THE ONSET OF A CRITICAL PERIOD FOR THE MATURATION OF THE ORBITOFRONTAL CORTEX AT THE END OF THE FIRST YEAR

"Enriched" or "growth-promoting" environments specifically influence the ontogeny of homeostatic self-regulatory and attachment systems (Greenspan, 1981). Bowlby (1969) pointed out that the maturation of control systems involved in attachment functions is open to influence by the particular environment in which development occurs. Cicchetti (1994) asserted that the capacity for attachment originates during early affect regulation experiences near the end of the first year of life. He also contended that caregiving plays a role in the ontogenesis of neuroregulatory processes during experience-dependent sensitive periods (Cicchetti & Toth, 1991). This leads to the next question: What specific areas of the brain are beginning a critical period of growth at 10 to 12 months, the time when attachment patterns are first reliably measured?

I suggest that dyadic communications that generate intense positive affective states and high levels of dopamine and endogenous opiates represent a growth-promoting environment for the prefrontal cortex, an area critically involved in Bowlby's imprinting processes (G. Horn, personal communication, August 9, 1994) that undergoes a major maturational change at 10 to 12 months (Diamond & Doar, 1989). An impressive body of neurobiological research indicates that increasingly complex self-regulatory structural systems are located in the frontal, especially orbital prefrontal, cortex (Damasio, 1994; Pribram, 1987). These systems are not ready-made at birth, and do not arise spontaneously in development, but are formed postnatally in the process of "social contact" and objective activity by the child (Luria, 1980). Indeed, the maturation of the prefrontal cortex, the largest area in the human cerebral cortex, is essentially postnatal, and the limbic orbital prefrontal areas are known to mature before the nonlimbic dorsolateral prefrontal areas (Pandya & Barnes, 1987). Neurons in the deep layers of the frontal polar regions of the human cortex mature at one year of age (Rabinowicz, 1979), and synaptic excess, an indicator of a critical period, has been observed to onset in the human prefrontal cortex at the end of the first year of life (Huttenlocher, 1979). Most importantly, there is now convincing evidence to show that orbitofrontal areas are critically involved in attachment processes (Steklis & Kling, 1985) and homeostatic regulation (Kolb, 1984).

In line with the principle that the postnatal growth of the brain is essentially influenced by events at the interpersonal and intrapersonal levels, attachment experiences, face-to-face transactions between caregiver and infant, directly influence the imprinting, the circuit wiring of this system. The onset of critical periods reflects the activation and expression of specific genes at particular times in development (Bateson & Hinde, 1987), and the expression of hereditary influences requires transactions with the environment (Plomin, 1983). In developing corticolimbic areas these transactions are specifically affective, and in them the mother regulates the neurochemistry of the infant's maturing brain and the neural substrates for infant emotion (Hofer, 1984, 1994). In the latest neurochemical models of critical period events, monoamine neurotransmitters and neurohormones are thought to regulate the temporal framework of developmental brain growth as well as mediate the effects of external influences on this process (Lauder & Krebs, 1986). Dopamine and endogenous opiates, neurochemicals that are increased in attachment experiences, are known to regulate neural growth and development (Le Moal & Simon, 1991; Hauser et al., 1989). Indeed, studies have shown that dopaminergic neurons innervate the orbital cortex (Levitt, Rakic, & Goldman-Rakic, 1984) and provide a trophic function in prefrontal development (Kalsbeek et al., 1987). (For a detailed discussion of the neurochemistry and neuroendocrinolgy of imprinting, see Schore [1994].)

The orbital area of the prefrontal cortex (so called because of its relation to the orbit of the eye) is "hidden" in the ventral and medial surfaces of the prefrontal lobe. This area of the cerebral cortex is so intimately interconnected into limbic areas that it has been conceived of as an "association cortex" for the limbic forebrain. It is functionally involved in the pleasurable qualities of social interaction, and contains the highest levels of opioids and dopamine in the cerebral cortex (Steklis & Kling, 1985). It also contains extremely high numbers of serotonin receptors (Raleigh & Brammer, 1993). In addition to receiving convergent multimodal input from all sensory areas of the posterior cortex, this frontolimbic structure uniquely projects extensive pathways to limbic areas in the temporal pole and the amygdala, to subcortical drive centers in the hypothalamus, and to dopamine neurons in reward centers in the ventral tegmental area (Nauta, 1964). In such an anatomical position, it hierarchically dominates the ventral tegmental limbic forebrain-midbrain circuit (Nauta & Domesick, 1982). Descending projections from the prefrontal cortex to subcortical structures mature during infancy, and the neural connections between the cortex and hypothalamus are established during the sensitive period for the development of social responses. This cortex also sends projections into motor areas, as its activity is associated with eye and head movements and motor responses of the face. In line with the proposal of orbitofrontal maturation at 10 to 12 months, distinct patterns of infant facial expressions, indicators of motor responses to emotion, are first reliably coded at the end of the first year (Malatesta, Culver, Tesmaa, & Shepard, 1989).

The orbitofrontal cortical area is especially expanded in the right cortex (Falk et al., 1990), the hemisphere which more so than the left, shows extensive reciprocal interconnections with limbic and subcortical regions. The right cortex is dominant for the processing, expression, and regulation of emotional information, is centrally involved in the memorial storage of emotional faces, and contains a representational system based on self-and-object images. In view of the fact that attachment experiences induce high levels of activity in neurons that selectively respond to faces (Horn & McCabe, 1984), it is important to note that this frontolimbic structure (like the amygdala and temporal cortex) contains neurons that specifically respond to the emotional expressions of faces. Furthermore, this prefrontal region is functionally implicated in appraisal processes, directed attention, and in the tracking of emotionally relevant objects in extrapersonal space, and is activated during the mental generation of images of faces. It also is known to play an important role in the processing of social signals necessary for the initiation of social interactions and affiliative behaviors. Activation of the mature orbitofrontal cortex elicits subcortical hormonal changes, such as an increase in pituitary endorphin and ACTH activity, as well as sympathetic nervous system adrenomedullary plasma noradrenaline and adrenaline release. Most significantly, in the cerebral cortex, the orbitofrontal region is uniquely involved in social and emotional behaviors and in the self-regulation of body and motivational states.

As the first year draws to a close, the initial phases of the anatomical maturation of the orbitofrontal cortex, a structural system that also subserves cognitive and memory functions (Stuss et al., 1982), allows for the developmental advances in cognition and attention that are observed at this time. The major cognitive functional output of the orbital cortex, the delayed response function, enables the individual to react to situations on the basis of stored representations, rather than on information immediately present in the environment. This also applies to socioemotional information—at 10 months infants are first able to construct abstract prototypes of human visual facial patterns (Strauss, 1979). As a result of attachment experiences the infant develops a schema, a mental image of the mother, especially her face. With the imprinting of a representational model of the primary attachment figure's emotionally expressive face, affective responses to an object can be maintained even in its absence. This emergent function results from the experience-dependent structural development of a corticolimbic system that can generate and store abstract templates of prototypical facial emotional expressions. Developmental neuroscience studies characterize the internalized regulatory capacities of the infant that develop in relation to the mother as a "mother icon" that acts as a "neurobiological guidance system" (Kraemer, Ebert, Schmidt, & McKinney, 1991).

Due to the organization of its dense connections with sites in both the cortex and subcortex, this corticolimbic system can begin to play an essential adaptive regulatory role. At the orbitofrontal level, cortically processed exteroceptive information concerning the external environment (such as visual and prosodic information emanating from an emotional face) is integrated with subcortically processed interoceptive information regarding the internal visceral environment (such as concurrent changes in the emotional or bodily state). As a result, this prefrontal system can now generate interactive representations—nonverbal internal working models of the infant's transactions with the primary attachment figure that dyadically maximize positive and minimize negative affect. Indeed, at the end of the first year internal working models of attachment are first encoded. These internal models are now viewed as mental representations that enable the individual to form expectations and evaluate the interactions that regulate his attachment system. Such "presymbolic" representations encode the infant's physiological-affective responses to the emotionally expressive face of the attachment figure. These interactive representations appear at the end of the first year, and in them the infant represents the expectation of being matched by, and being able to match the partner, as well as "participating in the state of the other" (Beebe & Lachmann, 1988b). By the end of the first year, the end of early infancy, they can now be accessed in the absence of the mother to appraise upcoming relational encounters, thereby allowing for the adaptive capacity of affect regulation.

AFFECT REGULATION IN THE SECOND YEAR

In optimal growth-promoting environments, the interactive mechanism for generating positive affect becomes so efficient that by the time the infant begins to toddle he is experiencing very high levels of elation and excitement. Developmental neuropsychological studies reveal a significant increase in positive emotion from 10 to 13.5 months (Rothbart, Taylor, & Tucker, 1989). As the practicing stage proceeds from early to late infancy, however, the socio-emotional environment of the caregiver-infant dyad changes dramatically, and the nature of their object relations is significantly altered. At 10 months, 90% of maternal behavior consists of affection, play, and caregiving. In sharp contrast, the mother of the 13- to-17-month-old toddler expresses a prohibition on the average of every 9 minutes. In the second year the mother's role now changes from a caregiver to a socialization agent, as she must now persuade the child to inhibit unrestricted exploration, tantrums, bladder and bowel function (i.e., activities that he enjoys).

Socialization Experiences and the Emergence of the Attachment Emotion of Shame

In other words, in order to socialize the child, she must now engage in affect regulation to reduce the heightened levels of positive affect associated with the pleasure of these activities. How does she do this? In fact there is one very specific inhibitor of accelerating pleasurable emotional states, one negative emotion that is more closely associated, both psychologically and neurologically with positive affects. Shame, a specific inhibitor of the activated ongoing affects of interest-excitement and enjoyment-joy, uniquely reduces self exposure or exploration powered by these positive affects (Tomkins, 1963). Indeed, shame, which has been described as "the primary social emotion" makes its initial appearance at 14 to 16 months (Schore, 1991).

In the second year the toddler continues to bring the things he/she is exploring and attempting to master to the mother's vicinity. However, at this point of social development the nature of the reunion exchanges is altered in that they now more than any time previously also engender intense stress. Face-to-face encounters that at one time elicited only joy become the principal context for shame experiences. As in the early practicing period, the late practicing senior toddler, in an activated state of stage-typical ascendant excitement and elation, exhibits itself during a reunion with the caregiver. Recall that the child now has access to presymbolic representations that encode the expectation of being matched by, and being able to match the partner, as well as "participating in the state of the other." Despite an excited expectation of a psychobiologically attuned shared positive affect state with the mother and a dyadic amplification of the positive affects of excitement and joy, the infant unexpectedly encounters a facially expressed affective misattunement. The ensuing break in an anticipated visual-affective communication triggers a sudden shock-induced deflation of positive affect. Shame represents this rapid state transition from a preexisting positive state to a negative state.

Psychobiological attunement drives the attachment process by acting as a mechanism that maximizes and expands positive affect and minimizes and diminishes negative affect. The negative affect of shame is thus the infant's immediate physiological-emotional response to an interruption in the flow of an anticipated maternal regulatory function, psychobiological attunement which generates positive affect, and to the maternal utilization of misattunement as a mediator of the socialization process. In other words, shame, which has been called an "attachment emotion" (Lewis, 1980), is the reaction to an important other's unexpected refusal to enter into a dyadic system that can recreate an attachment bond. It is well established that attachment bond disruptions precipitate an imbalance in the regulation of affect (Reite & Capitanio, 1985). Thus in the prototypical object relation of shame a separation response is triggered in the presence of and by the mother who spontaneously and unconsciously blockades the child's initial attempt to emotionally reconnect with her in a positive affective state. The impediment to anticipated positive affect is specifically a perception of a facial display which signals not joy and interest but disgust, and which precedes a sudden unanticipated break in social referencing, the process by which the toddler's affect and behavior are regulated by maternal facial expression. The misattunement in shame, as in other negative affects, represents a regulatory failure, and is phenomenologically experienced as a discontinuity in what Winnicott (1958) called the child's need for "going-on-being." How long and how frequently the child remains in this state is an important factor in her ongoing emotional development.

   This intense psychophysiological distress state, phenomenologically experienced as a "spiraling downward," is proposed to reflect a sudden shift from energy-mobilizing sympathetic- to energy-conserving parasympathetic-dominant autonomic nervous system activity, a rapid transition from a hyper-aroused to a hypoaroused state, a sudden switch from ergotropic high arousal to trophotropic low arousal (Scherer, 1986). In such a psychobiological state transition, sympathetically powered elation, heightened arousal, and elevated activity level instantly evaporate. This represents a shift into a low-keyed inhibitory state of parasympathetic conservation-withdrawal (Powles, 1992) that occurs in helpless and hopeless stressful situations in which the individual becomes inhibited and strives to avoid attention in order to become "unseen." This state is mediated by a different psychobiological pattern than positive states—corticosteroids are produced in a stress response, and these reduce opioid (endorphin) and corticotropin releasing factor in the brain. Physiologically there is an influx of autonomic proprioceptive and kinesthetic feedback into awareness, reflecting activation of medullary reticular formation activity in the brain stem. As opposed to the attuned state, shame elicits a painful infant distress state, manifest in a sudden decrement in mounting pleasure, a rapid inhibition of excitement, and cardiac deceleration by means of vagal impulses in the medulla oblongata. This shift reflects the reduced activation of the excitatory dopaminergic ventral tegmental limbic forebrain-midbrain circuit and increased activation of the inhibitory noradrenergic lateral tegmental (Robbins & Everitt, 1982) limbic forebrain-midbrain circuit.

Interactive Repair and the Origin
of Internal Shame Regulation

As a result of the interactive misattunement of socialization experiences the toddler is suddenly and unexpectedly propelled from an ongoing, accelerating positive affective state into a decelerating negative affective state, a stressful state transition that he cannot autoregulate. Prolonged states of shame are too toxic for older infants to sustain for very long, and although infants possess some capacity to modulate low-intensity negative affect states, these states continue to escalate in intensity and duration. Thus parental active participation in regulating the child's shame state is critical to enabling the child to shift from the negative affective state of deflation and distress to a reestablished state of positive affect. In early development, parents provide much of the necessary modulation of states, especially after a state disruption and across a transition between states, and this allows for the development of self-regulation. This transition involves and highlights the central role of stress recovery mechanisms in affect regulation. Stress has been defined as the occurrence of an asynchrony in an interactional sequence; further, a period of synchrony, following the period of stress, provides a "recovery" period (Chapple, 1970). The child's facial display, postural collapse, gaze aversion, and blushing act as nonverbal signals of his internal distress state. If the caregiver is sensitive, responsive, and emotionally approachable, especially if she reinitiates and reenters into synchronized mutual gaze visual-affect regulating transactions, the dyad is psychobiologically reattuned, shame is metabolized and regulated, and the attachment bond is reconnected. This repair is important to future emotional development. The key to this is the caregiver's capacity to monitor and regulate her own affect. Winnicott (1971a) described the "good enough" mother's "holding" or "containing" function as the capacity to "stay with" the child through its emotional/impulsive expressions, and Tomkins (1963) proposed that negative affect is reduced when the parent continues to maintain affective engagement with the child who is experiencing negative affect, thereby communicating tolerance of negative affect in both.

In this essential pattern of "disruption and repair," the "good-enough" caregiver who induces a stress response in her infant through a misattunement, reinvokes in a timely fashion her psychobiologically attuned regulation of the infant's negative affect state that she has triggered. This reattunement is mediated by the mother's reengagement in dyadic visuoaffective transactions that regenerate positive affect in the child. Her shame stress-regulating interventions allow for a state transition in the infant—the parasympathetic-dominant arousal of the shame state is supplanted by the reignition of sympathetic-dominant arousal that supports increased activity and positive affect. The latter effect is neurochemically mediated by a resumption of CRF-inducing endorphin production and a reactivation of the ventral tegmental dopaminergic limbic circuit. The mother and infant thus dyadically negotiate stressful state transitions of affect, cognition, and behavior. It is now thought that "the process of reexperiencing positive affect following negative experience may teach a child that negativity can be endured and conquered" (Malatesta-Magai, 1991, p. 218). Infant resilience is currently being characterized as the capacity of the child and the parent to transition from positive to negative and back to positive affect (Demos, 1991).

This recovery mechanism underlies the phenomenon of "interactive repair" in which participation of the caregiver is responsible for the reparation of dyadic misattunements. In this process the socializing mother who induces interactive stress and negative emotion in the infant is instrumental to the transformation of this affect into positive emotion. Although reregulating repair transactions begin in the first year, they are essential to emotional development in the second. Under the aegis of a caregiver who is sensitive and cooperative in this reparative process, the infant develops an internal representation of himself as effective, of his interactions as positive and reparable, and of the caregiver as reliable (Tronick, 1989). "Distress-relief sequences" initiated by the accessible mother facilitate a transition from distress to a state of quiet alertness, calmness, and responsiveness. They allow the infant to recover from negative affect states, to construct a multimodal nonverbal concept of the caregiver as predictable, and permit him to develop the capacity for anticipation of relief and a sense of his own efficacy.

The child's experiencing of an affect and the caregiver's response to this particular affect are internalized as an affect-regulating symbolic (as opposed to earlier presymbolic) interactive representation. A secure emotional attachment facilitates the transfer of regulatory capacities from caregiver to infant (Wilson, Passik, & Faude, 1990), that is, the experience of being with a self-regulating other is incorporated into an interactive representation. In these more complex schemata, interactions are represented as reparable; they encode an expectation that a transformation of state to a more comfortable range will occur. Security of attachment fundamentally relates to a physiological coding that "homeostatic disruptions will be set right" (Pipp & Harmon, 1987). These complex representations are equated with internal working models that arise in the context of parental responsiveness to the child's signal of distress. These models are guides for future interactions, and the term "working" refers to the individual's unconscious use of them to interpret and act on new experiences. They contain affective as well as cognitive components and are accessed and utilized in the generation of internal strategies of affect regulation, especially during times of stress.

THE FINAL MATURATION OF THE ORBITOFRONTAL CORTEX IN THE LAST HALF OF THE SECOND YEAR

It is now accepted that internal representations develop epigenetically through successive developmental stages (Blatt, Quinlan, & Chevron, 1990), and that developmental gradations of representational capacity have important implications for affective development (Trad, 1986). At the end of the first year, internal working models are first measured. I earlier equated these with presymbolic representations that mediate incipient affect regulatory functions. Under optimal conditions, in the latter part of the second year these are superceded by more highly complex symbolic representations that can be accessed in memory to more efficiently modulate distress related affects. I suggest that the developmental advance of internal representational functional regulatory capacity that occurs from early to late infancy is a reflection of a structural change in fronto-limbic systems, specifically a reorganization and maturation of the orbitofrontal cortex. A period of structural development in this cortex occurs in the first year of infancy, and a second period marked by further anatomical changes occurs in the second year of human life (Mrzljak, Uylings, van Eden, & Judas, 1990). This reorganization of the prefrontal region is "open to interactions with the external world" (Kostovic, 1990). In the second year these interactions are expressed in dyadic shame and disruption-repair transactions that are part of the socialization process. These experiences trigger specific psychobiological patterns of hormones and neurotransmitters, and the resultant biochemical alterations of brain biochemistry influence the experience-dependent final maturation of the orbitofrontal cortex.

Specifically, shame transactions produce low levels of endorphins and corticotropin releasing factor (CRF) and elevated levels of corticosteroids in the infant's brain. Stress-induced adrenocortical steroids are known to influence gene regulation and brain growth (Beato, Arnemann, Chalepakis, Slater, & Wilman, 1987). Although ventral tegmental dopamine is reduced, noradrenaline, responsible for a different type of arousal than dopamine, is released from catecholaminergic neurons in the nucleus of the solitary tract in the medulla. This noradrenergic source is distinct from plasma noradrenaline produced in the adrenals (and from another in the locus coeruleus). Noradrenergic axons specifically innervate the orbitofrontal cortex (Levitt et al., 1984). This catecholamine performs a neurotrophic role in the postnatal development of the cortex, plays an important role in the responsiveness of brain structures to environmental stimulation, has long-lasting effects on the biochemical processes that mediate developmental influences, and affects the ontogeny of cortical circuitry (Foote & Morrison, 1991). These and other socially induced biochemical alterations (see Schore, 1994) allow for further maturation of orbitofrontal regions, including the growth of prefrontal axons onto subcortical targets in autonomic areas of the medulla that receive vagal inputs (Yasui, Itoh, Kaneko, Shigemoto, & Mizuno, 1991) and hypothalamus (Nauta, 1964), thereby completing the organization of the parasympathetic lateral tegmental forebrain-midbrain limbic circuit that brakes arousal and activates the onset of an inhibitory state. This circuit is identical to the right- hemispheric vagal circuit of emotion regulation described by Porges, Doussard-Roosevelt, and Maiti (1994). Orbitofrontal stimulation, influenced by vagal activity, now produces increases of hypothalamico-pituitary-adrenocortical corticosteroid levels. Conversely, interactive repair transactions allow for a state transition in the infant—the parasympathetic-dominant arousal of the shame state is supplanted by the reignition of sympathetic-dominant arousal that supports increased activity and positive affect. This state transition is neurochemically mediated by a resumption of CRF-inducing endorphin production and a reactivation of the ventral tegmental limbic forebrain-midbrain circuit.

As a result of its structural maturation, the orbitofrontal regions are now capable of carrying out their unique adaptive role in socioemotional functioning. This frontolimbic system is connected into the two limbic forebrain-midbrain circuits (Nauta & Domesick, 1982) and is hierarchically involved in the dual excitatory and inhibitory functional mechanisms of the limbic system. It also acts as a major center of central-nervous-system (CNS) control over the sympathetic and parasympathetic branches of the automatic nervous system (ANS; Neafsey, 1990), as orbital stimulation leads to autonomic effects (e.g., changes in heart rate, skin temperature, blood pressure) that are involved in emotional behavior. The relationship of these two ANS components determines the individual's unique excitation-inhibition autonomic balance (Grings & Dawson, 1978) of this prefrontal system which regulates emotional responses. In optimal early environments, a system emerges in which the individual's rostral brain areas can modulate, under stress, an adaptive pattern of a coupled reciprocal autonomic mode of control, in which increases in the activity in one ANS division are associated with decreases in the other (Berntson, Cacioppo, & Quigley, 1991). This capacity to shift between states of ergotropic and trophotropic arousal allows for the reestablishment of autonomic balance after emotional stresses.

Limbic areas of the human cerebral cortex show anatomical maturation in the middle of the second year, suggesting that corticolimbic functional activity expressed in "emotional activities and mechanisms of memory" are operating at this specific time (Rabinowicz, 1979). This maturation reflects not only the growth of connections but also a pruning or parcellation (Ebbesson, 1980) of overproduced cortical synapses and redistribution of inputs that allows for the emergence of more complex function. This experience-influenced programmed cell death (apoptosis; Gerschenson & Rotello, 1992) results in a differentiated, dual circuit prefrontal system that is capable of an ontogenetic progression, the generation of a more efficient delayed response which supports symbolic representational capacity and a more complex affect regulatory function. Regulated and unregulated affective experiences with caregivers are imprinted and stored in the orbital prefrontal system and its cortical and subcortical connections as interactive representations. These internal representations of external human interpersonal relationships serve an important intrapsychic role as "biological regulators" that control physiological processes (Hofer, 1984). They are stored in representational memory, a prefrontal mechanism involved in regulatory processes that requires the collaborative processing of cortical and subcortical structures (Goldman-Rakic, 1987). Furthermore, such "dynamic representations" that generate cognitive expectations and program information about state transitions (Freyd, 1987) encode reciprocal modes of ANS control which allow for a more efficient regulation of energy dissipation in subsequent socioaffective transactions.

These enduring prototypical interactive representations can be accessed and regenerated in the future in order to trigger psychobiological state transitions and thereby discrete affective states in response to different types of emotionally stressful challenges of the social environment. Due to orbitofrontal connections with both cortical sensory and motor systems and subcortical limbic and auto-nomic centers, the mature orbitofrontal system performs an essential adaptive motivational function: the relatively fluid switching of internal bodily states in response to changes in the external environment that are appraised to be per-sonally meaningful. The orbital frontolimbic cortex performs an "appraisal" of "evaluative" function, and controls the allocation of attention to possible con-tents of consciousness. It is thus centrally involved in the operation of uncon-scious internal representations that encode interaction and motivational strate-gies, the generation of affective-cognitive schemata that regulate the processing of emotional information, and the regulation of visceral and bodily responses and internal states. The encoding of strategies of affect regulation is a primary function of internal working models of attachment (Kobak & Sceery, 1988) that encode expectations concerning the maintenance of basic regulation and positive affect even in the face of environmental challenge (Sroufe, 1989).

Success in regulating smoothness of transition between states is a principal indicator of the organization and stability of the emergent and core self. Emde (1983) identified the primordial central integrating structure of the nascent self to be the emerging "affective core" which functions to maintain positive mood and to regulate the infant's interactive behavior. (I equate this with LeDoux's [1989] "core of the emotional system" that computes the affective significance of environmental stimuli, Tucker's [1992] "paralimbic core" that functions in the evaluation of information for adaptive significance and in corticolimbic self-regulation, and Joseph's [1992] "childlike central core," localized in the right brain and limbic system that maintains the self image and all associated emotions, cognitions, and memories that are formed during childhood). I sug-gest that the orbitofrontal system is an essential component of the affective core. This prefrontolimbic region comes to act in the capacity of an executive control function for the entire right cortex, the hemisphere which modulates affect, nonverbal communication, and unconscious processes for the rest of the life-span. The "nonverbal, prerational stream of expression that binds the infant to its parent continues throughout life to be a primary medium of intuitively felt affective-relational communication between persons" (Orlinsky & Howard, 1986, p. 343). Most intriguingly, the activity of this hemisphere, and not the verbal-linguistic left, is instrumental to the capacity of empathic cognition and the perception of the emotional states of other human beings. Indeed, the right brain is thought to contain the essential elements of the self system (Mesulam & Geschwind, 1978).

From a clinical perspective, Krystal (1988) concluded that the development and maturation of affects represents the key event in infancy, and that the attainment of the essential adaptive capacity for the self-regulation of affect is a major developmental achievement. Thompson, an emotion researcher, asserted the fundamental principle that "Emotion is initially regulated by others, but over the course of early development it becomes increasingly self-regulated as a result of neurophysiological development" (1990, p. 371). Neurobiological studies show that the orbitofrontal system plays a major role in both the temporal organization of behavior (Fuster, 1985) and in the adjustment or correction of emotional responses (Rolls, 1986), that is, affect regulation. It acts as a recovery mechanism that efficiently monitors and autoregulates the duration, frequency, and intensity of not only positive but also negative affect states (mood regulation). This emergent function, in turn, enables the individual to recover from disruptions of state and to integrate a sense of self across transitions of state, thereby allowing for a continuity of experience. These capacities are critical to the operation of a self system that is both stable and adaptable. Sroufe (1989) concluded that the core of the self lies in patterns of affect regulation, and that this regulatory capacity is responsible for the maintenance of continuity despite changes in development and context.

It is now established that emotion expression changes developmentally as a function of the experience-dependent maturation of neural inhibitory mechanisms (Izard, Hembree, & Heubner, 1987), and that the maturation of the frontal region in the second year is responsible for affect regulation and the development of complex emotions (Fox, 1991). The emergence of the adaptive capacity to self-regulate affect is reflected in the appearance of more complex emotions that result from the simultaneous blending of different affects, and in an expansion in the "affect array." Developmental psychoanalytic researchers suggest that a psychic structural system involved in the self-regulation of affect and therefore of autonomous emotional functioning appears in the middle of the second year (Mahler et al., 1975). At this same time an internal signalling system emerges, in which affect, especially negative affect that conveys information about threat and lack of social success, can be used as a signal function. Affect tolerance, which allows for the experience of emotion to enter into consciousness, is related to the adaptive capacity to bear pain (Krystal, 1988). The external regulation of maternally induced intense negative affect states in this critical period facilitates the emergence of evocative memory at 18 months (Fraiberg, 1969). It is now accepted that the complex symbolic representational system of evocative memory allows the child to evoke an image of a comforting other when the other is not physically present and to gain access to "one's self-soothing, self-regulating functions." In light of the facts that affects in general serve the critical adaptive function of informing the individual who is tracking biologically relevant goals (Gilbert, 1992), and that specific emotions facilitate the preparation and sustenance for what must be done about the person-environment relationship (Lazarus, 1991a), successful emotional adaptation requires the capacity to tolerate both positive and negative affects of formidable intensity.

Not only the intensity but also the specific type of emotion that can be experienced is affected by these early experiences. According to Emde (1983), the biologically based affective core becomes biased with tendencies toward certain emotional responses, depending on early experiences in the caregiving relationship. Indeed, emotion biases in personality first appear in the second year of life, and are now understood to be due to the fact that certain neurophysiological and neuroanatomical "emotive circuits" may become more readily activated than others (Malatesta et al., 1989). I would identify these emotive circuits as the two forebrain-midbrain limbic circuits, the activation of which are hierarchically regulated by the orbitofrontal cortex. In attachment experiences, the output of the mother's corticolimbic regions, especially right frontal regions, serves as a template for the imprinting of the infant's developing corticolimbic regions. Dawson (1994) showed that the mother's attachment relationship with her child influences infant frontal brain activity. The right hemiphere is dominant for regulating autonomic activities, and both the postnatally maturing sympathetic and parasympathetic branches of the autonomic nervous system are modulated by the orbitofrontal region that is expanding in the right cortex. I suggest that the origin of mixed patterns of sympathetic and parasympathetic dominance that are found in individuals originates in the first 2 years of life. The developing individual's particular socioaffective imprinting experiences fine-tunes the final, mature distribution of the innervation pattern of orbitofrontal columns, emphasizing either early practicing, sympathetic, excitatory, ventral tegmental dopaminergic inputs, or late practicing, inhibitory, parasympathetic, lateral tegmental, noradrenergic inputs, thereby influencing the final excitation-inhibition balance of a particular prefrontolimbic regulatory system.

This dyadic psychoneurobiological mechanism ontogenetically sculpts the enduring temperamental features of the child's emerging personality. It is now held that the molding of temperamental traits into stable characteristics of personality is a transformation occurring in frontal, temporal, or limbic cortical areas (Carlson, Earls, & Todd, 1988), and that infant temperament can be defined as individual differences in tendencies to express the primary emotions (Goldsmith & Campos, 1982). Psychobiological studies of the development of temperament stress the importance of self-regulation (Rothbart, Derryberry, & Posner, 1994), and neurobiological studies focus on the role of the orbitofrontal cortex as a neural substrate of temperament in the first year-and-one-half of life (Nelson, 1994).

CRITICAL PERIOD AFFECTIVE EXPERIENCES AND
THE ONTOGENESIS OF INSECURE ATTACHMENTS

The ontogenetic attainment of an efficient internal system that can adaptively autoregulate various forms of arousal, and thereby affect, cognition, and behavior, only evolves in an optimal socioemotional environment. We now know that the environment of the child is contained within the specifically experienced caregiver relationship, one that allows the child to enter into a system of "reciprocal mutual influences" with an emotionally responsive mother. The mother's participation in interactive regulation during episodes of psychobiological attunement, misattunement, and reattunement not only modulates the infant's internal state, but also indelibly and permanently shapes the emerging self's capacity for self-organization. More specifically, access to her regulatory functions is a fundamental prerequisite to the emergence of those homeostatic structural systems that are neurobiologically maturing during a critical period of infancy. Caregivers vary in terms of being able to appraise and modulate not only their infants but also their own emotional states, and this potently influences the quality and style of infant attachment. In fact, different styles of maternal mutualization and regulation of infantile affect and different patterns of regulation of emotions during separation and reunion have been observed in the various attachment typologies.

Indeed, the affective experiences in the caregiver-infant relationship are very different in securely and insecurely attached dyads. The mother of the securely attached infant permits access to the child who seeks proximity at reunion and shows a tendency to respond appropriately and promptly to his/her emotional expressions, thereby engendering an expectation in the secure infant that during times of stress the primary attachment object will remain available and accessible. The psychobiologically attuned caregiver maintains the child's arousal within a moderate range that is high enough to maintain interactions (by stimulating the child up out of low arousal states) but not too intense as to cause distress and avoidance (by modulating high arousal states). This entails her actively initiating and participating in not only mirroring-refueling (arousal amplifying) and shame socializing (arousal braking) transactions, but also in interactive repair (optimal arousal recovering) transactions after attachment breaks. Optimal arousal refers to the maintenance of autonomic balance between sympathetic ergotropic and parasympathetic trophotropic states of arousal. It is known that moderate levels of arousal (within the optimal activation band) are associated with positive affect and focused attention, while extreme levels of arousal (high or low) are related to negative emotion and distracted attention.

In contrast to this scenario, the mother of an insecurely attached infant is inaccessible for reunions and reacts to her infant's expressions of emotions and stress inappropriately and/or rejectingly. This type of primary caregiver therefore shows minimal or unpredictable participation in the various types of arousal-modulating, affect-regulating processes. The next question is, what are the long-term structural and functional consequences of such events to those infants who are not fortunate enough to have optimal experiences with a "good enough," psychobiologically attuning caregiver during an early critical period?

The Developmental Neurobiology of Insecure-Avoidant Attachments

In order to understand the structural outcome of dyadic relationships that generate insecure-avoidant attachments, the maternal and infant patterns of affective exchanges of this interpersonal system must be understood. The mother of an insecure-avoidant infant exhibits very low levels of affect expression, and presents a maternal pattern of interaction manifested in withdrawal, hesitancy, and reluctance to organize the infant's attention or behavior. This caregiver typically experiences contact and interaction with her baby to be aversive and actively blocks access to proximity-seeking (attachment) behavior. Main and Weston (1982) observed that this mother manifests a general aversion to physical contact and at times expresses an unverbalizable physical response of withdrawing, or pushing the child away. This caregiver, when she rebuffs her infant, represents an assault from his haven of safety, and further, due to her aversion to physical contact, will not permit access to help him modulate environmentally induced stress, nor the painful emotions aroused by her behavior. Infant-initiated contacts thus elicit not empathic care but parental aversion, behaviorally expressed not only in the caregiver wincing and arching away from the infant's approach, but also in keeping the head at a different level from the infant's, thereby precluding mutual gaze transactions. Joseph stated, "[T]his feeling of aversion is communicated via the right half of the brain. The child responds accordingly because of its own right brain perceptions" (1992, p. 256).

With respect to the other member of the dyad, the insecure-avoidant toddler shows no interest in an adult who is attempting to attract his attention, and exhibits little motivation to maintain contact. This infant characteristically does not appear distressed by the mother's departure nor happy at her return; at reunion the child does not express distress or anger openly. However, there is evidence that it does experience anger during reunion episodes. The insecure avoidant infant, unlike the securely attached infant, does not stop experiencing anger once reunited with the mother, but unlike the insecure-resisitant child, does stop expressing it. This suppressed anger may represent a muffled protest response accompanying the infant's frustrated proximity need as he/she encounters the irritation, resentment, and sometimes outright anger and subsequent active blockade of the contact-aversive mother. In return, he actively avoids the mother, or in her presence ignores her by extensive use of gaze aversion, rather than seeking comfort from the interaction. That this avoidance reflects an expectation of an unsatisfying and rejecting dyadic contact. Reunited with the mother he actively turns away, looks away, and seems deaf and blind to her efforts to establish communication (Main & Stadtman, 1981). Main and

Stadtman interpreted avoidance as a mechanism to "modulate the painful and vacillating emotion aroused by the historically rejecting mother" (1981, p. 293).

As a result of the deprivational stress accompanying the lack of access to the mother's regulatory function, rather than using dyadic mutual gaze to modulate internal physiological disruptions that accompany separation, the insecure-avoidant child habitually utilizes averted (non-face-to-face) gaze, an arousal modulating mechanism. What is avoided is a disorganizing emotional communication expected to emanate from the mother's face. Gaze aversion and avoidance of (withdrawal from) the mother who herself withdraws from her infant is proposed to reflect a state of conservation-withdrawal (Bowlby's despair), a primary regulatory process for organismic homeostasis (Powles, 1992). The infant thus develops a bias toward this parasympathetic-dominant state, one characterized by heart rate deceleration, helplessness, and low levels of activity (McCabe & Schneiderman, 1985). It is interesting to note that the right frontal region is specifically activated during withdrawal-related negative affective states (Davidson, Ekman, Saron, Senulis, & Friesen, 1990).

This temperamental disposition could become permanent via a critical period of selective pruning of sympathetic ventral tegmental, and expansion of parasympathetic lateral tegmental innervation of orbitofrontal systems. Indeed, Izard and colleagues (1991) reported that the insecure-avoidant infant has a relatively high level of parasympathetic tone. Its autonomic balance is parasympathetically dominated and geared to respond maximally to low levels of socioemotional stimulation. Psychophysiologically, the overcontrolled and restrained nature of insecure-avoidant typologies reflects a vagotonic pattern (Eppinger & Hess, 1915) and a parasympathetically biased, inhibitory, orbitofrontal affective core that has a problem shiting out of parasympathetic trophotropic, low arousal states and in modulating sympathetic, ergotropic high-arousal states. This personality organization shows a pattern of "minimizing emotion expression" (Cassidy, 1994), a limited capacity to experience intense negative or positive affect, and is susceptible to overregulation disturbances and to overcontrolled (Lewis & Miller, 1990), internalizing (Cicchetti & Toth, 1991) developmental psychopathologies.

The Developmental Neurobiology
of Insecure-Resistant Attachments

As opposed to a withdrawing caregiver, Tronick and colleagues (1982) described a type of mother who is persistently engaging the infant even when the infant is looking away from her. Unlike the mother of the insecure-avoidant infant, she successfully serves as a source of high-intensity affective stimulation, enabling the characteristic high-arousal affects of the early practicing period. However, during these high-arousal states this type of intrusive caregiver does not sensitively and appropriately reduce her stimulation, and thereby interferes with the infant's attempt to disengage and gaze avert in order to modulate ergotropic arousal and high-intensity affect. Field (1985) noted that if the mother does not respond to the infant's dyadic affective cues of hyperarousal by diminishing her stimulation, especially during periods of infant gaze aversion, the child's aversion threshold will be exceeded and he/she will experience a distress state (Bowlby's protest). She thus does not alter the tempo or content of her stimulation in response to a monitoring of the infant's affective state; instead, she overloads him and interferes with his ability to assimilate new experiences. It is well known that the capacity of an organism to learn effective patterns of responses is negatively affected by heightened levels of arousal.

This type of mother inconsistently permits access to the infant who seeks proximity at reunion. She may engage in positive affect amplifying transactions, but be inefficient in limit setting, regulating shame induction, and aggression socialization in the late practicing period. Due to her lability and to the unpredictable nature of her emotional availability, even when she is present the infant is uncertain as to what to expect with regard to her being responsive to his/her signals and communication. However, in its heightened display of emotionality and dependence upon the attachment figure, this infant successfully draws the attention of the parent. The insecure-resistant infant thus intermixes proximity/contact seeking behaviors with angry, rejecting behaviors toward the mother at reunion; it is thus ambivalent. Additionally, during preseparation episodes the child is often so preoccupied with the mother and with monitoring the mother's face that he can not play independently, since the mother does not function as a reliable, secure base for refueling that enables exploration. This infant shows high separation distress and is notoriously difficult to comfort at reunion, and thus presents with "difficult temperament," the central attributes of which are tendencies to intense expressiveness and negative mood responses, slow adaptability to change, and irregularity of biological functions.

Most importantly, this type of caregiver does not provide an environment that is conducive to the expansion of lateral tegmental catecholaminergic system in the late practicing period. The autonomic balance of this affect regulating system is thus biased toward a predominance of the sympathetic, excitatory dopaminergic ventral tegmental, over the parasympathetic, inhibitory noradrenergic lateral tegmental limbic circuit. Insecure-resistant attachments are associated with undercontrolled and impulsive personality organizations, biochemically manifest by elevated mesolimbic dopamine activity during stress (King, 1985), which are biased toward ergotropic high-arousal states and avoid trophotropic low-arousal affects. The heightened display of emotionality and inefficient capacity to regulate the high levels of anger and distress which characterizes these infants reflects a sympatheticotonically biased affective core which displays a pattern of heightened emotion expression, one that poorly maintains positive mood in the face of stress. They are, therefore, susceptible to underregulation disturbances and to undercontrolled, externalizing developmental psychopathology.

AFFECT DYSREGULATION,
ORBITOFRONTAL DYSFUNCTION,
AND DEVELOPMENTAL PSYCHOPATHOLOGY

In 1978, Bowlby proposed that attachment theory can be used to frame specific hypotheses regarding the etiology of psychopathology. Indeed, this conceptual model is utilized as the central paradigm for developmental psychological research, especially in the emergent discipline of developmental psychopathology, whose primary goal is to characterize the ontological process whereby early patterns of individual adaptation evolve into later patterns of adaptation. This field is described as "a movement toward understanding the causes, determinants, course, sequelae, and treatment of psychopathological disorders by integrating knowledge from multiple disciplines within an ontogenetic framework" (Cicchetti, 1994, p. 286).

Developmental psychopathology provides a theoretical perspective for understanding atypical development in the context of typical development, of focusing on underlying mechanisms common to both. The most thoroughly studied of these is, of course, the mechanism underlying attachment, since this dyadic communicative system of mutual reciprocal influences is psychobiologically adaptive for the organization, equilibrium, and growth of the organism. I have specifically stressed the importance of reunion transactions, episodes of reattachment that occur after periods of separation or misattunement, since the rapid, "hidden" interactive regulation embedded in these reparative exchanges serves as an interpersonal matrix for the emergence of an internal system that can adaptively regulate affect, especially during periods of stress. It is now accepted that the effects of repeated separations are most debilitating when the reunion environment is not supportive (Coe, Wiener, Rosenberg, & Levine, 1985). This dynamic interface is thus also a critical site for the generation of stressful and thereby psychobiologically chaotic events that ultimately create a predisposition or vulnerability to future psychiatric and psychosomatic pathologies.

Functional Deficits Associated
with Developmental Psychopathology

More specifically, an essential adaptive capacity of a securely attached infant is that, when distressed by or during a separation, he/she can seek the caregiver for interactive regulation and be comforted at a reunion. The mother of this infant responds in a timely manner to a broad range of affective experiences and correctly assesses her baby's affect, whether it is positive or negative. Tronick (1989) demonstrated that an infant who is exposed to sensitive and cooperative maternal interactive repair of dyadic misattunements consequently shows self-regulatory skills in the form of persistent efforts to overcome an interactive stress. In such securely attached infants, stress-induced negative affect does not endure for long periods beyond the conditions that elicit them; rapid recovery to positively toned emotion is typical (Gaensbauer & Mrazek, 1981), reflective of efficient regulatory capacities. A cardinal feature of a "high-resilient" child and his/her parents is the capacity of the dyad to fluidly transition from positive to negative back to positive affect (Demos, 1991). Indeed, the ultimate indicator of attachment is seen as this resilience in the face of stress (Greenspan, 1981).

On the other hand, the reunion environment created by the insecure mother-infant dyad creates frequent and enduring high levels of negative and low levels of positive affect. As a result of the caregiver's inability to participate in dyadic affect-regulating functions that modulate extreme levels of stimulation and arousal, this infant shows a greater tendency for negative emotional states to endure beyond the precipitating stimulus events (Gaensbauer, 1982). Thomas and Chess (1982) characterized an infant with "difficult temperament" as manifesting poor adaptability to environmental changes, negative mood when challenged, and extreme intensity of these reactions over time and different situations. Malatesta-Magai (1991) reported that the young child of a depressed mother shows (like the mother) a difficulty in moving back from a negative affect state to a positive affect of interest.

As a result of the formation of an internal working model of a self-attuned-with-a-regulating-other, at later points in the lifespan the individual classified as securely attached in infancy actively and directly seeks and maintains contact with others when distressed, and finds this contact to be reassuring and effective in terminating distress. Early experiences of being with a psychobiologically dysregulating other who initiates but poorly repairs shame-associated misattunement are also incorporated in long-term memory as an interactive representation, a working model of the self-misattuned-with-a-dysregulating-other. Beebe and Lachmann (1988a) suggested that as a result of episodes of caregiver-infant "misregulation" or "misattunement," the infant comes to expect that he cannot benefit from the mother's participation in the management of his affect-arousal states. Furthermore, these representations are stored in memory "largely outside conscious awareness" as prototypical of all interactions. Clinical observers note that failures of early attachment invariably become sources of shame, that impairments in the parent-child relationship lead to pathology through an enduring disposition to shame, and that this results in chronic difficulties in self-esteem regulation found in all developmental psychopathologies. If an attachment figure frequently rejects or ridicules the child's requests for comfort in stressful situations, the child develops not only an internal working model of the parent as rejecting but also one of himself as unworthy of help and comfort (Bretherton, 1985). This precludes access to interactive regulation at times of emotional crisis.

There is now compelling evidence, from a number of separate disciplines at different levels of analysis, that all early forming psychopathology constitutes disorders of attachment and manifests itself as failures of self and/or interactional regulation (Grotstein, 1986). The functional indicators of this adaptive limitation are specifically manifest in recovery deficits of internal reparative mechanisms. This conceptualization fits well with recent models, which emphasize that loss of ability to regulate the intensity of feelings is the most far-reaching effect of early trauma and neglect (van der Kolk & Fisler, 1994), that all forms of psychopathology have concomitant symptoms of emotion dysregulation (Cole, Michel, & O'Donnell Teti, 1994), and that this dysfunction is manifest in more intense and longer lasting emotional responses (Oatley & Jenkins, 1992). Furthermore, a dysfunction of psychobiological regulatory systems is most obvious under stressful and challenging conditions that call for behavioral flexibility and affect regulation. Emde (1988) argued that a developmental orientation to pathology holds that what is not adaptive is a lack of variability in the individual faced with environmental demands that call for alternative choices and strategies for change. Rutter asserted that "environmental stresses tend to impinge most on those who have already exhibited psychological vulnerability and that the tendency is to accentuate pre-existing psychological characteristics, rather than change them" (1995, pp. 80–81). I conclude that these functional vulnerabilities reflect structural weaknesses in the affective core, the psychobiological system that regulates positive mood and interactive behavior, and defects in the organization of the orbitofrontal cortex, the neurobiological regulatory structure that is centrally involved in the adjustment or correction of emotional responses.

Orbitofrontal Structural Defects
and Developmental Psychopathology

An integration of neurobiological with psychological perspectives, of structure-function relationships, is absolutely essential to a deeper understanding of the dysfunctional outcomes of early failures of interactive regulation that contribute to pathological predispositions. Deficits in function must be associated with defects in dynamic structural systems, and a theory of the genesis of psychopathology needs to be tied into current developmental neurobiological models of the experience-dependent anatomical maturation of brain systems, especially systems involved in socioemotional functioning.

The developing infant is maximally vulnerable to nonoptimal and growth-inhibiting environmental events during the period of most rapid brain growth. During these critical periods of synapse overproduction followed by synapse elimination, the organism is sensitive to conditions in the external environment, and if these are outside the normal range a permanent arrest of development occurs. In view of the more extended ontogenetic development of prefrontal structures, cortical systems that perform control and regulatory functions, Goldberg and Bilder (1987) proposed that critical periods for pathogenic influences are prolonged in slowly maturing systems such as the prefrontal cortex. Greenspan (1981) refered to growth-inhibiting environments, which negatively influence the ontogeny of homeostatic self-regulatory and attachment systems. Social environments that provide less than optimal psychobiological attunement histories retard the experience-dependent development of frontolimbic regions, areas of the cortex that are influenced by attachment experiences and prospectively involved in homeostatic functions.

The causal relationship between these early experiences and the genesis of predispositions to pathology may be explained by the fact that the genetic systems that program the structural connections within the limbic system are extremely active during critical periods of infancy. Alterations in gene-regulating hormones, such as opioids, corticosteroids, and other neuropeptides, are induced and indeed regulated by interactions with the "external environment," and these changes trigger the activation of genetic programs and thereby the microarchitecture of growing brain regions in the "internal environment." The external environment is a social environment, specifically contained in the dyadic interaction, and if "psychotoxic" it can literally induce increased synapse destruction in the internal environment, especially in postnatally developing corticolimbic areas of the child's brain. Certain gene-environment interactions are therefore potential sources of pathological alterations of frontolimbic dual-circuit hard-wiring that mark developmentally immature and defective limbic systems. Joseph (1992) posited that the interaction of a noncuddling mother and a child who cannot respond appropriately to physical contact induces an atrophy of certain limbic nuclei in the infant's developing brain and a consequent social withdrawal and abnormal emotionality.

Early failures in dyadic regulation therefore skew the developmental trajectory of the corticolimbic systems that mediate the social and emotional functioning of the individual for the rest of the lifespan. What kinds of psychopathomorphogenetic mechanisms could account for such deflections of normal structural development? Disruption of attachment bonds in infancy leads to a regulatory failure expressed in an "impaired autonomic homeostasis," disturbances in limbic activity, and hypothalamic dysfunction (Reite & Capitanio, 1985). In situations where the caregiver routinely does not participate in reparative functions that reestablish homeostasis, the resulting psychobiological disequilibrium is expressed in a dysregulated and potentially toxic brain chemistry. Increased corticosteroid levels during infancy selectively induce neuronal cell death in "affective centers" in the limbic system (Kathol, Jaeckle, Lopez, & Meller, 1989) and produce permanent functional impairments of the directing of emotion into adaptive channels (DeKosky, Nonneman, & Scheff, 1982). Benes (1994) indicated that stress-induced increases of glucocorticoids during the postnatal period is associated with the induction of abnormal intrinsic circuitry within the corticolimbic system. In addition, a chaotic biochemical alteration of biogenic amines and neuropeptides in this critical period could also produce permanent modifications in the numbers and functional capacities of the frontolimbic receptors for these neuromodulatory agents, thereby causing long-enduring defects in this structural system that are later uncovered during particular types of socioemotional stress. Adverse social experiences during early

critical periods result in permanent alterations in, for example, opiate, dopamine, noradrenaline, and serotonin receptors (Lewis, Gluck, Beauchamp,
Keresztury, & Mailman,1990; Martin, Spicer, Lewis, Gluck, & Cork, 1991;
Rosenblum et al., 1994; van der Kolk, 1987). In light of the pharmacological
principle of receptor supersensitivity (Trendelenburg, 1963), such receptor alterations may be a central mechanism by which "early adverse developmental
experiences may leave behind a permanent physiological reactivity in limbic
areas of the brain" (Post, Weiss, & Leverich, 1994, p. 800).

Even more specifically, different types of unregulated experiences could lead
to distinct classes of psychopathologies. The caregiver's dysregulating effect on
the infant's internal state, and her poor capacity to psychobiologically regulate
excessive levels of low arousal and/or high arousal negative affect, defines a
pathogenetic influence, since such events interfere with the maturation of right
hemispheric structural systems that mediate socioaffective self-regulation. Reductions in the levels of neurotrophic catecholamines during critical periods of
corticolimbic maturation produce permanent alterations in the morphological
development of the orbitofrontal cortex, and extreme hormonal alterations induce a severe apoptotic parcellation of the sympathetic ventral tegmental and/
or parasympathetic lateral tegmental limbic circuits that it hierarchically dominates. For example, if the caregiver (such as a mother suffering a postpartum
depression) does not provide adequate opportunities of stimulation of infant
ergotropic arousal and does not engage in regulated positive affect generating
synchronized mirroring exchanges, levels of opiates and dopamine would be
very low during the critical period of growth of the ventral tegmental limbic
circuit. Such events could produce an enduring capacity to tolerate only low
levels of the positive affects of joy and excitement. Other types of nonoptimal
psychobiological experiences, such as traumatic episodes that maintain excessive states of hyperarousal, could lead to an extensive pruning of descending
orbital axons that synapse directly on ventral tegmental dopamine neurons
(Sesack & Pickel, 1992) via a kindling mechanism (Post et al., 1994), thereby
reducing the capacity of the cortex to effectively modulate subcortical excitatory
processes. It is known that postnatally maturing dopaminergic projections are a
critical potential site of developmental defects (Haracz, 1985).

On the other hand, interactive psychobiological environments that do not
provide regulated states of trophotropic arousal could alter levels of neurotrophic noradrenaline and interfere with the growth of orbitofrontal axons that
synapse on neurons in the dorsal motor nucleus of the vagal nerve in the medulla neurons (Yasui et al., 1991), thereby weakening cortical modulation of
and by brain stem inhibitory mechanisms. Or, chronic stressful dysregulating
states that alter hypothalamic peptide production could disrupt the formation
of orbitofrontal-hypothalamic connections, thus causing a permanent defect in
the capacity of higher cortical systems to influence the production of hypothalamic releasing factors that directly regulate the secretion of pituitary, thyroid,
adrenal, and gonadal hormones that are responsible for the somatic and visceral
components of emotional processes. Along this line, the recent findings that

the orbitofrontal cortex represents an anatomical substrate for psychosomatic disease (Neafsey, 1990) and that an underactivation of the right brain is associated with a high degree of physical health complaints (Wittling & Schweiger, 1993) may help explain a recently established relationship between avoidant attachment and a risk factor for health (Kotler, Buzwell, Romeo, & Bowland, 1994).

Thus, deprivation of empathic care, either in the form of chronic excessive arousal intensification or reduction, creates a growth-inhibiting environment that produces immature, physiologically undifferentiated orbitofrontal affect regulatory systems. Furthermore, extensive dysregulating experiences at this time are permanently etched into forming cortical-subcortical circuits in the form of right-hemispheric "pathological" representations of self-in-interaction-with-a-dysregulating-other. Instead of a dual circuit organization that generates adaptive coupled reciprocal modes, these unevolved frontolimbic systems that maintain weak bidirectional connections with the sympathetic and parasympathetic components of the peripheral nervous system are only capable of generating coupled or uncoupled nonreciprocal (Berntson et al., 1991) modes of autonomic control. They thus show a limitation in strategies of affect regulation. The result is an organization that cannot adaptively shift internal states and overt behavior in response to stressful external demands. Psychopathological regulatory systems contain poorly evolved frontolimbic switching mechanisms that are inefficient or incapable of uncoupling and recoupling the sympathetic and parasympathetic components of the autonomic nervous system in response to changing environmental circumstances. The inability to adapt to stress and the continued activation or inhibition of internal systems that is inappropriate to a particular environmental situation essentially defines the coping limitations of all psychiatric disorders.

I believe that every type of early forming primitive disorder involves, to some extent, altered orbital prefrontal function. Indeed, there is now evidence for impaired orbitofrontal activity in such diverse psychopathologies as autism (Baron-Cohen, 1995), mania (Starkstein, Boston, & Robinson, 1988), unipolar depression (Mayberg, Lewis, Regenold, & Wagner, 1994), phobic states (Rauch et al., 1995), drug addiction (Volkow et al., 1991), and borderline (Goyer, Konicki, & Schulz, 1994) and psychopathic (Lapierre, Braun, & Hodgins, 1995) personality disorders. Because the orbital system is centrally involved in the executive functions of the right cortex, these studies underscore the importance of the role of right hemisphere dysfunction in psychiatric disorders (Cutting, 1992). In light of the facts that this hemisphere mediates empathic cognition and the perception of the emotional states of other human beings (Voeller, 1986), and that orbitofrontal function is essential to the capacity of inferring the states of others (Baron-Cohen, 1995), regulatory dysfunctions of this prefrontal system would underlie the broad class of developmental psychopathologies that display "empathy disorders" (Trevarthen & Aitken, 1994).

1996

CHAPTER 2

The Experience-Dependent Maturation
of an Evaluative System in the Cortex

THE APPRAISAL OF CHANGES IN THE ENVIRONMENT within which an organism exists is a basic adaptive function of the nervous system. For humans, as for all other species, the most salient aspects of the environment are located in not so much the physical as in the social context, the realm of interactions between one individual and another. The transactions within human relationships are both verbal and nonverbal, and thereby contain both cognitive and emotional elements. These communications are not solely "psychological" but more correctly "psychobiological," and as mind-body events they involve activities in both the central and autonomic nervous systems. This means that although evaluative operations have usually referred to purely cognitive assessments of the external environment, they also involve concurrent appraisals of changes in the internal environment that are registered as emotional states. In addition to determining the significance of an environmental stimulus, the brain must also monitor feedback about the internal state in order to make assessments of coping resources, and it must update appropriate response outputs in order to make adaptive adjustments to particular environmental perturbations. Self-organizing appraisals thus involve feedback between social cognition and emotion, and they are a central component of a sequence of psychobiological processes that involve mind and body, cortex and subcortex.

There is now a consensus that appraisal systems assign value to current stimuli based on past experience, according to the accrued developmental history of an individual's preferences and aversions. But there has been some uncertainty about what particular types of early experiences are involved, and a vagueness about the mechanism by which these experiences influence the initial organization of appraisal systems. In light of the developmental principle articulated by Freud, Piaget, and others that the beginnings of living systems set the stage for every aspect of an organism's internal and external function for the rest of the lifespan, I suggest that a deeper understanding of the ontogeny of appraisal systems is an essential area of inquiry. This effort involves an integration of current information from a spectrum of disciplines—developmental psychology, developmental psychobiology, and developmental neurobiology.

In this chapter I will give a brief overview of my current work in this area (Schore, 1994, 1996), and suggest that certain specific early experiences, in conjunction with genetic factors (Schore, 1997a), occuring in particular critical periods of the individual's developmental history, are required for the organization of brain systems that come to mediate the appraisal of socioemotional information. These organismic-environmental experiences are embedded in the primordial interactions between a developing human and the first environment, the relationship between the infant and mother. Indeed, it is now clear that development can only be understood in terms of a continuing dialectic between an active and changing organism and an active and changing environment, and that the most important part of that environment is the interactions and relationships the child has with others (Hinde, 1990). The adaptive capacity to automatically and efficiently evaluate changes in the environment and in the self is an important ontogenetic goal, and its evolution is not only indelibly influenced by the first relationship with another human being, but its emergence also literally depends upon whether the infant has sufficient opportunities to be a coparticipant of an open dynamic system of reciprocal interchanges with an emotionally responsive caregiver.

In other words, the establishment of an attachment bond of emotional communication with the mother, the most important environmental object in early infancy, enables the child to receive the mother's affective appraisals of objects in the nonmaternal environment in late infancy. These interactively transmitted, affectively charged external appraisals provide the developing individual with the requisite experiences that ultimately allow for the organization, in the second year, of brain networks that can generate internal evaluations of the personal significance of what is happening in an encounter with the environment (Lazarus, 1991a) and can elicit emotions to actual or expected changes in events that are important to the individual (Frijda, 1988). A growing literature indicates that the attachment object acts as an external psychobiological regulator of the "experience-dependent" growth of the infant's nervous system, and that these attachment experiences are imprinted into the neurobiological structures that are maturing during the brain growth spurt of the first two years of life, and therefore have far-reaching and long-enduring effects.

This model fits well with Eisenberg's writings in the psychiatric literature on "the *social* construction of the human brain" (1995; italics added), and Tucker's (1992) assertion in the developmental psychological literature that the most important information for the successful development of the human brain is conveyed by the social rather than the physical environment. It has been suggested that "the best description of development may come from a careful appreciation of the brain's own self-organizing operations" (Cicchetti & Tucker, 1994, p. 544). There is widespread agreement that the brain is a self-organizing system, but there is perhaps less of an appreciation of the fact that the self-organization of the developing brain occurs in the context of a relationship with another self, another brain (Schore, 1996).

Here, I will present material on the psychobiology and neurobiology of attachment experiences, and then describe how social referencing experiences, a highly visual form of attachment behavior, serve as an interpersonal matrix for the development of the child's evaluative capacities. Next I will offer ideas about how these developmental interactive events influence the experience-dependent maturation of an evaluative system in the infant brain, especially in the right hemisphere which is undergoing a growth spurt in the first 18 months of life. This right brain system is characterized by particular cognitive, attentional, and arousal capacities that make it uniquely suited to respond to environmental events in an adaptive fashion (Heller, 1993). In light of the fact that the organization of this right hemispheric system operates in conjunction with a system localized to the frontal lobes that is involved in modulating the emotional valence of experience, I will emphasize the importance of the development of the paralimbic cortices, especially the orbitofrontal areas, which act, according to Pribram (1987), in an "evaluative" capacity. The orbitofrontal system is intimately involved in "cognitive-emotional interactions" (Barbas, 1995), a functional role that is relevant to the current emphasis on "cognition-emotion feedback" and self-organizing appraisals (Lewis, 1996).

MUTUAL GAZE AS A DYNAMIC MECHANISM FOR THE COORDINATION OF FACIAL APPRAISALS AND CHANGES IN PSYCHOBIOLOGICAL STATES

Although much has been written about cognitive development in infancy, until recently relatively few studies have specifically focused on the ontogeny of social cognition and emotional states. This development is closely tied into the maturation of sensory systems, especially visual systems. In fact, over the first year of life visual experiences play a paramount role in social and emotional development (Hobson, 1993; Preisler, 1995; Wright, 1991). The mother's emotionally expressive face is, by far, the most potent visual stimulus in the infant's environment, and the child's intense interest in her face, especially in her eyes, leads him to track it in space, and to engage in periods of intense mutual gaze. The infant's gaze, in turn, reliably evokes the mother's gaze, thereby acting as a potent interpersonal channel for the transmission of reciprocal mutual influences. These sustained face-to-face transactions are quite common and can be of very long duration, and they mediate the dialogue between mother and child. A body of research demonstrates that gaze represents the most salient channel of nonverbal communication and, indeed, the most intense form of interpersonal communication.

With the onset of increasing myelination of the visual areas of the infant's occipital cortex, mutual gaze interactions increase significantly over the second and third quarter of the first year. Since these interactions occur within the split second world of the mother and infant, they are therefore not easily visible. This dialogue is best studied by a frame-by-frame analysis of film, and in such work Beebe and Lachmann (1988a) observed a "mirroring sequence," synchronous rapid movements and fast changes in affective expressions within the dyad (Figure 2.1). In these mother-infant communications, each partner responds to the other extremely rapidly, in latencies ranging from simultaneous to one-half second. This affective mirroring is accomplished by a moment-by-moment matching of affective direction in which both partners increase together their degree of engagement and facially expressed positive affect. The fact that the coordination of responses is so rapid suggests the existence of a bond of unconscious communication. Notice that as the child breaks out in an intensely emotional "full gape smile" its attention is focused on one particular aspect of the environment—the visual image of the mother's face. I suggest that in light of the fact that the human face is a unique stimulus whose features display biologically significant information, these early mutual gaze episodes highlight the central role of emotionally charged facial expressions as a focus of appraisal processes.

This microregulation continues; soon after the "heightened affective moment" of an intensely joyful full gape smile, the baby will gaze avert in order to regulate the potentially disorganizing effect of this intensifying emotion (Figure 2.2). In order to maintain the positive emotion the psychobiologically attuned mother takes her cue and backs off to reduce her stimulation. She then waits for the baby's signals for reengagement. In this process of "contingent responsivity" the more the mother tunes her activity level to the infant during periods of social engagement, the more she allows him to recover quietly in periods of disengagement, and the more she attends to his reinitiating cues for reengagement, the more synchronized their interaction. The caregiver thus facilitates the infant's information processing by adjusting the mode, amount, variability, and timing of stimulation to the infant's actual integrative capacities. Facial mirroring thus illustrates interactions organized by ongoing regulations, and the development of mutually attuned synchronized interactions is fundamental to the ongoing affective development of the infant.

These facial mirroring exchanges generate much more than overt facial changes in the dyad; they represent a transformation of inner events. In these episodes of reciprocal facial signalling, as the mother and infant synchronize with each other's temporal and affective patterns, each recreates an inner psychophysiological state similar to the partner's. In this mutually attuned dynamic system, the crescendos and decrescendos of the infant's psychobiological state are in resonance with similar states of crescendos and decrescendos, cross-modally, of the mother. Consequently, both experience a state transition as they move together from a state of neutral affect and arousal to one of heightened positive emotion and high arousal. In physics, a property of resonance is sympathetic vibration, the tendency of one resonance system to enlarge and augment through matching the resonance frequency pattern of another resonance system. Infant researchers refer to a particular maternal social behavior that can "blast the infant into the next orbit of positive excitation" and generate "vitality affects" (Stern, 1985). The mother's face has been called the child's

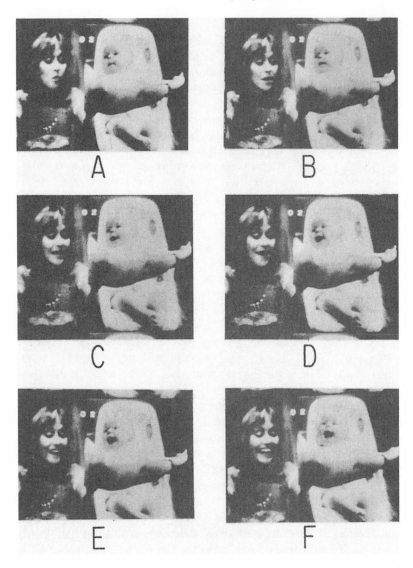

FIGURE 2.1. Photographs of a mirroring sequence. Mother and infant are seated face-to-face, looking at each other. (A) Mother shows a "kiss-face," and infant's lips are partially drawn in, resulting in a tight, sober-faced expression. (B) Mother's mouth has widened into a slightly positive expression, and infant's face has relaxed with a hint of widening in the mouth, also a slightly positive expression. (C) Both mother and infant show a slight smile, further widened at (D). (E) The infant breaks into a "full gape smile." (F) The infant has shifted the orientation of his head further to his left, and upward, which heightens the evocativeness of the gape-smile. Total time: under 3 seconds. (From Beebe & Lachmann, 1988a)

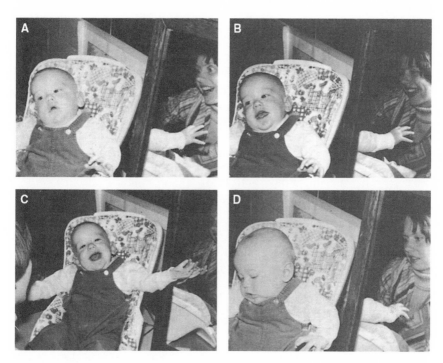

FIGURE 2.2. Sequence of an attuned interaction. (A) The infant looks at the mother and the mother shows an exaggerated facial expression. (B) The infant and the mother smile. (C) The infant laughs, the mother relaxes her smile. (D) The infant looks away, the mother ceases her smile and watches her infant. (From Field & Fogel, 1982)

"biological" or "emotional" mirror," but I suggest that it is not simply a reflective mirror, but rather an amplifying mirror. A major task of the first year is the evolution of affective tolerance for increasingly higher levels of arousal, and this is facilitated by the mother's modulation of the infant's highly stimulated states (Fogel, 1982).

Interactive transactions are also generating important events in the infant's bodily state. Hofer's (1990) developmental psychobiological research revealed that in the "symbiotic" state the adult's and infant's individual homeostatic systems are linked together in a superordinate organization, which allows for mutual regulation of vital endocrine, autonomic, and central nervous systems of both mother and infant by elements of their interaction with each other. Hofer emphasizes the importance of "hidden" psychobiological regulatory processes by which the caregiver's more mature and differentiated nervous system regulates the infant's "open," immature, internal homeostatic systems. His work reveals that the mother influences the neural substrates for infant emotion by directly regulating the neurochemistry of the infant's maturing brain, including arousal-regulating dopamine and noradrenaline levels, in order to generate high levels of positive affect (Hofer, 1984). The attachment relationship is thus essentially a regulator of arousal (van der Kolk & Fisler, 1994).

Indeed, regulatory processes are the precursors of psychological attachment and its associated emotions (Hofer, 1994), and psychobiological attunement is now thought to be the mechanism that mediates attachment bond formation (Field, 1985). These dialogues act as a crucible for the forging of an attachment bond that allows for the dyadic regulation of emotion (Sroufe, 1996). Infant research now suggests that the baby becomes attached to the modulating caregiver who expands opportunities for positive affect and minimizes negative affect (Demos & Kaplan, 1986). In other words, the affective state underlies and motivates attachment, and the central adaptive function of dyadic attachment dynamics is to interactively generate and maintain optimal levels of positively valenced states.

THE NEUROBIOLOGY OF DYADICALLY REGULATED PSYCHOBIOLOGICAL STATES

According to Bowlby (1969), vision is central to the establishment of a primary attachment to the mother, and imprinting is the learning mechanism that underlies attachment bond formation. Furthermore, attachment is more than overt behavior; it is internal, "being built into the nervous system, in the course and as a result of the infant's experience of his transactions with the mother" (Ainsworth, 1967, p. 429). Imprinting involves a state of mutually entrained central nervous system propensities and a synchrony between sequential infant-maternal stimuli and behavior (Petrovich & Gewirtz, 1985). This points to another level of analysis—the neurobiological level. How are developing systems of the organizing brain influenced by these interactions with the social environment?

The work of Trevarthen (1993) on maternal-infant protoconversations bears directly on this problem (Figure 2.3). Coordinated with eye-to-eye messages are auditory vocalizations (tone of voice, Motherese) and tactile and body gestures as a channel of communication. A traffic of visual and prosodic auditory signals induce instant emotional effects, namely excitement and pleasure builds within the dyad. The resonance of the dyad ultimately permits the intercoordination of positive affective brain states. His studies underscored the fundamental principle that the baby's brain is not only affected by these transactions, but also that its growth literally requires brain-brain interaction and occurs in the context of a positive affective relationship between mother and infant. Trevarthen concluded that the affective regulations of brain growth are embedded in the context of an intimate relationship, and that they promote the development of cerebral circuits. This interactive mechanism requires older brains to engage with mental states of awareness, emotion, and interest in younger brains, and involves a coordination between the motivations of the infant and the feelings of adults.

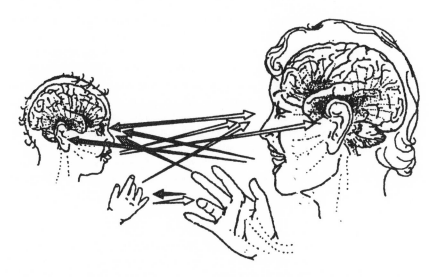

FIGURE 2.3. Channels of face-to-face communication in protoconversation. Protoconversation is mediated by eye-to-eye orientations, vocalizations, hand gestures, and movements of the arms and head, all acting in coordination to express interpersonal awareness and emotions. (From Aitken & Trevarthen, 1997)

In fact, there is consensus that interactions with the environment during sensitive periods are necessary for the brain as a whole to mature (Cicchetti & Tucker, 1994; Greenough, Black, & Wallace, 1987). But we know that different regions of the brain mature at different rates. Can we tell what specific parts of the growing brain are affected by these emotion-transacting events? In describing the dialogue, Trevarthen (1996) noted that the prosody of the voice of the mother is responded to by the infant's right hemisphere, which is "more receptive and self-regulatory." He also pointed out that the left side of the mother's face has a stronger expression of an attractive smile. It is thought that "The emotional experience of the infant develops through the sounds, images, and pictures that constitute much of an infant's early learning experience, and are disproportionately stored or processed in the right hemisphere during the formative stages of brain ontogeny" (Semrud-Clikeman & Hynd, 1990, p. 198). The right cortex, which matures before the left (Chi, Dooling, & Gilles, 1977; Crowell, Jones, Kapuniai, & Nakagawa, 1973; Geschwind & Galaburda, 1987), is known to be specifically impacted by early social experiences (Denenberg, Garbanti, Sherman, Yutzey, & Kaplan, 1978).

I suggest that in these psychobiologically attuned face-to-face transactions the infant's right hemisphere, which is dominant for the infant's recognition of the maternal face (de Schonen, Gil de Diaz, & Mathivet, 1986), and for the perception of arousal-inducing maternal facial affective expressions (Nelson, 1987), visual emotional information (Saxby & Bryden, 1985), and the prosody of the mother's voice (Fernald, 1989), is appraising the output of the mother's right hemisphere, which is dominant for nonverbal communication (Benowitz et al., 1983) and the processing and expression of emotional information (Bradshaw & Nettleton, 1983; Hellige, 1990; Natale, Gur, & Gur, 1983). The right hemisphere is known to be activated in intense states of elation (Tucker, 1981), to show an advantage in the recognition of positive facial expressions (Hugdahl, Iversen, & Ness, 1989), and to contribute to the development of reciprocal interactions within the mother-infant regulatory system (Taylor, 1987). The child is using the output of the mother's right cortex as a template for the imprinting, the hard wiring of circuits in his own right cortex that will come to mediate his expanding cognitive-affective capacities to appraise variations in both external and internal information. It has been said that in early infancy the mother is the child's "auxiliary cortex" (Diamond, Balvin, & Diamond, 1963). There is now solid evidence that the parenting environment influences the developing patterns of neural connections that underlie behavior (Dawson, 1994), including attachment behavior.

Indeed, the right hemisphere is centrally involved in attachment experiences (Henry, 1993; Schore, 1994, 1996). Developmental researchers have held for some time that as a result of attachment experiences the infant develops a schema, a mental image of the mother, especially her face (Mussen, Conger, & Kagan, 1969). Leventhal (1984) notes that the infant's automatic appraisals of the affective aspects of parental interactions, such as smiles, frowns, and vocalizations, are stored in memory along with the memory of emotional experience accompanying these events. These episodes produce prototypes which can then generate automatic and nonconscious affective attributions about environmental interactions. Along this same line of thinking, the internal working model of the attachment relationship is now understood to be a mental representation that guides appraisals of experience (Main, Kaplan, & Cassidy, 1985).

SOCIAL REFERENCING ATTACHMENT EXPERIENCES AND THE ORIGIN OF THE APPRAISAL OF EMOTIONALLY SIGNIFICANT ENVIRONMENTAL EVENTS

In the last quarter of the first year, a critical milestone in human development is reached—with the attainment of upright posture and independent locomotion the infant becomes a toddler. This capacity allows the child to now separate himself from the mother in order to begin to explore the nonmaternal physical environment. When the infant locomotes more widely in its environment, vision continues to be the primary mode of connection with the mother. The socioemotional function of gaze emerges at this very time, as the appearance of the infant's new cognitive capacity to "read" mother's face at reunions after separations coincides in time with the increase in motility.

At 10 to 12 months, social referencing experiences, a special form of attachment behavior (Bretherton, 1985), first appear (Walden & Ogan, 1988), in which the child searches the mother's face for emotional information about the physical environment and then follows her gaze (Scaife & Bruner, 1975). In these visuoaffective transactions, the mother's facially expressed emotional communications provide the infant with salient maternal appraisals of interactions and events (Hornik, Risenhoover, & Gunnar, 1987), especially of novel persons or objects. Also at this time "joint visual attention" becomes intensified and the child first exhibits communicative pointing (Butterworth, 1991), a social gesture (Leung & Rheingold, 1981) that occurs in the context of a shared activity (Murphy, 1978). In this sequence, the child points to an object in the environment but also looks at the other to check the person's gaze as well (Masur, 1983). This visually-driven dyadic mechanism, so synchronized that it has been described as a shared visual realiity (Scaife & Bruner, 1975), allows the infant to see from the adult's point of view, and therefore acts as an interactive matrix for cultural learning (Tomasello, 1993).

The child's first sorties into the world occur under the watchful eye of the caregiver, in which he uses the mother as a beacon of orientation. The infant, now at greater distances from the mother yet increasingly sensitive to her gaze, keeps an eye on the feelings expressed on the mother's face (Oatley & Jenkins, 1992), and uses this signal for evaluations of safety and danger in the nonmaternal environment. But even more than this, at the point when he returns to the secure base the mother's attention to the child's emotionally expressive face intensifies. With these facial cues the psychobiologically attuned mother is now able to appraise the child's internal state, and on the basis of this she reengages in synchronized patterns of visuoaffective communication. The toddler, in turn, attentively responds to the visual stimulation emanating from the mother's emotionally expressive face. These visuoaffective transactions that serve as episodes of "microregulation" are thus critical moments of reciprocal signaling that mediate emotional reconnection after separations. The dyad thus evolves into an operative practical system for processing high-intensity affective transmissions that rapidly maintains psychobiological attunement and sustains the attachment bond without the need for frequent and prolonged physical contact; these refueling transactions that cogenerate high levels of positive affect allow for exploration of the child's expanding world.

It is important to note that these developmental advances depend upon the earlier coconstruction of an attachment bond of emotional regulation within the dyad. In social referencing, an affectively charged dialogic process of the communication of "emotional vision" (Bauer, 1982), the mother induces a mood modification in the infant (Feinman, 1982), and is directly influencing the infant's learning of "how to feel," "how much to feel," and "whether to feel" about particular objects in the larger environment. With regard to the development of interest and curiosity, social referencing maternal attention-focusing strategies may also be essential to the caregiver's enduring effect on the infant's learning of "what to feel" about objects in the social environment, and "what to be interested in" among the objects in the physical environment. Developmental studies of 12-month-olds support the notion that social referencing accounts for the maternal emotional biasing of infant reactions to novel inanimate objects (Hornik et al., 1987). In a classic work, Vygotsky (1978) emphasized that the child's discovery of the physical environment is socially mediated. This seminal idea has been incorporated into and expanded upon in the latest models of emotion. Lazarus (1991b) contended that it is not the physical properties of the environment but the subjective meanings that count in the emotion process.

The visual-emotional communication of social referencing attachment transactions provides access to the mother's appraisal of objects in the animate and inanimate world, and this influences the development of an internalized system in the infant that can evaluate the personal emotional meaning of any particular environmental event. These critical period events may induce familiarization (Pribram, 1991) or "topographic familiarity" and begin to generate "personally relevant" aspects of the individual's world (Van Lancker, 1991). Emotions are currently understood to "arise in response to the meaning structures of given situations, to events that are important to the individual, and which importance he or she appraises in some way" (Frijda, 1988, p. 349), and they involve reactions to fundamental relational meanings that have adaptive significance (Lazarus, 1991a). In the current developmental literature, internal working models enable the individual to evaluate information relevant to attachment, and are unconsciously accessed to interpret and act on new experiences (Crowell & Feldman, 1991).

These internal working models are first measured at the end of the first year, and reflect the fact that psychobiological attachment experiences are imprinted into the early developing brain. Indeed, stable attachment bonds are vitally important for the infant's continuing neurobiological development (Trad, 1986). Main, perhaps the most influential current attachment researcher, concludes that the "formation of an attachment to a specified individual signals a quantitative change in infant behavioral (*and no doubt also brain*) organization" (1991, p. 214; italics added). Do we now know what parts of the brain begin a critical period of structural growth at 10 to 12 months and are involved in attachment, evaluative functions, and the regulation of emotion?

THE EXPERIENCE-DEPENDENT MATURATION OF AN EVALUATIVE SYSTEM IN THE FRONTOLIMBIC CORTEX OCCURS IN A CRITICAL PERIOD OF INFANCY

In my book, *Affect Regulation and the Origin of the Self: The Neurobiology of Emotional Development* (1994), I offered evidence to show that high intensity visual and auditory positive affective stimulation provided in face-to-face transactions represent a growth-promoting environment for the prefrontal cortex, an area that is known to undergo a major maturational change at 10 to 12 months (Diamond & Doar, 1989; Huttenlocher, 1979). It is established that the orbital (as opposed to the later maturing nonlimbic dorsolateral) prefrontal cortex (Figure 2.4) is critically and directly involved in attachment functions (Steklis & Kling, 1985), appraisal proceses (Pribram, 1987), and directed attention (King, Corwin, & Reep, 1989). This region (along with the anterior temporal area) is a central component of the paralimbic cortex whose structure surrounds the more medial and basal areas of the limbic forebrain and whose function involves the processing of social signals necessary for the initiation of social interactions (Raleigh & Steklis, 1981). Furthermore, this frontolimbic structure, which contains neurons that specifically respond to the emotional expressions of faces (Thorpe, Rolls, & Maddison, 1983), is part of a system that has evolved for the rapid and reliable identification of individuals from their faces, because of the importance of this in social behavior" (Rolls, 1986).

The orbitoinsular frontal cortex is "hidden" in the ventral and medial surfaces of the prefrontal lobe. Due to its location at the interface of cortex and subcortex (Figures 2.5, 2.6, & 2.7), it acts as a "convergence zone," and is one of the few brain regions that is "privy to signals about virtually any activity taking place in our beings' mind or body at any given time" (Damasio, 1994, p. 181). In addition to receiving input from all sensory association areas of the posterior cortex (including projections from the face and head region of the somatosensory cortex and from the inferior temporal regions related to central vision), as well as outputs to motor areas in the anterior cortex and ventral striatum, it uniquely projects extensive pathways to limbic areas in the temporal pole and the central nucleus of the amygdala, to glutamate receptors of mesocorticolimbic dopamine neurons in ventral tegmental areas of the anterior reticular formation, and to subcortical drive centers in the paraventricular hypothalamus

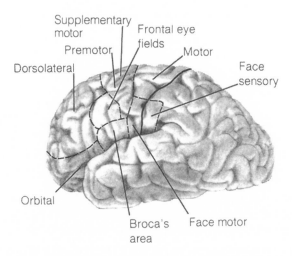

FIGURE 2.4. Approximate boundaries of functional zones of the human cerebral cortex, showing the dorsolateral and orbital prefrontal areas. (From Kolb & Whishaw, 1996)

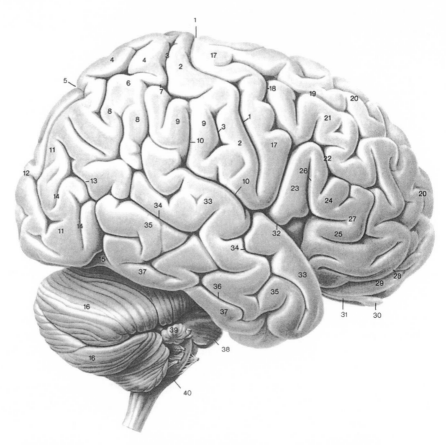

1 Sulcus centralis	15 Incisura praeoccipitalis	28 Sulci orbitales
2 Gyrus postcentralis	16 Hemisphaerium cerebelli	29 Gyri orbitales
3 Sulcus postcentralis	17 Gyrus praecentralis	30 Bulbus olfactorius
4 Lobulus parietalis superior	18 Sulcus praecentralis	31 Tractus olfactorius
5 Sulcus parieto-occipitalis	19 Sulcus frontalis superior	32 Sulcus lateralis
6 Lobulus parietalis inferior	20 Gyrus frontalis superior	33 Gyrus temporalis superior
7 Sulcus intraparietalis	21 Gyrus frontalis medius	34 Sulcus temporalis superior
8 Gyrus angularis	22 Sulcus frontalis inferior	35 Gyrus temporalis medius
9 Gyrus supramarginalis	23 Pars opercularis ⎫	36 Sulcus temporalis inferior
10 Sulcus lateralis, ramus posterior	24 Pars triangularis ⎬ Gyrus	37 Gyrus temporalis inferior
11 Gyri occipitales	25 Pars orbitalis ⎭ frontalis inferior	38 Pons
12 Sulcus lunatus	26 Sulcus lateralis, ramus ascendens	39 Flocculus
13 Sulcus occipitalis anterior	27 Sulcus lateralis, ramus anterior	40 Medula oblongata
14 Sulci occipitales		

FIGURE 2.5. Lateral view of the human right hemisphere. Note the position of the orbital sulci (28) and gyri (29) in the frontal undersurface. (From Nieuwenhuys, Voogd, & van Huijzen, 1981)

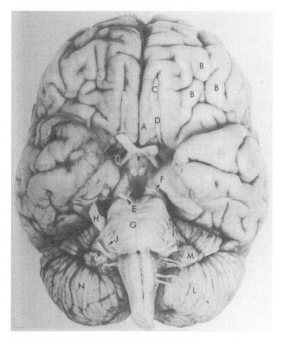

FIGURE 2.6. Photograph of the base of the human brain showing orbital gyri and sulci at sites labelled B. (From Watson, 1977)

that are associated with the sympathetic branch of the autonomic nervous system. This excitatory limbic circuit, what Nauta and Domesick (1982) termed the ventral tegmental limbic forebrain-midbrain circuit, is involved with the generation of positively valenced states associated with motivational reward and approach behavior. Orbitofrontal regions also send axons onto subcortical targets in parasympathetic autonomic areas of the hypothalamus, and to noradrenergic neurons in the medulla and the vagal complex in the brain stem caudal reticular formation, thereby completing the organization of another limbic circuit, the lateral tegmental limbic forebrain-midbrain circuit that activates the onset of an inhibitory, negatively valenced state associated with avoidance.

The orbital prefrontal system is so intimately interconnected into limbic areas that it has been conceived of as an "association cortex" (Martin, 1989; Pribram, 1981) for the limbic forebrain (see Figure 2.8). Indeed, it sits at the apex of the limbic system, the brain system responsible for the rewarding-excitatory and aversive-inhibitory aspects of emotion. This frontolimbic cortex acts as a major center of central nervous system (CNS) hierarchical control over the energy-expending sympathetic and energy-conserving parasympathetic branches of the autonomic nervous system (ANS), and due to its autonomic connections, it plays an important cortical role in the feedback from bodily systems and in the reception of what Damasio (1994) called "somatic markers."

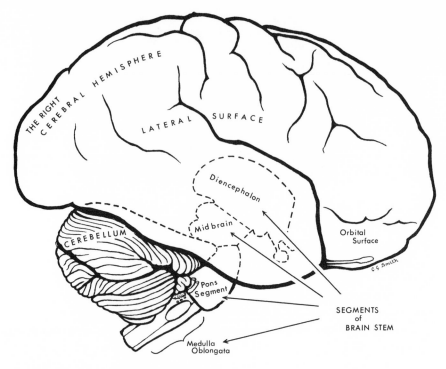

FIGURE 2.7. Relationships of brain stem structures to the orbital surface of the right hemisphere. (From Smith, 1981)

The orbitofrontal system is involved in, according to Luria, "the regulation of the body state and reflect changes taking place in that state" (1980, p. 262). At the orbitofrontal level, cortically processed information concerning the external environment (such as visual and auditory stimuli emanating from the emotional face of the object) is integrated with subcortically processed information regarding the internal visceral environment (such as concurrent changes in the emotional or bodily self state), thereby enabling incoming information to be associated with motivational and emotional states (Pandya & Yeterian, 1985). This far frontolimbic attentional system determines the "regulatory significance" of stimuli that reach the organism (Luria, 1980), and in such manner, "forebrain circuits concerned with the recognition and interpretation of life experiences are capable of influencing virtually all, if not all, regulatory mechanisms in the body" (Wolf, 1995, p. 90).

The orbital prefrontal region is especially expanded in the right cortex (Falk et al., 1990; Tucker, 1992), and it comes to act in the capacity of an "executive control system" (Pribram, 1991) for the entire right cortex, the "visuospatial" hemisphere that is centrally involved in selective attention to facial expressions (Etcoff, 1984), appraisal (Davidson et al., 1990), and unconscious processes

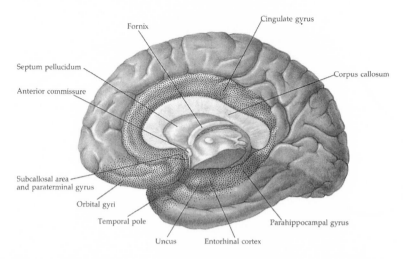

Fornix

Cingulate gyrus

Septum pellucidum

Corpus callosum

Anterior commissure

Subcallosal area and paraterminal gyrus

Orbital gyri

Temporal pole

Parahippocampal gyrus

Uncus   Entorhinal cortex

FIGURE 2.8. Midsagittal view of the right cerebral hemisphere, with brain stem removed. The limbic association cortex is indicated by the dotted region. Note the orbital gyri. (From Martin, 1989)

(Galin, 1974; Watt, 1990). The right cortex is dominant for evaluating emotional expressions (Ahern et al., 1991), perceiving briefly presented emotionally expressive faces (Suberi & McKeever, 1977), and eliciting autonomic responses after subliminal presentations of facial expressions (Johnson & Hugdahl, 1991). These operations define the implicit perception of affective information (Niedenthal, 1990), and they reflect the specialization of this hemisphere not only for detecting stimuli faster than the left (Anzola, Bertolini, Buchtel, & Rizzolatti, 1977), globally directed attention (Fink et al., 1996), processing novel information (Bever, 1983), and holistic analysis (Van Kleeck, 1989), but also for processing the autonomic correlates of emotional arousal (Wittling & Roschmann, 1993). According to Lazarus (Lazarus & Smith, 1988), rapid unconscious appraisals on the basis of the optic stimulus array are a necessary and sufficient condition of emotion. Bear (1983) argued that extensive direct corticolimbic connections of the right hemispheric "ventral pathway," which includes orbitofrontal and anterior temporal components, are responsible for its function in enabling a heightened autonomic response and an immediate, powerful affective reaction to particular stimuli.

Automatic emotional processes are a central element of nonverbal communicaton between humans, and their appraisal is essential to interpersonal functioning. In light of the fact that emotions can be facially expressed in as little as one-half second (Izard, 1991), an accurate perception of a facial stimulus must be rapidly evaluated in terms of its significance to the particular individual. Ohman (1986) described a very quick, involuntary, unconscious and holistic "preattentive stimulus analysis" of an emotionally expressive face; Broadbent

(1977) refered to a "hidden preattentive process" of analysis of incoming emotional stimuli, and Zajonc (1984) described an early, fast evaluation which computes the affective significance of an external stimulus. It is established that evaluative learning occurs without awareness (Baeyens, Eelen, & Van den Bergh, 1990), and that emotional stimuli (Wexler, Warrenburg, Schwartz, & Janer, 1992) and the recognition of familiar faces (De Haan, Young, & Newcombe, 1987) are processed unconsciously.

Socioaffective stimuli, especially patterns of change in visual and auditory stimuli emanating from an emotionally expressive face, are processed in the right posterior occipitoparietal (Bradshaw & Nettleton, 1983) and right parietotemporal (Ross, 1983) association cortices, respectively. The final steps in the discrimination of an incoming stimulus pattern takes place in multimodal or paralimbic association areas in the temporal and frontal cortices which register the motivational significance of the stimulus. In this manner the paralimbic system, via its role in visceroautonomic processing and valuation (Pribram, 1991), performs a "valence tagging" function, in which perceptions receive an affective charge of a positive (pleasurably toned, idealized, good) or negative (unpleasurable, dysphoric, bad) hedonic quality. LeDoux (1989) referred to the "core of the emotional system" that computes the affective significance of environmental stimuli, and Tucker (1992) spoke of frontal networks of the "paralimbic core" that function in the evaluation of information in terms of its motivational significance.

The developmental literature now indicates that the infant's "biologically organized affective core" becomes biased with tendencies toward certain emotional responses, depending on early experiences in the caregiving relationship (Emde, 1983). Emotion biases in personality, which first appear in the second year of life, may be due to the fact that certain neurophysiological and neuroanatomical emotive circuits become more readily activated than others (Malatesta et al., 1989). Ultimately, the affective core "biases the infant's evaluation of a new situation and his interactive patterns even before the information arising from the situation has been processed" (Tronick, Cohn, & Shea, 1986, p. 23). These experiences may permanently influence the types of information channels and the specific patterns of input used by a particular personality organization to receive and recognize idiosyncratically meaningful socioaffective signals that trigger particular motivational systems. The early interactional events that provide for the experience-dependent maturation of the orbital cortex thus permanently influence the unique manner by which this system augments and enhances sensitivities as to what to do in a particular environmental context (Deecke, Kornhuber, Long, & Schreiber, 1985; Pribram, 1991). It has been noted that "With progressively higher organizational levels in evaluative mechanisms, there appears to be a general expansion in the range and relational complexity of contextual controls and in the breadth and flexibility of adaptive response" (Cacioppo & Berntson, 1992, p. 1026).

Limbic areas of the human cerebral cortex show anatomical maturation at 15 months, suggesting that corticolimbic functions expressed in "emotional activities and mechanisms of memory" are operating at this specific time (Rabinowicz, 1979). The early affective experiences that occur during the critical period of growth of this frontolimbic system are imprinted and stored in implicit-procedural memory systems in the orbital prefrontal system and its cortical and subcortical connections as interactive representations. Damasio described dispositonal representations, stored in the ventromedial cortex, that "embody knowledge pertaining to how certain types of situations have usually been paired with emotional responses in [one's] individual experience" (1995, p. 22). These representations are repositories of stimulus appraisals and memories of somatic value acquired in the individual's experience, and when they are activated they create a bodily state that regulates approach or avoidance toward an object. Such representations also encode an appraisal of the organism's bodily state to generate energy in response to the challenge of a particular external context, that is an estimate of the individual's capacity to cope with a particular environmental situation (Schore, 1994).

The orbitofrontal system plays a major role in the internal state of the organism (Mega & Cummings, 1994), the temporal organization of behavior (Fuster, 1985), and in the adjustment or correction of emotional responses (Rolls, 1986), that is, affect regulation. Pribram (1987) proposed that the ventrolateral cortex, acting in an "evaluative" or "appraisal" capacity, functions to "refine" emotions in keeping with current sensory input and with the consequences of actions. I suggest that the essential activity of this psychic system is thus the adaptive switching of internal bodily states in response to changes in the external environment that are appraised to be personally meaningful. This emergent function, in turn, enables the individual to recover from disruptions of state and to integrate a sense of self across transitions of state, thereby allowing for a continuity of experience in various environmental contexts.

The orbital cortex matures in the middle of the second year, a time when the right hemisphere ends its growth phase and the left hemisphere begins one (Thatcher, 1994). Most intriguingly, infant observers report that in the course of the second year the infant acquires the capacity to generate a "theory of mind," in which an individual imputes mental states to self and to others and predicts behavior on the basis of such states (Bretherton, McNew, & Beeghly, 1981; Meltzoff, 1995a). Indeed, there is evidence that the orbital frontolimbic system functionally mediates the the capacity of empathizing (Mega & Cummings, 1994) and inferring the states of others (Baron-Cohen, 1995), and of reflecting on one's own internal emotional states, as well as others' (Povinelli & Preuss, 1995). The activity of the nondominant right hemisphere, and not the later maturing dominant verbal-linguistic left, is instrumental to the capacity of empathic cognition and the perception of the emotional states of mind of other human beings (Voeller, 1986). The human appraisal system, from its very beginnings throughout the rest of the life span, is not just directed toward evaluating the overt behavior of others, but also toward attempting to understand the mind of other humans.

1998

CHAPTER 3

Attachment and the Regulation
of the Right Brain

I N 1969, 29 YEARS AFTER HIS INITIAL PUBLICATION of an article on how the early environment could influence the development of character (1940), John Bowlby
integrated his career-spanning observations and theoretical conceptualizations
into the first of three influential volumes on *Attachment and Loss* (1969, 1973,
1981). This foundational volume, *Attachment* (1969), was groundbreaking for
a number of reasons. It focused upon one of the major questions of science,
specifically, how and why do certain early ontogenetic events have such an
inordinate effect on everything that follows? Bowlby presented these essential
problems in such a way that both a heuristic theoretical perspective and a
testable experimental methodology could be created to observe, measure, and
evaluate certain very specific mechanisms by which the early social environment interacts with the maturing organism in order to shape developmental
processes (Schore, 2000a).

But perhaps of even more profound significance was his carefully argued
proposition that an interdisciplinary perspective should be applied to the study
of developmental phenomena, as they exist in nature. In such an approach the
collaborative knowledge bases of a spectrum of sciences would yield the most
powerful models of both the nature of the fundamental ontogenetic processes
that mediate the infant's first attachment to another human being, and the
essential psychobiological mechanisms by which these processes indelibly influence the development of the organism at later points of the life cycle.

In response to this classic volume Ainsworth observed, "In effect what
Bowlby has attempted is to update psychoanalytic theory in the light of recent
advances in biology" (1969, p. 998). Bowlby's deep insights into the potential
synergistic effects of combining the literatures of what appeared on the surface
to be distantly related realms may now seem like a brilliant flash of intuition.
In actuality it represented a natural convergence of his two most important
intellectual influences, Darwin and Freud. In order to create a perspective that
could describe critical events in both the external and internal world, concepts
from both ethology (behavioral biology) and psychoanalysis are presented and

interwoven throughout the volume. In essence, a central goal of Bowlby's first book is to demonstrate that a mutually enriching dialogue can be organized between the biological and the psychological realms, something Darwin (1872/ 1965) had attempted in the first scientific treatise on the biology and psychology of emotion, *The Expression of Emotions in Man and Animals,* and Freud (1895/ 1966) had attempted in his endeavor to integrate neurobiology and psychology in order to create a "natural science," *Project for a Scientific Psychology* (Schore, 1997b).

Although both Darwin and Freud emphasized the centrality of early development as an important part of their overall work, each primarily focused his observational and theoretical lens on the adaptive and maladaptive functioning of fully matured adult organisms. In *Attachment* Bowlby (1969) argued that clinical observers and experimental scientists should intensively focus on developing organisms that are in the process of maturing. More specifically, he called for deeper explorations of the fundamental ontogenetic mechanisms by which an immature organism is critically shaped by its primordial relationship with a mature adult member of its species, that is, more extensive studies of how an attachment bond forms between the infant and mother. In this conception, Bowlby asserted that these developmental processes are the product of the interaction of a unique genetic endowment with a particular environment, and that the infant's emerging social, psychological, and biological capacities cannot be understood apart from its relationship with the mother.

BOWLBY'S ORIGINAL CHARTINGS
OF THE ATTACHMENT LANDSCAPE

Much has transpired since the original publication of Bowlby's *Attachment,* and the ensuing explosion of attachment research since 1969 is a testament to the power of the concepts it contains. And yet a (re)reading of this classic still continues to reveal more and more subtle insights into the nature of developmental processes, and to shine light upon yet to be fully explored areas of developmental research. In fact, in this seminal work of developmental science, the pioneering Bowlby (1969) presented a survey of what he saw to be the essential topographic landmarks of the uncharted territory of mother-infant relationally-driven psychobiological processes. The essential guideposts of this dynamic domain—the central phenomena that must be considered in any overarching model of how the attachment relationship generates both immediate and long-enduring effects on the developing individual—were presented by Bowlby in not only the subject matter but also the structural organization of the book. The reader will notice that the book is divided into four parts, "The Task," "Instinctive Behaviour," "Attachment Behaviour," and "Ontogeny of Human Attachment," and that Bowlby devoted ten chapters to the first two parts, and seven to the last two parts.

It is now more than 30 years since Bowlby called for "a far-reaching pro-
gramme of research into the social responses of man, from the preverbal period
of infancy onwards" (1969, p. 174). In the following, I want to offer a psychoneurobiological perspective of not only the original contents of Bowlby's guide-
book, but also some thoughts about the current and future directions of the
experimental and clinical explorations of attachment theory as they pass from
one century into the next. In doing so, I will specifically attend to not so much
the quality of attachment research, which has served as a standard in psychology, psychiatry, and psychoanalysis as a whole, nor to the breadth of the research, which spans developmental psychology, developmental psychobiology,
developmental neurochemistry, infant psychiatry, and psychoanalysis, but rather
to the foci of current investigations, as measured against the original prescriptions that were offered by Bowlby. And I will suggest that certain uninvestigated
areas of this attachment domain, sketched out in Bowlby's cartographic descriptions in his book, are now ready to be explored by interdisciplinary research
programs. For a broad overview of the field at the end of the century I refer
the reader to two excellent edited volumes, *Attachment Theory: Social, Developmental, and Clinical Perspectives* (Goldberg, Muir, & Kerr, 1995) and *Handbook of Attachment: Theory, Research, and Clinical Applications* (Cassidy &
Shaver, 1999).

In Bowlby's book, most current readers are very familiar (or even perhaps
only familiar) with the latter two sections on attachment, and most researchers
continue to focus their investigation upon the concepts outlined in these later
chapters. It is here, as well as in the introductory sections, that Bowlby presented his essential contributions on the infant's sequential responses to separation from the primary attachment figure—protest, despair, and detachment. In
the context of emphasizing the importance of studying the infant's behavior
specifically during the temporal interval when the mother returns, Bowlby introduced the methodology of Ainsworth, which would soon become the major
experimental paradigm for attachment research, the incrementally stress-
increasing "strange situation."

But in addition to theorizing on the nature of separation responses, stressful
ruptures of the mother-infant bond, Bowlby also described what he saw as the
fundamental dynamics of the attachment relationship. In stating that the infant
is active in seeking interaction, that the mother's maternal behavior is "reciprocal" to the infant's attachment behavior, and that the development of attachment is related both to the sensitivity of the mother in responding to her baby's
cues and to the amount and nature of their interaction, he laid a groundwork
that presents attachment dynamics as a "reciprocal interchange" (1969, p. 346),
a conceptualization that is perfectly compatible with recent advances in dynamic systems theory (Schore, 1997a; Lewis, 1995, 1999, 2000).

At the very beginning of the section on "Attachment Behavior" Bowlby
(1969) offered his earliest model of the essential characteristics of attachment:
It is instinctive social behavior with a biological function, "readily activated

especially by the mother's departure or by anything frightening, and the stimuli that most efficiently terminate the systems are sound, sight, or touch of the mother," and is "a product of the activity of a number of behavioural systems that have proximity to mother as a predictable outcome" (p. 179). Although the first three postulates remained unaltered in his later writings, in his second volume Bowlby (1973) attempted to more precisely define the set-goal of the attachment system as seeking not just proximity but also access to an attachment figure who is emotionally available and responsive.

A further evolution of this concept is now found in transactional theories that emphasize the central role of the primary caregiver in coregulating the child's facially expressed emotional states (Schore, 1994, 1998a, 2002a) and that define attachment as the dyadic regulation of emotion (Sroufe, 1996) and the regulation of biological synchronicity between organisms (Wang, 1997). The development of synchronized interactions is fundamental to the healthy affective development of the infant (Penman, Meares, & Milgrom-Friedman, 1983). Reite and Capitanio (1985) conceptualized affect as "a manifestation of underlying modulating or motivational systems subserving or facilitating social attachments" (p. 248) and suggest that an essential attachment function is "to promote the synchrony or regulation of biological and behavioral systems on an organismic level" (p. 235). In these rapid, regulated face-to-face transactions the psychobiologically attuned (Field, 1985) caregiver not only minimizes the infant's negative but also maximizes his positive affective states (Schore, 1994, 1996, 1998b). This proximate interpersonal context of "affect synchrony" (Feldman, Greenbaum, & Yirmiya, 1999) and interpersonal resonance (Schore, 1997a) represents the external realm of attachment dynamics.

But due to his interests in the inner world, Bowlby presented a model of events occurring within the internal realm of attachment processes. And so he offered his initial speculations about how the developing child constructs internal working models "of how the physical world may be expected to behave, how his mother and other significant persons may be expected to behave, how he himself may be expected to behave, and how each interacts with the other" (1969, p. 354). This initial concept has evolved into "process-oriented" conceptions of internal working models as representations that regulate an individual's relationship adaptation through interpretive/attributional processes (Bretherton & Munholland, 1999), and encode strategies of affect regulation (Kobak & Sceery, 1988; Schore, 1994). Psychobiological models refer to representations of the infant's affective dialogue with the mother which can be accessed to regulate its affective state (Polan & Hofer, 1999).

Interestingly, Bowlby (1969) also described internal working models in the first part of the volume, the eight chapters devoted to "instinctive behavior." I repeat my assertion that a deeper explication of the fundamental themes of this section of the book represents the frontier of attachment theory and research. In these opening chapters, the aggregate of which represents the foundation on which the later chapters on attachment are built, Bowlby posited that internal models function as "cognitive maps" in the brain, and are accessed "to transmit, store, and manipulate information that helps making predictions as to how . . . set-goals [of attachment] can be achieved" (p. 80). Furthermore, he states that "the two working models each individual must have are referred to respectively as his environmental model and his organismic model" (p. 82). This is because "sensory data regarding events reaching an organism via its sense organs are immediately assessed, regulated, and interpreted. . . . The same is true of sensory data derived from the internal state of the organism" (p. 109). Here Bowlby pointed to the need for a developmental theoretical conception of attachment that can tie together psychology and biology, mind and body.

And so at the very onset of his essay, he began "The Task" by describing a theoretical landscape that includes both the biological and social aspects of attachment, a terrain that must be described both in terms of its structural organization as well as its functional properties. Following the general perspective of all biological investigators he attempted to elucidate the structure-function relationships of a living system, but with the added perspective of developmental biology he was specifically focusing on the early critical stages within which the system first self-organizes. Thus the form of the book is to first outline the general characteristics of the internal structural system, and then to describe this system's central functional role in attachment processes.

Bowlby (1969) began the third chapter by quoting Freud's (1925/1959a) dictum that "There is no more urgent need in psychology than for a securely founded theory of the instincts." The attempt to do so in this book, an offering of an "alternative model of instinctive behavior," in essence represents Bowlby's conviction that what Freud was calling for was the creation of a model that could explicate the biology of unconscious processes. Toward that end, in the first of eight chapters on the topic he proposed that attachment is instinctive behavior associated with self preservation, and that it is a product of the interaction between genetic endowment and the early environment.

But immediately after a brief five-page introduction, Bowlby (1969) launched into a detailed description of a biological control system that is centrally involved in instinctive behavior. This control system is structured as a hierarchical mode of organization that acts as "an overall goal-corrected behavioral structure." Bowlby also gave some hints as to the neurobiological operations of this control system—its functions must be associated with the organism's "state of arousal" that results from the critical operations of the reticular formation, and with "the appraisal of organismic states and situations of the midbrain nuclei and limbic system" (p. 110). He even offered a speculation about its anatomical location—the prefrontal lobes (p. 156).

This control system, Bowlby wrote, is "open in some degree to influence by the environment in which development occurs" (p. 45). More specifically, it evolves in the infant's interaction with an "environment of adaptiveness, and especially of his interaction with the principal figure in that environment, namely his mother" (p. 180). Furthermore, Bowlby speculated that the "upgrading of control during individual development from simple to more sophisticated is no doubt in large part a result of the growth of the central nervous system" (p. 156). In fact he even went so far as to suggest the temporal interval that is critical to the maturation of this control system—9 to 18 months (p. 180).

In a subsequent chapter, "Appraising and Selecting: Feeling and Emotion," Bowlby quoted Darwin's (1872/1965) observation that the movements of expression in the face and body serve as the first means of communication between the mother and infant. Furthering this theme on the communicative role of feeling and emotion, Bowlby emphasized the salience of "facial expression, posture, tone of voice, physiological changes, tempo of movement, and incipient action" (p. 120). The appraisal of this input is experienced "in terms of value, as pleasant or unpleasant" (pp. 111–112) and "may be actively at work even when we are not aware of them" (p. 110), and in this manner feeling provides a monitoring of both the behavioral and physiological state (p. 121). Emotional processes thus, he wrote, lie at the foundation of a model of instinctive behavior.

In following chapters Bowlby concluded that the mother-infant attachment relation is "accompanied by the strongest of feelings and emotions, happy or the reverse" (p. 242), that the infant's "capacity to cope with stress" is correlated with certain maternal behaviors (p. 344), and that the instinctive behavior that emerges from the coconstructed environment of evolutionary adaptiveness has consequences that are "vital to the survival of the species" (p. 137). He also suggested that the attachment system is readily activated until the end of the third year, when the child's capacity to cope with maternal separation "abruptly" improves, due to the fact that "some maturational threshold is passed" (p. 205).

CONTRIBUTIONS FROM NEUROSCIENCE TO ATTACHMENT THEORY

So the next question is, 30 years after the appearance of this volume, at the end of the "decade of the brain," how do Bowlby's original chartings of the attachment domain hold up? In a word, they were prescient. In fact his overall bird's-eye perspective of the internal attachment landscape was so comprehensive that we now need to zoom in for close-up views of not just the essential brain structures that mediate attachment processes but also visualizations of how these structures dynamically self-organize within the developing brain. This includes neurobiological studies of Bowlby's control system, which I suggest may now be identified with the orbitofrontal cortex, an area that has been called the "senior executive of the emotional brain" (Joseph, 1996) and that has been shown to mediate "the highest level of control of behavior, especially in relation to emotion" (Price, Carmichael, & Drevets, 1996, p. 523). Keeping in mind Bowlby's previously presented theoretical descriptions, the following is an extremely brief overview of a growing body of studies on the neurobiology of attachment. (For more extensive expositions of these concepts and references see Schore, 1994, 1996, 1997a, 1998a, 1999a, 2000b, 2001a, 2001b, 2002a).

According to Ainsworth (1967, p. 429), attachment is more than overt behavior, it is internal, "being built into the nervous system, in the course and as a result of the infant's experience of his transactions with the mother." Following Bowlby's lead, the limbic system has been suggested to be the site of developmental changes associated with the rise of attachment behaviors (Anders & Zeanah, 1984). Indeed, the specific period from 7 to 15 months has been shown to be critical for the myelination and therefore the maturation of particular rapidly developing limbic and cortical association areas (Kinney, Brody, Kloman, & Gilles,1988) and limbic areas of the human cerebral cortex show anatomical maturation at 15 months (Rabinowicz, 1979). In a number of works I offered evidence to show that attachment experiences, face-to-face transactions of affect synchrony between caregiver and infant, directly influence the imprinting, the circuit wiring of the orbital prefrontal cortex, a corticolimbic area that is known to begin a major maturational change at 10 to 12 months and to complete a critical period of growth in the middle to end of the second year (Schore, 1994, 1996, 1997a, 1998a). This time frame is identical to Bowlby's maturation of an attachment control system that is open to influence of the developmental environment.

The cocreated environment of evolutionary adaptiveness is thus isomorphic to a growth-facilitating environment for the experience-dependent maturation of a regulatory system in the orbitofrontal cortex. Indeed, this prefrontal system appraises visual facial (Scalaidhe, Wilson, & Godman-Rakic, 1997) and auditory (Romanski et al., 1999) information, and processes responses to pleasant touch, taste, smell (Francis, Diorio, Liu, & Meaney, 1999) and music (Blood, Zatorre, Bermudez, & Evans, 1999) as well as to unpleasant images of angry and sad faces (Blair, Morris, Frith, Perrett, & Dolan, 1999). But this system is also involved in the regulation of the body state and reflects changes taking place in that state (Luria, 1980).

This frontolimbic system provides a high-level coding that flexibly coordinates exteroceptive and interoceptive domains and functions to correct responses as conditions change (Derryberry & Tucker, 1992), processes feedback information (Elliott, Frith, & Dolan, 1997), and thereby monitors, adjusts, and corrects emotional responses (Rolls, 1986) and modulates the motivational control of goal-directed behavior (Tremblay & Schultz, 1999). So after a rapid evaluation of an environmental stimulus, the orbitofrontal system monitors feedback about the current internal state in order to make assessments of coping resources, and it updates appropriate response outputs in order to make adaptive adjustments to particular environmental perturbations (Schore, 1998a). In this manner, "the integrity of the orbitofrontal cortex is necessary for acquiring very specific forms of knowledge for regulating interpersonal and social behavior" (Dolan, 1999, p. 928).

These functions reflect the unique anatomical properties of this area of the brain. Due to its location at the ventral and medial hemispheric surfaces, it acts as a convergence zone where cortex and subcortex meet. It is thus situated at the apogee of the "rostral limbic system," a hierarchical sequence of interconnected limbic areas in orbitofrontal cortex, insular cortex, anterior cingulate, and amygdala (Schore, 1997a, 2000b). The limbic system is now thought to be centrally involved in the capacity "to adapt to a rapidly changing environment" and in "the organization of new learning" (Mesulam, 1998, p. 1028). Emotionally focused limbic learning underlies the unique and fast-acting processes of imprinting, the learning mechanism associated with attachment, as this dynamic evolves over the first and second year. Hinde pointed out that "the development of social behavior can be understood only in terms of a continuing dialectic between an active and changing organism and an active and changing environment" (1990, p. 162).

But the orbitofrontal system is also deeply connected into the autonomic nervous system and the arousal-generating reticular formation, and due to the fact that it is the only cortical structure with such direct connections, it can regulate autonomic responses to social stimuli (Zald & Kim, 1996) and modulate "instinctual behavior" (Starkstein & Robinson, 1997). The activity of this frontolimbic system is therefore critical to the modulation of social and emotional behaviors and the homeostatic regulation of body and motivational states, affect-regulating functions that are centrally involved in attachment processes. The essential aspect of this function is highlighted by Westin who asserts that "The attempt to regulate affect—to minimize unpleasant feelings and to maximize pleasant ones—is the driving force in human motivation" (1997, p. 542).

The orbital prefrontal region is especially expanded in the right hemisphere, which is specialized for "inhibitory control" (Garavan, Ross, & Stein, 1999), and it comes to act as an executive control function for the entire right brain. This hemisphere, which is dominant for unconscious processes, computes, on a moment-to-moment basis, the affective salience of external stimuli. Keeping in mind Bowlby's earlier descriptions, this lateralized system performs a "valence tagging" function (Schore, 1998a, 1999a), in which perceptions receive a positive or negative affective charge, in accord with a calibration of degrees of pleasure-unpleasure. It also contains a "nonverbal affect lexicon," a vocabulary for nonverbal affective signals such as facial expressions, gestures, and vocal tone or prosody (Bowers, Bauer, & Heilman, 1993). The right hemisphere is thus faster than the left in performing valence-dependent, automatic, preattentive appraisals of emotional facial expressions (Pizzagalli, Regard, & Lehmann, 1999).

Because the right cortical hemisphere, more so than the left, contains extensive reciprocal connections with limbic and subcortical regions (Joseph, 1996; Tucker, 1992), it is dominant for the processing of "self-related material" (Keenan et al., 1999) and emotional information, and for regulating psychobiological states (Schore, 1994, 1998a, 1999a; Spence, Shapiro, & Zaidel, 1996).

Thus the right hemisphere is centrally involved in what Bowlby described as the social and biological functions of the attachment system (Henry, 1993; Schore, 1994; Shapiro, Jamner, & Spence, 1997; Siegel, 1999; Wang, 1997).

Confirming this model, Ryan, Kuhl, and Deci, using EEG and neuroimaging data, concluded that "The positive emotional exchange resulting from autonomy-supportive parenting involves participation of right hemispheric cortical and subcortical systems that participate in global, tonic emotional modulation" (1997, p. 719). And in line with Bowlby's assertion that attachment behavior is vital to the survival of the species, it is held that the right hemisphere is central to the control of vital functions supporting survival and enabling the organism to cope with stresses and challenges (Wittling & Schweiger, 1993).

There is a growing body of studies that shows that the infant's early maturing (Geschwind & Galaburda, 1987) right hemisphere is specifically impacted by early social experiences (Schore, 1994, 1998b). This developmental principle is now supported in a recent single photon emission computed tomographic (SPECT) study by Chiron and colleagues (1997), which demonstrated that the right brain hemisphere is dominant in preverbal human infants, and indeed for the first three years of life. I suggest that this ontogenetic shift of dominance from the right to left hemisphere after this time may explicate Bowlby's description of a diminution of the attachment system at the end of the third year that is due to an "abrupt" passage of a "maturational threshold."

Neuropsychological studies indicate that "the emotional experience(s) of the infant . . . are disproportionately stored or processed in the right hemisphere during the formative stages of brain ontogeny" (Semrud-Clikeman & Hynd, 1990, p. 198), that "the infant relies primarily on its procedural memory systems" during "the first 2–3 years of life" (Kandel, 1999, p. 513), and that the right brain contains the "cerebral representation of one's own past" and the substrate of affectively-laden autobiographical memory (Fink et al., 1996, p. 4275). These findings suggest that early forming internal working models of the attachment relationship are processed and stored in implicit-procedural memory systems in the right hemisphere.

In the securely attached individual, these models encode an expectation that "homeostatic disruptions will be set right" (Pipp & Harmon, 1987, p. 650). In discussing these internal models Rutter noted, "children derive a set of expectations about their own relationship capacities and about other people's resources to their social overtures and interactions, these expectations being created on the basis of their early parent-child attachments" (1987, p. 449). Such representations are processed by the orbitofrontal system, which is known be activated during "breaches of expectation" (Nobre, Coull, Frith, & Mesulam, 1999) and to generate affect regulating strategies for coping with expected negative and positive emotional states that are inherent in intimate social contexts.

The efficient operations of this regulatory system allow for cortically processed information concerning the external environment (such as visual and auditory stimuli emanating from the emotional face of the attachment object) to be integrated with subcortically processed information regarding the internal visceral environment (such as concurrent changes in the child's emotional or bodily self state). The relaying of sensory information into the limbic system allows incoming information about the social environment to trigger adjustments in emotional and motivational states, and in this manner the orbitofrontal system integrates what Bowlby termed environmental and organismic models. Findings that the orbitofrontal cortex generates nonconscious biases that guide behavior before conscious knowledge does (Bechara, Damasio, Tranel, & Damasio, 1997), codes the likely significance of future behavioral options (Dolan, 1999), and represents an important site of contact between emotional information and mechanisms of action selection (Rolls, 1996), are consonant with Bowlby's (1981) assertion that unconscious internal working models are used as guides for future action.

These mental representations, according to Main and colleagues (1985), contain cognitive as well as affective components and act to guide appraisals of experience. The orbitofrontal cortex is known to function as an appraisal mechanism (Pribram, 1987; Schore, 1998a) and to be centrally involved in the generation of "cognitive-emotional interactions" (Barbas, 1995). It acts to "integrate and assign emotional-motivational significance to cognitive impressions; the association of emotion with ideas and thoughts" (Joseph, 1996, p. 427) and in "the processing of affect-related meanings" (Teasdale et al., 1999).

Orbitofrontal activity is associated with a lower threshold for awareness of sensations of both external and internal origin (Goldenberg et al., 1989), thereby enabling it to act as an "internal reflecting and organizing agency" (Kaplan-Solms & Solms, 1996). This orbitofrontal role in "self-reflective awareness" (Stuss, Gow, & Hetherington, 1992) allows the individual's to reflect on one's own internal emotional states, as well as others (Povinelli & Preuss, 1995). According to Fonagy and Target (1997) the reflective function is a mental operation that enables the perception of another's state. The right hemisphere mediates empathic cognition and the perception of the emotional states of other human beings (Voeller, 1986) and orbitofrontal function is essential to the capacity of inferring the states of others (Baron-Cohen, 1995). This adaptive capacity may thus be the outcome of a secure attachment to a psychobiologically attuned, affect regulating caregiver. A recent neuropsychological study indicates that the orbitofrontal cortex is "particularly involved in theory of mind tasks with an affective component" (Stone, Baron-Cohen, & Knight, 1998, p. 651).

Furthermore, the functioning of the orbitofrontal control system in the regulation of emotion (Baker, Frith, & Dolan, 1997) and in "acquiring very specific forms of knowledge for regulating interpersonal and social behavior" (Dolan, 1999, p. 928) is central to self regulation, the ability to flexibly regulate emotional states through interactions with other humans—interactive regulation in interconnected contexts, and without other humans—autoregulation in autonomous contexts. The adaptive capacity to shift between these dual regulatory modes, depending upon the social context, emerges out of a history of secure attachment interactions of a maturing biological organism and an early attuned social environment.

ATTACHMENT THEORY IS FUNDAMENTALLY A REGULATORY THEORY

Attachment behavior is thought to be the output of "a neurobiologically based biobehavioral system that regulates biological synchronicity between organisms" (Wang, 1997, p. 168). I suggest that the characterization of the orbitofrontal system as a frontolimbic structure that regulates interpersonal and social behavior (Dolan, 1999), determines the regulatory significance of stimuli that reach the organism, and regulates body state (Luria, 1980), bears a striking resemblance to the behavioral control system characterized by Bowlby in the late 1960s. The Oxford English Dictionary defines control as "the act or power of directing or regulating."

Attachment theory, as first propounded in Bowlby's (1969) definitional volume, is fundamentally a regulatory theory. Attachment can thus be conceptualized as the interactive regulation of synchrony between psychobiologically attuned organisms. This attachment dynamic, which operates at levels beneath awareness, underlies the dyadic regulation of emotion. Emotions are the highest order direct expression of bioregulation in complex organisms (Damasio, 1998). Imprinting, the learning process associated with attachment, is described by Petrovich and Gewirtz (1985) as synchrony between sequential infant maternal stimuli and behavior (see Schore, 1994, and Nelson & Panksepp, 1998 for models of the neurochemistry of attachment).

According to Feldman, Greenbaum, and Yirmiya, "face-to-face synchrony affords infants their first opportunity to practice interpersonal coordination of biological rhythms" (1999, p. 223) and acts as an interpersonal context in which "interactants integrate into the flow of behavior the ongoing responses of their partner and the changing inputs of the environment" (p. 224). The visual, prosodic-auditory, and gestural stimuli embedded in these emotional communications are rapidly transmitted back and forth between the infant's and mother's face, and in these transactions the caregiver acts as a regulator of the child's arousal levels.

Because arousal levels are known to be associated with changes in metabolic energy, the caregiver is thus modulating changes in the child's energetic state (Schore, 1994, 1997a). These regulated increases in energy metabolism are available for biosynthetic processes in the baby's brain, which is in the brain growth spurt (Dobbing & Sands, 1973). In this manner, "the intrinsic regulators of human brain growth in a child are specifically adapted to be coupled, by emotional communication, to the regulators of adult brains" (Trevarthen 1990, p. 357).

In addition, the mother also regulates moments of asynchrony, that is, stressful negative affect. Social stressors can be characterized as the occurrence of an asynchrony in an interactional sequence (Chapple, 1970). Stress describes both the subjective experience induced by a distressing, potentially threatening, or novel situation, and the organism's reactions to a homeostatic challenge. It is now thought that social stressors are "far more detrimental" than nonsocial aversive stimuli (Sgoifo et al., 1999).

Separation stress, in essence, is a loss of maternal regulators of the infant's immature behavioral and physiological systems that results in the attachment patterns of protest, despair, and detachment. The principle that "a period of synchrony, following the period of stress, provides a 'recovery' period" (Chapple, 1970, p. 631) underlies the mechanism of interactive repair (Schore, 1994; Tronick, 1989). The primary caregiver's interactive regulation is therefore critical to the infant's maintaining positively charged as well as coping with stressful negatively charged affects. These affect regulating events are particularly impacting the organization of the early developing right hemisphere.

Bowlby's control system is located in the right hemisphere that is not only dominant for "inhibitory control" (Garavan et al., 1999), but also for the processing of facial information in infants (Deruelle & de Schonen, 1998) and adults (Kim et al., 1999), and for the regulation of arousal (Heilman & Van Den Abell, 1979). Because the major coping systems, the hypothalamo-pituitary-adrenocortical axis and the sympathetic-adrenomedullary axis, are both under the main control of the right cerebral cortex, this hemisphere contains "a unique response system preparing the organism to deal efficiently with external challenges," and so its adaptive functions mediate the human stress response (Wittling, 1997, p. 55). Basic research in stress physiology shows that the behavioral and physiological response of an individual to a specific stressor is consistent over time (Koolhaas et al., 1999).

These attachment transactions are imprinted into implicit-procedural memory as enduring internal working models, which encode coping strategies of affect regulation (Schore, 1994) that maintain basic regulation and positive affect even in the face of environmental challenge (Sroufe, 1989). Attachment patterns are now conceptualized as "patterns of mental processing of information based on cognition and affect to create models of reality" (Crittenden, 1995, p. 401). The "anterior limbic prefrontal network," which interconnects the orbital and medial prefrontal cortex with the temporal pole, cingulate, and amygdala, "is involved in affective responses to events and in the mnemonic processing and storage of these responses" (Carmichael & Price, 1995, p. 639), and "constitutes a mental control system that is essential for adjusting thinking and behavior to ongoing reality" (Schnider & Ptak, 1999, p. 680). An ultimate indicator of secure attachment is resilience in the face of stress (Greenspan, 1981), which is expressed in the capacity to flexibly regulate emotional states via autoregulation and interactive regulation. However, early social environments that engender insecure attachments inhibit the growth of this control system (Schore, 1997a) and therefore preclude its adaptive coping function in "operations linked to behavioral flexibility" (Nobre et al., 1999, p. 12).

In support of Bowlby's assertion that the child's capacity to cope with stress is correlated with certain maternal behaviors, developmental biological studies are exploring "maternal effects," the influence of the mother's experiences on her progeny's development and ability to adapt to its environment (Bernardo, 1996). This body of research indicates that "variations in maternal care can serve as the basis for a nongenomic behavioral transmission of individual differences in stress reactivity across generations" (Francis et al., 1999, p. 1155), and that "maternal care during infancy serves to 'program' behavioral responses to stress in the offspring" (Caldji et al., 1998. p. 5335).

Developmental neurobiological findings support the idea that "infants' early experiences with their mothers (or absence of these experiences) may come to influence how they respond to their own infants when they grow up" (Fleming, O'Day, & Kraemer, 1999, p. 673). I suggest that the intergenerational transmission of stress-coping deficits occurs within the context of relational environments that are growth-inhibiting to the development of regulatory corticolimbic circuits sculpted by early experiences. These attachment-related psychopathologies are thus expressed in dysregulation of social, behavioral, and biological functions that are associated with an immature frontolimbic control system and an inefficent right hemisphere (Schore, 1994; 1996; 1997a). This conceptualization bears directly upon Bowlby's (1978) assertion that attachment theory can be used to frame the early etiologies of a diverse group of psychiatric disorders and the neurophysiological changes that accompany them.

FUTURE DIRECTIONS OF ATTACHMENT RESEARCH ON REGULATORY PROCESSES

Returning to *Attachment*, Bowlby asserted, "The merits of a scientific theory are to be judged in terms of the range of phenomena it embraces, the internal consistency of its structure, the precision of the predictions it can make and the practibility of testing them" (1969, p. 173). The republication of this classic volume is occurring at a point in time, coincident with the beginning of the new millennium, when we are able to explore the neurobiological substrata on which attachment theory is based. In earlier writings I have suggested that "the primordial environment of the infant, or more properly of the commutual psychobiological environment shared by the infant and mother, represents a primal *terra incognita* of science" (Schore, 1994, p. 64). The next generation of studies of Bowlby's theoretical landscape will chart in detail how different early social environments and attachment experiences influence the unique microtopography of a developing brain.

Such studies will project an experimental searchlight upon events occurring at the common dynamic interface of brain systems that represent the psychological and biological realms. The right brain–right brain psychobiological transactions that underlie attachment processes are bodily-based, and critical to the adaptive capacities and growth of the infant. This calls for studies that concurrently measure brain, behavioral, and bodily changes in both members of the dyad. Autonomic measures of synchronous changes in the infant's and mother's bodily states need to be included in studies of attachment functions, and the development of coordinated interactions between the maturing central and autonomic nervous systems should be investigated in research on attachment structures.

It is accepted that internal working models that encode strategies of affect regulation act at levels beneath conscious awareness. In the *American Psychologist*, Bargh and Chartrand asserted that "most of moment-to-moment psychological life must occur through nonconscious means if it is to occur at all . . . various nonconscious mental systems perform the lion's share of the self-regulatory burden, beneficiently keeping the individual grounded in his or her current environment" (1999, p. 462). This characterization describes internal working models, and since their affective-cognitive components regulate the involuntary autonomic nervous system, these functions may very well be inaccessible to self-report measures that mainly tap into conscious thoughts and images.

The psychobiological mechanisms that trigger organismic responses are fast-acting and dynamic. Studying very rapid affective phenomena in real time involves attention to a different time dimension than usual, a focus on interpersonal attachment and separations on a microtemporal scale. The emphasis is less on enduring traits and more on transient dynamic states, and research methodologies will have to be created that can visualize the dyadic regulatory events occuring at the brain-mind-body interface of two subjectivities that are engaged in attachment transactions. Digital videotape recordings, analyzing split-second events in both members of an affect-transacting dyad, may be particularly suited for this purpose.

Because the human face is a central focus of these transactions, studies of right brain appraisals of visual and prosodic facial stimuli, even presented at tachistoscopic levels, may more accurately tap into the fundamental mechanisms that are involved in the processing of social-emotional information. And in light of the principle that dyadic regulatory affective communications maximize positive as well as minimize negative affect, both procedures that measure coping with negative affect (strange situtations), and those that measure coping with positive affect (play situations), need to be used to evaluate attachment capacities.

It is established that face-to-face contexts of affect synchrony not only generate positive arousal but also expose infants to high levels of social and *cognitive* information (Feldman et al., 1999). In such interpersonal contexts, including attachment-related "joint attention" transactions (Schore, 1994), the developing child is exercising early attentional capacities. There is evidence to show that "intrinsic alertness," the most basic intensity aspect of attention, is mediated by a network in the right hemisphere (Sturm et al., 1999). In light of the known impaired functioning of right frontal circuits in attention-deficit/hyperactivity disorders (Casey et al., 1997), developmental attachment studies may elucidate the early etiology of these disorders, as well as of right hemisphere learning disabilities (Gross-Tsur, Shalev, Manor, & Amir, 1995; Semrud-Clikeman & Hynd, 1990).

Furthermore, although most attachment studies refer to infants and toddlers, it is well known that the brain maturation rates of baby girls are significantly more advanced than boys. Gender differences in infant emotional regulation (Weinberg, Tronick, Cohn, & Olson, 1999) and in the orbitofrontal system that mediates this function (Overman, Bachevalier, Schuhmann, & Ryan, 1996) have been demonstrated. Studies of how different social experiences interact with different female-male regional brain growth rates could elucidate the origins of gender differences within the limbic system that are later expressed in variations of social-emotional information processing between the sexes. This research should include measures of "psychological gender" (see Schore, 1994). And in addition to maternal effects on early brain maturation, the effects of fathers, especially in the second and third years, on the female and male toddler's psychoneurobiological development can tell us more about paternal contributions to the child's expanding stress-coping capacities.

We must also more fully understand the very early pre- and postnatally maturing limbic circuits that organize what Bowlby calls the "building blocks" of attachment experiences (see Schore, 2000b, 2001a). Bowlby (1969) referred to a succession of increasingly sophisticated systems of limbic structures that are involved in attachment. Since attachment is the outcome of the child's genetically encoded biological (temperamental) predisposition *and* the particular caregiver environment, we need to know more about the mechanisms of gene-environment interactions. This work could elucidate the nature of the expression of particular genes in specific brain regions that regulate stress reactivity, as well as a deeper knowledge of the dynamic components of "non-shared" environmental factors (Plomin, Rende, & Rutter, 1991). It shoud be remembered that DNA levels in the cortex significantly increase over the first year, the period of attachment (Winick, Rosso, & Waterlow, 1970).

A very recent report of an association between perinatal complications (deviations of normal pregnancy, labor-delivery, and early neonatal development) and later signs of specifically orbitofrontal dysfunction (Kinney, Steingard, Renshaw, & Yurgelun-Todd, 2000) may elucidate the mechanism by which an interaction of a vulnerable genetically-encoded psychobiological predisposition interacts with a misattuned relational environment to produce a high-risk scenario for future disorders. Orbitofrontal dysfunction in infancy has also been implicated in a later appearing impairment of not only social but moral behavior (Anderson, Bechara, Damasio, Trahel, & Damasio, 1999).

Furthermore, developmental neuroscientific studies of the effects of attuned and misattuned parental environments will reveal the subtle but important differences in brain organization among securely and insecurely attached individuals, as well as the psychobiological mechanisms that mediate resilience to or risk for later-forming psychopathologies. Neurobiological studies now indicate that although the right prefrontal system is necessary to mount a normal stress response, extreme alterations of such activity are maladaptive (Sullivan & Gratton, 1999). In line with the association of attachment experiences and the development of brain systems for coping with relational stress, future studies need to explore the relationship between different adaptive and maladaptive coping styles of various attachment categories and correlated deficits in brain systems involved in stress regulation. Subjects, classified on the Adult Attachment Inventory (Hesse, 1999), could be exposed to a real-life, personally meaningful stressor, and brain imaging and autonomic measures could then evaluate the individual's adaptive or maladaptive regulatory mechanisms. Such studies can also elucidate the mechanisms of the intergenerational transmission of the regulatory deficits of different classes of psychiatric disorders (see Schore, 1994, 1996, 1997a).

In light of the fact that the right hemisphere subsequently reenters into growth spurts (Thatcher, 1994) and ultimately forms an interactive system with the later maturing left (Schore, 1994, 2002a; Siegel, 1999), neurobiological reorganizations of the attachment system and their functional correlates in ensuing stages of childhood and adulthood need to be explored. Psychoneurobiological research of the continuing experience-dependent maturation of the right hemisphere could elucidate the underlying mechanisms by which certain attachment patterns can change from "insecurity" to "earned security" (Phelps, Belsky, & Crnic, 1998).

The documented findings that the orbitofrontal system is involved in "emotion-related learning" (Rolls, Hornak, Wade, & McGrath, 1994) and that it retains plasticity throughout later periods of life (Barbas, 1995) may also help us understand how developmentally based, affectively focused psychotherapy can alter early attachment patterns. A functional magnetic resonance imaging study by Hariri, Bookheimer, and Mazziotta provided evidence that higher regions of specifically the right prefrontal cortex attenuate emotional responses at the most basic levels in the brain, that such modulating processes are "fundamental to most modern psychotherapeutic methods" (2000, p. 43), that this lateralized neocortical network is active in "modulating emotional experience through interpreting and labeling emotional expressions" (p. 47), and that "this form of modulation may be impaired in various emotional disorders and may provide the basis for therapies of these same disorders" (p. 48). This process is a central component of therapeutic narrative organization, of turning "raw feelings into symbols" (Holmes, 1993, p. 150). This "neocortical network," which "modulates the limbic system" is identical to the right-lateralized orbitofrontal system that regulates attachment dynamics. Attachment models of mother-infant psychobiological attunement may thus be used to explore the origins of empathic processes in both development and psychotherapy, and reveal the deeper mechanisms of the growth-facilitating factors operating within the therapeutic alliance (see Schore, 1994, 1997c, 2002a).

In a sense these deeper explorations into the roots of the human experience have been waiting for not just theoretical advances in developmental neurobiology and technical improvements in methodologies that can noninvasively image developing brain-mind-body processes in real time, but also for a perspective of brain-mind-body development that can bridge psychology and biology. Such interdisciplinary models can shift back and forth between different levels of organization in order to accomodate heuristic conceptions of how the primordial experiences with the external social world alters the ontogeny of internal structural systems. Ultimately, these psychoneurobiological attachment models can be used as a scientific basis for creating even more effective early-prevention programs.

In her concluding comments of a recent overview of the field, Mary Main, a central figure in the continuing development of attachment theory, writes "We are currently at one of the most exciting junctures in the history of our field. We are now, or will soon be, in a position to begin mapping the relations between individual differences in early attachment experiences and changes in neurochemistry and brain organization. In addition, investigation of physiological 'regulators' associated with infant-caregiver interactions could have far-reaching implications for both clinical assessment and intervention" (1999, pp. 881–882).

But I leave the final word to Bowlby himself, who in the last paragraph of his seminal book (1969), sums up the meaning of his work:

> The truth is that the least-studied phase of human development remains the phase during which a child is acquiring all that makes him most distinctively human. Here is still a continent to conquer.

2000

CHAPTER 4

Parent-Infant Communications
and the Neurobiology of
Emotional Development

A T THIS POINT IN TIME, although "the decade of the brain" has ended, it is clear that we are in the midst of a remarkable period in which dramatic new brain technologies continue to concentrate on certain basic problems of human psychology. And so, brain imaging studies are giving us a more comprehensive picture of how the mature brain performs it essential function — detecting changes in both the environment and in the body, so that internal alterations can also be made in order to adapt to different contexts. This research can do more than just detail the physical structure of the brain, it can also delve directly into how changes in brain structural organization are associated with various normal and abnormal functional states, thereby linking biological and psychological models of the brain/mind/body.

It is undoubtedly true that by far the greatest amount of current research is on the adult rather then the developing brain, and most of it is not on normal but abnormal brain function. Even so, neuroscience is becoming very interested in the early development of the brain. And so neurobiology is exploring "early beginnings for adult brain pathology" (Altman, 1997, p. 143) and describing "alteration[s] in the functional organization of the human brain which can be correlated with the absence of early learning experiences" (Castro-Caldas, Petersson, Reis, Stone-Elander, & Ingvar, 1998, p. 1060). But this same time period of expansion of developmental neuroscience has also seen an explosion of interdisciplinary infant research, as developmental studies are now actively exploring not just the origins of cognitive, language, and sensory motor functions, but also the early development of social and emotional processes.

The question of why the early events of life have such an inordinate influence on literally everything that follows is one of the fundamental problems of science. How do early experiences, especially emotionally charged attachment experiences with other humans, induce and organize the patterns of structural growth that result in the expanding functional capacities of a developing individual? Using an arsenal of different methodologies and studying different levels of analysis, investigators are inquiring into the fundamental mechanisms that underlie developmental processes. We know that the concept of "early experiences" connotes much more than an immature individual being a passive recipient of environmental stimulation. Rather, these events represent active transactions between the infant and the early environment. The most important aspect of the environment is the social environment, the relationship the infant has with its caregivers.

Development is "transactional," and is represented as a continuing dialectic between the maturing organism and the changing environment. This dialectic is embedded in the infant-maternal relationship, and emotion (affect) is what is transacted in these interactions. This very efficient system of emotional exchanges is entirely nonverbal, and it continues throughout life as the intuitively felt affective communications that occur within intimate relationships. Human development cannot be understood apart from this affect-transacting relationship. Indeed, it appears that the development of the capacity to experience, communicate, and regulate emotions may be the key event of human infancy.

Neuroscientists and developmental psychologists are converging on the common principle that "the best description of development may come from a careful appreciation of the brain's own self-organizing operations" (Cicchetti & Tucker, 1994, p. 544). There is widespread agreement that the brain is a self-organizing system, but there is perhaps less of an appreciation of the fact that "the self-organization of the developing brain occurs in the context of a relationship with another self, another brain" (Schore, 1996, p. 60). This relationship is between the developing infant and the social environment, and is mediated by affective communications and psychobiological transactions.

Furthermore, these early socioemotional events are imprinted into the biological structures that are maturing during the brain growth spurt that occurs in the first two years of human life, and therefore have far-reaching and long-enduring effects. The stupendous growth rate of brain structure in the first year of life is reflected in the increase of weight from 400g at birth to over 1000g at 12 months. The human brain growth spurt, which begins in the last trimester and is at least 83% postnatal, continues to about 18 to 24 months of age (Dobbing & Sands, 1973). Furthermore, interactive experiences directly impact genetic systems that program brain growth. DNA production in the cortex increases dramatically over the course of the first year (see Schore, 1994). We know that the genetic specification of neuronal structure is not sufficient for an optimally functional nervous system — the environment also has a powerful effect on the structure of the brain.

Thus, current models hold that development represents an experiential shaping of genetic potential, and that genetically programmed "innate" stuctural systems require particular forms of environmental input.

> The traditional assumption was that the environment determines only the
> psychological residuals of development, such as memories and habits,

while brain anatomy matures on its fixed ontogenetic calendar. Environmental experience is now recognized to be critical to the differentiation of brain tissue itself. Nature's potential can be realized only as it is enabled by nurture. (Cicchetti & Tucker, 1994, p. 538)

Neurobiology has established that the infant brain "is designed to be molded by the environment it encounters" (Thomas et al., 1997, p. 209). The brain is thought of as a "bioenvironmental" or "biosocial" organ (Gibson, 1996), and investigators are exploring the unique domains of the "social brain" (Brothers, 1990) and are speaking of "the social construction of the human brain" (Eisenberg, 1995). It is known that the accelerated growth of brain structure occurs during "critical periods" of infancy, is "experience-dependent," and is influenced by "social forces." Neuroscience is, however, unclear as to the nature of these "social forces." In fact, developmental psychology has much to say about the "social forces" that influence the organization of the baby's brain. The brain growth spurt exactly overlaps the period of attachment so intensely studied by contemporary researchers (Schore, 1998c, 1998d, 1998e, 1999b). And so it is thought that

within limits, during normal development a biologically different brain may be formed given the mutual influence of maturation of the infant's nervous system and the mothering repertory of the caregiver. (Connelly & Prechtl, 1981, p. 212)

My work integrates developmental psychology and infant psychiatry with neuroscience in order to formulate models of normal and abnormal emotional development. "The beginnings of living systems set the stage for every aspect of an organism's internal and external functioning throughout the lifespan" (Schore, 1994, p. 3). The central thesis of my ongoing work is that the early social environment, mediated by the primary caregiver, directly influences the final wiring of the circuits in the infant's brain that are responsible for the future socioemotional development of the individual. The "experience" that is required for the "experience-dependent" growth of the brain in the first two years of human life is specifically the social-emotional experiences embedded in the attachment relationship between the infant and the mother. Attachment is thus the outcome of the child's genetically encoded biological (temperamental) predisposition *and* the particular caregiver environment.

Since *Affect Regulation and the Origin of the Self* (1994) I have expanded this psychoneurobiological model and continue to cite a growing body of interdisciplinary studies, which suggest that these interpersonal affective experiences have a critical effect on, specifically, the early organization of the limbic system (Schore, 1994, 1996, 1997a, 1998a, 1999a, 2001a, 2001c), the brain areas specialized for not only the processing of emotion but for the organization of new learning and the capacity to adapt to a rapidly changing environment (Mesulam, 1998). The emotion-processing limbic system is expanded in the right brain (Tucker, 1992; Joseph, 1996), or what neuroscientist Ornstein (1997) called "the right mind." Most importantly, this right hemisphere, the neurobiological substrate of the emotional brain, is in a growth spurt in the first year and a half (see Figure 4.1) and dominant for the first three years of human life (Chiron et al., 1997).

According to attachment theory, the dominant theory of emotional development in international developmental psychology, the limbic system is the site of developmental changes associated with the rise of attachment behaviors (Schore, 1994, 2000a). But this theory also proposes that the mother directly influences the maturation of the infant's emerging coping capacities. In a number of writngs I offered evidence that attachment experiences specifically influence the experience-dependent maturation of the infant's right hemisphere (Schore, 1994, 1997a, 2000b, 2001a, 2001c, 2001d). The right brain acts "a unique response system preparing the organism to deal efficiently with external challenges and so" (Wittling, 1997, p. 55), and so its adaptive functions mediate the stress coping mechanisms. This psychoneurobiological conception thus highlights the critical role of attachment experiences in the development of life-long coping capacities. The finding that the right hemisphere is dominant in human infants, and indeed, for the first three years of life, thus has significant implications for Head Start, and particularly Early Head Start.

In this chapter, I will present an overview of recent psychological studies of the social-emotional development of infants and neurobiological research on the maturation of the early developing right brain. I want to focus on the structure-function relationships of an event in early infancy that is central to human emotional development—the organization, in the first year, of an attachment bond of interactively regulated affective communication between the primary caregiver and the infant. These experiences culminate, at the end of the second year, in the maturation of a regulatory system in the right hemisphere. The

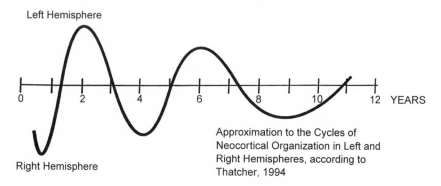

FIGURE 4.1. Hemispheric brain growth cycles continue asymmetrically throughout childhood, showing early growth spurt of the right hemisphere. (Trevarthen 1996, adapted from Thatcher, 1994)

failure of the dyad to create this system in the first two years is a developmental risk factor. These models are offered as heuristic proposals that can be evaluated by experimental and clinical research.

ATTACHMENT PROCESSES AND
EMOTIONAL COMMUNICATIONS

As soon as the child is born it uses its maturing sensory capacities, especially smell, taste, and touch, to interact with the social environment. But by the end of the second month, with the myelination of occipital areas involved in the visual perception of a human face, there is a dramatic progression of its social and emotional capacities. In particular, the mother's emotionally expressive face is, by far, the most potent visual stimulus in the infant's environment, and the child's intense interest in her face, especially in her eyes, leads him to track it in space, and to engage in periods of intense mutual gaze. The infant's gaze, in turn, evokes the mother's gaze, thereby acting as a potent interpersonal channel for the transmission of "reciprocal mutual influences." It has been observed that the pupil of the eye acts as a nonverbal communication device and that large pupils in the infant release caregiver behavior (Hess, 1975).

Face-to-face interactions begin at about two months, in the first context of social play, and they are patterned by an infant-leads-mother-follows sequence. These are "highly arousing, affect-laden, short interpersonal events that expose infants to high levels of cognitive and social information. To regulate the high positive arousal, mothers and infants . . . synchronize the intensity of their affective behavior within lags of split seconds" (Feldman, Greenbaum, & Yirmiya, 1999, p. 223). These authors observe that such experiences afford infants "their first opportunity to practice interpersonal coordination of biological rhythms, to experience the mutual regulation of positive arousal, and to build the lead-lag structure of adult communication" (p. 223).

A frame-by-frame analysis shows that this moment-to-moment state sharing represents an organized dialog occurring within milliseconds. In contexts of "mutually attuned selective cueing," the infant learns to send specific social cues to which the mother has responded, thereby reflecting "an anticipatory sense of response of the other to the self, concomitant with an accommodation of the self to the other" (Bergman, 1999, p. 96). Thus the best description of this exchange is "affect synchrony." According to Lester, Hoffman, and Brazelton, "synchrony develops as a consequence of each partner's learning the rhythmic structure of the other and modifying his or her behavior to fit that structure" (1985, p. 24).

This microregulation continues, as soon after the "heightened affective moment" of an intensely joyful full gape smile, the baby will gaze avert in order to regulate the potentially disorganizing effect of this intensifying emotion. In order to maintain the positive emotion the attuned mother takes her cue and backs off to reduce her stimulation. She then waits for the baby's signals for reengagement. In this way, not only the tempo of their engagement but also their disengagement and reengagement is coordinated. In this process of "contingent responsivity" the more the mother tunes her activity level to the infant during periods of social engagement, the more she allows him to recover quietly in periods of disengagement, and the more she attends to the child's reinitiating cues for reengagement, the more synchronized their interaction. The psychobiologically attuned caregiver thus facilitates the infant's information processing by adjusting the mode, amount, variability, and timing of the onset and offset of stimulation to the infant's actual integrative capacities. These mutually attuned synchronized interactions are fundamental to the healthy affective development of the infant.

Furthermore, in the visual and auditory emotional communications embedded within synchronized face-to-face transactions both members of the dyad experience a state transition as they move together from low arousal to a heightened energetic state of high arousal, a shift from quiet alertness into an intensely positive affective state. In physics, a property of resonance is sympathetic vibration, which is the tendency of one resonance system to enlarge and augment through matching the resonance frequency pattern of another resonance system. It is well established that the transfer of emotional information is intensified in resonant contexts, and that at the moment when a system is tuned at the "resonant" frequency it becomes synchronized. Such energy-infused moments allow for a sense of vitalization, and thereby increased complexity and coherence of organization within the infant (Schore, 1997a, 2000b).

Resonances often have chaos associated with them, and thus they are characterized by nonlinear dynamic factors — relatively small input amplitudes engender a response with a surprisingly large output amplitude. This amplification especially occurs when external sensory stimulation frequency coincides with the organism's own endogenous rhythms. The British pediatrician-psychoanalyst Winnicott (1971b) described the infant's expression of a "spontaneous gesture," a somatopsychic expression of the burgeoning "true self," and the attuned mother's "giving back to the baby the baby's own self."

In other words, when a psychobiologically attuned dyad cocreates a resonant context within an attachment transaction, the behavioral manifestation of each partner's internal state is monitored by the other, and this results in the coupling between the output of one partner's loop and the input of the other's to form a larger feedback configuration and an amplification of the positive state in both. Infant researchers refer to the delight the infant displays in reaction to the augmenting effects of his mother's playful, empathically attuned behavior, her mulitmodal sensory amplification, and resonance with the child's feelings. Stern (1985, p.53) described a particular maternal social behavior which can "blast the infant into the next orbit of positive excitation," and generate "vitality affects." In these transactions the dyad is cocreating "mutual regulatory systems of arousal."

In this system of nonverbal emotional communcation the infant and mother cocreate a context which allows for the outward expression of internal affective states in infants. In order to enter into this communication, the mother must be psychobiologically attuned not so much to the child's overt behavior as to the dynamic crescendos and decescendos of his internal states of arousal. She also must monitor her own internal signals and differentiate her own affective state, as well as modulating nonoptimal high levels of stimulation which would induce supraheightened levels of arousal in the infant. The burgeoning capacity of the infant to experience increasing levels of accelerating, rewarding affects is thus at this stage amplified and externally regulated by the psychobiologically attuned mother, and depends upon her capacity to engage in an interactive emotion-communicating mechanism that generates these in herself and her child.

But the primary caregiver is not always attuned — developmental research shows frequent moments of misattunement in the dyad, ruptures of the attachment bond. Although short-term dysregulations are not problematic, prolonged negative states are toxic for infants, and although they possess some capacity to modulate low-intensity negative affect states, these states continue to escalate in intensity, frequency, and duration. In early development an adult provides much of the necessary modulation of infant states, especially after a state disruption and across a transition between states, and this allows for the development of self regulation.

Studies of interactive attunement following dyadic misattunement, of "interactive repair," support a conception of the mother's "holding" or "containing" function as the capacity to "stay with" the child through its emotional/impulsive expressions, "to hold the situation in time." In this pattern of "disruption and repair" (Beebe & Lachmann, 1994), the "good enough" caregiver who induces a stress response in her infant through a misattunement, reinvokes in a timely fashion a reattunement, a regulation of the infant's negative state. If attachment is interactive synchrony, stress is defined as an *asynchrony* in an interactional sequence, and, following this, a period of reestablished *synchrony* allows for stress recovery. The mother and infant thus dyadically negotiate a stressful state transition. Infant resilience emerges from the child and parent's transitioning from positive to negative and back to positive affect. Again, the key is the caregiver's capacity to monitor and regulate her own arousal levels.

These arousal-regulating transactions, which continue throughout the first year, underlie the formation of an attachment bond between the infant and primary caregiver. An essential attachment function is "to promote the synchrony or regulation of biological and behavioral systems on an organismic level" (Reite & Capitanio, 1985, p. 235). Indeed, psychobiological attunement, interactive resonance, and the mutual synchronization and entrainment of physiological rhythms are fundamental processes that mediates attachment bond formation, and attachment can be defined as the interactive regulation of biological synchronicity between organisms. (Schore, 1994, 2000a, 2000c, 2001a, 2001d)

To put this another way, in forming an attachment bond of somatically expressed emotional communications, the mother is synchronizing and resonating with the rhythms of the infant's dynamic internal states and then regulating the arousal level of these negative and positive states. Attachment is thus the dyadic (interactive) regulation of emotion (Sroufe, 1996). The baby becomes attached to the psychobiologically attuned regulating primary caregiver who not only minimizes negative affect but also maximizes opportunties for positive affect.

These data underscore an essential principle overlooked by many emotion theorists — affect regulation is not just the reduction of affective intensity, the dampening of negative emotion. It also involves an amplification, an intensification of positive emotion, a condition necessary for more complex self-organization. Attachment is not just the reestablishment of security after a dysregulating experience and a stressful negative state; it is also the interactive amplification of positive affects, as in play states. Regulated affective interactions with a familiar, predictable primary caregiver create not only a sense of safety, but also a positively charged curiosity that fuels the burgeoning self's exploration of novel socioemotional and physical environments.

THE NEUROBIOLOGY AND
PSYCHOBIOLOGY OF ATTACHMENT

According to Ainsworth, attachment is more than overt; behavior; it is "built into the nervous system, in the course and as a result of the infant's experience of his transactions with the mother" (1967, p. 429). This brings us to another level of analysis — the neurobiological level. In this transfer of affect between mother and infant, how are developing brain systems influenced by these interactions with the social environment?

Trevarthen's work on maternal-infant protoconversations bears directly on this problem. Coordinated with eye-to-eye messages are auditory vocalizations (tone of voice, Motherese) as a channel of communication, and tactile and body gestures. A traffic of visual and prosodic auditory signals induce instant emotional effects, namely the positive affects of excitement and pleasure build within the dyad. But Trevarthen also focused on internal structure-function events, stating that "the intrinsic regulators of human brain growth in a child are specifically adapted to be coupled, by emotional communication, to the regulators of adult brains" (Trevarthen, 1990, p. 357).

According to Trevarthen (1993), the resonance of the dyad ultimately permits the intercoordination of positive affective brain states. His work underscored the fundamental principle that the baby's brain is not only affected by these transactions, but also that it's growth literally requires brain-brain interaction and occurs in the context of an intimate positive affective relationship between mother and infant. This interactive mechanism requires older brains to engage with mental states of awareness, emotion, and interest in younger brains, and involves a coordination between the motivations of the infant and the subjective feelings of adults. These findings support Emde's idea that "It is the emotional availability of the caregiver in intimacy which seems to be the most central growth-promoting feature of the early rearing experience" (1988, p. 32).

There is a consensus that interactions with the environment during critical periods are necessary for the brain as a whole to mature. But we know that different regions of the brain mature at different times. Can we tell what specific parts of the growing brain are affected by these emotion-transacting events? It is now thought that "The emotional experience of the infant develops through the sounds, images, and pictures that constitute much of an infant's early learning experience, and are disproportionately stored or processed in the right hemisphere during the formative stages of brain ontogeny" (Semrud-Clikeman & Hynd, 1990, p. 198). With regard to the unique nature of this memory store, it has been pointed out that "the infant relies primarily on its procedural memory systems" during "the first 2–3 years of life" (Kandel, 1999, p. 513). Recall the right hemsphere is dominant for the first three years.

These emotionally charged, psychobiologically attuned face-to-face interactions occur in the context of mother-infant play, and they increase over the second and third quarters of the first year. The learning mechanism of attachment, imprinting, is defined as *synchrony* between sequential infant-maternal stimuli and behavior (Petrovich & Gewirtz, 1985). I suggest that in these interactive regulatory transactions the infant's right hemisphere, which is dominant for the infant's recognition of the maternal face, and for the perception of arousal-inducing maternal facial affective expressions, visual emotional information, and the prosody of the mother's voice, is synchronizing with and thereby regulated by the output of the mother's right hemisphere, which is dominant for nonverbal communication, the processing of emotional information, the expression of spontaneous gestures, and the maternal capacity to comfort the infant.

In these transactions the attuned caregiver is "downloading programs" into the infant's brain by an optimal "chunking" of bits of sociaffective stimulation that the child's developing right hemispheric socioaffective information processing system can efficiently process and store in memory. In particular, as a result of attachment experiences the infant develops a representation of the mother, especially her face. We know that the infant's memory representation includes not only details of the learning cues of events in the external environment (especially those from a face), but also of reactions in his internal arousal state to changes in the external environment. These attachment experiences are imprinted into the early imagistic, visceral, and nonverbal implicit-procedural memory system of the right brain (Henry, 1993; Schore, 1994, 2000c; Siegel, 1999).

Furthermore, Tronick and his colleagues (1998) have described how micro-regulatory social-emotional processes of communication generate expanded intersubjective states of consciousness in the infant-mother dyad. In such there is "a mutual mapping of (some of) the elements of each interactant's state of consciousness into each of their brains" (Tronick & Weinberg, 1997, p. 75). Tronick argued that the infant's self-organizing system, when coupled with the mother's, allows for a brain organization that can be expanded into more coherent and complex states of consciousness. I suggest that Tronick was describing an expansion of what neuroscientist Edelman (1989) called primary consciousness, which relates visceral and emotional information pertaining to the biological self, to stored information processing pertaining to outside reality. Edelman lateralized primary consciousness to the right brain.

In light of research showing the involvement of the right hemisphere in attentional processes (e.g., Sturm et al., 1999), interactive experiences of "joint attention" may act as a growth-facilitating environment for the experience-dependent maturation of right hemispheric attentional capacities (Schore, 2000a, 2001a, 2001c). Notice that during the heightened affective moment the child's attention is riveted on the mother's face. But this hemisphere is also concerned with the analysis of direct information received from the body. Thus, in attachment transactions the child is using the output of the mother's right cortex as a template for the imprinting, the hard wiring of circuits in his own right cortex that will come to mediate his expanding cognitive-affective capacities to adaptively attend to, appraise, and regulate variations in both external and internal information. In support of this, Ryan and his colleagues, using EEG and neuroimaging data, reported that the "positive emotional exchange resulting from autonomy-supportive parenting involves participation of right hemispheric cortical and subcortical systems that participate in global, tonic emotional modulation" (1997, p. 719).

It is important to note that these dyadically synchronized affectively charged transactions elicit high levels of metabolic energy for the tuning of developing right-brain circuits involved in processing socioemotional information. An article in *Science* suggested "mothers invest extra energy in their young to promote larger brains" (Gibbons, 1998, p. 1346). In terms of self-organization theory, the mutual entrainment of their right brains during moments of affect synchrony triggers an amplified energy flow, which allows for a coherence of organization that sustains more complex states within both the infant's and the mother's right brains. In fact, evidence indicates that the organization of the mother's brain is also being influenced by these relational transactions. A study of early mammalian mother-infant interactions (Kinsley et al., 1999), reports increased dendritic growth in the mother's brain.

Interactive transactions, in addition to producing neurobiological consequences, are also generating important events in the infant's bodily state, that is, at the psychobiological level. Winnicott proposed that the "main thing is a communication between the baby and mother in terms of the anatomy and physiology of live bodies" (1986, p. 258). Developmental psychobiological research is revealing that when the dyad is in the mutually regulating "symbiotic" state, the adult's and infant's individual homeostatic systems are linked together in a superordinate organization which allows for mutual regulation of vital endocrine, autonomic, and central nervous systems of both mother and infant by elements of their interaction with each other. Psychobiologists emphasize the importance of "hidden" regulatory processes by which the caregiver's more mature and differentiated nervous system regulates the infant's "open," immature, internal homeostatic systems (Hofer, 1990).

These body-to-body communications also involve right-brain-to-right-brain interactions. Indeed, most human females cradle their infants on the left side of the body (controlled by the right hemisphere). This tendency is well developed in women but not in men, is independent of handedness, and is widespread in all cultures (Manning et al., 1997). Manning and colleagues suggested that this left-cradling tendency "facilitates the flow of affective information from the infant via the left ear and eye to the center for emotional decoding, that is, the right hemisphere of the mother" (p. 327). As Damasio (1994) indicated, this hemisphere contains the most comprehensive and integrated map of the body state available to the brain. Lieberman wrote that current models of development focus almost exclusively on cognition. In an article in the *Infant Mental Health Journal* she stated, "The baby's body, with its pleasures and struggles, has been largely missing from this picture" (1996, p. 289).

Even more specifically, psychobiological studies of attachment, the interactive regulation of biological synchronicity between organisms, indicate that the intimate contact between the mother and her infant is regulated by the reciprocal activation of their opiate systems—elevated levels of opiates (beta endorphins) increase pleasure in both (Kalin, Shelton, & Lynn, 1995). In these mutual-gaze transactions, the mother's face is also inducing the production of not only endogenous opiates but also regulated levels of dopamine in the infant's brain, which generates high levels of arousal and elation. The expanding attachment mechanism thus sustains increased regulated, synchronized, positive arousal in play episodes, and in them, the mother, in a state of excitement, is also stimulating regulated levels of corticotropin-releasing factor in the infant brain, which in turn increases ACTH, noradrenaline, adrenaline activity in the child's sympathetic nervous system (Schore, 1994, 1996, 2001a).

And in her soothing and calming functions, the mother is also regulating the child's oxytocin levels. It has been suggested that oxytocin, a vagally-controlled hormone with antistress effects, is released by "sensory stimuli such as tone of voice and facial expression conveying warmth and familiarity" (Uvnas-Moberg, 1997, p. 42). In regulating the infant's vagal tone and cortisol level, activities regulated by the right brain, she's also influencing the ongoing development of the infant's postnatally maturing parasympathetic nervous system. The sympathetic and parasympathetic components of the autonomic nervous system, important elements of the affect-transacting attachment mechanism, are centrally involved in the child's developing coping capacities.

ORGANIZATION OF A REGULATORY
SYSTEM IN THE RIGHT BRAIN

Attachment is "the apex of dyadic emotional regulation, a culmination of all development in the first year and a harbinger of the self regulation that is to come" (Sroufe, 1996, p. 172). A psychoneurobiological perspective suggests that the infant's emerging social, psychological, and biological capacities cannot be understood apart from its relationship with the mother. This is due to the fact that the maturation of the infant's right brain is experience-dependent, and that this experience is embedded in the affect-regulating transactions between the mother's right brain and the infant's right brain. This hemisphere contains the major regulatory systems of the brain (Schore, 1994, 1997a, 2000c, 2001a).

What are the unique functional capacities of this nondominant, nonverbal right hemisphere? Right cortical areas contain a "nonverbal affect lexicon," a vocabulary for nonverbal affective signals such as facial expressions, prosody (the emotional tone of the voice), and gestures (Bowers et al., 1993). Neuroimaging studies show that the right hemisphere is faster than the left in performing valence-dependent, automatic, preattentive appraisals of emotional facial expressions (Pizzagalli et al., 1999). But in addition, the representation of visceral and somatic states and body sense is under primary control of the nondominant hemisphere (Schore, 1998a).

Indeed, the right cortical hemisphere, more so than the left, contains extensive reciprocal connections with limbic and subcortical regions, and so it is dominant for the processing and expression of emotional information (Schore, 1994). Authors are referring to a "rostral limbic system," a hierarchical sequence of interconnected limbic areas in orbitofrontal, insular cortex, anterior cingulate, and amygdala (Devinsky, Morrell, & Vogt, 1995), and an "anterior limbic prefrontal network" interconnecting the orbital and medial prefrontal cortex with the temporal pole, cingulate, and amygdala (Carmichael & Price, 1995). These right limbic circuits allow for cortically processed information concerning the external environment (such as visual and auditory stimuli emanating from the emotional face of an attachment object) to be integrated with subcortically processed information regarding the internal visceral environment (such as concurrent changes in the bodily self state). This relaying of sensory information into the limbic system allows incoming social information to be associated with motivational and emotional states.

A growing body of work reveals that the right hemisphere is also more deeply connected into the ANS and that right hemisphere control exists over both parasympathetic and sympathetic responses, the somatic components of all emotional states (Spence et al., 1996). There is data to show that the hypothalamus, the head ganglion of the ANS, is right-lateralized (Kalogeras et al., 1996). The hypothalamic nuclei are considerably larger on the right side of the human brain (Sowell & Jernigan, 1998), and the right hemisphere is dominant for the production of corticotropin-releasing factor and cortisol (Wittling & Pfluger, 1990), the neurohormones that that mediate coping responses. For the rest of the life span the right brain plays a superior role in the regulation of physiological and endocrinological functions whose primary control centers are located in subcortical regions of the brain. The connections between the higher centers of this hemisphere and the hypothalamus are forged in infancy.

Because both the hypothalamo-pituitary-adrenocortical axis and the sympathetic-adrenomedullary axis that mediate the brain's coping mechanisms are under the control of the right cerebral cortex, the adaptive functions of this hemisphere mediate the human stress response (Wittling, 1997). It therefore is centrally involved in the vital functions that support survival and enable the organism to cope actively and passively with stress (Wittling & Schweiger, 1993). The attachment relationship thus directly shapes the maturation of the infant's right-brain stress-coping systems that act at levels beneath awareness.

The right hemisphere contains an affective-configurational representational system, one that encodes self-and-object images unique from the lexical-semantic mode of the left. It stores an internal working model of the attachment relationship that determines the individual's characteristic approach to affect regulation. In the securely attached individual, this representation encodes an expectation that homeostatic disruptions will be set right, allowing the child to self-regulate functions which previously required the caregiver's external regulation. For the rest of the life span these unconscious internal working models are used as guides for future action.

In the *American Psychologist*, Bargh and Chartrand (1999) asserted,

> most of moment-to-moment psychological life must occur through nonconscious means if it is to occur at all . . . various nonconscious mental systems perform the lion's share of the self-regulatory burden, beneficiently keeping the individual grounded in his or her current environment. (p. 462)

These regulatory systems are not innate, but a product of the attachment experience–dependent maturation of the right brain. Since the right hemisphere is centrally involved in the unconscious processing of emotional stimuli (Morris, Ohman, & Dolan, 1998; Wexler et al., 1992), and in implicit (procedural) learning (Hugdahl, 1995), this unconscious model is stored in right-cerebral implicit-procedural memory. A body of studies reveal that the right hemisphere, "the right mind," is the substrate of affectively-laden autobiographical memory (Fink et al., 1996).

Implicit learning is also a major mechanism for the incorporation of cultural learning, a process that initiates in infancy. Tucker asserted that social interaction, which promotes brain differentiation, is the mechanism for teaching "the epigenetic patterns of culture," and that successful social development requires a high degree of skill in negotiating emotional communication, "much of which is nonverbal" (1992, p. 122). Tucker concluded that such culturally transmitted social-emotional information engages specialized neural systems within the right hemisphere. I suggest that socialization is essential not only for advances in emotional-motivational development but also for expansion of the self. Recent neuropsychological studies conclude that self-related material is processed in the right hemisphere (Keenan et al., 1999).

Furthermore, the activity of this nondominant hemisphere, and not the later, maturing dominant verbal-linguistic left, is instrumental to the perception of the emotional states of other selves, that is, for empathy (Schore, 1994, 1996, 1999a, 2000c). Findings in neuroscience suggest that the right hemispheric biologically-based spontaneous emotional communications that occur within intimate interactions represent a "conversation between limbic systems" (Buck, 1994, p. 266) and that "while the left hemisphere mediates most linguistic behaviors, the right hemisphere is important for broader aspects of communication" (Van Lancker & Cummings, 1999, p. 95).

The right brain contains a circuit of emotion regulation that is involved in intense emotional-homeostatic processes (Porges et al., 1994), and in the modulation of not only the biologically primitive negative emotions such as rage, fear, terror, disgust, shame, and hopeless despair, but also intensely positive emotions such as excitement and joy (Schore, 1994, 1996, 1997a, 1999a). Neuroimaging studies show that the right hemisphere is particularly responsive to not only the positive aspects of touch, smell (Francis et al., 1999), music (Blood et al., 1999), facial expressions (Blair et al., 1999), and visual stimuli (Muller, Keil, Gruber, & Elbert, 1999), but also for the negative emotional/ motivational aspects of pain (Hari, Portin, Kettenmann, Jousmaki, & Kobal, 1997; Hsieh, Belfrage, Stone-Elander, Hansson, & Ingvar, 1995).

In securely attached individuals the highest levels of the right brain, the right orbitofrontal cortex (Schore, 1994; 1998a, 2001a, 2001c) acts as a recovery mechanism that efficiently monitors and autoregulates the duration, frequency, and intensity of not only positive but negative affect states. It's coping functions are most observable in contexts of uncertainty, in moments of emotional stress (Elliott, Dolan, & Frith, 2000). In a recent entire issue of *Cerebral Cortex* on "The mysterious orbitofrontal cortex," the editors conclude that "the orbitofrontal cortex is involved in critical human functions, such as social adjustment and the control of mood, drive and responsibility, traits that are crucial in defining the 'personality' of an individual" (Cavada & Schultz, 2000, p. 205). This right-lateralized self-system matures in the middle of the second year. The regulatory core of the self is thus nonverbal and unconscious.

The functioning of the "self-correcting" right hemispheric system is central to self-regulation, the ability to flexibly regulate emotional states through interactions with other humans (interactive regulation in interdependent, interconnected contexts), and without other humans — autoregulation in independent, autonomous contexts. The earliest cultural learning experiences, affective transactions in infancy, may influence the balance of these two modes within different cultures. On an individual basis, however, the adaptive capacity to shift between these dual regulatory modes, depending upon the social context, emerges out of a history of secure attachment interactions of a maturing biological organism and an early attuned social environment. Researchers are concluding that "The attempt to regulate affect — to minimize unpleasant feelings and to maximize pleasant ones — is the driving force in human motivation" (Westen, 1997, p. 542).

In closing, I want to point out that I have described an optimal developmental scenario, one that facilitates the experience-dependent growth of an efficient regulatory system in the right hemisphere that supports functions associated with a secure attachment. On the other hand, growth-inhibiting environments negatively impact the ontogeny of homeostatic self-regulatory and attachment systems. Social environments that provide less than optimal psychobiological attunement histories and generate prolonged episodes of unregulated interactive stress and heightened levels of negative affect retard the experience-dependent development of the higher levels of the right brain that are prospectively involved in affect regulating functions (Schore, 1994, 1997a, 1997d, 1998b, 1999c, 1999d, 2001c).

There is compelling evidence that all early forming psychopathology constitutes disorders of attachment and manifests itself as failures of autoregulation and/or interactive regulation. I propose that the functional indicators of this adaptive limitation are specifically manifest in recovery deficits of internal reparative coping mechanisms. This can take the form of either underregulation associated with externalizing psychopathologies, or overregulation and internalizing disturbances. Such coping deficits are most obvious under challenging conditions that call for behavioral flexibility and adaptive responses to socioemotional stress.

This conceptualization fits well with recent models, which emphasize that loss of ability to regulate the intensity of feelings is the most far-reaching effect of early trauma and neglect, that this dysfunction is manifest in more intense and longer-lasting emotional responses, and that defense mechanisms are forms of emotion-regulation strategies for avoiding, minimizing, or converting affects that are too difficult to tolerate. I suggest that these functional vulnerabilities reflect structural weaknesses and defects in the organization of the right hemispheric regulatory system that is centrally involved in the adjustment or correction of emotional responses.

The right hemisphere, the substrate of early attachment processes, ends its growth phase in the second year, when the left hemisphere begins one, but it cycles back into growth phases at later periods of the life cycle (Thatcher, 1994). This allows for the continuity of attachment mechanisms in subsequent functioning, and also for the potential continuing reorganization of the emotion-processing right brain throughout life. Future research of the continuing experience-dependent maturation of the right hemisphere could elucidate the underlying mechanisms by which certain attachment patterns can change from insecurity to earned security (Phelps et al., 1998). However, this system is most plastic during the early critical periods of its maturation. Current brain research indicates that efficient right brain function is centrally involved in the control of vital functions supporting survival. Early interventions that focus on social-emotional development would have enduring effects on the adaptive coping capacities of a developing self throughout the life span.

2001

PART II

DEVELOPMENTAL

NEUROPSYCHIATRY

The Early Organization of the Nonlinear Right Brain and the Development of a Predisposition to Psychiatric Disorders

A LTHOUGH THERE IS AGREEMENT within a wide spectrum of sciences that dynamic systems theory offers powerful insights into the organizational principles of all inanimate and animate systems, the application of its general tenets to specific problems of human psychology and biology has represented a difficult challenge. And yet this model of the mechanism of self-organization, of how complex systems that undergo discontinuous changes come to produce both emergent new forms yet retain continuity, clearly must be relevant to the study of normal and abnormal human development. Here I will suggest that in order to more deeply integrate nonlinear principles into the discipline of developmental psychopathology, they must not be used as just metaphors but rather directly incorporated in their literal form into the core of the developmental sciences. In particular, I will propose that multidisciplinary knowledge regarding three systems concepts—state changes, self-organization, and the central role of energy flows—can more deeply elucidate the mechanisms by which early development indelibly influences all later function and dysfunction.

A fundamental focus of nonlinear dynamic theory is the modeling of complex patterns of *state changes* in all physical and biological systems. This clearly implies that the basic unit of analysis of the process of human development is not changes in behavior, cognition, or even affect, but rather the ontogenetic appearance of more and more complex psychobiological states that underlie these state-dependent emergent functions (Schore, 1994). Lydic pointed out that "'studies that ignore organismic state are analogous to the experiments of physics that ignore time" and that the ubiquity of state-dependent organismic changes "reminds us that biological systems are highly dynamic and notoriously nonlinear" (1987, p. 14). He then concluded that the prospects for future progress in our understanding of state phenomena must include a deeper explication of the role played by the brain systems that biochemically regulate all brain and bodily state phenomena—various discrete groups of bioaminergic neurons of the subcortical reticular formation that innervate wide areas of the brain through diffuse projections. The unique anatomical capacities of these systems to affect large areas simultaneously allow for their central involvement in global, state-associated brain functions. (Flicker, McCarley, & Itabson, 1981; Foote, 1987).

The concept of psychobiological state lies at the common boundary of the psychological and biological sciences, and as such it can go far to overcome the myopia of "Descartes's error," "the separation of the most refined operations of mind from the structure and operation of a biological organism" (Damasio, 1994, p. 250). At all points of human development, but especially in infancy, the continually developing mind cannot be understood without reference to the continually maturing body, and their ongoing interactions become an important interface for the organizing self. This perspective necessitates an infusion of recent data from developmental psychobiology into the disciplines of developmental psychology and developmental psychopathology. Indeed, in a very recent text in this field, Michel and Moore declared that dynamic system theories are "good models on which to construct the developmental psychobiological approach" (1995, p. 31).

A second core assumption of systems theory is that *self-organization* is characterized by the emergence and stabilization of novel forms from the interaction of lower-order components and involves "the specification and crystallization of structure" (Lewis, 1995). I will argue that this mechanism also describes how hierarchical structural systems in the developing brain self-organize. The developmental neurosciences are now identifying the "lower" autonomic and "higher" central brain systems that organize in infancy and become capable of generating and regulating psychobiological states. These homeostatic structures that maintain stability are primarily lateralized in the right brain (Chiron et al., 1997), which is, more so than the left, well connected into the limbic system and the mechanisms of autonomic and behavioral arousal, and their maturation is experience-dependent. In light of the ontogenetic principle that the most important information for the successful development of the human brain is conveyed by the social rather than the physical environment, I have proposed that "the self-organization of the developing brain occurs in the context of another self, another brain" (Schore, 1996, p. 60). This organization, like all aspects of human brain maturation, is nonlinear and shows discontinuous developmental patterns.

And lastly, another cardinal feature of nonlinear theory is that it assigns the sources of new adaptive forms to the self-organizing properties of systems that use *energy* in order to faciliate the cooperativity of simpler subsystem components into a hierarchically structured complex system (Thelen, 1989). This model therefore emphasizes the central roles of thermodynamics, the science of energy flow, and bioenergetics, the study of how energy is used for the work of establishing biological order, toward the understanding of the creation of new complex structural forms. The functional activity of the brain is an energy-requiring process. One of the most striking aspects of development is found in the growing brain's rapidly increasing capacity to generate and sustain higher and higher levels of energy metabolism over the first two years of life.

The biosynthetic processes that underlie the proliferation of synaptic connections in the postnatally developing brain demand, in addition to sufficient quantities of essental nutrients, massive amounts of energy, so much so that the metabolic rate of the young child's brain is significantly greater than adults (Kennedy & Sokoloff, 1957). Sequential increments in metabolic rates take place in various regions of the brain during postnatal development, and this accounts for the finding that the brain matures in discontinuous discrete stages (Martin et al., 1988). Due to the relationship between energy metabolism and physiological function, this event is central to the emergence of "higher" brain systems and the appearance of more complex behaviors. A central principle of systems theory asserts that self-organization increases the rate of energy transfer, and the more ordered the complexity, the faster the energy flows (Goerner, 1995). In light of the fact that energy systems within the developing brain responsible for self-organization are themselves undergoing dramatic transformation, I will propose that knowledge of the gene-environment interactions responsible for the onset of aerobic energy metabolism in mitochondria, the preeminent source of biological energy in the brain, is relevant to an understanding of how neurons increase their synaptic connectivity and how energy fluxes organize new adaptive structures in development.

The energy metabolism of the brain is regulated and coordinated by biogenic amines that are delivered to widely distributed regions by ascending, unmyelinated projections from the brain stem. Ontogenetic changes in these monoaminergic systems result in progressive increases in organismic energy metabolism. These neuromodulators, in concert with different subtypes of their receptors that determine whether they augment local excitatory or inhibitory activity, alter and synchronize the input-output characteristics of brain cell populations in accord with changes in arousal. In human infancy these same bioagents that regulate central arousal and bodily states play an essential ontogenetic role—they also act as morphogenetic agents that induce the growth and organization of the developing brain. Most intriguingly, it is evident that these bioamines are regulated by the interaction between caregiver and infant. Neurobiological studies can thus offer us valuable information about how social factors modulate the effects of state organization on development, that is, how early interpersonal experiences induce the bioenergetic changes that support the growth of brain interconnections, and therefore more complex stuctures and emergent functions.

This latter problem is, of course, a central focus of models of self-organization. In order to further explore ths question, I will present an application of dynamic systems theory to normal development, and then to a conceptualization of atypical development, but I will address the underlying mechanisms common to both. Within this framework, I will propose models of the nonlinear phenomena of attachment dynamics, of the roles of bioamines and mitochondria in self-oganizational processes of synaptic connectivity, and of the energy-dependent imprinting of neural circuitry in the infant brain. In this application of self-organizational concepts to developmental models of both resistance against and vulnerability to mental disorders, I will particularly focus on the experience-dependent maturation of a frontolimbic system that regulates psychobiological states and organismic energy balance in a nonlinear fashion. This prefrontal system is expanded in the right hemisphere that plays a superior role in enabling the organism to cope actively and passively with stress. In the final section I will suggest that early forming microstructural pathology and energetic limitations of this specific system are associated with a predisposition to later appearing psychiatric disorders. This work is a continuation of recent writings in which I have contended that less than optimal gene-environment interactions that occur during the critical period of growth of this system produce a frontolimbic organization that is vulnerable to a spectrum of psychopathologies (Schore 1994, 1996).

FUNCTIONAL PROPERTIES OF SELF-ORGANIZING DEVELOPMENTAL SYSTEMS

A fundamental property of any developing living system is that it is open to and interactive with its particular environment. This applies to the human infant, who actively seeks environmental input, adjusts to the variations of this input, transforms it with its organizing properties, and incorporates it into its developing form. In such reciprocal interchanges the dynamic activity of the developing system, in turn, produces changes in the proximal environment. As a result of these continuous self-environment interactions the system establishes dynamic equilibria both within itself, and between itself and its environment (Michel & Moore, 1995). It is important to note that in the physical sciences, dynamic systems theories imply that "the environment" is singularly the physical environment. But in the case of a living system, one that proceeds through development to ultimately attain a mature form that can pass on its genomes, these primordial interactions are with the social environment—others of its species, and in particular, the primary caregiver.

A central tenet of dynamic systems theory prescribes that in these early transactions the developing biological system is openly exchanging both energy and matter with the environment. Indeed, ongoing development requires an open system, one that inputs free energy from the environment, uses it for matter-energy transformations, and exports it in degraded form. As a result of incorporating the dissipation of energy and matter of its environment into itself, the developing system moves away from equilibrium and remains for periods of time in a state of disequilibrium, one that exhibits negative entropy. In this manner the flow of energy through the system creates conditions for strong deviations from thermodynamic equilibrium, and this results in the phenomenon of self-organization. When a system is "far-from-equilibrium" (Prigogine & Stengers, 1984), energy is continually dissipated in the very process that binds the elements of the system together, allowing the elements to "behave in a sychrononous fashion, to couple with each other through ongoing feedback, and to act together in macroscopic entities rather than independent entities" (Lewis, 1995, p. 79).

As the patterns of relations among the components of a self-organizing system become increasingly interconnected and well-ordered, it is more capable of maintaining a coherence of organization in relation to variations in the environment. Given a particular organization and a particular environmental context, the system prefers a certain range of states. A system passes through a succession of a finite number of states, but it must eventually reenter a state that it has previously encountered. These cycles of contiguous states represent the dynamic attractors of the system, and the path taken by the system from one state to another defines a "trajectory" that describes the time evolution of the system. If the system is driven away from its stationary state, it will tend to return to that state; the time it takes to return to its stationary state is a function of the stability of the system. The stability of a system is dependent upon its capacity to transition between and thereby exist within a range of possible states, and this property is a consequence of its dynamic processes.

Self-organization, the process whereby order and complexity create more order and complexity, proceeds hierachically, as each level of self-organization builds on the level that precedes it. Different levels of organization are represented in heirarchical models of development, and maturation in infancy is best characterized by an alternation of rapid development and slower rates, even plateaus, which delimit "stages" (McGuiness, Pribram, & Pirnazar, 1990). Developmental change results from a series of states of stability and instability and phase transitions in the attractor landscape that irreversibly alter the trajectory of the system and allow for the organization of new states of matter-dissipative structures. These "points of bifurcation," when new states can potentially evolve from preceding ones, occur in the context of a "mutually determining organism-environment interaction" (Schwalbe, 1991). During these intervals, the open system, due to increasingly complex interconnections within its components and the creation of feedback mechanisms, can now act not only on the output of an environmental system with which it is interacting, but also iteratively to amplify its own output, and so it is sensitive to fluctuations of both external and internal processes. Complex systems thus show sensitive dependence on initial conditions, the state of the system when fluctuations first initiate change, and small differences can be amplified into large effects over many cycles of iteration. These fluctuations drive the system to explore new states.

Most importantly, environmental perturbations that occur during points of bifurcation create nonlinear breaks in organization and discontinuous changes in system states. According to Schwalbe (1991),

> Chaos ... arises at the point of phase transitions, when systems are "choosing" between different process structures. What occurs at these points is that random fluctuations in energy can be amplified throughout the entire system so that a new process structure is formed. Chaos in dynamical systems is thus a product of the same forces that create process structures and give rise to self-organization. (p. 276)

Nonlinearity, the source of rapid change and novel structure, is thus also the source of potential order and stability. It is now well established that nonlinearity can produce either positive (amplifying) or negative (dampening) feedback, stability or instability, convergence (coupling or entrainment) or divergence (Goerner, 1995). Along these same lines, Jackson, in chaos research in the physical sciences, argued that "entrainment" of a dynamic system is a precondition to control of dynamic flows, and that this allows for "hierarchical systems to adapt to environmental changes" (1991, p. 4839). Shinbrot, Grebogi, Ott, and Yorke (1993) reported that chaotic systems are extremely sensitive to small perturbations, and that these tiny feedback perturbations control their trajectories. These researchers experimentally demonstrate that small perturbations can be used both to stabilize regular dynamic behaviors and to direct chaotic trajectories rapidly to a desired state. They also showed that, using only tiny perturbations, one can switch between a rich variety of dynamical behaviors as circumstances change. Referring to "the advantage of chaos," Shinbrot and colleagues concluded that "Incorporating chaos deliberately into practical systems therefore offers the possibility of achieving greater flexibility in their performance" (1993, p. 411). These findings fit nicely with Thelen's (1995) assertion that times of instability are essential to give a developing system flexibility to select adaptive capacities.

Developing organisms internalize environmental forces by becoming appropriately structured in relation to them, and by incorporating an internal model of these exogenous signals they develop adaptive homeostatic regulatory mechanisms which allow for stability in the face of external variation. The regulation of the organism, which maintains internal stability and output regulation and enables an effective response to external stimuli, therefore depends on the formation of a dynamic model of the external environment. Self-organizing systems are thus systems that are able capable of generating new internal representations in response to changing environmental conditions.

These abstract self-organizational principles apply in a general way to all living systems. The next question is, how do these overarching principles specifically apply to ontogeny of the human infant, itself described as "very nonlinear" (Thelen, 1989)? Schwalbe (1991) portrayed the human as "a nonlinear dynamic system," an inherently dynamic energy-transformation regime that coevolves with its environment, one that self-organizes when exposed to an energy flux. In a scenario that resembles attachment dynamics, he postulated that the infant becomes attuned to an external object in its environment who consistently responds in a stimulating manner to the infant's spontaneous impulsive energy dissipating behaviors.

The concept of energy, central to dynamic systems theory, is rarely used in developmental psychology. In an article on the self-organization of developmental paths, Lewis (1995) asked, "What is the best analogy for energy in psychological systems?" He pointed out that the energy flow-through for self-organization has been conceived of as information, an idea that fits well with Harold's (1986) formulation that information is a special kind of energy required for the work of establishing biological order. He then went on to argue that information can be defined subjectively as that which is relevant to an individual's goals or needs, an idea that echoes recent concepts of emotion as adaptive functions that guide attention to the most relevant aspects of the environment, and of emotional appraisals that monitor and interpret events in order to determine their significance to the self. Lewis concluded that there is no better marker of such information than the emotion that accompanies it, that emotions amplify fluctuations to act in self-organization, and that the processing of relevant information in the presence of emotion may be analogous to the flowthrough of energy in a state of disequilibrium. Stability is a property of interpersonal attractors that maintain their organization by perpetuating equilibrium as well as resolving emotional disequilibrium.

In applying nonlinear systems concepts to development, Lewis emphasized the salience of "dyadic self-organization," which is epitomized by the creation of specific forms of communication between the mother and infant. When emotion is present in this dyadic interaction, each partner's behavior is monitored by the other, which results in the coupling between the output of one partner's loop and the input of the other's to form a larger feedback configuration. These transactions represent a flow of interpersonal information accompanying emotion, and critical fluctuations, amplified by positive feedback, lead to disequilibrium and self-organization. Attachment patterns are posited to arise through consolidating interpretations (working models) of caretaking contingencies, and such representations take into account emotional responses to caretaking fluctuations as well as maternal behavioral characteristics. Core attachment organizations stabilize with age and branch into attachment categories, and in this manner emotional experiences with caregivers set the course of the individual's behavioral style and emotional disposition (Lewis, 1995).

NONLINEAR STATE CHANGES AND THE ORGANIZATION OF ATTACHMENT DYNAMICS

In a previous work I proposed that emotional transactions involving synchronized ordered patterns of energy transmissions (directed flows of energy) represent the fundamental core of the attachment dynamic (Schore, 1994). This conception, congruent with nonlinear dynamic models, focuses on reciprocal affective exchanges in which the caregiver psychobiologically regulates changes in the infant's state. These interactions occur in sensitive periods of infancy, phases when energy is high in the infant and the parent for receptivity to each other's cues and for adapting to each other. The creation of this dynamic system of "contingent responsivity" occurs in the context of face-to-face interactions, and it relies heavily upon the processing of visual and auditory (prosodic) information emanating from the most potent source of stimulation in the infant's environment—the mother's face. The human face is a unique stimulus whose features display biologically significant information.

Indeed, over the first year of life visual experiences play a paramount role in social and emotional development (Preisler, 1995; Wright, 1991). These face-to-face dialogs create a match between the expression of arousal-accelerating, positively valenced internal states. For this to happen, the mother must monitor the infant's state as well as her own, and then resonate not with the child's overt behavior but with certain qualities of its internal state, such as contour, intensity, and temporal features. In physics, a property of resonance is sympathetic vibration, which is the tendency of one resonance system to enlarge and augment through matching the resonance frequency pattern of another resonance system. Dynamically fluctuating moment-to-moment state-sharing represents an organized dialog occurring within milliseconds, and acts as an interactive matrix in which both partners match states and then simultaneously adjust their social attention, stimulation, and accelerating arousal in response to the partner's signals. In this mutually synchronized attunement of emotionally driven facial expression, prosodic vocalization, and kinesic behaviors, the dyad coconstructs a mutual regulatory system of arousal which contains a "positively amplifying circuit mutually affirming both partners" (Wright, 1991, p. 12).

In such facial mirroring transactions (see Chapter 2, Figure 2.1) the caregiver facilitates a state transition, manifest in a change in patterns of "energetic arousal," and a shift from quiet alertness (A) into an intensely positive affective state (F). Stern (1990) describes exchanges of smiles in escalating overlapping waves that propel the other into "higher orbit." At resonance, energy transfer from the external agent to the resonant system is maximal (Katsuri, Amtey, & Beall, 1984). In accord with complex systems theory, an environmental perturbation triggers a rapid and discontinuous change in state, one far-from-equilibrium that leads to the potential for achieving novel states of temporal stability. Schwalbe (1991) posited that the nonlinear self acts iteratively, so that minor changes, occurring at the right moment, can be amplified in the system, thus launching it into a qualitatively different state. The caregiver is thus modulating changes in the child's energetic state, since arousal levels are known to be associated with changes in metabolic energy. Indeed, energy shifts are the most basic and fundamental features of emotion, discontinuous states are experienced as affect responses, and nonlinear psychic bifurcations are manifest as rapid affective shifts.

In light of the facts that in these interchanges the infant's and mother's homeostatic systems are "open" and linked together (Hofer, 1990) and are "semipermeable to regulation from the other" (Pipp, 1993), the transition embedded in the psychobiological attunement of the dyad involves an alteration in the infant's bodily state. These interactions increase over the first year, because the baby's ability to adjust the amount of interaction with the mother in accordance with internal states increases with physiological and psychological maturity. An essential attachment function is to promote the synchrony or regulation of biological and behavioral systems on an organismic level. Damasio (1994) concluded that primordial representations of body states are the building blocks and scaffolding of development. The infant's core sense of self is bodily based, and since body processes abide by the laws of nonlinear dynamics (Goldberger, Rigney, & West, 1990), the emerging self is grounded in biologically mediated self-organizing properties (Pipp, 1993). Even more specifically, synchronized gaze transactions induce changes in the infant's bodily states by maternal regulation of the child's autonomic nervous system, and this interactive mechanism represents a mutual entrainment of the mother's and infant's brains, including a coupling of the activation of subcortical areas responsible for the somatic components of emotion.

In support of this model, Trevarthen (1993) argued that the epigenetic program of brain growth requires brain-brain interaction and occurs in the context of a traffic of visual and prosodic auditory signals which induce instant positive emotional states in both infant and mother (see Chapter 2, Figure 2.3). The resonance of the dyad ultimately permits the intercoordination of positive affective brain states. Trevarthen concluded that "the affective regulations of brain growth" are embedded in the context of an intimate relationship, and that they promote the development of cerebral circuits.

CENTRAL ROLE OF BIOAMINES IN
THE REGULATION OF THE ENERGY METABOLISM
OF THE DEVELOPING BRAIN

Thelen (1995) asserted that dynamic systems theory needs to be more closely tied into a theory of brain development that addresses the fundamental question, How is the brain molded through experience? Although nonlinear systems theory has been used to model brain functions, the problem of what causes the infant brain to change, of how this organization is influenced by the interaction of genetic programming and environmental history, has not received much attention. Yet, Cicchetti and Tucker (1994) emphasized that the identification of the brain's self-organizing mechanisms is a primary challenge of science, and that indeed it may reveal the best description of development. These authors also pointed out that certain interactions between an "open homeostatic system" and the environment are critical to the differentiation of brain tissue, and that particular environmental experiences during sensitive periods are necessary for the induction of certain developmental changes that result from the maturation of the infant brain.

This leads to two fundamental questions: What specific kinds of experiences induce brain maturation, and How does this early experience influence the "social construction" (Eisenberg, 1995) of the human brain? Toward that end I have proposed that attachment experiences essentially represent affective transactions in which the caregiver modulates changes in the infant's arousal levels, and thereby in its energetic state. This is accomplished by her psychobiological regulation of neurohormones and catecholaminergic neuromodulators in the infant's developing brain (Hofer, 1990). In the context of face-to-face interactions, the mother triggers production of corticotropin releasing factor (CRF) in the infant's paraventricular hypothalamus that, in turn, raises plasma concentations of noradrenaline, activates the sympathetic nervous system, increases oxygen consumption and energy metabolism, and generates a state of emotional excitement. CRF, which controls endorphin and adrenocorticotropic hormone (ACTH) production in the anterior pituitary, also activates the ventral tegmental system and augments the activity of the other catecholamine, dopamine, thereby elevating dopaminergic arousal and an elated state in the infant.

These same catecholamines are known to be centrally involved in the regulation of brain metabolic energy levels, morphogenesis, and the maturation of cortical areas during different developmental stages (Berntman, Dahlgren, & Siesjo, 1978; Lauder & Krebs, 1986). For this reason, the energy transformations occuring in attachment bond formation are vitally important for the infant's continuing neurobiological development. Because the ascending bioaminergic "reticular" systems that are responsible for various states of arousal are in an intense state of active growth in infancy, the regulatory transactions embedded in the emotional relationship are occurring at a time when the infant's circuitry of the biological hardware of arousal is expanding. In fact, there are specific postnatal critical periods and developmental sequences for the regional expansion of the biogenic amines dopamine and noradrenaline. Central catecholaminergic neurons undergo an accelerated development in mammalian infancy, and their proliferating axonal terminals hyperinnervate distant cortical territories. In these same periods various types of regional catecholaminergic receptors are amplified, especially the D1 dopamine receptor that is found throughout the prefrontal cortex and limbic system associated with memory, learning, and cognitive processing (Huang et al., 1992), as well as the beta noradrenergic receptor that is activated in states of emotonal excitement (Cahill, Prins, Weber, & McGaugh, 1994). These events are experience-dependent, and they account for the evolution of an increasing tolerance for higher levels of arousal over the course of the first year.

During early critical periods, biogenic amines, the same agents that regulate emotion and motivation throughout the life span, play an important role in the responsiveness of the cortex to environmental stimulation and in the regulation of the temporal framework of developmental processes. These neuromodulators influence the ontogeny of cortical circuitry and have long-lasting effects on synaptic plasticity and on biochemical processes that mediate developmental influences (Foote & Morrison, 1987). Their activation of both glycogenolysis, a cascade of biochemical reactions that trigger the release of glucose in conditions of intense activity, and the hexose monophosphate shunt, a pathway that meditates biosynthetic processes, underscores their preeminent role in the regulation of energy substrate availability in the developing brain.

Catecholamines modulate cerebral circulatory systems and the blood-brain barrier that delivers and exports metabolic substrate to the brain, thereby regulating the responsivity of large areas of the brain to inputs in a coordinated manner (see Schore, 1994 for a detailed discussion). The growth and organization of the brain are highly dependent upon the continued availability of substrate, and in postnatal periods its production of energy shifts from anaerobic to aerobic oxidative metabolism, thereby enabling a significant increase in output that can sustain the very large energy requirement of brain cells for differentiation and the formation of connections. The brain's main metabolic fuel is glucose, which in the presence of oxygen undergoes complete combustion to CO_2 and H_2O:

$$C_6H_{12}O_6 + 6O_2 \rightarrow 6CO_2 + 6H_2O + energy$$

The free energy liberated in this exergonic reaction is partially trapped as adenosine triphosphate (ATP), the main source of energy in living matter, in glycolysis and oxidative phosphorylation (Erecinska & Silver, 1989). Adenosine triphosphate is generated both in glycolysis, a process located in Na^+,K^+-ATPase activity, especially at the plasma membrane surrounding the cell and in synaptic nerve endings (Erecinska, Nelson, & Silver, 1996), and in oxidative phosphorylation, the preeminent supplier of ATP in biological systems. This latter process occurs in mitochondria and reflects the activity of cytochrome oxidase, the enzyme that supports the high aerobic energy metabolism of the brain (Wong-Riley, 1989). The activity of these enzymes is coordinated (Hevner, Duff, & Wong-Riley, 1992) and influenced by catecholamines (Van der Krogt & Belfroid, 1980), and because they act as regulators, the effects of their action involve large amplification factors. The major inactivation of biogenic amines is performed by monoamine oxidase, an enzyme located solely in mitochondria.

Levels of Na^+,K^+-ATPase increase dramatically in early development during periods of neuronal arborization (Bertoni & Siegel, 1978), and cytochrome oxidase activity, regulated by oxygen concentrations, increases and peaks at the time of most rapid growth and maturation (Wong-Riley, 1989). During the critical period of a brain region, growth in neurons occurs essentially in dendrites, and is manifest in heightened levels of synaptogenesis. Na^+,K^+-ATPase and cytochrome oxidase are heightened in dendrites, and this accounts for the fact that dendritic metabolism makes the largest contribution to the metabolic activity of the brain. In postnatal development mitochondria are associated with the presynaptic and postsynaptic processes of developing synapses. In these same time periods catecholamines induce dynamic changes in the shape and branching patterns of dendrites and the growth of dendritic spines. These spines have the greatest energy requirements and density of mitochondria in the brain, and they act as potential sites of synaptic contact which modulate rapid changes in the nervous system throughout the course of its development.

It is well established that the the size and complexity of dendritic arbors increase in development and that dendritic growth and synaptogenesis of the postnatally developing brain is "experience-sensitive." Indeed, the neuro-developmental processes of dendritic proliferation and synaptogenesis, which are responsible for postnatal brain growth, are critically influenced by events at the interpersonal and intrapersonal levels. As mentioned, the events embedded in interpersonal transactions can be very fast-acting, yet structure-inducing. Indeed, modifications of dendritic spines occur "within minutes of a stimulus train that lasts for a fraction of a second" (Lynch, 1986, p. 7). Dopamine, regulated within rapid mother-infant affective transactions, activates excitatory NMDA receptors (Knapp, Schmidt, & Dowling, 1990) and modulates the excitability of prefrontal neurons by altering dendritic spine responses to excitatory inputs (Smiley, Levey, Ciliax, & Goldman-Rakic et al., 1994). Excitatory sensory input, including visual input, is required for the increases in mitochondrial cytochrome oxidase-driven oxidative metabolism in spines of growing dendrites of the developing cerebral cortex (Wong-Riley, 1979). Most intriguingly, catecholamines initiate protein synthesis and the maturation of energy transduction in mitochondria (Houstek et al., 1990), and infant animals exposed to early environments that allow for social experiences show larger mitochondrial populations, an indicator of metabolic energy activity, as well as increased dendritic volume, in developing cortical areas (Sirevaag & Greenough, 1987).

THE ENERGY-DEPENDENT IMPRINTING OF NEURAL CIRCUITS DURING CRITICAL PERIODS OF INFANCY

A central tenet of dynamic systems theory holds that at particular critical moments, a flow of energy allows the components of a self-organizing system to become increasingly interconnected, and in this manner organismic form is constructed in developmental processes. These moments occur in instances of imprinting, the very rapid form of learning that irreversibly stamps early experience upon the developing nervous system and mediates attachment bond formation. It is thought that a stimulus that elicits a high level of catecholamine-generated arousal facilitates the imprinting process and exerts an enduring influence on neural development (a perfect description of the emotionally expressive face of the attachment object), and that certain types of early learning experiences associated with new levels of arousal lead to rapid increases in the volume of hemispheric blood flow. Both imprinting and arousal are associated with increased metabolic activity, and both are regulated by catecholamines, agents that have pronounced effects on cerebral oxidative energy metabolism and cerebral blood flow.

During very early development, the neonatal cerebral metabolic rate that sustains early cortical function is very low. But as infancy proceeds, blood flow, known to correlate with changes in arousal, and to be an indicator of regional oxidative metabolism, rises to maximal levels and then declines (Kennedy, Grave, Jehle, & Sokoloff, 1972). Kennedy suggested that the peak elevation in early infancy specifically reflects the increased energy demands associated with biosynthetic processes essential for growth and development of differentiating cortical structures and their emergent functions. In this period of intense growth, the metabolic activity that supports this growth is heightened, so much so that the young child's cerebral metabolic rate consumes one-half of the total body oxygen consumption (Kennedy & Sokoloff, 1957).

In a similar dynamic scenario, Purves and LaMantia (1990) demonstrated that mitochondrial cytochrome oxidase-rich zones in the cerebral cortex increase in number in development, and propose that the pattern of high metabolic activity in these areas demarcates modular circuits. These researchers further suggested that novel circuits are constructed in a critical period of postnatal life, that modular and processing units are added progressively during the period of brain growth and maturation, and that modular circuit formation wanes in the later stages of postnatal development. Purves and LaMantia concluded that critical periods, "epochs in early life when the brain is particularly sensitive to the effects of experience" represent the normal duration of the construction of cytochrome oxidase-labeled circuits.

Indeed, the dramatic transformations of energy production that occur in particular portions of the maturing nervous system during specific postnatal temporal intervals represent the physiological basis of developmental stage and critical period phenomena, and these events allow for the onset of increasing complexity of structure and efficiency and integration of function, just as described by dynamic systems theory. I have proposed (see Chapters 11 and 36 in Schore, 1994) that the onset of a critical period of growth in a differentiating brain region is defined by a sudden switch from anaerobic to aerobic energy metabolism. A mature neuron has greater energy-consuming demands than an immature neuron, and this transformation is expressed at the intracellular level by a replication of the mitochondrial genome, a rapid multiplication of cellular mitochondria, an elevation of environmentally regulated mitochondrial protein synthesis, and a significant increase in cytochrome oxidase levels. These fast-onset, discontinuous changes that occur within "the period of rapid mitochondrial prolferation" (Pysh, 1970) result in an augmentation of cellular energy metabolism, since glycolysis alone only produces 2 mols of ATP per mol of glucose, while oxidative phosphorylation produces 36 (Erecinska & Silver, 1989).

The increased number and onset of aerobic metabolism in mitochondrial populations within maturing regions of the infant's developing brain allow for the generation of significantly higher levels of biological energy that are available for "morphogenesis," the generation of new forms during growth and development, that is for the processing of genetic information, biosynthesis, and the transport of building blocks to their final destination (Harold, 1986). The transient increase in the division and production of new mitochondria peaks just when the dendrites are growing out, a fact that may account for the finding that in a developing system, postsynaptic neurons respond initially to excitatory inputs by heightening their energy metabolism (Mjaatvedt & Wong-Riley, 1988). I suggest that during the critical period growth of a particular region, the peaks of heightened energy metabolism described by Wong-Riley (1989), Purves and LaMantia (1990), and Kennedy and coleagues (1972) represented a coordinated flow of energy through the components of a system that is now synaptically coupling into a circuit. This directed energy is continually dissipated in the very process that binds the elements of the system together, that is, it allows for the coordinated onset of mitochondrial energy metabolism among the neurons, glia, and endothelial cells within contemporaneously differentiating cortical columns. Most importantly, the dramatic increase in the number of mitochondria during a critical period results in larger and larger flows of energy within more and more interconnected elements that can be used for self-organizational processes.

Since these bioenergetic transformations are cooordinated over long distances, they also underlie the critical period construction of a neural circuit—a self-contained neuronal network that sustains a nerve impulse by channeling it repeatedly through the same network. In a discussion of the stabilization of excitatory Hebbian cell assemblies, Singer (1986) suggested that pathways are formed between elements that have a high probability of being active at the same time. This selection process serves to develop assemblies of reciprocally coupled neurons that allow for the organization of a reverberating circuit. He also stated that these experience-dependent processes rely upon both cortical sensory processing of information from the "outer" world, and internally generated signals involving catecholamines from the reticular formation, which reflect the central state of the organism during a postnatal period.

Hudspeth and Pribram (1992) proposed that a maturation period has three phases: (a) an accelerating edge that reflects a changing state in the brain region; (b) a peak that reflects the attainment of a new state; and (c) a decelerating edge, in which a stable equilibrium within the state is established. I deduce that the peak phase is identical to the metabolic peak described above, and that in its critical period of maturation a particular brain region is an object of an energy flux, which creates conditions for strong deviations from thermodynamic equilibrium that result in self-organization. The last phase may be related to the fact that in a developing system, neurons initially receive excitatory inputs that heighten energy metabolism followed by inhibitory inputs that lower metabolism. This developmental shift from excitation to inhibition may reflect an early overexpression of excitatory NMDA glutamate receptors to later maturing inhibitory GABAergic systems. Glutamate is metabolized in mitochondria, and GABA-T, the enzyme that degrades GABA, is located in this organelle. Overall, these phenomena are more accurately described by the second law of thermo-dynamics, which deals with the efficiency with which energy is used and the amount of useful work to which the energy is put, rather than to the first law, the conservation of energy.

In light of the facts that energy metabolism peaks in a critical period of a developing brain region when dendrites are growing and neurons are attaining a new state of organization, and that dendritic spines have the greatest energy requirements in the brain, I would characterize their local cellular environ-ment at this specific time as a "far-from-equilibrium system" (Prigogine & Stengers, 1984). It is held that energy-regulating bioamines modulate ion chan-nels in dendrites, and that excitatory events occurring in dendrites within a "narrow time window" produce a "much bigger response" than outside this window, thereby allowing for interactions among synapses to be "highly nonlin-ear" (Johnston, Magee, Colbert, & Christie, 1996). Expanding upon these ideas, I suggest that although dendritic spines represent a unique site for receiv-ing communications from other cells, these points of interface with the local environment, especially in critcal periods, also potentially expose the neuron to a state of "oxidative stress," thereby making the cell vulnerable to excitotoxic "apoptotic" or "programmed cell death" (Margolis, Chuang, & Post, 1994).

Apoptosis plays a crucial role in the early development and growth regula-tion of living systems. This same mechanism may underlie the developmental process of circuit pruning, the selective loss of connections and redistributions of inputs that allow for the appearance of an emergent function. Regressive events such as cell death and the elimination of long axon collaterals and den-dritic processes are essential mechanisms of brain maturation. A large body of evidence supports the principle that cortical networks are generated by a geneti-cally programmed initial overabundant production of synaptic connections, which is then followed by a process of competitive interaction to select those connections that are most effectively entrained to environmental information. "Parcellation," the activity-dependent fine tuning of connections and winnow-ing of surplus circuitry, dominates the third maturational phase described by Hudspeth and Pribram (1992).

Parcellation is responsible for the loss of early transient ontogenetic adapta-tions, but this same mechanism of functional segregation also allows the devel-oping brain to become increasingly complex, a property of a self-organizing system. Furthermore, this process has been described as analogous to natural selection. Changeux and Dehaene (1989) pointed out that the Darwinian se-lective stabilization of surviving synapses that have functional significance in a particular environment occurs in cortical areas during postnatal sensitive peri-ods. These findings imply that maternal behavior, the preeminent source of environmental information for the infant, functions as an agent of natural selec-tion that shapes the trajectory of the infant's emerging self. They may also bear upon the mechanism of "maternal effects" (Bernardo, 1996), the influence of the mother's experiences on her progeny's development and ability to adapt to its environment.

Studies of the infant brain thus have direct implications for a more precise elucidation of dynamic systems theories. A fundamental postulate of this model holds that a condition of chaos exists when a system must move from a previously ordered, yet obsolete adaptive state to a more flexible state in order to be better adapted to novel aspects of a currently changing environment. The term "self-organization" can be imprecise and misleading for two reasons: first, despite the implications of the two words used to describe this process, self-organization occurs in interaction with another self—it is not monadic but dyadic; and second, the organization of brain systems does not involve a simple pattern of increments but rather changes in organization. Development, the process of self assembly, thus involves both progressive and regressive phenomena, and is best characterized as a sequence of processes of organization, disorganization, and reorganization.

THE ORGANIZATION OF A REGULATORY SYSTEM IN THE ORBITOFRONTAL CORTEX THAT MANIFESTS CHAOTIC DYNAMICS

According to chaos theory, the stabilization of reverberating circuits in early development allows for the organization of a network that can amplify minor fluctuations over cycles of iteration, and thereby influence the system's trajectory. This reexcitational activity launches the system into a different state, but it also facilitates the "persistence" of a memory trace, an important advance, since "attractors might be thought of as either as memories held by the neural network or as concepts" (Kaufmann, 1993, p. 228). As previously mentioned, these attractors maintain the system's organization by acting as adaptive homeostatic regulatory mechanisms that allow for stability in the face of external variation.

Of particular importance to the regulation of nonlinear emotional states are cortical-subcortical circuits, especially those that directly link cortical areas that process current information about changes in the external social environment and subcortical information about concurrent alterations in internal bodily states. These systems are hierarchicaly arranged, and they develop in a fixed progression over the first year. Although the amygdala, a limbic structure that appraises only crude information about external stimuli, is on line at birth, a critical period for the development of corticolimbic association areas activates in the second and third quarter of the first year, invoving maturation of the anterior cingulate cortex, area involved in play and separation behaviors, laughing and crying vocalizations, face representations, and modulation of autonomic activity (MacLean, 1993; Paus, Petrides, Evans, & Meyer, 1993).

By the end of this year the orbitoinsular region of the prefrontal cortex, an area that contains neurons that fire in response to faces, first become preeminently involved in the processing of interpersonal signals necessary for the initiation of social interactions and in the regulation of arousal and body states, properties that account for its central involvement in attachment neurobiology. The orbitofrontal system matures in the last half of the second year, a watershed time for the appearance of a number of adaptive capacities. These advances reflect the role of the frontal lobe in the development of infant self-regulatory behavior (Dawson, 1994), and are relevant to Cicchetti and Tucker's (1994) assertion that the homeostatic, self-regulating structures of the mind are the major stabilities in the chaotic dynamics of psychological and neural development. Due to the fact that orbital activity is essentially implicated in maintaining organismic homeostasis, the operational nature of this prefrontal cortex is best described as a nonlinear dynamic system.

The functional properties of this structural system can only be understood in reference to its unique neuroanatomical characteristics. The orbital frontal cortex is "hidden" in the ventral (areas 11–14 and 47) and medial (areas 24, 25, and 32) surfaces of the prefrontal lobe (Price et al., 1996). Because of its location at the interface of cortex and subcortex, this ventromedial prefrontal cortex acts as a "convergence zone," and is one of the few brain regions that is "privy to signals about virtually any activity taking place in our beings' mind or body at any given time" (Damasio, 1994, p. 181). In addition to receiving input from all sensory association areas of the posterior cortex as well as outputs to motor areas in the anterior cortex and ventral striatum, it uniquely projects extensive pathways to limbic areas in the temporal pole, central nucleus of the amygdala, and olfactory areas, to glutamate responsive N-methyl-D-aspartate (NMDA) receptors of mesocorticolimbic dopamine neurons in ventral tegmental areas of the anterior reticular formation, and to subcortical drive centers in the paraventricular hypothalamus that are associated with the sympathetic branch of the autonomic nervous system. This excitatory limbic circuit, the ventral tegmental limbic forebrain-midbrain circuit, is involved with the generation of positively valenced states associated with motivational reward. Orbitofrontal regions also send axons onto subcortical targets in parasympathetic autonomic areas of the hypothalamus, and to noradrenergic neurons in the medullary solitary nucleus and the vagal complex in the brain stem caudal reticular formation, thereby completing the organization of another limbic circuit, the lateral tegmental limbic forebrain-midbrain circuit that activates the onset of an inhibitory, negatively valenced state (see Schore, 1994).

The orbital corticolimbic system, along with the amygdala, insular cortex, and anterior cingulate, is a component of the "rostral limbic system" (Devinsky et al., 1995). Even more, it sits at the hierarchical apex of the emotion-generating limbic system, and regulates not only anterior temporal and amygdala activity, but indeed all cortical and subcortical components of both the excitatory and inhibitory reverberating circuits of the limbic system. In addition, it acts as a major center of CNS hierarchical control over the energy-expending sympathetic and energy-conserving parasympathetic branches of the ANS, thereby regulating respectively, ergotropic high arousal and trophotropic low arousal bodily states (Gellhorn, 1970). With such autonomic connections, it plays an important cortical role in both the nonlinear mechanisms of visceral regulation (Skinner, Molnar, Vybiral, & Mitra, 1992) and the feedback from bodily systems, what Damasio (1994) called "somatic markers." These reciprocal connections with autonomic areas allow for an essential orbitofrontal role in the control of emotional behavior (Price et al., 1996), the repesentation of highly integrated information on the organismic state (Tucker, 1992), and the modulation of energy balance (McGregor & Atrens, 1991).

By being directly connected into heteromodal areas of the cortex as well as into both limbic circuits, the sensory perception of an environmental perturbation can be associated with the adaptive switching of bioaminergic-peptidergic regulated energy-expending and energy-conserving bodily states in response to changes (or expected changes) in the external environment that are appraised to be personally meaningful (Schore, 1988a). These rapid-acting orbitofontal appraisals of the social environment are accomplished at levels beneath awareness by a visual and auditory scanning of information emanating from an emotionally expressive face, and they act as nonconscious biases that guide behavior before conscious knowledge does (Bechara, Damasio, Tranel, & Damasio, 1997). The paralimbic orbitofrontal cortex performs a "valence tagging" function, in which perceptions receive a positive or negative affective charge. The orbitofrontal system, the "administrator of the basolimbic forebrain circuitry" (Nelson, 1994, p. 52), is a central component of the mechanism by which "forebrain circuits concerned with the recognition and interpretation of life experiences are capable of influencing virtually all, if not all, regulatory mechanisms in the body" (Wolf, 1995, p. 90).

In such organism-environment interactions there is a sensitive dependence on initial conditions, and these heightened affective moments represent "points of bifurcation" of the potential activation of the two limbic circuits. Marder, Hooper, and Eisen demonstrated that "a given circuit might easily express a variety of states, depending on the presence or absence of one or more peptides or amines" (1987, p. 223). The output of each circuit and the interaction between the circuits are influenced by one or more bioaminergic neurotransmitters, thereby allowing for an adaptive flexible control of multiple states or output patterns. Indeed, in the orbitofrontal areas, dopamine excites and noradrenaline inhibits neuronal activity (Aou, Oomura, Nishino, Inokuchi, & Mizuno, 1983). Mender (1994) pointed out that in a competitive system, steep gain increases in response to stimulus input, combined with arousal, can create explosive bursts of neural activity and hence discontinuous jumps between discrete aggregate states of neuronal networks. As a result, distributed aggregates of neurons can shift abruptly and simultaneously from one complex activity pattern to another in response to the smallest of inputs. It is interesting to note that dopamine neurons involved in emotional states show a nonlinear relationship between impulse flow and dopamine release, and shift from single spike to "burst firing" in response to environmental stimuli that are associated with a quick behavioral reaction (Gonon, 1988), and that this effect is induced by medial prefrontal activity (Gariano & Groves, 1988).

Von Bertalanffy asserted that a small change in an anterior "higher" controlling center "may by way of amplification mechanisms cause large changes in the total system. In this way a hierarchical order of parts or processes may be established" (1974, p. 1104). I suggest that the orbitofrontal cortex represents this controlling center, and that it is intimately involved in the mechanism by which affect acts as an "analog amplifier" that extends the duration of whatever activates it (Tomkins, 1984). In accord with chaos theory, "Tiny differences in input could quickly become overwhelming differences in output" (Gleick, 1987, p. 8). These "tiny differences" refer to extremely brief events perceived at levels below awareness—although facially expressed emotions can be appraised within 30 miliseconds, spontaneously expressed within seconds, and continue to amplify within less than a half minute, it can take hours, days, even weeks or longer, for certain personalities experiencing extremely intense negative emotion to get back to a "normal" state again.

Chaotic behavior within the excitatory and inhibitory limbic circuits is thus expressed in sudden psychobiological state transitions. Orbitofrontal activity is associated with affective shifts, the alteration of behavior in response to fluctuations in the emotional significance of stimuli (Dias, Robbins, & Roberts, 1996). In optimal frontolimbic operations, these shifts from one emotional state to another are are experienced as rhythms in feeling states and are fluid and smooth, a flexible capacity of a coherent dynamic system. The adaptive aspects of these nonlinear phenomena were stressed by Hofer (1990):

> To accomplish various age-specific tasks, the brain must be able to shift from one state of functional organization to another and thus form one mode of information processing to others within an essentially modular structure. These organized states constitute an important component of motivational systems, and they can be considered to provide the neural substrates of affect—both the internal experience of affect and the communicative aspects that are embedded in the form and patterning of the behavior that is produced during these states. (p. 74)

The activity of this prefrontal system is responsible for the regulation of motivational states and the adjustment or correction of emotional responses. It is specialized for generating and storing cognitive interactive representations (internal working models) that contain information about state transitions, and for physiologically coding that state changes associated with homeostatic disruptions will be set right. The infant's memory representation includes not only details of the learning cues of events in the external environment, but also of reactions in his internal state to changes in the external environment. The dampening of emotional discomfort and the performance of previously re-warded actions are now thought to be specifically stored in infant procedural memory (Meltzoff, 1995b). Regulated emotional states represent desired attract-ors that maintain self-organization by perpetuating emotional equilibrium and resolving emotional disequilibrium. Chaotic variability in brain self-regulatory activity is thus necessary for flexibility and adaptability in a changing environ-ment. According to Ciompi under certain conditions feedback processes in "affective cognitive systems" are capable of "provoking sudden nonlinear jumps, far away from equilibrium, leading to chaotic conditions or to the for-mation of new 'dissipative structures'" (1991, p. 98). Further research has indi-cated that the orbitofrontal system is specialized for "cognitive-emotional inter-actions" (Barbas, 1995), and that neurons in the right prefrontal cortex with balanced excitatory and inhibitory inputs show chaotic behavior (van Vreeswijk & Sompolinsky, 1996).

RIGHT BRAIN AS A NONLINEAR SYSTEM

The fact that the orbital prefrontal area is expanded in the right hemisphere (in contrast to the later maturing nonlimbic dorsolateral prefrontal area, which is larger in the left [White, Lucas, Richards, & Purves, 1994]) has been sug-gested to account for the dominance of this hemisphere in the processing of emotional information (Falk et al., 1990). The early developing right cerebral cortex plays an important role in the processing of individual faces early in life, in the infant's recognition of arousal-inducing maternal facial affective expres-sions, and in its response to the prosody of motherese. In describing the greater involvement of the right hemisphere in infancy, Semrud-Clikeman and Hynd (1990) pointed out that the

> emotional experience of the infant develops through the sounds, images, and pictures that constitute much of an infant's early learning experi-ence, and are disproportionately stored or processed in the right hemi-sphere during the formative stages of brain ontogeny. (p. 198)

Indeed, the right hemisphere is centrally involved in human bonding and at-tachment (Henry, 1993) and in the development of reciprocal interactions within the mother-infant regulatory system (Schore, 1994, 1998b). In earlier work I presented a substantial body of multidisciplinary evidence that indicates the high-intensity affective communications that culminate in the development of the attachment system are essentially right-hemisphere-to-right-hemisphere arousal regulating energy transmissions between the primary caregiver and infant. Attachment dynamics continue in ongoing development, and the ven-tromedial region of the right cortex that neurobiologically mediates these dy-namics plays a crucial role in the processing of information emanating from the human face throughout the life span (Sergent, Ohta, & MacDonald, 1992).

Descending projections from the prefrontal cortex to subcortical structures are known to mature during infancy, and the "primitive" right hemisphere, more than the left, has dense reciprocal interconnections with limbic and subcortical structures, and contains an increased emphasis on paralimbic networks. These reciprocal right frontal-subcortical connections, especially with bioaminergic and hypothalamic subcortical nuclei, account for the unique contribution of the right hemisphere in regulating homeostasis and modulating physiological state in response to internal and external feedback. The representation of visceral and somatic states is under primary control of the right hemisphere, and the somatic marker mechanism, tuned by critical learning interactions in development, is more connected into the right ventromedial area. Wittling and Pfluger concluded that the right hemisphere is dominant for "the metacontrol of fundamental physiological and endocrinological functions whose primary control centers are located in subcortical regions of the brain" (1990, p. 260). This cortical asymmetry is an extension of an autonomic asymmetry—at all levels of the nervous system the right side of the brain stem provides the primary central regulation of homeostasis and physiological reactivity (Porges et al., 1994).

Expanding upon these neurophysiological and neuroanatomical relationships, Porges proposed that the right vagus is involved in the regulation of emotion and communication. Porges also discussed the relationship between "shifts" in emotion regulation and oxygen demands within the ANS. Based on further research (1995) Porges presented a neuroanatomical schema in which he proposed that the input site into this right brain circuit of emotional regulation is the nucleus of the solitary tract. This site, in turn, is fed by unnamed higher central structures that promote either immediate mobilization of energy resources or calming. I deduce that the orbitofrontal-insular cortex, the anterior cingulate, and the central amygdala, which all send axons directly into the noradrenergic neurons of the nucleus of the solitary tract and into the hypothalamus, are these structures. Indeed, orbitofrontal-vagal interconnections are demonstrated in studies showing that vagal stimulation induces a cortical evoked response only in the orbito-insular cortex, and that orbitofrontal stimulation triggers an almost instantaneous inhibition of gastrointestinal motility, respiratory movements, and somatic locomotor activity, and a dramatic precipitous fall in blood pressure (see Schore, 1994).

In other words, Porges's right brain circuit of emotion regulation is identical to the inhibitory lateral tegmental noradrenergic limbic circuit that is hierarchically dominated by the right orbitofrontal cortex. As opposed to sympathetically driven "fight-flight" active coping strategies, parasympathetically mediated passive coping mechanisms expressed in immobility and withdrawal allow for conservation-withdrawal, the capacity that improves survival efficiency through inactive disengagement and unresponsiveness to environmental input in order "to conserve resources." In contrast to "problem-focused coping," which entails direct action on the self or on the environment to remove the source of stress, this "emotion-focused coping" is directed toward the reduction of the emotional impact of stress through psychological processes (Folkman & Lazarus, 1980).

With regard to the other ventral tegmental dopaminergic limbic circuit, psychopharmacological research shows that emotionally stressful experiences result in greater dopaminergic activation of the right over the left prefrontal cortex (Fitzgerald, Keller, Glick, & Carlson, 1989). In a study of the mesocortical dopaminergic system, Sullivan and Szechtman (1995) concluded that the right cortex is at the top of a hierarchy for the processing of prolonged emotionally stressful inputs, and that endogenous dopaminergic modulation facilitates adaptive responses. Furthermore, the researchers posited that under intense inputs, a left-to-right shift occurs in intrinsic neural activity. These ideas correspond with the assertion that this nondominant (!) hemisphere plays a central role in the control of vital functions supporting survival and enabling the organism to cope with stressors (Wittling & Schweiger, 1993). In line with the principle that the right cortex operates in conjunction with a frontal system that is involved in modulating the emotional valence of experience (Heller, 1993), I suggest that upon its maturation in the middle of the second year, the orbitofrontal area of the right hemisphere acts as an "executive control system" for the entire right brain.

These findings bear upon an ongong debate concerning hemispheric asymmetry and the regulation of emotions. There is now general agreement that right cortical posterior association regions are centrally involved in the perception of all emotional information. However, with regard to the production and experience and thereby the regulation of emotion, there is a controversy as to whether the right hemisphere regulates all emotions or the right is specialized for negative and the left for positive emotions. In general, studies examining hemispheric lateralization for emotional *nonverbal* stimuli (e.g., faces) have provided support for the right hemispheric model of emotional lateralization (Ali & Cimino, 1997), a finding that fits with the conception that the right hemisphere contains a "nonverbal affect lexicon," a vocabulary for nonverbal affective signals such as facial expressions, gestures, and prosody (Bowers et al., 1993). Conditioned autonomic responses after subliminal presentations of facial expressions only occur when faces are presented to the right hemisphere (Johnsen & Hugdahl, 1991), clearly implying that future studies should use tachistoscopic facial stimuli. Furthermore, the majority of these studies have been done with adults. Infant studies (e.g., Nass & Koch, 1991) reported that the right hemisphere plays a crucial role in mediating emotional expression from a very early point in development. (Note in Figure 2.1, at [F], in the high-arousal elated state, the infant turns the head to the left, indicating right hemispheric activation.) Further, infants with right posterior brain damage show a persistent deficit in the expression of *positive* affect (Reilly, Stiles,

Larsen, & Trauner, 1995). These latter researchers concluded that the development of infant emotions represent "primitives" of affective communication.

It is important to note that emotions have, in addition to a valence (hedonic) dimension, an intensity or arousal (energetic) dimension. Many of the "primary" emotions are ergotropic-dominant, energy-expending high-arousal, or trophotropic-dominant, energy-conserving low-arousal affects, and these "primitive" affects appear early in development, arise automatically, are expressed in facial movements, and are correlated with differentiable ANS activity. Due to the lateralization of catecholaminergic systems in the right hemisphere, it is dominant in the regulation of arousal and is more closely associated with regulation of heart rate than the left. This hemisphere is specialized for processing the autonomic correlates of emotional arousal, and activation of the right orbitofrontal area occurs during classical conditioning of an emotional response, the learning of the relationship between events that allows the organism to represent its environment (Hugdahl et al., 1995). The structural and functional qualities of the right cortex, which has a higher metabolic rate than the left, thus account for its essential role in highly arousing emotional processes.

The developmental approach presented here is compatible with a model in which the early maturing right hemisphere modulates all nonverbal "primary" emotions, regardless of valence, while the later maturing left (which does not begin its growth spurt until the last half of the second year) modulates verbal "social" emotions and enhances positive and inhibits negative emotional behavior (Ross, Hohman, & Buck, 1994). It also supports the views that the right hemisphere mediates pleasure and pain and the more intrinsically primitive emotions, and that although the left cortex acts to inhibit emotional expression generated in the limbic areas of the right half of the brain, the right brain contains a circuit of emotion regulation that is involved in the modulation of "primary" emotions and "intense emotional-homeostatic processes" (Porges, 1995). Thus, the experience and regulation of affects mediated by extremes of arousal, both high (like terror, excitement, and elation) and low (like shame), would involve more right hemispheric activity, in contrast to their left hemispheric-driven counterparts, anxiety, interest, enjoyment, and guilt.

The right cortex is also specialized for globally directed attention, holistic analysis, and the processing of novel information. As opposed to the left hemisphere's "linear" consecutive analysis of information (Tucker, 1981), the processing style of the right hemisphere has been described as "nonlinear" based on multiple converging determinants rather than on a single causal chain (Galin, 1974). I conclude that the orbitofrontal cortex, especially in the right brain, is particularly suited to amplify appraisals of short-acting, small fluctuations of initial conditions into larger effects, and that it is primarily activated in far-from-equilibrium states of heightened ergotropic and/or trophotropic emotional arousal that create a potential for achieving novel states and a new stability.

CRITICAL PERIOD GENE-ENVIRONMENT
INTERACTIONS AND THE DEVELOPMENT
OF A VULNERABILITY TO PSYCHOPATHOLOGY

The development, in the first two years of life, of a right hemispheric dynamic system that adaptively regulates psychobiological states is a product of the interaction of genetic systems and early experience. Transactional models view the organization of brain systems as a product of interaction between (a) genetically coded programs for the formation of structures and connections among structures and (b) environmental influence (Fox, Calkins, & Bell, 1994). The onset and offset of sensitive periods, "unique windows of organism-environment interaction," are attributed to the activation and expression of families of programmed genes which synchronously turn on and off during infancy, thereby controlling the transient enhanced expression of enzymes of biosynthetic pathways which allow for growth in particular brain regions. In light of the established principles that early postnatal development represents an experiential shaping of genetic potential (Kendler & Eaves, 1986) and that visual experience regulates gene expression in the developing cortex (Neve & Bear, 1989), I suggest that gene-environment mechanisms are embedded within face-to-face visuo-affective interactions.

These socioemotional interactions thus directly impact the growth of limbic regions. The right cerebral cortex, densely interconnected into limbic structures, is specifically impacted by early social experiences, is primarily involved in attachment experiences, and is more vulnerable to early negative environmental influences than the left. Bowlby (1969) pointed out that the development of a late-maturing control system associated with attachment is influenced by the particular environment in which development occurs. This implies that during sensitive periods of right hemispheric growth less than optimal early environments in interaction with genetic factors are important forces in compromised brain organization and the pathogenesis of disorders of affect regulation.

The brain growth spurt spans from the end of prenatal life through the end of infancy, a time period when the right hemisphere is rapidly expanding. During this exact interval the total amount of DNA in the cerebral cortex increases dramatically and then levels off (Winick, Rosso, & Waterlow, 1970). It is in this period that timed gene action systems, which program the structural growth and connections of the higher structures of the limbic system, are activated. Although it is established that these hereditary expressions require transactions with the environment, the question arises as to what mechanism embedded in the early caregiver-infant relationship could act to experientially shape genetic potential? Hofer's (1990) research showed that the mother acts as a "hidden" regulator of not only infant brain catecholamines, agents that activate the hexose monophosphate shunt and ribonucleic acid synthesis (Cummins, Loreck, & McCandless, 1985), but also of ornithine decarboxylase, a key enzyme in the control of nucleic acid synthesis in the developing brain (Morris, Seidler, & Slotkin, 1983). These events influence not only catecholaminergic-driven maturation of the amygdala, but also later-maturing paralimbic areas in the temporal pole and then orbitofrontal cortices.

There is an increasing amount of evidence indicating that the underlying genetic defect in psychiatric disorders is in the hereditary systems involved in the synthesis and catabolism of biogenic amines which trophically regulate maturation in subcortical and cortical information processing centers, and that such mutations lead to a disruption of normal synaptogenesis and circuit formation. The genes that encode the production of bioamines and their receptors continue to be activated postnatally, causing a dramatic expansion of these systems over the stages of human infancy. Aminergic neuromodulators regulate both the responsiveness of the developing cortex to environmental stimulation and the organization of cortical circuitry, and because their activity is highly heritable (Clarke et al., 1995), altered genetic systems that program the key enzymes in their biosynthesis are now considered to represent potential contributors to high-risk scenarios (Mallet, 1996). Indeed, the genes for tyrosine hydroxylase, the rate-limiting enzyme in both dopamine and noradrenaline production, are essential to both fetal development and postnatal survival (Zhou, Quaife, & Palmiter, 1995). Alterations in the genetic systems that program bioamines and their receptors, agents that directly influence morphogenesis, would thus negatively effect the critical period organization and functioning of ventral tegmental dopaminergic and lateral tegmental noradrenergic neurons that regulate the metabolic capacities of their corticolimbic terminal fields.

As previously mentioned, the construction of modular circuits in critical periods is associated with linkages between areas of high activity of the energy generating enzyme cytochrome oxidase. This implies that early mitochondrial pathology would underlie defective brain circuitry. Nuclear and mitochondrial genes that encode cytochrome oxidase (Hevner & Wong-Riley, 1993), especially in bioaminergic (and hypothalamic neuroendocrine) systems and their receptors, may turn out to be an important locus for the development of "faulty" circuit wirings that mediate a predisposition to later forming psychiatric disorders. In fact, brain mitochondrial abnormalities are implicated in the etiology of a childhood neurological disorder of the right frontal lobe (Rett syndrome) that shows socialization deficits at 9 months and onset of autisitic-appearing regression of interpersonal interaction at 18 months (Cornford, Philippart, Jacobs, Scheibel, & Vintners, 1994). Alterations of oxidative metabolism due to mutations of genes that encode isoforms of cytochrome oxidase are being explored in the pathogenesis of the schizophrenic brain (Marchbanks, Mulcrone, & Whatley, 1995).

Mitochondrial gene expression is involved in "the mechanisms by which mammalian cells adapt to the changing energetic demands in response to functional, developmental and pathological factors" (Attardi et al., 1990, p. 509). The genetic system encoded in mitochondrial DNA is maternally inherited, is governed by non-Mendelian mechanisms, and has a mutagenicity rate ten times that of nuclear DNA. A mutation of these genes may occur in utero, but the amplification of mitochondrial DNA (which occurs from infancy onward; Simonetti, Chen, DiMauro, & Schon, 1992) during a critical period of rapid mitochondrial proliferation in actively growing brain regions represents a mechanism by which the number of local genetic mutations could increase. It is now thought that once the mutant mitochondrial DNAs reach a critical level, cellular phenotype changes rapidly from normal to abnormal, and the resultant impairment of oxidative phosphorylation and ATP production leads to disease expression. Shoffner stated "disease expression seems to be influenced by poorly understood genetic and environmental interactions" (1996, p. 1284).

Models of the genetic analysis of complex diseases prescribe an interaction between a susceptibility gene with a predisposing environmental agent. In these studies, "environmental" usually refers to factors in the physical environment, but I propose that in the case of the transmission of psychiatric diseases stressors in the social environment interact with genetic mechanisms to amplify a genetic predisposition and create a vulnerability to later forming mental illness. I further suggest that these interactions occur between the developing organism and the "nonshared" (Plomin et al., 1991) environment with which it interacts, responding first to the environmental signals provided by the internal body of the mother, and then after birth, to the environmental signals provided by the external body of the mother. The brain growth spurt, from the last trimester of pregnancy through the second year, spans both of these periods, emphasizing the principle that the genes that program its regional organization are expressed in two very different environments: first, a totally anaerobic environment and then an increasingly aerobic cellular environment. Gene expression is regulated by oxygen levels in the cell as well as by neurohormones and bioaminergic neuromodulators.

During critical periods of regional maturation, prolonged perturbations in the social environment lead to dysregulated levels of stress-responsive catecholamines, thereby altering gene-environment interactions and providing for potential sites of pathomorphogenesis. Dopamine, acting at excitatory glutamatergic NMDA and D1 receptors triggers c-*fos* immediate-early genes (Berretta, Robertson, & Graybiel, 1992) that turn on other genes within the cell, ultimately leading to long-term structural changes associated with early imprinting experiences. But dopamine increases under stress (Bertolucci-D'Angio, Serrano, Driscoll, & Scatton, 1990), and can induce neurotoxic inhibition of mitochondrial respiration and defective energy metabolism (Ben-Shachar, Zuk, & Glinka, 1994) and DNA mutations in brain tissue (Spencer et al., 1994). An early stressful environment thus detrimentally and irreversibly impacts the genetic systems of catecholaminergic neurons and their receptors (including receptors on astroglial and endothelial cells, near dendritic spines) that trophically regulate the critical period growth and metabolism of widespread cortico-limbic areas.

Indeed, animal studies show that early postnatal stress, such as maternal deprivation, produces permanent changes in dopamine receptor function (Lewis et al., 1990), especially in cortical areas, as well as a significant reduction in the number of dopaminergic neurons in the ventral tegmental area, long-lasting effects that result in "abnormalities of social and affective function" (Martin et al., 1991) and a reduced capacity to respond to aversive experiences in adulthood (Cabib, Puglisi-Allegra, & D'Amato, 1993). It is well established that postnatally maturing dopaminergic projections are potential sites of developmental defects. In light of the principle that "developing mesencephalic dopamine neurons may display varying subpopulation specific vulnerability to outside pathological influences over the course of postnatal ontogeny" (Wang & Pitts, 1994, p. 27), genetic systems, both nuclear and mitochondrial DNA, of the dopamine neurons within the ventral tegmental area, particularly the medial, rostral linear nucleus (as opposed to other mesencephalic dopaminergic subnuclei that innervate mesolimbic areas) would be particularly important, because these project collaterals to the cortex, including the ventral prefrontal areas (see Schore, 1994).

In addition, early social experiences play a significant role in the development of the other catecholamine, noradrenaline. Attachment stress induces alterations in mammalian infant noradrenaline levels (Clarke et al., 1996) that become permanent (Higley, Suomi, & Linnoila, 1991). The enduring changes in noradrenergic system function that result from disturbed mother-infant relations represent a biological substrate or "risk factor" for a vulnerability to despair in later life (Kraemer, 1992) and a susceptibility to affective and anxiety disorders (Rosenblum et al., 1994). In human studies, Rogeness and McClure (1996) reported lowered noradrenaline levels in children exposed to neglect, suggesting that this psychosocial stress modifies the genetic expression of the noradrenaline system. These authors concluded that early experience has long-lasting effects on neuromodulator functioning, and that genetic-environmental factors, especially during early critical periods of development, are important in psychopathogenesis.

EXCESSIVE DEVELOPMENTAL PARCELLATION AND THE PATHOMORPHOGENESIS OF FRONTOLIMBIC CIRCUITS

As opposed to an adaptive stable dynamic system that can flexibly transition between states, a pathological system lacks variability in the face of environmental challenge. What early factors could produce such an organization? According to the classical diathesis-stress model, psychiatric disorders are caused by the interaction of genetic-constitutional vulnerability *and* environmental psychosocial stressors. The interface of nature and nurture is now thought to occur in the psychobiological interaction between mother and infant, "the first encounter between heredity and the psychological environment" (Lehtonen, 1994, p. 28). In such transactions the primary caregiver is providing experiences that shape genetic potential by acting as a psychobiological regulator (or dysregulator) of hormones that directly influence gene transcription. This mechanism mediates a process by which psychoneuroendocrinological changes during critical periods initiate permanent effects at the genomic level. The final developmental outcome of early endocrine-gene interactions is expressed in the imprinting of evolving brain circuitry.

Of particular importance to the creation of a brain system which is "invulnerable" or "vulnerable" to future psychopathology are steroid hormones associated with stress responses. These bioagents regulate gene expression, and, depending upon the cell type, induce or repress sets of genes, and in this manner they act as an essential link between "nature and nurture." Levels of corticosteroids in the infant's brain are directly influenced by the maternal-infant interaction. In beneficial experiences the infant's glucocorticoid stress response is modulated by the psychobiologically attuned mother, thereby inhibiting the infant's pituitary-adrenal response to stress. As a result of these experiences, the infant, in the face of a subsequent novel stimulus, shows a lesser corticoid output and a more rapid return of corticosterone to baseline levels, characteristics of a resilient coping mechanism. These critical period experiences also have long-term structural consequences—they permanently enhance glucocorticoid-receptor concentrations in neurons in the frontal cortex that are involved in terminating the adrenocortical stress response.

On the other hand, stressful dyadic interactions that generate enduring states of painful negative affect are associated with elevated levels of corticosteroids in the infant brain. Deprivation of early maternal stress modulation is known to trigger an exaggerated release of corticosteroids upon exposure to novel experiences which, in adulthood, persists for a longer period of time. Elevated levels of this stress hormone in prenatal and postnatal periods inhibit dendritic branching, reduce brain nucleic acid synthesis, and permanently decrease brain corticosteroid receptors. Critical periods are times of heightened energy production, and these neurohormones specifically inhibit brain energy metabolism, a condition that enhances the toxicity of excitatory neurotransmitters (Novelli, Reilly, Lysko, & Henneberry, 1988) and produces alterations in mitochondrial structure and function (Kimberg, Loud, & Wiener, 1968). Glucocorticoids within the high physiological range impact both DNA and energy systems, and profoundly effect areas of the brain that are organizing in infancy.

As I have noted (Schore, 1994, 1996), the developing brain of an infant who experiences frequent intense attachment disruptions is chronically exposed to states of impaired autonomic homeostasis which he/she shifts into in order to maintain basic metabolic processes for survival. These disturbances in limbic activity and hypothalamic dysfunction are accompanied by increased levels of "stress proteins" in the developing brain (Schore, 1994). In addition to an extensive history of misattunement in the first year, stressful socialization experiences in the second that elicit shame represent a traumatic interruption of interpersonal synchronizing processes, a rupture of attachment dynamics that triggers a state transition from energy-mobilizing sympathetic to energy-conserving parasympathetic dominant ANS activity, a sudden switch from ergotropic to trophotropic arousal that is accompanied by elevated levels of cortisol (Schore 1991; 1998b). Both catecholamines are released in response to stressful disruptions of the attachment bond. If the caregiver does not participate in reparative functions that reduce stress and reestablish psychobiological equilibrium, limbic connections in a critical stage of growth are exposed for extended periods of time to heightened levels of circulating corticosteroids and catecholamines. This toxic brain chemistry induces synapse destruction and death in "affective centers" in the maturing limbic system and therefore permanent functional impairments of the directing of emotion into adaptive channels. More specifically, I suggest that the postnatal development of the affect-regulating orbitofrontal cortex, the corticolimbic system, which directly connects into the hypothalamus and influences corticosteroid levels (Hall & Marr, 1975), is specifically and permanently negatively impacted by high levels of circulating corticosteroids that accompany stressful socioemotional environmental interactions.

In support of this, there is evidence to show that that stress-induced increases of glucocorticoids in postnatal periods induce an abnormal intrinsic circuitry within the corticolimbic system. Benes (1994) suggested that the neurotoxic effects of glucocorticoids are associated with simultaneous hyperactivation of the excitotoxic NMDA-sensitive glutamate receptor, a critical site of synapse elimination and neurotoxicity during early development. It is now known that not only glucocorticoids (Wyllie, 1980) but also glutamate (Ankarcrona et al., 1995) and dopamine (Offen, Ziv, Sternin, Melamed, & Hochman, 1996) can induce apoptotic cell death. Dopamine activates NMDA receptors, and excessive NMDA receptor stimulation generates the superoxide free radicals associated with oxidative stress (Lafon-Cazal, Pietri, Culcasi, & Bockaert, 1993). Both Na^+,K^+-ATPase (Jamme et al., 1995) and mitochondria (Vercesi & Hoffmann, 1993) can sustain damage from the potentially toxic effects of the extremely reactive free radicals, especially hydroxyl radicals that destroy cell membranes and induce mutations in mitochondrial DNA (Giulivi, Boveris, & Cadenas, 1995). Defective mitochondrial biogenesis and energetic activity are early events in apoptosis (Vayssiere, Petit, Risler, & Mignotte, 1994; Zamzimi et al., 1995). Impaired mitochondrial function would result in reduced ATP synthesis levels, which in turn is associated with synaptic transmission failure (Lipton & Whittingham, 1982). These events, occurring during a critical period, could produce a permanently diminished local metabolic capacity and therefore reduced functional activity within and between particular brain regions, especially under challenging conditions that require sustained energy levels.

In fact, this same interaction between corticosteroids and excitatory transmitters is thought to mediate programmed cell death and to represent a primary etiological mechanism for the pathophysiology of neuropsychiatric disorders (Margolis et al., 1994). Although the critical-period overproduction of synapses is genetically driven, the pruning and maintenance of synaptic connections is environmentally driven. This clearly implies that the developmental overpruning of a corticolimbic system that contains a genetically-encoded underproduction of synapses represents a scenario for high risk conditions. Carlson and colleagues (1988) emphasized the importance of "psychological" factors in the "pruning" or "sculpting" of neural networks in specifically the postnatal frontal, limbic, and temporal cortices. Excessive pruning is thought to a be primary mechanism in such "neurodevelopmental" disorders as autism and schizophrenia (Keshavan, Anderson, & Pettegrew, 1994), where large reductions in frontal connectivity are associated with the emergence of circuit pathology that mediates dysfunctional symptoms (Hoffman & Dobscha, 1989).

In most models of psychiatric disorders the concept of "pruning in parallel circuits" (Mender, 1994) has been applied to circuits within the cortex, but it is the pruning of hierarchical cortical-subcortical circuits that is central to the psychoneurodevelopmental origins of the corticolimbic defects that underlie a vulnerability to psychopathology. Of special importance to the emergence of adaptive affect regulation are the reciprocal connections between the orbitoinsular cortex and not only all sensory areas of the cortex, but also with subcortical dopamine neurons in the ventral tegmental area, noradrenaline neurons in the medulla, and various neuroendocrine neurons in the hypothalamus. Critical period interactive experiences, which lead to excessive pruning of catecholaminergic axonal terminals that innervate cortical areas, or of cortical cholinergic axons that project to different subcortical bioaminergic or hypothalamic nuclei, would have long-enduring negative effects.

These interactive experiences are embedded in different types of dyadic attachment transactions, and if these are less than optimal they can induce an excessive apoptotic parcellation (e.g., elimination of long axon collaterals, cell death, dendritic regression) of the components of either one or both of the dual limbic circuits (Schore, 1994; 1996). Frontolimbic parcellation is mediated by the same mechanism described above—excitotoxins have been shown to destroy orbitofrontal neurons (Dias et al., 1996), and this would produce modifications in the microstructural organization and thereby metabolic limitations of areas that hierarchically dominate the two limbic circuits. Different amounts and types of connectional degenerations of the maturing orbitofrontal cortex, an area intimately involved in attachment dynamics, would account for the different patterns in biobehavioral organizations of securely and insecurely attached infants (Spangler & Grossmann, 1993).

More specifically, infants with a history of "disorganized-disoriented" insecure attachments show a high rate of exposure to abuse experiences (Main & Solomon, 1986). Perry, Pollard, Blakely, Baker, and Vigilante (1995) asserted that the abused infant responds to this threatening interpersonal environment with states of hyperarousal that induce long-lasting elevations of sympathetic catecholaminergic activty, and states of parasympathetic vagal-associated dissociation associated with hypoarousal, and that these states are internalized as a sensitized neurobiology. The latter effect is revealed in the finding that this group of toddlers exhibits higher cortisol levels than all other attachment classifications (Hertsgaard, Gunnar, Erickson, & Nachmias, 1995). These dysregulating environmental events trigger extreme and rapid alterations of ergotropic and trophotropic arousal that create chaotic biochemical alterations in the infant brain, a condition conducive to extensive oxidative stress and apoptotic destruction of developing synaptic connections within both limbic circuits. This psychoneurobiological mechanism may mediate the effects by which exposure of an infant to emotional trauma results in a sensory-affecto-motor "emotional-instinctual recordings" of the experience that are inscribed in the neurotransmitter patterns in the limbic system (Weil, 1992).

Early abuse experiences of neglect and/or trauma thus create abnormal critical period microenvironments for the development of corticolimbic areas. Critical period cell death of orbitofrontal and/or temporal cortical neurons that respond to emotional facial displays would lead to permanent deficits in reading the facially expressed emotional states of others. Deficits in emotion-decoding ability are seen in abused children (Camras, Grow, & Ribordy, 1983). Because the orbitofrontal areas are tied into both limbic circuits and both branches of the autonomic nervous system, an extensive developmental parcellation of both circuits would result in a poorly evolved frontolimbic cortex, one in which sympathetic and parasympathetic components could not operate reciprocally (Berntson, Cacioppo, & Quigley, 1991). This organization of autonomic control prevents the integration of lower more primitive autonomic states that allows for the elaboration of new higher states. Due to its fragile regulatory capacities, under even moderate stress, it is vulnerable to disorganization and to affect shifts that are extremely discontinuous and labile.

It is established that structural alterations of the developing hypothalamic-pituitary-adrenal system are responsible for a vulnerability to pathology in later life and that chronically elevated levels of corticosteroids are associated with psychiatric disturbance. Exposure of the right hemisphere to extensive and long-enduring traumatic alterations of arousal during its critical period of organization may predispose the disorganized-disoriented infant to a vulnerability to post traumatic stress disorders (Rauch et al., 1996). This hemisphere is dominant for the regulation of the secretion of cortisol (Wittling & Pfluger, 1990) and shows heightened activity in overwhelming and uncontrollable panic states marked by terror and intense somatic symptoms (Heller, Etienne, & Miller, 1995) and during recall of traumatic memories (Schiffer, Teicher, & Papanicolaou, 1995).

In contrast, different attachment histories indelibly influence the dual limbic components of the "organized" forms of insecure attachments. An insecure-resistant (ambivalent) attachment organization reflects an experience-dependent expansion of the excitatory ventral tegmental circuit and an extensive parcellation of the inhibitory lateral tegmental circuit. The final wiring of this type of orbitofrontal system is sympathetically biased toward states of ergotropic high

arousal and heightened emotionality, but it lacks in "vagal restraint" and therefore has a reduced functional capacity of, under stress, stimulating the parasympathetic and inhibiting the sympathetic components of limbic function. This
system manifests a susceptibility to the underregulation disturbances that underlie externalizing psychopathologies. Such personalities show difficulty in re-
pressing negative affects and easy access to negative memories, and an inability
to inhibit emotional spreading (Mikulincer & Orbach, 1995).

On the other hand, insecure-avoidant attachment histories experientially
shape an expansion of the inhibitory lateral tegmental and excessive parcellation of the excitatory ventral tegmental limbic circuits. In the middle of the
second year, a point of orbitofrontal maturation, insecure-avoidant infants of
depressed mothers, during separation stress, exhibit reduced right frontal EEG
activity (Dawson, 1994). This type of frontolimbic system is biased toward parasympathetic states of trophotropic low arousal and reduced overt emotionality,
but under stress it is inefficient in regulating high arousal states, and is vulnerable to overregulation disturbances and internalizing psychopathologies. These
personalities show defensiveness and low accessibility to negative memories, as
well as high levels of "deactivating strategies" (Dozier & Kobak, 1992). A finding of gender differences in orbital functions that are established in the second
year but thought to persist across the life span (Overman et al., 1996) suggested
differences in wiring of the limbic system between the sexes, and may be relevant to the well-known susceptibility of males to externalizing and females to
internalizing disorders.

Frontal functions have long been known to be associated with personality
functioning. An important emphasis of the chaotic systems approach is a shift
away from the study of traditional group-oriented procedures toward a new
emphasis on individual differences of personality. In neuroscience literature,
authors are proclaiming that, rather than concentrating on a singular "'average"
neuroanatomic design, attention should be focused on the large range of
variation that "normal" stuctures can exhibit, and that the variability in the
morphology of the frontal lobe may underlie individual differences in functional capacities. These principles equally apply to the ontogenesis of "abnormal" organizations, and particularly to the experience-dependent evolution of
frontal and limbic microarchitectures and metabolic limitations that are associated with emotional dysfunction and a vulnerability to psychiatric disorders.
According to Rutter (1995), environmental stresses impinge most on those who
have already exhibited psychological vulnerability and accentuate preexisting
psychological characteristics.

The question is, which specific structural systems exhibit this vulnerability?
I am suggesting that the orbital frontolimbic system, the "executive control
system" for the entire right cortex, the primary cortical hemisphere involved in
attachment functions, the processing of socioemotional information, and the
regulation of psychobiological states, is sensitive to prolonged aversive experiences during its critical period of growth, and that different types of alterations

of its organization account for its adaptive limitations and dysfunctional operations. This formulation is congruent with Main's (1996) assertion that "disorganized" and "organized" forms of insecure attachment are primary risk factors for the development of mental disorders.

EARLY-FORMING STRUCTURAL PATHOLOGY OF THE NONLINEAR RIGHT HEMISPHERE AND THE ORIGINS OF A PREDISPOSITION TO PSYCHIATRIC DISORDERS

At the beginning of this chapter, I presented a general model of self-organization, one that emphasizes the central role of synchronized energy exchanges between a developing living system and its environment. These patterned energy fluctuations, associated with nonlinear changes in state, allow for more complex interconnections between the system's components, and therefore constitute a salutary primordial matrix for self-organization and the emergence of a hierarchical structural system that is capable of dynamically transitioning between a range of possible states and exploring new states. This allows for the operation of a stable and resilient system, one that can adaptively change in response to environmental perturbations yet retain continuity. I then applied this general model to the developmental organization of the orbitiofrontal cortex and its subcortical and cortical connections, a homeostatic system that dynamically regulates organismic energy balance and transitions between psychobiological states in response to internal and external alterations. This hierarchical regulatory structure acts as an executive control system for the nonlinear right brain.

As opposed to growth-promoting environments, growth-inhibiting environments negatively influence the ontogeny of homeostatic self-regulatory and attachment systems. Nonoptimal environments do not supply sufficient quantities of nutritive matter and modulated levels of energy to the growing brain, and these circumstances, especially in interaction with a genetically encoded lowered limbic threshold and hyperreactivity to novel environmental events, give rise to a developing system that is poorly equipped to enter into a dyadic open homeostatic system with the human environment. This precludes exposure to a variety of socioemotional experiences that are required for experience-dependent brain maturation, and therefore negatively influences the stabilization of interconnections within subcortical and cortical areas of the infant's brain that are in a critical period of growth. Furthermore, the infant's transactions with an emotionally unresponsive or misattuned environment that provides poor interactive repair are stored in the infant's developing corticolimbic circuitries as imagistic, visceral, and nonverbal procedural memories. As opposed to a secure interactive representation of a regulated-self-in-interaction-with-an-attuning-other, these "pathological" working models of attachment encode an enduring prototypical cognitive-affective schema of a dysregulated-self-in-interaction-with-a-misattuning-other (see Schore 1994, 1998b).

Early attachment experiences represent psychobiological transactions between the mother's and infant's right hemispheres. The child's growing brain imprints the output of the mother's right cortex which contains the mechanism for the maternal capacity to comfort the infant (Horton, 1995). Structural limitations in the mother's emotion-processing right brain are reflected in a poor ability to comfort and regulate the infant's negative affective states, and these experiences are stamped into the infant's right orbitofrontal system and its cortical and subcortical connections. Exposure to such conditions throughout a critical period of corticolimbic marturation results in inefficient coping systems that cannot adaptively switch internal states in response to stressful external environmental challenges. The functional indicators of this intergenerationally transmitted adaptive limitation are specifically manifest in recovery deficits of internal reparative coping mechanisms, a poor capacity for the state regulation involved in self-comforting in times of stress.

Such deficits are most obvious under highly emotional and challenging conditions that call for behavioral flexibility and affect regulation. The adaptive limitation of all psychopathologies is manifest in more intense and longer lasting emotional responses and the amplification of negative states. This characterization describes the dysfunction of a structurally impaired frontal ventromedial system that results in "emotional response perseveration" (Morgan & LeDoux, 1995), that is, an inefficiency in the temporal organization of behavior (Fuster, 1985) and in the adjustment and correction of emotional states (Rolls, 1986). Neurobiological studies indicate that due to its unique neurobiological characteristics, the orbital cortex shows a "preferential vulnerability" to a spectrum of psychiatric disorders (Barbas, 1995). In previous work, I chronicled a number of studies that implicated orbitofrontal metabolic dysfunction in autism, schizophrenia, bipolar disorder, unipolar depression, posttraumatic stress disorder, drug addiction, alcoholism, and psychopathic, borderline, and narcissistic personality disorders (for references, see Schore, 1994, 1996).

A fundamental postulate of clinical psychiatry holds that the major source of stress precipitating psychiatric disorders involves the affective response to a rupture or loss of a significant relationship. It is thought that an environmental event, appraised to be emotionally meaningful, may be the direct cause of a neurochemical change that then becomes the psychopathogenic mechanism of the illness (Gabbard, 1994). Due to the "patterning of the nervous system," psychiatric patients show an inability to adapt internally to stress, and this is symptomatically expressed in a continuing activation or inhibition of organ systems in a manner inappropriate to the immediate environmental situation. In neuropsychiatric models, defective modulators are viewed as causal agents for mental abnormalities that are characterized by a disturbance in the continuity of successive stable memory states (Mender, 1994). According to dynamic systems theory, a stable yet resilient dynamic open system can return to a previous stationary state within an appropriate time period (Thelen, 1989), but a dysfunctional system shows poor capacity to recover after stressful departures from homeostatic equilibrium. Systems that exhibit good primitive organization become more complex (Schwalbe, 1991), but those with a compromised early ontogeny are inefficient at state regulation and therefore exhibit an abnormality in the dimensionality of state transitions, specifically an overreliance on an oversimplified set of transition paths among attractors which constrains the individual's flexibility to adapt to challenging situations with new strategies.

Research in biological psychiatry is focusing on the relationships between the disturbed emotions and cognitions of psychopathological states and neurotransmitter dysfunctions (Maas & Katz, 1992) and is emphasizing the functional role of monoaminergic neuromodulators in psychiatric disorders (Dolan & Grasby, 1994). Indeed, the limbic receptors of these bioamines are the primary target of the psychopharmacological agents that are currently being used by clinical psychiatrists. Contemporary psychiatry is also delving more deeply into the role of right hemispheric dysfunction in psychiatric disorders (Cutting, 1992), such as schizophrenia (Cutting, 1994), autism (Ozonoff & Miller, 1996), depression (Liotti & Tucker, 1992), mania (Starkstein et al., 1988), and posttraumatic stress disorder (Rauch et al., 1996). This hemisphere is deeply connected into the two forebrain-midbrain limbic circuits, the noradrenergic vagal brain circuit of emotion regulation and the mesocortical dopaminergic system that processes emotionally stressful inputs. The dysfunction of these limbic circuits is central to the affect regulatory deficits of all psychiatric disorders.

A major contribution of the discipline of developmental psychopathology to the study of psychiatric disorders is its emphasis on the elucidation of the early ontogenetic factors that predispose high-risk individuals to later psychopathologies. In consonance with dynamic systems theory, this developmental perspective underscores the fact that a more detailed knowledge of the self-organization of the developing brain is essential to a deeper understanding of specifically how genetic and environmental factors interact to generate an enduring vulnerability to stress-induced disorganizations of adaptive functions. Developmental neurobiological studies indicate that the right brain system, which more than the left is deeply interconnected into the limbic system and is fundamentally involved in responding to and coping with stress, is in a growth spurt in early infancy. The limbic areas of the cortex are in an intense state of myelination from the middle of the first through the middle of the second year (Kinney et al., 1988) and show an anatomical maturation at the end of this period. Most importantly, the biogenic aminergic systems that regulate the growth and activity of the limbic system are in an active state of experience-dependent growth in these same stages of human infancy.

This clearly implies that various patterns of alterations of right-brain bioamine activity should be exhibited in the high-risk infant. Indeed, there is interest in identifying the critical involvement of dopamine in development, before signs and symptoms are expessed (Winn, 1994). Psychobiological research indicates that prenatally stressed developing systems show, soon after birth, an alteration of dopamine levels in the right hemisphere and alterations of emotionality (Friede & Weinstock, 1988). Children diagnosed as high-risk for schizophrenia exhibit early neurointegrative deficits, reflecting dysregulation of hypothalamic and reticular activating systems (Fish, Marcus, Hans, Auerbach, & Perdue, 1992). Under challenge, these infants show left-sided postural and movement abnormalities, reflecting overactivity of ascending dopaminergic systems in the right hemisphere (Walker, 1994). This developmental syndrome may reflect an early inefficient orbitocortical modulation of ascending excitatory influences, which results in an overactivity of right brain ascending dopaminergic systems and enhanced responsiveness of subcortical mesolimbic dopaminergic systems to stress (Deutsch, 1992). High-risk offspring of schizophrenic parents show EEG abnormalities in the right, rather than left hemisphere (Itil, Hsu, Saletu, & Mednick, 1974), and disturbances in facial expressions of emotion are seen in preschizophrenic infants in the first year of life (Walker, Grimes, Davis, & Smith, 1993). These early events may play a critical role in the "'developmental disconnection of temporolimbic prefrontal cortices" seen in the hypometabolic prefrontal areas of the schizophrenic brain (Weinberger & Lipska, 1995).

This model of early right-brain deficits is also supported in another high-risk population. Three-to-6-month-old infants of depressed mothers show a right frontal EEG asymmetry (Field, Fox, Pickens, & Nawrocki, 1995), which has been interpreted as reflecting a subcortical asymmetry in the amygdala (Calkins & Fox, 1994). At 10 months, infants who express more intense distress to maternal separation display a greater right- than left-frontal activation (Davidson & Fox, 1989), and this asymmetry has been related to emotional reactivity and vulnerability to psychopathology in both infants and adults (Davidson et al., 1990). Individuals with extreme right-frontal activation are thought to exhibit a negative affective response to a very low intensity negative affect elicitor, and to be impaired in the ability to terminate a negative emotion once it has begun (Wheeler, Davidson, & Tomarken, 1993). Fox, Schmidt, Calkins, Rubin, & Coplan (1996) report that young children with internalizing *and* externalizing problems show greater right- than left-frontal EEG activation, and suggest that this pattern reflects difficulties with affect regulation, whether the affect arousal is extremely negative or positive. These findings fit nicely with the model of right hemispheric regulation of intense emotional states presented earlier.

There is convincing evidence that the deficits of an early compromised right cortex persist as the individual passes into early childhood. A loss of interconnections (extensive parcellation) within the infant's early developing right hemisphere is associated with an impairment of social perception, that is, difficulty in evaluating facial expression, gestures, or prosody. These children are at high risk for the nonverbal learning disabilities (Semrud-Clikeman & Hynd, 1990) associated with a "developmental right hemisphere syndrome" (Gross-Tsur et al., 1995). The latter authors enumerate specific emotional and interpersonal problems that are present early in development but frequently not recognized until the child begins school. These include maladaptation to new situations, difficulties in maintaining friendships, withdrawn and excessively shy behaviors, and avoidance of eye contact. A "developmental social-emotional processing disorder" associated with electrophysiological abnormalities of the right hemisphere has been reported by Manoach, Sandson, Mesulam, Price, and Weintraub (1993). In a previous study these authors concluded that early right hemisphere dysfunction is expressed in later life as introversion, poor social perception, chronic emotional difficulties, inability to display affect, and impairment in visuospatial representation (Weintraub & Mesulam, 1983).

These deficits endure into adulthood. Longitudinal studies have shown that undercontrolled and inhibited disturbances in early childhood predict adult psychiatric disorders (Caspi, Moffitt, Newman, & Silva, 1996). In adults "greater right hemisphericity" is associated with a history of more frequent negative affect and lower self-esteem (Persinger & Makarec, 1991), that is, chronic difficulties in affect regulation. Functional limitations of affect regulation reflect structural and metabolic impairments in right frontolimbic distributed systems that contain connections between cortical and subcortical areas, and these prefrontal organizations represent primary sites of psychopathogenesis. This is because early relational environments that inhibit the organization of this control system generate an unstable right cortical capacity to evaluate and guide behavior, a metabolically inefficient one that under stress is easily displaced by an inflexible subcortical mechanism. The uncoupling of the two right-brain limbic circuits would occur in response to high levels of interactive stress in episodes of "expressed emotion," intense levels of humiliation, criticism, hostility, and emotional overinvolvement within a close relationship (Vaughn & Leff, 1976). This uniquely potent psychobiological stressor for the induction of all classes of psychiatric disorders triggers extremely high levels of sympathetic ergotropic and parasympathetic trophotropic arousal that are beyond the individual's regulatory capacities. The resultant "transient frontolimbic imbalance" elicits subcortical limbic kindling, subjectively experienced as a sudden transition into rapidly shifting and intensely affective states, that is, "emotional chaos" (Grotstein, 1990).

The right hemisphere, which is preferentially activated in stress, is specialized to process intensely negative states (Otto, Yeo, & Dougher, 1987). PET (Positron Emission Tomography) imaging studies that measure energy metabolism are now revealing the preeminent role of right-hemispheric paralimbic activity as traumatic emotional memories are activated (Rauch et al., 1996), and are documenting the changes in orbitofrontal metabolic activity during the evocation of a phobic state (Frederikson, Wik, Annas, Ericson, & Stone-Elander, 1995). The importance of these studies is that they can do more than simply "localize" psychiatric impairments in the brain. Rather, they offer information regarding the temporal organization of dysregulated dynamic systems, and can therefore elucidate a deeper understanding of the state changes that underlie the various forms of emotional dysregulation manifest in different classes of psychiatric disorders. The fact that a broad spectrum of psychiatric disorders show disturbances of the right hemisphere, the hemisphere that is centrally influenced by attachment experiences, accounts for the principle that all early forming psychopathology constitutes disorders of attachment and manifests itself as failures of interactional and/or self-regulation.

DYNAMIC SYSTEMS THEORY AND ONGOING RIGHT-HEMISPHERIC DEVELOPMENT

Attachment is "the apex of dyadic emotional regulation, a culmination of all development in the first year and a harbinger of the self-regulation that is to come" (Sroufe, 1996, p. 172). The attachment dynamic continues throughout the life span as an unconscious mechanism that mediates the interpersonal and intrapsychic events of all relationships, especially intimate relationships. By the second year, the infant can construct accurate representations of events that endure and are accessible over time (Bauer, 1996), and these experiences are imprinted into right-hemispheric networks that store autobiographical memory (Fink et al., 1996). In this manner, "dispositional characteristics that appear to be linked to right hemisphere activity are a product of a developmental process involving cognitive and memory structures" (Heller, 1993, p. 484). The ability to access an internal working model of relationships that encodes strategies of affect regulation and expectations of future interactions, to interact with a meaningful other in order to share positive affect and reduce negative affective states, to develop a theory of mind of the intentions of others, and to be psychobiologically attuned and thereby empathic to the internal states of an other self, are fundamental prerequisites of an adaptive capacity to enter into satisfying interactions with other humans. Affect-regulating interactions are essential to the development of the infant's coping skills, but at later points in the life span they continue to be necessary for the continued growth of the brain and the expanding capacity to experience more complex psychobiological states.

The nonlinear right hemisphere, the substrate of early attachment processes, ends its growth phase in the second year, when the linear left hemisphere begins one, but it cycles back into growth phases at later periods of the life cycle (Thatcher, 1994). This allows for the continuity of attachment mechanisms in subsequent functioning, and yet also for the potential continuing reorganization of the emotion-processing right brain throughout life. The orbitofrontal regions, centrally involved in the regulation of psychobiological state and energy balance, are unique in that they retain the neuroanatomic and biochemical features of early development, and for this reason they are the most plastic areas of the cortex (Barbas, 1995). If, however, an infant, especially one born with a genetically encoded altered neurophysiologic reactivity, does not have adequate experiences of being part of an open dynamic system with an emotionally responsive adult human, its corticolimbic organization will be poorly capable of coping with the stressful chaotic dynamics that are inherent in all human relationships. Such a system tends to become static and closed, and invested in defensive structures to guard against anticipated interactive assaults that potentially trigger disorganizing and emotionally painful psychobiological states. Because of its avoidance of novel situations and diminished capacity to cope with challenging situations, it does not expose itself to new socioemotional learning experiences that are required for the continuing experience-dependent growth of the right brain. This structural limitation, in turn, negatively impacts the future trajectory of self-organization.

1997

CHAPTER 6

The Effects of a Secure Attachment Relationship on Right Brain Development, Affect Regulation, and Infant Mental Health

THE FUNDAMENTAL IMPORTANCE of the psychological as well as the biological health of the infant has long been held as a cardinal principle by every clinical discipline that deals with young children — infant psychiatry, behavioral pediatrics, child psychology, developmental psychoanalysis, and more recently the emerging fields of developmental psychopathology and infant mental health. And yet a more precise characterization of the concept of infant mental health, like the definition of "mental health" itself, has been elusive. Theoretically, it is clear that there must be links between infant and adult mental health, yet these too have been ill-defined. Although there is a large body of clinical knowledge in psychiatry, abnormal psychology, and psychoanalysis affirming the centrality of early relational experiences on enduring adaptive and maladaptive aspects of personality, there has been some question as to the structural mechanisms by which such events positively or negatively influence the process of development as it continues over the life span. In other words, How do the earliest interactions between a maturing biological organism and the social environment influence infant mental health? What are the central functions that define infant mental health? How does infant mental health influence mental health at later stages of development?

The defined mission of *The Infant Mental Health Journal* is to focus upon infant social-emotional development, caregiver-infant interactions, contextual and cultural influences on infant and family development, and all conditions that place infants and/or their families at risk for less-than-optimal development.* In this two-part work I suggest that although the unique importance of

*This chapter was written as an article for a Special Edition of the *Infant Mental Health Journal*. "Contributions from the Decade of the Brain to Infant Mental Health." Its companion piece, also published in *Infant Mental Health Journal*, appears here as Chapter 7.

"optimal development" has long been addressed by the psychological sciences, due to the advances of "the decade of the brain," developmental neuroscience is now in a position to offer more detailed and integrated psychoneurobiological models of normal and abnormal development. The incorporation of this information into developmental psychological models could forge closer links between optimal brain development and adaptive infant mental health, as well as altered brain development and maladaptive mental health.

A theoretical concept that is shared by an array of basic and clinical sciences is the concept of regulation (Schore, 1994, 1996, 1998e, 1999e, 2000c), and because it integrates both the biological and psychological realms, it can also be used to further models of normal and abnormal structure-function development, and therefore adaptive and maladaptive infant mental health. Interdisciplinary research and clinical data are affirming the concept that in infancy and beyond, the regulation of affect is a central organizing principle of human development and motivation. In the neuroscience literature, Damasio asserted that emotions are the highest order direct expression of bioregulation in complex organisms (1998), and that primordial representations of body states are the building blocks and scaffolding of development (1994). Brothers argued that emotion occurs "in the context of evolved systems for the mutual regulation of behavior, often involving bodily changes that act as signals" (1997, p. 123). Emotions and their regulation are thus essential to the adaptive function of the brain, which is described by Damasio (1994):

> The overall function of the brain is to be well informed about what goes on in the rest of the body, the body proper; about what goes on in itself; and about the environment surrounding the organism, so that suitable survivable accommodations can be achieved between the organism and the environment. (p. 90)

In a number of works I have described the earliest ontogeny of these adaptive brain functions, and have argued that the essential events that allow for the emergence of the regulatory systems that control such functions occur during the brain growth spurt (Schore, 1994, 1996, 1997a, 1998a, 1998b, 2000b, 2000c). Moreover, I have offered data that suggests that the inceptive stages of development represent a maturational period of specifically the early maturing right brain, which is dominant in the first three years of human life (Chiron et al., 1997; Schore, 1994). The right brain is centrally involved in not only processing social-emotional information, facilitating attachment functions, and regulating bodily and affective states (Schore, 1994, 1998a), but also in the control of vital functions supporting survival and enabling the organism to cope actively and passively with stress (Wittling & Schweiger, 1993).

Furthermore, in a series of contributions I have proposed that the maturation of these adaptive right brain regulatory capacities is experience-dependent, and that this experience is embedded in the attachment relationship between the infant and primary caregiver (Schore, 1994, 1999b, 2000a, 2000c). But it is important to point out that this experience can positively or negatively influence the maturation of brain structure, and therefore the psychological development of the infant. This developmental psychoneurobiological model clearly suggests direct links between secure attachment, development of efficient right brain regulatory functions, and adaptive infant mental health, as well as between traumatic attachment, inefficient right-brain regulatory function, and maladaptive infant mental health.

In an attempt to forge these conceptual links more tightly, in this two-part work I will address the problem of operationally defining adaptive and maladaptive infant mental health by integrating very recent data from attachment theory, developmental neuroscience, and developmental psychopathology. The primary goal of this latter field is to characterize the ontological processes whereby early patterns of individual adaptation evolve into later patterns of adaptation (Cicchetti, 1994), and thereby it investigates the early development of the individual's coping systems. In generating models of how early ontogenetic factors predispose high-risk individuals to later psychopathologies, this rapidly growing interdisciplinary approach is directly inquiring into the mechanisms that account for the continuity between infant mental health and mental health at later points in the life span.

An essential principle of the developmental psychopathology perspective is that atypical development can only be understood in the context of typical development, and so the focus is on underlying mechanisms common to both. This model suggests that any overarching conception of early development needs to integrate both the biological and psychological realms, and that it must incorporate models of both adaptive and maladaptive infant mental health. It also implies that infant mental health cannot be defined solely as a "psychological" construct — rather, it is more precisely characterized as "psychobiological."

Utilizing such a perspective, in these two papers I will contrast the neurobiology of a secure attachment, an exemplar of adaptive infant mental, with the neurobiology of an insecure disorganized/disoriented ("type D") attachment, the most severe form of attachment pathology. This attachment category is associated with early trauma, and will be presented as a prototype of maladaptive infant mental health. Throughout I shall underscore the effects of the caregiver's stress regulating and dysregulating psychobiological interactions on the infant's maturing coping systems that are organizing in the limbic circuitries of the early developing right hemisphere. An increasing body of evidence indicates that "maternal care during infancy serves to 'program' behavioral responses to stress in the offspring" (Caldji et al., 1998, p. 5335).

And so in the first of this two-part contribution I will offer an overview of an interdisciplinary perspective of development, outline connections between attachment theory, stress regulation, and infant mental health, describe the neurobiology of a secure attachment, present models of right-brain, early limbic system, and orbital frontolimbic development, and suggest links between continued orbitofrontal and right-brain development and adaptive mental health. In the second part I will offer ideas about how early relational traumatic assaults of the developing attachment system inhibit right brain development, impair affect-regulating capacities, and negatively impact infant and adult mental health. These models are presented for further experimental testing and clinical validation.

OVERVIEW OF AN INTERDISCIPLINARY
PERSPECTIVE OF DEVELOPMENT

To date, infant mental health has mostly been described in terms of the presence or absence of certain psychological functions, but it should be pointed out that these functions are, in turn, the product of biological structural systems that are organizing over the stages of infancy. Such internal systems are clearly located in the developing brain, which mediates more complex functions, and it is known that the conditions and events occurring in "critical" or "sensitive" early periods of brain development have long-enduring effects. Brazelton and Cramer (1990) noted that in critical phases energy is high in the infant and the parent for receptivity to each other's cues and for adapting to each other.

From late pregnancy through the second year, the brain is in a critical period of accelerated growth, a process that consumes higher amounts of energy than any other stage in the life span, and so it requires sufficient amounts of not only nutrients, especially long-chain polyunsaturated fatty acids (Dobbing, 1997), but also regulated interpersonal experiences for optimal maturation (Levitsky & Strupp, 1995; Schore, 1994). The critical period concept, now firmly established in biology (Katz, 1999), prescribes that "specific critical conditions or stimuli are necessary for development and can influence development only during that period" (Erzurumlu & Killackey, 1982, p. 207). But it also suggests that during critical periods brain growth is exquisitely susceptible to adverse environmental factors such as nutritional deficits and dysregulating interpersonal affective experiences, both of which negatively impact infant mental health.

The human brain growth spurt, which is at least 5/6 postnatal, begins in the third trimester in utero and continues to about 18 to 24 months of age (Dobbing & Sands, 1973). During this period the brain is rapidly generating nucleic acids that program developmental processes at a rate that will never again be attained. This massive production of both nuclear and mitochondrial genetic material in the infant's brain is directly influenced by events in specifically the social-affective environment (Schore, 1994). Indeed, recent conceptions of development utilize a "transactional model," which views development and brain organization as "a process of transaction between (a) genetically coded programs for the formation of structures and connections among structures and (b) environmental influence" (Fox et al., 1994, p. 681). And so Sander (2000) formulated a key question for deeper understandings of infant mental health:

To what extent can the genetic potentials of an infant brain be aug-
mented or optimized through the experiences and activities of the infant
within its own particular caregiving environment? (p. 8)

The interface of nature and nurture occurs in the psychobiological interaction between mother and infant, "the first encounter between heredity and the
psychological environment" (Lehtonen, 1994, p. 28). According to Cicchetti
and Tucker (1994), "Environmental experience is recognized to be critical to
the differentiation of brain tissue itself. Nature's potential can be realized only
as it enabled by nurture" (p. 538). The evolution and specification of this potential is described by Gomez-Pinilla, Choi, and Ryba, (1999):

> [O]ne of the most fundamental strategies for biological adaptation in or-
> ganisms is the ability of the central nervous system (CNS) to react and
> modify itself to environmental challenges. There is general agreement
> that the genetic specification of neuronal structure is not sufficient for an
> optimally functional nervous system. Indeed, a large variety of experimen-
> tal approaches indicate that the environment affects the structure and
> function of the brain. (p. 1051)

A large body of evidence supports the principle that cortical and subcortical
networks are generated by a genetically programmed initial overabundant production of synaptic connections, which is then followed by an environmentally
driven process of competitive interaction to select those connections that are
most effectively entrained to environmental information. This parcellation, the
activity-dependent fine-tuning of connections and pruning of surplus circuitry,
is a central mechanism of the self-organization of the developing brain
(Chechik, Meilijson, & Ruppin, 1999; Schore, 1994). It is important to emphasize, however, that environmental experience can either enable or constrain
the structure and function of the developing brain. In other words, early interpersonal events positively or negatively impact the structural organization of
the brain and its expanding adaptive functional capacities. This clearly implies,
in the broadest of terms, a direct relationship between an enabling socioemotional environment, an optimally developing brain, and adaptive infant mental
health.

A major conclusion of developmental neuroscience research in the 1990s
was that there is agreement that the infant brain "is designed to be molded by
the environment it encounters" (Thomas et al., 1997, p. 209). The brain is
thus considered to be a bioenvironmental or biosocial organ (Gibson, 1996),
and investigators are now exploring the unique domains of the "social brain"
(Brothers, 1990), and the central role of emotions in social communication
(Adolphs, 2000). In applying this principle to social-emotional development,
the connections between the neurobiological concept of "enriched environ-

ment" and the psychological concept of "optimal development" can be more closely coupled in the psychoneurobiological construct of a "growth-facilitating" (as opposed to "growth-inhibiting") interpersonal environment (Greenspan, 1981; Schore, 1994) that positively (or negatively) effects the experience-dependent maturation of the brain.

This interdisciplinary model is compatible with conceptions which emphasize that developmental processes can best be understood in terms of a context in which evolving biological systems are interacting with the social realm. As Cairns and Stoff (1996) described:

> It is necessary to go beyond the conventional notion that biological variables not only influence behavior and environment to the more modern notion that behavioral and environmental variables also impact on biology. Maturation and developmental processes may provide the common ground for understanding the process of biological social integration. On the one hand, it is virtually impossible to conceptualize developmental changes without recognition of the inevitable internal modifications that occur within the organism over time. On the other hand, it is misleading to focus on the individual's biology in the absence of detailed information about the interaction and social circumstances in which the behavior occurs. (p. 349)

This integration of biology and psychology in order to understand development has a rich tradition in science. In *The Expression of Emotion in Man and Animals*, Darwin (1872/1965) established the scientific study of emotions and proposed that movements of expression in the face and body serve as the first means of communication between the mother and her infant (Schore, 2000a, 2000c, 2001d). In *The Project for a Scientific Psychology*, Freud (1895/1966), in an attempt to link neurology and psychology, first presented both his models of early development and ideas on how early traumatic events could heighten the risk of later forming psychopathology (Schore, 1995, 1997b, 1997c). Although others have followed this line of integrating the biological and psychological realms, perhaps the most important scientist of the late twentieth century to apply an interdisciplinary perspective to the understanding of how early developmental processes influence later mental health was Bowlby. He asserted that attachment theory can frame specific hypotheses that relate early family experiences to different forms of psychiatric disorders, including the neurophysiological changes that accompany these disturbances of mental health. It is thus no coincidence that attachment theory, the dominant theoretical model of development in contemporary psychology, psychoanalysis, and psychiatry, is the most powerful source of hypotheses about infant mental health.

ATTACHMENT, STRESS REGULATION,
AND INFANT MENTAL HEALTH

In his classic work of developmental science, Bowlby (1969) called for deeper explorations of how an immature organism is critically shaped by its primordial relationship with a mature adult member of its species, that is, more extensive studies of how an attachment bond forms between the infant and mother (Schore, 2000a, 2000c). In this conception, developmental processes are the product of the interaction of a unique genetic endowment with a particular "environment of adaptiveness, and especially of his interaction with the principal figure in that environment, namely his mother" (Bowlby 1969, p. 180). Thus, the infant's emerging social, psychological, and biological capacities can not be understood apart from its relationship with the mother.

More specifically, in *Attachment* Bowlby (1969) inquired into the mechanisms by which the infant forms a secure attachment bond of emotional communication with the mother, and how this early socioemotional learning is then internalized in the form of an enduring capacity to regulate and thereby generate and maintain states of emotional security. He observed that the mother-infant attachment relationship is "accompanied by the strongest of feelings and emotions, happy or the reverse" (p. 242), that this interaction occurs within a context of "facial expression, posture, tone of voice, physiological changes, tempo of movement, and incipient action" (p. 120), that attachment interactions allow for the emergence of a *biological control system* that functions in the organism's "state of arousal" (pp. 152–157), that the instinctive behavior which constitutes attachment emerges from the coconstructed environment of evolutionary adaptiveness has consequences that are "vital to the survival of the species" (p. 137), and that the infant's "capacity to cope with stress" is correlated with certain maternal behaviors (p. 344). These last two factors, adaptiveness and coping capacity, are obviously central components of infant mental health.

I have contended that attachment theory is, in essence, a regulatory theory (Schore, 2000a, 2000c, 2001d). More specifically, in such attachment transactions the secure mother, at an intuitive, nonconscious level, is continuously regulating the baby's shifting arousal levels and therefore emotional states. Emotions are the highest order direct expression of bioregulation in complex organisms (Damasio, 1998), and attachment can thus be defined as the dyadic regulation of emotion (Sroufe, 1996). As a result of being exposed to the primary caregiver's regulatory capacities, the infant's expanding adaptive ability to evaluate on a moment-to-moment basis stressful changes in the external environment, especially the social environment, allows him or her to begin to form coherent responses to cope with stressors. It is important to note that not just painful experiences but also novel events are stressors. This means that the capacity to orient toward not only the familiar but to approach, tolerate, and incorporate novelty is fundamental to the expansion of a developing system's adaptive capacity to learn new information and therefore to move toward more complexity.

Furthermore, because the maturation of the brain systems that mediate this coping capacity occurs in human infancy, the development of the ability to adaptively cope with stress is directly and significantly influenced by the infant's early interaction with the primary caregiver (Schore, 1994, 1997a; 2000c). In support of Bowlby's speculations on the association of attachment with coping mechanisms, recent interdisciplinary studies indicate that "even subtle differences in maternal behavior can affect infant attachment, development, and physical well-being" (Champoux, Byrne, DeLizio, & Suomi, 1992, p. 254), and that "variations in maternal care can serve as the basis for a nongenomic behavioral transmission of individual differences in stress reactivity across generations" (Francis et al., 1999, p. 1155).

In other words, the same interactive regulatory transactions that cocreate a secure attachment bond also influence the development and expansion of the infant's regulatory systems involved in appraising and coping with stress, and therefore essential to organismic survival. According to McEwen and Stellar, "A stressful stimulus results in a severe perturbation of an organism's physiological systems, and the degree of the perceived or real threat determines the magnitude of the stress response to an internal or external challenge" (1993, p. 2093). In describing stress, a concept that lies at the interface of the biological and psychological realms, Weinstock (1997) stated:

> The survival of living organisms depends upon the maintenance of a harmonious equilibrium or homeostasis in the face of constant challenge by intrinsic or extrinsic forces or stressors. Stress is a term that is widely used to describe both the subjective experience induced by a novel, potentially threatening or distressing situation, and the behavioral or neurochemical reactions to it. These are designed to promote adaptive response to the physical and psychological stimuli and preserve homeostasis . . . Successful equilibrium is reflected by a rapid neurochemical response to these stimuli which is terminated at the appropriate time, or gives way to counter-regulatory measures to prevent an excessive reaction. (p. 1)

There is now agreement that these critical functions are mediated by the sympathetic-adrenomedullary (SAM) axis and the hypothalamo-pituitary-adrenocortical (HPA) axis. Furthermore, a growing body of studies indicates that the threshold for stimulation of the SAM axis is lower than that for stimulation of the HPA axis (Malarkey, Lipkus, & Cacioppo, 1995), and that the neurochemistry of the former is regulated by the major stress hormone, corticotropin releasing factor (CRF), which regulates catecholamine release in the sympathetic nervous system (Brown et al., 1982), and of the latter by the glucocorticoid cortisol, the major "anti-stress" hormone (Yehuda, 1999). Yehuda pointed out that the greater the severity of the stressor, the higher the levels of these neurochemicals, and also that the actions of these two systems are synergistic: "whereas catecholamines facilitate the availability of energy to the body's vital organs, cortisol's role in stress is to help contain, or shut down sympathetic activation" (1999, p. 257).

In other words, the energy-expending sympathetic and energy-conserving parasympathetic components of the autonomic nervous system (ANS) regulate the autonomic, somatic aspects of not only stress responses but also emotional states. This adaptive function was stressed by Porges (1997):

> Emotion depends on the communication between the autonomic nervous system and the brain; visceral afferents convey information on physiological state to the brain and are critical to the sensory or psychological experience of emotion, and cranial nerves and the sympathetic nervous system are outputs from the brain that provide somatomotor and visceromotor control of the expression of emotion. (p. 65)

But in addition to the ANS, there is a growing appreciation of the role of the central nervous system (CNS) limbic circuits in coping capacities, because this emotion-processing system is specialized to appraise social information from facial expressions implicitly, without conscious awareness (Critchley, Daly, et al., 2000), to represent motivationally salient stimuli in order to adapt to a rapidly changing environment (Mesulam, 1998), and to alter the activity of brain-stem neuromodulatory systems responsible for emotional states and arousal (Tucker, 1992). These subcortically produced neuromodulatory bioamines, especially the catecholamines dopamine and noradrenaline, regulate brain state (Flicker, McCarley, & Hobson, 1981), energy metabolism (Huang et al., 1994), and blood flow microcirculation (Krimer, Mully, Williams, & Goldman-Rakic, 1998). By activating cAMP-response-element-binding protein (CREB; Walton & Dragunow, 2000), they also act as internal clocks to coordinate the timing of developmental processes (Lauder & Krebs, 1986) and mediate both trophic growth-promoting and stress-related functions (Morris et al., 1983; O'Dowd, Barrington, Ng, Hertz, & Hertz, 1994; Schore, 1994). The limbic system is involved in stress functions (Seyle, 1956), and various components of this system are responsible for appraising the salience of a stressor, and then initiating and organizing a psychobiological response.

Developmental research indicates that individual differences in peripheral and central autonomic balance emerge in early development, and that these are reflected in the affective and cognitive domains (Friedman & Thayer, 1998). The "lower," subcortical sympathetic and parasympathetic components of the ANS, as well as the "higher" cortical limbic components of the CNS, are organizing pre- and postnatally, and their maturation is experience-dependent (Schore, 1996; 2000b). In fact it is thought that an early postnatal period represents a "critical period" of limbic-autonomic circuit development, during which time experience or environmental events might participate in shaping ongoing synapse formation. (Rinaman, Levitt, & Card, 2000, p. 2739)

This organization is especially expressed in the early maturing (Chiron et al., 1997) right hemisphere, which, more so than the later developing left, deeply connects into both the limbic system (Tucker, 1992) and the ANS (Spence et al., 1996), and is therefore dominant for the human stress response (Wittling, 1997) and organismic survival (Wittling & Schweiger, 1993). The environmental events that influence ANS-limbic circuit development are embedded in the infant's ongoing affect-regulating attachment transactions. Bowlby suggested that the limbic system is intimately tied to attachment, an idea furthered by Anders and Zeanah (1984). But these circuits are emphasized in specifically the right brain, because compared to the left, "the right limbic system may be better connected with subcortical neurochemical systems associated with emotion" (Buck, 1994, p. 272).

It is accepted that in a growth-facilitating social enviornment, the attachment interactions the child has with its mediators influences the maturation of connections within her developing limbic system (Schore, 1994), and that cortical paralimbic networks are formed through "ontogenetic plasticity, that is, through a natural selection of those connections that match the data in the environment" (Tucker, 1992, p. 109). On the other hand, current developmental neurobiological research reveals that growth-inhibiting, adverse early-rearing experiences "have longstanding and complex effects on a range of neurochemicals relevant to emotion regulation" (Coplan et al., 1998, p. 473). Severely compromised attachment histories are thus associated with brain organizations that are inefficient in regulating affective states and coping with stress (Schore, 1997a), and therefore engender maladaptive infant mental health. This deficit is expressed in a failure to move away from homeostasis in order to turn on neurochemical stress responses when needed, and/or to turn them off and reestablish homeostasis when they are no longer needed.

As Emde (1988) has pointed out, a developmental orientation indictates that maladaptive functioning is specifically manifest as a lack of variability when an individual is faced with environmental demands that call for alternative choices and strategies for change. In light of the principle that the process of reestablishing homeostasis in the face of challenge allows for the adaptive capacity of "achieving stability through change" (Schulkin, Gold, & McEwen, 1998, p. 220), this deficit results in not just an unstable self system but also one with a poor capacity to change, a limited ability to continue to develop at later points in the life cycle. Crittenden and DiLalla (1988) described how:

Adaptive development can be considered a product of the interaction of a changing biological organism with its environment such that the organism is effective in using the resources of its environment to meet its present needs without jeopardizing its future development. Maladaptive developmental courses either do not meet the organism's present needs as well as others or they reduce the organism's responsiveness to future change. (p. 585)

This relationship between events in early development and a later capacity for change is due to the fact that the early social environment directly impacts the experience-dependent maturation of the limbic system, the brain areas specialized for the organization of new learning and the capacity to adapt to a rapidly changing environment (Mesulam, 1998). Because limbic areas in the cortex and subcortex are in a critical period of growth in the first two years and these same neurobiological structures mediate stress-coping capacities for the rest of the the the life span, early interpersonal stress-inducing and stress-regulating events have long-enduring effects.

Indeed, developmental psychobiological studies suggested that:

An individual's response to stressful stimuli may be maladaptive producing physiological and behavioral responses that may have detrimental consequences, or may be adaptive, enabling the individual to better cope with stress. Events experienced early in life may be particularly important in shaping the individual's pattern of responsiveness in later stages of life. (Kehoe, Shoemaker, Triano, Hoffman, & Arons, 1996, p. 1435)

This conception proposes direct links between infant and adult mental health.

Integrating these conceptualizations, I suggest that adaptive infant mental health can be fundamentally defined as the earliest expression of efficient and resilient strategies for coping with novelty and stress, and maladaptive infant mental health as a deficit in these same coping mechanisms. The former is a resilience factor for coping with psychobiological stressors at later stages of the life cycle, the latter is a risk factor for interruptions of developmental processes and a vulnerability to the coping deficits that define later-forming psychopathogies. Both are attachment outcomes, and so this formulation is congruent with Main's (1996) assertion that "disorganized" and "organized" forms of insecure attachment are primary risk factors for the development of mental disorders.

AFFECT SYNCHRONY, RESONANCE, AND ATTACHMENT COMMUNICATIONS

The ontogeny of adaptive infant mental health is positively correlated with the ongoing development of attachment experiences over the first year. This is due to the fact that the experience-dependent maturation of the baby's brain allows for the emergence of more complex functional capacities for coping with stressors, especially those from the social environment. This developmental advance is an outcome of the cocreation of a secure attachment bond of emotional communication between infant and mother. It has been said that "learning how to communicate represents perhaps the most important developmental process to take place during infancy" (Papousek & Papousek, 1997, p. 42). What do we know about the relationships between the earliest development of socioemotional communication and the organization of adaptive brain systems?

From birth onward, the infant is using its expanding coping capacities to interact with the social environment. In the earliest proto-attachment experiences, the infant is utilizing its maturing motor and developing sensory capacities, especially smell, taste, and touch, to interact with the social environment. As described by Trevarthen (2001) and confirmed in recent research on rhythmic discriminations in newborns (Ramus, Hauser, Miller, Morris, & Mehler, 2000), auditory stimuli are also impacting the infant's developing sensory systems. But by the end of the second month there is a dramatic progression of its social and emotional capacities. In two functional magnetic resonance imaging (fMRI) studies, Yamada and colleagues (1997, 2000) demonstrated a milestone for normal development of the infant brain occurs at about 8 weeks. At this point a rapid metabolic change occurs in the primary visual cortex of infants. These authors interpret this rise to reflect the onset of a critical period during which synaptic connections in the occipital cortex are modified by visual experience.

With this maturational advance, the visual stimuli emanating from the mother's emotionally expressive face becomes the most potent stimulus in the infant's social environment, and the child's intense interest in her face, especially in her eyes, leads him to track it in space, and to engage in periods of intense mutual gaze. The infant's gaze, in turn, evokes the mother's gaze, thereby acting as a potent interpersonal channel for the transmission of "reciprocal mutual influences." In the developmental psychological literature Fogel and Branco characterized infant emotional metacommunication in parent-infant interaction expressed in nonverbal gaze direction, facial expression, posture, and body movements that are "mutually coordinated to create emergent social patterns" (1997, p. 68). And writing in the neurobiological literature, Allman and Brothers asserted, "When mutual eye contact is established, both participants know that the loop between them has been closed . . . and this is the most potent of all social situations" (1994, p. 613).

In very recent basic research on 3-month-old infants, Feldman, Greenbaum, and Yirmiya (1999) described the following:

> Face-to-face interactions, emerging at approximately 2 months of age, are highly arousing, affect-laden, short interpersonal events that expose infants to high levels of cognitive and social information. To regulate the high positive arousal, mothers and infants . . . synchronize the intensity of their affective behavior within lags of split seconds. (p. 223)

These episodes of "affect synchrony" occur in the first expression of social play, and at this time they are patterned by an infant-leads-mother-follows sequence.

This highly organized dialogue of visual and auditory signals is transacted within milliseconds, and is composed of cyclic oscillations between states of attention and inattention in each partner's play. In this interactive matrix both partners match states and then simultaneously adjust their social attention, stimulation, and accelerating arousal to each other's responses.

Feldman, Greenbaum, Yirmiya, and Mayes (1996) asserted:

> Synchronicity is defined as a match between mother's and infant's activities that promotes positivity and mutuality in play. By synchronizing with the child's attentive states, mothers structure playful interactions, regulate infant attention, facilitate the development of verbal dialogue, and promote the infant's capacity for self-regulation . . . mutual synchrony exists when both partners simultaneously adjust their attention and stimulation in response to the partner's signals. (p. 349)

These are critical events, because they represent a fundamental opportunity to practice the interpersonal coordination of biological rhythms. According to Lester, Hoffman, and Brazelton "synchrony develops as a consequence of each partner's learning the rhythmic structure of the other and modifying his or her behavior to fit that structure" (1985, p. 24).

In this process of "contingent responsivity," not only the tempo of their engagement but also their disengagement and reengagement is coordinated. The more the psychobiologically attuned mother tunes her activity level to the infant during periods of social engagement, the more she allows him to recover quietly in periods of disengagement, and the more she attends to the child's reinitiating cues for reengagement, the more synchronized their interaction. The period immediately after a "moment of meeting," when both partners disengage, provides "open space," in which both can be together, yet alone (autoregulating) in the presence of the other (Sander, 1988). The synchronizing caregiver thus facilitates the infant's information processing by adjusting the mode, amount, variability, and timing of the onset and offset of stimulation to the infant's actual integrative capacities. These mutually attuned synchronized interactions are fundamental to the healthy affective development of the infant (Penman et al., 1983).

In these exchanges of affect synchrony, as the mother and infant match each other's temporal and affective patterns, each recreates an inner psychophysiological state similar to the partner's. Stern (1983a) described moment-to-moment state sharing, feeling the same as the other, and state complementing, responding in one's unique way to stimuli coming from the other. In contexts of "mutually attuned selective cueing," the infant learns to preferentially send social cues to which the mother has responded, thereby reflecting "an anticipatory sense of response of the other to the self, concomitant with an accommodation of the self to the other" (Bergman, 1999, p. 96).

In describing the unique nature of an emotionally communicationg mother-infant dyad, a number of prominent theoreticians have been drawn to the concept of resonance. Trevarthen (1993) stated:

> Corresponding generative parameters in . . . two subjects enable them to resonate with or reflect on one another as minds in expressive bodies. This action pattern can become "entrained," and their experiences can be brought into register and imitated. These are the features that make possible the kind of affectionate empathic communication that occurs, for instance, between young infants and their mothers. (p. 126)

Simliarly, Sander (1991) emphasized the critical importance of the context of a specifically fitted interaction between the infant and mother as a resonance between two systems attuned to each other by corresponding properties. Such energy-infused moments allow for a sense of vitalization, and thereby increased complexity and coherence of organization within the infant.

Furthermore, in the visual and auditory emotional communications embedded within synchronized face-to-face transactions, both members of the dyad experience a state transition as they move together from low arousal to a heightened energetic state of high arousal, a shift from quiet alertness into an intensely positive affective state. In physics, a property of resonance is sympathetic vibration, which is the tendency of one resonance system to enlarge and augment through matching the resonance frequency pattern of another resonance system. It is well established that energy shifts are the most basic and fundamental features of emotion, that the transfer of emotional information is intensified in resonant contexts, and that at the moment when a system is tuned at the "resonant" frequency it becomes synchronized (Schore, 1997a, 2000b; 2002a).

Resonances often have chaos associated with them, and thus they are characterized by nonlinear dynamical factors — relatively small input amplitudes engender a response with a surprisingly large output amplitude. This amplification especially occurs when external sensory stimulation frequency coincides with the organism's own endogenous rhythms. In other words, when a psychobiologically attuned dyad cocreates a resonant context within an attachment transaction, the behavioral manifestation of each partner's internal state is monitored by the other, and this results in the coupling between the output of one partner's loop and the input of the other's to form a larger feedback configuration and an amplification of the positive state in both.

In demonstration of this principle, emotion theorists describe "affect bursts," nonverbal expressions of synchronized facial and vocal activity triggered by an external stimulus (Scherer, 1994). And infant researchers refer to the delight the infant displays in reaction to the augmenting effects of his mother's playful, empathically attuned behavior, her mulitmodal sensory amplification and resonance with the child's feelings. Stern described how the mother can "blast the infant into the next orbit of positive excitation," and generate "vitality affects"

(1985, p. 53). In these transactions the dyad is cocreating "mutual regulatory systems of arousal" (Stern, 1983b).

In this interactive context, the infant's attachment motivation synergistically interacts with the caregiver's maternal motivation. In psychobiological models, maternal motivation is conceptualized as the outcome of the interaction between external visual and auditory infant stimuli and the central state of maternal arousability (Pryce, 1992). In order to act as a regulator of the infant's arousal, she must be able to regulate her own arousal state. The burgeoning capacity of the infant to experience increasing levels of accelerating, rewarding arousal states is thus at this stage amplified and externally regulated by the psychobiologically attuned mother, and depends upon her capacity to engage in an interactive emotion communicating mechanism that generates these in herself and her child.

Reciprocal facial signalling, mutual rhythmic entrainment, and dyadic resonance thus act as a psychobiological context for an open channel of social communication, and this interactive matrix promotes the outward expression of internal affective states in infants. Sander (1997) asserted that the parent expresses a behavior that is particularly fitted to catalyze a shift in the infant's state, and Tronick and colleagues (1998) stated that the complexity of the infant's state is expandable with input from an external source—the caregiver. In order to enter into this communication, the mother must be psychobiologically attuned not so much to the child's overt behavior as to the reflections of the rhythms of his internal state.

Because affect attunements are "spontaneous, nonverbal responses to . . . children's expressed emotions" (Polan & Hofer, 1999, p. 176), the moment-to-moment expressions of the mother's regulatory functions occur at levels beneath awareness. Even so, the attuned mother can self-correct by accessing her reflective function whereby she monitors not only her infant's but also her own internal signals and differentiates her own affective state. As a regulator of the infant's arousal levels, she also modulates nonoptimal high levels of stimulation, which would induce supra-heightened levels of arousal in the infant. Thus, she regulates not just the type but also the intensity of socioaffective information within the dyad's communication system.

But the primary caregiver is not always attuned—developmental research shows frequent moments of misattunement in the dyad, ruptures of the attachment bond. In early development an adult provides much of the necessary modulation of infant states, especially after a state disruption and across a transition between states, and this allows for the development of self-regulation. Again, the key to this is the caregiver's capacity to monitor and regulate her own affect, especially negative affect. The regulation of her own affective state, as well as the child's, may be an emotionally demanding task.

In this essential regulatory pattern of "disruption and repair" (Beebe & Lachmann, 1994; Schore, 1994) the "good-enough" caregiver who induces a stress response in her infant through a misattunement, reinvokes in a timely fashion her psychobiologically attuned regulation of the infant's negative affect state that she has triggered. The reattuning, comforting mother and infant thus dyadically negotiate a stressful state transition of affect, cognition, and behavior. This recovery mechanism underlies the phenomenon of "interactive repair" (Lewis, 2000; Tronick, 1989), in which participation of the caregiver is responsible for the reparation of stressful dyadic misattunements.

If attachment is interactive synchrony, stress is defined as an asynchrony in an interactional sequence, but a period of synchrony following this allows for stress recovery (Chapple, 1970). It is now thought that the process of reexperiencing positive affect following negative experience may teach a child that negativity can be endured and conquered. Infant resilience emerges from an interactive context in which the child and parent transition from positive to negative and back to positive affect, and resilience in the face of stress is an ultimate indicator of attachment capacity and therefore adaptive mental health.

These arousal-regulating transactions, which continue throughout the first year, underlie the formation of an attachment bond between the infant and primary caregiver. An essential attachment function is "to promote the synchrony or regulation of biological and behavioral systems on an organismic level" (Reite & Capitanio, 1985, p. 235). Indeed, psychobiological attunement and the interactive mutual entrainment of physiological rhythms are fundamental processes that mediate attachment bond formation, and attachment can be defined as the regulation of biological synchronicity between organisms (Schore, 2000c; Wang, 1997). The mechanism of attachment dynamics is thus an example of the regulation of rhythm, which is a fundamental organizing principle of all living systems (Iberal & McCulloch, 1969).

To put this another way, the infant's developing regulatory and control systems create spontaneous physiological rhythms that are manifest in arousal fluctuations, which are in turn expressed in fluctuating psychobiological affective states, what Stern (1985) called "vitality affects." It is accepted that affects reflect an individual's internal state and have an hedonic (valenced) dimension and an arousal (intensity) dimension. The crescendos and decrescendos of the infant's peripheral (ANS) and central (CNS) arousal systems underlie emotions, and so the mutual entrainment of affective states in attachment transactions can be defined as the dyadic regulation of emotion (Sroufe, 1996). Thus, Damasio (1998) was correct in characterizing emotions as the highest order direct expression of bioregulation in complex organisms, but it should be emphasized that the efficient bioregulation of internal emotional states can take the form of both interactive regulation and autoregulation.

These data underscore an essential principle overlooked by many emotion theorists: affect regulation is not just the reduction of affective intensity, the dampening of negative emotion; it also involves an amplification, an intensification of positive emotion, a condition necessary for more complex self-organization. Attachment is not just the reestablishment of security after a dysregulating experience and a stressful negative state, it is also the interactive amplification of positive affects, as in play states. Regulated affective interactions with a familiar, predictable primary caregiver create not only a sense of safety, but also a positively charged curiosity that fuels the burgeoning self's exploration of novel socioemotional and physical environments (Grossman, Grossman, & Zimmerman, 1999; Schore, 1994). This ability is a marker of adaptive infant mental health.

ATTACHMENT AND THE INTERACTIVE
REGULATION OF THE RIGHT BRAIN

In a number of contributions I have offered evidence that indicates that the emotional communications of evolving attachment transactions directly impact the experience-dependent maturation of the infant's developing brain. Trevarthen (1993) also observed that the growth of the baby's brain literally requires brain-brain interaction and occurs in the context of a positive affective relationship (see Chapter 2, Figure 2.3). But in light of the fact that the early maturing right hemisphere is in a growth spurt in the first year-and-a-half, and that it is dominant for the first three (Chiron et al., 1997), I have contended that attachment experiences specifically impact the development of the infant's right brain. Confirming this model, Ryan, Kuhl, and Deci (1997), using EEG and neuroimaging data, reported:

> The positive emotional exchange resulting from autonomy-supportive parenting involves participation of right hemispheric cortical and subcortical systems that participate in global, tonic emotional modulation. (p. 719)

In an elegant phrase, Trevarthen asserted that "the intrinsic regulators of human brain growth in a child are specifically adapted to be coupled, by emotional communication, to the regulators of adult brains" (1990, p. 357). But again, I would amend this general statement to suggest that the regulators of both the infant and mother's brains are located in specifically the right limbic brain (Schore, 1994). Furthermore, Trevarthen's description of "emotional communication" as a traffic of visual, prosodic auditory, and gestural signals that induce instant emotional effects is paralleled by Buck's (1994) characterization of "spontaneous emotional communication":

> Spontaneous communication employs species-specific expressive displays in the sender that, given attention, activate emotional preattunements and are directly perceived by the receiver . . . The 'meaning' of the display is known directly by the receiver . . . This spontaneous emotional communication constitutes a *conversation between limbic systems* . . . It is a biologically-based communication system that involves individual organisms *directly* with one another: *the individuals in spontaneous commu-*

nication constitute literally a biological unit... The direct involvement with the other intrinsic to spontaneous communication represents an attachment that may satisfy deeply emotional social motives. (p. 266; italics added)

Buck (1994) emphasized the importance of the right limbic system, and localizes this biologically based spontaneous emotional communication system to the right hemisphere, in accord with other research that indicated a right lateralization of spontaneous gestures (Blonder, Burns, Bowers, Moore, & Heilman, 1995) and emotional communication (Blonder, Bowers, & Heilman, 1991).

Recall Winnicott's (1971b) description of the infant's expression of a "spontaneous gesture," a somato-psychic expression of the burgeoning "true self," and the attuned mother's "giving back to the baby the baby's own self." Winnicott contended that as a result of its transactions with the mother, the infant, through identification, internally creates a "subjective object." Recent research indicates that the right hemisphere is specialized for "the detection of subjective objects" (Atchley & Atchley, 1998), and for the processing and regulation of self-related information (Keenan, Wheeler, Gallup, & Pascual-Leone, 2000; Ryan et al., 1997; Schore, 1994).

Furthermore, developmental neuroscientists have proposed that engrams related to emotional voices are more strongly imprinted into the early maturing, more active right hemisphere (Carmon & Nachson, 1973), and that particular areas of the right hemisphere are timed to be in a plastic and receptive state at the very time when polysensory information that emanates from faces is being attended to most intensely by the infant (Deruelle & de Schonen, 1998; de Schonen, Deruelle, Mancini, & Pascalis, 1993). These latter authors reported that right-hemisphere activation in face processing shows a significant structural advance at 2–3 months, in line with the previously cited work of Yamada and colleagues (1997, 2000) and Feldman and others (1999). With ongoing episodes of affective synchrony, attachment functions mature later in the first year, and it has been suggested that "there is earlier maturation of right hemisphere inhibition over subcortically mediated emotional expressions in infancy, once cortical influences over this behavior come into play" (Best & Queen, 1989, p. 273).

An accumulating body of evidence indicates that the infant's right hemisphere is involved in attachment and the mother's right hemisphere in comforting functions (Henry, 1993; Horton, 1995; Schore, 1994, 1998a, 1998b, 1999f; Shapiro et al., 1997; Siegel, 1999; Wang, 1997). Attachment represents the regulation of biological synchronicity between organisms, and imprinting, the learning process that mediates attachment, is defined as synchrony between sequential infant-maternal stimuli and behavior (Petrovich & Gewirtz, 1985). During the sequential signalling of play epsiodes, mother and infant show sympathetic cardiac acceleration and then parasympathetic deceleration in response to the smile of the other (Donovan, Leavitt, & Balling, 1978). Imprinting is thus not a unidirectional learning process by which attachment experiences are passively absorbed into an empty template; rather it is an active dyadic process that occurs between two brains that are cogenerating synchronized emotional communications with each other.

I suggest that when two right brain systems are mutually entrained in affective synchrony, they create a context of resonance, which is now thought to play a fundamental role in brain organization, CNS regulatory processes, and the organization of connectivity properties that are tuned by function (Salansky, Fedotchev, & Bondar, 1998). Earlier I described how in face-to-face contexts resonant amplification occurs when the frequency patterns of the mother's exogenous sensory stimulation coincides with the infant's own endogenous organismic rhythms. Trevarthen (1993) pointed out that the resonance of the dyad ultimately permits the intercoordination of positive affective brain states.

In current neuroscience, resonance refers to the ability of neurons to respond selectively to inputs at preferred frequencies, and "amplified resonance" or "amplifying currents" serve as a substrate for coordinating (synchronizing) patterns of network (circuit) activity. Basic research establishes that different behavioral and perceptual states are associated with different brain rhythms, that a resonant system evolves continuously into a spontaneously oscillatory system as the amplifying conductance is increased, and that amplified resonance can "tune networks to operate in frequency ranges of special biological meaning" (Hutcheon & Yarom, 2000, p. 220).

These general principles apply to face-to-face transactions, where patterns of information emanating from the caregiver's face, especially of low visual and auditory frequencies, are specifically processed by the infant's right hemisphere (Ornstein, 1997). The ventral stream (Ungerleider & Haxby, 1994) of this hemisphere is specialized to analyze low frequencies of visual perception that convey the general outlines of faces and low frequencies of auditory tones that express the emotional intonation of language—prime examples of biologically meaningful information. Fernald (1992) described human maternal vocalizations to infants as "biologically relevant signals." Furthermore, these dyadically synchronized, affectively charged transactions elicit high levels of metabolic energy for the tuning of right-brain cortical-subcortical circuits involved in processing socioemotional information (Schore, 1994, 1997a, 2000b). An article in *Science* suggested that, "mothers invest extra energy in their young to promote larger brains" (Gibbons, 1998, p. 1346).

Lewis (1995) pointed out that the best example of the flow-through of energy in a developing system is the processing of relevant information in the presence of emotion. Thus, as a result of synchronized emotional transactions, the organization of the infant's right brain shows increased coherence, as the flow of energy between the hierarchically organized higher right cortical and lower right subcortical components increase their connectivity, allowing the right brain to act as a self-regulating integrated whole, and therefore capable of increasing complexity. This conception is consonant with models that emphasize that the brain is a self-organizing system (van Pelt, Corner, Uylings, & Lopes da Silva, 1994), and that age increases brain complexity (Anokhin, Birnbaumer, Lutzenberger, Nikolaev, & Vogel, 1996). In applying dynamic systems principles to attachment theory, Siegel (1999) proposed a similiar scenario.

The infant's right brain is tuned to dynamically self-organize upon perceiving certain patterns of facially expressed exteroceptive information, namely the visual and auditory stimuli emanating from the smiling and laughing joyful face of a loving mother. In face-to-face interactive affect-amplifying transactions, the relational context triggers facially expressed "affect bursts" in the infant. According to Scherer, these highly emotionally charged events lead to a "strong synchronization of various organismic subsystems, particularly the various expressive channels, over a very brief period of time" (1994, p. 181).

What psychoneurobiological mechanism could underlie this caregiver-induced organization of the infant's brain? In earlier work, I have suggested that the appearance of the mother's face in dyadic play experiences generates high levels of dopaminergic-driven arousal and elation in the infant's right brain (Schore, 1994). Dopamine neurons in the ventral tegmental area of the anterior reticular formation are involved in reward and emotionality (Wise & Rompre, 1989), and they respond to visual, auditory, and tactile stimuli by switching from "pacemaker-like firing" to "burst firing" (Gonon, 1988; Overton & Clark, 1997) in response to an environmental stimulus that is "ethologically salient" (a good definition of sensory stimulation emanating from the mother). This pacemaker firing of a subnuclei of arousal-generating ventral tegmental dopamine neurons may represent an important component of the infant's genetically encoded endogenous organismic rhythms.

The bursting of these neurons to salient, arousing environmental stimuli contributes to an orienting response, the setting of a motivational state, and the onset of exploratory behavior (Horvitz, Stewart, & Jacobs, 1997). Furthermore, "electrical coupling among bursting dopamine neurons may provide a mechanism for further amplification of the effects of synchronously firing dopamine cells on their target areas" (Freeman, Meltzer, & Bunney, 1985, p. 1993). Evidence also indicates that the evaluation of an environmental stimulus as affectively positive is associated with dopaminergic activation of specifically the right brain (Besson & Louilot, 1995).

An integration of these data may give us a model of the critical right brain events by which psychobiologically attuned attachment communications generate amplified resonance that tunes reward circuits to certain forms of human visual and auditory patterns of stimulation. In affectively charged face-to-face transactions, the biologically significant information that emanates from the mother's face is imprinted into the infant's developing right inferior temporal areas that process familiar faces (Nakamura et al., 2000), and thereby takes on "special biological meaning." The right hemisphere is also dominant for the perception of "biological motion" (Grossman et al., 2000). These psychoneurobiological events of mother-infant play sequences drive the "affective bursts" embedded within moments of affective synchrony, in which positive states of interest and joy are dyadically amplified. Panksepp contended that "play may have direct trophic effects on neuronal and synaptic growth in many brain systems" (1998, p. 296), and suggests that play serves the adaptive role of organizing affective information in emotional circuits, a function also performed by rapid eye movement (REM) dream sleep. This fits nicely with current neuroscience conceptions of the important role of REM sleep in brain maturation (Marks et al., 1995) and imaging studies showing a preferential activation of limbic regions in REM sleep (Braun et al., 1997; Maquet et al., 1996).

How can we account for the trophic effects of early play episodes? Again, in a previous contribution (Schore, 1994), I have proposed that in these face-to-face emotional communications, the visual input of the mother's face is also inducing the production of neurotrophins in the infant's brain, such as brain-derived neurotrophic factor (BDNF). Maternal care has been shown to increase N-methyl-D-aspartate (NMDA) receptor levels, resulting in elevated BDNF and synaptogenesis in the infant's brain (Liu, Diorio, Day, Francis, & Meaney, 2000). This trophic factor, which is regulated by visual input (Gomez-Pinilla et al., 1999), promotes synaptic plasticity during postnatal critical periods (Huang et al., 1999). BDNF is also a growth-promoting factor for mesencephalic dopamine neurons (Hyman et al., 1991), and dopamine, which activates NMDA receptors (Knapp et al., 1990), is known to perform a growth-promoting role in the postnatal development of the cortex (Kalsbeek et al., 1987), especially in corticolimbic areas that send axons down to the dendrites of these dopamine neurons, and thereby come to regulate their activity (Sesack & Pickel, 1992; Schore, 1994). Dopamine acts as a trophic agent via regulation of the developing blood brain barrier (Schore, 1994) and microcirculation (Krimer et al., 1998) of developing target areas.

Other psychobiological data may explicate the mechanisms that mediate attachment, the interactive regulation of biological synchronicity between organisms. Despite the intrinsic dyadic nature of the attachment concept, hardly any research has concurrently measured mother and infant in the process of interacting with each other. In one of the few studies of this kind, Kalin, Shelton, and Lynn (1995) showed that the intimate contact between the mother and her infant is mutually regulated by the reciprocal activation of their opiate systems—elevated levels of beta endorphins increase pleasure in both brains. It is established that opioids enhance play behavior (Schore, 1994) and that endorphins increase the firing of mesolimbic dopamine neurons (Yoshida et al., 1993).

Furthering these ideas, the developmental principle of "reciprocal mutual influences" refers to more than mutual behavior changes; indeed it specifically implies that there are simultaneous changes within the right brains of *both* members of the dyad. In terms of self-organization theory, the mutual entrainment of their right brains during moments of affect synchrony triggers an amplified energy flow that allows for a coherence of organization that sustains more complex states within both the infant's and the mother's right brains. In this manner, "the self-organization of the developing brain occurs in the context of a relationship with another self, another brain" (Schore, 1996, p. 60).

Evidence supports the idea that the organization of the mother's brain is also influenced by these relational transactions. A neurobiological study of early mammalian mother-infant interactions, published in *Nature*, reported increased dendritic growth in the mother's brain (Kinsley et al., 1999). Kinsley and colleagues concluded that events in late pregnancy and the early postpartum period

> may literally reshape the brain, fashioning a more complex organ that can accomodate an increasingly demanding environment . . . To consider the relationship of a mother caring for her young as unidirectional disregards the potentially rich set of sensory cues in the opposite direction that can enrich the mother's environment. By providing such stimuli, [infants] may ensure both their own and their mother's development and survival. (p. 137)

Hofer's (1990) developmental psychobiological work also emphasized the bidirectional brain events of the mother-infant interaction. He describes, in detailed fashion, how the infant's immature and developing internal homeostatic systems are coregulated by the caregiver's more mature and differentiated nervous system. In this "symbiotic" pleasurable state, the adult's and infant's individual homeostatic systems are linked together in a superordinate organization, which allows for "mutual regulation of vital endocrine, autonomic, and central nervous systems of both mother and infant by elements of their interaction with each other" (Hofer, 1990, p. 71).

These matters bear upon the concept of symbiosis, which has had a controversial history in recent developmental psychoanalytic writings. This debate centers around a reference, made by Mahler, Pine, and Bergman, to a normal symbiotic phase during which the infant "behaves and functions as though he and his mother were a single omnipotent system-a dual unity within one common boundary" (1975, p. 8). Although the symbiotic infant is dimly aware that the mother is the source of his pleasurable experiences, he is in a "state of undifferentiation, a state of fusion with the mother, in which the 'I' is not differentiated from the 'not-I' " (p. 9).

This latter defintion of symbiosis departs from the classical biological concept and is unique to psychoanalytic metapsychology. Current evidence may not directly support any inferences about the limits of the infant's awareness, nor about an entire stage that describes the infant's behavior only with this characterization. However, moments of face-to-face affective synchrony do begin at 2–3 months, the advent of Mahler's symbiotic phase, they do generate high levels of positive arousal, and such mutually attuned sequences can be portrayed as what Mahler and colleagues (1975) called instances of "optimal mutual cueing."

But even more importantly, Hofer's work as well as recent brain research called for a return of the definition of symbiosis to its biological origins. The Oxford English Dictionary offers the derivation from the Greek, "living together," and defines symbiosis as an interaction between two dissimilar organisms living in close physical association, especially *one in which each benefits the other.* An even more basic definition from biological chemistry suggests that "symbiosis is an association between different organisms that leads to a reciprocal enhancement of their ability to survive" (Lee, Severin, Yokobayashi, & Ghadiri, 1997, p. 591). Recall Buck's (1994) description of an emotionally communicating dyad as "literally a biological unit," a conception that echoes Polan and Hofer's (1999) description of the dyad as a self-organizing regulatory system composed of mother and infant as a unit. These conceptions suggest that instances of secure attachment bonding are an example of biological symbiosis. Interestingly, the Oxford English Dictionary also defines symbiosis as "companion," which suggests that Trevarthen's concept refers to this same psychobiological phenomenon.

The construct of symbiosis is reflected in the conception of attachment as the interactive regulation of biological synchronicity between organisms. In discussing the central role of facial signalling in attachment, Cole asserted, "It is through the sharing of facial expressions that mother and child become as one. It is crucial, in a more Darwinian biological context, for the infant to bond her mother to ensure her own survival" (1998, p. 11). Recall Bowlby's (1969) assertion that the development of attachment has consequences that are vital to survival and that the infant's capacity to cope with stress is correlated with certain maternal behaviors. The right hemisphere is dominant for both attachment functions and for the control of vital functions supporting survival and enabling the organism to cope actively and passively with stress. These capacities are surely critical indices of adaptive infant mental health.

ATTACHMENT TRANSACTIONS
AND THE HIERARCHICAL ORGANIZATION
OF THE LIMBIC SYSTEM

Main concluded, "The formation of an attachment to a specified individual signals a quantitative change in infant behavioral (*and no doubt also brain*) organization" (1991, p. 214; italics added). As a result of advances in the "decade of the brain" can we now identify what specific brain areas mediate this function? In his initial outline of attachment theory, Bowlby speculated that a "succession of increasingly sophisticated systems" involving the limbic system and brain arousal-regulating areas mediate attachment processes (1969, p. 154). It is well established that regions of the brain mature in stages, so the question is, what parts of the postnatally developing brain are maximally impacted by emotionally charged attachment experiences? As previously mentioned, the emotion-processing limbic system has been implicated in attachment functions.

Indeed, the first 18 months of human life are critical for the myelination and therefore the maturation of particular rapidly developing limbic and cortical association areas and limbic areas of the human cerebral cortex show anatomical maturation at about 15 months. It has long been thought that the limbic system is fundamentally associated with emotional functions. But, as I stated previously, recent conceptions emphasize that limbic system function underlies the organization of new learning and the capacity to adapt to a rapidly changing environment (Mesulam, 1998). This concept relates to Hinde's assertion that "the development of social behavior can be understood only in terms of a continuing dialectic between an active and changing organism and an active and changing environment" (1990, p. 162).

Within the first year perhaps no organismic system is changing as rapidly as the brain, especially a sequence of ontogenetically appearing limbic circuits. These systems are organized from the simplest to the most complex, and they commence in a fixed progression over the first year, with the later maturing hierarchical cortical structures adaptively regulating the earlier maturing subcortical systems. This general ontogentic principle is articulated by Werner, who suggested that "the development of biological forms is expressed in an increasing differentiation of parts and an increasing subordination, or hierarchization . . . an ordering and grouping of parts in terms of the whole (1948, p. 44). This hierarchical model has been significantly advanced in the psychoanalytic literature in the groundbreaking work of Gedo (1999; Gedo & Wilson, 1993).

In the current neuroscience literature, Toates (1998) described the importance of hierarchical control systems in development:

> Development is associated with gaining autonomy from sensory control and acquisition of top-down control over behavior that is organized at a lower level. Reflexes can become integrated into cortical control. Such control will be perhaps most usually inhibition, but excitation might also occur . . . acquisition of higher-level control is not merely a process of more inhibition being exerted since the new forms of reacting to the environment also emerge and it is assumed that these are mediated at the higher level. (p. 73)

In classical ego psychology psychoanalytic writings, Hartmann (1939) proposed that adaptation is primarily a reciprocal relationship of the organism and its environment, and that development is a differentiation in which primitive regulatory systems are increasingly replaced or supplemented by more effective regulatory systems. The progression and reorganization of the infant's regulatory, control systems is described by Brazelton and Cramer (1990):

> The central nervous system, as it develops, drives infants towards mastery of themselves and their world. As they achieve each level of mastery, they

seek a kind of homeostasis, until the nervous system presses them on to their next level. Internal equilibrium is always being upset by a new imbalance created as the nervous system matures. Maturation of the nervous system, accompanied by increasing differentiation of skills, drives infants to reorganize their control systems. (p. 98)

Fischer and Rose (1994) concluded that the development of higher order control system allows for the emergence of "dynamic skills," that a developmental stage is a point at which a new level of control systems emerge, and that emotions fundamentally shape the ways that control systems develop.

These control systems can now be identified. In current neuroscience, the neuroanatomy of the limbic system is characterized as a hierarchical system of vertically organized circuits within the brain (see Figure 6.1). Authors are now referring to the "rostral limbic system," a hierarchical sequence of interconnected limbic areas in the orbitofrontal and insular cortices, anterior cingulate, and amygdala (Devinsky et al., 1995); an "anterior limbic system" composed of the orbitofrontal cortex, basal forebrain, amygdala, and hypothalamus (Schnider & Ptak, 1999); a "paralimbic circuit," containing orbitofrontal, insu-

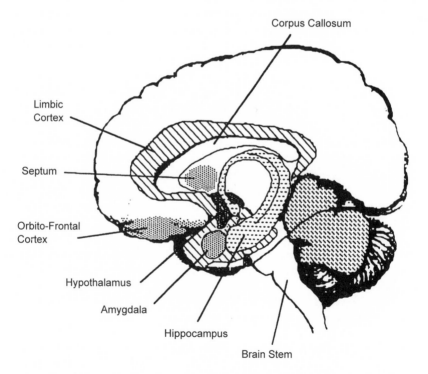

FIGURE 6.1. Limbic structures of the right hemisphere, lateral view. The cingulate is labeled *limbic cortex*. (From Trevarthen, Aitken, Papoudia, & Robarts, 1998)

lar, and temporopolar cortices (Mesulam & Mufson, 1982); an "anterior limbic prefrontal network," interconnecting the orbital and medial prefrontal cortex with the temporal pole, cingulate, and amygdala (Carmichael & Price, 1995); and a complex circuit of emotion regulation, consisting of the orbitolfrontal cortex, anterior cingulate, and amygdala (Davidson, Putnam, & Larson, 2000).

A body of evidence shows that the orbitofrontal-insula, medial-frontal anterior cingulate, and amygdala systems all interconnect with each other and with brain-stem bioaminergic neuromodulatory and hypothalamic neuroendocrine nuclei (see Figure 6.2). Although each has reciprocal connections with dopamine neurons in the ventral tegmental area of the anterior reticular formation and noradrenaline neurons of the caudal reticular formation, each limbic subsystem maintains connections with different monoaminergic subnuclei (Halliday & Tork, 1986; Halliday et al., 1988).

Because they are all components of the limbic system, each processes and imprints a positive or negative hedonic charge on current exteroceptive information about changes in the external social environment and then integrates it with interoceptive information about concurrent alterations in internal bodily states. Due to the facts that they each directly interconnect with the ANS (Neafsey, 1990) and that autonomic activity is controlled by multiple integrative sites within the CNS that are heirarchically organized (Lane & Jennings, 1995), all are involved in the regulation of bodily-driven affective states. Although all components process exteroceptive and interoceptive information, the later-maturing systems in the cortex will process this information in a more complex fashion than the earlier subcortical components. The output of the lowest level limbic levels have the character of automatic innate reflexes, while higher processing produces more flexible intuitive responses that allow fine adjustment to environmental circumstances.

In optimal socioemotional environments, each limbic level has bidirectional connections with the others, and in this manner information can both be forwarded up and down the limbic axis for further appraisal and hierarchical modulation. The earliest and simplest appraisals of exteroceptive and interoceptive affective stimuli would be hedonic and aversive affective core processes in the amygdala (Berridge, 2000), the later and most complex subjective experiences of pleasure and pain in the orbitofrontal areas (Blood et al., 1999; Francis et al., 1999; Petrovic, Petersson, Ghatan, Stone-Elander, & Ingvar, 2000). These operations are primarily lateralized to the right limbic system, which is preferentially connected downward to the right neurochemical systems associated with emotion (Buck, 1994) and upward to the ipsilateral right neocortex (Wilson et al., 1991).

The concept of a hierarchically organized brain that develops through an increasingly complex coordination of lower and higher levels was first introduced by British neurologist Hughlings Jackson at the end of the nineteenth century. Jackson conceived of three levels of organization, including the lowest and most primitive, middle, and last to evolve, highest centers. Each of these

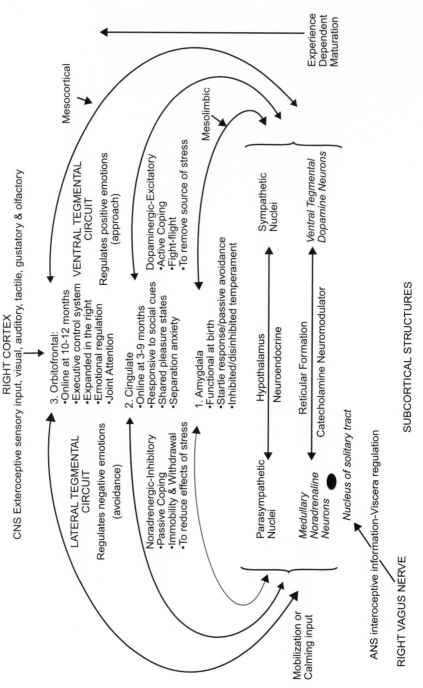

FIGURE 6.2. The right brain dual cortical-limbic circuits. (From Schore 2001a)

levels is a representing system, with the highest level of integration and coordination dependent upon prefrontal activity that allows the organism as a whole to adjust to the environment (Jackson, 1931). A similar trilevel model is also seen in MacLean's (1990) triune brian. As applied to the developmental organization of the right limbic system of the right brain, this conception suggests a three-tiered self-organizing dynamic system. Increased interconnectivity (energy flow) among the three component circuits would allow for information stored at one level to be transferred to the others. The top level that receives feedback from the lower performs an executive function (Toates, 1998), and this allows for emergent properties, that is, novel combinations of more complex emotional states.

In line with the Jacksonian ontogenetic concept of vertical brain organization (Luu & Tucker, 1996) and the principle of caudal to rostral brain development, a model of the ontogeny of the limbic system can be offered. Keeping in mind that in humans this development continues postnatally, reversing the sequence of the rostral limbic system (amygdala, anterior cingulate, insular-orbitofrontal) could offer specific ideas about how a number of discrete limbic components could come on line in a defined sequence in the first year. Recall Bowlby's speculation that the limbic system is centrally involved in attachment and that the "upgrading of control during individual development from simple to more sophisticated is no doubt in large part a result of the growth of the central nervous system" (1969, p. 156).

The following sequence represents Bowlby's "succession of increasingly sophisticated systems" that mediates attachment development. I further propose that the ontogenetic progression of each of these limbic subsystems progresses from an initial sympathetic-dominant excitatory phase followed by a latter parasympathetic-dominant inhibitory phase and ultimately excitation-inhibition balance (Schore, 1994).

At birth only the amygdala (see Figure 6.1), a primitive limbic regulatory system that appraises crude information about external stimuli and modulates autonomic and arousal systems, is on line (Chugani, 1996). The right amygdala is known to be implicated in the processing of olfactory stimuli (Zald, Lee, Fluegel, & Pardo, 1998) within the mother and the perinatal infant relationship (Van Toller & Kendal-Reed, 1995). This suggests that right amygdala–driven processes underlie the infant's recognition of the mother's scent as well as the mother's recognition of neonates through olfactory cues (Porter, Cernoch, & McLaughlin, 1983).

Amygdala memorial systems also mediate the organization of the earliest representations of the infant maternal relationship that allow 6-day-old infants to discriminate the scent of their mother's breast pad (MacFarlane, 1977) or axillary odor (Cernoch & Porter, 1985) from that of another woman. This early appearing subcortical limbic control system is thus a central component of the protoattachment mechanisms that are driven by the unique salience of olfactory signals (Porter & Winberg, 1999). These data further suggest that dyadic "human olfactory communication" (Russell, 1976) occurs between the mother's and infant's right brains. Limbic areas of the right hemisphere are also centrally involved in human gustation (Small et al., 1999).

The fact that the processing of olfactory/gustatory information is dominant in the perinatal period is also documented by developmental researchers. The primary organ of the body that specializes in the latter function is, of course, the mouth. According to Hernandez-Reif, Field, Del Pino, & Diego (2000):

> The infant mouth, including the tongue, is a highly specialized multi-functional sensory-motor system designed to receive nutrients and to express discomfort, such as by varied cries that relay hunger or pain (van den Boom & Gravenhorst, 1995) . . . Recent research revels that the newborn's mouth is also a well-developed perceptual organ. Upon contacting a non-nutritive object, the tactile receptors of the mouth generate positive presssure, presumably for the purpose of detecting object information (Butterworth & Hopkins, 1988; Rochat, 1983). (p. 205)

These authors pointed out that newborns exhibit a transfer of learning from information detected by the mouth to other sensory modalities, citing studies that show newborns suck harder in order to see the visual (Walton, Bower, & Bower, 1992) and hear the auditory stimulation (DeCasper & Fifer, 1980) emanating from the mother's face. They also mentioned that at a later point of development (the second quarter of the first year; Morange-Majoux, Cougnot, & Bloch, 1997), exploration of objects shifts from the mouth to the hands (Bloch, 1998).

In the cerebral hemispheres only the primary somatosensory cortex is metabolically active at birth (Chugani, 1996), and this area is known to process tactile and kinesthetic sensations. If the olfactory and gustatory systems are connecting into the amygdala prenatally, I suggest that specific somatosensory connections into the amygdala are also forming by the end of the first two months. Sufficient levels of tactile stimulation are provided by the maternal environment in the form of maternal contact comfort that releases early protoattachment behavior. Taylor noted, "The sensations impinging on the infant's skin presumably help regulate aspects of the infant's behavior and physiology" (1987, p. 164). In accord with this, the classical work of Harlow (1958) demonstrated that skin-to-skin contacts come on line early and that the infant actively seeks to adhere to as much skin surface on the mother's body as possible.

Most human females cradle their infants on the left side of the body (Harris, Almergi, & Kirsch, 2000; Manning et al., 1997). This tendency is well developed in women but not in men, is independent of handedness, and is widespread in all cultures. It has been suggested that this left-cradling tendency "facilitates the flow of affective information from the infant via the left ear and eye to the center for emotional decoding, that is, the right hemisphere of the mother" (Manning et al., 1997, p. 327). It also has been observed that "the language of mother and infant consist of signals produced by the autonomic, involuntary nervous system in both parties" (Basch, 1976, p. 766). This hemisphere, deeply connected into the ANS, is specialized for tactile perception on both sides of the body (Carmon & Benton, 1969) and for the perception and recall of spatial patterns of touch in nonverbal memory (Milner & Taylor, 1972). Again, the overt expressions of right hemisphere-to-right hemisphere communications are manifest from the very beginnings of infancy.

Neurobiological research indicates that "in early postnatal life, maintenance of critical levels of tactile input of specific quality and emotional content is important for normal brain maturation" (Martin et al., 1991, p. 3355). Indeed, the sensory input derived from contact with the mother during nursing has been suggested to shape dendritic growth (Greenough & Black, 1992). Infantile handling, tactile stimulation associated with comforting "holding" and "containing" experiences provided by the mother, induces permanent modifications of later hypothalamic CRF levels (Campbell, Zarrow, & Denenberg, 1973). Again, these experiences are right-laterlized—Kalogeras and colleagues (1996) demonstrate that the right side of the human hypothalamus is dominant for neuropeptide secretion, including CRF activity.

I further propose that areas of the amygdala in the medial temporal lobe, especially the central and medial nuclei, are in a critical period of maturation that begins in the last trimester of pregnancy and continues through the first two months of human life, the earliest period of bonding. In growth-facilitating perinatal environments, the experience-dependent maturation of interconnections between the infant's right amygdala and right paraventricular hypothalamic nuclei allow for coregulation of vasopressin and the antistress hormone oxytocin in early maternal-infant interactions (Panksepp, 1998). This is a critical period of organization of the amygdalar-hypothalamic system, in which sensory information processed by the amygdala receives a positive or negative hedonic charge and is then relayed to various hypothalamic nuclei (Fonberg, 1986). These events occur in what Bowlby (1969) called the "preattachment phase" of the first two months, the same time period of the evolution of Stern's (1985) "emerging self," and the time frame of the first-to-mature homeostatic control system described by Brazelton (2000) that is on line in the first weeks of life.

I previously cited a finding of a milestone for normal development in a rapid change in brain maturation at 8 weeks, reflecting the onset of a critical period during which synaptic connections in the primary visual cortex are modified by visual experience (Yamada et al., 1997, 2000). At this time infant visual-preference behavior shifts from subcortical to cortical processing (Hoffmann, 1978), and face-to-face interactions, occurring within the primordial experiences of human play, first appear (Cohn & Tronick, 1987). Fogel and Branco (1997) observed:

Three-month old-infants signal their willingness to engage in play by both gazing at mother and smiling, and they use gaze away and the cessation of smiling or the onset of crying to indicate their desire to end a bout of play. Before 3 months, infants do not have the ability to do this. (p. 76)

In these play sequences of affective synchrony, dyadically amplified elevations in sympathetic arousal occur in gaze engagements, followed by infant increases in parasympathetic activity (vagal nucleus ambiguus) in gaze aversion disengagements. The vagally controlled hormone, oxytocin, now is released by "sensory stimuli such as tone of voice and facial expression conveying warmth and familiarity" (Uvnas-Molberg, 1997, p. 42). Vagal tone (Porges, 1991) is undeveloped and weak in the first quarter of the first year, but increases significantly at 2 to 4 months (Kagan, 1994), a time when primary intersubjectivity and delight and laughter first appear (Sroufe, 1996).

This same interval represents the onset of a critical period for the development of the anterior cingulate areas (see Figure 6.1) of the medial-frontal cortex, a region involved in play and separation behaviors, laughing and crying vocalizations, face representations, and modulation of autonomic activity (MacLean, 1993; MacLean & Newman, 1988; Paus, Petrides, Evans, & Meyer, 1993). MacLean (1987) provided evidence to show that this cortex is responsible for vocalizations that "maintain maternal-offspring contact." The anterior cingulate is also known to contribute to maternal behavior (Slotnick, 1967). A fMRI study revealed that the mother's cingulate and right orbitofrontal cortex respond to both pain and separation cries of an infant (Lorberbaum et al., n.d. With regard to the infant's expanding capacities, the right cingulate and parietal areas have been implicated in exploratory attentional movements (Gitelman et al., 1996) in the generation of a subjective prediction, and in the anticipation of being tickled (Carlsson, Petrovic, Skare, Petersson, & Ingvar, 2000).

Recall the earlier depiction of mutually regulated states of maternal-infant high arousal, attention, and vocalizations occuring in play experiences that emerge at this time (Feldman et al., 1999). This is also the onset of the positive resonances that occur within the mother-infant protoconversations that induce what Trevarthen called primary intersubjectivity (Trevarthen et al., 1998). In this relational context, the primary caregiver's anterior cingulate–driven maternal behavior would be socially tuning the infant's medial frontal cortex, thereby influencing the parcellation and final circuit wiring of the baby's developing anterior cingulate. During this critical period of the onset the infant's anterior cingulate-right temporal (Nakamura et al., 2000) face processing, which Mahler and colleagues (1975) called the symbiotic period, the infant forms a discriminate attachment to the mother's face.

The later occurring parasympathetic phase of the critical period of growth of this limbic component would occur in the third quarter, a time of cingulate-driven expressions of separation-anxiety (Joseph, 1992b; MacLean, 1990), responses to attachment ruptures. At 7 to 10 months infants show fear (Sroufe, 1996) and stranger anxiety, in which they inhibit ongoing behavior and withdraw when exposed to novel and threatening situations and unfamiliar people. The emergence of this more complex defensive behavior, inhibited approach, represents the parasympathetic maturation of the cingulate.

Furthermore, in light of the known role of the cingulate in consciousness (Kennard, 1955), it is tempting to speculate that the experience-dependent maturation of this limbic structure may be activated in moments of dyadically expanded states of consciousness that onset in the middle of the first year. Tronick and colleagues (1998) described how microregulatory social-emotional processes of communication literally expand intersubjective states of consciousness in the infant-mother dyad. They argued that the baby's self-organizing system, when coupled with the mother's, allows for a brain organization which can be expanded into more coherent and complex states of consciousness. The interpersonal context of a coregulated dyadic system allows for "a mutual mapping of (some of) the elements of each partner's state of consciousness into the other partner's brain" (p. 296).

I suggest that Tronick was describing an expansion of what Edelman (1989) called primary consciousness. Edelman stated primary consciousness relates visceral and emotional information pertaining to the biological self to stored information pertaining to outside reality, and that it is lateralized to the right brain. Activity of limbic cingulate areas are known to be associated with primary consciousness (Denton et al., 1999). This developmental work supports the idea that consciousness is a product of that part of the brain that handles human relations, and is a property of a brain that is and has been in communication with other brains (Barlow, 1980; Schore, 1994). It also suggests that indices of the maturation of the infant's capacity for primary consciousness needs to be included in our models of infant mental health.

The critical period of anterior cingulate–driven limbic maturation thus overlaps Bowlby's (1969) phase of "attachment-in-the-making," and mediates what Stern (1985) termed, "the core self." Brazelton (2000) described the emergence in the second quarter of the first year of a second homeostatic control system, one associated with a mutual reciprocal feedback system. Though an advance of the former control system it is still "an immature psychophysiological system." I suggest this system can be identified as a maturing anterior cingulate, which now hierarchically controls the earlier amygdala-dominated limbic configuration.

The right insula, a limbic structure involved in emotional and facial processing (Berthier, Starkstein, & Leiguarda, 1987), in integrating tonal structure with a speaker's emotions and attitudes (Riecker, Ackermann, Wildgruber, Dogil, & Grodd, 2000), and in visceral and autonomic functions that mediate the generation of an image of one's physical state (Craig, Chen, Bandy, & Reiman, 2000), is also activated in primary consciousness (Denton et al., 1999). This limbic structure is implicated in pain processing and serves as an alarm center, "alerting the individual to potentially distressing interoceptive stimuli, investing them with negative emotional significance" (Banzett et al., 2000, p. 2120). It is tempting to speculate that the experience-dependent maturation of this system is associated with both the more complex representation of body image and "stranger anxiety" that emerges in the second half year of life.

In the last quarter of the first year the quality of the infant's social relatedness changes dramatically (see Schore, 1994), due to the concurrent rapid myelination and maturation of developing limbic and cortical association areas. If earlier face-to-face interactions contain only spontaneous communication processes, after 9 months the infant can engage in "joint attention," the ability to shift attention between an object and a person. In this form of nonverbal communication the infant coordinates his visual attention with that of the caregiver, and is now not only aware of an object but also simultaneously aware of the mother's attention to the object. In such instances of what Trevarthen and colleagues (1998) called "secondary intersubjectivity," each member of the dyad coaligns separable, yet related forms of consciousness.

Joint attention occurs within highly affectively charged social referencing transactions, an attachment process that mediates a resonance of positive affect (Schore, 1994). This dyadic mechanism allows the infant to appreciate that "the other person is a locus of psychological attitudes toward the world, that the other is 'attending' in such a way that shared experiences are possible" (Hobson, 1993, p. 267). In this manner the child comes to understand others "as intentional beings, that is, as subjects of experience possessing internal states such as interest and attention" (Tomasello & Camaioni, 1997, p. 20). In order to get an adult to tune into his attentional and intentional focus on the world, the infant now uses an expanded repertoire of bidirectional communicative gestures, an important cognitive advance that communicates intention (Goldin-Meadow, 2000). It is also in this period, the last quarter of the first year, when "the infant starts to adopt a mentalistic strategy to interpret and predict the behavior of other agents" and is "capable of taking the intentional stance" (Gergely, Nadasdy, Csibra, & Biro, 1995, p. 184). In developmental neurobiological research, Caplan and colleagues suggested that "the development of joint attention might reflect maturation of the prefrontal cortex" (1993, p. 589).

These critical advances represent a further maturation of the right hemisphere, since current research suggests it contributes to attention and intention (Mattingley, 1999; Sturm et al., 1999). Studies of joint attention demonstrate that the right (and not left) hemisphere shifts attention to where someone is looking to follow the gaze of another (Kingstone, Friesen, & Gazzaniga, 2000). In fact there is evidence for "a special role for the right frontal lobe in sustaining attention over time" (Rueckert & Grafman, 1996, p. 952). Studies reveal that the right orbitofrontal and right anterior insula cortices are components of a neural circuit that "enables integration of adaptive bodily responses with ongoing emotional and attentional states of the organism" (Critchley, Elliott, Mathias, & Dolan, 2000, p. 3033). But in addition this right prefrontal cortex is fundamentally involved in "regulating emotional responses" (Hariri et al., 2000).

THE MATURATION OF AN
ORBITOFRONTAL REGULATORY SYSTEM

In *Affect Regulation and the Origin of the Self* (1994) I offered evidence to show that the orbital prefrontal cortex enters a critical period of growth that spans the last quarter of the first through the middle of the second year, an interval that corresponds with the beginnings of human socialization. The critical period of orbitofrontal-driven limbic maturation thus overlaps and mediates what Stern (1985) termed the developmental achievement of "the subjective self." This prefrontal limbic structure is reciprocally interconnected with other limbic areas in the insula (Augustine, 1996), anterior cingulate (Devinsky et al., 1995), and the amygdala (Barbas & de Olmos, 1990), and represents the hierarchical apex of the limbic system.

Brothers (1995, 1997) described a limbic circuit of orbitofrontal cortex, anterior cingulate gyrus, amygdala, and temporal pole which functions as a social "editor," that is "specialized for processing others' social intentions" by appraising "significant gestures and expressions" (1997, p. 27) and "encourages the rest of the brain to report on features of the social environment" (1997, p. 15). The editor acts as a unitary system "specialized for responding to social signals of all kinds, a system that would ultimately construct representations of the mind" (p. 27). Mesulam pointed out that the prefrontal areas involved in emotional modulation and attentional functions help to create "a highly edited subjective version of the world" (1998, p. 1013). This emergent subjective function is the outcome of a secure attachment.

In an entire issue of *Cerebral Cortex* on "The mysterious orbitofrontal cortex," the editors concluded that "the orbitofrontal cortex is involved in critical human functions, such as social adjustment and the control of mood, drive and responsibility, traits that are crucial in defining the 'personality' of an individual" (Cavada & Schultz, 2000, p. 205). Referring back to Brazelton and Cramer's (1990) conception of the developmental reorganization of control systems, neurobiological studies show that the mature orbitofrontal cortex acts in "the highest level of control of behavior, especially in relation to emotion" (Price et al., 1996, p. 523). This prefrontal system, which functions in "emotional control" (Roberts & Wallis, 2000), and acts to "control autonomic responses associated with emotional events" (Cavada, Company, Tejedor, Cruz-Rizzolo, & Reinoso-Suarez-Suarez, 2000), is identical to Bowlby's control system of attachment (for a further characterization of this prefrontal system see Schore, 1994, 1996, 1997a, 1997b, 1998a, 1998b, 1999a, 2000b, 2000c, 2001b, 2002a).

This control system integrates the psychological and biological spheres of mind and body. The orbitofrontal cortex is known to play an essential role in the processing of interpersonal signals necessary for the initiation of social interactions between individuals (Schore, 1994). This cortex, along with the superior temporal sulcus and amygdala, comprises a circuit that mediates social gaze (Emery, 2000). Orbitofrontal neurons specifically process visual and auditory information associated with emotionally expressive faces and voices (Romanski et al., 1999; Scalaidhe et al., 1997). But this frontolimbic system is also involved in the representation of highly integrated information on the organismic state (Tucker, 1992). The systems that biochemically regulate all brain and bodily state phenomena are located in discrete groups of arousal-regulating bioaminergic neurons of the subcortical reticular formation that innervate wide areas of the brain through diffuse projections (Lydic, 1987). It is now thought that the most basic level of regulatory process is the regulation of arousal (Tucker, Luu, & Pribram, 1995). The orbitofrontal cortex, especially in the right hemisphere, "is involved in "both generation and afferent feedback representation of arousal" (Critchley, Elliott, et al., 2000b, p. 3037).

This prefrontal area regulates dopaminergic arousal (Iversen, 1977) via its direct reciprocal connections with dopamine neurons in the ventral tegmental area of the anterior reticular formation. It also projects to the ventral striatum and the core of the nucleus accumbens, a basal ganglia structure innervated by dopamine neurons and centrally involved in motivated behavior (Haber Kunishio, Mizobuchi, & Lynd-Balta, 1995; Mogenson, Jones, & Yim, 1980), in the nonverbal decoding of positive facial expressions (Morris, Robinson, Raphael, & Hopwood, 1996), and in mechanisms of pleasant reward and motivation (Robbins & Everitt, 1996). The right nucleus accumbens (and the right cingulate) are activated in the encoding of pleasant emotional stimuli (Hamann, Ely, Grajon, & Kilts, 1999).

This excitatory limbic circuit, the ventral tegmental limbic forebrain-midbrain circuit (Schore, 1994, 1996), is involved with the generation of positively valenced states associated with approach behavior, motivational reward, and active coping strategies. Neuroimaging data indicate that the lateral orbital prefrontal areas (which is irrigated by the middle cerebral artery) are specialized for regulating excitement (Elliott et al., 2000) and other positive emotional states (Northoff et al., 2000). Midbrain dopamine neurons are known to be preferentially activated by positively valenced appetitive rather than negatively valenced aversive stimuli (Mirenowicz & Schultz, 1996) and to exert an inhibitory influence on cortisol receptors (Casolini et al., 1993).

Phasic increases in dopamine activity allow the individual to immediately appraise the salience of biologically important stimuli in the environment (Berridge & Robinson, 1998). It is important to note, however, that there is an optimal range of stimulation of the dopamine (D_1) receptor that mediates working memory in the prefrontal cortex (Williams & Goldman-Rakic, 1995), and that dopamine levels that are either too low or too high impair its functional output (Zahrt, Taylor, Mathew, & Arnsten, 1997; Arnsten & Goldman-Rakic, 1998). Optimal activation of the ventral tegmental limbic forebrain-midbrain circuit is described not by a linear function but by an inverted "U" relationship. I suggest that an individual's unique narrow or broad optimal orbitofrontal ventral tegmental dopaminergic profile is set up during its critical period of development in positively valenced attachment transactions.

Orbitofrontal regions also have reciprocal connections with arousal-regulating noradrenergic neurons in the medulla oblongata solitary nucleus and the vagal complex in the brain stem caudal reticular formation, and onto subcortical targets in parasympathetic autonomic areas of the lateral hypothalamus, thereby completing the organization of another later maturing limbic circuit, the lateral tegmental limbic forebrain-midbrain circuit that activates the onset of an inhibitory state, regulates negative affect, and is associated with avoidance and passive coping (see Schore, 1994, 1996). Orbital-amygdala interactions allow the individual "to avoid making choices associated with adverse outcomes, without their first having to experience these adverse conditions" (Baxter, Parker, Lindner, Izquierdo, & Murray, 2000, p. 4317). Stimulation of orbitofrontal noradrenergic inhibitory circuits results in "behavioral calming" (Arnsten, Steere, & Hunt, 1996). Optimal activity is also described by an inverted "U" relationship, one organized in critical period attachment transactions of interactive repair of negative states. Neuroimaging studies show the medial orbitofrontal areas (irrigated by the anterior cerebral artery) are specialized for processing negative emotional states (Northoff et al., 2000; Paradiso, Chemerinski, Yazici, Tartaro, & Robinson, 2000).

The functioning of the two limbic circuits (see Figure 6.2) underlies the observation that emotions organize behavior along a basic appetitive-aversive dimension associated with either a behavioral set involving approach and attachment, or a set disposing avoidance, escape, and defense (see Schore, 1994, 1996, 1997a). A number of theorists have suggested that positive and negative affect are mediated by different neural circuitries (e.g., Cacioppo & Berntson, 1994; Gray, 1990), and neuroimaging data demonstrate that the neural activation pattern of happiness is "remarkably distinct" from sadness (Damasio et al., 2000).

The orbitofrontal system has been termed the "senior executive of limbic arousal" (Joseph, 1996). This is due to the fact that it has reciprocal connections with both dopaminergic neurons in the ventral tegmental area of the anterior reticular formation, as well as noradrenergic neurons in the solitary tract of the medullary areas of the caudal reticular formation (and serotonin neurons in the raphe nucleus). In the orbitofrontal areas dopamine excites and noradrenaline inhibits neuronal activity (Aou et al., 1983). These opposing mechanisms of excitation and inhibition provide for rapid regulation of graded metabolic output and thereby functional activity. Subtle external perturbations would trigger changes in this control parameter, preferentially activating the excitatory lateral orbitofrontal subsystem and its connections into dopamine neurons that modulate large areas of the brain and/or the inhibitory medial orbitofrontal subsystem and its connections into noradrenaline neurons which also innervate widely separated brain regions (Foote, 1987). In this manner small changes in the excitation-inhibition balance of the dual orbitofrontal system lead to large changes in the activity of state-regulating neuromodulators that regulate far-reaching neural networks.

The structural connections within and between the lateral and medial orbitofrontal subsystems and the excitation-inhibition balance between them are a product of both genetic and environmental factors, specifically the caregiver's attachment function as a regulator of the infant's arousal. Bowlby speculated that the functions of the attachment control system are associated with the organism's "state of arousal" that results from the critical operations of the reticular formation, and with "the appraisal of organismic states and situations of the midbrain nuclei and limbic system" (1969, p. 110).

Furthermore, due to the interconnections of the orbitofrontal system into the cervical, thoracic, lumbar, and sacral divisions of the spinal cord (Burstein & Potrebic, 1993) and into the vagal nerve that delivers autonomic information, it receives (like the amygdala and anterior cingulate) moment-to-moment interoceptive information from the entire body, especially information concerning changes in autonomic arousal and in bodily or "somatic" states. Because of its intimate connections with the hypothalamus (Ongur, An, & Price, 1998), the head ganglion of the ANS and the brain's major control center for energy expenditure (Levin & Routh, 1996), the orbital prefrontal area acts as a major center of CNS hierarchical control over the energy-expending sympathetic and energy-conserving parasympathetic branches of the ANS. The ANS is responsible for the somatic aspects of all affective states. In optimal early environments, a system emerges in which higher brain areas can modulate a flexible coping pattern of coupled reciprocal autonomic control, in which increases in one ANS division are associated with decreases in the other (Berntson et al., 1991).

This frontolimbic system is particularly involved in situations in which internally generated affective representations play a critical role (Zald & Kim, 1996), and in the implicit processing (Critchley, Daly, et al., 2000; Rolls, 1996) and procedural learning (de Guise et al., 1999) of socioemotional information. The orbitofrontal system has been described as "a nodal cortical region that is important in assembling and monitoring relevant past and current experiences, including their affective and social values" (Cavada et al., 2000, p. 238). Orbitofrontal neurons are specialized for working memory, a sequential processing of information in real time, that is, on a moment-to-moment basis (Goldman-Rakic, Muly, & Williams, 2000). These procedures include encoding a facially expressed affective stimulus, maintaining it on line, and directing an adaptive memory-guided response. As a result of such operations, the orbitofrontal cortex is centrally involved in "acquring very specific knowledge for regulating interpersonal and social behavior" (Dolan, 1999, p. 928).

There is evidence that the right inferior frontal regions mediate nonverbal memorial encoding and retrieval (Wagner et al., 1998). The operations of the right orbitofrontal control system involve a rapid subcortical evaluation of the regulatory significance of an external environmental stimulus, a processing of feedback information about the current internal state in order to make assessments of coping resources, and an adaptive updating of context-appropriate autonomic response outputs in order to make adaptive adjustments to particular environmental perturbations (Schore, 1998a). In this manner the orbitofrontal areas are involved in the regulation of autonomic responses to social stimuli (Zald & Kim, 1996), the spontaneous gut feelings to others.

The orbitofrontal cortex is situated at the hierarchical apex of an "anterior limbic prefrontal network" that interconnects it with the temporal pole, cingulate, and amygdala, and through these linkages it plays an essential role in affect regulation (Davidson et al., 2000; Schore, 1994). The early maturing amygdala acts as a sensory gateway to the limbic system, but amygdala processing, although very rapid, is crude compared to the more complex processing of affective stimuli by later maturing corticolimbic areas. A fMRI study (Teasdale et al., 1999) demonstrated that while the subcortical amygdala responds to emotional stimuli at a direct perceptual level, its operations are less relevant to cognitively elicited emotions. In contrast, the ventromedial cortex is known as "the thinking part of the emotional brain." In optimal contexts the orbitofrontal cortex takes over amygdala functions (Rolls, 1996), and "provides a higher level coding that more flexibly coordinates exteroceptive and interoceptive domains and functions to correct responses as conditions change" (Derryberry & Tucker, 1992, p. 335).

Operating at levels beneath awareness, it is activated "when there is insufficient information available to determine the appropriate course of action" (Elliott et al., 2000, p. 308), but subsequently this regulatory system monitors, adjusts, and corrects emotional responses and regulates the motivational control of goal-directed behavior. It thus functions as a recovery mechanism that efficiently monitors and regulates the duration, frequency, and intensity of positive and negative affect states, from high intensity joy and excitement (Schore, 1994) to the affective-motivational aspects of pain (Gyulai, Firestone, Mintun, & Winter, 1997; Petrovic et al., 2000).

The functioning of this system thus allows for "the emotional modulation of experience" (Mesulam, 1998). Orbitofrontal areas function to "integrate and assign emotional-motivational significance to cognitive impressions; the association of emotion with ideas and thoughts" (Joseph, 1996, p. 427) and in "the processing of affect-related meanings" (Teasdale et al., 1999). A neuropsychological study indicated that the orbitofrontal cortex is "particularly involved in generating a theory of mind tasks with an affective component" (Stone et al., 1998, p. 651). These adaptive capacities are the outcome of a secure attachment.

The orbitofrontal system is specialized to act in contexts of "uncertainty or unpredictability" (Elliott et al., 2000, p. 308), an operational definition of stress. Its functions mediate affective shifts, the alteration of behavior in response to fluctuations in the emotional significance of stimuli (Dias et al., 1996). In optimal frontolimbic operations, these shifts from one emotional state to another are experienced as rhythms in feeling states and are fluid and smooth, a flexible capacity of a coherent dynamic system. Efficient orbitofrontal operations organize the expression of a regulated emotional response and an appropriate motivational state for a particular social environmental context, and in this fashion it contributes to "judicious, adapted behavior" (Cavada et al., 2000). These coping capacities define an optimally functioning limbic system, the brain network responsible for the organization of new learning and the capacity to adapt to a rapidly changing environment. The right limbic system is centrally involved in complex attachment functions and interpersonal coping strategies, and its operations are instrumental to adaptive infant mental health.

The efficient functioning of this frontolimbic cortex is thus manifest in its capacity to mediate between the external environment and the internal milieu. At 18 months, the time of orbitofrontal maturation, toddlers have been observed to have a "vastly enhanced capacity for experiencing the internal milieu" (Greenspan, 1979). Lieberman has emphasized that, "in the last two decades . . . efforts at understanding the subjective world of the infant have focused primarily on mental representations as the building blocks of inner experience. The baby's body, with its pleasures and struggles, has largely been missing from this picture" (1996, p. 289). These findings suggest that bodily intactness, somatic and physical functioning, mechanisms for coping with illness and pain, and general psychobiological integrity need to be included in operational definitions of infant mental health.

REGULATORY FUNCTIONS OF THE RIGHT BRAIN

The orbital prefrontal region, the "senior executive" of the social-emotional brain (Joseph, 1996), is especially expanded in the right cortex (Falk et al., 1990), and indeed it comes to act in the capacity of an executive control function for the entire right brain. Because the early maturing and "primitive" right cortical hemisphere contains extensive reciprocal connections with limbic and subcortical regions (Tucker, 1992), it is dominant for the processing and expression of emotional information (Schore, 1994, 1999a, 2000a, 2002a). The extensive reciprocal right frontal-subcortical connections, especially with bioaminergic and hypothalamic subcortical nuclei, account for the unique contribution of this hemisphere in regulating homeostasis and modulating physiological state in response to internal and external feedback.

It has been known for some time that arousal systems are right-lateralized (Heilman & Van Den Abell, 1979), and now there is data to show that the hypothalamus, the core brain system where hormonal control and visceral-emotional reactions are regulated (Kupferman, 1985), is also right-lateralized (Kalogeras et al., 1996). MRI research reveals that the right anterior temporal lobe is larger than the left from early infancy (Utsunomiya, Takano, Okazaki, & Mitsudome, 1999), and that the diencephalic hypothalamic nuclei are considerably larger on the right side of the human brain (Sowell & Jernigan, 1998). The right hemisphere, more so than the left, is deeply connected into the ANS (Erciyas, Topalkara, Topaktas, Akyuz, & Dener, 1999; Lane & Jennings, 1995; Yoon, Morillo, Cechetto, & Hachinski, 1997), and so the representation of interoceptive information, the dynamic flows of visceral and somatic states, is under primary control of this hemisphere.

But this hemisphere is also specialized for processing significant patterns of exteroceptive information. The right hemisphere is faster than the left in performing valence-dependent, automatic, preattentive appraisals of emotional facial expressions (Pizzagalli et al., 1999) and in assessing visual or auditory emotional communicative signals (Nakamura et al., 1999). The right cortex is responsive to not only the positive aspects of facial expressions (Blair et al., 1999), visual stimuli (Muller et al., 1999), touch, smell (Francis et al., 1999), and music (Blood et al., 1999), but also for the negative emotional/motivational aspects of pain (Hari et al., 1997; Hsieh et al., 1995). In fact, this hemisphere plays an essential role in the nonconscious appraisal of the positive or negative emotional significance of social stimuli via a mechanism similar to Freud's pleasure-unpleasure principle (Schore, 1998a, 1998f; 1999a, 1999e, 2001b). These findings are not consonant with earlier models, which held that positive approach-related emotions are lateralized to the left hemisphere and negative withdrawal-related emotions to the right (Davidson et al., 1990), a position not supported by recent brain imaging techniques (Canli, 1999). Citing only one example, Damasio's group (2000) reported a PET study revealing that happiness is associated with activation of the right orbitofrontal, right insula, right somatosensory, right anterior cingulate, and right hypothalamus.

The coprocessing of exteroceptive and interoceptive information is possible when the higher cortical limbic regions of the right hemisphere are actively and bidirectionally communicating with the different levels of the right subcortical limbic regions. This organizational mode allows for the operation of right-lateralized (dual) circuit of emotion regulation that is involved in "intense emotional-homeostatic processes" and in the modulation of "primary" emotions (Porges et al., 1994). These authors describe a vagal circuit of emotion regulation lateralized on the right side of the brain.

Vagal tone is defined as "the amount of inhibitory influence on the heart by the parasympathetic nervous system" (Field, Pickens, Fox, Nawrocki, & Gonzalez, 1995, p. 227), and although it is present at birth it evolves in an experience-dependent manner over the first two years. A functional progression in vagal tone occurs from the middle of the first to the middle of the second year (Sweet, McGrath, & Symons, 1999). The progressive postnatal assembly of this limbic-autonomic circuit (Rinaman et al., 2000) is reflected in a developmental shift from interactive regulation to autoregulation of negative affective states. This ontogenetic achievement represents the evolution, at 18 months, of the right lateralized orbitofrontal-dominated lateral tegmental limbic forebrain-midbrain parasympathetic inhibitory circuit.

Current studies indicate that "right hemisphere control exists over both para-sympathetic and sympathetic responses" (Spence et al., 1996, p. 118), the autonomic somatic components of all emotional states. For the rest of the life span the right brain plays a superior role in the regulation of fundamental physiological and endocrinological functions whose primary control centers are located in subcortical regions of the brain. There is also now evidence to show that the right hemisphere is dominant for the production of cortisol (Wittling & Pfluger, 1990), CRF and ACTH (Kalogeras et al., 1996), and indeed for immune, neuroendocrine, and cardiovascular functions (Hugdahl, 1995; Sullivan & Gratton, 1999).

Because the hypothalamo-pituitary-adrenocortical axis and the sympathetic-adrenomedullary axis that mediate coping capacities are both under the main control of the right cerebral cortex, this hemisphere contains "a unique response system preparing the organism to deal efficiently with external challenges," and so its adaptive functions mediate the human stress response (Wittling, 1997, p. 55). It therefore is centrally involved in the vital functions that support survival and enable the organism to cope actively and passively with stress. The attachment relationship thus directly shapes the maturation of the infant's right brain stress-coping systems that act at levels beneath awareness. In line with Bowlby's description of a "control system" that regulates attachment behavior, the right hemisphere is dominant for "inhibitory control" (Garavan et al., 1999).

Furthermore, the right brain stores an internal working model of the attachment relationship, which encodes strategies of affect regulation that maintain basic regulation and positive affect even in the face of environmental challenge (Schore, 1994). Since this hemisphere is centrally involved in unconscious processes (Joseph, 1992b; Schore, 1998f; 1999a; 2001b, 2002a) and in "implicit learning" (Hugdahl, 1995), nonconsciously processed socioemotional information is stored in right cerebral implicit-procedural memory. Neuropsychological studies reveal that this hemisphere, and not the later forming verbal-linguistic left, is the substrate of autobiographical memory (Fink et al., 1996).

Continuing these ideas, I suggest that the expansion of the earlier maturing ventral stream (Ungerleider & Haxby, 1994) in the right hemisphere accounts for its role in "implicit," or "procedural" learning, while the predominance of the later maturing dorsal stream in the left underlies its emphasis in "explicit" or "declarative" functions. Zaidel, Esiri, and Beardsworth's proposal that "human memory systems in the two sides are wired up differently to support separate but complementary functional specialization in the hemispheres" (1998, p. 1050) suggests that the storage of right hemispheric implicit-procedural learning (Hugdahl, 1995) of affective information may be mediated by very different operations than explicit learning and memorial systems of the left (Gabrieli, Poldrack, & Desmond, 1998).

The right hemisphere contributes to the development of reciprocal interactions within the mother-infant regulatory system (Taylor, 1987) and mediates the capacity for biological synchronicity, the regulatory mechanism of attachment. In further support of its role in organismic synchronicity, the activity of this hemisphere is instrumental to the empathic perception of the emotional states of other human beings (Schore, 1994, 1999a, 2002a). The right hemisphere decodes emotional stimuli by "actual felt [somatic] emotional reactions to the stimuli, that is, by a form of empathic responding" (Day & Wong, 1996, p. 651). According to Adolphs, Damasio, Tranel, Cooper, & Damasio, "recognizing emotions from visually presented facial expressions requires right somatosensory cortices," and in this manner "we recognize another individual's emotional state by internally generating somatosensory representations that simulate how the individual would feel when displaying a certain facial expression" (2000, p. 2683). The interactive regulation of right brain neuropsychology and attachment psychobiology is thus the substrate of empathy, another fundamental aspect of adaptive infant metal health.

CONTINUED ORBITOFRONTAL AND RIGHT-BRAIN DEVELOPMENT AND ADAPTIVE MENTAL HEALTH

The orbital cortex matures in the middle of the second year, a time when the average child has a productive vocabulary of less than 70 words. The core of the self is thus nonverbal and unconscious, and it lies in patterns of affect regulation. This structural development allows for an internal sense of security and resilience that comes from the intuitive knowledge that one can regulate the flows and shifts of one's bodily-based emotional states either by one's own coping capacities or within a relationship with caring others. As a result of developmental neurobiological studies, Ryan and colleagues (1997) concluded that the operation of the right prefrontal cortex is integral to autonomous regulation, and that the activation of this system facilitates increases in positive affect in response to optimally challenging or personally meaningful situations, or decreases in negative affect in response to stressful events.

The activities of the "self-correcting" orbitofrontal system are central to self-regulation, the ability to flexibly regulate emotional states through interactions with other humans — interactive regulation in interconnected contexts via a two-person psychology, and without other humans — autoregulation in autonomous contexts via a one-person psychology. As Sander (1997) noted, in health both poles are primarily suffused with positive affects. The adaptive capacity to shift between these dual regulatory modes, depending upon the social context, emerges out of a history of secure attachment interactions of a maturing biological organism and an attuned social environment. The essential aspect of this function is highlighted by Westen who asserted that "The attempt to regulate affect — to minimize unpleasant feelings and to maximize pleasant ones — is the driving force in human motivation" (1997, p. 542). The efficient functioning of the orbitofrontal system is thus necessary for adaptive infant (and adult) mental health.

But this system is also necessary for later mental health. In the *American Psychologist*, Bargh and Chartrand (1999) asserted,

> most of moment-to-moment psychological life must occur through nonconscious means if it is to occur at all . . . various nonconscious mental systems perform the lion's share of the self-regulatory burden, beneficiently keeping the individual grounded in his or her current environment. (p. 462)

These regulatory mental systerms care not innate, but a product of the experience-dependent maturation of the orbitofrontal system, which generates nonconscious biases that guide behavior before conscious knowledge does (Bechara et al., 1997). Such nonconscious regulatory mechanisms are embedded in implicit-procedural memory in unconscious internal working models of the attachment relationship that encode strategies of affect regulation. The orbitofrontal cortex is involved in procedural learning (de Guise et al., 1999) and the right cerebral hemisphere is dominant for implicit learning (Hugdahl, 1995), and so at all points of the life span this "senior executive of the social-emotional brain" is centrally involved in "emotion-related learning" (Rolls et al., 1994). Current defitions of intuition as "the subjective experience associated with the use of knowledge gained through implicit learning" (Lieberman, 2000, p. 109) clearly suggest that intuitive thinking is a right-brain process.

Implicit learning is also a major mechanism for the incorporation of cultural learning, a process that initiates in infancy. Tucker (1992) asserted that social interaction, which promotes brain differentiation, is the mechanism for teaching "the epigenetic patterns of culture," and that successful social development requires a high degree of skill in negotiating emotional communication, "much of which is nonverbal." He also stated that the important brain systems in such functions are those that are involved in affective communication processes and mediate socialization. Tucker concluded that such emotional information engages specialized neural networks in humans, within the right hemisphere. Socialization is essential to advances in emotional-motivational development and to expansion of the self. A recent neuropsychological study concludes that "self-related material is processed in the right hemisphere" (Keenan et al., 1999, p. 1424).

The right hemisphere subsequently reenters into growth spurts (Thatcher, 1994) and ultimately forms an interactive system with the later-maturing left (Schore, 1994; Siegel, 1999). This structural attainment, at 15 to 30 months, allows for the emergence of what Stern (1985) called "the verbal self." The term "verbal self" connotes a purely left-brain mechanism, and yet it may really be an emergent function of an early maturing and expanding right brain and its connections into the later maturing left.

In describing a model of lingusitic development, Locke (1997) proposed:

The first phase is indexical and affective; the infant is strongly oriented to the human face and voice, and learns caregivers' superficial characteristics. The second phase is primarily affective and social: its function is to collect utterances, a responsibility that is subserved largely by mechanisms of social cognition sited primarily in the right hemisphere. (pp. 265–266)

Thus, both the first stage, which spans the last trimester of pregnancy to 5–7 months, and the second, which continues to 20–37 months, are heavily driven by the right hemisphere. Although the left hemisphere begins a growth spurt at around 18 months, the right hemisphere is dominant through 36 months (Chiron et al., 1997).

Indeed, despite a pervasive tendency for scientists and clinicians to automatically assume that language involves operations solely of the left hemisphere, there is now a growing body of evidence underscoring the important roles of the early developing right hemisphere at later points in the life span for processing prosodic information in infants (Snow, 2000), children (Cohen, Branch, & Hynd, 1994), and adults (George et al., 1996; Schmidt, Hartje, & Willmes, 1997), for comprehension of language (Beeman & Chiarello, 1998), lexical emotional stimuli (Cicero et al., 1999), and communicative pragmatics (Van Lancker, 1997), and for emotional communication (Blonder et al., 1991).

Neurobiological studies indicated that "while the left hemisphere mediates most linguistic behaviors, the right hemisphere is important for broader aspects of communication" (Van Lancker & Cummings, 1999, p. 95). Buck noted that "language is not simply a matter of 'cold cognition': strong motivational and emotional forces invigorate the learning of language and infuse its application with intensity and energy," and emphasizes the adaptive nature of right hemispheric "spontaneous emotional communication" (1994, p. 266). At all points of the life span nonverbal and verbal spontaneous emotional communications are outputs of the right brain attachment system.

It is important to point out that these communications are positively and negatively valenced, and so in addition to "satisfying" the attachment system, they can also stress it. In other words, they are also sources of interpersonal stressors and stress regulation, processes that tap directly into the unique functions of the right brain. Scherer (1994) described facially and vocally expressed "highly emotionally charged affect bursts" associated with activation of the ANS. These events, although lasting for very brief periods, accommodate the needs of information processing and behavioral adaptation. Scherer wrote:

> One of the fundamental characteristics of an emotional episode . . . is the synchronization of the different components in the organism's efforts to recruit as much energy as possible to master a major crisis situation (in a positive or negative sense). (p. 186)

I suggest that this principle applies to the developmental crises that must be mastered as one moves along the life span. The continuing growth spurts of the right hemisphere (Thatcher, 1997) that mediate attachment, the synchronization of right-brain activities between and within organisms, thus occur as the developing individual is presented with the stresses that are intrinsic to later stages of life, childhood, adolescence, and adulthood (Erikson, 1950; Seligman & Shahmoon-Shanok, 1995). The expanding ability of the individual to cope with interpersonal and bodily stressors is an important achievement in continuing human development, and it represents an expansion of the right brain, the hemisphere dominant for the human stress response. In terms of interpersonal stressors, this hemisphere is specialized for processing not only facially expressed auditory (Snow, 2000) but also visual emotional information in infants (de Schonen et al., 1993), children (de Haan, Nelson, Gunnar, & Tout, 1998), and adults (Kim et al., 1999). These right-brain capacities are essential to all interactions between humans, including the social bonding between "companions" (Trevarthen, 2001). Panksepp (2000), noted, the underlying neurobiological mechanisms for bonding are quite similar to those that sustain the affective side of friendships. Such interpersonal experiences facilitate future growth of the brain and therefore personality.

Attachment theory is fundamentally a theory of the development of the personality over the life span (Ainsworth & Bowlby, 1991). Weinfeld, Sroufe, Egeland, and Carlson (1999) offered a number of possible explanations for why early attachment experiences influence development at later stages of life: the early attachment relationship may serve as a foundation for learning affect regulation; it may influence subsequent development through behavioral regulation and behavioral synchrony; or through the continuing presence, over the course of the ensuing developmental trajectory, of early forming internal representations. But Weinfeld and colleagues offered one other mechanism:

> [I]t is possible that the experiences within the early attachment relationaship influence the developing brain, resulting in lasting influences at a neuronal level (Schore, 1994). This possibility . . . (is) compelling. (1999, p. 75)

In parallel writings in the neuroscience literature on the concept of development, Pandya and Barnes (1987) asserted the principle that:

> Each stage in development is marked by a more differentiated cytoarchitecture and a new set of connections, which together might reasonably be expected to subserve a new, and more advanced, behavior. (p. 66)

Thatcher (1994, 1997) provided evidence to show that the right hemisphere, especially its frontal areas, continues subsequent growth spurts. I suggest that the ongoing maturational potential of an individual right brain is related to its attachment-influenced early organization, and that as in infancy, this further growth of right-lateralized cortical-subcortical systems is experience-dependent.

For example, as the toddler becomes a young child, age-appropriate interactions with peers depend upon an efficient right-hemispheric ability to engage in processes of affective synchrony with other children. This capacity involves the abilities to nonconsciously yet efficiently read faces and tones and therefore the intentionalities of peers and teachers, to empathically resonate with the states of others, to communicate emotional states and regulate interpersonal affects, and thus to cope with the novel ambient interpersonal stressors of early childhood. In light of the fact that both the right and left hemispheres enter into subsequent growth spurts from ages 4 through 10 and that the frontal lobes continue to reorganize (Thatcher, 1997), the cognitive-emotional advances of late childhood reflect more complex connections within the right and between the emotional right and verbal-lingusitic left hemisphere.

In a chapter on attachment in adolescence, Allen and Land (1999) offered sections on "continuity in the meaning and status of attachment from infancy through adolescence" and on "emotion-regulating functions of adolescent attachment organization." In parallel writings in neuroscience, Spear (2000) presented a rapidly growing body of studies to show that the brain undergoes a significant reorganization during adolescence, and that this maturation contributes to the multiple psychological changes seen at this time of transition between childhood and adulthood. She noted, "adolescence is second only to the neonatal period in terms of both rapid biopsychosocial growth as well as changing environmental characteristics and demands" (p. 428), and that after a relatively long period of slowed growth during early childhood, the adolescent brain undergoes a prominent developmental transformation.

Indeed, overproduction and pruning of synapses, as in the postnatal period, is a hallmark of adolescence (Huttenlocher, 1984). It has been estimated that, over the adolescent period, 30,000 synapses are lost per second in the primate cortex resulting in an ultimate reduction of almost one-half of the number of synapses per neuron in the preadolescent period (Rakic, Bourgeois, & Goldman-Rakic, 1994). During this time, as in human infancy, hypothalamic-regulated gonadal hormones reach very high levels, and Spear (2000) suggested that the reorganization of amygdala and prefrontal limbic areas that innervate the hypothalamus and modulate emotional reactivity, as well as alterations in the balance between mesocortical and mesolimbic dopamine systems involved in stress regulation, may drive the reorganization of the adolescent brain. Indeed, an increase in the volume of the right hypothalamus (Sowell & Jernigan, 1998) is seen in late adolescence.

An fMRI study indicates that adolescents exhibit greater activation in the amygdala than in the frontal lobe during the identification of an emotional state from a facial expression, in contrast to adults who show greater frontal over amygdala activation (Yurgelun-Todd, 1998). These data suggest that the right brain hierarchical dual corticolimbic-autonomic circuits that support self-regulation and stress-coping mechanisms are significantly reorganized in adolescence (see Figure 6.2). This allows for early imprinted internal working models of attachment that encode strategies of affect regulation to become more complex over the course of the Eriksonian stages of the life cycle.

The stress literature clearly shows that exposing the personality to learning from novel stressors and challenges is "pivotal for emotional and intellectual growth and development" (Chrousos, 1998, p. 312). Yet in addition to being potentially growth enhancing, these same events can be emotionally overwhelming and disorganizing. However, during disequilibrating stage transitions when right-lateralized autoregulatory systems are reorganizing, the child-adolescent with a secure attachment can access emotionally available parents for interactive regulation. In this manner, the original attachment objects can continue to scaffold the individual's developing nascent regulatory capacities.

This same principle is articulated in the neuropsychological literature by Lane, Kivley, Du Bois, Shamasundara, and Schwartz (1995):

> [I]ndividuals who are naturally right hemispheric dominant may be better able to perceive and integrate emotion cues from the environment and thus take full advantage of an emotionally nurturing environment in promoting emotional development. (p. 535).

Each of these ontogenetic continuations allows for more complex right and right-left representations, yet the earliest-forming strategies of affect regulation, cocreated in attachment transactions of affective synchrony, provide the coping mechanisms for dealing with the stressors inherent in these later novel, more challenging socioemotional environments. In securely attached individuals, or those in interaction with securely attached individuals who can act as interactive regulators, unconscious internal working models can become more complex.

The experience-dependent expansion of the right brain is reflected in the growth of the unconscious over the life span (Schore, 1999f). This reorganization is accompanied by more complex interconnections with the also expanding left brain, especially the anterior sections of the corpus callosum which include axons of the orbitofrontal areas that "participate in interhemispheric integration on a broad scale" (Cavada et al., 2000). The orbitofrontal and amygdalar areas are the most plastic areas of the cortex (Barbas, 1995), and thus capable of future dendritic and synaptogenetic growth. This major stress coping system in the brain, activated in contexts of uncertainty, can potentially accrue more complexity.

During the transitions between later developmental stages, the individual is presented with the challenge of retaining continuity while changing in response to environmental pressures. These challenges are associated with positive and negative affective states, and they call for a resilient right orbitofrontal regulated capacity that can read the facially expressed states of others, access a theory of mind, as well as cope with, regulate, and thereby tolerate the uncertainty and stress that are inherent in the attachment separation and exploratory dynamics of these transitional periods. Such regulated interpersonal and intrapersonal experiences allow for the further experience-dependent maturation of the emotion processing right brain at later stages of development. The evolutionary progression of the right-lateralized frontolimbic "social editor" (Brothers, 1997) can now reedit more complex yet coherent and adaptive internal working models that can flexibly process greater amounts of information in more complex subjective states. The continuing ontogeny of this self-regulating and self-correcting dynamic system allows for an expansion of the boundaries of the emotion communicating self. The early right brain capacities of processing socioemotional information and bodily states are not only central to the origin of the self, they are also required for the ongoing development of the self over the life span.

This evolution of the developmental trajectory allows for an elaboration and increased complexity of the known functions of the right brain: the storage of internal working models of the attachment relationship (Schore, 1994), the processing of socioemotional information that is meaningful to the individual (Schore, 1998a), the ability to empathize with the emotional states of other humans beings (Schore, 1996), the mediation of emotional-imagistic processes in moral development (Vitz, 1990), the appreciation of humor, a mechanism for coping with daily stress (Shammi & Stuss, 1999), the cerebral representation of one's own past and the activation of autobiographical memory (Fink et al., 1996), the establishment of a "personally relevant universe" (Van Lancker, 1991), and "the capacity to mentally represent and become aware of subjective experiences in the past, present, and future" (Wheeler, Stuss, & Tulving, 1997, p. 331).

On the most fundamental level, however, the emotion-processing right hemisphere is dominant for the control of vital functions that support survival and enable the organism to cope with stressors (Wittling & Schweiger, 1993). There is agreement that, fundamentally, "emotion is a mechanism that enables an organism to adapt psychologically, physiologically and behaviorally to meet organismic challenges" (Lane, Chua, & Dolan, 1999, p. 996). These stressors include interoceptive challenges, since it has been demonstrated that individuals express emotional responses to immunological stimuli like bacteria (Kusnecov, Liang, & Shurin, 1999). Recall, the emotion-processing right hemisphere is primarily involved with the analysis of direct information received from the body (Luria, 1973). But in addition, the ability of the right brain to process exteroceptive socioemotional stimuli may underlie the mechanism by which an individual can recognize and respond to social support that beneficiently alters physiological processes (Uchino, Cacioppo, & Kiecolt-Glaser,

1996). In an earlier work, I have proposed that the attachment relationship directly influences the development of right brain psychosocial-neuroendo-crine-immune communications (Schore, 1994).

Writing on the relationship between emotional states and physical health, Salovey, Rothman, Detweiler, and Steward (2000) concluded,

> In general, negative emotional states are thought to be associated with unhealthy patterns of physiological functioning, whereas positive emotional states are thought to be associated with healthier patterns of responding in both cardiovascular activity and the immune system. (p. 111)

Salovey and Mazer also contended that in order to mount an adaptive coping response to preserve mental (and physical) health, the individual must be able to access "emotional intelligence," defined as the processing of emotional information and accurate perception and appraisal of emotions in oneself and others, appropriate expression of emotion, and adaptive regulation of emotion in such a manner as to enhance living (Salovey & Mayer, 1989/1990).

This psychological description is echoed in neuroscience, where Lane and colleagues concluded, "as right hemispheric dominance in the perception of facial emotion increases, the ability to perceive complexity during the processing of emotional information increases" (1995, p. 525). In a direct counterpart to psychological emotional intelligence, Brothers (1990) offered the neurobiological concept of "social intelligence," a product of the "social brain" that is composed of limbic areas of the orbitofrontal cortex and amygdala, and face processing systems in the temporal lobe. This model is also advanced by Baron-Cohen and colleagues (2000), who differentiated general intelligence from social intelliegence, the latter decribed as:

> our ability to interpret others' behaviour in terms of mental states (thoughts, intentions, desires and beliefs), to interact both in complex social groups and in close relationships, to empathize with others' states of mind, and to predict how others will feel, think, and act. (p. 355)

Recall that limbic circuits are emphasized in specifically the right brain, that the right limbic system is more directly connected with subcortical neuochemical systems associated with emotion, and that the limbic system is intimately tied to attachment functions. The data offered in this work suggest that emotional or social intelligence relies heavily upon right-brain function, and that this capacity is an outcome of a secure attachment and a central component of adaptive infant, child, adolescent, and adult mental health.

In a related conception, Gardner (1983) spoke of "personal" intelligence, which has two forms, intrapersonal intelligence, the ability to access one's feeling life, and interpersonal intelligence, the ability to read the moods, intentions, and desires of others. These dual modes refer to, respectively, right brain autoregulatory and interactive regulatory capacities. As described above, these two abilities are available to the securely attached individual, and for this reason such early appearing coping capacities of adaptive infant mental health are positive factors for "optimal development" and the ability to increase the complexity of the brain/mind/body self system and thereby enhance and vitalize the experience of being alive over all of the stages of the life span.

2001

The Effects of Relational Trauma on Right Brain Development, Affect Regulation, and Infant Mental Health

I N THE FIRST PAPER OF THIS SERIAL CONTRIBUTION,* I suggested that an interdisciplinary approach that focuses upon attachment experiences and their effects on regulatory structures and functions can offer us more comprehensive models of normal development. This conception evolves directly from the central tenets of attachment theory. In his groundbreaking volume, *Attachment*, Bowlby (1969) argued that developmental processes could best be understood as the product of the interaction of a unique genetic endowment with a particular environment. Integrating then current biology with developmental psychoanalytic concepts, he proposed that the infant's "environment of adaptiveness" has consequences that are "vital to the survival of the species," and that the attachment relationship directly influences the infant's "capacity to cope with stress" by impacting the maturation of a "'control system" in the infant's brain that comes to regulate attachment functions. From the very start, Bowlby contended that a deeper understanding of the complexities of normal development could only be reached through an integration of developmental psychology, psychoanalysis, biology, and neuroscience (Schore, 2000a).

Over the course of (and since) the "Decade of the Brain," the amount of scientific information concerning the unique psychological, psychobiological, and neurobiological phenomena that occur in the early stages of human life has rapidly expanded (Schore, 1996, 1997a, 1998a, 1998b, 1999a, 2000c). With an eye to these data, at the end of the very same decade Main (1999) proclaimed:

> We are now, or will soon be, in a position to begin mapping the relations
> between individual differences in early attachment experiences and

*This chapter was written as an article for a Special Edition of the *Infant Mental Health Journal*, "Contributions from the Decade of The Brain to Infant Mental Health." Its companion piece, also published in *Infant Mental Health Journal*, appears here as Chapter 6.

changes in neurochemistry and brain organization. In addition, investigation of physiological "regulators" associated with infant-caregiver interactions could have far-reaching implications for both clinical assessment and intervention. (pp. 881–882)

This current confluence of attachment theory, psychobiology, and neurobiology, the one that Bowlby predicted, offers us a real possibility of creating more complex interdisciplinary conceptions of attachment and social and emotional development. The field of infant mental health specifically focuses upon social emotional development, and so more detailed psychoneurobiological understandings of attachment can generate a more overarching model of the normal development of the human mind/brain/body at the earliest stage of the life span and therefore more precise definitions of adaptive infant mental health.

With that goal in mind, in Chapter 6 I argued that in attachment transactions of affective synchrony, the psychobiologically attuned caregiver interactively regulates the infant's positive and negative states, thereby coconstructing a growth-facilitating environment for the experience-dependent maturation of a control system in the infant's right brain. The efficent functioning of this coping system is central to the infant's expanding capacity for self-regulation, the ability to flexibly regulate stressful emotional states through interactions with other humans — interactive regulation in interconnected contexts, and without other humans — autoregulation in autonomous contexts. The adaptive capacity to shift between these dual regulatory modes, depending upon the social context, is an indicator of normal social emotional development. In this manner a secure attachment relationship facilitates right brain development, promotes efficient affect regulation, and fosters adaptive infant mental health.

But from the beginning, attachment theory has also had a parallel interest in the etiology of abnormal development. In applying the theory to the links between stress coping failures and psychopathology, Bowlby (1978) proposed:

In the fields of etiology and psychopathology [attachment theory] can be used to frame specific hypotheses which relate different family experiences to different forms of psychiatric disorder and also, possibly, to the neurophysiological changes that accompany them.

These germinal ideas have lead to the field of developmental psychopathology, an interdisciplinary approach that conceptualizes normal and aberrant development in terms of common underlying mechanisms (Cicchetti, 1994). This field is also now incorporating current data from neuroscience into more complex models of psychopathogensis.

This is because contemporary neuroscience is now producing more studies of not just the pathology of the mature brain, but also the early developmental failures of the brain. And so neurobiology is currently exploring "early beginnings for adult brain pathology" (Altman, 1997, p. 143) and describing "alteration[s] in the functional organization of the human brain which can be correlated with the absence of early learning experiences" (Castro-Caldas et al., 1998, p. 1060). These data are also relevant to the field of infant mental health, with its interest in all early conditions that place infants and/or their families at risk for less than optimal development.

These trends indicate that an integration of current attachment theory, neuroscience, and infant psychiatry can offer more complex models of psycho-pathogenesis (Schore, 1994, 1997d, 1998h). Toward that end, in this second part, I will offer interdisciplinary data in order to strenghthen the theoretical connections between attachment failures, impairments of the early development of the brain's stress coping systems, and maladaptive infant mental health. And so I will present ideas on the effects of traumatic attachment experiences on the maturation of brain regulatory systems, the neurobiology of relational trauma, the neuropsychology of a disorganized/disoriented attachment pattern, the inhibitory effects of early trauma on the development of control systems involved in affect regulation, the links between early relational trauma and a predisposition to postraumatic stress disorder, a neurobiological model of dissociation, the connections between traumatic attachment and enduring right hemisphere dysfunction, and implications for early intervention.

In the course of this work I will use the disorganized/disoriented ("type D") attachment pattern as a model system of maladaptive infant mental health. This attachment category is found predominantly in infants who are abused or neglected (Carlson, Cicchetti, Barnett, & Braunwald, 1989; Lyons-Ruth, Repacholi, McLeod, & Silva, 1991) and is associated with severe difficulties in stress management and dissociative behavior in later life (van Ijzendoorn, Schuengel, & Bakermans-Kranenburg, 1999). In the broadest sense, this work utilizes a psychoneurobiological perspective to attempt to explicate "how external events may impact on intrapsychic structure and development for infants and children already burdened by high psycho-social risk" (Osofsky, Cohen, & Drell, 1995, p. 596). These models are offered as heuristic proposals that can be evaluated by experimental and clinical research.

AN OVERVIEW OF TRAUMATIC ATTACHMENTS
AND BRAIN DEVELOPMENT

Development may be conceptualized as the transformation of external into internal regulation. This progression represents an increase of complexity of the maturing brain systems that adaptively regulate the interaction between the developing organism and the social environment. The experiences necessary for this experience-dependent maturation are created within the attachment context, the dyadic regulation of emotions. More specifically, as outlined in Chapter 6, the primary caregiver of the securely attached infant affords emotional access to the child and responds appropriately and promptly to his or her positive and negative states. She allows for the interactive generation of high levels of positive affect in coshared play states, and low levels of negative affect in the interactive repair of social stress, that is, attachment ruptures.

Because stable attachment bonds are vitally important for the infant's continuing neurobiological development, these dyadically regulated events scaffold an expansion of the child's coping capacities, and therefore adaptive infant and later adult mental health. In psychobiological research on mother-infant affiliative processes, Kalin, Shelton, and Lynn (1995) described the long-enduring effects of such transactions:

> The quality of early attachment is known to affect social relationships later in life. Therefore, it is conceivable that the level of opiate activity in a mother and her infant may not only affect behaviors during infancy, but may also affect the development of an individual's style of engaging and seeking out supportive relationships later in life. (pp. 740–741)

In contrast to this scenario, the abusive caregiver not only shows less play with her infant, she also induces traumatic states of enduring negative affect. Because her attachment is weak, she provides little protection against other potential abusers of the infant, such as the father. This caregiver is inaccessible and reacts to her infant's expressions of emotions and stress inappropriately and/ or rejectingly, and shows minimal or unpredictable participation in the various types of arousal regulating processes. Instead of modulating she induces extreme levels of stimulation and arousal, either too high in abuse or too low in neglect, and because she provides no interactive repair the infant's intense negative emotional states last for long periods of time. Such states are accompanied by severe alterations in the biochemistry of the immature brain, especially in areas associated with the development of the child's coping capacities (Schore, 1996, 1997a).

There is agreement that repetitive, sustained emotional abuse is at the core of childhood trauma (O'Hagan, 1995), and that parental maltreatment or neglect compromises cognitive development (Trickett & McBride-Chang, 1995). In line with the established general principle that childhood abuse is a major threat to children's mental health (Hart & Brassard, 1987), a context of very early relational trauma serves as a matrix for maladaptive infant (and later adult) mental health. Current developmental research is delving into the most severe forms of attachment disturbances, reactive (Boris & Zeanah, 1999) and disorganized (Lyons-Ruth & Jacobvitz, 1999; Solomon & George, 1999) attachment disorders, and are offering neurobiological models that underlie these early appearing psychopathologies (Hinshaw-Fuselier, Boris, & Zeanah, 1999). Such massive attachment dysfunctions are clearly prime examples of maladaptive infant mental health.

It has been said that "sexual trauma and childhood abuse may simply be the most commonly encountered severely aversive events inherent in our culture" (Sirven & Glosser, 1998, p. 232). Trauma in the first two years, as at any point in the life span, can be inflicted upon the individual from the physical or interpersonal environment. It is now established, however, that social stressors are "far more detrimental" than nonsocial aversive stimuli (Sgoifo et al., 1999). For this reason I will use the term "relational trauma" throughout this work. Because such trauma is typically ambient, the stress embedded in ongoing relational trauma is therefore not single-event but cumulative. Because attachment status is the product of the infant's genetically encoded psychobiological predisposition and the caregiver experience, and attachment mechanisms are expressed throughout later stages of life, early relational trauma has both immediate and long-term effects, including the generation of risk for later-forming psychiatric disorders.

Within the biopsychosocial model of infant psychiatry, the diathesis-stress concept prescribes that psychiatric disorders are caused by a combination of a genetic-constitutional predisposition and environmental or psychosocial stressors that activate the inborn neurophysiological vulnerability. In light of the fact that the brain growth spurt begins in the third trimester in utero (Dobbing & Smart, 1974), genetic-constitutional factors can be negatively impacted during this period by adverse conditions within the uterine maternal-infant environment. For example, research shows that maternal hormones regulate the expression of genes in the fetal brain, and that acute changes in maternal hormone induce changes in gene expression in the fetal brain that are retained when it reaches adulthood (Dowling, Martz, Leonard, & Zoeller, 2000). Other studies reveal that high levels of maternal corticotropin-releasing hormone during pregnancy negatively affects fetal brain development (Glynn, Wadhwa, & Sandman, 2000) and reduces later postnatal capacities to respond to stressful challenge (Williams, Hennessey, & Davis, 1995).

These and other data indicate that certain maternal stimuli that impinge upon the fetus negatively impact the hypothalamo-pituitary-adrenocortical (HPA) axis (Glover, 1997; Sandman et al., 1994; Weinstock, 1997) and thereby produce an enduring neurophysiological vulnerability. There is convincing evidence of the enduring detrimental effects of maternal alcohol (Streissguth et al., 1994), drug (Espy, Kaufman, & Glisky, 1999; Jacobson, Jacobson, Sokol, Martier, & Chiodo, 1996), and tobacco (Fergusson, Woodward, & Horwood, 1998) use during pregnancy on the child's development. These risk factors in part reflect a delay in postnatal brain development (Huppi et al., 1996), which is expressed not only in prematurity and low birth weight, but also in poor infant interactive capacities (Aitken & Trevarthen, 1997). These limitations in social responsiveness may be aligned with parental avoidance or rejection (Field, 1977), and even physical abuse of the premature infant (Hunter, Kilstom, Kraybill, & Loda, 1978).

Various maternal behaviors may severely dysregulate the homeostasis and even future development of the developing fetus, yet these are not usually considered to be instances of trauma. On the other hand, caregiver abuse and neglect of the postnatal infant are viewed as clear examples of relational trauma.

Again, in neonatal phases, both genetic factors that influence stress responsivity and detrimental environmental effects interact to contribute to a behavioral outcome, that is stress exaggerates the effects of a developmental lesion (Lipska & Weinberger, 1995). This biopsychosocial model suggests that high-risk infants born with delayed brain development and poor interactive capacites, and thereby a vulnerable predisposition, would experience even low levels of relational stress as traumatic, while an infant with a more durable constitution would tolerate higher levels of dyadic misattunement before shifting into dysregulation. There is no one objective threshhold at which all infants initiate a stress response, rather this is subjectively determined and created within a unique organismic-environmental history. Even so, the severe levels of stress associated with infant abuse and neglect are pathogenic to all immature human brains, and the latter may be even more detrimental to development than the former.

These principles suggest that caregiver-induced trauma is qualitatively and quantitatively more potentially psychopathogenic than any other social or physical stressor (aside from those that directly target the developing brain). In an immature organism with undeveloped and restricted coping capacities, the primary caregiver is the source of the infant's stress-regulation, and therefore sense of safety. When not safety but danger emanates from the attachment relationship, the homeostatic assaults have significant short- and long-term consequences on the maturing psyche and soma. The stress regulating systems that integrate mind and body are a product of developing limbic-autonomic circuits (Rinaman et al., 2000), and since their maturation is experience-dependent, during their critical period of organization they are vulnerable to relational trauma. Basic research is revealing that perinatal distress leads to a blunting of the stress response in the right (and not left) prefrontal cortex that is manifest in adulthood (Brake, Sullivan, & Gratton, 2000), and that interruptions of early cortical development specifically affect limbic association areas and social behavior (Talamini, Koch, Luiten, Koolhaas, & Korf, 1999).

The nascent psychobiological structures that support the primordial motive systems to attach are located in subcortical components of the limbic system. These brain stem neuromodulatory and hypothalamic neuroendocrine systems that regulate the HPA axis are in a critical period of growth pre- and postnatally, and they regulate the maturation of the later-developing cerebral cortex (Aitken & Trevarthen, 1997; Bear & Singer, 1986; Durig & Hornung, 2000; Osterheld-Haas, Van der Loos, & Hornung, 1994; Schore, 1994). Severe attachment problems with the caregiver negatively impact the postnatal development of these biogenic amine systems (Kraemer & Clarke, 1996).

In human infancy, relational trauma, like exposure to inadequate nutrition during the brain growth spurt (Levitsky & Strupp, 1995; Mendez & Adair, 1999), to biological pathogens or chemical agents that target developing brain tissue (Connally & Kvalsvig, 1993), and to physical trauma to the baby's brain (Anderson et al., 1999), interferes with the experience-dependent maturation of the brain's coping systems, and therefore have a long-enduring negative impact on the trajectory of developmental processes.

NEGATIVE IMPACT OF RELATIONAL TRAUMA
ON INFANT MENTAL HEALTH

The neuropsychobiological literature underscores a central finding of developmental science — that the maturation of the infant's brain is experience-dependent, and that these experiences are embedded in the attachment relationship (Schore, 1994, 2000c; Siegel, 1999). If there is truth to the dictum that security of the attachment bond is a primary defense against trauma-induced psychopathology, then what about the infant who doesn't have such an experience, but its antithesis? And because attachment transactions occur in a period in which the brain is massively developing, what is the future course of the brain/mind/body of an infant who does not have the good fortune of engaging with a caregiver who cocreates the child's internal sense of emotional security? What if the brain is evolving in an environment not of interpersonal security, but of danger? Is this a context for the intergenerational transmission of psychopathology, and the origins of maladaptive infant mental health? Will early trauma have lasting consequences for future mental health, in that the trajectory of the developmental process will be altered?

This portrait of infancy is usually not presented by the media, or even in current books on the effects of early experience on brain development (e.g., Bruer, 1999; Gopnik, Meltzoff, & Kuhl, 1999). This is not the image of a "scientist in the crib," but rather of "ghosts in the nursery" (Fraiberg, Adelson, & Shapiro, 1975). In fact, this infant was depicted in Karr-Morse and Wiley's *Ghosts from the Nursery: Tracing the Roots of Violence* (1997). These authors asked, what is the effect of early trauma, abuse and/or neglect, on developing brain anatomy? And how does this effect the future emotional functioning of the individual as he or she passes into the next stages of the life span?

In his last work Freud (1940/1964) observed that trauma in early life effects all vulnerable humans because "the ego . . . is feeble, immature and incapable of resistance." In recent thinking, this dictum translates to the principle that the infant's immature brain is in a state of rapid development, and is therefore exquisitely vulnerable to early adverse experiences, including adverse social experiences. An entire issue of the journal *Biological Psychiatry* is devoted to development and vulnerability, and in it De Bellis and colleagues writing on developmental traumatology, concluded on developmental traumatology, "the overwhelming stress of maltreatment in childhood is associated with adverse influences on brain development" (1999, p. 1281).

A number of scientific and clinical disciplines are focusing on not only the interactional aspects of early trauma, but also the untoward effects of abuse and deprivational neglect on the development of the infant brain. In a major advance of our knowledge, discoveries in the developmental sciences now clearly show that the primary caregiver acts as an external psychobiological regulator of the "experience-dependent" growth of the infant's nervous system (Schore, 1994, 1996, 1997a, 2000b). These early social events are imprinted into the neurobiological structures that are maturing during the brain growth spurt of the first two years of life, and therefore have far-reaching effects. Eisenberg (1995) referred to "the social construction of the human brain," and argues that the cytoarchitectonics of the cerebral cortex are sculpted by input from the social environment. The social environment can positively or negatively modulate the developing brain.

Early relational trauma, which is usually not a singular event but ambient and cumulative, is of course a prime example of the latter. These events may not be so uncommon. In 1995 over 3 million children in this country were reported to have been abused or neglected (Barnet & Barnet, 1998), and the *Los Angeles Times* reported (September 26, 1999) that in California, in 1997, there were 81,583 reported cases of neglect and 54,491 reported cases of physical abuse. Although these sources did not specify how many infants were in these categories, other evidence indicates that in the United States the most serious maltreatment occurs to infants under 2 years of age (National Center on Child Abuse and Neglect, 1981). Homicide (Karr-Morse & Wiley, 1997) and traumatic head injury (Colombani, Buck, Dudgeon, Miller, & Miller, 1985) are the leading causes of death for children under the age of 4.

A 1997 issue of *Pediatrics* contains a study of covert videorecordings of infants hospitalized for life-threatening events, and it documents, in a most careful and disturbing manner, the various forms of child abuse that are inflicted by caregivers on infants as young as 3 months *while they are in the hospital* (Southall, Plunkett, Banks, Falkov, & Samuels, 1997). These experiences are recorded and stored in the infant. Terr has written that "literal mirroring of traumatic events by behavioral memory [can be] established at any age, including infancy" (1988, p. 103). According to Luu and Tucker, "To understand neuropsychological development is to confront the fact that the brain is mutable, such that its structural organization reflects the history of the organism" (1996, p. 297).

Because early abuse negatively impacts the developing brain of these infants, it has enduring effects. There is extensive evidence that trauma in early life impairs the development of the capacities of maintaining interpersonal relationships, coping with stressful stimuli, and regulating emotion. A body of interdisciplinary research demonstrates that the essential experiences that shape the individual's patterns of coping responses are forged in the emotion-transacting caregiver-infant relationship (Schore, 1994, 2000c). We are beginning to understand, at a psychobiological level, specifically how beneficial early experiences enhance and detrimental early histories inhibit the development of the brain's active and passive stress coping mechanisms.

The explosion of developmental studies are highly relevant to the problem of how early trauma uniquely alters the ongoing maturation of the brain/mind/

body. As Gaensbauer and Siegel have written, prolonged and frequent episodes of intense and unregulated interactive stress in infants and toddlers have devastating effects on "the establishment of psychophysiological regulation and the development of stable and trusting attachment relationships in the first year of life" (1995, p. 294). Perhaps even more revealing is the fact that these early dysregulating experiences lead to more than an insecure attachment; they also trigger a chaotic alteration of the emotion processing limbic system that is in a critical period of growth in infancy. The limbic system has been suggested to be the site of developmental changes associated with the rise of attachment behaviors (Anders & Zeanah, 1984) and to be centrally involved in the capacity "to adapt to a rapidly changing environment" and in "the organization of new learning" (Mesulam, 1998, p. 1028). These limbic circuits are particularly expressed in the right hemisphere (Joseph, 1996; Tucker, 1992), which is in a growth spurt in the first two years of life (Schore, 1994).

There is agreement that, in general, the enduring effects of traumatic abuse are due to deviations in the development of patterns of social information processing. I suggest that, in particular, early trauma alters the development of the right brain, the hemisphere that is specialized for the processing of socioemotional information and bodily states. The early maturing right cerebral cortex is dominant for attachment functions (Henry, 1993; Schore, 1994, 2000b, 2000c; Siegel, 1999) and stores an internal working model of the attachment relationship. An enduring developmental impairment of this system would be expressed as a severe limitation of the essential activity of the right hemisphere — the control of vital functions supporting survival and enabling the organism to cope actively and passively with stressors (Wittling & Schweiger, 1993).

Davies and Frawley (1994) described the immediate effects of parent-inflicted trauma on attachment:

> The continued survival of the child is felt to be at risk, because the actuality of the abuse jeopardizes (the) primary object bond and challenges the child's capacity to trust and, therefore, to securely depend. (p. 62)

In contexts of relational trauma the caregiver, in addition to dysregulating the infant, withdraws any repair functions, leaving the infant for long periods in an intensely disruptive psychobiological state that is beyond her immature coping strategies. In studies of a neglect paradigm, Tronick and Weinberg (1997) wrote:

> When infants are not in homeostatic balance or are emotionally dysregulated (e.g., they are distressed), they are at the mercy of these states. Until these states are brought under control, infants must devote all their regulatory resources to reorganizing them. While infants are doing that, they can do nothing else. (p. 56)

In other words, infants who experience chronic relational trauma too frequently forfeit potential opportunities for socioemotional learning during critical periods of right-brain development.

But there is also a pernicious long-term consequence of relational trauma — an enduring deficit at later points of the life span in the individual's capacity to assimilate novel (and thus stressful) emotional experiences. At the beginning of the twentieth century, Janet (1911) speculated:

> All [traumatized] patients seem to have the evolution of their lives checked; they are attached to an unsurmountable object. Unable to integrate traumatic memories, they seem to have lost their capacity to assimilate new experiences as well. It is . . . as if their personality development has stopped at a certain point, and cannot enlarge any more by the addition of new elements. (p. 532)

The functional limitations of such a system are described by Hopkins and Butterworth: "Undifferentiated levels of development show relatively rigid but unstable modes of organization in which the organism cannot adapt responses to marked changes coming from within or without" (1990, p. 9). From a psychoanalytic perspective, Emde (1988) defined pathology as a lack of adaptive capacity, an incapacity to shift strategies in the face of environmental demands. In psychiatric writings, van der Kolk (1996) asserted that under ordinary conditions traumatized individuals adapt fairly well, but they do not repond to stress the way others do, and Bramsen, Dirkzwager, and van der Ploeg observed that in the aftermath of trauma, certain personality traits predispose individuals to engage in less successful coping strategies. All of these all descriptions characterize an immature right brain, the locus of the human stress response (Wittling, 1997).

This structural limitation of the right brain is responsible for the individual's inability to regulate affect. As van der Kolk and Fisler (1994) have argued, the loss of the ability to regulate the intensity of feelings is the most far-reaching effect of early trauma and neglect. I further suggest that significantly altered early right brain development is reflected in a "type D" pattern (Main & Solomon, 1986), the disorganized/disoriented attachment seen in abused and neglected infants (Carlson et al., 1989; Lyons-Ruth et al., 1991). This severe right brain attachment pathology is involved in the etiologies of a high risk for both posttraumatic stress disorder (Schore, 1997a, 1998d, 1998g, 1998i; 1999g; 2000e) and a predisposition to relational violence (Lyons-Ruth & Jacobvitz, 1999; Schore, 1999c). In discussing the characteristics of toddlers and preschoolers exhibiting severe psychiatric disturbance, Causey, Robertson, and Elam (1998) reported that a large number of these young patients were neglected and/or physically or sexually abused. Main (1996) argued that "disorganized" and "organized" forms of insecure attachment are primary risk factors for the development of mental disorders.

THE NEUROBIOLOGY OF INFANT TRAUMA

Although the body of studies on childhood trauma is growing, there is still hardly any research on infant trauma. A noteworthy example is the work of Perry and his colleagues, which is extremely valuable because it includes not just behavioral but also developmental neurobiological and psychobiological data. Perry and others (1995) demonstrated that the human infant's psychobiological response to trauma is comprised of two separate response patterns, hyperarousal and dissociation. In the initial stage of threat, a startle or alarm reaction is initiated, in which the sympathetic component of the autonomic nervous system (ANS) is suddenly and significantly activated, resulting in increased heart rate, blood pressure, respiration, and muscle tone, as well as hypervigilance. Distress is expressed in crying and then screaming.

This dyadic transaction is described by Beebe (2000) as "mutually escalating overarousal" of a disorganized attachment pair:

> Each one escalates the ante, as the infant builds to a frantic distress, may scream, and, in this example, finally throws up. In an escalating overarousal pattern, even after extreme distress signals from the infant, such as ninety-degree head aversion, arching away . . . or screamimg, the mother keeps going. (p. 436)

The infant's state of "frantic distress," or what Perry termed fear-terror is mediated by sympathetic hyperarousal, known as ergotropic arousal (Gellhorn, 1967. It reflects excessive levels of the major stress hormone corticotropin releasing factor (CRF) which regulates catecholamine activity in the sympathetic nervous system (Brown et al., 1982). Noradrenaline is also released from the locus coeruleus (Aston-Jones, Valentino, Van Bockstaele, & Meyerson, 1996; Butler., Weiss, Stout, & Nemeroff, 1990; Svensson, 1987). The result is rapid and intensely elevated noradrenaline and adrenaline levels which trigger a hypermetabolic state within the brain. In such "kindling" states (Adamec, 1990; Post, Weiss, Smith, & McCann, 1997), very large amounts of CRF and glutamate, the major excitatory neurotransmitter in the brain (Chambers et al., 1999), are expressed in the limbic system (Schore, 1997a). Harkness and Tucker (2000) stated that early traumatic experiences, such as childhood abuse, literally kindle limbic areas.

But Perry's group described a second, later-forming reaction to infant trauma, dissociation, in which the child disengages from stimuli in the external world and an attends to an "internal" world. The child's dissociation in the midst of terror involves numbing, avoidance, compliance, and restricted affect. Traumatized infants are observed to be staring off into space with a glazed look. This behavioral strategy is described by Tronick and Weinberg (1997):

> [W]hen infants' attempts to fail to repair the interaction infants often lose postural control, withdraw, and self-comfort. The disengagement is

profound even with this short disruption of the mutual regulatory process and break in intersubjectivity. The infant's reaction is reminiscent of the withdrawal of Harlow's isolated monkey or of the infants in institutions observed by Bowlby and Spitz. (p. 66)

The state of conservation-withdrawal (Kaufman & Rosenblum, 1967, 1969; Schore, 1994) is a parsympathetic regulatory strategy that occurs in helpless and hopeless stressful situations in which the individual becomes inhibited and strives to avoid attention in order to become "unseen." This state is a primary hypometabolic regulatory process, used throughout the life span, in which the stressed individual passively disengages in order "to conserve energies . . . to foster survival by the risky posture of feigning death, to allow healing of wounds and restitution of depleted resources by immobility" (Powles, 1992, p. 213). It is this parasympathetic mechanism that mediates the "profound detachment" (Barach, 1991) of dissociation. If early trauma is experienced as "psychic catastrophe" (Bion, 1962), dissociation represents "detachment from an unbearable situation" (Mollon, 1996), "the escape when there is no escape" (Putnam, 1997), and "a last resort defensive strategy" (Dixon, 1998).

Most importantly, the neurobiology of the later-forming dissociative reaction is different than the initial hyperarousal response. In this passive state, pain numbing and blunting endogenous opiates are elevated. These opioids, especially enkephalins, instantly trigger pain-reducing analgesia and immobility (Fanselow, 1986) and inhibition of cries for help (Kalin, 1993). In addition, the behavior-inhibiting steroid, cortisol, is elevated. The inhibition produced by cortisol results from the rapid modulation of gamma-aminobutyric acid (GABA) receptors by cortisol metabolites (Majewska, Harrison, Schwartz, Barker, & Paul, 1986; Orchinik, Murray, & Moore, 1994). GABA is the principal inhibitory neurotransmitter in the brain.

Furthermore, vagal tone increases dramatically, decreasing blood pressure and heart rate, despite increases in circulating adrenaline. This increased parasympathetic trophotropic hypoarousal (Gellhorn, 1967) allows the infant to maintain homeostasis in the face of the internal state of sympathetic ergotropic hyperarousal. In the traumatic state, and it may be long-lasting, both the sympathetic energy-expending and parasympathetic energy-conserving components of the infant's developing ANS are hyperactivated.

In the developing brain states organize neural systems, resulting in enduring traits. That is, traumatic states in infancy trigger psychobiological alterations that effect state-dependent affect, cognition, and behavior. But since they are occurring in a critical period of growth of the emotion regulating limbic system, they negatively impact the experience-dependent maturation of the structural systems that regulate affect, thereby inducing characterological styles of coping that act as traits for regulating stress. In light of the principle that "critical periods for pathogenic influences might be prolonged in these more slowly maturing systems, of which the prefrontal cortex is exemplary" (Goldberg &

Bilder, 1987, p. 177), prefrontolimbic areas would be particularly vulnerable. What psychoneurobiological mechanism could account for this?

The brain of an infant who experiences frequent intense attachment disruptions is chronically exposed to states of impaired autonomic homeostasis which he/she shifts into in order to maintain basic metabolic processes for survival. If the caregiver does not participate in stress-reparative functions that reestablish psychobiological equilibrium, the limbic connections in the process of developing are exposed to high levels of excitotoxic neurotransmitters, such as glutamate (Choi, 1992; Moghaddam, 1993) as well as cortisol (Moghaddam, Bolinao, Stein-Behrens, & Sapolsky, 1994; Schore, 1997a) for long periods of time. The neurotoxic effects of glucocorticoids are synergistcally amplified by simultaneous activation of the excitotoxic N-methyl-D-aspartate (NMDA)-sensitive glutamate receptor, a critical site of neurotoxicity and synapse elimination in early development (McDonald, Silverstein, & Johnston, 1988; Guilarte, 1998).

It is known that stress-induced increases of glucocorticoids in postnatal periods selectively induce neuronal cell death in "affective centers" in the limbic system (Kathol et al., 1989), imprint an abnormal limbic circuitry (Benes, 1994), and produce permanent functional impairments of the directing of emotion into adaptive channels (DeKosky et al., 1982). The interaction between corticosteroids and excitatory transmitters is now thought to mediate programmed cell death and to represent a primary etiological mechanism for the pathophysiology of neuropsychiatric disorders (Margolis et al., 1994). Here is a template for impaired limbic morphogenesis, a structural alteration that will reduce future adaptive coping functions. This is a context for psychopathogenesis.

The major environmental influence on the development of the limbic structures involved in organismic coping is the attachment relationship. Severe disruption of attachment bonds in infancy leads to a regulatory failure expressed in disturbances in limbic activity, hypothalamic dysfunction, and impaired autonomic homeostasis (Reite & Capitanio, 1985). The dysregulating events of abuse and neglect produce extreme and rapid alterations of ANS sympathetic ergotropic hyperarousal and parasympathetic trophotropic hypoarousal that create chaotic biochemical alterations, a toxic neurochemistry in the developing brain.

The neurochemistry of brain growth is essentially regulated by the monoaminergic neuromodulators, especially the biogenic amines dopamine, noradrenaline, and serotonin, and the neuropeptide and steroid neurohormones. In critical periods, increased production of these agents, many of which are trophic, are matched by increased production of the receptors of such agents. Prenatal stress is known to alter biogenic amine levels on a long-lasting basis (Schneider et al., 1998). Postnatal traumatic stress also induces excessive levels of dopamine, activating excitatory NMDA receptor binding of glutamate (Knapp et al., 1990). Excitatory neurotransmitters regulate postsynaptic calcium influx in developing neocortex (Yuste & Katz, 1991) and glutamate acting at

NMDA receptors increases intracellular calcium in neurons (Burgoyne, Pearce, & Cambray-Deakin, 1988), which, if uncontrolled, leads to intracelluar damage or cell death (Garthwaite & Garthwaite, 1986).

In other words, intense relational stress alters calcium metabolism in the infant's brain, a critical mechanism of cell death (Farber, 1981). Dopamine (Filloux & Townsend, 1993; McLaughlin, Nelson, Erecinska, & Chesselet, 1998) and glutamate (Tan, Sagara, Liu, Maher, & Schubert, 1998) can be neurotoxic, by generating superoxide free radicals associated with oxidative stress (Lafon-Cazal et al., 1993), especially hydroxyl radicals which destroy cell membranes (Lohr, 1991). These events greatly enhance "apoptotic" or "programmed cell death" (Margolis et al., 1994; Schore, 1997a). During a critical period of growth of a particular brain region, DNA production is highly increased, and so excitotoxic stress, which is known to cause oxidative damage to DNA, lipid membrane, and protein (Liu et al., 1996), also negatively impacts the genetic systems within evolving limbic areas.

Indeed, there is evidence to show that adverse social experiences during early critical periods result in permanent alterations in opiate, corticosteroid, corticotropin releasing factor, dopamine, noradrenaline, and serotonin receptors (Coplan et al., 1996; Ladd, Owens, & Nemeroff, 1996; Lewis et al., 1990; Martin et al., 1991; Rosenblum et al., 1994; van der Kolk, 1987). Such receptor alterations are a central mechanism by which "early adverse developmental experiences may leave behind a permanent physiological reactivity in limbic areas of the brain" (Post et al., 1994, p. 800).

It is established that "dissociation at the time of exposure to extreme stress appears to signal the invocation of neural mechanisms that result in long-term alterations in brain functioning" (Chambers et al., 1999, p. 274). In other words, infants who experience states of terror and dissociation and little interactive repair, especially those with a genetic-constitutional predisposition and an inborn neurophysiological vulnerability, are high risk for developing severe psychopathologies at later stages of life. Bowlby (1969) asserted,

> since much of the development and organization of [attachment] behavioral systems takes place whilst the individual is immature, there are plenty of occasions when an atypical environment can divert them from developing on an adaptive course. (p. 130)

Recall that attachment involves limbic imprinting, and so infant trauma will interfere with the critical period organization of the limbic system, and therefore impair the individual's future capacity to adapt to a rapidly changing environment and to organize new learning (Mesulam, 1998). Maladaptive infant mental health is therefore highly correlated with maladaptive adult mental health.

The infant posttraumatic stress disorder of hyperarousal and dissociation thus sets the template for later childhood, adolescent, and adult posttraumatic stress disorders (PTSD), all of which show disturbances of autonomic arousal (Prins, Kaloupek, & Keane, 1995) and abnormal catecholaminergic function (Southwick et al., 1993). In each, "chronic, inescapable or uncontrollable stress may lead to impairment of the normal counter-regulatory mechanisms producing hyperactivity of the hypothalamic-pituitary-adrenal and sympathetic nervous systems, which could lead to excessive anxiety, feelings of hopelessness and defeat, and depression" (Weinstock, 1997, p. 1). The latter symptomatic triad represents unregulated parasympathetic activity that is associated with dissociation. At any point of the lifespan, dissociative defensive reactions are elicited almost instantaneously.

This continuity in infant and adult coping deficits is described by Nijenhuis, Vanderlinden, and Spinhoven (1998):

> The stress responses exhibited by infants are the product of an immature brain processing threat stimuli and producing appropriate responses, while the adult who exhibits infantile responses has a mature brain that, barring stress-related abnormalities in brain development, is capable of exhibiting adult response patterns. However, there is evidence that the adult brain may regress to an infantile state when it is confronted with severe stress. (p. 253)

But, as we have seen, developmental neurobiological studies now demonstrate that "the overwhelming stress of maltreatment in childhood is associated with adverse influences on brain development" (De Bellis et al., 1999, p. 1281), and that "early adverse experiences result in an increased sensitivity to the effects of stress later in life and render an individual vulnerable to stress-related psychiatric disorders" (Graham, Heim, Goodman, Miller, & Nemeroff, 1999, p. 545).

THE NEUROPSYCHOLOGY AND NEUROPSYCHOANALYSIS OF A DISORGANIZED/ DISORIENTED ATTACHMENT PATTERN

The next question is, how would the trauma-induced psychobiological and neurobiological alterations of the developing brain be expressed in the behavior of an early traumatized toddler? We have the data. In a classic study, Main and Solomon (1986) studied the attachment patterns of infant's who had suffered trauma in the first year of life. This lead to the discovery of a new attachment category, type D, an insecure disorganized/disoriented pattern. (This work is updated and summarized by Solomon and George [1999].)

The type D pattern is found in over 80% of maltreated infants (Carlson et al., 1989). Indeed Spangler and Grossman (1999) demonstrated that this group of toddlers exhibits the highest heart rate activation and most intense alarm reaction in the strange situation procedure (see Figure 7.1). They also show higher cortisol levels than all other attachment classifications and are at greatest risk

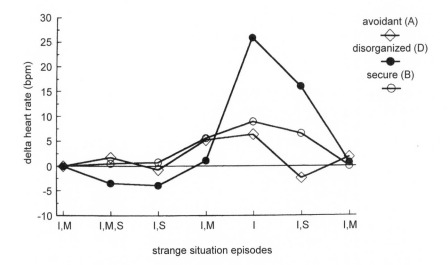

FIGURE 7.1. Changes in heart rate during strange situation episodes for different attachment groups (M, mother; I, infant; S, stranger). (From Spangler & Grossman, 1993)

for impaired hypothalamo-pituitary-adrenocortical axis stress responding (Herts-gaard et al., 1995). Main and Solomon concluded that "these infants are experiencing low stress tolerance" (1986, p. 107). These authors contend that the disorganization and disorientation reflect the fact that the infant, instead of finding a haven of safety in the relationship, is alarmed by the parent. They noted that because the infant inevitably seeks the parent when alarmed, any parental behavior that directly alarms an infant should place it in an irresolvable paradox in which it can neither approach, shift its attention, or flee. At the most basic level, these infants are unable to generate a coherent behavioral coping strategy to deal with this emotional challenge.

Main and Solomon (1986) documented, in some detail, the uniquely disturbing behaviors these 12-month-old infants show in "strange situation" reunion transactions. These episodes of interruptions of organized behavior and low stress tolerance are often brief, frequently lasting 10–30 seconds, yet they are highly significant. For example, Main and Solomon show a simultaneous display of contradictory behavior patterns, such as backing toward the parent rather than approaching face-to-face.

> The impression in each case was that approach movements were continually being inhibited and held back through simultaneous activation of avoidant tendencies. In most cases, however, proximity-seeking sufficiently "over-rode" avoidance to permit the increase in physical proximity. Thus, contradictory patterns were activated but were not mutually inhibited. (p. 117)

Notice the simultaneous activation of the energy expending sympathetic and energy conserving parasympathetic components of the ANS.

Maltreated infants also show evidence of apprehension and confusion, as well as very rapid shits of state during the stress-inducing strange situation.

> One infant hunched her upper body and shoulders at hearing her mother's call, then broke into extravagent laugh-like screeches with an excited forward movement. Her braying laughter became a cry and distress-face without a new intake of breath as the infant hunched forward. Then suddenly she became silent, blank and dazed. (Main & Solomon, 1986, p. 119)

A dictionary definition of apprehension is distrust or dread with regard to the future. These apprehensive behaviors generalize beyond just interactions with the mother. The intensity of the baby's dysregulated affective state is often heightened when the infant is exposed to the added stress of an unfamiliar person. At a stranger's entrance, two infants moved away from both mother and stranger to face the wall, and another "leaned forehead against the wall for several seconds, looking back in apparent terror" (Main & Solomon, 1986, p. 120).

These maltreated infants also showed "behavioral stilling" — that is, "dazed" behavior and depressed affect (again a hyperactivation of the PNS). One infant "became for a moment excessively still, staring into space as though completely out of contact with self, environment, and parent" (Main & Solomon, 1986, p. 120) Another showed "a dazed facial appearance . . . accompanied by a stilling of all body movement, and sometimes a freezing of limbs which had been in motion" (p. 120). And yet another "fell face-down on the floor in a depressed posture prior to separation, stilling all body movements" (p. 120).

Furthermore, Main and Solomon pointed out that the type D behaviors take the form of stereotypies that are found in neurologically impaired infants. It should be emphasized that these behaviors are overt manifestations of an obviously impaired regulatory system, one that rapidly disorganizes under stress. Notice that these observations are taking place at 12 to 18 months, a critical period of corticolimbic maturation, and they reflect a severe structural impairment of the orbitofrontal control system that is involved in attachment behavior and state regulation. The orbitofrontal areas, like other limbic structures in the anterior temporal areas and the amygdala, contains neurons that fire to emotionally expressive faces. The mother's face is the most potent visual stimulus in the child's world, and it is well known that direct gaze can mediate powerful aggressive messages.

During the trauma, the infant is presented with an aggressive expression on the mother's face. The image of this aggressive face, as well as the chaotic alterations in the infant's bodily state that are associated with it, is indelibly imprinted into subcortical limbic circuits as a "flashbulb memory" (Brown & Kulik, 1977) and thereby stored in implicit-procedural memory in the visuospatial right hemisphere. These are stored memories of what Lieberman (1997) called "negative maternal attributions" that contain an intensely negative affective charge, and therefore rapidly dysregulate the infant.

In the course of the traumatic interaction, the infant is presented with another affectively overwhelming facial expression, a maternal expression of fear-terror. Main and Solomon (1986) noted that this occurs when the mother withdraws from the infant as though the infant were the source of the alarm, and they report that dissociated, trancelike, and fearful behavior is observed in parents of type "D" infants. Current studies show a link between frightening maternal behavior and disorganized infant attachment (Schuengel, Bakersmans-Kranenburg, & Van Ijzendoorn, 1999). I suggest that during these episodes the infant is matching the rhythmic structures of the mother's dysregulated states, and that this synchronization is registered in the firing patterns of the stress-sensitive corticolimbic regions of the infant's brain that are in a critical period of growth. This is the context of the down-loading of programs of psychopathogenesis.

Mothers of children with disorganized attachment describe themselves as unable to care for or protect their infants, inflicting harsh punishments, feeling depressed, and being out of control. In general, high-risk and physically abusive mothers, relative to comparison mothers, differ in the types of perceptions, attributions, evaluations, and expectations of their children's behavior, engage in fewer interactions and communicate less with their children, use fewer positive parenting behaviors, and use more aversive disciplinary techniques, (Nayak & Milner, 1998). Role reversal (Mayseless, 1998) and a subjective feeling of helplessness (George & Solomon, 1996) are commonly found mothers of disorganized infants. In light of the fact that many of these mothers have suffered from unresolved trauma themselves (Famularo, Kinscherff, & Fenton, 1992a), this spatiotemporal imprinting of the chaotic alterations of the mother's dysregulated state may be a central mechanism for the "intergenerational transmission child abuse" (Kaufman & Zigler, 1989).

Research on the neurobiology of attachment is revealing that the early experiences of female infants with their mothers (or absence of these experiences) influence how they respond to their own infants when they later become mothers, and that this provides a psychobiological mechanism for the intergenerational transmission of adaptive and maladaptive parenting styles and responsiveness (Fleming et al., 1999). This psychobiological principle is advanced in the clinical writings of Silverman and Lieberman, who concluded that although the mother's caregiving system has an instinctual basis, it is expressed through the filter of her own representational templates, "which derive from her sense of being cared and protected in her relationship with her own parents" (1999, p. 172). This experience did not occur in the abusive mother's early attachment.

In a recent biosocial model of the determinants of motherhood, Pryce (1995) viewed parenting as varying on a continuum between the extremes of maximal care and infant/abuse and neglect. Expanding upon these ideas,

Maestripieri (1999) asserted that although models of parenting are often presented in terms of social and cognitive processes, recent biological studies in primates of the neurobiological regulation of parental responsivess and the determinants of infant abuse indicate that human parenting is much more sensitive to neuroendocrine mechanisms than previously thought. Maestripieri portrays maximal parental care, as represented in a mother

> with a genotype for a secure and sensitive personality, a developmental environment that included a secure attachment to an adequate caregiver and experience of "play-mothering," a stress-free pregnancy and postpartum period, optimal neurobiological priming and control, and considerable social support. Such a female will be highly attracted to her infant and made anxious by its crying, but will not averse to her infant or its novelty per se. (p. 417)

In contrast, the mother characterized as expressing minimal parental care and maximal neglect presents

> with a genotype for a insecure . . . personality, a developmental environment that included a insecure attachment to a caregiver and no experience with infants, a stressful pregnancy and postpartum period, a suboptimal neurobiological priming and control, and little or no social support. Such a female will be weakly attracted to her infant and will be averse to the infant, including its crying, its physical burden, and its novelty. (Maestripieri, 1999, p. 417)

Maestripieri also suggested that high vulnerability to stress and emotional disorders are common among abusive parents.

Indeed, a vulnerability to dissociation in the postpartum period has been reported by Moleman, van der Hart, and van der Kolk (1992). In a number of cases they described women panic-striken with the anticipation of losing their babies:

> Panic ceased when they dissociated from both their subjective physical experience and from contact with their surroundings. They all continued to experience dissociative phenomena, intrusive recollections about some aspects of the delivery, and amnesia about others, and *they all failed to attach to their children.* (p. 271; my italics)

These symptoms lasted months after the delivery. Notice the authors' contention that maternal dissociation blocks infant attachment.

What would be the effect if the mother's dissociative episodes continued as a clinical depression well through the first year of the infant's life? I suggest that in certain critical stressful dyadic moments, this same individual will show a vulnerability for a suboptimal neurobiological priming in the form of dissociation. In light of the fact that infant cries produce elevated physiological reactivity and high levels of negative affect in abusing mothers (Frodi & Lamb, 1980), episodes of "persistent crying" (Papousek & von Hofacker, 1998) may be a potent trigger of dissociation. The caregiver's entrance into a dissociative state represents the real-time manifestation of neglect. Such a context of an emotionally unavailable, dissociating, unresolved/disorganized mother and a disorganized/disoriented infant is evocatively captured by Fraiberg (cited in Barach, 1991), who provided a painfully vivid description of a dissociative mother and her child's detachment:

> The mother had been grudgingly parented by relatives after her mother's postpartum attempted suicide and had been sexually abused by her father and cousin. During a testing session, her baby begins to cry. It is a hoarse, eerie cry . . . On tape, we see the baby in the mother's arms screaming hopelessly; she does not turn to her mother for comfort. The mother looks distant, self-absorbed. She makes an absent gesture to comfort the baby, then gives up. She looks away. The screaming continues for five dreadful minutes. In the background we hear Mrs. Adelson's voice, gently encoraging the mother. "What do you do to comfort Mary when she cries like this?" (The mother) murmurs something inaudible . . . As we watched this tape later . . . we said to each other incredulously, "It's as if this mother doesn't hear her baby's cries." (p. 119)

Ultimately, the child will transition out of hyperexcitation-protest into hyperinhibition-detachment, and with the termination of protest (screaming), she'll become silent. She will shift out of the hyperarousal, and she'll dissociate and match the mother's state. This regulatory failure is experienced as a discontinuity in what Kestenberg (1985) referred to as dead spots in the infant's subjective experience, an operational definition of the restriction of consciousness of dissociation. Winnicott (1958) held that a particular failure of the maternal holding environment causes a discontinuity in the baby's need for going-on-being, and that this is a central factor in psychopathogensis. And so not just trauma but the infant's posttraumatic response to the relational trauma, the parasympathetic regulatory strategy of dissociation, is built into the personality.

There is a long tradition in the classical psychoanalytic literature of the severely detrimental effects of the traumatic effects of a sudden and unexpected influx of massive external stimulation (sympathetic hyperexcitation) that breaches the infant's stimulus barrier (Freud, 1920/1955) and precludes successful self-regulation (Freud, 1926/1959b). This has lead to an emphasis of the role of overstimulation and annihilation anxieties in classical, object relational, and self psychological models of trauma. I suggest that "screaming hopelessly" is the vocal expression of annihilation anxiety, the threat to one's bodily wholeness and survival, the annihilation of one's core being.

However, Freud (1926/1959b) also described the psychic helplessness associated with the ego's immaturity in the first years of childhood, and postulated
that the passively experienced reemergence of the trauma is "a recognized,
remembered, expected situation of helplessness." In writings on psychic trauma
and "emotional surrender" Anna Freud (1951/1968; 1967/1969) also referred
to helplessness, defined as a state of "disorientation and powerlessness" that the
organism experiences in the traumatic moment. Although almost all psychoanalytic theoreticicans have overlooked or undervalued this, Krystal (1988) and
Hurvich (1989) emphasized that at the level of psychic survival helplessness
constitutes the first basic danger. This helplessness is an early appearing primitive organismic defense against the growth inhibiting effects of maternal over-
or understimulation.

What has been undetermined in this literature is how, as Mahler (1958)
stated, trauma interferes with psychic structure formation. This question can
only be answered with reference to current neurobiological models of developing psychic structure. Translating this into developmental neurobiological concepts, evidence now shows that the neurobiological alterations of traumatic
sympathetic hyperexcitation and parasympathetic hyperinhibition on the developing limbic system are profound. Perry and colleagues state that sympathetically
driven early terror states lead to a "sensitized" hyperarousal response. Due to the
alterations of maturing catecholamine systems, "critical physiological, cognitive,
emotional, and behavioral functions which are mediated by these systems will
become sensitized" (Perry et al., 1995). According to Perry and colleagues,

> Everyday stressors that previously may not have elicited any response now
> elicit an exaggerated reactivity . . . This is due to the fact that . . . the child
> is in a persisting fear state (which is now a "trait"). Furthermore, this
> means that the child will very easily be moved from being mildly anxious
> to feeling threatened to being terrorized. (p. 278)

Thus, not only is the onset of sympathetically driven fear-alarm states more
rapid, but their offset is prolonged, and they endure for longer periods of time.
This permanent dysregulation of CRF-driven fear states is described by Heim
and Nemeroff who, on the basis of a study of adult survivors of childhood abuse
suggested that "stress early in life results in a persistent sensitization of these
CRF circuits to even mild stress in adulthood, forming the basis for mood and
anxiety disoders" (1999, p. 1518).

But, in addition, due to the chaotic parasympathetic alterations that accompany trauma to the early self, this branch of the ANS also is dysregulated.
Deprivation of early maternal stress modulation is known to trigger not only an
exaggerated release of corticosteroids upon exposure to novel experiences, but,
in addition, inhibitory states that persist for longer periods of time. The result
is a quicker access into and a longer duration of dissociated states at later points
of stress. This represents a deficit, since adaptive coping is reflected by the

termination of a stress response at an appropriate time in order to prevent an excessive reaction (Weinstock, 1997).

Sroufe and his colleagues concluded that early more so than later trauma has a greater impact on the development of dissociation. They wrote, "The vulnerable self will be more likely to adopt dissociation as a coping mechanism because it does not have either the belief in worthiness gained from a loving and responsive early relationship or the normal level of defenses and integration that such a belief affords" (Ogawa, Sroufe, Weinfield, Carlson, & Egeland, 1997, p. 875).

CRITICAL PERIOD TRAUMA AND DEFICIENT ORBITOFRONTAL CONNECTIVITY

In an editorial of a special issue of *Biological Psychiatry*, Foote wrote, "Combining developmental and affective approaches, it may even be possible to test hypotheses regarding the components of stress and affective circuitry that can exhibit dysregulation following traumatic and/or harmful events, especially early in life" (1999, p. 1457). A developmental perspective can tell us when adverse experiences have the greatest disorganizing impact on evolving adaptive functions, and a neurobiological approach can give us clues as to which limbic circuits that mediate these functions are in a critical period of growth, and therefore most vulnerable. Clearly, attachment neurobiology is centrally involved. This leads to the question, specifically what brain systems involved in attachment are negatively impacted by early abuse and neglect?

Relational trauma in the first, second, and third quarters of the first year negatively impacts the experience-dependent maturation of the amygdala and anterior cingulate limbic circuits (see previous article). But by the end of this year and into the second, the higher corticolimbic circuits are in a critical period of growth, and therefore negatively impacted. Referring back to Main and Solomon's (1986) studies, these involved infants of 12 to 18 months, a time when internal working models of the attachment relationship are first assessed by the strange situation. Research documents that disorganized infant attachment strategies increase in frequency from 12 to 18 months (Lyons-Ruth, Alpern, & Repacholi, 1993). In fact, this interval is a critical period for the experience-dependent maturation of the orbitofrontal areas of the cortex (see Figure 7.2).

Perry and colleagues (1995) contended that early traumatic environments that induce atypical patterns of neural activity interfere with the organization of cortical-limbic areas and compromise, in particular, such brain-mediated functions as attachment, empathy, and affect regulation. These very same functions are mediated by the frontolimbic areas of the cortex, and because of their dysfunction, affective disturbances are a hallmark of early trauma. Teicher, Ito, and Glod (1996) reported that children with early physical and sexual abuse show EEG abnormalities in frontotemporal and anterior brain regions. They

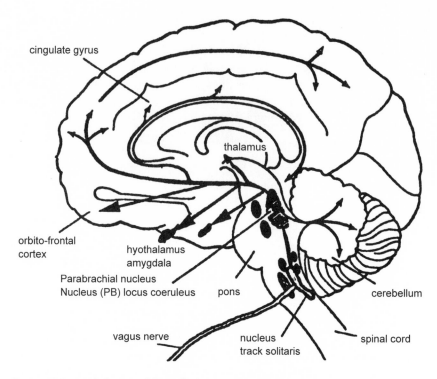

FIGURE 7.2. Medial view of the right hemisphere, showing limbic structures and connections of the vagus nerve into the medulla. (From George et al., 2000).

concluded that stress alters the development of the prefrontal cortex, arrests its
development, and prevents it from reaching a full adult capacity. So the next
question is, what kind of psychoneurobiological mechanism could account for
this prefrontal developmental arrest?

The developing infant is maximally vulnerable to nonoptimal and growth-
inhibiting environmental events during the period of most rapid brain growth.
During these critical periods of intense synapse production, the organism is
sensitive to conditions in the external environment, and if these are outside
the normal range a permanent arrest of development occurs. In Chapter 6 I
proposed that the amygdala, anterior cingulate, and insula limbic structures
play a role in preattachment experiences that begin early in the first year, and
thus trauma during each of their critical periods would interfere with the
experience-dependent maturation of these limbic structures (see Figure 7.3).

Indeed, neurobiological studies indicate that damage to the amygdala in
early infancy is accompanied by profound changes in the formation of social
bonds and emotionality (Bachevalier, 1994). These socioemotional effects are
long-lasting and appear even to increase in magnitude over time (Malkova,

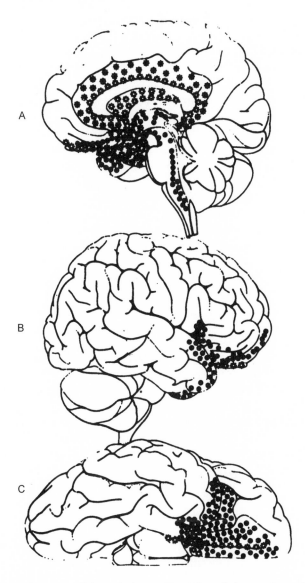

FIGURE 7.3. Limbic areas of the right brain. Top (A) medial view; front of the brain at left. Middle (B) lateral view; front of the brain is to the right. Bottom (C) ventral view; front of the brain is to the right. (From Brothers, 1997)

Mishkin, Suomi, & Bachevalier, 1997). Abnormalities of the social functions of the amygdala are implicated in autism (Baron-Cohen et al., 2000), and this would include autistic posttraumatic developmental disorder (Reid, 1999), a subgroup of children in which trauma in the first two years of life precipitates autism. Even more specifically to the model outlined here, abnormally large right (and not left) amygdala volumes have been reported in children and adolescents with generalized anxiety disorders (De Bellis, Casey, et al., 2000).

Relational traumatic events in the middle of the first year act as a growth-inhibiting environment for the anterior cingulate limbic network. This would interfere with the ongoing development of the infant's coping systems, since impairments in anterior cingulate functions are known to lead to prolonged glucocorticoid and ACTH release during stress (Diorio, Viau, & Meaney, 1993) and later deficits in emotional arousal and an impoverished conscious experience of emotion (Lane, Ahern, Schwartz & Kazniak, 1997). Indeed, maltreated children diagnosed with PTSD manifest metabolic abnormaliites of the anterior cingulate (De Bellis, Keshavan, Spencer, & Hall, 2000). And early relational trauma that interferes with the experience-dependent maturation of the insula negatively impacts its role in generating an image of one's physical state (body image), a process that underlies the experiencing of basic emotions (Craig et al., 2000).

But in addition, abuse and/or neglect over the first two years negatively impacts the major regulatory system in the human brain, the orbital prefrontolimbic system. In classic basic research, Kling and Steklis (1976) found that orbitofrontal lesions critically disrupt behaviors of "social bonding." More recently, Damasio's group reported that early neurological damage of this prefrontal cortex caused a failure "to acquire complex social knowledge during the regular developmental period" and an enduring impairment of social and moral behavior due to a "disruption of the systems that hold covert, emotionally related knowledge of social situations" (Anderson et al., 1999, p. 1035). Interestingly, a 20-year-old female patient, who at 15 months sustained ventromedial prefrontal damage due to a car accident, was unable to experience empathy, and "her maternal behavior was marked by dangerous insensitivity to (her) infant's needs" (p. 1032).

In these cases, damage to the orbitofrontal system is of neurological causation. It should be pointed out that relational trauma may be accompanied by physical trauma to not only the body (Southall et al., 1997) but also to the developing brain. In either case, the developmental trajectories of the brain's regulatory systems are negatively altered. In other words failures of structural development occur in relational trauma that includes or does not include physical trauma to the brain. In human infancy, purely "psychological" relational trauma leads to altered brain development, and purely "neurological" trauma negatively impacts relational development. Indeed, type D behaviors are found in neurologically impaired infants (Barnett et al., 1999), and infants who experience perinatal complications show orbitofrontal dysfunction in adolescence

(Kinney et al., 2000). Sapolsky has pointed out that exposure to acute of chronic stress may be associated with *either* psychological disorders (such as child abuse) *or* neurological disorders (Moghaddam et al., 1994).

Earlier, I suggested that physical trauma to the baby's head and brain have a long-enduring negative impact on the trajectory of developmental processes. Infant/toddler abuse in the form of violent shaking of the head or forceful impact to the skull are sources of traumatic brain injury. The potential for such catastrophic outcomes of relational trauma may increase as the toddler becomes ambulatory in the second year, and account for the increase of type D attachments at this time. Although direct studies of such relationally induced brain injuries have not been done, information about the deleterious effects on brain function can be extrapolated from two sources, brain magnetic resonance imaging (MRI) human studies of closed head injuries (Mamelak, 2000), and animal studies of traumatic brain injuries (Gennarelli, 1994; McIntosh et al., 1989). This research may give a model of the metabolic dysregulation occurring within the orbitofrontal areas of a physically traumatized infant/toddler.

Due to the topography of the brain as it sits within the bony skull, orbitofrontal contusions on the ventral surface are particularly common following impact-type closed head injury (Adams, Graham, Scott, Parker, & Doyle, 1980). Studies of the biomechanics of traumatic head injury in mature humans demonstrated that the sudden forceful movement of the brain within the skull causes inertial strain and tissue deformation that are greatest at the orbital surfaces of the frontal and temporal lobes, and that these areas are common sites of contusion (Mamelak, 2000). The ensuing anatomical and functional damage occurs whether or not there is impact on the skull or loss of consciousness. The response to orbitofrontal injury is a sudden increase in metabolic energy utilization followed by a prolonged period of metabolic energy depression.

Parallel studies in animal models demonstrated that the neurochemical consequences of closed-head injury occur even without signs of gross morphologic damage. This profile shows an initial significant rise in extracellular levels of excitatory amino acids, glutamate and aspartate, which trigger an initial hypermetabolic response. This in turn elevates intracellular calcium levels, which may last for days, and leads to a prolonged posttraumatic depression. This pattern of initial hypermetabolism followed by hypometabolism (Yoshino, Hovda, Kawamata, Katayama, & Becker, 1991) is identical to that described by Perry. The later shut down of cerebral metabolism has been suggested to be due to the action of a sensor in the dorsal medullary region that functions as an energy conservation system which protects the brain against the detrimental consequences of energy depletion (Pazdernik, Cross, & Nelson, 1994).

It has been suggested that the symptoms of cerebral physical trauma take the form of a change in emotional functions, personality, and indeed psychiatric disorders, and can be explained as consequences of the impairment of specifically orbitofrontal functions (Mamelak, 2000). As mentioned earlier, Anderson and colleagues (1999) documented the enduring psychosocial deficits that result from orbitofrontal damage (car accident and tumor resection) in the first and second year. These studies of orbitofrontal injury in infancy and adult-hood suggested a similar pattern of impairments of energy metabolism in re-sponse to both intense physical and psychosocial stressors. The developing brain, which requires large amounts of energy during the brain growth spurt, reacts with massive bioenergetic alterations in response to traumatic assaults of brain and/or body. What would be the common outcome of either physical trauma or relational trauma-induced energy impairments during a critical pe-riod of energy-dependent growth of corticolimbic systems?

The postnatal organization of the brain and the progressive postnatal assem-bly of limbic-autonomic circuits (Rinaman et al., 2000) occur in a very specific pattern. During a critical period of regional brain growth, genetic factors are expressed in an initial overproduction of synapses. This is followed by a process that is environmentally-driven, the pruning and maintenance of synaptic con-nections and the organization of functional circuits. This process of genetic-environmental organization of a brain region is energy dependent (Schore, 1994, 1997a, 2000b), and can be altered, especially during its critical period of growth. The construct of developmental instability (Moller & Swaddle, 1997) has been invoked to describe the imprecise expression of the genetic plan for development due to genetic (e.g., mutations) and environmental effects (e.g., toxins). I suggest that the psychotoxic contexts of early relational trauma acts as an inducer of developmental instability, which has been shown to contribute to alterations of cerebral lateralization (Yeo, Gangestad, Thoma, Shaw, & Repa, 1997a) and to a vulnerability factor in the etiology of neurodevelopmental dis-orders (Yeo, Hodde-Vargas, et al. 1997).

In a magnetic resonance spectroscopy (^{1}H-MRS) study of the right frontal lobe, Yeo, Hill, Campbell, Vigil, and Brooks (2000) concluded that develop-mental instability

> may lead to a greater need for energy-requiring, stabilizing forces in de-velopment. Hence, there may be less in the way of metabolic resources left for metabolic growth. (p. 155)

These very same conditions are produced in the patterns of initial hypermetabo-lism followed by enduring hypometabolism of relational trauma described earlier. This disruption of energy resources for the biosynthesis of right lateralized limbic connections would be expressed in a critical period developmental overpruning of the corticolimbic system, especially one that contains a genetically-encoded underproduction of synapses. This psychopathomorphogentic mechanism acts a generator of high-risk conditions.

It is accepted that psychological factors "prune" or "sculpt" neural networks in specifically the postnatal frontal, limbic, and temporal cortices (Carlson et al., 1988). I propose that excessive pruning of cortical-subcortical limbic-autonomic circuits occurs in early histories of trauma and neglect, and that this severe growth impairment represents the mechanism of the genesis of a developmental structural defect. Because this defect is in limbic organization, the resulting functional deficit will specifically be in the individual's maturing stress coping systems. The dysregulating events of abuse and neglect create chaotic biochemical alterations in the infant brain, a condition that intensifies the normal process of apoptotic programmed cell death. Post and his colleagues reported a study of infant mammals entitled, "Maternal deprivation induces cell death" (Zhang, Xing, et al., 1997). Maternal neglect is the behavioral manifestation of maternal deprivation, and this alone or in combination with paternal physical abuse is devastating to developing limbic subsystems.

In its critical period the orbitofrontal areas are synaptically connecting with other areas of the cerebral cortex, but they are also forging contacts with subcortical areas. And so the orbitofrontal cortex is a "convergence zone" where cortex and subcortex meet. In earlier writings I have proposed that it is the severe parcellation (excessive pruning) of hierarchical cortical-subcortical circuits that is central to the developmental origins of the regulatory deficits that are the sequelae of early trauma (Schore, 1997a). Caregiver-induced trauma exacerbates extensive destruction of synapses in this "senior executive" of limbic arousal (Joseph, 1996), which directly connects into the dopaminergic and noradrenergic systems in the anterior and caudal reticular formation. Exposure to fear cues provokes enhanced dopamine metabolism in the ventral tegmental areas (Deutsch et al., 1991), which activates the locus coeruleus (Deutsch, Goldstein, & Roth, 1986) and increases noradrenaline activty (Clarke et al., 1996; Tanaka et al., 1990). Both catecholamines are released in response to stressful disruptions of the attachment bond, and elevated levels of these bioamines result in regression of synapses and programmed cell death (McLaughlin et al., 1998; see Schore 1994 and 1997a for a description of dopaminergic disruptions of mitochondrial energy metabolism).

The mechanism of this parcellation, the activity-dependent winnowing of surplus circuitry, has been previously described in terms of hyperactivation of the dopamine-sensitive excitotoxic NMDA-sensitive glutamate receptor, a critical site of synapse neurotoxicity and elimination during early development. As opposed to this hypermetabolic response, cortisol release triggers hypometabolism, a condition that enhances the toxicity of excitatory neurotransmitters (Novelli et al., 1988). During critical periods, dendritic spines, potential points of connection with other neurons, are particularly vulnerable to long pulses of glutamate (Segal, Korkotian, & Murphy, 2000) that trigger severely altered calcium metabolism and therefore "oxidative stress" and apoptotic damage (Park, Bateman, & Goldberg, 1996; Schore, 1997a). It is known that stress causes oxidative damage to brain lipid membranes, protein, and DNA (Liu et al., 1996), including mitochondrial DNA (Bowling et al., 1993; Schinder, Olson, Spitzer, & Montal, 1996; Schore, 1997a), that stress increases levels of excitatory amino acids such as glutamate in the prefrontal cortex (Moghaddam, 1993), and that excitotoxins can destroy orbitofrontal neurons (Dias et al., 1996).

Developmental parcellation, experience-dependent circuit pruning, is associated with a selective loss of connections and redistribution of inputs via an elimination of long axon collaterals and dendritic processes, and such regressive events are essential mechanisms of brain maturation. But excessive parcellation during a critical period of synaptogenesis leads to a stress-induced shrinkage of dendritic fields, which are exquisitely vulnerable to oxidative damage (Schore, 1997a). Due to the massive bioenergetic alterations that accompany relational trauma, orbitofrontal dendritic fields are virulently overpruned and extremely retracted, thus reducing potential sites of synaptic connectivity with distant cortical and subcortical inputs into this major convergence zone of the brain. Such smaller dendritic surface areas would lead to reduced current flow through orbitofrontal regulatory circuits.

In writings on brain plasticity and behavior Kolb and Whishaw (1998) articulated the general principle:

> [Individuals] with extensive dendritic growth . . . show facilitated performance on many types of behavioral measures . . . In contrast, individuals with atrophy in dendritic arborization show a decline in behavioral capacity. Similar factors that enhance dendritic growth . . . facilitate behavioral outcome, whereas factors that block dendritic growth (e.g., brain injury at birth) retard functional outcomes. (p. 59)

Relational trauma not only blocks critical period dendritic growth, but also astrocyte proliferation that occurs in these intervals. These glial cells surround the most active regions of neurons, and thereby regulate the metabolic activity and connectional plasticity of all synapses in the brain (Laming et al., 2000). The postnatal proliferation and surface area of astrocytic processes that surround synapses is directly influenced by events in early the social environment (Jones & Greenough, 1996), including traumatic events.

Under conditions of continual traumatic assaults, more than dendritic fields may be lost, rather the neuronal components of one or both of the limbic circuits may undergo extensive programmed cell death. In describing the mechanism of neurotoxicity, Fornai, Vaglini, Maggio, Bonuccelli, & Corsini (1997) stated:

> [W]hen acute insults are repeated, the neuronal loss progresses downstream to synaptically linked neurons. This trans-synaptic progression of neuronal death . . . resembles . . . neurodegenerative diseases in which the "systemic degeneration" consists of spreading cell loss to neurons interconnected in functional circuits. (p. 402)

An overly extensive developmental pruning of particularly, vertically-organized limbic circuits would result in an inefficent regulation of subcortical systems by cortical inputs. Excessive parcellation of the lateral orbitofrontal areas and the excitatory ventral tegmental forebrain-midbrain limbic circuit would severely alter the capacity to experience positive states, and underlie a vulnerability to hypoarousal, that is anhedonia and depression. On the other hand, a severe parcellation of the medial orbitofrontal areas and the inhibitory medial tegmental forebrain-midbrain circuit would result in a limited capacity to inhibit stressful hyperaroused states, such as terror and rage (Schore, 1996, 1997a).

It is important to point out that these disorganized insecure attachment psychopathologies are defined by an impairment of both limbic circuits. In less severe dysfunctions, such as those in the organized insecure attachments, only one circuit of the dual circuit limbic system is developmentally structurally immature and functionally inefficent (see Schore, 1994, 1996). But in these most severe attachment disturbances the regulatory failures are manifest in the individual's limited capacity to modulate, either by autoregulation or interactive regulation, the intensity and duration of biologically primitive sympathetic-dominant affects like terror, rage, excitement, and elation, or parasympathetic-dominant affects like shame, disgust, and hopeless despair. Notice that intense positive affect, excitement and joy, is also a stressor to these personalities (Litz, Orsillo, Kaloupek, & Weathers, 2000).

This early-appearing adaptive dysfunction of internal reparative coping mechanisms endures in later developmental stages, and is most obvious under stressful and challenging conditions that call for behavioral flexibility. In this manner the coping deficits of maladaptive infant mental health endure as inefficient stress regulating deficts of maladaptive adult mental health.

RELATIONAL TRAUMA, ORBITOFRONTAL DYSFUNCTION, AND A PREDISPOSITION TO POSTTRAUMATIC STRESS DISORDERS

In fact, this hierarchical apex of the limbic system manifests a "preferential vulnerability" to psychiatric disorders (Barbas, 1995). The limbic system is described as the border zone where psychiatry meets neurology (Mega & Cummings, 1994). In updated psychiatric models, not severity of the trauma but characteristics of the individual, including his or her reactions to a trauma, are viewed as the essential factors that contribute to PTSD (American Psychiatric Association, 1994). An individual's repertoire of stress-coping strategies is directly affected by the attachment relationship, and a disorganized/disoriented attachment interferes with this ontogenetic achievement. In this manner, there are direct connections between infant posttraumatic stress disorder and child, adolescent, and adult stress disorders. Indeed, traumatic childhood events are commonly reported by adult PTSD patients with neurologic soft signs (Gurvitz et al., 2000).

Because the loss of the ability to regulate the intensity of affect is the most far-reaching effect of early trauma and neglect, this deficit involves a developmentally impaired inefficient orbitofrontal regulatory system. Neurobiological research on PTSD reveals dysfunctional frontal-subcortical systems (Sutker, Vasterling, Brailey, & Allain, 1995; Uddo, Vasterling, Brailey, & Sutker, 1993), and altered orbitofrontal (Bremner et al., 1997; Shin et al., 1999), anterior cingulate (Hamner, Lorberbaum, & George, 1999), and amygdala (Rauch et al., 1996) functions. So the next question is, how would a severe developmental pruning of the connections between the higher and lower levels of vertical limbic circuits be expressed in the functional deficits of PTSD?

Of special importance are the connections between the orbitofrontal areas and the hypothalamus, the head ganglion of the ANS and control system of visceral-somatic emotional reactions, and the amygdala, the major fear center in the brain. The right amygdala is known to process frightening faces and to mediate the "nonconscious processing" (Whalen et al., 1998) of "unseen fear" (Morris, Ohman, & Dolan, 1999), but when adequately functioning the right frontotemporal cortex exerts inhibitory control over intense emotional arousal (Kinsbourne & Bemporad, 1984). According to Rolls "although the amygdala is concerned with some of the same functions as the orbitofrontal cortex, and receives similar inputs, there is evidence that it may function less effectively in . . . very rapid learning" (1996, p. 1443). In optimal contexts the orbitofrontal cortex takes over amygdala functions.

The connections between the orbitofrontal areas and the amygdala form postnatally, and are negatively impacted by the adverse environmental events of relational trauma (see Figure 7.4). A severe experientially driven pruning of these interconnections would allow for amygdala-driven states, such as fear-flight states to be later expressed without cortical inhibition. It is now established that a pathological response to stress reflects the functions of a hyperexcitable amygdala (Halgren, 1992) and that the memory processes of the amygdala are amplified by extreme stress (Corodimas, LeDoux, Gold, & Schulkin, 1994). Even subliminally processed low intensity interpersonal stressors could activate unmodulated terrifying and painful emotional experiences of the individual's early history that are imprinted into amygdalar-hypothalamic circuits. These fear-freeze responses would be intense, because they are totally unregulated by the orbitofrontal areas that are unavailable for the correction and adjustment of emotional responses.

In optimal contexts, both the amygdala and the orbital prefrontal cortex have direct connections with the lateral hypothalamus (Kita & Oomura, 1981), an area known to activate parasympathetic responses through interconnections with the vagus nerve in the medulla (Brownstein, 1989). The anterior regions of the lateral hypothalamus are involved in "tonic immobility," defined as an inborn behavioral inhibition and terminal defense characterized by profound

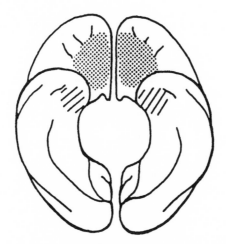

FIGURE 7.4. Undersurface of the brain. Front of the brain at top. Dotted area shows: the orbitofrontal cortex; hatched area, the amygdala. (From George et al., 2000)

physical inactivity and lack of responsiveness to the environment that is triggered by fear generated during prey-predator confrontation (de Oliveira, Hoffmann, & Menescal-de-Oliveira, 1997). Notice the similarity of this to the immobility of the infant's conservation-withdrawal response, to dissociation, the escape when there is no escape, the detachment from an unbearable situation, and to Bowlby's terminal separation response, "profound detachment."

The lateral hypothalamus develops postnatally (Fisher & Almli, 1984). Relational trauma in this period could result in weaker orbitofrontal and stronger amygdala connections into this structure, leading to amygdala-dominant behavioral inhibition. The higher corticolimbic areas would inefficiently regulate the immobility response, that is, there would be a tendency to dissociate under stress, and this response would be long-lasting. Morgan and LeDoux (1995) described such a condition:

> while the amygdala determines the emotional significance of threatening stimuli, the ventromedial prefrontal cortex uses this information to monitor and give feedback about the internal state of the [organism] and to update response outputs dependent on this internal state. Without the internal feedback as to the level of threat posed by the stimulus at any given time, the [organism] might, for adaptive purposes, remain in the defensive response state longer than necessary. (p. 687)

In other work LeDoux suggested that a defective orbitofrontal system results in an inability to shift cognitive strategies and a reduction in behavioral flexibility, and that this "emotional perseveration" would lead to an increased resistance to extinction of fear behaviors, such as found in "anxiety, phobic, panic, and post-traumatic stress disorders." (Morgan, Romanski, & LeDoux, 1993, p. 112).

An inefficient orbitofrontal reparative function is expressed in a poor capacity for the state regulation that is necessary for self-comforting in times of stress. In such unstable systems, small disruptions associated with interpersonal stresses too easily become rapidly amplified into intense distress states. This is subjectively experienced as a sudden transition into rapidly shifting negative affective states. A failure of orbitofrontal modulation of limbic arousal and an uncoupling of both the ventral tegmental and lateral tegmental forebrain-midbrain limbic circuits results in a cycling between intrusive hypersympatheti-cally driven terrifying flashbacks and traumatic images and parasympathetically driven dissociation, avoidance, and numbing. Models of PTSD refer to stressor-induced oscillations between traumatic and avoidant states, and cycling between the bidirectional symptoms of emotional reexperiencing and emotional constrictedness (Antelman et al., 1997).

Functional magnetic imaging (fMRI) research conducted by Hariri, Book-heimer, and Mazziotta (2000) suggested an inability of the orbitofrontal areas, specifically in the right hemisphere, to modulate the amygdala's fear response to emotionally valent stimuli would underlie the emotional disturbances of posttraumatic stress disorder. These authors emphasized the adaptive importance of this network by which higher right frontal brain regions attenuate emotional stimuli mediated by more primitive brain regions. It is exactly this higher network that is rendered dysfunctional by early relational trauma and disorganized/disoriented attachments.

It is important to note that type D attachments are associated with another form of psychopathology, one of hostile-aggressive behavior (Lyons-Ruth et al., 1993). PTSD patients also show dysregulation of aggression, and so in addition to unmodulated hypothalamic hypersympathetic fear-freeze states, these individuals also manifest dysregulated hypothalamic hypersympathetic fight states. Basic neurobiological studies indicate that the orbitofrontal cortex exerts an inhibitory control over hypothalamic sites from which aggression can be elicited by electrical stimulation (Kruk, Van der Poel, & De Vos-Freichs, 1979), and that this cortex is implicated in the suppression of aggression in dyadic encounters (de Bruin, 1990).

A substantial body of neurological studies also indicate that aggression dysregulation is associated with specifically altered orbitofrontal function (Fornazzari, Farenik, Smith, Heasman, & Ischise, 1992; Grafman et al., 1996; Miller, Darby, Benson, Cummings, & Miller, 1997; Raine, Stoddard, Bihrle, & Buchsbaum, 1998; Starkstein & Robinson, 1997). Davidson and colleagues (2000) implicated a dysregulation of an orbitofrontal-anterior cingulate-amygdala circuit of emotion regulation in a risk for violence and aggression. Right orbitofrontal impairment is associated with difficulties in emotional recognition of angry and disgusted facial expressions, autonomic responding, and social cognition, as well as with high levels of aggression (Blair & Cipolotti, 2000).

There is evidence that there are two types of aggression, predatory or "stalking" attack and defensive or "affective" rage (Panksepp, 1998; Siegel, Roeling, Gregg, & Kruk, 1999). Positron emission tomography (PET) studies revealed that both predatory and affective murderers show reduced prefrontal and increased subcortical activity (Raine, Meloy, et al., 1998). Increased metabolic rate in the right hemisphere is also seen in affective, impulsive muderers. Affective rage is mediated by the hypothalamic ventromedial nucleus, a structure associated with elevated sympatho-adrenal and cardiovascular activity (Stoddard-Apter, Levin, & Siegel, 1983), increases in anxiety (Adamec & McKay, 1993), and parasympathetic vagal suppression (Colpaert, 1975). This system is also involved in maternal rage that is part of maternal protectiveness, and so, in line with the finding that maternal aggression shares similarities with hypothalamic attack (Siegel et al., 1999), it is tempting to speculate that a functional dysregulation of this system occurs in maternal abuse.

Sympathetic ventromedial hypothalamic neurons continue to develop in a postnatal critical period (Almli & Fisher, 1985), a time when their dendrites receive frontolimbic axonal projections. These neurons also receive input from the amygdala (Adamec, 1998), and thus an excessive developmental parcellation of the orbitofrontal (and cingulate-insular) inhibitory pathway to the sympathetic ventromedial hypothalamic nucleus (Ohta & Oomura, 1979) would seriously interfere with the ability of higher limbic inputs to regulate amygdala-driven affective rage. This deficit represents the outcome of early relational trauma, and it mediates the intermittent states of relationally triggered uncontrolled aggression seen in certain traumatized populations.

Furthermore, a large body of studies indicates disrupted early attachments and early trauma and abuse in the histories of children and adults diagnosed as borderline personality disorder (Lyons-Ruth & Jacobvitz, 1999), and thus there is a high correlation of PTSD and borderline diagnoses (Famularo et al., 1992a; Herman, Perry, & van der Kolk, 1989; van der Kolk, Hostetler, Heron, & Fisler, 1994). Zanarini and colleagues (1997) report that 91% of borderline patients report childhood abuse, and 92% reported some type of childhood neglect. In an overview of the literature Paris, summarized the developmetal data and asserts "the weight of the research evidence supports the hypothesis that abuse during childhood is an important risk factor for borderline personality disorder" (1995, p. 15). Herman and van der Kolk (1987) asserted that PTSD and borderline personality disorders both share massive disturbances in affect regulation, impulse control, interpersonal difficulties, self-integration, and a bias to use dissociation when under stress. Neurobiological studies revealed altered amygdala (Corrigan, Davidson, & Heard, 2000) and orbitofrontal function (Goyer et al., 1994) in borderline personality disorder.

Brain imaging research also demonstrated decreased orbitofrontal metabolism in another class of psychiatric patients with a history of violent behavior (Raine, Stoddard, et al., 1998), that is, sociopathic personality disorder. These authors implicated a defective orbitofrontal system in a "predisposition to violence," a finding of numerous studies. Such personalities show the second type of aggression, predatory or stalking attack (Panksepp, 1998; Siegel et al., 1999). This type of aggression is also associated with hypothalamic activity, but from different areas in the parasympathetic lateral hypothalamus, an area also innervated by amygdala inputs. In natural settings, predatory attacks are released when modulatory brain mechanisms, such as those in the amygdala and prefrontal cortex, are suppressed (Siegel et al., 1999). These authors reported that stimulation of the medial prefrontal cortex blocks predatory attack elicited from the lateral hypothalamus.

The orbital prefrontal cortex has direct connections with lateral hypothalamus, and thereby regulates its activity (Kita & Oomura, 1981). Because this hypothalamic system also continues to develop in a postnatal critical period (Fisher & Almli, 1984), an excessive experience-dependent parcellation of prefrontal-lateral hypothalamic connections would result in an inefficient higher cortical regulation of not just the immobility response, but under extremely intense stressful levels, predatory attack. This predisposition to relational violence, which may result from a toxic growth-inhibiting combination of early maternal neglect and later paternal abuse, is expressed in type D attachments (Lyons-Ruth et al., 1993; Lyons-Ruth & Jacobvitz, 1999). This model suggests that a sociopathic personality organization is frequently another manifestation of developmental posttraumatic stress disorder.

In an earlier work, I presented ideas on the regulation of infantile rage reactions and on how structural impairments associated with attachment failures can be incorporated into models of primitive personality disorders (Schore, 1994). Continuing this, in Chapter 9 I offer data to show that type D disorganized/disoriented attachments and severe orbitofrontal pruning and apoptotic programmed cell death represent the developmental origins of both the affective aggression of various levels of borderline personality disorders and the predatory or stalking type of aggression of sociopathic personality disorders.

THE NEUROBIOLOGY OF THE DISSOCIATIVE DEFENSE

In severe attachment pathologies the developing infant/toddler is repeatedly exposed to the ambient cumulative trauma that emanates from an interactive dysregulating context with a misattuning caregiver. Because this growth-inhibiting context generates dense and prolonged levels of negative affect in the infant, for self-protective purposes it severely restricts it's overt expressions of an attachment need for dyadic regulation. The child thus significantly reduces the output of its emotion-processing, limbic-centered attachment system. And so for defensive functions it shifts from interactive regulatory modes into long-enduring, less complex autoregulatory modes. These subcortical-limbic organizational patterns are primitive strategies for survival, and therefore they become self-organizing attractor states. This sets the stage for primitive autoregulation, for the habitual use of dissociation. Indeed the type D attachment classification utilizes dissociative behaviors in later life (van Ijzendoorn et al., 1999).

The principle that severe attachment psychopathologies frequently access more primitive modes of autoregulation can be translated into the clinical tenet that more severe psychiatric disorders use dissociation as a characterological defense. In the parasympathetic-dominant state of dissociation, the individual is cut off (dis-associated) from both the external and the internal environment. This clearly implies a dysfunction of the orbitofrontal cortex, a site at which cortically processed exteroceptive information concerning the external environment is integrated with subcortically processed interoceptive information regarding the internal visceral environment.

The orbitofrontal system directly connects into the body via its direct connections into the ANS (Neafsey, 1990), and its modulation of the ANS is achieved via descending axons that synapse on dendritic fields of the hypothalamus, the head ganglion of the ANS, and vagal areas of the medulla. An extensive parcellation or thinning of these synaptic connections would lead to an inefficient regulation of the ANS by higher centers in the CNS. This loss means that under stress there would be not be a counterbalancing mechanism between the sympathetic-excitatory and parasympathetic-inhibitory components of the ANS, a loss of a coupled reciprocal mode of autonomic control, in which increases in activity in one ANS division are associated with a decrease in the other (Berntson et al., 1991).

Under stress, a developmentally immature orbitofrontal regulatory system would give way to a coupled nonreciprocal mode of autonomic control (Berntson et al., 1991). The result is an intensely high state of sympathetic ergotropic plus parasympathetic trophotropic arousal, the same pattern of Perry's infant trauma response. Although right vagal and sympathetic innervation of the heart elicits, respectively, decreased and increased cardiac activity, simultaneous stimulation produces an even greater cardiac output and aortic blood flow (Koizumi, Terui, Kolloui, & Brooks, 1982). Behaviorally this is like "riding the gas and the brake at the same time," and the simultaneous activation of hyperexcitation and hyperinhibition results in the "freeze response."

In classic neurological primate research, Ruch and Shenkin (1943) lesioned the orbitofrontal cortex (area 13) and observed a "definite reduction in emotional expression," and an elimination of "fear" and aggressive" behaviors that were replaced by "gazing into the distance with a blank expression." Such behavior was interpreted as an "over-reactive" response to the presence of the experimenter-observer. This is identical to the blank, dazed behavior of the freeze or surrender reaction of type D infants, to the frozen watchfulness observed in the abused child who waits warily for parental demands, responds quickly and compliantly, and then returns to her previous vigilant state, and to the frozen state of speechless terror seen in adult PTSD patients. Primate studies by Kalin, Shelton, Rickman, and Davidson (1998) showed that freezing in infants, which is elicited by eye contact, correlates with extreme right frontal

EEG activity and high basal cortisol levels. This pattern, first measured in late infancy, endures for the rest of the lifespan as a fearful temperament. Extremely inhibited fearful children show heightened sympathetic activity as well as increased cortisol levels (Kagan, Reznick, & Snidman, 1987).

But in addition, due to a loss of a counterbalancing functions of the ANS, severe attachment pathologies also show an inefficient orbitofrontal capacity in coordinating the two branches of the ANS and therefore in regulating affective shifts. Henry and colleagues (1992) pointed out that a simultaneous activation of the sympathetic-adrenal medullary and hypothalamic-pituitary adrenal axes typically occurs in the initial phases of overwhelming stress, but these systems can operate also independently. In PTSD, they noted, these two systems can undergo an "increasing separation," and this "dissociation" is the basis for the emotional psychopathology of this disorder. This represents what Berntson and colleagues (1991) called an uncoupled nonreciprocal mode of autonomic control, in which responses in one division of the ANS occur in absence of change in the other.

A resultant rapid uncoupling of the two frontolimbic circuits would occur in response to even low levels of interactive stress, and be expressed in emotional lability and rapid state shifts. Putnam (1997) described pathological "dissociative switches" between states, which occur rapidly, and are manifest in "inexpliable shifts in affect," changes in facial appearance, mannerisms and speech, and discontinuities in train of thought. Recall that in trauma, sympathetic hyperarousal is suddenly followed by hyperparasympathetic dissociation. Meares also concluded that "dissociation, at its first occurrence, is a consequence of a 'psychological shock' or high arousal" (1999, p. 1853).

A habitual tendency to shift into primitive parasympathetic states is a characterstic of a developmentally immature regulatory system with weak connections between the highest level of the limbic system and the ANS. Of particular importance is the experience-dependent maturation of orbital areas that regulate the parasympathetic system, a development that is slower and later than the sympathetic (Schore, 1994). The orbitofrontal areas, like the amygdala, have direct inputs into the medulla (Mizuno, Sauerland, & Clemente, 1968; Yasui et al., 1991), including the medullary reticular formation (Travers, Dinardo, & Karimnamazi, 1997) and medullary noradrenergic neurons in the nucleus of the solitary tract (see Figure 7.2).

These are the sites of the medullary vagal system, but it is now known that there are two parasympathetic vagal systems, a late developing "mammalian" or "smart" system in the nucleus ambiguus which allows for the ability to communicate via facial expressions, vocalizations, and gestures via contingent social interactions, and a more primitive early developing "reptilian" or "vegetative" system in the dorsal motor nucleus of the vagus that acts to shutdown metabolic activity during immobilization, death feigning, and hiding behaviors (Porges, 1997). Both of these vagal systems are right lateralized (Porges et al., 1994). The central nucleus of the amygdala has extensive connections into the dorsal motor vagal nucleus (Schwaber, Kapp, Higgins, & Rapp, 1982) and is involved in passive coping, immobile behavior, and parasympathetic activity (Roozendaal, Koolhaas, & Bohus, 1997).

In an earlier discussion of traumatic brain injury, I referred to this same dorsal medullary region that functions as an energy conservation system. I posit that in growth-facilitating socioemotional environments, the orbitofrontal system enhances its inputs into the nucleus ambiguus vagal system and therefore expands its affect regulatory capacities, but in traumatic growth inhibiting environments, this "smart" system never optimally develops, and the vegetative system dominates. I suggest that the longer enduring "developmental vegetative state" (Multi-Society Task Force, 1994) of trauma-induced widespread hypometabolism would interfere with the growth of the developing brain, which requires massive amounts of energy for the biosynthetic processes of the brain growth spurt (Schore, 1994, 1997a, 2000b).

In neurological patients the vegetative state is characterized as a "complete loss of attention to the external world" (Laureys et al., 2000), a description that echoes the psychiatric concept of dissociation. I propose that the massive inhibition of the dorsal motor vegetative vagal system mediates dissociation, a primitive defensive mechanism which has long been implicated in trauma-induced psychopathogenesis (Chu & Dill, 1990; Janet, 1889/1973). Porges stated that the dorsal motor nucleus of the vagus "contributes to severe emotional states and may be related to emotional states of 'immobilization' such as extreme terror" (1997, p. 75). Perry's description of the traumatized infant's sudden state switch from sympathetic hyperarousal into parasympathetic dissociation is reflected in Porges's (1997) characterization of

the sudden and rapid transition from an unsuccessful strategy of struggling requiring massive sympathetic activation to the metabolically conservative immobilized state mimicking death associated with the dorsal vagal complex (p. 75).

Clinically, dissociation is described as "a submission and resignation to the inevitability of overwhelming, even psychically deadening danger" (Davies & Frawley, 1994, p. 65).

Dissociation is a primitive defense, and in early traumatized developmental psychopathologies more complex defenses never organize. The inhibitory vagal brake in such systems is predominantly provided by the rigid, fixed vegetative dorsal motor vagus, and not the more evolved and flexible "smart" nucleus ambiguus that allows for social communication. The vagal brake must be withdrawn when the individual shifts from a state of low to high metabolic demand, an operation that is adaptive for engaging and disengaging with the dynamically changing environment (Porges, 1997). This precludes involvement in dyadic play states and loss of a context for interactively creating high levels of arousal and metabolic energy for brain biosynthesis (see earlier section on developmental instability). The lack of the ability to engage in interactive play is an indicator of maladaptive infant health.

DISSOCIATION AND BODY-MIND PSYCHOPATHOLOGY

Dissociation is a common symptom of a spectrum of severe psychopathologies, from reactive attachment disorder of infants (Hinshaw-Fuselier et al., 1999), to dissociative identity disorders (Putnam, 1989), psychotic experiences (Allen & Coyne, 1995), borderline personality disorders (Golynkina & Ryle, 1999), and posttraumatic stress disorders of adults (van der Kolk, McFarlane, & Weisaeth, 1996). The *DSM-IV* lists five dissociative disorders: dissociative amnesia, dissociative fugue, depersonaliztion disorder, dissociative identity disorder, and dissociative disorder not otherwise identified (American Psychiatric Association, 1994).

Because dissociation appears in the earliest life stage, a developmental psychopathology perspective is being utilized to understand its etiology (Putnam, 1997), and disorganization of attachment is now proposed as a model system to understand dissociative psychopathology (Liotti, 1992, 1999). However, these models are purely psychological, and do not refer to the neurobiological mechanisms that underlie the phenomena. An integration of neuroscience and clinical data can offer such a model.

It is important to emphasize that in traumatic abuse the individual dissociates not only from the external world, from processing external stimuli associated with terror, but also from the internal world, that is, painful stimuli originating within the body. It is sometimes difficult to keep in mind the fact that the body of an abused infant is physically assaulted, and therefore in pain. Darwin, in the work that began the scientific study of emotion, asserted that "Pain, if severe, soon induces extreme depression or prostration but it is first a stimulant and excites to action . . . Fear again is the most depressing of all emotions, and it soon induces utter helpless prostration" (1872/1965, p. 31). Krystal (1998), in a classic text on trauma, also described the state switch from sympathetic hyperaroused-terror into parasympathetic hypoaroused conservation-withdrawal hopelessness and helplessness:

> The switch from anxiety to the catatonoid response is the subjective evaluation of the impending danger as one that cannot be avoided or modified. With the perception of fatal helplessness in the face of destructive danger, one surrenders to it. (pp. 114–115)

Using interdisciplinary data, Krystal further explained how the catatonoid reaction is the affective response to unavoidable danger, a pattern of surrender, and equates it with the "freeze" response and state of cataleptic immobility: "in the state of surrender and catatonoid reaction, all pain is stilled and a soothing numbness ensues" (1988, p. 117). As previously described, this numbness is due to a sudden massive elevation of endogenous opioids in stress-induced catalepsy or immobility (Fanselow, 1986). A clinical description of the trauma-tized child state is offered by Nijenhuis and colleagues (1988):

> [I]ndividuals tend to hide in dark places, freeze there, and prefer to physi-cally disappear when they feel threatened. Adopting a fetal position, they seem to be unresponsive to external stimuli. (p. 251)

Bodily stiffening frequently accompanies these incidents, and the passive de-fense of dissociation increases with the severity of abuse.

The long-term effect of infantile psychic trauma is the arrest of affect devel-opment and the process of desomatization (Krystal, 1997). The ultimate end-point of experiencing catastrophic states of relational-induced trauma in early life is a progressive impairment of the ability to adjust, take defensive action, or act on one's own behalf, and, most importantly, a blocking of the capacity to register affect and pain. Lane and colleagues asserted that "traumatic stress in childhood could lead to self-modulation of painful affect by directing atten-tion away from internal emotional states" (1997, p. 840), a principle consonant with the well-documented association between traumatic childhood events and proneness to dissociation (Irwin, 1996; Ogawa et al., 1997).

In an earlier section of this chapter, I offered a psychoneurobiological model of the developmental events that lead to such maladaptive coping strategies. The pattern of cataleptic immobility described by Krystal is normally seen in the first two months of life of human infants: "[In] dangerous situations a sud-den behavioral change in the infant may occur . . . the infant lies motionless with non-converging, staring eyes and sleep-like respiration" (Papousek & Papousek, 1975, p. 251). The right lateralized dorsal motor "vegetative vagus" is involved with respiration (Porges et al., 1994). Recall traumatized infants are observed to be staring off into space with a glazed look, and the child's dissocia-tion and immobility in the midst of terror result from elevated levels of cortisol and vagal tone, while opiates induce pain numbing and blunting. The state of conservation-withdrawal occurs in hopeless and helpless contexts, and is behav-iorally manifest as feigning death (Powles, 1992). Krystal (1988) noted that in German catalepsy is called totstell-reflex, or death-posturereflex.

The purpose of this primitive defensive reaction is to protect the developing organism against the overwhelming psychobiological pain of the attachment disruptions induced by early relational trauma. MacLean pointed out that "nature appears to have ensured that maternal-offspring separation in mam-mals results in distress comparable to pain" (1987, p. 136). This implies that maternal regulation of pain-distress occurs as a normal attachment function. But what if the caregiver is a source of intense noxious and painful stimula-tion? There is an increasing consensus that both the child's reactivity and the parenting context contribute to changes in the infant's pain response (Sweet,

McGrath, & Symons, 1999). According to Grunau, Whitfield, Petrie, and Fryer (1994):

> [N]on-optimal parenting may contribute to the development of inappropriate strategies for coping with common pains in childhood, or of chronic pain patterns, in some children who have experienced prolonged or repeated pain as neonates. (p. 353)

Because these are attachment experiences occurring in a critical period of limbic ontogeny, they alter the organization of the brain circuits that process pain. What do we know of these circuits?

Basic research reveals that persistent pain experiences during the early neonatal period, a critical period for the organization of nociceptive neuronal circuits, rewires immature pain circuits, and leads to lasting and potentially detrimental alterations in the individual's response to pain in adulthood (Ruda, Ling, Hohmann, Peng, & Tachibana, 2000). These studies tracked the long-term effects of physical pain, but the effects of pain associated with relational trauma may lead to even more adverse consequences. It is established that a traumatic painful event, in contrast to nontraumatic pain, triggers an intense emotional experience with concomitant autonomic/somatic outflow, and activates increased sympathetic activity and prominent responses in the limbic, system, that is, hypothalamus, periaqueductal gray, anterior cingulate, insula, posterior parietal and prefrontal cortex (Hsieh et al., 1995; Hutchison, Harfa, & Dostrovsky, 1996). Positron emission tomography (PET) studies showed that the right anterior cingulate plays a central role in the sensorial/affective aspect of pain (Hsieh, Belfrage, et al., 1995; Price, 2000) and that the orbitofrontal regions modulate distant processing of pain and therefore coping with a painful stimulus (Petrovic et al., 2000).

Neurobiological studies indicated that through its hierarchical connections with the pain processing areas in the periaqueductal gray, hypothalamus, anterior cingulate, and insula, the orbitofrontal areas are involved in both the perception (Y-U. Zhang et al., 1997) and the regulation (Gyulai et al., 1997) and therefore coping with pain, especially the affective-motivational aspects of pain (Petrovic et al., 2000). The latter authors concluded that increased orbitofrontal activation is necessary for coping "during pain with a relevant threat to the organism" (p. 28). Such a context occurs in relational traumatic abuse.

An efficient mature orbitofrontal system can adaptively regulate both sympathoadrenomedullary catecholamine (Euler & Folkow, 1958) and corticosteroid levels (Hall & Marr, 1975), and therefore hyper- and hypoarousal. It can also facilitate or inhibit the defense reactions of the amygdala (Timms, 1977). But stress may also take the prefrontal areas "off-line," allowing the more habitual responses mediated by the subcortical structures to regulate behavior (Arnsten, & Goldman-Rakic, 1998). This occurs all too frequently in a severely developmentally compromised immature frontolimbic system, especially one with an inefficient medial orbitofrontal area involved in processing and regulating negative emotional states (Northoff et al., 2000).

When optimally functioning, the orbitofrontal cortex is one of the few brain regions that is "privy to signals about virtually any activity taking place in our beings' mind or body at any given time" (Damasio, 1994, p. 181). This implies that an inefficient frontolimbic system will not process pain signals that come from the body, an adaptive loss. Indeed, inactivation of the medial orbitofrontal cortex produces an analgesic effect (Cooper, 1975), and its removal elicits a suppression of pain-related behaviors and an increased threshold of pain associated with affect (Reshetniak & Kukushkin, 1989). Patients with neurological damage in this cortex report that they know a stimulus is pain-producing, but that the pain does not feel very bad (Melzack & Wall, 1996).

These studies suggest that an inefficient orbitofrontal-cingulate higher limbic circuit (Dostrovsky, Hutchison, Davis, & Lozano, 1995) would be unable to adaptively sense and regulate pain, and a lower amygdala limbic level-driven dissociation would dominate. Cutting, a common form of self-destructive behavior associated with early trauma (Russ et al., 1992; van der Kolk, Perry, & Herman, 1991), may be an attempt to autoregulate out of the altered pain sensitivity associated with the elevated opioid activity of the dissociative state.

Dissociation is a common symptom in PTSD patients, and its occurrence at the time of a trauma is a strong predictor of this disorder (Koopman, Classen, & Spiegel, 1994; Shalev, Peri, Canetti, & Schreiber, 1996). At the moment of feeling threatened, individuals who characterlogically dissociate switch into a trancelike state, freeze, become analgesic, and later report out-of-body experiences and dissociative amnesia. Total amnesia for traumatic events is now increasingly documented (Elliott, 1997; van der Hart & Nijenhuis, 1995).

Markowitsch and colleagues (2000) reported a case of "dissociative amnesia" triggered by reexposure to a traumatic scene, a fire in the patient's house. For the next two months he exhibited a severe memory impairment, barely recognized his partner, and failed to remember any friends. He showed flat affect and lack of interest, and his mood was sad and helpless. After 3 weeks of psychotherapy he recalled an early memory of childhood, a car crash in which he witnessed the driver's screams and death in flames. PET (positron emission tomagraphy) studies at 2 months after the trauma showed an "unusually drastic" hypometabolism in memory-sensitive regions, which improved upon recovery at 12 months. Markowitsch and colleagues concluded that early emotionally negative childhood events and prolonged stress lead to a dissociative (functional) amnesia, that acute stress can trigger posttraumatic stress disorder, and that "even sporadic environmental stress can apparently induce long-lasting brain dysfunction with subsequent cognitive deterioration" (2000, p. 65).

In considering possible factors for generating the hypometabolic state these authors point to the memory-influencing role of dopamine under stress conditions and alterations within the hypothalamo-hypophysal-adrenocortical axis, specifically excessive release of glucocorticoids. I suggest the finding of these researchers that psychic trauma can grossly reduce brain metabolism and thereby cognitive deterioration describes the hypometabolic mechanism of vagal-induced conservation-withdrawal and the mechanism of dissociation in response to trauma.

The characterological use of dissociation by certain personalities underlies the description offered by Allen and Coyne (1995):

> Although initially they may have used dissociation to cope with traumatic events, they subsequently dissociate to defend against a broad range of daily stressors, including their own posttraumatic symptoms, pervasively undermining the continuity of their experience. (p. 620)

These "initial traumatic events" are embedded in infant relational trauma, the first context in which dissociation is used to autoregulate massive stress.

Dissociation represents a disruption of the monitoring and controlling functions of consciousness. Fonagy and colleagues (1996) described:

> victims of childhood abuse who coped by refusing to conceive of the contents of their caregiver's mind and thus successfully avoided having to think about their caregiver's wish to harm them. This initially defensive disruption of the capacity to depict feelings and thoughts in themselves and others becomes a characteristic response to all subsequent intimate relationships . . . It also drastically limits their capacity to come to terms with these abusive experiences in later life and creates a vulnerability to interpersonal stress. (p. 29)

Furthermore,

> [T]rauma victims who lack the cognitive and emotional structures to immediately assimilate the experience use the state of consciousness known as dissociation to escape from the full psychological impact of the event. (Classen, Koopman, & Spiegel, 1993, p. 179)

It should be pointed out that dissociation may be a more common phenomenon of the psychopathology of everyday life than previously thought. On the Adult Attachment Interview a classification of unresolved (the adult disoriented/disorganized analog) is made when an individual's narrative of his or her early experiences shows lapses in monitoring, prolonged silences of 20 seconds, and "micro-dissociative processes" (Schuengel et al., 1999). Under a series of dyadic emotional stressors these characterolgical microstates, however, become stabilized attractor macrostates of dissociation.

Such clinical descriptions describe impaired activity of the orbitofrontal system, which acts in the highest level of control of behavior, especially in relation to emotion (Price et al., 1996), plays a fundamental role in monitoring relevant

past and current experiences (Cavada et al., 2000) and in controlling the allocation of attention to possible contents of consciousness (Goldenberg et al.,
1989), and allows for choosing appropriate actions in a flexible and purposeful
manner in stressful contexts of uncertainty (Elliott et al., 2000). These and the
above data clearly suggest that a developmentally immature and metabolically
inefficient orbitofrontal regulatory system is found in immature personalities
who characterolgically use dissociation.

In 1893 Breuer and Freud, citing the work of Janet (1889/1973), described
dissociation as the major mechanism for "strangulations of affect," but by 1900
and *The Interpretation of Dreams* Freud discarded this notion and favored repression as the major force of the unconscious. In later writings Freud (1915/
1957) again hinted of its existence in asserting:

> [U]nconscious ideas continue to exist after repression as actual structures
> in the system Ucs, whereas all that corresponds in that system to uncon-
> scious affects is a potential beginning which is prevented from developing
> (p. 178).

With an eye to Freud's ideas on the negative effects of early truama, Winnicott (1960) postulated:

> If maternal care is not good enough, then the infant does not really come
> into existence, since there is no continuity in being; instead, the personal-
> ity becomes built on the basis of reactions to environmental impinge-
> ment. (p. 54)

Tustin (1981) described this impingement as a "psychological catastrophe,"
which is responded to by "autistic withdrawal" or "encapsulation," an innate
defensive measure against bodily hurt that involves a "shutting out of mind"
what can not be handled at the moment. This is an operational definition of
the growth inhibiting defense of dissociation, the generator of unconscious affects and the block against potential affective development and the ongoing
continuity of existence.

What is maladaptive about this psychic-deadening defense is not only that
the individual shifts into dissociation at lower levels of stress, but also that it
finds difficulty in exiting the state of conservation-withdrawal. Once dissociated
it stays in this massive autoregulatory mode for long periods of time. During
these intervals it is shut down to the external environment, and thus totally
closed and impermeable (encapsulated) to attachment communications and
interactive regulation. If this becomes a basal state, the avoidance of emotional
contexts, especially those containing novel and more complex affective information, prevents emotional learning, which in turn precludes any advances of
right brain emotional intelligence or what Janet (1889/1973) called an "enlargement" of personality development. The habitual use of this primitive defense

against affect is thus another manifestation of maladaptive infant (and adult) mental health.

EARLY RELATIONAL TRAUMA AND ENDURING RIGHT HEMISPHERIC DYSFUNCTION

The orbitofrontal system, which is expanded in the right hemisphere (Falk et al., 1990), acts as an executive control function for the entire right brain. The right prefrontal cortex is critical to the processing and regulation of self functions (Keenan et al., 2000; Schore, 1994). During its critical period of maturation in the first two years, prolonged episodes of intense and unregulated interactive traumatic stress induce not only heightened negative affect, but chaotic biochemical alterations that produce a developmentally immature, structurally defective right brain. Although very few neuropsychobiological studies on traumatized human infants have yet been done, basic research on trauma in infant mammals and adult humans strongly implicates dysfunction in the right hemisphere, the hemisphere that is dominant in human infancy (Chiron et al., 1997).

And yet compelling theoretical, research, and clinical links have been made between right hemisphere functions and attachment behaviors (Henry, 1993; Schore, 1994), attachment transactions and the regulation of the right brain (Schore, 2000b, 2000c), traumatic stress, attachment and right brain function (Wang, 1997), and the role of impaired right hemispheric activity in very early-forming reactive attachment disorders (Hinshaw-Fuselier et al., 1999), personality disorders (Horton, 1985), and various psychiatric syndromes (Cummings, 1997; Cutting, 1992). The development of attachment, the interactive regulation of biological synchronicity between organisms (Schore, 2000c), allows for the development of emotions, the highest order direct expression of bioregulation in complex organisms (Damasio, 1998).

At the beginning of this two-paper series, (see Chapter 6), I cited Damasio's (1994) description of the fundamental adaptive function of the brain—to be well informed about its own activities, the rest of the body, and the environment so that suitable survivable accommodations can be achieved between the organism and the environment. Although the existence of not one but two brains, a left brain and a right brain, was discovered at the dawn of neurology (Harrington, 1985), neuroscience, armed with neuroimaging technologies, is detailing the unique functions of the right brain and its critical roles. These systems that contribute to the forementioned adaptive functions are maturing before the advent of language, and are influenced by the attachment relationship.

The right hemisphere, more so than the left, is deeply connected into the limbic system and the sympathetic and parasympathetic components of the ANS, and therefore it plays a predominant role in the physiological and cognitive components of emotional processing (Spence et al., 1996). This nondomi-

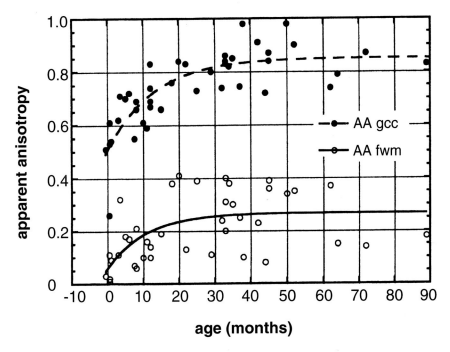

FIGURE A-1 Diffusion-weighted magnetic resonance imaging study of brain development in infants and children. During early brain maturation changes in water diffusion in white matter (apparent anisotropy, AA) precedes myelination. Graph shows low AA values and therefore little myelination in frontal white matter (fwm) at birth, which increases significantly by 20 months, reflecting myelination of this area in the first two years. Age-dependent changes in the genu of the corpus callosum are seen above. See Chapters 1, 2, and 6 for details of the development of the frontal lobes in infancy.

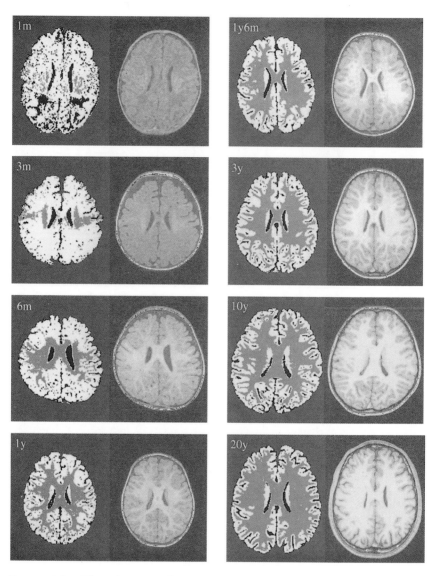

FIGURE A-2A Three-dimensional magnetic resonance imaging (MRI) of healthy children aged 1 month to 10 years, compared to a 20-year-old adult; this is the first report including volumetric analysis of infants and toddlers under 2 years of age. Original image at right, images at left segmented into white matter (colored gray), gray matter (colored white), and cerebrospinal fluid (colored black). The volumes of the whole brain and frontal and temporal lobes increase rapidly during the first 2 years after birth. The authors conclude that the appearance of brain structures is similar to that of adults by the end of 2 years and all major fiber tracts can be identified in brains of 3-year-old children.

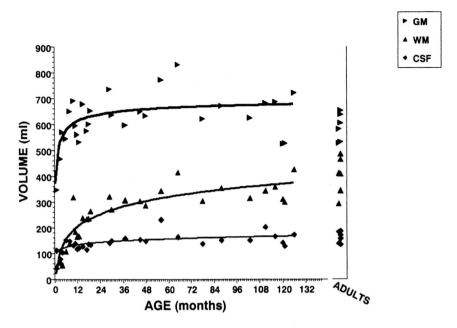

FIGURE A-2B Age-related volumetric changes of three tissue compartments (GM, gray matter; WM, white matter; CSF, cerebrospinal fluid). The volumes of both GM and WM increase rapidly during the first 2 years after birth. The volume of the right hemisphere is larger than the left in infants due largely to increases in the white matter. See Chapters 8 and 9 for a discussion.

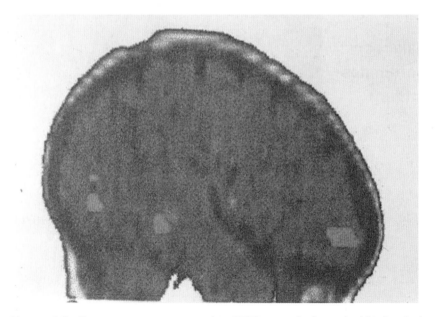

FIGURE A-3 Positron emission tomographic (PET) scan of a 2-month-old infant looking at the image of a woman's face. Activation is shown in the right fusiform gyrus, the visual associative cortex specialized for processing human faces. At this age, infants first recognize their mother's face and distinguish it from among others.

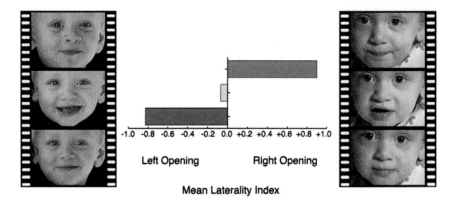

Left Opening   **Right Opening**

Mean Laterality Index

FIGURE A-4 Consecutive frames from video recordings show a baby's left mouth open-ing (reflecting right hemisphere activation) while smiling (left) and right mouth opening (reflecting left hemisphere activation) while babbling (right). A standard Laterality Index was calculated for infants 5 to 12 months. These data suggest that, like adults, the emotional expression of 5-month-old infants might be more controlled by the right hemisphere.

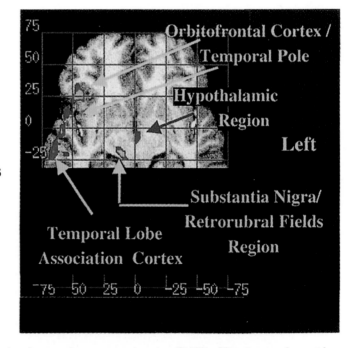

FIGURE A-5 Functional magnetic resonance imaging (fMRI) of first-time mothers with 4- to 8-week-old infants when they listened to the cry of a 3-day-old infant. Brain regions uniquely active when new mothers listen to infant cries include the right lateral orbito-frontal cortex and the right temporal lobe. Yellow indicates more activity (in comparison to areas colored red).

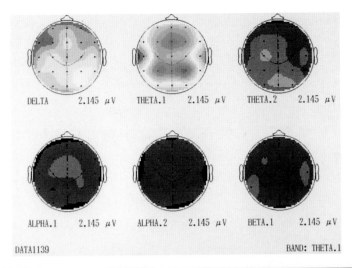

DELTA   2.145 μV   THETA.1   2.145 μV   THETA.2   2.145 μV

ALPHA.1   2.145 μV   ALPHA.2   2.145 μV   BETA.1   2.145 μV

DATA1139   BAND: THETA.1

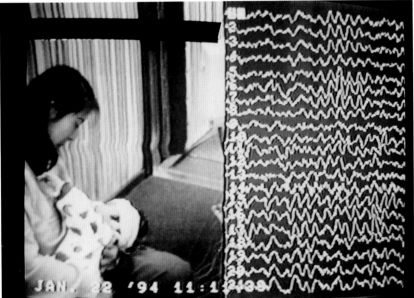

JAN. 22 '94 11:1

FIGURE A-6 Simultaneous electroencephalogram (EEG) and video recording with power spectral map analysis of handling while the infant was gazing (bottom). The result of power spectral map analysis (top). While this 7-month-old female infant was sucking her mother's breast, rhythmic theta appeared in posterior temporal regions. When the infant and mother were gazing at each other's faces, theta appeared in the parietal regions. Shortly after the gazing, the infant reached her hand to her mother's hair and fingered it, when the rhythmic theta appeared also in the frontal areas.

FIGURE A-7   Representation of the fundamental psychobiological nature of the attach-ment bond, a communication between the baby and mother in terms of the anatomy and physiology of live bodies. In such moments of biological synchronicity the mother's and infant's individual homeostatic systems are linked, thereby allowing for the mutual regulation of their endocrine, autonomic, and central nervous systems by elements of their interaction with each other. The artist's caption reads, "The bonding of mother and child is a miraculous outpouring of unobstructed love channeled through the mor-tal coil. Between mother and child, there are also bio-electromagnetic bonds, emotional and psychic bondings, and ultimately the spiritual bond that brought them together."

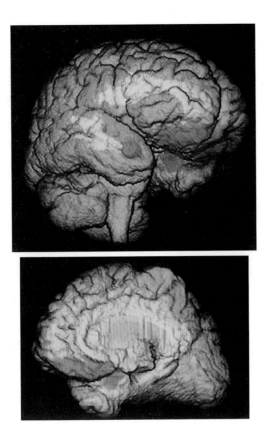

FIGURE A-8   Neuroanatomy of human social cognition represented in a partially transparent brain (right lateral view of whole brain at top, medial view of the right hemisphere at bottom). Some of the most central structures are shown: the amygdala (blue), the ventromedial (orbital) prefrontal cortex (red), the cingulate cortex (yellow), and the somatosensory-related cortices in the right hemisphere (green).

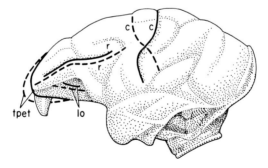

FIGURE A-9   Asymmetrical features of the primate frontal lobe, left lateral see-through view. Dashed features are in right hemisphere, solid lines are from left hemisphere. The right lateral orbital (lo) sulci are significantly longer than the left.

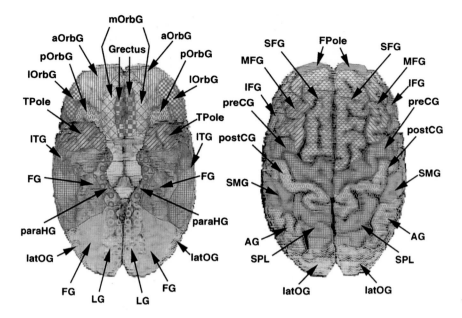

FIGURE A-10A   Computerized image of the inferior (left) and superior (right) views of the normal human brain with identification of major sulci. Note medial (m), anterior (a), posterior (p), and lateral (l) orbital gyrus (OrbG), gyrus rectus (Grectus), frontal (F) and temporal (T) poles, inferior temporal gyrus (ITG), fusiform gyrus (FG), parahippocampal gyrus (paraHG), superior (S), medial (M), and inferior (I) frontal gyrus (FG), pre- and post-central gyrus (CG), supramarginal (SMG), angular (AG), and lateral occipital gyrus (latOG).

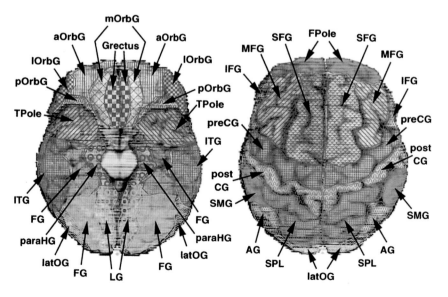

FIGURE A-10B   Another normal brain. Note variations from the brain illustrated above (Figure A-10a).

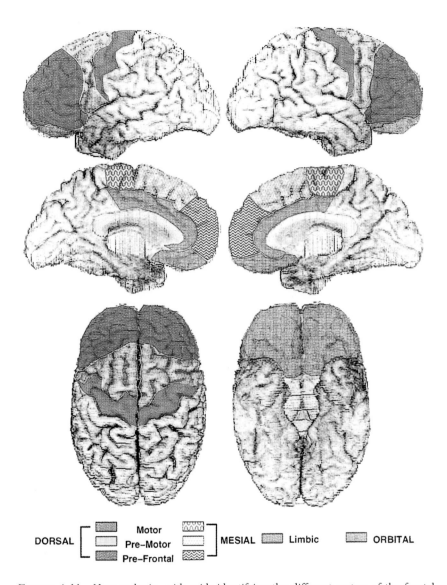

DORSAL ⸤ ▨ Motor ▨ ⸣ MESIAL ▨ Limbic ▨ ORBITAL
        □ Pre–Motor □
        ▨ Pre–Frontal ▨

FIGURE A-11 Human brain, with grids identifying the different sectors of the frontal lobe.

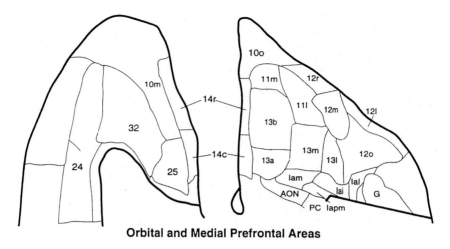

Orbital and Medial Prefrontal Areas

FIGURE A-12   A map of architectonic areas recognized in the orbital (to the right) and medial (to the left) prefrontal cortex.

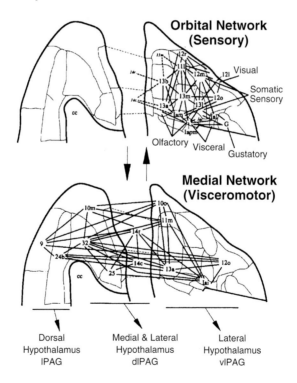

FIGURE A-13   Corticocortical connections within the orbitomedial prefrontal cortex, which forms the basis for the division of the area into the 'orbital' and 'medial' network (which also includes several orbital areas), although there are points of interaction. The orbital network receives several sensory inputs and functions as a system for sensory integration. The medial network projects to the hypothalamus and periaqueductal gray (PAG), and functions as a visceromotor system.

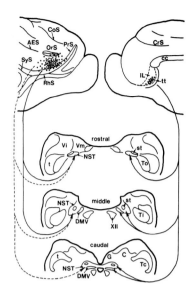

FIGURE A-14 Schematic of direct cerebral connections from the orbital gyrus (OrG) and infralimbic (IL) to the nucleus of the solitary tract (NTS) and the dorsal motor nucleus of the vagal nerve (DMV) in the cat medulla.

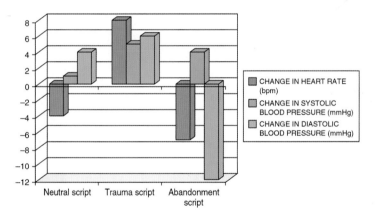

FIGURE A-15 Heart rate and blood pressure reactivity in a patient with posttraumatic stress disorder (PTSD) and borderline personality disorder, manifest in suicide attempts, self-injurious behavior, and severe emotional instability. This 36-year-old woman, with a history of childhood abuse, listened to a personalized script of child abuse and abandonment situations. When the trauma script was read to her, she displayed an intense emotional reaction and her heart rate increased 7bpm. While listening to the abandonment script she dissociated. During this period her heart rate fell by 7bpm and her diastolic blood pressure decreased by 12mmHg. See Chapters 7 and 8 for the same shift from hyperarousal heart rate increase to dissociation hypoarousal heart rate decrease in infant relational trauma.

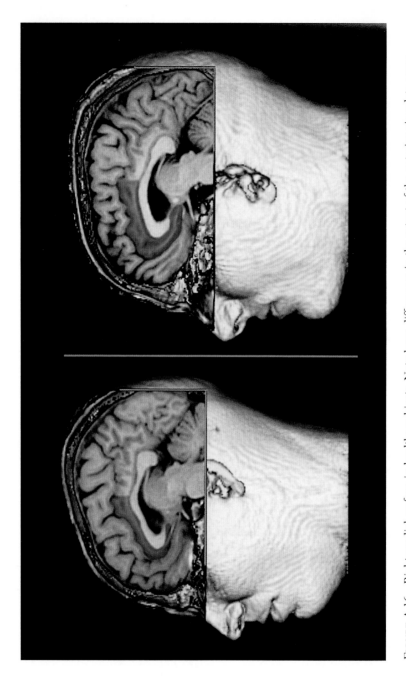

FIGURE A-16 Right medial surface in healthy subjects. Note large differences in the extent of the anterior cingulate gyrus (shaded in red) in these two subjects. The authors suggest that a large right anterior cingulate is related to a temperamental disposition to fear and anticipatory worry.

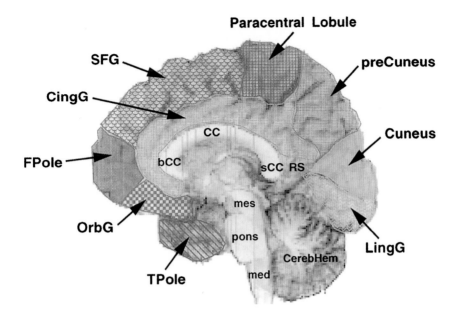

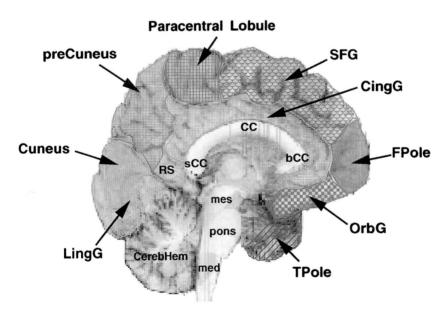

FIGURE A-17   Computerized image of the mesial view of the right (top) and left (bottom) hemispheres. Note orbital gyri (OrbG), cingulate gyrus (CingG), temporal (T) and frontal (F) pole, superior frontal gyrus (SFG), corpus callosum (CC), mesencephalon (mes), pons, and medulla (med).

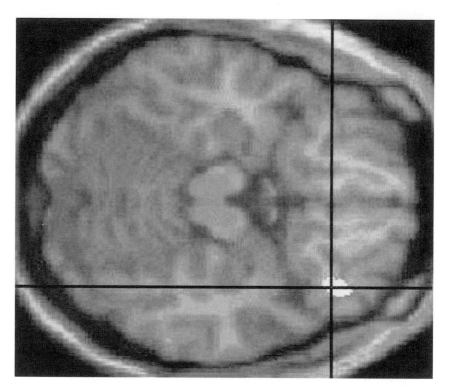

FIGURE A-18 A positron emmision tomography (PET) image of activation of the right lateral orbitofrontal cortex when viewing an angry face. The top is the left side of brain, bottom is the right; the left is the posterior, right the anterior. See Chapter 9 for further discussion.

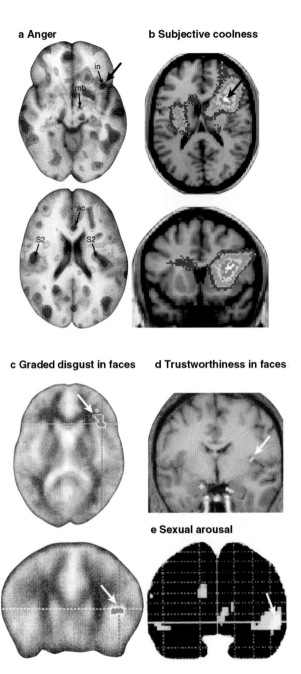

FIGURE A-19 Activation of the right hemisphere, including the right anterior insular cortex associated with different subjective feelings. (A) Recall-induced anger in which activation is also visible in the right orbitofrontal, anterior cingulate (ac), and interoceptive (S2) cortices (in = insular cortex; mb = mammillary bodies). (B) Regression analysis of subjective ratings of the intensity of cooling the hand. (C) Activation after exposure to a disgusted face. (D) Activation elicited by subjective ratings of trustworthiness in faces. (E) Activation elicited by sexual arousal.

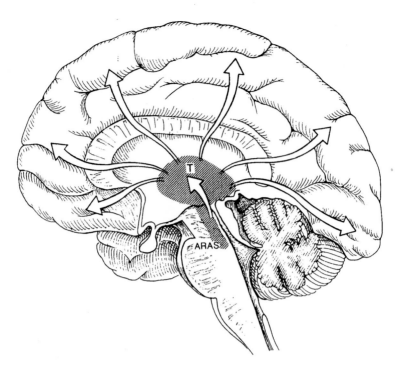

FIGURE A-20A Drawing of the brain in the midsagittal plane illustrating the major structures responsible for arousal and attention (T = thalamus).

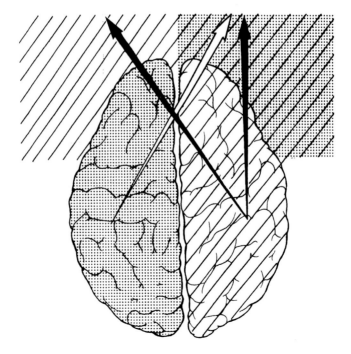

FIGURE A-20B Drawing of the superior surface of the brain that schematically represents the dominance of the right hemisphere for directed attention. The right side of the cerebrum has the capacity to survey both sides of extrapersonal and intrapersonal space, whereas the left side can only survey the contralateral space.

AUDITORY: LEFT > RIGHT

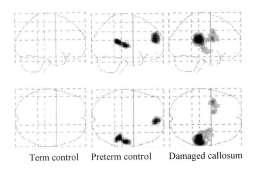

Term control   Preterm control   Damaged callosum

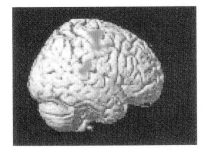 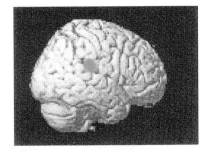

FIGURE A-21   Neuroimaging study of adults born very preterm who sustained corpus callosum damage. Functional magnetic resonance image (fMRI) was performed while patients carried out auditory and visual tasks requiring callosal transfer. On the auditory task a deficit of activity was seen in the right temporal lobe of the callosum group. This is significantly different from the term control group (left panel) and preterm control group (right panel). The authors concluded that both the structure and function of the adult brain are influenced by events occurring perinatally. Other research indicates that the right hemisphere is in a critical period of growth pre- and postnatally (see Chapters 1, 3, and 6).

Amygdala Response: s Group > l Group

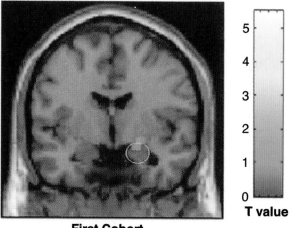

**First Cohort
(N = 14)**

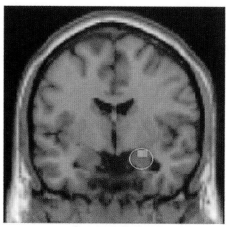

**Second Cohort
(N = 14)**

FIGURE A-22 Individuals with variations in the serotonin transporter gene, which has been associated with increased fear and anxiety behaviors, show greater right amygdala activity in response to angry or fearful faces. The authors note that the laterality of the amygdala difference is consistent with the general role of the right hemisphere in processing faces and of the right amygdala in processing angry and fearful facial expressions. See Chapters 8 and 9. Functional magnetic resonance image (fMRI) responses in the right amygdala are outlined in the white circle.

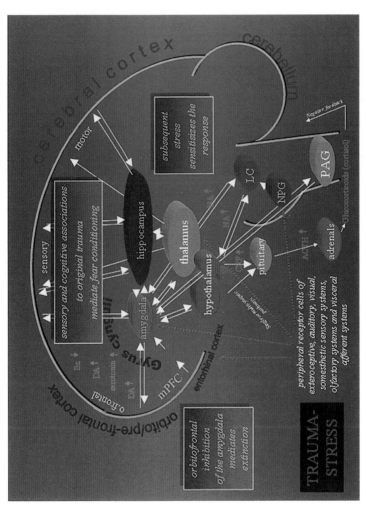

FIGURE A-23   Schema of a comprehensive overview of the brain circuits involved in stress processing. Multiple brain areas mediate stress and fear responses, including orbitofrontal and medial prefrontal cortex, cingulate, amygdala, hippocampus, brain stem, periaqueductal gray, hypothalamus, pituitary, and adrenals. These regions are functionally interrelated. Long-term changes in function and structure of these regions can lead to symptoms of posttraumatic stress disorder (PTSD). See Chapters 7 and 8.

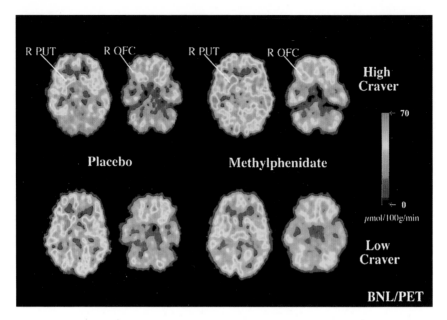

FIGURE A-24 Regional brain metabolic images of a cocaine abuser, one in whom methylphenidate induced intense craving and one in whom it did not. Notice the activation of the right orbitofrontal cortex (R OFC) and of the right putamen (R PUT) in the subject reporting intense craving.

nant(!) hemisphere is specialized for neuroendocrine and autonomic activation (Sullivan & Gratton, 1999), for the secretion of the stress hormones, CRF (Kalogeras et al., 1996) and cortisol (Wittling & Pfluger, 1990), for the human stress response (Wittling, 1997), and for controlling the vital functions supporting survival and enabling the organism to cope with stresses and challenges (Wittling & Schweiger, 1993). Severe developmental impairments of these right brain structure-function relationships are manifest in inefficient and vulnerable coping mechanisms, and they occur in the attachment pathology of disorganized infant and toddlers. I would amend Main's (1996) assertion that disorganized attachment is a primary risk factor for the development of mental disorders to specifically posttraumatic stress, borderline, and sociopathic personality disorders.

Throughout these two chapters I have offered interdisciplinary data indicating a developmental right brain etiology of these severe regulatory disorders. Continuing this theme, a juxtaposition of trauma-associated functional deficits in coping strategies and stress tolerance of type D infants found in attachment research, right lateralized structural defects from developmental psychobiological studies, and findings on the right brain of normal and abnormal adults from neuroscience can offer more powerful models of the mechanisms by which early relational trauma in the first two years alters the experience-dependent maturation of the right brain and thereby induces a high risk for psychopathogenesis.

Evidence of this lateralization effect is provided by human studies showing that conditioned fear acquisition and extinction are associated with amygdala function, and that this activation is right hemisphere dominant (La Bar, Gatenby, Gore, LeDoux, & Phelps, 1998). In a series of basic psychobological studies Adamec reported that partial kindling of the right and not left amygdala induces long-lasting increases in anxiety-like behavior (1997, 1999), that NMDA receptors mediate transmission from the right amygdala to the ventromedial hypothalamus (Adamec, 1998), and that right amygdala kindling also induces elevated production of the stress hormone CRF (Adamec & McKay, 1993). In parallel research, type D infants showed direct indices of apprehension regarding the parent, as manifest in fearful facial expressions (Solomon & George, 1999). The latter authors documented that such infants show asymmetries of facial expression, as in an extremely swift "tic" which lifts only the left side of the facial musculature, indicating right hemispheric dysfunction. They also described freezing lasting 20 seconds or more, accompanied by dazed or trance-like facial expressions in type D infants. Recall that freezing in primate infants is associated with high basal cortisol levels and extreme right frontal EEG activity (Kalin et al., 1998).

In fact, EEG studies of 1-month-old (Jones, Field, Fox, Lundy, & Davalos, 1997) and 3- to 6-month-old (Field, Fox, et al., 1995) infants of depressed (and therefore potentially neglectful) mothers showed this same right frontal EEG asymmetry, a finding that has been interpreted as reflecting a subcortical asymmetry in the amygdala (Calkins & Fox, 1994). At 10 months, infants who express more intense distress to maternal separation display a greater right than left frontal activation (Davidson & Fox, 1989), and this asymmetry is related to emotional reactivity and vulnerability to psychopathology in both infants and adults (Davidson et al., 1990). At 3 to 6 years, children of depressed mothers show a right frontal EEG asymmetry and lack of empathy (Jones, Field, & Davalos, 2000).

Individuals with extreme right frontal activation are thought to exhibit a negative affective response to a very low intensity negative affect elicitor, and to be impaired in the ability to terminate a negative emotion once it has begun (Wheeler, Davidson, & Tomarken, 1993). Fox and colleagues (1996) reported that young children with internalizing and externalizing problems show greater right than left frontal EEG activation, and suggest that this pattern reflects difficulties with affect regulation, whether the affect arousal is extremely negative or positive. At later ages "greater right hemisphericity" is associated with a history of more frequent negative affect and lower self esteem (Persinger & Makarec, 1991), that is, chronic difficulties in affect regulation.

With respect to the association of type D attachments and a predisposition to relational violence (Lyons-Ruth & Jacobvitz, 1999), impaired right hemispheric functioning has also been reported in disinhibited aggressive patients with orbitofrontal brain damage (Starkstein & Robinson, 1997), autonomic physiological studies of high-hostility subjects (Demaree & Harrison, 1997), and neuroimaging research of murderers, where Raine, Stoddard, and colleagues (1998) concluded, "reductions in right orbitofrontal functioning may be a particularly important predisposition to violence" (p. 6).

The right-brain circuitry that is involved in the regulation of "primary" emotions (Ross et al., 1994) and in "intense emotional-homeostatic processes" (Porges et al., 1994) is organized in the first two years of life. Exposure to extensive and long-enduring traumatic states interferes with this organization and predisposes the disorganized/disoriented infant (later, the unresolved/disorganized adult) to a vulnerability, at later points of stress, to develop chronic difficulties in affect regulation. Due to its unique anatomical connections into the reticular formation, the right hemisphere is dominant for the bilateral regulation of arousal (Heilman & Van Den Abell, 1979) and its dysfunction is therefore central to the arousal dysregulation that characterizes the severe coping deficits of fear dysregulation of posttraumatic stress disorders. The right cortex is responsible for maintaining important controls over autonomic activities (Heilman, Schwartz, & Watson, 1977) and for generating the most comprehensive and integrated map of the body state available to the brain (Damasio, 1994). An impairment of the right brain is thus central to the disordered mind-body functions that are found in children and adults who continue to experience the relational trauma of their infancy.

Indeed, van der Kolk (1996) specifically implicated right brain dysfunction in posttraumatic stress disorders, and this lateralization effect is observed in studies that expose the patient to a personal high arousal stressor (Rauch et al., 1996; Shin et al., 1997) and those that induce a stressful startle response (Morgan, Grillon, Lubin, & Southwick, 1997). Patients with panic disorders show greater activation of a right frontal avoidance-withdrawal system in negatively valenced situations (Wiedemann et al., 1999) and altered GABAergic receptor patterns in the right insula and orbitofrontal cortices (Malizia et al., 1998).

Research may also tell us more about the triggers of right hemispheric dysregulation. It is thought that traumatic early life events predispose certain individuals to later psychiatric disturbance when they are "rechallenged" with a "matching event" or recurrence of the stressor. Previously I wrote of the right-brain imprinting into procedural memory of the abusive caregiver's threatening face. Evidence shows that the right amygdala (Morris et al., 1999) is involved in the storage of fearful faces (vs. the left in linguistic threat; Isenberg et al., 1999). The right amygdala is also implicated in the expression of emotionally influenced memory of aversive experiences (Colman-Mensches & McGaugh, 1995). Similarly, the right orbitofrontal cortex shows an enhanced response to anger expressions that correlate with expression intensity (Blair et al., 1999).

The "visuospatial" right hemisphere contains a "nonverbal affect lexicon" of facial expressions (Bowers et al., 1993), and these are imprinted in mother-infant affective transactions. This hemisphere appraises facial expression at levels beneath awareness (Schore, 1994, 1998b, 1999a, 2001b, 2002a), and if a match is registered with a stored image an affective response occurs. Autonomic changes in the body are evoked when angry facial expressions are subliminally presented to the right, and not the left hemisphere (Johnsen & Hugdahl, 1991). Right-hemispheric impairments in processing facial (Deldin, Keller, Gergen, & Miller, 2000) and vocal affective-prosodic (Snow, 2000) interpersonal stimuli have profound consequences for interpersonal behavior, isolating the individual from the social environment. A growing literature demonstrates that neglected children have difficulty in recognizing emotion in faces, and that physically abused children display a response bias for angry facial expressions (Pollak, Cicchetti, Hornung, & Reed, 2000).

I suggest that visual and auditory stressors that are nonconsciously processed (Mogg, Bradley, Williams, & Mathews, 1993) in an inefficient right hemisphere, especially the perception or memory of images and sounds of threatening and humiliating faces, are potent triggers of dysregulation and dissociation in early traumatized patients. In support of this, Main (1995) reported the dissociative responses of disorganized/disoriented children to the faces of a family photograph:

> One child, happily interacting with the examiner just previously, bent silently over the photograph for 12 seconds, then looked up, silent and depressed. Another looked into the photograph for some time then murmured softly, "Where are you, Mama?" For children who had been disorganized/disoriented with mother in infancy, then, the visual presen-

tation of the parent, self, or family presented within the photograph seemed to have an overwhelming and absorbing quality that drew attention away from the immediate situation. (p. 435)

Furthermore, the infant's transactions with an emotionally misattuned and unresponsive caregiver who induces traumatic states and provides poor interactive repair are stored in the infant's developing corticolimbic circuitries as imagistic, visceral, and nonverbal implicit-procedural memories. Interpersonal contexts of interactive repair contain facially expressed safety signals that can be associated with "switching off" the traumatized state, and so the lack of such internal representations deprives the traumatized individual of an internal regulatory mechanism that can terminate the traumatic reaction.

Kiersky and Beebe (1994) stated that nonverbal presymbolic forms of relating constitute adult versions of the early interaction structures that protected the infant from trauma and continue to be used by patients to avoid retraumatization. Fonagy (1991) asserted that the mental representations of early traumatic interactions with an abusive parent lead the child to defensively disregard perceptions of the thoughts and feelings of the parent. These unconscious working models of disorganized-disoriented attachment encode an enduring prototypical cognitive-affective schema of a dysregulated-self-in-interaction-with-a-misattuning-other (Schore, 1994, 1997b, 1997c, 2002a).

Such "pathological" representations are accessed when the individual is stressed, and they are stored in the right hemisphere which is dominant for unconscious processes (Schore, 1994, 1997b, 1999f, 1999h, 2001b) and for episodic and autobiographical memory (Fink et al., 1996). Early abusive memories are recorded in the right hemisphere outside of conscious awareness, and this realm represents the traumatic memories in imagistic form along with the survival behavior employed as a result of the abuse. The cortical hemispheres contain two different types of representational processes and separate, dissociable memory systems (Zaidel, Esiri, & Beardsworth, 1998), and this allows for the fact that early emotional learning of the right, especially of stressful, threatening experiences, can be unknown to the left (Joseph, 1982). In clinical psychoanalytic writings Bromberg (1991) described:

> Dissociated experience thus tends to remain unsymbolized by thought and language, exists as a separate reality outside of self-expression, and is cut off from authentic human relatedness and deadened to full participation in the life of the rest of the personality. (p. 405)

A limited representational capacity is thus another deficit derived from early relational trauma. According to Reid (1999),

> Where trauma has occurred in infancy, before there is adequate differentiation of self from other, and before the development of the capacity to

symbolize, the child cannot withdraw into daydreaming and fantasy, which has been noted in adults and children suffering from post-traumatic stress disorders. (pp. 99–100)

In a similar description, Meares (1993) demonstrated that in cases of early abuse, the older child's capacity for positively charged symbolic play is not adequately established. Slade reported that insecurely attached children have fewer episodes, shorter periods, and less complex symbolic play (1994), and emphasizes the links between play, the consolidation of affect, meaning, and representation (1987). These essential capacities to generate and maintain positively charged autoregulatory representations heavily depend upon efficient right hemispheric activity.

Another right hemispheric cognitive activity may be detrimentally affected by relational trauma during its initial period of maturation. In light of the known involvement of the right hemisphere in attention (Coule, Frith, Frackowiak, & Grasby, 1996; Posner & Peterson, 1990; Sturm et al., 1999; Tucker & Derryberry, 1994) and joint attention (Kingstone et al., 2000), it is tempting to speculate that joint attention experiences in the first year tune the attentional mechanisms of these right laterlized circuits. Unmedicated children with attention-deficit/hyperactivity disorder (ADHD) show a disruption of right hemispheric attentional systems, due to a difficulty sustaining attention over short time intervals and a failure of inhibition (Carter, Krener, Chaderjian, Norhtcutt, & Wolfe, 1995; Castellanos et al., 1996; Epstein, Conners, Erhardt, March, & Swanson, 1997; Pliszka, Liotti, & Woldorff, 2000). Elevated dopamine levels in right midbrain areas that control attention are correlated with symptom severity (Ernst et al., 1999).

Evidence suggests that developmental dyslexia is a left hemispheric dysfunction, while developmental hyperactivity is a right hemispheric dysfunction (Braun, Archambault, Daigneault, & Larocque, 2000). A number of researchers have described this latter clinical entity. In early work Weintraub and Mesulam (1983) documented right hemispheric learning disability as:

a syndrome of early right hemisphere dysfunction . . . that is associated with introversion, poor social perception, chronic emotional difficulties, inability to display affect, and impairments in visuospatial representation. (p. 468)

In more recent work, this group differentiated children with left-hemisphere dyslexia from right hemisphere social emotional processing disorder, the latter displaying difficulties in interpreting and producing nonverbal aspects of communication including prosody, facial expression, and gesture, as well as poor emotional adjustment and psychiatric disorder (Manoach, Weintraub, Daffner, & Scinto, 1997). Similar descriptions are seen in patients with developmental right-hemisphere syndrome, expressed in emotional and interpersonal problems and avoidance of eye contact (Gross-Tsur et al., 1995), right hemispheric learning disability, showing episodic dyscontrol and psychiatric disorders (Grace & Malloy, 1992), and nonverbal learning disability, who in adolescence are at high risk for depression and suicide (Rourke, Young, & Leenars, 1989). Neuroimaging research indicates that the metabolic rate of the right amygdala correlates with negative affect in depressed patients (Abercrombie et al., 1998). I suggest that these more severely disturbed right brain learning disabilities are type D attachments.

One other defining clinical feature occurs in individuals who are at high risk for later developing pathological traumatic reactions. Relational trauma in the second year would induce a severe pruning of the right hemispheric orbitofrontal callosal axons that are growing toward their counterparts in the left hemisphere. This would produce an interhemispheric organization in which facial expressions, bodily states, and affective information implicitly processed in the right brain would be inefficiently transmitted to the left hemisphere for semantic processing. Maltreated toddlers show a dramatic inability to talk about their emotions and internal states (Cicchetti, Ganiban, & Barnett, 1991).

This represents the early expression of alexithymia, "no words for feelings," a common symptom of trauma patients (Taylor, Bagby, & Parker, 1997; Taylor, Parker & Bagby, 1999). Neuropsychological studies of alexithymia now demonstrate a right hemispheric dysfunction (Jessimer & Markham, 1997) and a specific right to left deficit of callosal transfer (Dewarja & Sasaki, 1990). A physiological disconnection of the two hemispheres results in an inability of the affective and symbolic energies of the right hemisphere to be externalized through the verbal expression of the left hemisphere. A hyporesponsivity in the prefrontal and orbital circuits has been suggested to underlie alexithymia (Hommer et al., 1997).

Indeed, both alexithymia and PTSD share similar altered neuroendocrine patterns (Henry et al., 1992), and the extensive overlap between the two has been emphasized (Taylor et al., 1997). Alexithymic personalities manifest a deficit in the capacity for symbolization of emotions, a tendency for impulsive behavior, avoidance of social relationships, abnormal physiology resulting in disease, and an impaired capacity for self-care and self-regulation. Miller (1986, p. 138) pointed out that the noninsightful constricted mental state of the alexithymic resembles "the retraction of the field of consciousness" discussed by Janet (1924), as well as the dissociative reactions described in hysterical patients by Breuer and Freud (1893–1985/1955). Right hemisphere involvement in hysterical paresthesia (Tiihonen, Kuikka, Viinamaki, Lehtonen, & Partanen, 1995) and somatization (Min & Lee, 1997) is also reported.

Alexithymic individuals become disorganized under stress, and the regulatory disturbance is manifest in dramatic outbursts of emotion that end as quickly as they begin as though a valve is turning on and off (Nemiah & Sifneos, 1970), affective blocking in the face of unbearably intense pain during overwhelming experiences (Krystal, 1988), and deficits in spontaneous nonverbal expressions of negative affect (McDonald & Prkachin,1990). Alexithymia is thus fundamentally an impairment in emotional information processing (Lane et al., 1997), specifically a deficit in the cognitive processing and regulation of emotions (Taylor, 2000), and is manifest in posttraumatic stress disorder, borderline personality disorders, substance abuse disorders, and somatoform disorders (Taylor et al., 1997). Developmental traumatic stress and neurobiological deficits in the anterior cingulate and orbitofrontal cortices (Lane et al., 1997) and in the right hemisphere (Taylor et al., 1997) have been implicated in alexithymic symptomatology.

In discussing the etiology of alexithyma Rotenberg (1995) concluded:

[The] functional deficiency of the right hemisphere . . . may be caused by the lack of emotional relationships between the child and the parents. Such emotional relationships . . . stimulate the development of the right hemisphere functions and correspond to these functions as a key to the lock. If these emotional relationships are insufficient, the right hemisphere will become inefficient, its contribution in psychological defense mechanisms and emotional stabilization will be lost, and there will be a general predisposition to subsequent mental and psychosomatic disorders. (p. 59)

The right hemisphere ends its growth phase in the second year, when the left hemisphere begins one, but it cycles back into growth phases at later periods of the life cycle (Thatcher, 1994). This allows for potential continuing reorganization of the emotion-processing right brain. The orbitofrontal regions, which are involved in "emotion-related learning" (Rolls et al., 1994) are unique in that they retain the neuroanatomic and biochemical features of early development, and for this reason they are the most plastic areas of the cortex (Barbas, 1995). If, however, in its earliest organizational history this system is exposed to frequent and intense caregiver-induced dysregulation, its primordial organization will be poorly capable of coping with the stresses inherent in human relationships. Maladaptive infant mental health describes a system that early on becomes static and closed, and due to its inability to respond to novel stimuli and challenging situations it does not expose itself to new forms of socioemotional experiences that are required for the continuing experience-dependent growth of the right brain.

IMPLICATIONS FOR MODELS OF EARLY INTERVENTION

It is important to remember that type D behaviors are found in neurologically impaired infants, and infants with early neurological insults to the orbitofrontal cortex show long-term deficits, despite optimal environments. This means that relational trauma cannot be automatically inferred from deflections, even severe deflections of a normal developmental course. That being the case, the opportunity for a maturing individual, even one with a constitutional deficit, to optimize its developmental trajectory is greatly enhanced by forming a dyadic system with a primary caregiver who is sensitive to its unique strategies of processing and expressing social emotional information.

Orbitofrontal deficiencies and affect regulatory disturbances are not solely found in patients with severe relational trauma. This system is also impaired in neurological patients (Brazzelli, Colombo, Della Sala, & Spinnler, 1994), schizophrenia (Norman et al., 1997), autism (Baron-Cohen, 1995), manic state of bipolar disorder (Blumberg et al., 1999), unipolar (Biver et al., 1994) and major (Biver et al., 1997) depression, obsessive-compulsive disorder (McGuire et al., 1994; Rauch et al., 1994), and, indeed, Alzheimer's disease (van Hoesen, Parvizi, & Chu, 2000). It is also dysfunctional in alcoholism (Hommer et al. 1997; Volkow et al., 1999; Volkow et al., 1997) and drug addiction (London, Ernst, Grant, Bonson, & Weinstein, 2000; Volkow & Fowler, 2000), and it is tempting to speculate that the origins of a predisposition to addiction lie in prenatal exposure to maternal drug use during pregnancy (Espy et al., 1999; Jacobson et al., 1996) and postnatal relational stressors embedded in type D parenting (O'Connor, Sigman, & Brill, 1987).

Abnormalities in the limbic system, in the frontal lobe, temporal lobe, basal ganglia, reticular formation, and the hypothalamic-pituitary-adrenal axis connectivity play a critical role in the pathophysiology of each of these disorders, but which limbic circuit and what point in a circuit is metabolically unstable and inefficient would determine the particular expression of affect dysregulation of a specific psychiatric syndrome. The most severe disturbances would involve cell death of dopamine or noradrenaline or hypothalamic neurons at the base of the hierarchical circuits, since disruption of their trophic functions would lead to widespread alterations of subcortical and cortical structures. Less severe would be loss of the receptors for these bioagents, many of which are found on astrocyes that regulate the metabolic activity and connectional plasticity of brain synapses (Laming et al., 2000). The postnatal proliferation and growth of astrocytic processes that surround synapses is influenced by events in the social environment (Jones & Greenough, 1996).

It should also be remembered that the process of prefrontal-subcortical parcellation continues over the life stages (Keshavan et al., 1994), and this process, for example, as the brain reorganizes in adolescence, may pare down an already thinned cortical-subcortical system, and therefore result in the massive dysregulatory symptoms of the psychopathologies that "first appear" at this time. Yet the early regulatory deficts of social-emotional information processing of these disorders are manifest in attachment disturbances in infancy, and may be treatable at this early time.

Although I have focused upon disorganized insecure attachments, what of the the other insecure categories? Insecure organized attachments also express partial orbitofrontal hypo- or hypermetabolic disturbances under stress (see Schore, 1994 & 1996, for insecure resistant/ambivalent and avoidant brain organizations). However, these involve stress impairments of only one of the two limbic circuits, the sympathetic ventral tegmental limbic forebrain-midbrain circuit or the parasympathetic lateral tegmental limbic forebrain-midbrain circuit. The insecure avoidant infant/dismissing adult and insecure resistant-ambivalent/preoccupied adult organizations show inhibitory or excitatory biased orbitofrontal systems. Under stress the former can access a passive coping strategy of autoregulation, the latter an active coping capacity of interactive regulation, while the disoriented, neither. The availability of single circuit strategy is limiting, yet it allows for an organized if limited coping mechanism. The affect regulating dysfunctions of insecure organized personalities are not as severe as the disorganized-disoriented insecures, but as Main (1996) pointed out, these attachments are also high risk for psychiatric disorders.

I want to stress the point that I do not believe that only trauma in the first two years of life is psychopathogenic or self-disorganizing. I also am not undervaluing the long-term negative impact that an abusing father can have on the the developing child. Indeed, most forms of sexual abuse are perpetrated by the father. What I am saying is that what a particular individual appraises to be stressful, how he or she characteristically consciously and especially unconsciously responds to stressors, and how efficiently he or she psychobiologically copes with these stressors, are uniquely and indelibly influenced by events in early and late infancy, especially events that involve abuse by the primary caregiver, who in the vast majority of cases is the mother. What's more, these early interactive experiences determine whether, in later times of crisis, the individual can allow himself to go to others for interpersonal support, that is, to avail himself of interactive regulation within an intimate or psychotherapeutic relationship when his own autoregulatory mechanisms have temporarily failed.

The promotion of affect regulation is now seen as a common mechanism in all forms of psychotherapy (Bradley, 2000). Furthermore, developmental models suggest that psychotherapeutic treatment for severe attachment disorders should begin as early in the life span as possible. Osofsky and her colleagues demonstrated that effective therapeutic interventions can be made in traumatized 2-year-olds. They concluded, "Helping young children acquire self-regulation through reciprocal management of affects with an emotionally available therapist" can allow for a "return to a healthy developmental pathway" (1995, p. 605). The interactive regulation embedded in the therapeutic relationship functions as a "growth-facilitating environment," specifically for the experience-dependent maturation of right orbitofrontal systems (Schore, 1994, 1997a, 2001d, 2001b, 2002a). This context can alter attachment patterns from "insecurity" to "earned security" (Phelps et al., 1998).

A fMRI study conducted by Hariri and colleagues provided evidence that higher regions of specifically the right prefrontal cortex attenuate emotional responses at the most basic levels in the brain, that such modulating processes are "fundamental to most modern psychotherapeutic methods" (2000, p. 43), that this lateralized neocortical network is active in "modulating emotional experience through interpreting and labeling emotional expressions" (p. 47), and that "this form of modulation may be impaired in various emotional disorders and may provide the basis for therapies of these same disorders" (p. 48). Furthermore, the coconstruction of a coherent narrative of the trauma may emerge in a relational context which promotes a callosal transfer of affective information from the right to left orbitofrontal regions. This structural advance allows for left hemispheric retrieval and explicit semantic processing of right hemispheric emotional states encoded in implicit-procedural memory (Schore, 2002a).

This model also has practical implications for programs of early prevention. A logical outcome of psychological, psychoanalytic, and psychiatric theories that emphasize the centrality of early development to later functioning is that early prevention is an essential goal. In accord with clinical findings (e.g., Eckenrode et al., 2000), the latest psychoneurobiological developmental models which focus on the effects of early environmental interactions on evolving brain-behavior relationships also emphatically stress the fundamental importance of early intervention. A core postulate of classical developmental biology and now of developmental neurobiology is the concept of critical periods. This construct emphasizes that certain detrimental early influences lead to particular irreversible or only partially reversible enduring effects, highlighting the fact that limitations of biological organization set into place once systems differentiate.

It is important to remember, however, that the flip side of the critical period concept emphasizes the extraordinary sensitivity of developing dynamic systems to their environment, and asserts that these systems are most plastic in periods when they are in the process of differentiating. The right hemisphere, which is centrally involved in both the capacity to perceive the emotional states of other human beings and the control of vital functions supporting survival and enabling the individual to cope actively and passively with stress, is in a growth spurt in the first 18 months of life and is dominant for the first three years. Its maturation is "experience-dependent," and this experience is embedded in the attachment relationship between caregiver and infant. Developmentally focused clinicians are familiar with the various patterns of emotional transactions of securely and insecurely attached dyads, but they also have extensive clinical knowledge of how the relationship between the patient and therapist cocreates a safe environment that facilitates what Emde (1990) called a mobilization of the patient's "biologically prepared positive developmental thrust." These same interpersonal skills and intersubjective sensitivities are valuable assets in preventive programs.

Attachment researchers in association with infant mental health workers are devising interventions that effectively alter the affect-communicating capacities of mother-infant systems, and thereby the attachment experiences of high-risk dyads. By providing an optimal context for the cocreation of a system of interactive regulation that is timed to critical periods of socioemotional development, such interventions can facilitate the maturation of neurobiologically adaptive regulatory systems. Early interventions thus have lifelong effects on the adaptive capacities of a developing self. These efforts, if expanded onto a larger scale, could make deep inroads into not only altering the intergenerational transmission of psychiatric disorders but improving the quality of a life throughout the life span. A deepening social and political commitment to early treatment and prevention programs would thus be a major contribution to the problems our societies are now facing.

2001

Dysregulation of the Right Brain: A Fundamental Mechanism of Traumatic Attachment and the Psychopathogenesis of Posttraumatic Stress Disorders

A LARGE, NATIONALLY REPRESENTATIVE STUDY reported that 60% of men and 50% of women experience a traumatic event at some point in their lives (Kessler, Sonnega, Bromet, Hughes, & Nelson, 1995). And yet this same study found that estimates of lifetime posttraumatic stress disorder (PTSD) are 5% for men and 10% for women. Other research indicated that roughly one half of those who have an episode of PTSD develop chronic symptoms of the disorder (Zlotnick et al., 1999). These data underscore a central problem: although trauma is a common element of many if not most lives, why do only a certain minor proportion of individuals exposed to the various forms of trauma develop chronic pathological reactions of mind and body to catastrophic life events?

A major change in our approach to this problem is reflected in the shift from *DSM-III-R*, where the severity of the trauma was considered to be the key factor in precipitating PTSD, to the *DSM-IV*, where characteristics of the victim, including the reaction to the trauma, is emphasized. In other words, the etiology of PTSD is best understood in terms of what an individual brings to a traumatic event as well as what he or she experiences afterward, and not just the nature of the traumatic event itself (Schnurr & Friedman, 1997). This implies that certain personality patterns are specifically associated with the unique ways individuals cope or fail to cope with stress.

Psychobiological research on PTSD (Morgan et al., 2001) echoed this principle:

> Although many people are exposed to trauma, only some individuals develop PTSD; most do not. It is possible that humans differ in the degree to which stress induces neurobiological perturbations of their threat re-

sponse systems, which may result in a differential capacity to cope with aversive experiences. (p. 412)

These individual differences exist before trauma exposure and may be used to test constructs of stress hardiness and stress vulnerability in humans. (p. 420)

There is agreement that the developmental stage at the time of exposure (Pynoos, 1993) and the specific type of trauma exposure (Davidson & Foa, 1993) are essential factors in PTSD, and yet they have been deemphasized in the recent literature (McFarlane & Yehuda, 2000). Highlighting these factors, however, brings into the foreground a number of fundamental issues: What are the effects of trauma in the earliest developmental stages? Why does this developmental exposure impact the differential capacity to cope with stress, and how is this related to the genesis of premorbid personality organizations vulnerable to posttraumatic stress disorder? These questions, which lie at the core of trauma theory, direct clinical psychiatry into the realms of child and especially infant psychiatry.

ATTACHMENT AND THE DEVELOPMENT OF RIGHT BRAIN STRESS-COPING MECHANISMS

The exploration of the early development of adaptive coping mechanisms and of the personality is at the core of attachment theory, "the dominant approach to understanding early socioemotional and personality development during the past quarter-century of research" (Thompson, 2000, p. 145). In his ground-breaking volume, *Attachment*, Bowlby (1969) hypothesized that the infant's "capacity to cope with stress" is correlated with certain maternal behaviors, that the developing emotion processing limbic system is impacted by attachment transactions, and that attachment outcome has consequences that are "vital to the survival of the species." Bowlby's speculation that, within the attachment relationship, the mother shapes the development of the infant's coping responses is now supported by a large body of basic experimental studies that characterize maternal care and the development of stress responses (Anisman, Zaharia, Meaney, & Merali, 1998; Essex, Klein, Cho, & Kalin, 2002; Francis & Meaney, 1999; Kuhn & Schanberg, 1998), and the influence of maternal factors on the ontogeny of the limbic-hypothalamic-pituitary-adrenal axis (Hennessy, 1997; Levine, 1994; Suchecki, Nelson, Van Oers, & Levine, 1995).

Recent developmental psychobiological models indicate that,

An individual's response to stressful stimuli may be maladaptive producing physiological and behavioral responses that may have detrimental consequences, or may be adaptive, enabling the individual to better cope with stress. Events experienced early in life may be particularly important in shaping the individual's pattern of responsiveness in later stages of life. (Kehoe et al., 1996, p. 1435)

These "events" are attachment experiences, shaped by the interaction of the infant's innate psychophysiological predispositions and the social environment of maternal care (Helmeke, Ovtscharoff, Poeggel, & Braun, 2001; Henry & Wang, 1998; Nachmias, Gunnar, Mangelsdorf, Parritz, & Boss, 1996; Ovtsharoff & Braun, 2001; Schore, 1994; 1998b, 1999b, 2000a, 2000d, 2001a; Siegel, 1999; Streeck-Fischer & van der Kolk, 2000; Suomi, 1995; Valent, 1998).

Furthermore, basic stress research suggests that deprivation of maternal care represents a source of "stressful environmental information" for the developmental, maturational pattern of the neural circuitry of the infant's stress system (Korte, 2001). This complements studies indicating that pre- or postnatal stressors negatively impact later mental health, especially when maternal care is absent (Korfman, 2002; Schore, 2001c). Such work is derivative of attachment theory's deep interest in the etiology of not only normal but abnormal development. In applying the theory to links between stress coping features and psychopathology Bowlby (1978) proposed:

> In the fields of etiology and psychopathology [attachment theory] can be used to frame specific hypotheses which relate different family experiences to different forms of psychiatric disorder and also, possibly, to the neurophysiological changes that accompany them.

With respect to the etiology of PTSD, a large body of studies implicates childhood abuse, and suggests that early life trauma produces specific patterns of developmental neurobiolial alterations, especially in the limbic system (Kaufman, Plotsky, Nemeroff, & Charney, 2000; Teicher, Glod, Surrey, & Swett, 1993; Vermetten & Bremner, 2002).

In this chapter I will apply the above central principle of attachment theory to the etiology of posttraumatic stress disorder. Although etiological models of PTSD have centered primarily on childhood sexual abuse, I will suggest that an increased focus on the neurobiological consequences of relational abuse and dysregulated infant attachment can offer a deeper understanding of the psychoneurobiological stress coping deficits of both mind and body that define the symptomatic presentation of the disorder, especially chronic forms of PTSD.

STRESS AND THE RIGHT HEMISPHERE

A growing body of evidence shows that the neural circuitry of the stress system is located in the early developing right brain, the hemisphere that is dominant for the control of vital functions that support survival and the human stress response (Wittling, 1997). Because stress-coping strategies are deeply connected into essential organismic functions, they begin their maturation pre- and post-natally, a time of right-brain dominance (Chiron et al., 1997). An MRI study of infants reported that the volume of the brain increases rapidly during the first two years, that normal adult appearance is seen at 2 years and all major fiber tracts can be identified by age 3, and that infants under 2 years show higher right than left hemispheric volumes (Matsuzawa et al., 2001). Attachment experiences of the first 2 years thus directly influence the experience-dependent maturation of the right brain (Henry, 1993; Schore, 1994, 1996, 1997c, 2000c; Siegel, 1999; Wang, 1997). These include experiences with a traumatizing caregiver, which are well known to negatively impact the child's attachment security, stress-coping strategies, and sense of self (Crittenden & Ainsworth, 1989; Erickson, Egeland, & Pianta, 1989).

Recent research is describing pediatric and maltreatment-related post-traumatic stress disorder in childen (Carrion et al., 2001, 2002; Beers & De Bellis, 2002). These studies in developmental traumatology concluded that "the overwhelming stress of maltreatment in childhood is associated with adverse influences on brain development" (De Bellis et al., 1999, p. 1281). This "maltreatment" specifically refers to the severe affect dysregulation of the two dominant forms of infant trauma — abuse and neglect. It is established that social stressors are far more detrimental than nonsocial aversive stimuli (Sgoifo et al., 1999), and therefore attachment or "relational trauma" from the social environment has more negative impact upon the infant brain than assaults from the nonhuman or inanimate, physical environment.

And so it is now being emphasized that specifically a dysfunctional and traumatized early *relationship* is the stressor that leads to PTSD, that severe trauma of interpersonal origin may override any genetic, constitutional, social, or psychological resilience factor, and that the ensuing adverse effects on brain development and alterations of the biological stress systems may be regarded as "an environmentally induced complex developmental disorder" (De Bellis, 2001). Furthermore, these relational perspectives on PTSD in early childhood emphasize the importance of understanding young children's traumatic responses in the context of their primary caregiving relationships. These efforts call for a deeper exploration of "the mechanism of how parental functioning impinges on child adaptation" (Scheeringa & Zeanah, 2001, p. 812).

The fact that early relational trauma is "ambient" clearly suggests that the infant is frequently experiencing not single-episode or acute stress, but cumulative and chronic unpredictable traumatic stress in his very first interactions with another human. The stress literature, which is investigating "determinants of individual differences in stress reactivity in early development" clearly shows that acute stress produces short-term and reversible deficits, while repeated, prolonged, chronic stress is associated with long-term patterns of autonomic reactivity, expressed in "neuronal structural changes, involving atrophy that might lead to permanent damage, including neuronal loss" (McEwen, 2000, p. 183). Consonant with this principle, in earlier writings I have suggested that early relational trauma has a significant negative impact on the experience-dependent maturation of the right brain, which is in a critical period of growth during the same temporal intervals as dyadic attachment experiences (Schore, 1994, 1997a, 1998h, 1998i; 1999d, 1999g; 2001c).

Because the early developing right hemisphere is, more so than the later maturing left, deeply interconnected into the autonomic, limbic, and arousal systems, it is dominant for the processing of social emotional and bodily information (Devinsky, 2000; Schore, 1994, 2000b, 2001b). A large number of studies indicated that this hemisphere is dominant not only for the reception (Adolphs, Damasio, Tranel, & Damasios, 1996; Adolphs, 2002; Borod et al., 1998; George et al., 1996; Keil et al., 2002; Nakamura et al., 1999; Pizzagalli et al., 2002), expression (Borod, Haywood, & Koff, 1997), and communication (Blonder et al., 1991) of emotion, but also for the control of spontaneously evoked emotional reactions (Dimberg & Petterson, 2000), the modulation of "primary emotions" (Ross et al., 1994), and the adaptive capacity for the regulation of affect (Schore, 1994, 1998a, 2001a).

It has been said that the most significant consequence of the stressor of early relational trauma is the lack of capacity for emotional self-regulation (Toth & Cicchetti, 1998), expressed in the loss of the ability to regulate the intensity and duration of affects (van der Kolk & Fisler, 1994). Basic developmental neuropsychobiological studies indicated that perinatal distress leads to a blunting of the stress regulating response of the right (and not left) prefrontal cortex that is manifest in adulthood (Brake et al., 2000; Sullivan & Gratton, 2002). In light of the essential role of the right hemisphere in the human stress response, this psychoneurobiological conception of trauma-induced right brain pathogenesis bears upon recent data which suggest that early adverse experiences result in an increased sensitivity to the effects of stress later in life and render an individual vulnerable to stress-related psychiatric disorders (Graham et al., 1999). Affect dysregulation is now seen to be a fundamental mechanism of all psychiatric disorders (Taylor et al., 1997).

A developmental neuropsychopathological perspective dictates that to "understand neuropsychological development is to confront the fact that the brain is mutable, such that its structural organization reflects the history of the organism" (Luu & Tucker, 1996, p. 297). A history of early relational traumatic stress is specifically imprinted into the right brain, which is dominant for "autobiographical" (Fink et al., 1996) or "personal" (Nakamura et al., 2000) memory. Terr (1988) wrote that literal mirroring of traumatic events by behavioral memory can be established at any age, including infancy. In fact it is now thought that preverbal children, even in the first year of life, can establish and retain an internal representation of a traumatic event over significant periods of time (Gaersbauer, 2002), and that young children and adults are able to re-enact traumatic experiences that occurred in their infancy (Fogel, in press). This developmental model suggests that traumatic attachments, occurring in a critical period of organization of the right brain, will create an enduring vulnerability to dysfunction during stress and a predisposition to posttraumatic stress disorders.

RIGHT BRAIN DYSREGULATION, DISSOCIATION, AND PTSD PATHOGENESIS: INTRODUCTION

Indeed, in 1996 van der Kolk proposed that the symptoms of PTSD fundamentally reflect an impairment of the right brain, known to be dominant for inhibitory control (Garavan et al., 1999). This hypothesis subsequently received experimental support in a number of studies (e.g., Rauch et al., 1996; Schuff et al. 1997; Shin et al., 1999; Spivak, Segal, Mester, & Weizman, 1998). In this same period dysfunction of the frontal lobes, specifically the orbitofrontal system that is expanded in the right hemisphere (Falk et al., 1990) and controls instinctive emotional responses through cognitive processes, was also implicated in PTSD (Bremner et al., 1997; Charney, Deutch, Southwick, & Krystal, 1995; Deutch & Young, 1995; Semple et al., 1992). This line of research has continued in studies that show right hemispheric and orbitofrontal dysfunction in PTSD (e.g., Berthier, Posada, & Puentes, 2001; Galletly, Clark, McFarlane, & Weber, 2001; Koenen et al., 2001; Shin et al., 1999; Vasterling, Brailey, & Sutker, 2000).

The emotional disturbances of PTSD have been suggested to have their origins in the inability of the right prefrontal cortex to modulate amygdala functions (Hariri et al., 2000; Schore, 1999h; 2001a, 2001c), especially activity of the right amygdala (Adamec, 1997), known to process frightening faces (Adolphs, Tranel, & Damasio, 2001; Whalen et al., 1998) and "unseen fear" (Morris, Ohman, & Dolan, 1999). Morgan and LeDoux (1995) conclude that without orbital prefrontal feedback regarding the level of threat, the organism remains in an amygdala-driven defensive response state longer than necessary, that in humans, conditioned fear acquisition and extinction are associated with right hemisphere dominant amygdala function (La Bar et al., 1998), and that a defective orbitofrontal system operates in PTSD (Morgan et al., 1993).

We are also seeing a parallel interest in developmental research on the etiology of the primitive defense that is used to cope with overwhelming affective states — dissociation. In part this has been driven by PTSD models that suggest that individuals with a history of early childhood abuse may develop more dissociative responses to subsequent traumas (Bremner, 1999). From the perspective of developmental psychopathology, an outgrowth of attachment theory that conceptualizes normal and aberrant development in terms of common underlying mechanisms, dissociation is described as offering "potentially very rich models for understanding the ontogeny of environmentally produced psychiatric conditions" (Putnam, 1995, p. 582). Disorganized-disoriented insecure attachment, a primary risk factor for the development of psychiatric disorders (Main, 1996), has been specifically implicated in the etiology of the dissociative disorders (Barach, 1991; Liotti, 1992). Intriguingly, clinical psychiatric research suggests that specifically maternal dysfunction contributes to the etiology of adult dissociative psychopathology (Draijer & Langeland, 1999).

Neuroscience is beginning to delve into the neurobiology of dissociation, especially in infancy (Schore, 2001b, 2001e). It is now thought that dissociation at the time of exposure to extreme stress signals the invocation of neural mechanisms that result in long-term alterations in brain functioning (Chambers et al., 1999). This principle applies to long-term alterations in the developing brain, especially the early maturing right brain, the locus of dissociation (Laniusetal, 2002; Schore, 2001c; Weinberg, 2000), activation during acquisition of conditioned fear (Fischer et al., 2002), withdrawal and avoidance (Davidson & Hugdahl, 1995), and a spectrum of psychiatric disorders (Cutting, 1992; Schore, 1996, 1997a).

TRAUMATIC ATTACHMENT, DYSREGULATION, AND THE PATHOGENESIS OF PTSD

Bowlby (1969) postulated that the major negative impact of early traumatic attachments is an alteration of the organism's normal developmental trajectory:

> [S]ince much of the development and organization of [attachment] behavioral systems takes place whilst the individual is immature, there are plenty of occasions when an atypical environment can divert them from developing on an adaptive course. (p. 130)

And sixty years earlier, Janet (1911) proposed:

> All [traumatized] patients seem to have the evolution of their lives checked; they are attached to an unsurmountable object. Unable to integrate traumatic memories, they seem to have lost their capacity to assimilate new experiences as well. It is . . . as if their personality development has stopped at a certain point, and cannot enlarge any more by the addition of new elements. (p. 532)

Janet further postulated that the psychological consequence of trauma is the breakdown of the adaptive mental processes leading to the maintenance of an integrated sense of self. Again, recent studies indicate that the right hemisphere is central to self-recognition (Keenan, Nelson, O'Connor, & Pascual-Leone, 2001) and the ability to maintain a coherent, continuous, and unifed sense of self (Devinsky, 2000), but it also is the locus of various self-regulation pathologies (Schore, 1994, 1996, 1997c).

The concept of regulation — shared by the attachment, PTSD, neuroscience, and psychiatric literatures — may be a bridging concept for expanding a biopsychosocial model of psychiatry. According to Taylor, Bagby, and Parker (1997),

> The concept of disorders of affect regulation is consistent with a growing realization in medicine and psychiatry that most illnesses and diseases are the result of dysregulations within the vast network of communicating systems that comprise the human organism. (p. 270)

A model of the interactive genesis of psychobiological dysregulation also supports and provides a deeper understanding of the diathesis-stress concept — that psychiatric disorders are caused by a combination of a genetic-constitutional predisposition and environmental or psychosocial stressors that activate the inborn neurophysiological vulnerability. The unique contributions of the intrinsic psychobiological perspective of trauma studies to both clinical psychiatry and neuroscience is articulated by McFarlane (2000):

> [T]he origins of psychiatry in medicine tie the discipline strongly to its biological roots. The field of traumatic stress has the potential to bridge this divide. (p. 900)
> Traumatic stress as a field, has the capacity to show the future direction of functional neurobiology. (p. 901)

In an editorial in the *American Journal of Psychiatry*, Rapoport (2000) called for deeper studies of the association between pre/perinatal adverse events or stressors and adult psychiatric outcomes. Toward that end, in the following I will suggest that recent theoretical models linking developmental affective neuroscience and attachment theory, updated basic research in biological psychiatry on stress mechanisms, and current advances in psychophysiology on the survival functions of the autonomic nervous system may offer us a deeper understanding of the underlying mechanisms by which early childhood trauma massively dysregulates and thereby alters the developmental trajectory of the right hemisphere. This results in an immature personality organization with vulnerable coping capacities, one predisposed to the pathological hyperarousal and dissociation that characterizes PTSD at later points of stress. These psycho-neurobiological models, which link infant, child, and adolescent psychiatry, are offered as heuristic proposals that can be evaluated by experimental and clinical research.

OVERVIEW OF THE NEUROBIOLOGY
OF A SECURE ATTACHMENT

The essential task of the first year of human life is the creation of a secure attachment bond of emotional communication between the infant and the primary caregiver. In order to enter into this communication, the mother must be psychobiologically attuned to the dynamic crescendos and decescendos of the infant's bodily-based internal states of autonomic arousal. During the sequential signalling of play epsiodes, mother and infant show sympathetic cardiac acceleration and then parasympathetic deceleration in response to the smile of the other, and thus the language of mother and infant consist of signals produced by the autonomic, involuntary nervous system in both parties (Basch, 1976). The attachment relationship mediates the dyadic regulation of emotion (Sroufe, 1996), wherein the mother coregulates the infant's postnatally developing autonomic nervous system. Also known as the "vegetative" nervous system (from the Latin *vegetare*, to animate or bring to life), it is responsible for the generation of what Stern (1985) called "vitality affects."

In heightened affective moments each partner learns the rhythmic structure of the other and modifies his or her behavior to fit that structure, thereby co-creating a specifically fitted interaction. In play episodes of affect synchrony, the pair are in affective resonance, and in such, an amplification of vitality affects and a positive state occurs especially when the mother's psychobiologically attuned external sensory stimulation frequency coincides with the infant's genetically encoded endogenous rhythms. And in moments of interactive repair the "good-enough" caregiver who induces a stress response in her infant through a misattunement, reinvokes in a timely fashion a reattunment, a regulation of the infant's negative state. Maternal sensitivity thus acts as an external organizer of the infant's biobehavioral regulation (Spangler, Schieche, Ilg, Maier, & Ackerman, 1994).

If attachment is the regulation of interactive synchrony, stress is defined as an asynchrony in an interactional sequence, and, following this, a period of reestablished synchrony allows for stress recovery and coping. The regulatory processes of affect synchrony that creates states of positive arousal and interactive repair that modulates states of negative arousal are the fundamental building blocks of attachment and its associated emotions, and resilience in the face of stress is an ultimate indicator of attachment security. Attachment, the outcome of the child's genetically encoded biological (temperamental) predisposition and the particular caregiver environment, thus represents the regulation of biological synchronicity between organisms, and imprinting, the learning process that mediates attachment, is defined as synchrony between sequential infant-maternal stimuli and behavior.

It is now thought that "attachment relationships are formative because they facilitate the development of the brain's major self-regulatory mechanisms" (Fonagy & Target, 2002, p. 328). The optimally regulated communications embedded in secure attachment experiences directly influence the maturation of both the postnatally maturing central nervous system (CNS) limbic system that processes and regulates social-emotional stimuli and the autonomic nervous system (ANS) that generates the somatic aspects of emotion (Braun & Poeggel, 2001; Helmeke, Poeggel, & Braun, 2001; Ovtscharoff & Braun, 2001; Poeggel & Braun 1996; Schore 1994). The limbic system derives subjective information in terms of emotional feelings that guide behavior (MacLean, 1985), and functions to allow the brain to adapt to a rapidly changing environment and organize new learning (Mesulam, 1998). As mentioned, the higher regulatory systems of the right hemisphere form extensive reciprocal connections with the limbic and autonomic nervous systems (Spence et al., 1996; Tucker, 1992). Both the ANS and the CNS continue to develop postnatally, and the assembly of these limbic-autonomic circuits (Rinaman et al., 2000) is directly influenced by the interactive regulatory transactions embedded in the attachment relationship (Schore, 1994, 2001a). In this manner, the internalized regulatory capacities of the infant develop in relation to the mother, and thus, as Bowlby suggested, the mother shapes the infant's stress coping systems.

ATTACHMENT AND RIGHT CORTICAL REGULATION
OF THE AUTONOMIC NERVOUS SYSTEM

In his original formulation Bowlby (1969) described a neurophysiological control system that is centrally involved in regulating instinctive attachment behavior (Schore, 2000c, 2001d). In a number of writings, I indicated that this system is located in the right orbitofrontal area and its cortical and subcortical connections (Schore, 1994, 1996, 1998a, 2000a, 2000b, 2000c, 2001a). Due to its position at the interface of the cortex and subcortex, this ventromedial cortex sits at the hierarchical apex of the limbic system. This frontolimbic system directly connects into the subcortical reticular formation, thus regulating arousal, a central component of all emotional states. Its lateral and medial divisions process positive and negative emotions (Northoff et al., 2000). Indeed this prefrontal system acts the highest level of control of behavior, especially in relation to emotion (Price et al., 1996). Referred to as "the thinking part of the emotional brain," it is situated at the hierarchical apex of what is now refered to as the "rostral limbic system" (Devinsky et al., 1995), or "anterior limbic prefrontal network" (Carmichael & Price, 1995), which also includes the anterior cingulate (medial frontal cortex) and the amygdala (see Schore, 2000b, 2001a). This "senior executive" of the social-emotional brain comes to act in the capacity of an executive control function for the entire right brain, the locus of what Devinsky (2000) called the "emotional self," and LeDoux (2002) termed the "implicit self."

But in addition, the orbitofrontal cortex also represents the apex of the hierarchy of control of autonomic functions (Pribram, 1981). Due to its direct connections into the hypothalamus, the head ganglion of the ANS, it functions as a cortical control center of involuntary bodily functions that represent the somatic components of all emotional states, and acts to control autonomic responses associated with emotional events (Cavada et al., 2000). Recent studies demonstrated that the right orbitofrontal cortex represents the highest level of organization for processing interoceptive state, and thus is responsible for the subjective evaluation of the physiological condition of the entire body (Craig,

2002). Indeed, the right hemisphere is dominant for the regulation of self-related information and the corporeal self (Devinsky, 2000; Keenan et al., 2001; Ryan, Kuhl, & Deci, 1997; Schore, 1994).

In optimal early environments that promote secure attachments, a right-lateralized regulatory system organizes with a capacity to modulate, under stress, a flexible coping pattern of shifting out of autonomic balance into a coupled reciprocal autonomic mode of control in which homestatic increases in the activity in one ANS division are associated with decreases in the other (Berntson et al., 1991). The two components of the centrally regulated ANS are known to be distinct modular circuits that control arousal expressions, with the catabolic sympathetic branch responsible for energy-mobilizing excitatory activity and the anabolic parasympathetic branch involved in energy-conserving inhibitory activity. These dissociable autonomic functions reflect the sympathetic catecholaminergic stimulation of glycogenolysis and parasympathetic vagal and cortisol stimulation of glycogenesis (Hilz, Tarnowski, & Arend, 1963; Shimazu, 1971; Shimazu & Amakawa, 1968).

In light of the fact that primordial representations of body states are the building blocks and scaffolding of development (Damasio, 1994), the current intense interest in emotional development is leading researchers to focus attention upon changes in bodily state, mediated by the ANS, that are crucial to ongoing emotional experience. The right hemisphere, dominant for somatosensory processing (Adolph, 2001; Coghill, Gilron, & Iadorola, 2001), predominantly controls both sympathetic and parasympathetic activity (Erciyas et al., 1999; Wiltling, Block, Schweiger, & Genzel, 1998; Yoon et al., 1997). The ANS, by regulating the strength of the heartbeat and controlling vascular caliber, perfroms a critical role in ensuring that bloodflow is adequate to supply oxygen and nutrients to the bodily organs and the brain, according to their relative needs.

A quick review of the ANS indicates that the sympathetic branch is activated by any stimulus above an organsmic threshold, and that it functions to increase arousal, trigger an immediate anticipatory state, and rapidly mobilize resources in response to appraised stressors. Physiological activation is expressed in the conversion of glycogen to glucose and elevation of blood sugar for increased energy, quicker and stronger heart beat, increased blood supply to the muscles, dilation of bronchii and increases in breathing rate, dilation of the pupils, increased sweating, and speeding up of mental activity. The opposing parasympathetic branch has a higher threshold of activation and thus initiates its operations after the sympathetic, and its adaptive functions are expressed in slowing the heart rate, relaxing the muscles, lowering blood pressure, and pupillary constriction. Its operations allow for breathing to return to normal rates, increases in digestion, onset of bowel and bladder activities, and reestablishment of immune functions.

An autonomic mode of reciprocal sympathetic-parasympathetic control is behaviorally expressed in an organism that responds alertly and adaptively to a personally meaningful (especially social) stressor, yet as soon as the context is appraised as safe, immediately returns to the relaxed state of autonomic balance. The ANS is not only sensitive to environmental demands and perceived stresses and threats, but will, in a predictable order, also rapidly reorganize to different neural-mediated states (Porges, 2001). These ANS changes are regulated by "higher" limbic structures in the CNS. Indeed, the orbitofrontal cortex acts as a major center of CNS control over the sympathetic and parasympathetic branches of the ANS (Neafsey, 1990), and thereby regulales autonomic responses to social stimuli (Zald & Kim, 1996), the intuitive "gut feelings" than an individual has to other humans. These right lateralized connections also mediate the adaptive capacity of empathically perceiving the emotional states of other human beings (Adolphs et al., 2000; Schore 1994, 1996, 2001a, 2001d).

The early forming right hemisphere stores an internal working model of the attachment relationship (Schore, 1994; Siegel, 1999) that determines the individual's characteristic strategies of affect regulation for coping and survival (Schore, 1994; Valent, 1998). This working model is encoded in implicit memory, which is primarily regulatory, automatized, and unconscious (Bargh & Chartrand, 1999) and right-lateralized (Hugdahl, 1995). This right frontal system thus plays a unique role in the regulation of motivational states and the adjustment or correction of emotional responses. It acts as a recovery mechanism that monitors and regulates the duration, frequency, and intensity of not only positive but negative affect states.

In the securely attached individual the representation of the attachment relationship with the primary caregiver encodes an implicit expectation that homeostatic disruptions will be set right, allowing the child to self-regulate functions which previously required the caregiver's external regulation. In this manner, emotion is initially regulated by others, but over the course of early development it becomes increasingly self-regulated as a result of neurophysiological development (Thompson, 1990). These adaptive capacities are central to self-regulation, the ability to flexibly regulate emotional states through interactions with other humans — interactive regulation in interconnected contexts, and without other humans — autoregulation in autonomous contexts.

The orbitofrontal system, shaped in its critical period by interpersonal attachment transactions, is fundamentally involved in the regulation of interpersonal behavior (Eslinger, 1999). This control system is specialized to play a critical role in strategic memory by supporting the early mobilization of effective behavioral strategies in novel or ambiguous situations (Savage et al., 2001). Operating at levels beneath awareness, it is activated when there is insufficient information available to determine the appropriate course of action, and is specialized to act in contexts of "uncertainty or unpredictability" (Elliott et al., 2000), an operational definition of stress. Efficient orbitofrontal operations organize the expression of a regulated emotional response and an appropriate motivational state for a particular social environmental context, and in this fashion it contributes to "judicious, adapted behavior" (Cavada et al., 2000). Anatomical, electrophysiological, and imaging studies indicate that the orbitofrontal functions are central to "the integration of past, present, and future experiences, enabling adequate performance in behavioral tasks, social situation, or situations involving survival" (Lipton, Alvarez, & Eichenbaum, 1999, p. 356). As mentioned earlier, neuroscience research indicates that these same adaptive stress-survival capacities are severely impaired in infant, child, and adult post-traumatic stress disorders.

THE NEUROBIOLOGY OF INFANT TRAUMA

It is important to stress that the developmental attainment of an efficient internal system that can adaptively regulate various forms of arousal and psychobiological states, and thereby affect, cognition, and behavior, only evolves in a growth-facilitating emotional environment. The good-enough mother of the securely attached infant permits access to the child after a separation and shows a tendency to respond appropriately and promptly to his/her emotional expressions. She also allows for the interactive generation of high levels of positive affect in shared play states. These regulated events allow for an expansion of the child's coping capacities, and account for the principle that security of the attachment bond is the primary defense against trauma-induced psychopathology.

In contrast to this scenario is a relational growth-inhibiting early environment, in which the abusive caregiver not only shows less play with her infant, but also induces traumatic states of enduring negative affect in the child. Because her attachment is weak, she provides little protection against other potential abusers of the infant, such as the father. This caregiver is inaccessible and reacts to her infant's expressions of emotions and stress inappropriately and/or rejectingly, and therefore shows minimal or unpredictable participation in the various types of arousal regulating processes. Instead of modulating she induces extreme levels of stimulation and arousal, very high in abuse and/or very low in neglect. And because she provides no interactive repair the infant's intense negative states last for long periods of time.

The enduring detrimental effects of parent-inflicted trauma on the attachment bond is now well-established:

> The continued survival of the child is felt to be at risk, because the actuality of the abuse jeopardizes (the) primary object bond and challenges the child's capacity to trust and, therefore, to securely depend. (Davies & Frawley, 1994, p. 62)

Freyd (1996), describing the effects of childhood abuse and attachment, referred to "betrayal trauma theory."

In contexts of relational trauma, the caregiver(s), in addition to dysregulating the infant, withdraws any repair functions, leaving the infant for long periods in an intensely disruptive psychobiological state that is beyond her immature coping strategies. In studies of a neglect paradigm, Tronick and Weinberg (1997) described:

> When infants are not in homeostatic balance or are emotionally dysregu-lated (e.g., they are distressed), they are at the mercy of these states. Until these states are brought under control, infants must devote all their regu-latory resources to reorganizing them. While infants are doing that, they can do nothing else. (p. 56)

The "nothing else" these authors refer to is a failure to continue to develop. These infants forfeit potential opportunities for socioemotional learning during critical periods of right brain development (Schore, 2001c).

Indeed, we now know that trauma causes biochemical alterations within the developing brain (Bremner et al., 1999; Schore, 1997a). The infant's psychobio-logical response to trauma is comprised of two separate response patterns, hy-perarousal and dissociation (Perry et al., 1995; Schore, 2001c), the same two responses of adult PTSD (Bremner, 1999). In the initial stage of threat, a startle or an alarm reaction is initiated, in which the sympathetic component of the ANS is suddenly and significantly activated, resulting in increased heart rate, blood pressure, and respiration. Distress is expressed in crying and then scream-ing. In very recent work, this dyadic transaction is described by Beebe (2000) as "mutually escalating overarousal" of a disorganized attachment pair:

> Each one escalates the ante, as the infant builds to a frantic distress, may scream, and, in this example, finally throws up. In an escalating overarous-al pattern, even after extreme distress signals from the infant, such as ninety-degree head aversion, arching away . . . or screamimg, the mother keeps going. (p. 436)

The infant's state of "frantic distress," or what Perry and colleagues (1995) termed fear-terror is mediated by sympathetic hyperarousal, expressed in in-creased levels of the brain's major stress hormone, corticotropin releasing factor, which in turn regulates sympathetic catecholamine activity (Brown et al., 1982), and so brain adrenaline, noradrenaline, and dopamine levels are signifi-cantly elevated. Noradrenaline is also released from the locus coeruleus (Aston-Jones et al, 1996; Butler et al., 1990; Svensson, 1987). The resultant rapid and intensely elevated catecholamine levels trigger a hypermetabolic state within the developing brain. Catecholamines are among the first neurochemicals to respond to stressors in response to perceived threat, and repeated stress triggers their persi-sent activation (Sabban & Kvetnansky, 2001). Prolonged stress and elevated levels of catecholamines in turn induce high levels of thyroid hormones that accompany hyperarousal (Galton, 1965; Wang, 1997). Thyroid hormones are known to be active agents in brain differentiation and in the regulation of critical period phenomena (Nunez, 1984; Lauder & Krebs, 1986; see Schore, 1994).

Furthermore, increased amounts of vasopressin are expressed, a hypothalamic neuropeptide associated with sympathetic activation (Kvetnansky et al., 1989, 1990). This condition is specifically triggered when an environment is perceived to be unsafe and challenging, and resultant high levels of vasopressin potentiate immobilization responses via sympathetic activation, behaviorally expressed as fear (Porges, 2001). Interestingly, high levels of this neuropeptide are associated with nausea (Koch, Summy-Long, Bingaman, Sperry, & Stern, 1990), a finding that may explain the hyperarousal behaviors observed by Beebe. In addition, when the body of the abused infant is physically assaulted, she is in pain, another state accompanied by sympathetic hyperarousal.

But a second later-forming reaction to infant trauma is seen in dissociation, in which the child disengages from stimuli in the external world and attends to an internal world. The child's dissociation in the midst of terror involves numbing, avoidance, compliance, and restricted affect (the same pattern as adult PTSD). Traumatized infants are observed to be "staring off into space with a glazed look." This behavioral strategy is described by Tronick and Weinberg (1997):

> [W]hen infants' attempts fail to repair the interaction infants often lose postural control, withdraw, and self-comfort. The disengagement is profound even with this short disruption of the mutual regulatory process and break in intersubjectivity. The infant's reaction is reminiscent of the withdrawal of Harlow's isolated monkey or of the infants in institutions observed by Bowlby and Spitz. (p. 66)

This parasympathetic dominant state of conservation-withdrawal occurs in helpless and hopeless stressful situations in which the individual becomes inhibited and strives to avoid attention in order to become "unseen" (Schore, 1994, 2001c). This metabolic shutdown state is a primary regulatory process, used throughout the life span, in which the stressed individual passively disengages in order "to conserve energies . . . to foster survival by the risky posture of feigning death, to allow healing of wounds and restitution of depleted resources by immobility" (Powles, 1992, p. 213). It is this parasympathetic mechanism that mediates the "profound detachment" (Barach, 1991) of dissociation. If early trauma is experienced as "psychic catastrophe" (Bion, 1962), dissociation represents "detachment from an unbearable situation" (Mollon, 1996), "the escape when there is no escape" (Putnam, 1997), and "a last resort defensive strategy" (Dixon, 1998).

Most importantly, the neurobiology of the later-forming dissociative reaction is different than the initial hyperarousal response. In this passive state pain numbing and blunting endogenous opiates (Fanselow, 1986; Liberzon et al.,

2002; Zubieta et al., 2002) and behavior-inhibiting stress hormones, such as cortisol, are elevated. Furthermore, activity of the dorsal vagal complex in the brain stem medulla increases dramatically, decreasing blood pressure, metabolic activity, and heart rate, despite increases in circulating adrenaline. This elevated parasympathetic arousal, a survival strategy (Porges, 1997), allows the infant to maintain homeostasis in the face of the internal state of sympathetic hyperarousal.

It is now known that there are two parasympathetic vagal systems that lower heart rate (Cheng, & Powley, 2000; Cheng, Powley, Schwaber, & Doyle, 1999), a late developing mammalian or "smart" system in the nucleus ambiguous which allows for the ability to communicate via facial expressions, vocalizations, and gestures via contingent social interactions, and a more primitive early developing reptillian or "vegetative" system in the dorsal motor nucleus of the vagus that acts to shutdown metabolic activity during immobilization, death feigning, and hiding behaviors (Porges, 1997, 2001). Porges described that as opposed to the ventral vagal complex that can rapidly regulate cardiac output to foster engagament and disengagement with the social environment, the dorsal vagal complex "contributes to severe emotional states and may be related to emotional states of 'immobilization' such as extreme terror" (1997, p. 75). Perry and colleagues' (1995) description of the traumatized infant's sudden state switch from sympathetic hyperarousal into parasympathetic dissociation was reflected in Porges's (1997) characterization of

> the sudden and rapid transition from an unsuccessful strategy of struggling requiring massive sympathetic activation to the metabolically conservative immobilized state mimicking death associated with the dorsal vagal complex. (p. 75)

Meares (1999) also concluded that in all stages "dissociation, at its first occurrence, is a consequence of a 'psychological shock' or high arousal" (p. 1853). Notice that in the traumatic state, and this may be of long duration, both the sympathetic energy-expending and parasympathetic energy-conserving components of the infant's developing ANS are hyperactivated.

DISORGANIZED/DISORIENTED
ATTACHMENT NEUROPSYCHOLOGY

The next question is, how would the trauma-induced neurobiological and psychobiological alterations of the developing right brain be expressed in the socioemotional behavior of an early traumatized toddler? In a classic study, Main and Solomon (1986) studied the attachment patterns of infant's who had suffered trauma in the first year of life. This lead to the discovery of a new attachment category, Type D, an insecure-disorganized/disoriented pattern, found in 80% of maltreated infants (Carlson et al., 1989). Indeed this group of toddlers exhibits higher cortisol levels and higher heart rates than all other attachment classifications (Hertsgaard et al., 1995; Spangler & Grossman, 1999).

Main and Solomon concluded that these infants are experiencing low stress tolerance and that the disorganization and disorientation reflect the fact that the infant, instead of finding a haven of safety in the relationship, is alarmed by the parent. They note that because the infant inevitably seeks the parent when alarmed, any parental behavior that directly alarms an infant should place it in an irresolvable paradox in which it can neither approach, shift its attention, or flee. At the most basic level, these infants are unable to generate a coherent behavioral coping strategy to deal with this emotional challenge.

Main and Solomon documented, in some detail, the uniquely bizarre behaviors these 12-month-old infants show in strange situation observations. They note that these episodes of interruptions of organized behavior are often brief, frequently lasting only 10–30 seconds, yet they are highly significant. For example, they show a simultaneous display of contradictory behavior patterns, such as "backing" toward the parent rather than approaching face-to-face.

> The impression in each case was that approach movements were continually being inhibited and held back through simultaneous activation of avoidant tendencies. In most cases, however, proximity-seeking sufficiently "over-rode" avoidance to permit the increase in physical proximity. Thus, contradictory patterns were activated but were not mutually inhibited. (Main & Solomon, 1986, p. 117)

Notice the simultaneous activation of the energy expending sympathetic and energy conserving parasympathetic components of the ANS.

Maltreated infants also show evidence of apprehension and confusion, as well as very rapid shifts of state during the stress-inducing strange situation:

> One infant hunched her upper body and shoulders at hearing her mother's call, then broke into extravagent laugh-like screeches with an excited forward movement. Her braying laughter became a cry and distress-face without a new intake of breath as the infant hunched forward. Then suddenly she became silent, blank and dazed. (Main & Solomon, 1986, p. 119)

These behaviors generalize beyond just interactions with the mother. The intensity of the baby's dysregulated affective state is often heightened when the infant is exposed to the added stress of an unfamiliar person. At a stranger's entrance, two infants moved away from both mother and stranger to face the wall, and another "leaned forehead against the wall for several seconds, looking back in apparent terror" (p. 120).

These infants exhibit "behavioral stilling"—that is, dazed behavior and depressed affect, behavioral mainfestations of dissociation. One infant "became for a moment excessively still, staring into space as though completely out of contact with self, environment, and parent" (p. 120). Another showed "a dazed facial appearance . . . accompanied by a stilling of all body movement, and sometimes a freezing of limbs which had been in motion" (p. 120). Yet another "fell face-down on the floor in a depressed posture prior to separation, stilling all body movements" (p. 120).

Furthermore, Main and Solomon pointed out that the type D behaviors take the form of stereotypies that are found in neurologically impaired infants. These behaviors are overt manifestations of an obviously impaired regulatory system, one that rapidly disorganizes under stress. Notice that these observations are taking place at 12 to 18 months, a critical period of corticolimbic maturation (Schore, 1994), and they reflect a severe structural impairment of the orbitofrontal control system that is involved in attachment behavior and state regulation. The orbitofrontal areas specialize in encoding information (Frey & Petrides, 2000), especially information contained in emotionally expressive faces and voices, including angry and fearful faces (Elliott et al., 2000; Kawasaki et al., 2001).

The mother's face is the most potent visual stimulus in the child's world, and it is well known that direct gaze can mediate not only loving but powerful aggressive messages. In coding the mother's frightening behavior Hesse and Main described "in non-play contexts, stiff-legged 'stalking' of infant on all fours in a hunting posture; exposure of canine tooth accompanied by hissing; deep growls directed at infant" (1999, p. 511). Thus, during the trauma, the infant is presented with an aggressive expression on the mother's face. The image of this aggressive face, as well as the chaotic alterations in the infant's bodily state that are associated with it, are indelibly imprinted into limbic circuits as a "flashbulb memory," and thereby stored in imagistic procedural memory in the visuospatial right hemisphere, the locus of implicit (Hugdahl, 1995) and autobiographical (Fink et al. 1996) memory.

But in traumatic episodes the infant is presented with another affectively overwhelming facial expression, a maternal expression of fear-terror. Main and Solomon noted that this occurs when the mother withdraws from the infant as though the infant were the source of the alarm, and they report that dissociated, trancelike, and fearful behavior is observed in parents of type D infants. Studies have shown a link between frightening maternal behavior and disorganized infant attachment (Schuengel et al., 1999).

I suggest that during these episodes the infant is matching the rhythmic structures of the mother's dysregulated states, and that this synchronization is registered in the firing patterns of the stress-sensitive corticolimbic regions of the infant's brain that are in a critical period of growth. In light of the fact that many of these mothers have suffered from unresolved trauma themselves, this spatiotemporal imprinting of the chaotic alterations of the mother's dysregulated state facilitates the down-loading of programs of psychopathogenesis, a context for the intergenerational transmission of trauma. This represents a fundamental mechanism by which maladaptive parental behavior mediates the association between parental and offspring psychiatric symptoms (Johnson, Cohen, Kasen, Smailes, & Brook, 2001), and parental PTSD and parental trauma exposure impact the child's development of a risk factor for PTSD (Yehuda, Halligan, & Grossman, 2001). Posttraumatic stress disorder, defined by the *DSM-IV* as "actual or threatened death or serious injury, or threat to the physical integrity of the individual" that invokes "feelings of horror and intense fear" (APA, 1994), thus occurs in the nonverbal infant.

IMPACT OF RELATIONAL TRAUMA
ON RIGHT-BRAIN DEVELOPMENT

In an early history of traumatic attachment, the developing infant/toddler is too frequently exposed to a massively misattuning primary caregiver who triggers and does not repair long-lasting intensely dysregulated states. These negative states reflect severe biochemical alterations in the rapidly maturing right brain, and because they occur during the brain growth spurt which ends in the second year (Dobbing & Sands, 1973; Ferrie et al., 1999), the effect of ambient cumulative trauma is enduring. In the infant brain, states become traits (Perry et al., 1995), and so the effects of early relational trauma as well as the defenses against such trauma are embedded into the core structure of the evolving personality. According to Bowlby (1969) the effect of an atypical environment is that development is diverted from its adaptive course. This leads to the question, what do we now know about the psychopathomorphogenetic mechanisms that underlie such deflections of normal structural development?

The developing infant is maximally vulnerable to nonoptimal environmental events in the period of most rapid brain growth. During these critical periods of genetically encoded synapse overproduction followed by environmentally driven synapse elimination, the organism is sensitive to conditions in the external environment, and if these are outside the normal range a permanent or semi-permanent arrest of development occurs. Of particular importance is the identification of various stressful growth-inhibiting environments that negatively influence the critical period organization of limbic cortical and subcortical connections that mediate homeostatic self-regulatory and attachment systems. Disruption of attachment bonds in infant trauma leads to a regulatory failure, expressed in an impaired autonomic homeostasis, disturbances in limbic activity, and hypothalamic and reticular formation dysfunction. Intense stress modulates transcriptional regulation of gene expression in the developing brain (Hatalski & Baram, 1997; Mayer et al., 2002). Hyperaroused attachment stressors are correlated with elevated levels of the arousal-regulating catecholamines and hyperactivation of the excitotoxic N-methyl-D-aspartate (NMDA)-sensitive glutamate receptor, a critical site of neurotoxicity and synapse elimination in early development (Chaparro-Huerta, Rivera-Cervantes, Torres-Mendoza, & Beas-Zárate, 2002; Guilarte, 1998; McDonald et al., 1988).

The relational trauma of infant abuse also triggers significant alterations in the major stress-regulating neurochemicals, corticotropin releasing factor (which induces catecholamines) and the glucocorticoid, cortisol, especially in the right hemisphere that is dominant for the secretion of these hormones (Kalogeras et al., 1996; Wittling & Pfluger, 1990). Yehuda pointed out that the actions of these two systems are synergistic: "whereas catecholamines facilitate the availability of energy to the body's vital organs, cortisol's role in stress is to help contain, or shut down sympathetic activation" (1999a, p. 257). It is well established that stress hormones are protective in the short run and yet cause damage when they are overproduced or not shut off when no longer needed (McEwen, 2000). These is a large body of basic research to show that both stress hormones are regulated (for better or worse) within the mother-infant relationship (Gunnar & Donzella, 2002; Schore, 1994).

In situations where the caregiver routinely does not participate in reparative functions that reestablish homeostasis, the resulting psychobiological disequilibrium is expressed in a dysregulated and potentially toxic brain chemistry, especially in limbic areas that are in a critical period of synaptogenesis. Indeed, this same interaction between high levels of catecholamines, excitatory transmitters, and corticosteroids is now thought to mediate programmed cell death, and to represent a primary etiological mechanism for the pathophysiology of neuropsychiatric disorders. (See Schore 1997a & 2001c for a detailed account of trauma-induced altered calcium metabolism and oxidative stress damage in neurons and astroglia in the developing brain, and Schore 1994 & 1997a for free radical damage of brain mitochondria.)

But in addition, when the attachment trauma exhausts the infant's active coping mechanisms, she shifts into hypoarousal and accesses the ultimate survival strategy, dissociation, "a submission and resignation to the inevitability of overwhelming, even psychically deadening danger" (Davies & Frawley, 1994). If this primary metabolic shutdown becomes a chronic condition, it will have devastating effects on the morphogenesis of limbic structures. Dissociation and conservation-withdrawal, functional expressions of heightened dorsal vagal activity, induce an extreme alteration of the bioenergetics of the developing brain. During critical periods of regional synaptogenesis this would have growth-inhibiting effects, especially in the right brain which specializes in withdrawal and contains a vagal circuit of emotion regulation (Davidson & Hugdahl, 1995; Porges et al., 1994). This is because the biosynthetic processes that mediate the proliferation of synaptic connections in the postnatally developing brain demand, in addition to sufficient quantities of essental nutrients, massive amounts of energy (Schore, 1994, 1997a; 2000b). An infant brain that is chronically shifting into hypometabolic survival modes and decreased heart rate has little energy available for brain growth.

In describing the dorsal vagal complex Porges (2001) stated that when all else fails, the nervous system elects a metabolically conservative course; this strategy may be adaptive in the short term, but lethal if maintained. He also noted that high levels of dorsal vagal activation are associated with potentially life-threatening bradycardia, apnea, and cardiac arrhythmias. This may describe stresses on the infant's cardiovascular during and after relational trauma. I have suggested that in the developing brain this "lethality' is expressed in intensified apoptotic cell death in "affective centers" in the limbic system (Schore, 1997a, 2001c). The neonatal brain is much more prone to excitoxicity than the adult brain, and apoptotic neurodegeneration following trauma is markedly enhanced in the immature brain (Bittigau et al., 1999; Johnston, 2001; Portera-Cailliau, Price, & Martin, 1997).

As opposed to the excitotoxic cell death associated with elevated levels of corticosteroids, prolonged and intense dorsal vagal activity may be associated with profoundly low corticosteroid levels, also known to impair brain development in limbic structures (Gould, Wooley, & McEwen, 1991). Hypocortisol-ism develops subsequent to extended periods of elevated cortisol in response to trauma, and adverse conditions in early life that induce elevated levels of cortisol are now proposed to contribute to the development of hypocortisolism in adulthood (Gunnar & Vazquez, 2001), a known predictor of PTSD (Yehuda, McFarlane, & Shalev, 1998). Recall that abused type D infants show higher cortisol levels than all other attachment classifications (Hertsgaard et al., 1995). It should be pointed out that infants raised in a neglectful environment show a low cortisol pattern of circadian cortisol production (Gunnar & Vazquez, 2001). This suggests different neurobiological impairments and neurophysiological deficits in the two types of infant trauma — abuse and neglect.

In other words, the caregiver's dysregulating effect on the infant's internal state, and her poor capacity to psychobiologically regulate excessive levels of high and/ or low arousal negative affect, defines a pathomorphogenetic influence. Structural limitations in the mother's emotion processing right brain are reflected in a poor ability to comfort and regulate her child's affective states, and these experiences, central to the intergenerational transmission of psychopathology, are stamped into the insecurely attached infant's right orbitofrontal system and its cortical and subcortical connections. Stuss and Alexander (1999) described that experiences are "affectively burnt in" the right frontal lobe. Harkness and Tucker (2000) stated that the early traumatic experiences of childhood abuse, literally kindle limbic areas. In this manner, severe early adverse developmental experiences may imprint "neurological scars" (Poeggel et al., 1999) that leave behind a permanent physiological reactivity in limbic areas of the brain (Post et al., 1994), thereby inhibiting its capacity to cope with future stressors.

In light of the fact that males, due to delayed rates of cerebral maturation, are more susceptible than females to a large number of conditions that impair the developing brain, and that the limbic system of males and females show different connectivity patterns, gender differences in developmental traumatology must be considered. These factors indicate that by nature of their CNS and ANS immaturity, males may be more susceptible to relational abuse, and that the dysregulation of early abused males is psychobiologically biased more toward hyperarousal, while females are biased more toward dissociation. These would endure as permanent limbic reactivities that underlie gender predispositions to externalizing and internalizing disorders.

The infant posttraumatic stress disorder episodes of hyperarousal and dissociation imprint the template for later childhood, adolescent, and adult posttraumatic stress disorders, all of which show disturbances of autonomic arousal (Prins et al., 1995), abnormal catecholaminergic function (Geracioti et al., 2001; Southwick et al., 1993), neurologic soft signs (Gurvits et al., 2000), and dissociation (Schore, 2001c). This would be sympomatically expressed as a cycling between intrusive hypersympathetically driven terrifying flashbacks and traumatic images and parasympathetically driven dissociation, avoidance, and numbing. More recent models of PTSD refer to stressor-induced oscillations between traumatic and avoidant states, and cycling between the bidirectional symptoms of emotional reexperiencing and emotional constrictedness (Antelman et al., 1997).

TRAUMA-INDUCED EXCESSIVE PRUNING OF RIGHT-BRAIN CIRCUITS

Even more specifically, social-emotional environments that provide traumatizing attachment histories retard the experience-dependent development of frontolimbic regions, especially the right cortical areas that are prospectively involved in affect regulating functions. These descending projections from the prefrontal cortex to subcortical structures are known to mature during infancy (Bouwmeester, Smits, & van Ree, 2002; Nair, Berndt, Barrett, & Gonzalez-Lima, 2001), and relational traumatic experiences could induce a severe and extensive pruning of higher limbic connections (orbitofrontal, anterior cingulate, and amygdala) into the arousal centers in the reticular formation and autonomic centers in the hypothalamus via a "kindling" (Post et al., 1997) mechanism (see Chapter 6, Figure 6.2).

Relational trauma-induced developmental overpruning of a corticolimbic system, especially one that contains a genetically encoded underproduction of synapses, represents a scenario for high-risk conditions. It is now established that psychological factors "prune" or "sculpt" neural networks in the postnatal brain. In earlier works, I have suggested that excessive pruning of hierarchical cortical-subcortical circuits operates in the etiology of a vulnerability to later extreme disorders of affect regulation (Schore, 1994, 1996, 1997a, 2001c). In the last decade, a growing body of neurobiological research on PTSD has uncovered dysfunctional frontal-subcortical systems (Sutker et al., 1995; Uddo et al., 1993), and altered functional activity of the orbitofrontal cortex (Berthier, Posada, & Puentes, 2001; Bremner et al., 1997; Galletly, Clark, Mcfarlane, & Weber, 2001; Koenen et al., 2001; Shin et al., 1999), anterior cingulate (Bremner et al., 1999; Hamner et al., 1999; Lanius et al., 2001; Shin et al., 2001), and amygdala (Rauch et al., 1996). This represents an uncoupling of components of the rostral limbic system.

An extensive parcellation of axonal-dendritic connections between orbito-frontal and catecholaminergic areas of the midbrain and medullary reticular formation would lead to a predisposition for arousal dysregulation under stress. At the same time severe pruning of its hypothalamic connections would lead to inefficient regulation of the ANS by higher centers in the CNS (Schore, 1997c, 2001c), functionally expressed in a dissociation of central regulation of sympathetic and hypothalamic-pituitary-adrenal systems (Young, Rosa, & Landsberg, 1984). The orbitofrontal cortex, in normal circumstances, represents the apex of a hierarchy of control of autonomic functions. Recall that this system is specialized to show a flexible response in stressful contexts of uncertainty. A loss of these functions means that under stress a coupled reciprocal mode of autonomic control would give way to a coupled nonreciprocal mode of auto-nomic control, resulting in an intensely high state of sympathetic plus parasym-pathetic arousal. Severe dysregulation of both central and autonomic arousal is a hallmark of posttraumatic stress disorders.

The right orbitofrontal cortex is thought to act as the neural basis by which humans control their instinctive emotional responses through cognitive processes, and the emotional disturbances of PTSD are now proposed to have their origins in the inability of the right prefrontal cortex to modulate amygdala functions (Hariri et al., 2000). What could be the origin of a defec-tive "rostral limbic system"? The answer may lie in early development. Amygdala-driven aversive conditioning has been shown to operate in the early attachment to an abusive caregiver (Sullivan, Landers, Yeaman, & Wilson, 2000).

Over the course of postnatal development connections between the orbito-frontal cortex and amygdala increase (Bouwmeester, Wolterink, & van Ree, 2002), and this hierarchical organization allows this prefrontal system to take over amygdala functions (Rolls, 1996), and for the right frontotemporal cortex to maintain inhibitory control over intense emotional arousal (Kinsbourne & Bemporad, 1984). But early traumatic attachment intensifies the parcellation of these right lateralized connections, and so in posttraumatic stress disorders, when orbitofrontal inhibitory control is lost, activity of the right amygdala (Ada-mec, 1999), known to nonconsciously process frightening faces (Whalen et al., 1998) and "unseen fear" (Morris et al., 1999) drives the right brain system. Work on the neurobiology of stress suggests that chronic stress contributes to atrophy of specifically the prefrontal cortex and amygdala (McEwen, 2000).

It is established that a pathological response to stress reflects the functions of a hyperexcitable amygdala (Halgren, 1992), that fear-potentiation of startle is mediated through the amygdala (Angrilli et al., 1996), which directly projects to the brainstem startle center (Davis, 1989), and that the memory processes of the amygdala are amplified by extreme stress (Corodimas et al., 1994). These amygdala-driven startle and fear-freeze responses would be intense, because they are totally unregulated by the orbitofrontal (and medial frontal) areas that are unavailable for the correction and adjustment of emotional responses. Loss of modulating function of the right anterior cingulate, anterior and inferior to the amygdala, would interfere with its known role in inducing a relaxation of bodily states of sympathetic arousal (Critchley, Melmed, Featherstone, Mathias, & Dolan, 2001). In poorly evolved right brain systems of PTSD-vulnerable personalities even low intensity interpersonal stressors could activate unmodulated terrifying and painful bodily-based dysregulated experiences of the individual's early history that are imprinted into amygdalar-hypothalamic limbic-autonomic circuits. According to Valent (1998) early handling and mis-attunements may be deeply remembered physiologically in later life in the form of disconnected physiological responses, emotions, and acting out, a description that mirrors Van der Kolk's (1996) assertion that "the body keeps the score."

In light of the findings that autonomic changes in the body are evoked when angry facial expressions are subliminally presented at levels beneath awareness to the right and not the left hemisphere (Johnsen & Hugdahl, 1991), and that the right amygdala is preferentially activated by briefly presented, subliminal faces (Morris et al., 1998) and specialized for the expression of memory of aversively motivated experiences (Colman-Mensches & McGaugh, 1995), I suggest that subliminal (Mogg et al., 1993) visual and auditory stressors emanating from faces, processed in an inefficient right hemisphere, the locus of the startle mechanism (Bradley, Cuthbert, & Lang, 1996), are potent triggers of dysregulation and dissociation in early traumatized patients. Of special importance is the very rapid right brain perception (Braeutigam, Bailey, & Swithenby, 2001; Funayama, Grillon, Davis, & Phelps, 2001; Nakamura et al., 1999) and memory retrieval (Funnell, Corballis, & Gazzamiga, 2001; Keil et al., 2002; Simons, Graham, Owen, Patterson, & Hodges, 2001) of visual images and prosodic tones of voice that emanate from subjectively perceived threatening and humiliating faces (Schore, 1994, 2001c, 2002a).

These neuropsychological deficits in social cognition underlie the severe interpersonal difficulties in PTSD patients. It is often overlooked that such individuals experience severe social-emotional deficits, including problems in self-disclosure, intimacy, and affection, as well as in the control of interpersonal hostility and aggression (Beckham et al., 1996; Calhoun, Beckham, & Bosworth, 2002; Carroll, Foy, Cannon, & Zwier, 1991). The orbital frontolimbic cortex is centrally involved in not only the regulation of interpersonal behavior (Eslinger, 1999) but also in the regulation of aggression (Schore, 1994). Impairments of the right orbitofrontal region are known to be associated with violence (Blaire & Cipolotti, 2000; Raine et al., 2001). The rapid shifts in mood, aggressive impulses, and interpersonal violence (Beckham et al., 1997; Savarese, Suvak, King, & King, 2001; Yehuda, 1999b) in PTSD paients thus may trace back to early relational trauma-induced limbic dysfunction.

Furthermore, the right, as opposed to the left, amygdala is activated when the individual is not consciously aware of the aversive nature of a nonverbal eliciting stimulus, one that still triggers an immediate negative representation

(Phelps et al., 2001). Loss of function of the right anterior cingulate would preclude its function in attentional processes (Casey et al., 1997). Loss of higher orbital corticolimbic regulation would lead to a deficit in distinguishing between mental representations of ongoing reality and currently irrelevant memories (Schnider, Treyer, & Buck, 2000). When dissociated from these "top-down" influences, an "exaggerated amygdala" response to masked facially expressed fearful reminders of traumatic events occurs in PTSD patients (Rauch et al., 2000).

It is well established that individuals with PTSD show a selective memory and attention for trauma-related experiences (Reynolds & Brewin, 1998). Much has been written about the memory mechanisms of PTSD, and until recently the focus has been upon deficits in hippocampal function and impairments of conscious explicit memory. Stress-induced elevations of cortisol impair declarative memory (Kirschbaum, Wof, May, Wippich, & Hellhammer, 1996). But PTSD models are shifting from the later developing hippocampus to the early developing amygdala, from "cool" to "hot" memory systems (Metcalfe & Jacobs, 1998), from the explicit memory of places to the implicit memory of faces. Very recent research demonstrates that chronic stress induces contrasting patterns of dendritic remodeling in hippocampal and amygdaloid neurons, leading to a loss of hippocampal inhibitory control as well as a gain of excitatory control by the amygdala, and thereby an imbalance in HPA axis function (Vyas, Mitra, Shankaranarayana Rao, & Chattarji, 2002).

This work is complemented by curent neuropsychological models of PTSD which suggest that amygdala inhibition of hippocampal function at high levels of arousal mediates the diminution of conscious explicit memory in peritraumatic events (Layton & Krikorian, 2002). These neurobiological mechanisms may account for the retention of implicit memory yet amnesia for the explicit memory of the traumatic event (Krikorian & Layton, 1998). Indeed, the amygdala is centrally inolved in the consolidation of the traumatic experience and in the storage of perceptual implicit memory for trauma-related information (McNally & Amir, 1996). Recall that the right amygdala is activated in experiences of "unseen fear" (Morris et al., 1999) and that this hemisphere is specialized for the processing of implicit memory (Hugdahl, 1995).

Thus in peritraumatic flashback moments, a right subcortically-driven traumatic re-enactment encoded in implicit memory would occur in the form of a strong physiological autonomic dysregulation and highly aversive motivational state for "no apparent reason." In other words, the person would not be aware that his fear has any origin in space, place, and time. This bears upon McFarlane and Yehuda's observation, "Essentially, the core of traumatic syndromes is the capacity of current environmental triggers (real or symbolic), to provoke the intense recall of affectively charged traumatic memory structures, which come to drive current behaviour and perception" (2000, p. 900). I would add that a focus on cumulative relational instead of "single-hit" trauma emphasizes that the traumatic event of the PTSD patient originated as a personal and social process, thereby suggesting that the "affectively charged traumatic memory" is not of a specific overwhelming experience with the physical environment as much as a reevocation of a prototypical disorganized attachment transaction with the misattuning social environment that triggers an intense arousal dysregulation. The right brain, at nonconscious levels, both appraises trauma-related conditioned social stimuli and (re-)organizes the traumatic "conditioned emotional response" (Kolb & Multipassi, 1982).

Indeed, there is evidence that early relational trauma is particularly expressed in right hemisphere deficits. Studies revealed that maltreated children diagnosed with PTSD manifest right-lateralized metabolic limbic abnormalites (De Bellis, Keshaven, et al., 2000; De Bellis et al., 2002a) and smaller right temporal lobe volumes (De Bellis et al., 2002b), and that right brain impairments associated with severe anxiety disorders are expressed in childhood (De Bellis, Casey, et al., 2000). Adults severely abused in childhood (Raine et al., 2001) and diagnosed with PTSD (Galletly et al., 2001) show reduced right hemisphere activation during a working memory task. Neurological studies of adults confirmed that dysfunction of the right frontal lobe is involved in PTSD symptomatology (Freeman & Kimbrell, 2001) and dissociative flashbacks (Berthier et al., 2001). Neuropsychiatric research indicated that the paralimbic areas of the right hemisphere are preferentially involved in the storage of traumatic memories (Schiffer et al., 1995), that right lateralized activation occurs during acquisition of conditioned fear (Fisher et al., 2002), that altered right-sided activity occurs in panic and social phobic anxiety states (Davidson et al., 2000; Galderisi et al., 2001), and that dissociation is associated with a deficiency of the right brain (Lanius et al., 2002; Weinberg, 2000). Neurobiological research thus suggests a continuity in the expression of the stress coping deficits of posttraumatic stress disorders over the course of the life span.

CONTINUITY AMONG INFANT, CHILDHOOD, AND ADULT PTSD

In parallel work, clinical researchers described a continuity in infant and adult coping deficits:

> The stress responses exhibited by infants are the product of an immature brain processing threat stimuli and producing appropriate responses, while the adult who exhibits infantile responses has a mature brain that, barring stress-related abnormalities in brain development, is capable of exhibiting adult response patterns. However, there is evidence that the adult brain may regress to an infantile state when it is confronted with severe stress. (Nijenhuis et al., 1998, p. 253)

This "infantile state" is a disorganized-disoriented state of insecure attachment. As in infancy, children, adolescents, and adults with posttraumatic stress disorders can not generate an active coherent behavioral coping strategy to confront subjectively perceived overwhelming, dysregulating events, and thus they quickly access the passive survival strategy of disengagement and dissociation.

Indeed, the type D attachment classification has been observed to utilize dissociative behaviors in later stages of life (van Ijzendoorn et al., 1999), and to be implicated in the etiology of the dissociative disorders (Liotti, 1992). The characterological use of dissociation over developmental stages is discussed by Allen and Coyne (1995):

> Although initially they may have used dissociation to cope with traumatic events, they subsequently dissociate to defend against a broad range of daily stressors, including their own posttraumatic symptoms, pervasively undermining the continuity of their experience. (p. 620)

These initial traumatic events are embedded in the abuse and neglect experienced by type D infants, the first relational context in which dissociation is used to autoregulate massive stress. In developmental research, Sroufe and his colleagues concluded that early trauma more so than later trauma has a greater impact on the development of dissociative behaviors (Ogawa et al., 1997). Dissociation, like hyperarousal and elevated heart rate, is a common symptom in PTSD patients, and their occurrence at the time of a trauma is a strong predictor of the disorder (Bremner et al., 1992; Koopman et al., 1994; Shalev et al., 1996, 1998). Although initially an acute response, a chronic pattern of dissociation to even minor stressors develops in these individuals (Bremner & Brett, 1997).

The fact that dissociation becomes a trait in posttraumatic stress disorders has devastating effects on self, and therefore psychobiological functions. In neurological studies of trauma Scaer referred to somatic dissociation, and concluded, "Perhaps the least appreciated manifestations of dissociation in trauma are in the area of perceptual alterations and somatic symptoms" (2001, p. 104). He further pointed out that distortion of proprioceptive awareness of the trauma patient's body is a most common dissociative phenomena. Similarly, in clinical psychiatric studies Nijenhuis (2000) described not just psychological (e.g., amnesia) but "somatoform dissociation," which is associated with early onset traumatization, often involving physical abuse and threat to life by another person. Somatoform dissociation is expressed as a lack of integration of sensorimotor experiences, reactions, and functions of the individual and his/her self-representation.

Clinical research suggests a link between between childhood traumatic experiences and somatoform dissociation in chronic PTSD (and borderline and somatoform disorders) (Waller et al., 2000). The dissociation is manifest as a suppression of autonomic physiological responses (e.g., heart rate and skin conductance), especially when recalling traumatic experiences (Carrey, Butter, Persinger, & Bialek 1995; Griffin, Resick, & Mechanic, 1997; Lanius et al., 2000). A study of psychophysiological reactivity in adults with childhood abuse demonstrated a significant decline in heart rate and diastolic blood pressure in a PTSD patient, while she was dissociating (Schmahl, Elzinga, & Bremner, 2002). Recall that in the previous description of early relational trauma, the infant's dissociative response is mediated by heightened dorsal vagal activity that dramaticaly decreases heart rate and blood pressure. These data suggest that somatic dissociation ontogenetically precedes psychological dissociation.

This shift from the cognitive to the affective-somatic aspects of dissociation is echoed in the neuroscience literature, which describes "a dissociation between the emotional evaluation of an event and the physiological reaction to that event, with the process being dependent on intact right hemisphere function" (Crucian et al., 2000, p. 643). Posttraumatic stress disorders therefore reflect a severe dysfunction of the right brain's role in attachment, regulatory functions, the stress response, and in maintaining a coherent, continuous, and unifed sense of self. Although the right brain's growth spurt is maximal in the first two years, it continues to enter into experience-dependent growth (Thatcher, 1994) and forms connections with the later developing left, which would be impacted by later relational trauma such as sexual abuse in childhood (e.g., Teicher et al., 1997). It is thought that the effectiveness of newly formed and pruned networks in these later stages is limited by the adequacy of already-formed, underlying networks, and therefore maturation is optimal only if the preceding stages were installed optimally (Epstein, 2001).

Traumatic attachment experiences negatively impact the early organization of the right brain, and thereby produce deficits in its adaptive functions of emotionally understanding and reacting to bodily and environmental stimuli, identifying a corporeal image of self and its relation to the environment, distinguishing the self from the other, and generating self-awareness (Devinsky, 2000; Keenan et al., 2001; Ruby & Decety, 2001; Schore, 1994). Optimal attachment experiences allow for the emergence of self-awareness, the adaptive a capacity to sense, attend to, and reflect upon the dynamic changes of one's subjective self states, but traumatic attachments in childhood lead to self-modulation of painful affect by directing attention away from internal emotional states.

From a psychoneurobiological perspective, dissociation reflects the inability of the right brain cortical-subcortical system to recognize and coprocess (integrate) external stimuli (exteroceptive information coming from the environment) and internal stimuli (interoceptive information from the body, the corporeal self). According to van der Kolk and McFarlane (1996), a central feature of PTSD is a loss of the ability to physiologically modulate stress responses which leads to a reduced capacity to utilize bodily signals as guides to action, and this alteration of psychological defense mechanisms is associated with an impairment of personal identity.

These deficits are the expression of an malfunctioning orbitofrontal cortical-subcortical system, the senior executive of the right brain (Schore, 1994, 1996, 1998a, 2000b, 2000c, 2001a). In light of the finding that the orbitofrontal cortex is involved in critical human functions that are crucial in defining the 'personality' of an individual (Cavada & Schultz, 2000), personality organizations that characterologically access dissociation can be described as possessing an inefficient orbital frontolimbic regulatory system and a developmentally immature coping mechanism. And because adequate limbic function is required to allow the brain to adapt to a rapidly changing environment and organize new learning (Mesulam, 1998), a metabolically altered orbitofrontal system would interfere with ongoing social emotional development. Early failures in attachment thus skew the developmental trajectory of the right brain over the rest of the life span, thereby engendering what Bowlby described as a diverting of development from its adaptive course, and precluding what Janet called an "enlargement" of personality development.

DE-EVOLUTION OF RIGHT BRAIN LIMBIC CIRCUITS AND PTSD PATHOGENESIS

According to Krystal (1988), the long-term effect of infantile psychic trauma is the arrest of affect development. Because emotions involve rapid nonconscious appraisals of events that are important to the individual (Frijda, 1988) and represent reactions to fundamental relational meanings that have adaptive significance (Lazarus, 1991a), this enduring developmental impairment is expressed in a variety of critical dysfunctions of the right brain. PTSD patients, especially when stressed, show severe deficits in the preattentive reception and expression of facially expressed emotion, the processing of somatic information, the communication of emotional states, the maintaining of interactions with the social environment, the use of higher level more efficient defenses, the capacity to access an empathic stance and a reflective function, and the psychobiological ability to regulate, either by autoregulation or interactive regulation, and thereby recover from stressful affective states. Most of these dysfunctions represent pathological alterations of implicit, unconscious mechanisms. Note that they also describe the deficits of borderline personality disorders, a condition that correlates highly with PTSD and shares both a history of early attachment trauma and orbitofrontal and amygdala dysfunction (see Schore, 2001c).

Furthermore, the observations that in human infancy, the right brain, the neurobiological locus of the stress response, organizes in an affective experience-dependent fashion, and that the emotion processing and stress coping limbic system evolves in stages, from the amygdala, to anterior cingulate, to orbitofrontal cortex (Schore, 1994, 2001a), supports the concept of de-evolution as a mechanism of symptom generation in PTSD. Wang, Wilson, and Mason (1996) described "stages of decompensation" in chronic PTSD, reflected in incremental impairments in amplified hyperarousal symptoms and defensive dissociation, decreased range of spontaneity and facial expression, heightened dysregulation of self-esteem, deepening loss of contact with the environment, reduced attachment and insight, and increased probability of destruction and suicide. Intriguingly, they posited the existence of specifically three stages beneath a level of good to maximum functioning, and suggest each stage is physiologically distinct.

The concept of "decompensation" describes a condition in which a system is rapidly disorganizing over a period of time. This construct derives from Jackson's (1931) classic principle that pathology involves a "dissolution," a loss of inhibitory capacities of the most recently evolved layers of the nervous system that support higher functions (negative symptoms), as well as the release of lower, more automatic functions (positive symptoms). This principle applies to the dissolution or disorganization of the brain's complex circuit of emotion regulation of orbital frontal cortex, anterior cingulate, and amygdala (Davidson et al., 2000; Schore, 2000b, 2001a).

And so it is tempting to speculate that the stage model of Wang and her colleagues describes a Jacksonian deevolution of the "rostral limbic system" (Devinsky et al., 1995), in reverse developmental order, from orbitofrontal loss, to anterior cingulate loss, and finally to amygdala dysfunction. At a certain threshold of stress, the frontolimbic systems of PTSD patients would be unable to perform a higher regulatory function over lower levels, thereby releasing lower level right amygdala activity, without the adaptive capacity of flexibly reinitiating higher control functions. Heightened baseline right amygdala metabolism is found in patients with major depressive disorder (Abercombie et al., 1998). The amygdala is activated in states of helplessness (Schneider et al., 1996), and thus may be the key brain system that triggers the onset of conservation-withdrawal.

In addition, in light of the fact that the orbitofrontal, anterior cingulate, and amygdala systems each connect into the ANS (Schore, 2001a), the mechanism of deevolution dynamics would also apply to the hierarchical disorganization of the autonomic nervous system. This would be manifest in long-lasting episodes of a coupled nonreciprocal mode of autonomic control, in which concurrent increases (or decreases) occur in both sympathetic and parasympathetic components, or uncoupled nonreciprocal mode of autonomic control, in which responses in one division of the ANS occur in absence of change in the other. In other words, the ANS would too easlily be displaced from a state of autonomic balance, and once displaced, have difficulty in re-establishing balance, that is, show a poor capacity for vagal rebound and recovery from psychological stress (Mezzacappa, Kelsey, Katkin, & Sloan, 2001).

This deevolution would also be manifest in a stress-associated shift down from the higher ventral vagal complex (which is known to be defective in posttraumatic stress disorder; Sahar, Shalev, & Porges, 2001) to the dorsal vagal complex that mediates severe emotional states of terror, immobilization, and dissociation. Ultimately higher vagal functions would be metabolically compromised, and dorsal vagal activity would predominate even in a resting state. This lowest level may be seen in infants raised in a neglectful environment (Gunnar & Vazquz, 2001), mothers of child cancer survivors with PTSD (Glover &

Poland, 2002), chronic PTSD patients with low cortisol levels (Mason et al., 1990, 2001), suicidal patients with severe right brain deficiencies experiencing intense despair (Weinberg, 2000), and Wang and colleagues' (1996) final stage of depression — hopelessness. I suggest low levels are also found in coronary patients showing "vital exhaustion" (Kop et al., 1994). This conception therefore suggests qualitative physiological as well as symptomatic differences between acute and chronic PTSD populations, and it relates developmental models of early organization to later clinical models of disorganization.

At the beginning of the this chapter, I suggested that a developmental psychoneurobiologial perspective can deepen our understanding of the deficits of mind and body seen in chronic PTSD. I then outlined how early physical abuse and relational trauma induce central and autonomic hyperarousal, the latter associated with severe states of bodily dysregulation and subjecive pain. It is established that the child's reactivity and the parenting context contribute to changes in the infant's pain response (Sweet, McGrath, & Symons, 1999), that non-optimal parenting contributes to chronic pain patterns in certain children who have experienced prolonged or repeated pain as neonates (Grunau, Whitfield, Petrie, & Fryer, 1994), and that persistent pain experiences during the early neonatal period, a critical period for the organization of nociceptive neuronal circuits, rewires immature pain circuits, and leads to lasting and potentially detrimental alterations in the individual's response to pain in adulthood (Ruda, Ling, Hohmann, Peng, & Tachibana, 2000).

These effects may reflect an alteration of the experience-dependent maturation of the right hemisphere, specifically the right insular cortex that is dominant for the representation of somatic sensation and pain (Ostrowsky et al., 2002), the right anterior cingulate that plays a central role in the sensorial/affective aspect of pain (Hsieh et al., 1995b; Price, 2000), and the right lateral orbitofrontal regions that modulate distant processing of pain and therefore coping with a painful stimulus (Petrovic, Petersson, Ghatan, Stone-Elander, & Ingvar, 2000). This relational trauma-induced structural limitation of right limbic circuits in processing pain may be exposed under later stress, and play a critical role in PTSD pathogenesis. Indeed, there is extensive documentation that persistent pain is frequently associated with symptoms of PTSD (Benedikt & Kolb, 1986; Chibnall & Duckro, 1994; Geissner, Roth, Bachman, & Eckert, 1996; Perry et al., 1987; Smith, Egert, Winkel, & Jacobson, 2002).

The endpoint of chronically experiencing catastrophic states of relational-induced trauma in early life is a progressive impairment of the ability to adjust, take defensive action, or act on one's own behalf, and a blocking of the capacity to register affect and pain, all critical to survival. These individuals perceive themselves as different from other people and outside of, as well as unworthy of, meaningful attachments (Lansky, 1995). Henry (cited in Wang, 1997) echoed this conclusion:

> The ability to maintain personally relevant bonds is vital for our evolutionary survival. The infant's tie to the mother's voice and odor is recog-

nized even by the newborn (van Lancker, 1991), yet this personal relevance and recognition of the familiar can be impaired by anxious insecurity resulting from difficult early experiences or traumatic stress. The vital task of establishing a personally relevant universe and the solace derived from it depend on right hemispheric functioning. If this function is indeed lost in the insecurely attached, much has been lost. (p. 168)

These survival limitations may negatively impact not just psychological but also essential organismic functions in coping with physical disease. Studies are linking attachment, stress, and disease (Maunder & Hunter, 2001; Schmidt, Nachtigall, Wuethrich-Martone, & Strauss, 2002) and childhood attachment and adult cardiovascular and cortisol function (Luecken, 1998), as well documenting effects of childhood abuse on multiple risk factors for several of the leading causes of death in adults (Fellitti et al., 1998).

This developmental neurobiological model has significant implications for psychiatry and the other mental health professions. The organization of the brain's essential coping mechanisms occurs in critical periods of infancy. The construct of critical periods implies that certain detrimental early influences lead to particular irreversible or only partially reversible enduring effects. But the flip side of the critical period concept emphasizes the extraordinary sensitivity of developing dynamic systems to their environment, and asserts that these systems are most plastic in these periods. The development of the right brain is experience-dependent, and this experience is embedded in the attachment relationship between caregiver and infant.

Attachment researchers in association with infant mental health workers are devising interventions that effectively alter the affect-communicating capacities of mother-infant systems, and thereby the attachment experiences of high risk dyads. Early interventions that are timed to critical periods of development of the right brain, the locus of the human stress response, can facilitate the maturation of neurobiologically adaptive stress coping systems, and thereby have lifelong effects on the adaptive capacities of a developing self. Early treatment and prevention programs, if expanded onto a societal scale, could significantly diminish the number of individuals who develop pathological reactions of mind and body to catastrophic life events. These efforts could, in turn, make deep inroads into not only altering the intergenerational transmission of post-traumatic stress disorders but improving the quality of many lives throughout all stages of human development.

2002

CHAPTER 9

Effect of Early Relational Trauma on Affect Regulation: The Development of Borderline and Antisocial Personality Disorders and a Predisposition to Violence

I N THE INTRODUCTION TO ROBIN KARR-MORSE and Meredith Wiley's landmark book on the early roots of violence, *Ghosts From the Nursery*, pediatrician Berry Brazelton stated, "experiences in infancy which result in the child's *inability to regulate strong emotions* are too often the overlooked source of violence in children and adults" (1997, p. xiii; italics added). When a child commits a violent act, it means that his or her developmental trajectory has gone seriously askew so very early in the life span. The fact that he can not even make it through the next developmental stage (much less the later challenges of adulthood) is a direct outcome of a severe growth-inhibiting environment in his very beginnings, in his first relationship, the one in the nursery. In their book, Karr-Morse and Wiley turned to new findings in what was then "the Decade of the Brain" that directly related to the problem of why interpersonal deprivations and failures in the earliest stages of human development serve as a primordial matrix for a personality that is high-risk for violence.

Despite overall decreases in violent crime in this country, statistics document that increases in the juvenile homicide rate have surpassed those of adults (Helmuth, 2000). A large proportion of current referrals to child and adolescent clinical services involve serious antisocial behaviors (Kazdin, Siegel, & Bass, 1990). This alarming trend compels us to look for the underlying causal mechanisms of violence, mechanisms that are already fully operational in childhood. A growing body of studies indicates that traumatic childhood experiences provide the contexts for the roots of adult violence. But now we're confronted with an increasing number of violent offenders who are still in their first decade of life, "early onset antisocial youth" (Loeber & Farrington, 2000), and this is telling us that we must look even earlier, indeed to the literal beginnings for the essential causal factors.

In this work I focus on the events in the nursery, not metaphorically, but through the lenses of developmental neuroscience, attachment theory, and infant psychiatry. In recent contributions I have modeled how severe traumatic attachments result in structural limitations of the early developing right brain, expressed in a number of enduring functional deficits, including a fundamental inability to regulate emotional states under stress (Schore, 1998g, 1998i, 1999d, 1999g, 2000b, 2001c, 2001e, 2002b). It is well established that the loss of the ability to regulate the intensity of affects is the most far-reaching effect of early traumatic abuse and neglect. Theoretical and clinical studies are focusing upon the direct connections between early traumatic attachment experiences and the inability of certain personalities to regulate fear-terror states, and therefore to developing a high risk for posttraumatic stress disorders (Schore, 1997a, 2001c, 2002b).

But here I want to suggest that another affect that can become dysregulated by early relational trauma is aggression. If the intense fear of PTSD represents a dysregulation of the brain "flight" systems, aggression disorders represent a dysregulation of the brain's "fight" centers. Each reflects a dysregulation of a pattern of autonomic nervous system (ANS) sympathetic hyperarousal, one associated with intense terror, the other with intense rage. These impairments are manifest at early ages in personalities who are high-risk for psychiatric disorders. Research now indicates that "exposure to early life stress is associated with neurobiological changes in children and adults, which may underlie the increased risk of psychopathology" (Heim & Nemeroff, 2001, p. 1023).

This general principle also applies to early trauma-associated psychopathologies of aggression dysregulation, including borderline and antisocial personality disorders. The American Psychiatric Association (1994) described antisocial (psychopathic) personality disorder as showing irritability and aggressiveness, as indicated by frequent physical fights and assaults, while borderline personality disorder manifests inappropriate, intense anger or difficulty controlling anger (e.g., frequent displays of temper, constant anger, recurrent physical fights). Both are therefore capable of violence, episodes of intense aggressive emotional states, psychobiologically driven by a hyperactive subcortical psychobiological core, that are dysregulated in both intensity and duration and cut off from feedback systems in the internal and external environment.

The interpersonal aspect of violence is highlighted in its definition as "aggression that has extreme harm as its goal (e.g., death)" and the intrapersonal aspect in its association with aggressive personalities (Anderson & Bushman, 2002, p. 29). I shall later argue that the psychopathic personality is susceptible to "cold blooded" predatory proactive aggression, while the borderline personality to "hot blooded" impulsive reactive aggression. The excessively impulsive, undermodulated state of blind rage is described by Horowitz (1992):

Not thinking, all feeling. He wants to demolish and destroy persons who frustrate him. He is not aware of ever loving or even faintly liking the object. He has no awareness that his rage is a passion that will decline. He believes he will hate the object forever. (p. 80)

I further propose that it is impossible to make definitive statements about the early roots of violence without considering what we now know about the early roots of human life, the process of development itself (Karmiloff-Smith, 1998; Schore, 1994). Why are the experiences that take place in the nursery, the very earliest events of human life, so critical to everything that follows? But in addition, I argue that we know enough about the structural biological development of the brain that we must go beyond purely functional psychological theories of the development of a predisposition to violence. A recent consensus statement on an understanding of violence concluded, "As is the case of all human behaviors, it is crucial to remember that an understanding of the organ producing the behavior cannot be overlooked" (Filley et al., 2001, p. 12).

This leads to the questions: How do early attachment experiences positively impact maturing brain structures and thereby the developmental process? By what mechanisms do early relational traumatic attachment experiences negatively impact brain development and deflect the developmental trajectory? Childhood traumatic maltreatment not only results in enduring brain deficits, but also acts as a risk factor for both the development of personality disorders in early adulthood (Johnson, Cohen, Brown, Smailes, & Bernstein, 1999). In other words, a deeper understanding of the genesis of a high risk for personality disorders of aggression dysregulation must integrate both the psychological and biological realms. The concept of trauma, which is by definition psychobiological, is a bridge between the domains of both mind and body.

INTRODUCTION

The idea that early trauma has an indelible negative impact upon the developing personality has a long history in psychology. In his last writings Freud (1981/1940) asserted that trauma in early life affects all vulnerable humans because "the ego . . . is feeble, immature and incapable of resistance." It should be emphasized that trauma in human infancy includes both abuse and neglect (Schore, 2001b, 2002b). Both are underreported with neglect and abandonment less likely to be ascertained than violent maltreatment (Crume, DiGuisoppi, Byers, et al., 2002). Physically abused infants show high levels of negative affect, while neglected infants demonstrate flattened affect (Gaensbauer & Hiatt, 1984). There is evidence indicating that neglect may be even more damaging than abuse (Hildyard & Wolfe, 2002), and that there is a link between neglect in childhood and antisocial personality disorders in later life (Lang, af Klinteberg, & Alm, 2002; Luntz & Widom, 1994). But the worst case scenario is, not infrequently, found in a child who experiences both abuse and neglect (Post & Weiss, 1997). There is agreement that severe trauma of inter-

personal origin may override any genetic, constitutional, social, or psychological resilience factor (De Bellis, 2001).

Furthermore, the perpetrator of abuse or neglect is most often one of the
primary caregivers (Graham et al., 1999). Such developmental trauma is relational, usually not a singular event but cumulative, a characteristic feature of
an impaired attachment relationship (Schore, 2001b). The ongoing repetitive
relational stressors embedded in a severely misattuned attachment relationship
means that the infant is experiencing not acute but chronic stress in the first
two years of life. In an editorial on child abuse in the *Journal of Trauma and
Dissociation*, Chu (2001) asserted,

> The child protective service statistics do not differentiate cases of single
> episodes of abuse from repetitive abuse, and it is particularly important
> to identify children who are chronically abused and victims of multiple
> types of abuse. These traumatized children are the most likely to go on
> to develop impairments in psychological functioning, specific psychiatric
> symptomatology, and changes in brain function. (p. 3)

Similarly, the consensus statement of the panel on an understanding of violence at the Aspen Neurobiobehavioral Conference concludes that violence in
children may be a product of "negative experiences such as early maternal
rejection and unstable family environment" and that "child abuse, particularly
that involving physical injury, may be especially damaging." Furthermore,
"exposure to emotionally traumatic or violent experiences may exert a profound
effect on behavior, presumably through their actions on the developing brain"
(Filley et al., 2001, p. 7). These authors then go on to specify the brain systems
involved in violence, specifically the temporolimbic areas of the subcortical
amygdala that are involved in the expression of aggressive states, and the corticolimbic areas in the orbitofrontal (ventromedial) cortex that control aggression.

A large body of studies in neurobiology indicates that an impairment of the
orbitofrontal cortex is a central mechanism in the behavioral expression of violence (e.g., Best, Williams, & Coccaro, 2002; Brower & Price, 2000; Dinn &
Harris 2000; Dolan & Park, 2002; Fornazzari et al., 1992; Grafman et al.,
1996; Miller et al., 1997; Raine, Meloy, et al., 1998; Raine, Stoddard, et al.,
1998; Schore, 1994, 1999c, 2001c, 2001d; Starkstein & Robinson, 1997; Volavka, 1999). It is well established that neurological damage of this system is
associated with "neurologically acquired sociopathy" (Blair & Cipolotti, 2000;
Tranel, 1994), that focal damage to the orbitofrontal cortex represents a neural
basis of sociopathy (Damasio, 2000), and that neurological impairment of this
prefrontal system in the first 18 months of life is associated with abnormal
development of social and moral behavior and a syndrome, later in life, resem-
bling psychopathy (Anderson et al., 1999).

I have suggested that the neurological trauma embedded in early relational
abuse and neglect can also produce an impaired orbitofrontal system, and

therefore a "developmentally acquired sociopathy" (Schore, 1999c, 2001f). An entire issue of the journal *Biological Psychiatry* is devoted to development and vulnerability, and in it De Bellis and colleagues concluded, "the overwhelming stress of maltreatment in childhood is associated with adverse influences on brain development" (1999, p. 1281l). We know that early psychosocial stressors, specifically from a severely missattuned maternal environment, can negatively impact brain development, including brain systems involved in aggression regulation (Glaser, 2000; Schore, 1994, 1996, 1997a, 1997d, 1998g, 2000e, 2001c, 2002b).

In current writings on the origins of violence, Cairns and Stoff (1996) stated,

> It is highly unlikely that the problem of aggression and violence can be reduced to a single gene or dysfunction . . . of a nerve cell. More than likely, multiple biological systems are involved and these systems act in concert with . . . the social realm. (p. 349)

The most in-depth investigations of the "social realm" occur within the province of attachment theory, "the dominant approach to understanding early socioemotional and personality development during the past quarter-century of research" (Thompson, 2000, p. 145). Recall that the first work published by Bowlby, the creator of attachment theory, was a study of the early histories of "Forty-four juvenile thieves" (1944).

The explosion of developmental studies is relevant to why certain personalities are high-risk for violence. Prolonged and frequent episodes of intense and unregulated stress in infants and toddlers have devastating effects on "the establishment of psychophysiological regulation and the development of stable and trusting attachment relationships in the first year of life" (Gaensbauer & Siegel, 1995, p. 294). These effects endure — a "type D" disorganized/disoriented insecure attachment pattern seen in abused and neglected infants predicts later chronic disturbances of affect regulation, stress management, and hostile-aggressive behavior (Lyons-Ruth & Jacobovitz, 1999). Although other organized insecure attachment patterns are associated with limitations in coping with aggressive states, this attachment pattern is involved in the etiologies of a high-risk for both posttraumatic stress disorder and a predisposition to relational violence (Schore, 1997a, 1998i, 1999c, 1999d, 1999g, 2000e, 2001c, 2001e, 2001f, 2002b). Main (1996) argued that "disorganized" forms of insecure attachment are primary risk factors for the development of psychiatric disorders. This includes disorders of aggression dysregulation (Schore, 1994).

RELATIONAL TRAUMA AND
RIGHT-BRAIN DEVELOPMENT

My own work in developmental affective neuroscience and developmental neuropsychiatry integrates psychological data of attachment theory and the data of developmental neurobiology. This psychoneurobiological perspective focuses on the first two years of life, when the human brain grows faster than any other stage of the life cycle. This interval exactly overlaps the period of attachment so intensely studied by contemporary developmental psychology. A fundamental tenet of Bowlby's (1969) model is that for better or worse, the infant's "capacity to cope with stress" is correlated with certain maternal behaviors.

The central thesis of my ongoing work is that the early social environment, mediated by the primary caregiver, directly influences the final wiring of the circuits in the infant brain that are responsible for the future social and emotional coping capacities of the individual. The attachment relationship thus directly shapes the maturation of the infant's right brain, which performs essential functions in both the assessment of visual or auditory emotional communicative signals (Nakamura et al., 1999) and the human stress response (Wittling, 1997). The ultimate product of this social-emotional development is a particular system in the prefrontal areas of the right brain that is capable of regulating emotions (Hariri et al., 2000; Schore, 1994, 1996, 1998a, 1998e, 1999b, 2000a, 2000b, 2000d, 2000e, 2001a, 2001d), including positive emotions such as joy and interest as well as negative emotions such as fear and aggression.

This work bears directly upon the problem of the etiology of violent personalities. The early traumatic dysregulating transactions with the social environment lead to more than an insecure attachment, they negatively impact the maturation of the brain during its growth spurt from the last trimester of pregnancy through the middle of the second year (Dobbing & Sands, 1973). This exact interval represents a period of accelerated growth of the right hemisphere:

> The right hemisphere is more advanced than the left in surface features from about the 25th (gestational) week and this advance persists until the left hemisphere shows a post-natal growth spurt starting in the second year. (Trevarthen, 1996, p. 582)

Thus, traumatic attachments act as a growth-inhibiting environment for the experience-dependent maturation of the right hemisphere, which is in a critical period of growth in the first year of life and dominant for the first three (Chiron et al., 1997). A MRI study of infants reported that the volume of the brain increases rapidly during the first two years, that normal adult appearance is seen at 2 years and all major fiber tracts can be identified by age 3, and that infants under 2 years show higher right than left hemispheric volumes (Matsuzawa et al., 2001).

There is agreement that the enduring effects of early abuse are specifically reflected in the impaired processing of both social and bodily information. In a number of works I offered data that indicates early trauma alters the development of the right brain, the hemisphere that is dominant for the unconscious processing of socioemotional information, the regulation of bodily states, the capacity to cope with emotional stress, and the corporeal and emotional self

(Schore 1994, 1996, 2000b, 2000c, 2001a). The right brain is specialized to process socioemotional information at levels beneath awareness, and so it is dominant for unconscious processes and fast-acting regulatory operations.

It is clear that threat-related cues associated with danger are nonconsciously processed (LeDoux, 1996) and that the autoregulation of aggression involves the operation of a self-regulatory mechanism operating at a preconscious level (Berkowitz, 1990). And so an enduring developmental impairment of the right brain would be expressed as a severe limitation in the ability, at levels beneath conscious awareness, to self-regulate negative states, such as fear and aggression. As opposed to nondestructive aggression, hostile destructiveness is associated with the dysregulated experience of excessive bodily pain and distress, is self-protective, and is present in its most primitive form in infancy (Parens, 1987).

In over two dozen contributions, I continued to offer experimental and clinical data characterizing the central role of the highest limbic level of the right brain, the right hemispheric orbitofrontal system, in the regulation of adaptive affective, motivational, and cognitive functions. Referring back to Brazelton's (1997) suggestion that the child's inability to regulate strong emotions is associated with violence, a growing body of evidence implicates the central role of the prefrontal areas of the right brain in affect regulation. A developmentally mature hierarchical orbitofrontal system regulates lower areas in the right brain that generate positive and negative affective states, including aggressive states, but a developmentally impaired right prefrontal cortex is vulnerable, especially under interpersonal stress, to disorders of aggression regulation. Thus,

> [D]epending on the presence of other social triggers and *early stressful environmental circumstances*, increased right hemisphere subcortical activity could predispose the individual to experience negative affect which fosters aggressive feelings and which in turn act as a general predisposition to violent behavior. (Raine, Meloy, et al., 1998, p. 329; italics added)

The maturation of the orbitofrontal areas, the brain's central emotion-regulating system, occurs completely postnatally, and their development is positively or negatively shaped by attachment experiences. The functional coping deficits of the disorganized/disoriented insecure attachment pattern thus reflect a severe structural defect of the orbitofrontal cortex (Schore, 2001c, 2002b), the brain system involved in "critical human functions, such as social adjustment and the control of mood, drive and responsibility, traits that are crucial in defining the 'personality' of an individual" (Cavada & Schultz, 2000, p. 205). But it is also thought that the "orbitofrontal cortex represents a brain region of particular interest with respect to violence because dysfunction in this brain area results in personality and emotional deficits that parallel criminal psychopathic behavior" (Raine, Stoddard, et al., 1998, p. 5).

This frontolimbic cortex is expanded in the right hemisphere (Falk et al., 1990), and is known as the "senior executive" of the social emotional right brain. A structural limitation of the right brain is responsible for the individual's inability to regulate emotion, which is a central deficit in aggressive personalities. Converging research indicates that activation of the right hemishere is associated with negative emotions (Hellige, 1993), that the self-regulation of negative emotions is low in aggressive personalities, and that antisocial personality disorders show greater activation of the resting electroencephalogram in the right hemisphere relative to the left (Deckel, Hasselbroock, & Bauer, 1996).

Furthermore, neurological studies with adult patients revealed that lesions in the right, but not left, orbitofrontal areas produce increased unregulated aggression (Grafman et al., 1996), and that "acquired sociopathy" results from neurological trauma to the right orbitofrontal region (Blair & Cipolotti, 2000). In neuropsychological research Raine and colleagues found that "reductions in right orbitofrontal functioning may be a particularly important predisposition to violence" (1998, p. 6), and observed reduced right hemisphere activation during a working memory task in severely abused violent offenders (Raine et al., 2001). In his review of biosocial studies of antisocial and violent behavior, Raine concluded that "a biological risk factor (initial right hemisphere dysfunctional), when combined with a psychosocial risk factor (severe early physical abuse) predisposes to serious violence" (2002, p. 319).

With this introduction, in the following I will elaborate upon this psychoneurobiological model of the early etiology of a predisposition to violence. A fundamental principle of the discipline of developmental psychopathology is that we need to understand normal development in order to understand abnormal development. Abuse and neglect not only expose the immature infant to threatening experiences, they also deprive the developing brain/mind/body of vital growth-facilitating interpersonal experiences that are requisite for the continuing experience-dependent maturation of the right brain.

In this chapter I will briefly outline the brain events of a secure attachment and the resultant organization of an adaptive regulatory system in the prefrontal areas of the right hemisphere. I will then describe the neuropsychology of a disorganized/disoriented *in*secure attachment pattern found in traumatized infants and children with aggressive behavior problems, the inhibitory effects of early trauma on the development of prefrontal systems involved in aggression regulation, the continuity of aggression dysregulation over the course of the life span, and a model of the etiology of the patterns of violence potential in borderline and antisocial personality disorders. And I will conclude with a few words on the implications of this model for early intervention programs. These psychoneurobiological models are offered as heuristic proposals that can be evaluated by experimental and clinical research.

OVERVIEW OF THE AFFECTIVE PSYCHOLOGY
OF A SECURE ATTACHMENT

The essential task of the first year of human life is the creation of a secure attachment bond of emotional communication between the infant and the primary caregiver. Within mutual gaze episodes of affect synchrony (Feldman et al., 1999) parents engage in intuitive, nonconscious, facial, vocal, and gestural preverbal communications. These experiences, which the parent carries out "unknowingly and can hardly control consciously,"

> provide young infants with a large amount of episodes — often around
> 20 per minute during parent-infant interactions — in which parents make
> themselves contingent, easily predictable, and manipulatable by the infant. (Papousek et al., 1991, p. 110)

In order to do this, the mother must be psychobiologically attuned to the dynamic crescendos and decrescendos of the infant's bodily-based internal states of arousal. Within a context of visual-facial, auditory-prosodic, and gestural preverbal communication, each partner learns the rhythmic structure of the other and modifies his or her behavior to fit that structure, thereby cocreating a specifically fitted interaction. The synchronizing caregiver facilitates the infant's unique information-processing capacities by adjusting the mode, amount, variability, and timing of the onset and offset of stimulation to the infant's actual integrative capacities, his "windows of tolerance" (Siegel, 1999).

In this interactively regulated context the more the mother tunes her activity level to the infant during periods of social engagement, the more she allows him to recover quietly in periods of disengagement, and the more she attends to the child's reinitiating cues for reengagement, the more synchronized their interaction. In play episodes, the pair are in affective resonance, and in such, an amplification of vitality affects and a positive state occurs especially when the mother's psychobiologically attuned external sensory stimulation frequency coincides with the infant's genetically encoded endogenous rhythms.

When an attuned dyad cocreates a resonant context within an attachment transaction, the behavioral manifestation of each partner's internal state is monitored by the other, and this results in the coupling between the output of one partner's loop and the input of the other's to form a larger feedback configuration and an amplification of the positive state in both. In order to enter into this communication, the primary caregiver must also monitor her own internal signals and differentiate her own affective state, as well as modulating nonoptimal high or low levels of stimulation which would induce supra-heightened or extremely low levels of arousal in the infant.

In these exchanges of affect synchrony, as the mother and infant match each other's temporal and affective patterns, each recreates an inner psychophysiological state similar to the partner's. Stern (1983a) described moment-to-moment state sharing, feeling the same as the other (interactive regulation), and state complementing, responding in one's unique way to stimuli coming from the other (autoregulation). In contexts of "mutually attuned selective cueing," the infant learns to preferentially send social cues to which the mother has responded, thereby reflecting "an anticipatory sense of response of the other to the self, concomitant with an accommodation of the self to the other" (Bergman, 1999, p. 96).

And in moments of interactive repair the "good-enough" primary caregiver who induces a stress response in her infant through a misattunement, reinvokes in a timely fashion a reattunement, a regulation of the infant's negative state. Active parental participation in state regulation is critical to enabling the child to shift from the negative affective states of hyperaroused protest or hypoaroused despair to a re-established state of positive affect. Again, the key to this is the caregiver's capacity to monitor and regulate her own affect, especially negative affect. Maternal sensitivity thus acts as an external organizer of the infant's biobehavioral regulation (Spangler et al., 1994).

If attachment is the regulation of interactive synchrony, stress is defined as an asynchrony in an interactional sequence, and, following this, a period of reestablished synchrony allows for stress recovery and coping. The regulatory processes of affect synchrony that creates states of positive arousal and interactive repair that modulates states of negative arousal are the fundamental building blocks of attachment and its associated emotions, and resilience in the face of stress is an ultimate indicator of attachment security. Attachment, the outcome of the child's genetically encoded biological predisposition and the particular caregiver environment, thus represents the regulation of biological synchronicity between organisms, and imprinting, the learning process that mediates attachment, is defined as synchrony between sequential infant-maternal stimuli and behavior (Schore, 2000a, 2000c, 2001c). The attachment mechanism, the dyadic regulation of emotion, thus psychobiologically modulates positive states, such as excitement and joy, but also negative states, such as fear and aggression.

In regard to the developmental regulation of aggression, it is especially important to emphasize that subsequent to the child's formation of attachment to the mother in the first year, the child forms another, in the second year to the father (Schore, 1994). According to Herzog, "the biorhythmicity of man with infant and woman with infant" affords the infant to have "interactive, state-sharing, and state-attuning experiences with two different kinds of caregivers" (2001, p. 55). He further asserted that this paternal function is "entirely contingent on the presence of homeostatic-attuned caregiving by the mother" (p. 260). Indeed, developmental researchers observe the formation of a second attachment system to the father emerges in the second year (Schaffer & Emerson, 1964), as the child now expresses a separation response to the absence of either parent. Research demonstrates that the quality of the toddler's attachment to the father is independent of that to the mother (Main & Weston, 1981), and that at 18 months both a "mother attachment system" and a "father attachment system" are operational (Abelin, 1971).

In parallel work, classical developmental psychoanalytic observational research indicates that in the second year the child shows more intense interest in the father's emotional availability (Mahler et al., 1975), and that an early experience of being protected by the father and caringly loved by him becomes internalized as a lifelong sense of safety (Blos, 1984). At this point he takes over from the early mother some significant portions of infantile attachment emotions, but in particular, he is critically involved in the development of the toddler's regulation of aggression. This is true of both sexes, but particularly boys, who are born with a greater aggressive endowment (Maccoby, 1966). Herzog pointed out that through the father's careful use of his own aggression he helps the boy to modulate and integrate his own burgeoning aggression, and states that his "stimulating, gear-shifting, disruptive, limit-setting play" mobilizes intense affect, and facilitates "radical reorganization and further developmental progression" (2001, p. 261).

OVERVIEW OF THE NEUROBIOLOGY OF A SECURE ATTACHMENT

The developmental progressions of emerging functions observed in the first two years of human life occur during during stages of the brain growth spurt. It is thought that "the intrinsic regulators of human brain growth in a child are specifically adapted to be coupled, by emotional communication, to the regulators of adult brains" (Trevarthen, 1990, p. 357). And so the emotional communications embedded within mutual gaze transactions impact the developing brain, especially early maturing limbic areas (Kinney et al., 1988) and cortical association areas of the right brain that myelinate in the first two years. These structures are specialized for assessing familiar faces, gaze direction, and processing visual or auditory emotional communicative signals (Acerra, Burnod, & de Schonen, 2002; Deruelle & de Schonen, 1998; Dimberg & Patterson, 2000; Nakamura et al., 1999, 2000; Ricciardelli, Ro, & Driver, 2002; Watanabe, Miki, & Kakigi, 2002; Wicker, Michel, Henaff, & Decety, 1998). According to Buck (1994),

> This spontaneous emotional communication constitutes a conversation between limbic systems . . . It is a biologically based communication system that involves individual organisms directly with one another: the individuals in spontaneous communication constitute literally a biological unit. The direct involvement with the other intrinsic to spontaneous communication represents an attachment that may satisfy deeply emotional social motives. (p. 266)

Neuroimaging studies demonstrate that infants as young as two months show right hemispheric activation when exposed to a woman's face (Tzourio-Mazoyer et al., 2002), that 5-month-old infants show a spontaneous smile on the left face reflecting right hemispheric control of emotional expression (Holowka & Petitto, 2002), and that the human maternal response to an infant's cry, a fundamental behavior of the attachment dynamic, is accompanied by an activation of the mother's right brain (Lorberbaum et al., n.d.).

These moments of imprinting, the very rapid form of learning that irreversibly stamps early experience upon the developing nervous system and mediates attachment bond formation, are described in the current neuroscience literature:

> When the child is held and hugged, brain networks are activated and strengthened and firing spreads to associated networks; when the child is sung to, still other networks are strengthened to receive sounds and interpret them as song. The repeated appearance of the mother provides a fixation object . . . as in imprinting. (Epstein, 2001, p. 45)

More specifically, during the imprinting of play episodes mother and infant show sympathetic cardiac acceleration and then parasympathetic deceleration in response to the smile of the other, and thus the language of mother and infant consist of signals produced by the autonomic, involuntary nervous system in both parties (Schore, 2000c, 2002a). The attachment relationship mediates the dyadic regulation of emotion (Sroufe, 1996), wherein the mother coregulates the infant's postnatally developing autonomic nervous system. Also known as the vegetative nervous system, from the Latin *vegetare*, to animate or bring to life, its variations of form, intensity, and timing are responsible for the generation of what Stern (1985) called vitality affects.

In this manner, the optimally regulated communications embedded in secure attachment experiences directly imprint postnatally maturing central nervous system (CNS) limbic system that processes and regulates social-emotional stimuli and the autonomic nervous system (ANS) that generates the somatic aspects of emotion. The limbic system derives subjective information in terms of emotional feelings that guide behavior (MacLean, 1985), and functions to allow the brain to adapt to a rapidly changing environment and organize new learning (Mesulam, 1998). The higher regulatory systems of the right hemisphere form extensive reciprocal connections with the limbic and autonomic nervous systems (Erciyas et al., 1999; Spence et al., 1996; Tucker, 1992; Yoon et al., 1997). Both the ANS and the CNS continue to develop postnatally, and the assembly of these limbic-autonomic circuits (Rinaman et al., 2000) in the right hemisphere, which is dominant for the human stress response (Wittling, 1997), is directly influenced by the attachment relationship (Schore, 1994; 2000a, 2000c, 2000d, 2001a, 2001d). In this manner, maternal care regulates the development of the infant's stress response:

> [T]he transmission of individual differences in stress reactivity from mother to offspring can provide an adaptive level of "preparedness" for the offspring . . . These responses promote detection of potential threats, avoidance learning, and the mobilization of energy reserves that are essential under the increased demands of the stressor. (Caldji, Diorio, & Meaney, 2000, p. 1170)

As Bowlby suggested, the mother shapes the infant's stress coping systems.

Developmental researchers have observed that a consequence of the attachment is the infant's development of a finely articulated schema, a mental image of the mother, especially her face (Mussen et al., 1969). Furthermore, studies of the psychobiology of attachment indicate,

> The mother initially provides an external regulating mechanism for many of the physiological mechanisms that the infant possesses but does not regulate itself. These effects are mediated by effects of the mother on the infant's neurobiological processes. At some point in development the infant becomes self-regulating through the development of internal regulatory mechanisms entrained to the stimuli that the mother provides. (Kraemer et al., 1991, p. 561)

THE DEVELOPMENT OF AN AGGRESSION-REGULATION SYSTEM IN THE ORBITOFRONTAL CORTEX

Bowlby also asserted that attachment behavior is organized and regulated by means of a "control system" in the brain, and that the maturation of this control system is influenced by the particular environment in which development occurs (Schore, 2000a, 2000c). In a number of works, I offered evidence to show that the right hemisphere is dominant for inhibitory control (Garavan et al., 1999), and that the orbitofrontal cortex, which acts in "the highest level of control of behavior, especially in relation to emotion" (Price et al., 1996, p. 523) is the attachment control system.

The observations that the right orbitofrontal region is centrally involved in self-regulation (Schore, 1994; Stuss & Levine, 2002) and in the short-term storage of icon-like representations of visual objects (Szatkowska, Grabowska, & Szymanska (2001), and that the human orbitofrontal cortex encodes a primary reinforcer that can produce affectively positive emotional responses (Rolls, 2000), support the idea that the visual image of the loving mother's positive emotional face as well as the imprint of the mother's regulatory capacities are inscribed into the circuits of this lateralized prefrontal system.

The orbitofrontal regions are not functional at birth, but as a result of attachment experiences this system begins to mature in the last quarter of the first year, the same time that internal working models of attachment are first measured. Socialization experiences in the second year also influence its maturation, a period when the toddler develops a second attachment, to the father, and these lead to further orbitofrontal development.

This ventromedial prefrontal cortex is a convergence zone, where the lower subcortical areas of the brain that generate emotional states interface with the higher cortical areas that regulate these states. The fact that it receives multimodal visual, auditory, and tactile input from all sensory areas of the posterior cortex enables this prefrontal cortex to be responsive to events in the external environment, especially the social environment. But in addition, due to its direct connections into dopaminergic, noradrenergic, and serotonergic nuclei in the subcortical reticular formation, it processes information from the internal environment, by acting acts as a senior executive of arousal, an essential component of all emotional states.

This regulation of internal states is also due to orbitofrontal connections into the subcortical hypothalamus, the head ganglion of the ANS, thereby allowing for cortical control of the autonomic sympathetic and parasympathetic somatic responses associated with emotional experiences (Papousek & Schulter, 2001; Schore, 1994). An efficient mature orbitofrontal system can adaptively regulate both sympathoadrenomedullary catecholamine (Euler & Folkow, 1958) and corticosteroid levels (Hall & Marr, 1975), and therefore autonomic hyper- and hypoarousal. In this manner, this prefrontal system is centrally involved in the regulation of autonomic responses to social stimuli (Zald & Kim, 1996), and in the control of autonomic responses associated with emotional events (Cavada et al., 2000).

More specifically, the orbital prefrontal cortex is situated at the hierarchical apex of the emotion-processing limbic system, above lower limbic centers in the anterior cingulate and insula, and the amygdala (see Chapter 6, Figure 6.2). All these limbic structures interconnect into the hypothalamus and the reticular formation, centers that generate arousal and psychobiological state. Although the early maturing amygdala acts as a sensory gateway to the limbic system, amygdala processing, although very rapid, is crude compared to the more complex processing of affective stimuli by later maturing corticolimbic areas. In optimal developmental environments the orbitofrontal cortex takes over amygdala functions and "provides a higher level coding that more flexibly coordinates exteroceptive and interoceptive domains and functions to correct responses as conditions change" (Derryberry & Tucker, 1992, p. 335). The interactions between the cortical orbital prefrontal cortex and the subcortical amygdala enables individuals "to avoid making choices associated with adverse outcomes, without their first having to experience adverse outcomes" and therefore this circuit is of "immense biological significance" (Baxter et al., 2000, p. 4317).

Right limbic-autonomic circuits allow for cortically processed information concerning the external environment (such as visual, auditory, tactile stimuli emanating from an attachment object) to be integrated with subcortically processed information regarding the internal visceral environment (such as concurrent changes in the bodily self state). The operations of the right orbitofrontal control system involve a rapid subcortical evaluation of the regulatory significance of an external environmental stimulus, a processing of feedback information about the current internal state in order to make assessments of coping resources, and a moment-to-moment updating of context-appropriate response outputs in order to make adaptive adjustments to particular environmental perturbations (Schore, 1998a).

This cortical-subcortical system also specializes in coping with threatening environmental stressors that trigger aggressive states, products of the fight-flight centers in the hypothalamus. Studies show that orbitofrontal areas specifically respond to angry faces (Elliott et al., 2000), yet are also involved in the regulation of "motivational control of goal-directed behavior" (Tremblay & Schultz, 1999). Indeed, the orbitofrontal region is centrally involved in the regulation of motivational states, including aggressive states. More specifically, basic neurobiological studies indicate that the orbitofrontal cortex exerts an inhibitory control over hypothalamic sites from which aggression can be elicited by electrical stimulation (Kruk et al., 1979), and that it is implicated in the suppression of aggression in dyadic encounters (de Bruin, 1990). Notice that the same system that is shaped by the attachment relationship regulates aggression.

The orbital prefrontal region is expanded in the right cortex, and it comes to act in the capacity of a "senior executive" of the social-emotional right brain. Current studies now demonstrate that self-related material and self-recognition are processed in the right hemisphere (Keenan et al., 2001; Kircher et al., 2001; Ruby & Decety, 2001) and that the right brain plays a fundamental role of in the maintenance of "a coherent, continuous, and unified sense of self" (Devinsky, 2000). The right brain, the locus of the corporeal and emotional self is also dominant for the ability to understand the emotional states of other human beings, that is, empathy (Perry et al., 2001; Schore, 1994). Empathy, an outcome of attachment (Mikulincer et al., 2001), is a moral emotion, and so attachment experiences thus directly impact the neurobiological substrate of moral development. The orbitofrontal regions mediate empathy (Tekin & Cummings, 2002), and the prefrontal areas are now referred to as a "frontal moral guidance system" (Bigler, 2001).

The right hemisphere stores, in implicit-procedural memory (Hugdahl, 1995), an internal working model of the attachment relationship that determines the individual's characteristic strategies of affect regulation (Schore, 1994). Unconscious internal working models of the maternal (and paternal) attachment relationship thus function as right hemispheric coping strategies for dealing with stressors in the social environment (Schore, 1994, 2000a, 2000c). In light of the principle that coping strategies have the greatest potential when they are initiated before the actual stimulus (Tulving, 1985), these models, acting at nonconscious levels, act to guide appraisals of experience (Main et al., 1985) before conscious knowledge does (Bechara et al., 1997).

The right hemisphere contains "a unique response system preparing the organism to deal efficiently with external challenges," and so its adaptive functions mediate the human stress response (Wittling, 1997, p. 55). It, and not the "rational" left hemisphere, is centrally involved in the vital functions that support survival and enable the organism to cope actively and passively with stress. The right brain contains a circuit of emotion regulation that is involved in "intense emotional-homeostatic processes" (Porges et al., 1994), and in the regulation of not only the biologically primitive positive emotions such as excitement and joy, but also negative emotions of terror, disgust, shame, hopeless despair and rage. The dysregulation of rage states is, of course, central to the expression of violence.

The orbitofrontal system that is centrally involved in "the emotional modulation of experience" (Mesulam, 1998) plays a unique role in the adjustment or correction of emotional responses, that is, affect regulation. Orbitofrontal coping functions are most observable in contexts of uncertainty, in moments of emotional stress (Elliott et al., 2000), when it supports "the early mobilization of effective behavioral strategies in novel or ambiguous situations" (Savage et al., 2001, p. 219). It acts as a recovery mechanism that efficiently monitors and regulates the duration, frequency, and intensity of not only negative but also positive states. The functioning of the "self-correcting" right hemispheric system is central to self-regulation, the ability to flexibly regulate emotional states through interactions with other humans in interconnected contexts via a two-person psychology, or autoregulation in independent, autonomous contexts via a one-person psychology.

It is thought that the "nonconscious mental systems perform the lion's share of the self-regulatory burden" (Bargh & Chartrand 1999, p. 462), that the autoregulation of aggression involves the operation of a self-regulatory mechanism operating at a preconscious level (Berkowitz, 1990), and that aggression dysregulation is associated with specifically altered orbitofrontal function (Best et al., 2002; Butter, Snyder, & McDonald, 1970; Fornazzari et al., 1992; Grafman et al., 1996; Miller et al., 1997; Raine, Meloy, et al., 1998a; Raine, Stoddard, et al., 1998; Raleigh, Steklis, Ervin, Kling, & McGuire, 1979; Schore, 1994; Starkstein & Robinson, 1997). The data lead to the questions, how does attachment trauma impair the development of this regulatory system, and how does an early relational envrionment of abuse and/or neglect engender personality organizations that are unable to adaptively regulate aggressive states?

THE NEUROBIOLOGY OF THE DISORGANIZED/ DISORIENTED ATTACHMENT

It is important to stress the fact that the developmental attainment of a secure attachment bond of emotional communication and an efficient internal system that can adaptively regulate various emotional states only evolves in a growth-facilitating emotional environment. The good-enough mother of the securely attached infant permits access after a separation and shows a tendency to respond appropriately and promptly to his or her emotional expressions. She also allows for the interactive generation of high levels of positive affect in shared play states. These regulated events allow for an expansion of the child's coping capacities, and thus security of the attachment bond is the primary defense against trauma-induced psychopathology (Glaser, 2000; Schore, 2001c).

In contrast to this scenario of a contingent, easily predictable, and manipulatable primary caregiver, the abusive and/or neglecting caregiver not only shows less play with her infant, she also induces traumatic states of enduring negative affect in the child. Affective communications, so central to the attachment dynamic, are distorted in the abused/neglected infant-caregiver relationship (Gaensbauer & Sands, 1979). Because her attachment is disorganized, she provides little protection against other potential abusers of the infant, such as the father. This caregiver is inaccessible and reacts to her infant's stressful emotions inappropriately and/or rejectingly, and shows minimal or unpredictable participation in the various types of affect regulating processes. Instead of modulating she induces extreme levels of stimulation and arousal, and because she provides no interactive repair the infant's intense negative states last for long periods of time. Prolonged negative states are toxic for infants, and although they possess some capacity to modulate low intensity negative affect states, these states continue to escalate in intensity, frequency, and duration.

It is established that the infant's psychobiological response to trauma is composed of two sequential response patterns, hyperarousal and dissociation (Schore, 2001c). Infant researchers observed instances of "mutually escalating over-arousal" between mother and infant, an experimental analog of abuse:

> Each one escalates the ante, as the infant builds to a frantic distress, may scream, and, in this example, finally throws up. In an escalating over-arousal pattern, even after extreme distress signals from the infant, such as ninety-degree head aversion, arching away . . . or screaming, the mother keeps going. (Beebe, 2000, p. 436)

In this initial stage of threat, the intensity, amount, and timing of the mother's stimulation shatters the upper boundary of the infant's window of tolerance. Extremely high visual, auditory, and tactile (pain) levels breach the infant's still fragile stimulus barrier, thereby suddenly inducing a startle reaction. This intensely stressful dysregulation triggers an alarm response, in which the sympathetic component of the ANS is suddenly and significantly activated, resulting in increased heart rate, blood pressure, and respiration. This same pychobiological pattern is expressed in states of pain (Liebeskind, 1991). Distress is vocally expressed in crying and then screaming.

This state of fear-terror, dysregulated sympathetic hyperarousal, reflects increased levels of the major stress hormone, corticotropin releasing factor, which in turn up-regulates central monoaminergic activity (Graham et al., 1999) as well as sympathetic catecholamine activity (Brown et al., 1982), and so brain adrenaline, noradrenaline, and dopamine levels are significantly elevated. The resultant rapid and intensely elevated catecholamine levels trigger a hypermetabolic state within the developing brain. Catecholamines are among the first neurochemicals to respond to stressors in response to perceived threat, and repeated stress triggers their persistent activation (Sabban & Kvetnansky, 2001). In such "kindling" states high levels of the excitatory neurotransmitter, glutamate, are also released in the limbic system.

In addition, increased amounts of vasopressin are expressed, a hypothalamic neuropeptide associated with sympathetic activation (Kvetnansky et al., 1989, 1990). This condition is specifically triggered when an environment is perceived to be unsafe and challenging, and resultant elevated levels of vasopressin potentiate immobilization responses via sympathetic activation, behaviorally expressed as fear (Porges, 2001).

But a second later forming reaction to infant trauma is seen in dissociation, in which the overwhelmed child disengages from stimuli in the external world and escapes "by altering his or her internal organization, i.e., by inward flight" (Kluft, 1992, p. 143). Tronick and Weinberg (1997) characterized contexts of hypoarousal and dissociation in the still-face procedure, an experimental analog of neglect:

> [W]hen infants' attempts fail to repair the interaction infants often lose postural control, withdraw, and self-comfort. The disengagement is profound even with this short disruption of the mutual regulatory process and break in intersubjectivity. The infant's reaction is reminiscent of the withdrawal of Harlow's isolated monkey or of the infants in institutions observed by Bowlby and Spitz. (p. 56)

Guedeney and Fermanian (2001) reported an infant assessment scale of sustained withdrawal, associated with disorganized attachment, manifest in a fixed, frozen, absent facial expression, total avoidance of eye contact, immobile level of activity, absence of vocalization, absence of relationship to others, and the impression that the child is beyond reach.

This massive disengagement is mediated by the parasympathetic dominant state of conservation-withdrawal (Kaufman & Rosenblum, 1967; Schore, 1994), one that occurs in helpless and hopeless stressful situations in which the individual becomes inhibited and strives to avoid attention in order to become "unseen." This primitive defensive state is a primary hypometabolic regulatory process, used throughout the life span, in which the stressed individual passively disengages in order "to conserve energies . . . to foster survival by the risky posture of feigning death, to allow healing of wounds and restitution of depleted resources by immobility" (Powles, 1992, p. 213). It is this parasympathetic mechanism that mediates the "profound detachment" (Barach, 1991) of dissociation.

The neurobiology of the later forming dissociative reaction is different than the initial hyperarousal response. In this passive state, pain numbing and blunting endogenous opiates (Matthes et al., 1996; Terman, Shavit, Lewis & Liebeskind, 1984) and behavior-inhibiting stress hormones, such as cortisol, are elevated. Furthermore, activity of the dorsal vagal complex in the brainstem medulla increases dramatically, decreasing blood pressure, metabolic activity, and heart rate, despite increases in circulating adrenaline (Schore, 2001c, 2002b). This elevated parasympathetic arousal, a basic survival strategy (Porges, 1997), allows the infant to maintain homeostasis in the face of the internal state of sympathetic hyperarousal. The traumatized infant's sudden state switch from sympathetic hyperarousal into parasympathetic dissociation is reflected in Porges's (1997) characterization of

> the sudden and rapid transition from an unsuccessful strategy of struggling requiring massive sympathetic activation to the metabolically conservative immobilized state mimicking death associated with the dorsal vagal complex. (p. 75)

The massive autonomic dysregulation of both hyperarousal and dissociation induce severe disturbances in the infant's nascent psychophysiological systems, especially the cardiovascular system. Sympathetic hyperarousal is accompanied by significant increases in heart rate, while dissociation involves severe alterations of parasympathetic dorsal vagal tone that dramatically decreases heart rate and blood pressure. Basic research shows that simultaneous stimulation of both autonomic components produces an even greater cardiac output and aortic blood flow (Koizumi et al, 1982). Behaviorally this is like "riding the gas and the brake at the same time," and the simultaneous activation of hyperexcitation and hyperinhibition results in the "freeze response" (Schore, 2001c, 2001g, 2002b).

But cumulative, ambient relational trauma also negatively impacts brain development — "dissociation at the time of exposure to extreme stress appears to signal the invocation of neural mechanisms that result in long-term alterations in brain functioning" (Chambers et al., 1999, p. 274). Because trauma in infancy occurs in a critical period of growth of the emotion regulating limbic system, it negatively effects the maturation of the brain systems that modulate stress and regulate affect, including aggressive affective states. In other words, infants who experience abuse and/or neglect and little interactive repair are high-risk for developing aggression dysregulation in later stages of life. An early relational environment of maternal neglect and paternal abuse (insecure maternal *and* paternal attachments) would be a particularly potent matrix for generating inefficient control systems that would be high-risk for developing later disorders of aggression dysregulation.

THE NEUROPSYCHOLOGY OF MATERNAL
AND PATERNAL ABUSE AND NEGLECT

As mentioned earlier a type D disorganized/disoriented insecure attachment pattern occurs in abused and neglected infants, and it predicts later hostile-aggressive behavior (Lyons-Ruth & Jacobovitz, 1999). This pattern is found in 80% of maltreated infants (Carlson et al., 1989). The infant, instead of finding a haven of safety in the relationship, is alarmed by the parent, and thereby in an irresolvable paradox in which it can neither approach, shift its attention, or flee (Main & Solomon, 1986). At 12 months in the strange situation attachment measure, type D infants show contradictory behavior patterns, such as backing towards the parent rather than approaching face-to-face, apprehension and confusion, and behavioral stilling and freezing.

This disorganization and disorientation is a collapse of behavioral and attentional strategies, and phenotypically resembles dissociative states (Hesse & Main, 2000; Main & Morgan, 1996). These infants are experiencing low stress tolerance, and at the most basic level, they are unable to generate a coherent behavioral coping strategy to deal with this interactive stress (Main & Solomon, 1986). Indeed, in the strange situation this group of toddlers exhibits higher heart rates and stress hormones than all other attachment classifications (Spangler & Grossman, 1999), and are at greatest risk for impaired hypothalamo-pituitary-adrenocortical axis stress responding (Hertsgaard et al., 1995).

More specifically, as episodes of relational trauma commence, the infant is processing information from the external and internal environment. The mother's face is the most potent visual stimulus in the child's world, and it is well known that direct gaze can mediate not only loving but powerful aggressive messages. In coding the mother's frightening behavior Hesse and Main described "in non-play contexts, stiff-legged 'stalking' of infant on all fours in a hunting posture; exposure of canine tooth accompanied by hissing; deep growls directed at infant" (1999, p. 511).

The image of the mother's aggressive face, as well as the chaotic alterations in the infant's autonomic (bodily) state and the disengagement-dissociative defenses that are associated with it, are indelibly imprinted into the infant's developing limbic circuits as a "flashbulb memory," and affectively burnt into the right frontal lobe (Stuss and Alexander, 1999). These episodes are processed and stored in imagistic implicit-procedural memory in the visuospatial right hemisphere, the hemisphere dominant for the autonomic conditioning of aggressive facial emotional expressions (Johnsen & Hugdahl, 1993), and the sympathetic and parasympathetic components of the physiological and cognitive components of emotional processing (Spence et al., 1996). Recall, dysregulated aggression reflects intense activation of subcortical fight centers, and sympathetic hyperarousal.

But, within the traumatic interaction the infant is presented with another affectively overwhelming facial expression, a maternal expression of fear-terror that represents a different pattern of sympathetic hyperarousal associated with hyperactivation of subcortical flight centers in the mother's brain. Main and Solomon (1986) noted that this occurs when the mother withdraws from the infant as though the infant were the source of the alarm, and they report that dissociated, trancelike, and fearful behavior is observed in parents of type D infants. Current studies show a specific link between frightening, intrusive maternal behavior and "unsolvable fear" and disorganized infant attachment (Schuengel et al., 1999). Again, dissociation, the escape when there is no escape (Mollon, 1996), is inscribed into the right hemisphere, which is specialized for withdrawal and avoidance (Davidson & Hugdahl, 1995).

In both cases, dysregulated maternal aggressive and fearful states, the infant is propelled into massive sympathetic hyperarousal, the immediate precipitant of dissociation. It is thought that "dissociation, at its first occurrence, is a consequence of a 'psychological shock' or high arousal" (Meares, 1999, p. 1853). From the moment of the switch into the dissociative state, the infant loses the capacity to efficiently process information from the external environment (the abusive caregiver's face and voice) and the internal environment (his chaotic bodily state). It is important to note that these dysfunctional coping patterns persist—the type D attachment classification has been observed to utilize dissociative behaviors in later stages of life (van Ijzendoorn et al., 1999), and are found in over 70% of hostile-aggressive preschoolers (Lyons-Ruth et al., 1993).

These instances of maternal relational trauma in the first year may be continue, in different form, in the second. In discussing maladaptive manifestations of aggression in relation to attachment, Lieberman (1996) described "aggressive" attributions of sons of single mothers with a history of abusive relationships:

> These mothers tend to attribute to their sons the same violent impulses acted out by the adult males in their lives . . . [T]hey distort the meaning of (age-appropriate) discrete angry behaviors on the son's part as evidence that the boy has an aggressive core to his personality and will grow up to be violent. These mothers exert very direct pressure on their sons to comply with their attributions. They tease the boy until he loses control and strikes out . . . they ignore or ridicule his signals of anxiety and vulnerability . . . and they are consistently rough and bossy with him. Paradoxically, when the boy does strike out . . . the mother is at a loss to put an effective stop to his behavior. (p. 287)

Lieberman pointed out that these mothers are giving their toddlers the early training to become violent when they grow up.

Or, where the mother continues in an abusive marital relationship, the child's maternal abuse may be compounded by later paternal trauma. Aggression dysregulation disorders are, of course, more common in males than females, and so it necessary to further elaborate the role of the father's abuse and/or neglect in the etiology of aggression dysregulation in males. For the toddler, paternal abuse again involves terror, but perhaps even more physical pain than in maternal abuse. Herzog (2001) reported a study of infants seen in the emergency room for croup, or vaginal or anal infection in cases of suspected abuse: In the context of a play group, abused children who did not suffer physical pain during abuse, termed "therapists," assisted other children in distress in a precocious fashion. In contrast, Herzog found that those who had been physically hurt the most and dissociated during the abuse, labeled "abusers," "seem to fall on an injured or otherwise compromised child and thus inflict even greater burden . . . In such a situation, identification with the aggressor seemed to be the resultant patterning" (2001, p. 90).

In a secure paternal-infant attachment system, the father serves as an interactive regulator of fear and aggression, thereby providing a growth-facilitating environment for the maturation of the boy's regulatory system that is responsible for "a lifelong sense of safety" (Blos, 1984). Thus, paternal neglect and an insecure attachment with the father would preclude the boy's access to this regulation, and therefore be manifest as "father thirst" (Abelin, 1971) or "father hunger" (Herzog, 1980). Increased paternal attachment activation has been observed in toddlers who are deprived of contact with father.

Also recall Herzog's (2001) description of "the biorhythmicity of man with infant and woman with infant." During episodes or maternal and paternal relational trauma, both abuse and neglect, the infant is matching the rhythmic structures of these states, and this synchronization is registered in the firing patterns of the right corticolimbic brain regions that are in a critical period of growth. Importantly, it is not just the trauma but the infant's defensive response to the trauma, the regulatory strategy of dissociation that is inscribed into the infant's right brain implicit-procedural memory system. According to Mollon (2001),

> If childhood trauma or abuse is repeated, and if the abuser is a caregiver, so that the child has nowhere to run and no one to turn to, then internal escape is resorted to — the child learns to dissociate more easily and in a more organized way. (p. 218)

In light of the fact that many of these parents have suffered from unresolved trauma themselves (Famularo, Kinscherff, & Fenton, 1992b; McCauley et al., 1997), this spatiotemporal imprinting of terror, rage, and dissociation is a primary mechanism for the intergenerational transmission of violence (see Schore, 2001c for a detailed discussion).

In an earlier work (Schore, 1997a) I sketched out the long-term effects of a severely compromised attachment relationship on the future developmental trajectory of the self system:

> If . . . an infant, especially one born with a genetically-encoded altered neurophysiologic reactivity, does not have adequate experiences of being part of an open dynamic system with an emotionally responsive adult human, its corticolimbic organization will be poorly capable of coping with the stressful chaotic dynamics that are inherent in all human relationships. Such a system tends to become static and closed, and invested in defensive structures to guard against anticipated interactive assaults that potentially trigger disorganizing and emotionally painful psychobiological states. Due to its avoidance of novel situations and diminished capacity to cope with challenging situations, it does not expose

itself to new socioemotional learning experiences that are required for the continuing experience-dependent growth of the right brain. This structural limitation, in turn, negatively impacts the future trajectory of self-organization. (p. 624)

CORTICOLIMBIC PSYCHOPATHOGENESIS AND AGGRESSION DYSREGULATION

The disorganized/disoriented attachment represents a pathological attachment pattern, and this pathology is expressed in both function and structure. Type D behaviors often take the form of stereotypies that are found in neurologically impaired infants. Indeed, relational trauma interferes with the maturation of, particularly, the right brain. A fundamental precept of developmental neurology is that the developing infant is maximally vulnerable to nonoptimal and growth-inhibiting environmental events during the period of most rapid brain growth. During a critical period of regional brain growth, genetic factors are expressed in an initial overproduction of synapses. This is followed by an environmentally driven process, the pruning and maintenance of synaptic connections and the organization of circuits. The principle is, "cells that fire together, survive together, and wire together," but in the case of inadequate environmental input, increased programmed cell death (apoptosis) occurs (Voigt, Baier, & de Lima, 1997). Apoptosis is a fundamental biological process under normal physiological conditions, "but under pathological conditions, there can be a failure to control the extent of cell death" (Chaparro-Huerta et al., 2002, p. 97). Relational trauma and maternal deprivation represent pathological conditions during a critical period of experience–dependent brain growth. Post and his colleagues reported a study of infant mammals entitled, "Maternal deprivation induces neuronal death" (Zhang, Xing, et al., 1997). Maternal neglect is the most profound behavioral manifestation of maternal deprivation, and so this research on cell death may explicate the psychoneurobiological mechanism by which severe attachment trauma massively alters the trajectory of brain growth.

Programmed cell death is a basic mechanism of brain development, in that the removal of overproduced cells allows for an optimization of synaptic connections and the sculpting of patterned functional circuits (Burek & Oppenheim, 1996; Kaufmann & Hengartner, 2001). Research now reveals that maternal behavior regulates apoptosis and synaptic survival in the infant's postnatally developing brain by directly impacting the genes that encode the proteins that regulate the apoptotic pathways and induce DNA fragmentation (Weaver, Grant, & Meaney, 2002). These effects are enduring, that is, maternal care is shown to directly influence hippocampal and therefore limbic neuronal survival and death during the offspring's adulthood.

The mechanism of maternal regulation of apoptosis may involve the mother's regulation of corticosteroid levels and numbers of corticosteroid receptors in the infant's brain, especially the developing limbic system (see Schore, 1994). Activation of these receptors directly influences the expression of the key regulatory molecules of the apoptotic pathway, the death suppressor Bcl-2, and the death inducer Bax (Almeida et al., 2000; Amsterdam, Tajima, & Sasson, 2002; Korsmeyer, Shutter, Veis, Merry, & Oltvai, 1993; Oltvai & Korsmeyer, 1994; Wyllie, 1997). These proto-oncogenes are located in energy-generating brain mitochondria that control apoptosis (Hockenberry, Nuncz, Milliman, Schreiber, & Korsmeyer, 1990; Kroemer, Zamzami, & Susin, 1997). They are active in the postnatally developing brain (Gonzalez-Garcia et al., 1995; Parsadanian et al., 1998; Schore, 1994) and preferentially expressed in limbic structures of the primate brain (Bernier & Parent, 1998). This research may elucidate the processes that underlie the "social control" of cell survival and cell death (Raff, 1992), and the mechanism by which the primary caregiver acts as an agent of natural selection that influences the stabilization or elimination (parcellation) of developing limbic connections (Schore, 1994).

This work is also delving into the basic question of how maternal deprivation (and therfore relational trauma) affects infant brain development (Zhang et al., 2002). These authors demonstrate that maternal deprivation during an early critical period increases the rate of apoptotic cell death in the infant brain, doubling the number of cells undergoing cell death in the cortex. These effects are especialy heightened in brain regions "where postnatal development is prominent" (p.8). In the human brain the first 18 months are critical for the myelination and therefore the maturation of particular rapidly developing limbic and cortical association areas (Kinney, Brody, Kloman, & Gilles, 1988; Rabinowicz, 1979; Yakovlev & Lecours, 1967).

Integrating this data, I propose that relational trauma-induced programmed cell death would be intensified in the developing limbic system, the brain circuits involved in attachment functions (Anders & Zeanah, 1984; Bowlby, 1969; Schore, 1994). Elevated corticosteroid levels that accompany relational trauma would induce increased activity of the proapoptotic death inducer, Bax, known to accelerate programmed cell death (Oltvai, Milliman, & Korsmeyer, 1993), in the developing limbic system, particularly in the early developing right brain. The amplified programmed cell death mechanism thus underlies the pathogenetic process by which "maternal deprivation during critical periods in development can alter brain development which may impact on the long-term cognitive and behavioral sequelae of maternal deprivation" (Zhang et al., 2002, p. 10). I would add that social-emotional attachment functions of the early developing right brain would also be negatively impacted, especially by the more severe forms of early maternal deprivation, neglect, and abuse.

The brain of an infant who experiences frequent intense attachment disruptions and little interactive repair is chronically exposed to states of impaired homeostasis which he or she shifts into in order to maintain basic metabolic processes for survival. If the caregiver does not participate in reparative functions that reduce stress and reestablish psychobiological equilibrium, the limbic connections that are in the process of developing are exposed to a toxic chemistry that negatively impacts a developing brain. Developmental psychobiological studies indicate that hyperaroused attachment stressors are correlated with elevated levels of the arousal-regulating catecholamines and hyperactivation of the excitotoxic N-methyl-D-aspartate (NMDA)-sensitive glutamate receptor, a critical site of neurotoxicity and synapse elimination in early development (McDonald et al., 1988; Guilarte, 1998). Research now indicates that apoptotic degeneration is intensified in the immature brain during the NMDA receptor hypersensitivity period (Johnston, 2001), and that the neonatal brain is more prone to excitotoxicity than the adult brain (Bittigau et al., 1999). High levels of glutamate and cortisol are known to specifically alter the growth of the developing limbic system. During critical periods, dendritic spines, potential points of connection with other neurons, are particularly vulnerable to long pulses of glutamate (Segal et al., 2000) that trigger severely altered calcium metabolism and therefore "oxidative stress" and cellular damage (Park et al., 1996; Schore, 1994, 1997a, 2001c).

Furthermore, basic research shows that adverse social experiences during early critical periods result in permanent alterations in opiate, corticosteroid, corticotropin releasing factor, dopamine, noradrenaline, and serotonin receptors (Coplan et al., 1996; Ladd et al., 1996; Lewis et al., 1990; Martin et al., 1991; Meerlo et al., 2001; Rosenblum et al., 1994; van der Kolk, 1987). Such receptor alterations are a central mechanism by which "early adverse developmental experiences may leave behind a permanent physiological reactivity in limbic areas of the brain" (Post et al., 1994, p. 800). Impairments in the limbic system, and in dopamine, noradrenaline, and serotonin receptors have all been implicated in aggression dysregulation (Dolan, Deakin, Roberts, & Anderson, 2002; Oquendo & Mann, 2000; Siever & Trestman, 1993).

Because the early maturing (Geschwind & Galaburda, 1987; Schore, 1994) right hemisphere is more deeply connected into the limbic system than the left (Borod, 2000; Gainotti, 2000; Tucker, 1992), this enduring reactivity is "burnt" into corticolimbic circuits of the right brain, the hemisphere dominant for the regulation of the stress hormones cortisol and corticotropin releasing factor (Kalogeras et al., 1996; Wittling & Pfluger, 1990). Studies show that the effects of CRF, including increased glucose metabolism in limbic areas, depend upon the social context (Strome et al., 2002), and that stressful postnatal contexts negatively impact the immature limbic system and lead to long-term cell loss (Brunson et al., 2001). Elevated corticotropin releasing factor is known to initiate seizure activity in the developing brain (Hollrigel, Chen, Baram, & Soltesz, 1998; Wang, Dow, & Fraser, 2001), and so this circuit hyperreactivity may be expressed at later periods as "psychogenic nonepileptic seizures," a syndrome etiologically associated with "physical assault or other extreme trauma" and "traumatic loss in childhood" (Sirven & Glosser, 1998). Partial seizure-like symptoms are associated with a low discharge threshold in kindled limbic areas, and the resultant psychosensory symptoms are found in PTSD patients with early childhood abuse (Roca & Freeman, 2002; Teicher et al., 1993).

The right frontal cortex is at the top of a cortical hierarchy for the processing of prolonged emotionally stressful inputs, where it adaptively modulates the activity of subcortical dopamine neurons (Sullivan & Gratton, 2002; Sullivan & Szechtman, 1995). But dopamine rapidly increases under stress (Bertolucci-D'Angio et al., 1990), and can induce DNA mutations and apoptosis in brain tissue (Simantov et al., 1996; Spencer et al., 1994). Perinatal distress leads to dopamine hypofunction and a blunting of the stress regulating response of the right (and not left) prefrontal cortex that is manifest in adulthood (Brake et al., 2000). A study in *Molecular Psychiatry* reports that 12-month-old type D infants, categorized in the strange situation, show a less sensitive D4 dopamine receptor, and the authors conclude that this leads to a blunted dopamine response that reduces the value of the mother and prevents the infant from organizing an appropriate coping response (Lakatos et al., 2000).

ORBITOFRONTAL-AMYGDALA DYSFUNCTION AND RAGE STATES

The dysregulating events of both abuse and neglect create chaotic biochemical alterations in the infant brain that intensify the normal process of apoptotic programmed cell death (Schore, 1994, 1997a, 1997d, 2001c, 2002b). A trauma-induced developmental overpruning of a corticolimbic system, especially one that contains a genetically encoded underproduction of synapses, represents a scenario for high-risk conditions. It is established that psychological factors "prune" or "sculpt" neural networks in the postnatal brain (Schore, 1994). Trauma-induced excessive pruning of hierarchical right cortical-subcortical circuits operates in the etiology of a vulnerability to later extreme disorders of affect regulation, including disorders of aggression dysregulation.

Earlier in this work, I described a hierarchical sequence of interconnected limbic areas in the orbitofrontal cortex, anterior cingulate-insula, and amygdala (Devinsky et al., 1995) that acts as a complex circuit of emotion regulation (Davidson et al., 2000; Schore, 1997a, 2000b, 2001c). The three components of this "rostral limbic system" all interconnect with each other and with brainstem bioaminergic neuromodulatory and hypothalamic neuroendocrine nuclei. These corticolimbic circuitries ontogenetically progress from the simplest system in the amygdala, which is on-line at birth, through the cingulate (areas 24, 25, and 32), which matures at the end of the second month, to the orbitofrontal cortex, which matures at the end of the first year (Schore, 1994, 2001c). This means that excessive prenatal stressors would most negatively impact the amygdala (Cratty, Ward, Johnson, Azzaro, & Birkle, 1995) via elevated levels of corticotropin releasing factor, a neuropeptide that contributes to shorter gestational lengths and altered fetal development (Glynn et al., 2000). Relational trauma in the second and third quarters of the first year would impair the development of the right insula, an area involved in representing bodily state (Craig, 2002), and the anterior cingulate, an area involved in social behavior and gating of amygdala activity.

The orbitofrontal areas of the right hemisphere undergo an experience-dependent maturation from the last quarter of the first through the last of the second year (Schore, 1994). Research documents that disorganized infant attachment strategies increase in frequency from 12 to 18 months (Lyons-Ruth et al., 1993). Relational trauma at this time interferes with the organization of the orbitofrontal regions and compromises such functions as attachment, empathy, the capacity to play, and affect regulation. In other words, due to a poor orbitofrontal organization, the achievement of emotional control, including aggression control, is precluded in these infants. As previously mentioned an impressive body of neurological evidence now indicates that at all points in the life span aggression dysregulation is associated with specifically altered orbitofrontal function (Anderson et al., 1999; Best et al., 2002; Brower & Price, 2001; Fornazzari et al., 1992; Grafman et al., 1996; Miller et al., 1997; Starkstein & Robinson, 1997; Tekin & Cummings, 2002).

A rapidly growing number of converging studies from psychiatry and neuroscience now underscore the centrality of the orbitofrontal cortex in the regulation and dysregulation of aggression. In an entire edition of the journal *Science* devoted to "Violence: A New Frontier for Scientific Research," Davidson and his colleagues (2000) concluded that dysregulation of an orbitofrontal-anterior cingulate-amygdala circuit of emotion regulation is associated with a risk for violence and aggression. An article in the *American Journal of Psychiatry* reported that a functional alteration of the orbitofrontal cortex is present in individuals with pathological aggressive behavior (Pietrini, Guazzelli, Basso, Jaffe, & Grafman, 2000). And, in the neuroscience journal *Brain*, a study described right orbitofrontal impairment is associated with difficulties in emotional recognition of angry facial expressions, as well as with high levels of aggression (Blair & Cipolotti, 2000).

More specifically, an inefficient right orbitofrontal system would be unable to regulate subcortical limbic structures through an early excessive parcellation of right cortical-subcortical connections. Of special importance are the connections between the orbitofrontal areas and the hypothalamus, the head ganglion of the ANS and control system for fight-flight responses, and the amygdala, a major fear (La Bar et al., 1998) and aggression (Bear, 1989) center in the brain. Studies show two types of aggression: affective, impulsive reactive, defensive, or hot blooded aggression (an uncontrolled and emotionally charged response to physical or verbal aggression initiated by another), in contrast to predatory, proactive, stalking, attack, or cold blooded aggression (controlled, purposeful aggression lacking in emotion), and each is mediated by a distinct neuroanatomical pathway (see Schore, 2001c, 2002b). Affective rage involves the hypothalamic sympathetic ventromedial nucleus, and predatory attack the parasympathetic lateral hypothalamus, an area also involved in "tonic immobility" or dissociation (Adamec, 1990; Panksepp, 1998; Siegel et al., 1999). An excessive developmental parcellation of either of these orbitofrontal-hypothalamic circuitries would thus lead to a limited capacity of the higher corticolimbic system to modulate these hypothalamically-driven aggressive states (Egger & Flynn, 1967).

The reciprocal connections between the orbitofrontal areas in the prefrontal lobe, the amygdala in the temporal lobe, and the diencephalic hypothalamus develop postnatally, and are directly influenced by attachment transactions (Schore, 1994). An excessive developmental parcellation of the orbitofrontal and cingulate inhibitory pathways that gate the amygdala would seriously interfere with the ability of higher limbic inputs to regulate amygdala-driven affective rage. In this manner,

> Temporolimbic dysfunction could conduce to hyperarousal in response to environmental stimuli, while prefrontal deficits might lead to inhibitory failures, with either or both contributing to aggressive dyscontrol. (Brower & Price, 2000, p. 147)

An efficient mature orbitofrontal system can facilitate or inhibit the defense reactions of the amygdala (Timms, 1977), and thereby adaptively regulate amygdala-driven autonomic hyperarousal or hypoarousal. But stress may also take the prefrontal areas "off-line," allowing the "more habitual" responses mediated by the subcortical structures to regulate behavior (Arnsten, & Goldman-Rakic, 1998). This occurs all too frequently in a severely developmentally compromised immature frontolimbic system, one that can not shift back to orbitofrontal dominance in a timely fashion:

> In the absence of the contribution from orbitofrontal cortex, the original encoding is more difficult to alter and exerts a stronger control over behavior. In other words, behavior becomes more rigid and less amenable to control by changing contingencies and more subtle contextual features of the enviroment. (Schoenbaum, Chiba, & Gallagher, 2000, p. 5189)

In light of the fact that social stressors are more detrimental than nonsocial aversive stimuli, relational trauma, perceived in facially expressed aggressive signals at even nonconscious levels, may expose this impaired cortical-subcortical regulatory system. According to Adolphs, Tranel, and Damasio (1998),

> The amygdala's role appears to be of special importance for social judgement of faces that are normally classified as unapproachable and untrustworthy, consistent with the amygdala's demonstrated role in processing threatening and aversive stimuli. (p. 472)

Previously I spoke of the infant's right-brain temporolimbic imprinting of the abusive, untrustworthy caregiver's threatening face into implicit-procedural memory in the right hemisphere, the hemisphere dominant for evaluating the trustworthiness of faces (Winston, Strange, O'Doherty, & Dolan, 2002) and the nonconscious processing of fearful and aggressive facial emotional expressions (Johnsen & Hugdahl, 1993; Peper & Karcher, 2001). But the abused infant also imprints the defenses against the arousal dysregulating abuse or neglect, and this operation also involves the amygdala. The amygdala's connections with the dorsolateral periaqueductal gray mediates the freeze response (Vianna, Graeff, Brandao, & Landeira-Fernandez, 2001) and its connections with the vagal complexes mediates the dissociative response (Schore, 2001c). The mothers periaqueductal gray, involved in both maternal nurturance and the modulation of maternal aggression (Lonstein & Stern, 1997), may be an essential structure in relational trauma.

The amygdala interacts with and modulates the fusiform gyri, the visual area that decodes facial patterns (George et al., 1999). It is now established that the right amygdala, a dynamic emotional stimulus detection system (Wright et al., 2001) that is specialized to respond to high arousal negative stimuli (Garavan, Pendergras, Ross, Stein, Risinger, 2001), is activated by the nonverbal facial and vocal expressions of fear (Phillips et al., 1998) and involved in the representations of fearful faces and the expression of emotionally influenced memory of aversive experiences (Colman-Mensches & McGaugh, 1995; Morris et al., 1999). Partial kindling of the right and not left amygdala induces long-lasting increases in anxiety-like behavior (Adamec, 1999). Research demonstrates that the right prefrontal cortex processes fear (Kalin, Larson, Shelton, & Davidson, 1998), that single neurons in the human right ventromedial cortex respond to facial expressions of fear in 120–160 ms (Kawasaki et al., 2001), and that the right orbitofrontal cortex shows an enhanced response to anger expressions which correlate with expression intensity (Blair, Morris, Frith, Perretti, & Dolan, 1999). The automatic emotional associative learning of threat-related facial stimuli is now understood to be the combined effect of opponent mechanisms that include both a right amygdalocortical excitatory process as well as prefrontal inhibitory influences (Peper & Karcher, 2001).

Thus an inefficient right orbitofrontal system would be unable to modulate the response of the right amygdala to emotionally significant and stressful stimuli, such as an aggressive face. These findings suggest that, under stress, the limbic system of these patients is regulated not by the right cortical areas, but by the subcortical right amygdala, a structure that also connects into the reticular formation and hypothalamus and is specialized to process "unseen fear" (Morris et al., 1999). This enduring pattern, associated with destructive, defensive rage, was imprinted into an immature, inefficient orbitofrontal system in contexts of early relational trauma: "If, during early childhood, the lower brain has been overstimulated through exposure to continual traumatic stress, while the upper brain has received scant amounts of nurturing, the scales will be tipped strongly in favor of violence" (Verny, 2002, p. 199).

CONTINUITY BETWEEN INFANT, CHILDHOOD, ADOLESCENT, AND ADULT AGGRESSION DYSREGULATION

Earlier I contended that severe disorders of aggression regulation may have their roots in not only neurological damage in infancy (neurologically acquired sociopathy) but in relational trauma of abuse and neglect (developmentally acquired sociopathy). Barnett and his colleagues (1999) found that infants with congenital conditions involving nervous system damage are also classified as disorganized/disoriented attachments. They concluded,

> [C]hildren with neurological disorders demonstrate indices of disorgani-
> zation under lower levels of stress that are typically required to evoke
> such behaviors in children with normal nervous systems. It also may be
> the case that living under chronically stressful conditions in which com-
> fort is rarely present contributes to congenitally healthy children develop-
> ing neurological damage. (pp. 205–206)

The origin of an environmentally impaired right brain system for regulating aggressive affective states thus all too frequently lies in early relational trauma and the intergenerational transmission of an insecure disorganized/disoriented attachment pattern.

Furthermore, attachment outcome is the result of the genetically encoded psychobiological predisposition of the infant and the nature of the caregiver environment (Schore, 1994, 2000c). Basic research shows that the degree of genetic predisposition interacts with the extent of early induced environmental defect, and that environmental stress exaggerates a "developmental lesion" to produce an enduring vulnerability to stress (Lipska & Weinberger, 1995). A particularly potent negative caregiver environment for generating high risk for aggression dysregulation would be pre- and/or postnatal maternal alcohol or cocaine use, a documented generator of disorganized/disoriented attach-ments (Espinosa, Beckwith, Howard, Tyler, & Swanson, 2001; O'Connor et al., 1987). Another would be maternal neglect followed by paternal abuse and humiliation.

This means that a type D attachment results from a combination of genetic-constitutional vulnerability *and* psychosocial environmental stressors, and that this interaction is involved in the genesis of a high-risk scenario for future aggression dysregulation. Indeed, birth complications combined with maternal rejection at age 1 predispose to violent crime at 18 years, and both early neuro-motor deficits and unstable family environments are associated with high rates of violence, crime, and behavioral and academic problems in adolescent and adult males (Raine, Brennan, & Mednick, 1994).

The aggression dysregulation of such personalities may be detected early in life. Infants who experience intense amounts of negative emotion (Dawson, Panagiotides, Grofer-Klinger, & Hill, 1992) and crying (Fox & Davidson, 1988) present a pattern of right frontal EEG activation at 10 months. A pattern of hitting, biting, and kicking, and temper tantrums common to all toddlers, peaks at 18 to 24 months and then declines. This maturational decline would not be seen in personalities, especially males, with severe attachment pathologies. Thus early warning signs are specifically disruptive behaviors, such as temper tantrums and aggression that persist beyond the first 2 to 3 years of life, and that are more frequent and severe than children of the same age (Loeber & Farrington, 2000).

Indeed, toddlers who exhibit severe disturbances are observed to physically assault others, and to engage in self-destructive behaviors (Causey et al., 1998). Children maltreated as toddlers are more angry, hyperactive, distractible, inattentive, noncompliant, and aggressive in preschool and kindergarten (Erikson, Egeland, & Pianta, 1989). Continuity between disorganized/disoriented attachment in infancy and hostile-aggressive behavior in the preschool classroom has been well-documented (Lyons-Ruth et al., 1993). Preschool 4-½-year-old girls, diagnosed with oppositional defiant disorder, show greater right than left frontal EEG activation (Baving, Laucht, & Scmidt, 2000).

In an important body of research on early markers of risk, Raine, Reynolds, Venables, Mednick and Farrington (1998) found that fearlessness, stimulation seeking, and large body size predispose to childhood aggression at age 11. This group (Raine, Venables, & Mednick, 1997) also reported that, at 3 years, low arousal, reflected in low resting heart rate, is a diagnostically specific early biological marker for later aggressive behavior. (Recall that dissociation, the infant's response to relational trauma, is reflected in decreased heart rate). Raine and colleagues pointed out that low heart rate, which is found in no other psychiatric disorder, is also a marker of fearless behavior; according to these researchers,

> [L]ow arousal represents an aversive physiological state . . . antisocial, aggressive individuals seek out stimulation to increase their arousal levels back to optimal or normal levels. Aggressive behavior may be viewed as a form of stimulation seeking in that behaviors such as outbursts of anger, fighting, swearing, and cruelty could be stimulating to some children. (1997, p. 1463)

These outbursts, dysfunctions of affect regulation, are most obvious under stressful and challenging conditions that call for behavioral flexibility. In such unstable systems, small disruptions associated with interpersonal stresses could too easily become rapidly amplified into intense negative states. This would be subjectively experienced as a sudden transition into rapidly shifting and intensely affective states. A good example of this occurs in the rapid escalation of rage seen in response to humiliation and in aggressive eye gaze, a very common trigger of interpersonal rage. Exposure to shame-humiliation is an all too frequent accompaniment of early child abuse, and it may serve as an interpersonal matrix for dissociated rage (shame-rage, Schore, 1994, 1998b).

The recent studies of Blair and his colleagues demonstrated that boys with psychopathic tendencies, as young as 9 years, show impairments in processing fearful and sad (but not aggressive) faces (Blair, Colledge, Murray, & Mitchell, 2001) and orbitofrontal dysfunction (Blair, Colledge, & Mitchell, 2001). As mentioned, this prefrontal cortex is centrally involved in the individual's appraisal of the safety or danger of interactive contexts. Early traumatic experiences bias this system toward insecurity and aggression, and this negatively tinged perceptual bias powerfully influences the way in which a male, abused early in childhood, would see the world during moments of stress. A growing literature demonstrates that neglected children have difficulty in recognizing emotion in faces, and that physically abused children display a response bias for angry facial expressions (Pollak et al., 2000).

Developmental research also reveals that "hostile attributional biases" among aggressive boys are specifically exacerbated under conditions of threat to the self. Dodge and Somberg (1987) suggested that early experiences of physical abuse, exposure to aggressive models, and insecure attachments lead a child to develop memory structures that contain a hostile world schema and an aggressive response repertoire. Later, when the child is presented with provocative stimuli, such as peer teasing and humiliation, these structures lead him to attend to hostile cues and to engage in aggressive behavior. These dynamics characterize "early onset antisocial youth," which spans 7 through 11 years (Loeber & Farrington, 2000).

Multiple psychological changes are seen in adolescence, a time in the life span when the commission of violence is highest (Reiss & Roth, 1993). The brain undergoes a significant reorganization during this period. Adolescence is second only to the neonatal period in terms of both rapid biopsychosocial growth as well as changing environmental characteristics and demands. After a relatively long period of slowed growth during early childhood, the adolescent brain undergoes extensive repruning and a prominent developmental transformation. It has been suggested that the reorganization of amygdala and prefrontal limbic areas that innervate the hypothalamus and modulate emotional reactivity drive the reorganization of the adolescent brain (Spear, 2000). Notice that these systems are the same ones involved in aggression and its regulation.

Although adolescence can be being potentially growth enhancing for certain personalities, for others with developmentally overly pruned cortical-subcortical circuits, this stage of the life span can be emotionally overwhelming and disorganizing. A brain that in infancy had to chronically shift into hypometabolic survival modes had little energy available for growth, and a repruning of already developmentally thinned-down cortical-subcortical connections exposes earlier forming regulatory deficits. This would be particularly so for type D personalities (identified on the Adult Attachment Interview as "unresolved/disorganized") who show inefficient capacities for regulating rage states. Excessive pruning is thought to a be primary mechanism in other "neurodevelopmental" disorders, where large reductions in frontal connectivity are associated with the emergence of circuit pathology that mediates dysfunctional symptoms (Hoffman & Dobscha, 1989).

In other words, early structural defects of aggression regulation circuits would become even more apparent during this stressful transitional period. In support of this principle, neurological damage of the orbitofrontal cortex in the first year-and-a-half results, in adolescence, in a syndrome that resembles psychopathy (Anderson et al., 1999), and infants who experience perinatal complications show orbitofrontal dysfunction in adolescence (Kinney et al., 2000). Psychiatric diagnoses of sociopathy are also first made at this time. The "frontal lobe maturational lag" of juvenile delinquents (Pontius & Ruttiger, 1976) thus reflects what Anderson, Damasio, Tranel, and Demasio (2000) describe as a "long-term sequelae of prefrontal cortex damage acquired in early childhood" (p. 281) that results in "a failure to ever develop specific cognitive and behavioral competencies," and what Bechara and colleagues (2001) term "a developmentally hypo-functioning ventromedial cortex" (p. 388). A "developmentally hypo-functioning ventromedial cortex" thus underlies a "developmentally acquired sociopathy."

BORDERLINE PERSONALITY DISORDER AND AFFECTIVE-IMPULSIVE VERSUS ANTISOCIAL PERSONALITY DISORDER AND PREDATORY-STALKING AGGRESSION

Teicher and colleagues (1996) reported that children who have suffered early physical abuse show EEG abnormalities in frontal brain regions, and concludes that stress alters the development of the prefrontal cortex, arrests its development, and prevents it from reaching a full adult capacity. I suggest that the ambient relational trauma embedded in type D disorganized/disoriented attachments induces an apoptotic excitotoxic alteration of neural circuitry (Mattson & Duan, 1999), a severe overpruning of reciprocal orbitofrontal (and anterior cingulate) connections with the amygdala. In earlier works I have outlined the role of this mechanism in the etiology of posttraumatic stress disorders and borderline personality disorders. Both of these groups show abnormal orbitofrontal and amygdala function (Herpetz et al., 2001; Schore, 2001c, 2002b). This conception further suggests that like PTSD, borderline and antisocial personality organizations that manifest dysregulated aggression each represent an "environmentally induced complex developmental disorder" (De Bellis, 2001).

A large body of studies demonstrates disrupted early attachments and early trauma and abuse in the histories of children and adults diagnosed as borderline personality disorder (Lyons-Ruth & Jacobvitz, 1999). Zanarini and colleagues (1997) reported that 91% of borderline patients report childhood abuse. Clinical studies document a high rate of PTSD among patients with borderline personality disorder (Zanarini et al., 1998) and a high rate of borderline personality disorder among PTSD patients (Shea, Zlotnick, & Weisberg, 1999). Like borderline personalities who show affective instability, including labile anger (Koenigsberg et al., 2002), PTSD patients exhibit "irritability or outbursts of anger" (American Psychiatric Association, 1994, p. 428), and anger regulation deficits (Chemtob, Novaco, Hamada, Gross, & Smith, 1997; Feeney, Zoellner, & Foa, 2000). In addition to maladaptive deficits in affect regulation, borderline personalities, in common with PTSD patients, show high frequencies of dissociation (Shearer, 1994; Brodsky, Cloitre, & Dulit, 1995; Golynkina & Ryle, 1999; Zanarini, Ruser, Frankenburg, & Hennen, 2000).

In the trauma literature Herman and van der Kolk (1987) asserted that borderline personality organization manifests a bias to use dissociation when under stress, and experiences massive disturbances in affect regulation, interpersonal difficulties, self-integration, and impulse control. The impulse control and aggression dysregulation deficits of borderline personality disorders have been well documented in the psychoanalytic literature by Kernberg (1975), who later stated that the excess (unregulated) endogenous aggression of this group of patients is due to "severe chronic traumatic experiences" (1988).

I suggest that such early traumatic attachments induce significantly increased rates of apoptosis and circuit overpruning in the developing limbic system and represent the origins of the enduring structural impairments of both borderline and antisocial (sociopathic) personality disorders. This would lead to a deficit of the higher right brain regulation of lower right subcortically driven aggressive states. Indeed, neuroimaging studies now confirm that both predatory and affective murderers show excessively high right subcortical activity (Raine, Meloy, et al., 1998). Furthermore, the severe disturbances in affect regulation and impulse control of borderline personality disorders are manifestations of aggression dysregulation, specifically of affective, impulsive, reactive aggression. On the other hand, predatory, stalking, proactive aggression characterizes antisocial (sociopathic) personality disorders.

Indeed, borderline personality disorder is now specifically being linked to labile anger and impulsive aggression (Dougherty, Bjork, Huckabee, Moeller, & Swann, 1999; Gurvits, Koenigsberg, & Siever, 2000; Koenigsberg et al., 2002; Oquendo & Mann, 2000), children manifesting reactive relative to proactive aggression show higher levels of physical abuse (Dodge, Lochman, Harnish, & Bates, 1997), and psychopathic adults are known to exhibit predatory violence, while nonpsychopathic adults manifest affective-impulsive violence (Raine, Meloy, et al., 1998). These differences would be seen most clearly not in a basal resting state, but under exposure to a personally meaningful stressor.

I also hypothesize that although both experience disorganized-disoriented insecure attachments and severe alterations of arousal, a history of maternal abuse-hyperarousal is dominant in the borderline, and neglect-hypoarousal in the antisocial personality. During a critical period of corticolimbic limbic-hypothalamic connectivity, an excessive developmental parcellation and/or cell death in the hypothalamic sympathetic ventromedial nuclei would lead to a borderline organization and a predisposition to affective-reactive rage, while a severe parcellation of the parasympathetic lateral hypothalamus would lead to an antisocial personality organization and a predisposition to predatory-proactive rage.

In addition, excessive developmental cell death in specific groups of face processing neurons in the developing right fusiform gyrus, the area that decodes facial stimuli (George et al., 1999), would be associated with the borderline's inability to efficiently process aggressive faces and the psychopath's mind-blindness to fearful faces. Relational trauma-induced excessive developmental cell death of neurons in the human right ventromedial cortex that respond to facial expressions of fear (Kawasaki et al., 2001) would also account for this mindblindness. Deficits in processing aggressive faces are seen in impulsive aggressive disorders, known to be associated with a dysfunctional orbital/medial prefrontal circuit (Best et al., 2002). These authors noted that facial expressions of anger (and disgust) are potential warning signals of impending physical and psychological danger. They also suggest that such individuals miss these signals until a dangerous situation has escalated. Children who exhibit reactive aggression also show increased skin conductance reactivity, a physiological pattern of emotional arousal (Hubbard et al., 2002).

On the other hand, children displaying proactive aggression, a trait of psychopathy, do not show a pattern of autonomic arousal. Indeed, children with psychopathic tendencies can respond appropriately to angry facial expressions, but not to fearful (or sad) expressions (Blair, 1999). Adult psychopaths also show impaired recognition of fearful vocal affect (Blair et al., 2002) and facial expressions of disgust (Kosson, Suchy, Mayer, & Libby, in press). The orbito-frontal system in such personalities may not receive feedback from right poste-rior processing areas regarding facial displays and auditory expressions of fear (submission), and thereby be unable to inhibit the subcortical autonomic com-ponents of aggression. This mechanism has been proposed by Blair (1995) to account for the observation that psychopaths show abnormal aggression even in the face of submissive displays.

The etiology of a failure to mobilize an appropriate autonomic response to fearful or aggressive facial expressions traces back to the previously described traumatic episodes of sympathetic hyperarousal triggered by maternal aggressive and fearful states, and the infant's defensive switch into dissociation. Extended periods of hypometabolism during a critical period of face processing neuron connectivity could later mediate a dissociative response to fearful or aggressive faces.

Furthermore, different patterns of critical period parcellation of various orbitofrontal connections into subcortical autonomic arousal systems would account for the high resting arousal of borderline and low resting arousal of socio-pathic personalities. In other words, although the borderline would oscillate between supra-low arousal (abandonment depression) and supra-high arousal (uncontrolled rage), the psychopath's ANS would fix at low arousal levels. Ear-lier I mentioned that physically abused infants show high levels of negative affect, while neglected infants demonstrate flattened affect (Gaensbauer & Hiatt, 1984) and low cortisol levels (Gunnar & Vazquez, 2001). This psycho-biological alteration endures — habitually violent offenders with antisocial per-sonality show low cortisol levels (Virkkunen, 1985).

In this conceptualization, infant neglect would be associated with severe hypoarousal, the same low arousal found in children who are high-risk for later fearless aggressive behavior (Raine et al., 1997). Recall the idea that maternal neglect is the most severe form of maternal deprivation, and the principles that "maternal deprivation induces cell death" (Zhang, Xing, et al., 1997), and "cells that fire together, survive together, and wire together." I suggest that severe neglect induces an overpruning of CNS-ANS limbic-autonomic connec-tions, producing the unique pattern of low resting heart rate, the best-replicated biological marker for antisocial personalities who are high-risk for aggression (see Schore, 2002b for a model of the de-evolution of the autonomic nervous system).

This reduced autonomic arousal has been hypothesized by Blair (1999) to be associated with the psychopath's "failure to develop" a "violence inhibition mechanism." Furthering Blair's developmental speculation, in the earlier dis-cussion of the psychobiology of relational trauma, I described the infant's intense disengagement during dissociation, psychobiologically expressed as a severe alteration of vagal tone and a dramatic decrease of heart rate and blood pressure. Vagal tone is defined as "the amount of inhibitory influence on the heart by the parasympathetic nervous system" (Field, Pickens, et al., 1995, p. 227). Vagal activity has long been known to decelerate heart rate, but it is now established that there are two parasympathetic vagal systems, a late devel-oping mammalian or "smart" system in the nucleus ambiguus which allows for the ability to communicate via facial expressions, vocalizations, and gestures via contingent social interactions, and a more primitive early developing reptil-ian or vegetative system in the dorsal motor nucleus of the vagus that acts to shutdown metabolic activity (Porges, 1997, in press). The former lowers heart rate in a fast, beat-by-beat short term manner, the latter in a slower, less phasic manner (Cheng & Powley, 2000). Both the ventral and dorsal vagal systems are right lateralized (Porges et al., 1994), and so during early critical periods of regional synaptogenesis prolonged episodes of dorsal vagal dissociation have growth-inhibiting effects, especially in the right brain which specializes in with-drawal and contains a vagal circuit of emotion regulation (Davidson & Hug-dahl, 1995; Porges et al., 1994).

I have suggested that in growth-facilitating socioemotional environments, the orbitofrontal system enhances its connections with the nucleus ambiguus vagal system and therefore expands its affect regulatory capacities, but in traumatic growth inhibiting environments, this "smart" system never optimally develops, and the vegetative system dominates (Schore, 2001c). I propose that Blair's adaptive violence inhibition mechanism is driven by a ventral vagal dominant parasympathetic mechanism, while the low arousal system of the psychopath reflects elevated levels of dorsal vagal activity.

The orbitofrontal system directly connects into the body via its direct connections into the ANS (Neafsey, 1990), and its modulation of the parasympathetic branch of the ANS is achieved via descending axons that synapse on dendritic fields of the hypothalamus, the head ganglion of the ANS, and vagal areas of the medulla. An extensive parcellation or developmentally impoverished synaptic connections in adolescence would lead to reduced orbitofrontal ventral vagal connectivity, and thereby a loss of higher cortical inhibition of subcortical sympathetic hyperexcitatory states. Panic attacks in late adolecence, accompanied by a subjective fear of madness or dying, are associated with high rates of antisocial personality disorder (Goodwin & Hamilton, 2002). Parcellation could also lead to increased prefrontal neuronal death and a predominance, especially under stress, of hypometabolic dorsal vagal over ventral vagal systems. This conception fits nicely with recent observations of reduced prefrontal gray matter, severely altered autonomic activity, and significantly reduced heart rate in individuals diagnosed with antisocial personality disorder (Raine, Lencz, Bihrle, LaCasse, & Colletti, 2000).

Thus, developmentally acquired sociopathy, like neurologically acquired sociopathy, would result in an adult orbitofrontal system that is unable to express autonomic responses (somatic markers) to social stimuli, and therefore a lack of empathy (Damasio, Tranel, & Damasio, 1990; van Honk et al., 2002). Impairments in this prefrontal system are also responsible for a personality organization that is primarily guided by immediate prospects and insensitive to future consequences, a "myopia for the future," one that has "difficulties learning from previous mistakes, as reflected by repeated engagement in decisions that lead to negative consequences" (Bechara, Tranel, & Damasio, 2000, p. 2189). They are also associated with a high-risk for drug and alcohol dependence, both of which show amygdala and orbitofrontal impairment (Bechara & Damasio, 2002; Bechara, Dolan, & Hindes, 2002; Franklin et al., 2002; Goldstein et al., 2001; Hill et al., 2001; Wang et al., 1999). Very recent studies suggest that childhood trauma affects HPA axis formation and thus predisposes to addiction disorders (De Bellis, 2002; Gordon, 2002), and that drugs of abuse impact substantially the same systems that affect aggressive behavior (Schlussman, Nyberg, & Kreck, 2002).

In an earlier work I presented ideas on the association between dysregulation of attachment-associated infantile rage reactions and the structural impairments of the orbitofrontal cortex seen in "primitive" personality disorders (Schore, 1994). In total, this body of work supports the hypothesis that the orbital cortex, the prefrontal system that is central to "defining the 'personality' of an individual" (Cavada & Schultz, 2000), shows a "preferential vulnerability" to psychiatric disorders (Barbas, 1995), including borderline and psychopathic personality disorders (Blair, 2001; Dinn & Harris, 2000; Goyer, Konicki, & Schulz, 1994; Lapierre et al., 1995; Mitchell, Colledge, Leonard, & Blair, 2002). Interestingly, the American Psychiatric Association (1994) listed "inability of function as a responsible parent" as a characteristic of psychopathic personality. Child abuse and neglect is the most direct expression of irresponsible parenting. With regard to borderline personalities, parents who attempt suicide and kill their children manifest impulsive aggression (Lindberg et al., 1984).

At the beginning of this chapter, I cited research that indicates reductions in right orbitofrontal functioning may be a particularly important predisposition to violence (Raine, Stoddard, et al., 1998), and that reduced right hemisphere activation during a working memory task in severely abused violent offenders (Raine et al., 2001). In this latter, recent work Raine and his colleagues (2001) concluded,

> A critical but unaddressed question in violence and abuse research concerns why some, but not all, physically abused children become violent .... Abused individuals who go on to perpetrate serious violence have right hemisphere dysfunction that predisposes to violence via poor fear conditioning, reduced pain perception, faulty processing of emotions, and a deficit in the withdrawal system. In contrast, abused individuals who refrain from violence ... have particularly good right temporal functioning, which may facilitate fear conditioning, processing of emotions, the withdrawal system, and pain perception. It is possible therefore that relatively good right hemisphere functioning protects individuals predisposed to violence (by virtue of being abused) from manifesting serious violence in adulthood. (p. 126)

EPILOGUE AND IMPLICATIONS
FOR EARLY INTERVENTION

Within the context of the preceding information it is extremely important to emphasize the point made by the pre- and perinatal psychiatrist Thomas Verny (2002):

> Most emotionally neglected or traumatized children do not turn into violent criminals or sociopaths. Usually, if these children have had some positive relationships-for example with a grandparent or cherished teacher — they will manage to function, even prosper. However, those not so lucky will most likely suffer a sense of emptiness and loneliness, because they are unable to connect with others. Others connect, but only through relationships that are destructive or disturbed. (p. 201)

This observation underscores the critical import of even a single timely, attuned, benign positive relationship in both altering a developmental trajectory away from violence, and diverting a child from a pathway leading to the fixed organization of a sociopathic personality that is unable to emotionally connect or a borderline personality that forms pathological connections with other humans.

Returning to Raine's proposition that an optimally functioning right hemisphere is a protective factor against a risk for violence, recall that this hemisphere is dominant for the first years of human life, the time of the human brain growth spurt. The critical period hypothesis (Schore, 1994), which applies to the experience-dependent maturation of the right brain systems that regulate aggression, strongly supports the notion that "treatment and intervention studies need to begin much earlier in life than hitherto in order for success to be maximized in preventing violence" (Raine et al., 1997, p. 1463).

Neurobiological, neuropsychiatric, and attachment data clearly indicate that prevention and intervention should commence even before the nursery, prenatally, during pregnancy. Right brain destruction in mid-pregnancy that precludes normal development of the right hemisphere has been shown to be associated with later disinhibition and impulsive aggressive attack (De Long, 2002). In light of the principle that birth insult and stress interact and impair later stress regulation (El-Khodor & Boksa, 2002), early right amygdala function, including impaired olfactory contributions to proto-attachment communications, shoud be evaluated in the perinatal period. In the early postnatal period and beyond, shaken infant syndrome (Marin-Padilla, Paris, Armstrong, Sargent, & Kaplan, 2002) and other apparent life-threatening events should be assessed by retinal hemorrhage screens, a reliable tool for detecting child abuse (Pitetti et al., 2002). During postnatal periods, standardized psychobiological protocols for identifying maternal and infant social-emotional risk factors and dyads that experience intense and prolonged negative affective states need to be established on a broad basis. These standards should take gender differences into account (see Schore, 2000c).

Following Brazelton's suggestion that the "inablity to regulate strong emotions" is the source of violence, developing right brain regulatory functions and coping capacities need to be assessed. Classification of disorganized/disoriented insecure infants must be made well before 12 months, and these high-risk infants need to be followed throughout the stages of infancy. Although postpartum depression has been well-studied, research is only now beginning to explore anger after childbirth (Graham, Lobel, & Stein-DeLuca, 2002). Very high levels of maternal anger are associated with rejecting or aggressive behavior towards infants (Dix, 1991). Because "harsh touch" in infancy is implicated in the genesis of later aggressive behavior (Weiss, Wilson, St. John Seed, & Paul, 2001), early tactile experience of low birth weight children should be evaluated. Screenings for sustained withdrawal and dissociation (Guedeney & Fermanian, 2001) and low resting heart rate are obviously essental in high-risk children. This calls for more precise measures of the separate mechanisms of dorsal vagal versus ventral vagal inhibition.

In light of the known function of the right frontal system is mobilizing an adaptive stress reponse, a neurobiologically oriented diagnostic program should include infant right frontal EEG risk markers. Indeed, Field and her colleagues now assert that greater relative right frontal EEG activation may be a marker for nonoptimal biochemical behavioral profiles in newborns and can serve as a risk index for targeting newborns needing early intervention (Field, Diego, Hernandez-Reif, Schonberg, & Kuhn, 2002). In addition, neuroimaging investigations of cortical and subcortical limbic structures (orbitofrontal, cingulate, insula, amygdala) under resting and attachment stress conditions at different critical periods would give a neurobiological picture of the developmental process.

Digital videotape assessments of the infant's capacity for recognition of positive and negative visual and auditory facial expressions need to measure the high-risk infant's autonomic responses to the mother's face in the first and to her own face in the second year. Ultimately, assessments that concurrently measure brain, behavioral, and bodily changes in both members of the dyad will give the most clinically relevant information about the adaptive and maladaptive nature of the right brain regulatory functions mediated by the attachment relationship (for further ideas on this theme see Schore, 2000c).

Interventions directed towards ameliorating relational trauma should focus on improving the efficiency of psychobiological communications within the bodily based attachment relationship, and on optimizing the maturation of limbic-autonomic circuits and the higher right brain prefrontal systems involved in affect regulation. Treatment programs that impact the early intergenerational transmission of traumatic abuse and neglect also transform a growth-inhibiting interpersonal context that generates dense negative affect and frequent episodes of aggression dysregulation, thereby reducing the incidence of personality disorders that are high-risk for violence. These programs should also include home visitations (Eckenrode et al., 2000).

In fact, infant mental health workers are devising interventions that effectively alter the regulatory capacities of effective parenting, and thereby the attachment experiences and psychobiological functions of high-risk infants (Cohen, Lojkasek, Muir, Muir, & Parker, 2002; Lieberman & Zeanah, 1999; van Ijzendoorn, Juffer, & Duyvesteyn, 1995). These programs are creating a developmental context for the transformation of insecure into secure attachments, thereby facilitating the experience-dependent neurobiological maturation of the right brain, which is centrally involved in the adaptive regulation of motivational states, including aggressive states, and in enabling the individual to cope with stress. This effort must involve a joint cooperation of developmental researchers and the spectrum of clinicians from pediatrics, child psychiatry, child psychology, social work, as well as the other professions that constitute the interdisciplinary field of infant mental health.

The mental health field must move from late intervention to early prevention in order to address the problem of violence in children, a growing concern of a number of societies. In these tragic cases the seemingly invisible "ghosts from the nursery" reappear in horrifyingly sharp outline during the ensuing stages of childhood, where they haunt and destroy not only individual lives but negatively impact entire communities and societies. The "ghosts from the nursery" that are associated with the early roots of violence, described by Karr-Morse and Wiley, are in essence the enduring right brain imprints of the nonconscious intergenerational transmission of relational trauma. According to a recent study, there are 3 million diagnosed antisocial personality disorders in this country (Narrow, Rae, Robins, & Reiger, 2002), about 1.7% of the population. And yet they represent 15%–25% of the U.S. prison inmates, and are common among child abusers, gang members, and terrorists (Hare, 1993). The answer to the fundamental question of why certain humans, can, in certain contexts, commit the most inhuman of acts, must include practical solutions to how we can provide optimal early social-emotional experiences for larger and larger numbers of our infants, the most recent embodiments of our expression of hope for the future of humanity.

2003

Permissions

ESSAYS

Schore, A. N. (1996), The experience-dependent maturation of a regulatory system in the orbital prefrontal cortex and the origin of developmental psychopathology, *Development and Psychopathology* 8: 59–87. Reprinted with permission of Cambridge University Press.

Schore, A. N. (1998), The experience-dependent maturation of an evaluative system in the cortex, *Brain and Values: Is Biological Science of Values Possible?* (Ed. K. Pribram), 337–358: Erlbaum.

Copyright 2000 from Attachment and the regulation of the right brain, by Allan N. Schore, *Attachment and Human Development* 2: 23–47. Reproduced by permission of Taylor & Francis, Inc., http://www.routledge-ny.com

Lamb-Parker, F., Hagen, J., & Robinson, R. (Eds.). (2001), in *Developmental and Contextual Transitions of Children and Families: Implications for Research, Practice, and Policy* (pp. 49–73). Summary of Conference Proceedings. Washington, D.C.: Administration for Children, Youth and Families (DHHS).

Schore, A. N. (1997), Early organization of the nonlinear right brain and the development of a predisposition to psychiatric disorders, *Development and Psychopathology* 9: 595–631. Reprinted with permission of Cambridge University Press.

Schore, A. N. (2001), The effects of a secure attachment relationship on right brain development, affect regulation, and infant mental health, *Infant Mental Health Journal* 22: 201–269: Michigan Association for Infant Mental Health.

Schore, A. N. (2001), The effects of relational trauma on right brain development, affect regulation, and infant mental health, *Infant Mental Health Journal* 22: 201–269: Michigan Association for Infant Mental Health.

From A. N. Schore (2002), Dysregulation of the right brain: A fundamental mechanism of traumatic attachment and the psychopathogenesis of posttraumatic stress disorders, *Australian and New Zealand Journal of Psychiatry*, 36 (1): 9–30. Reproduced with permission.

A. N. Schore (2003), Early relational trauma, disorganized attachment, and the development of a predisposition to violence, in *Healing Trauma: Attachment, Trauma, and the Brain* (Solomon, M. and Siegel, D., Eds.): New York: W. W. Norton.

FIGURES

Figure 2.1   Beebe, B. and Lachmann F. (1988), "Mother-infant mutual influence and precursors of psychic structure," *Frontiers in Self Psychology: Progress in Self Psychology* 3. Copyright The Analytic Press, 1988.

Figure 2.2   Field, T. and Fogel, A. (Eds.) (1982), "Affective displays of high-risk infants during early interactions," *Emotion and Early Interaction*, 101–125: Lawrence Erlbaum.

Figure 2.3   Aitken, K. J. and Trevarthen, C. (1997), "Self/other organization in human psychological development," *Development and Psychopathology* 9: 653–677. Reprinted with permission of Cambridge University Press.

Figure 2.4   Human Neuropsychology by Bryan Kolb and Ian Q. Whishaw © 1980, 1985, 1990, 1996 by Worth Publishers. Used with permission.

Figure 2.5   Nieuwenhuys, Voogd, and van Huijzen (1981), *The Human Central Nervous System, Second Revised Edition*: Springer-Verlag.

Figure 2.6   Watson (1977), *Basic Human Neuroanatomy, An Introductory Atlas, Second Edition*: Little, Brown & Company.

Figure 2.7   Smith, C. G. (1981), *Serial Dissections of the Human Brain*: Urban & Schwarzenberg.

Figure 2.8   Martin, J. (1989), *Neuroanatomy: Text and Atlas*: McGraw-Hill Education.

Figure 4.1   Reprinted from *Neuroscience and Biobehavioral Reviews* 20, C. Trevarthen, "Lateral asymmetries in infancy: Implications for the development of the hemispheres," 571–586, copyright 1996, with permission from Elsevier Science.

Figure 6.1   Trevarthen, Aitken, Papoudia, and Robarts (1998), *Children with Autism, Second Edition: Diagnosis and Interventions to Meet Their Needs*: Jessica Kingsley Publishers.

Figure 6.2   Schore, A. N. (2001), "Effects of a secure attachment relationship on right brain development, affect regulation, and infant mental health," *Infant Mental Health Journal 22*, 7–77: Wiley Interscience.

Figure 7.1   Spangler and Grossman (1993), "Biobehavioral organization in securely and insecurely attached infants," *Child Development 64*: Society for Research in Child Development.

Figure 7.2   Baron-Cohen, Simon, *Mindblindness: An essay on autism and theory of mind*, copyright 1995, The MIT Press.

Figure 7.3   From *Friday's Footprint: How Society Shapes the Human Mind* by Leslie Brothers, copyright © 1997 by Oxford University Press, Inc. Used by permission of Oxford University Press, Inc.

Figure 7.4   Reprinted by permission of Elsevier Science from "Vagus nerve stimulation: A new tool for brain research and therapy," by George et al., *Biological Psychiatry 47*: 287–295, copyright 2000 by the Society of Biological Psychiatry.

Color Insert

Figure A-1   Englebrecht, V. et al. (2002). "Diffusion-weighted MRI imaging in the brain in children: Findings in the normal brain and in the brain with white matter diseases." *Radiology 222*: 410–418. With permission of the Radiological Society of North America.

Figure A-2a/b   Matsuzawa, J. et al. (2001), "Age-related volumertric changes of brain grey and white matter in healthy infants and children." *Cerebral Cortex 11*: 335–342, by permission of Oxford University Press.

Figure A-3   Tzourio-Mazoyer, N. et al. (2002), "Neural correlates of woman's face processing by 2-month-old infants." *Neuroimage 15*: 454–461. New York: Elsevier.

Figure A-4   Reprinted with permission, from Holowka, S. and L. A. Petitto
                  (2002), "Left hemisphere cerebral specialization for babies
                  while babbling," *Science* 297: 1515. Copyright 2002 American
                  Association for the Advancement of Science.

Figure A-5   Reprinted by permission of Elsevier Science from "A potential
                  role for thalamocingulate circuitry in human maternal behav-
                  ior," by J. P. Lorberbaum et al., *Biological Psychiatry* 51: 431–
                  445, copyright 2002 by the Society of Biological Psychiatry.

Figure A-6   Reprinted from *Electroencephalography and Clinical Neuro-
                  physiology* 106, by Y. Futagi et al., "Theta rhythms associated
                  with sucking, crying, gazing, and handling in infants," 392–
                  399, copyright 1998, with permission from Elsevier Science.

Figure A-7   Gray, Alex, *Sacred Mirrors: The Visionary Art of Alex Grey*,
                  Rochester, NY: Inner Traditions.

Figure A-8   Reprinted from *Current Opinion in Neurobiology* 11, by R.
                  Adolphs, "The neurobiology of social cognition," 231–239,
                  copyright 2001, with permission from Elsevier Science.

Figure A-9   Reprinted from *Brain Research 512*, by Falk et al., "Cortical
                  asymmetries in frontal lobes of Rhesus monkeys," 40–45, copy-
                  right 1990, with permission from Elsevier Science.

Figure A-10   From *Human Brain Anatomy in Computerized Images* by
                  Hanna Damasio, copyright 1995 by Oxford University Press,
                  Inc. Used by permission of Oxford University Press, Inc.

Figure A-11   *The Neurobiology of Decision-Making*, by A. R. Damasio, page
                  6, figure 3, 1996, copyright notice of Springer-Verlag.

Figure A-12   Price, J. L. et al. (1996), "Networks related to the orbital and
                  medial prefrontal cortex: A substrate for emotional behavior?
                  Progress in Brain Research 107: 523–536. Reprinted with per-
                  mission of author.

Figure A-13   Ongur, D. and J. L. Price (2000), "The organization of net-
                  works within the orbital and medial prefrontal cortex of rats,
                  monkeys, and humans," *Cerebral Cortex* 10: 206–219, by per-
                  mission of Oxford University Press.

Figure A-14   From *Experimental Brain Research*, "Topographical projec-
                  tions from the cerebral cortex to the nucleus of the solitary tract

in the cat," by Y. Yasui et al., volume 85, 75–84, figure 15, 1991, copyright notice of Springer-Verlag.

Figure A-15 Schmahl, C. G., B. E. Elzinga, and J. D. Bremner (2002), "Individual differences in psychophysiological reactivity in adults with childhood abuse," *Clinical Psychology and Psychotherapy* 9: 271–276. Copyright 2002 © John Wiley & Sons Limited. Reproduced with permission.

Figure A-16 Pujol et al., "Anatomical variability of the anterior cingulated gyrus and basic dimensions of human personality." *Neuroimage* 15: 847–855. Copyright 2002 Elsevier Science.

Figure A-17 From *Human Brain Anatomy in Computerized Images* by Hanna Damasio, copyright 1995 by Oxford University Press, Inc. Used by permission of Oxford University Press, Inc.

Figure A-18 Elliott, R. et al. (2000), "Dissociable functions in the medial and lateral orbitofrontal cortex: Evidence from human neuroimaging studies," *Cerebral Cortx* 10: 308–317. Used by permission of Oxford University Press, Inc.

Figure A-19 Reprinted by permission from Nature Reviews Neuroscience. A. D. Craig (2002), "How do you feel? Interoception: The sense of the physiological condition of the body," *Nature Reviews Neuroscience* 3: 655–666. Figures 5a–d. Copyright 2002 Macmillan Magazines Ltd.

Figure 5e reprinted by permission of Kluwer Academic/Plenum Publishers. S. Stoleru, et al. (1999), "Neuroanatomical correlates of visually evoked sexual arousal in human males," *Arch. Sex. Behav.* 28: 1–21.

Figure A-20 Filley, C. M. (2002), "The neuroanatomy of attention," *Seminars in Speech and Language* 23: 89–98. Used by permission of Thieme Medical Publishers.

Figure A-21 Santhouse, A. M. et al. (2002), "The functional significance of perinatal corpus callosum damage: An fMRI study in young adults," *Brain* 125: 1782–1792, by permission of Oxford University Press.

Figure A-22 Hariri A. R. et al. (2002), "Serotonin transporter genetic variation and the response of the human amygdala," *Science* 297: 400–403. Reprinted from Science.

Figure A-23   Vermetten, E. and J. D. Bremner (2002), "Circuits and Sys-
                tems in stress. II. Application in neurobiology and treatment in
                posttraumatic stress disorder," *Depression & Anxiety* 16: 14–38.
                Reprinted by permission of Wiley-Liss, Inc., a subsidiary of
                John Wiley & Sons, Inc.

Figure A-24   Volkow, N. D. and J. S. Fowler (2000), "Addiction, a disease of
                compulsion and drive: Involvement of the orbitofrontal cortex,"
                Cerebral Cortex 10: 318–325, by permission of Oxford Univer-
                sity Press.

References

Abelin, E. (1971). The role of the father in the separation-individuation process. In J. B. McDevitt & C. F. Settlage (Eds.), *Separation-individuation* (pp. 229–252). New York: International Universities Press.

Abercrombie, H. C., Schaefer, S. M., Larson, C. L., Oakes, T. R., Lindgren, K. A., & Holden, J. E. (1998). Metabolic rate in the right amygdala predicts negative affect in depressed patients. *NeuroReport, 9*, 3301–3307.

Acerra, F., Burnod, Y., & de Schonen, S. (2002). Modelling aspects of face processing in early infancy. *Developmental Science, 5*, 98–117.

Adamec, R. (1990). Kindling, anxiety and limbic epilepsy: Human and animal perspectives. In J. A. Wada (Ed.), *Kindling* 4 (pp. 329–341). New York: Raven.

Adamec, R. (1997). Transmitter systems involved in neural plasticity underlying increased anxiety and defense — implications for understanding anxiety following traumatic stress. *Neuroscience and Biobehavioral Reviews, 21*, 755–765.

Adamec, R. E. (1998). Evidence that NMDA-dependent limbic neural plasticity in the right hemisphere mediates pharmacological stressor (FG-7142)-induced lasting increases in anxiety-like behavior: Study 1 — Role of NMDA receptors in efferent transmission from the cat amygdala. *Journal of Psychopharmacology, 12*, 122–128.

Adamec, R. E. (1999). Evidence that limbic neural plasticity in the right hemisphere mediates partial kindling induced lasting increases in anxiety-like behavior: Effects of low frequency stimulation (quenching?) on long-term potentiation of amygdala efferents and behavior following kindling. *Brain Research, 839*, 133–152.

Adamec, R. E., & McKay, D. (1993). Amygdala kindling, anxiety, and corticotopin releasing factor (CRF). *Physiology and Behavior, 54*, 423–431.

Adams, J. H., Graham, D. I., Scott, G., Parker, L. S., & Doyle, D. (1980). Brain damage in non-missile head injury. *Journal of Clinical Pathology, 33*, 1132–1145.

Adolphs, R., (2000). Is reward an emotion? *Behavioral and Brain Sciences, 23*, 177–234.

Adolphs, R. (2001). The neurobiology of social cognition. *Current Opinions in Neurobiology, 11*, 231–239.

Adolphs, R. (2002). Recognizing emotion from facial expressions: Psychological and neurological mechanisms. *Behavioral and Cognitive Neuroscience Reviews, 1*, 21–62.

Adolphs, R., Damasio, H., Tranel, D., Cooper, G., & Damasio, A. R. (2000). A role for somatosensory cortices in the visual recognition of emotion as revealed by three-dimensional lesion mapping. *Journal of Neuroscience, 20*, 2683–2690.

Adolphs, R., Damasio, H., Tranel, D., & Damasio, A. R. (1996). Cortical systems for the recognition of emotion in facial expressions. *Journal of Neuroscience, 23*, 7678–7687.

Adolphs, R., Tranel, D., & Damasio, A. R. (1998). The human amygdala in social judgment. *Nature, 393*, 470–474.

Adolphs, R., Tranel, D., & Damasio, H. (2001). Emotion recognition from faces and prosody following temporal lobectomy. *Neuropsychology, 15,* 396–404.

Ahern, G. L., Schomer, D. L., Kleefield, J., Blume, H., Rees Cosgrove, G., Weintraub, S., & Mesulam, M-M. (1991). Right hemisphere advantage for evaluating emotional facial expression. *Cortex, 27,* 193–202.

Ainsworth, M. D. S. (1967). *Infancy in Uganda: Infant care and the growth of love.* Baltimore: Johns Hopkins University Press.

Ainsworth, M. D. S. (1969). Object relations, dependency and attachment: A theoretical review of the infant-mother relationship. *Child Development, 40,* 969–1025.

Ainsworth, M. S., & Bowlby, J. (1991). An ethological approach to personality development. *American Psychologist, 46,* 333–341.

Aitken, K. J., & Trevarthen, C. (1997). Self/other organization in human psychological development. *Development and Psychopathology, 9,* 653–677. New York: Cambridge University Press.

Ali, N., & Cimino, C. R. (1997). Hemispheric lateralization of perception and memory for emotional verbal stimuli in normal individuals. *Neuropsychology, 11,* 114–125.

Allen, J. G., & Coyne, L. (1995). Dissociation and vulnerability to psychotic experience. The dissociative experiences scale and the MMPI-2. *Journal of Nervous and Mental Disease, 183,* 615–622.

Allen, J. P., & Land, D. (1999). Attachment in adolescence. In J. Cassidy & P. R. Shaver (Eds.), *Handbook of attachment: Theory, research, and clinical applications* (pp. 319–335). New York: Guilford.

Allman, J., & Brothers, L. (1994). Faces, fear and the amygdala. *Nature, 372,* 613–614.

Almeida, O. F. X., Condé, G. L., Crochemore, C., Demeneix, B. A., Fischer, D., Hassan, A. H. S., Meyer, M., Holsboer, F., & Michaelidis, T. M. (2000). Subtle shifts in the ratio between pro- and antiapoptotic molecules after activation of corticosteroid receptors decide neuronal fate. *FASEB Journal, 14,* 779–790.

Almli, C. R., & Fisher, R. S. (1985). Postnatal development of sensory influences on neurons in the ventromedial hypothalamic nucleus of the rat. *Developmental Brain Research, 18,* 13–26.

Altman, J. (1997). Early beginnings for adult brain pathology. *Trends in Neuroscience, 20,* 143–144.

American Psychiatric Association. (1994). *Diagnostic and statistical manual of mental disorders* (4th ed.). Washington DC: Author.

Amsterdam, A., Tajima, K., & Sasson, R. (2002). Cell-specific regulation of apoptosis by glucocorticoids: Implication to their anti-inflammatory action. *Biochemical Pharmacology, 64,* 843–850.

Anders, T. F., & Zeanah, C. H. (1984). Early infant development from a biological point of view. In J. D. Call, E. Galenson, & R. L. Tyson (Eds.), *Frontiers of infant psychiatry* (Vol. 2, pp. 55–69). New York: Basic.

Anderson, C. A., & Bushman, B. J. (2002). Human aggression. *Annual Review of Psychology, 53,* 27–51.

Anderson, S. W., Bechara, A., Damasio, H., Tranel, D., & Damasio, A. R. (1999). Impairment of social and moral behavior related to early damage in human prefrontal cortex. *Nature Neuroscience, 2,* 1032–1037.

Anderson, S. W., Damasio, H., Tranel, D., & Damasio, A. R. (2000). Long-term sequelae of prefrontal cortex damage acquired in early childhood. *Developmental Neuropsychology, 18,* 281–296.

Angrilli, A., Mauri, A., Palomba, D., Flor, H., Birbaumer, N., Sartori, G., & de Paola, F. (1996). Startle reflex and emotion modulation impairment after a right amygdala lesion. *Brain, 119,* 1991–2000.

Anisman, H., Zaharia, M. D., Meaney, M. J., & Merali, Z. (1998). Do early-life events permanently alter behavioral and hormonal responses to stressors? *International Journal of Developmental Neuroscience, 16*, 149–164.

Ankarcrona, M., Dypbukt, J. M., Bonfoco, E., Zhivotovsky, B., Orrenius, S., Lipton, S. A., & Nicotera, P. (1995). Glutamate induced neuronal death: A succession of necrosis or apoptosis depending on mitochondrial function. *Neuron, 15*, 961–973.

Anokhin, A. P., Birnbaumer, N., Lutzenberger, W., Nikolaev, A., & Vogel, F. (1996). Age increases brain complexity. *Electroencephalography and Clinical Neurophysiology, 99*, 63–68.

Antelman, S. M., Caggiula, A. R., Gershon, S., Edwards, D. J., Austin, M. C., Kiss, S., & Kocan, D. (1997). Stressor-induced oscillation. A possible model of the bidirectional symptoms in PTSD. *Annals of the New York Academy of Sciences, 821*, 296–304.

Anzola, G. P., Bertolini, G., Buchtel, H. A., & Rizzolatti, G. (1977). Spatial compatibility and anatomical factors in simple and choice reaction times. *Neuropsychologia, 15*, 292–302.

Aou, S., Oomura, Y., Nishino, H., Inokuchi, A., & Mizuno, Y. (1983). Influence of catecholamines on reward-related neuronal activity in monkey orbitofrontal cortex. *Brain Research, 267*, 165–170.

Arnsten, A. F. T., & Goldman-Rakic, P. S. (1998). Noise stress impairs prefrontal cortical cognitive function in monkeys: Evidence for a hyperdopaminergic mechanism. *Archives of General Psychiatry, 55*, 362–368.

Arnsten, A. F. T., Steere, J. C., & Hunt, R. D. (1996). The contribution of a_2-noradrenergic mechanisms to prefrontal cortical cognitive function. Potential significance for attention-deficit hyperactivity disorder. *Archives of General Psychiatry, 53*, 448–455.

Aston-Jones, G., Valentino, R. J., Van Bockstaele, E. J., & Meyerson, A. T. (1996). Locus coeruleus, stress, and PTSD: Neurobiological and clinical parallels. In M.M. Marburg (Ed.), *Catecholamine function in PTSD* (pp. 17–62). Washington, DC: American Psychiatric Press.

Atchley, R. A., & Atchley, P. (1998). Hemispheric specialization in the detection of subjective objects. *Neuropsychologia, 36*, 1373–1386.

Attardi, G., Chomyn, A., King, M. P., Kruse, B., Polosa, P. L., & Murdter, N. N. (1990). Biogenesis and assembly of the mitochondrial respiratory chain: Structural, genetic and pathological aspects. *Biochemical Society Transactions, 18*, 509–513.

Augustine, J. R. (1996). Circuitry and functional aspects of the insular lobe in primates including humans. *Brain Research Reviews, 22*, 229–244.

Bachevalier, J. (1994). Medial temporal lobe structures and autism: A review of clinical and experimental findings. *Neuropsychologia, 32*, 627–648.

Baeyens, F., Eelen, P., & Van den Bergh, O. (1990). Contingency awareness in evaluative conditioning: A case for unaware affective-evaluative learning. *Cognition and Emotion, 4*, 3–18.

Baker, C. C., Frith, C. D., & Dolan, R. J. (1997). The interaction between mood and cognitive function studied with PET. *Psychological Medicine, 27*, 565–578.

Banzett, R. B., Mulnier, H. E., Murphy, K., Rosen, S. D., Wise, R. J. S., & Adams, L. (2000). Breathlessness in humans activates insular cortex. *NeuroReport, 11*, 2117–2120.

Barach, P. M. M. (1991). Multiple personality disorder as an attachment disorder. *Dissociation, 4*, 117–123.

Barbas, H. (1995). Anatomic basis of cognitive-emotional interactions in the primate prefrontal cortex. *Neuroscience and Biobehavioral Reviews, 19*, 499–510.

Barbas, H., & de Olmos, J. (1990). Projections from the amygdala to basoventral and mediodorsal prefrontal regions in the Rhesus monkey. *Journal of Comparative Neurology, 300,* 549–571.

Bargh, J. A., & Chartrand, T. L. (1999). The unbearable automaticity of being. *American Psychologist, 54,* 462–479.

Barlow, H. B. (1980). Nature's joke: A conjecture on the biological role of consciousness. In B. D. Josephson & V. S. Ramachandran (Eds.), *Consciousness and the physical world* (pp. 81–94). Oxford: Pergamon.

Barnet, A. B., & Barnet, R. J. (1998). *The youngest minds: Parenting and genes in the development of intellect and emotion.* New York: Simon & Schuster.

Barnett, D., Hunt, K., Butler, C. M., McCaskill, J. W., Kaplan-Estrin, M., & Pipp-Siegel, S. (1999). Indices of attachment disorganiztion with neurological and non-neurological problems. In J. Solomon, C. George (Eds.), *Attachment disorganization* (pp. 189–212). New York: Guilford.

Baron-Cohen, S. (1995). *Mindblindness: An essay on autism and theory of mind.* Cambridge: MIT Press.

Baron-Cohen, S., Ring, H. A., Bullmore, E. T., Wheelwright, S., Ashwin, C., & Williams, S. C. R. (2000). The amygdala theory of autism. *Neuroscience and Biobehavioral Reviews, 24,* 355–364.

Bartolome, J. V., Bartolome, M. B., Lorber, B. A., Dileo, S. J., & Schanberg, S. M. (1991). Effects of central administration of beta-endorphin on brain and liver DNA synthesis in preweanling rats. *Neuroscience, 40,* 289–294.

Basch, M. F. (1976). The concept of affect: A re-examination. *Journal of the American Psychoanalytic Association, 24,* 759–777.

Bateson, P., & Hinde, R. A. (1987). Developmental changes in sensitivity to experience. In M. H. Bornstein (Ed.), *Sensitive periods in development: Interdisciplinary perspectives* (pp. 19–34). Hillsdale, NJ: Lawrence Erlbaum.

Bauer, P. J. (1996). What do infants recall of their lives? Memory for specific events by one-to-two-year-olds. *American Psychologist, 51,* 29–41.

Bauer, R. M. (1982). Visual hypoemotionality as a symptom of visual-limbic disconnection in man. *Archives of Neurology, 39,* 702–708.

Baving, L., Laucht, M., & Scmidt, M. H. (2000). Oppositional children differ from healthy children in frontal brain activation. *Journal of Abnormal Child Psychology, 28,* 267–275.

Baxter, M. G., Parker, A., Lindner, C. C. C., Izquierdo, A. D., & Murray, E. A. (2000). Control of response selection by reinforcer value requires interaction of amygdala and orbital prefrontal cortex. *Journal of Neuroscience, 20,* 4311–4319.

Bear, D. (1989). Hierarchical neural regulation of aggression: Some predictable patterns of violence. In D.A. Britzer & M. Crowner (Eds.), *Current approaches to the prediction of violence* (pp. 85–100). Washington, DC: American Psychiatric Press.

Bear, D. M. (1983). Hemispheric specialization and the neurology of emotion. *Archives of Neurology, 40,* 195–202.

Bear, M. F., & Singer, W. (1986). Modulation of visual cortical plasticity by acetylcholine and noradrenaline. *Nature, 320,* 172–176.

Beato, M., Arnemann, J., Chalepakis, G., Slater, E., & Wilman, T. (1987). Gene regulation by steroid hormones. *Journal of Steroid Biochemistry, 27,* 9–14.

Bechara, A., & Damasio, H. (2002). Decision-making and addiction (part I): Impaired motivation of somatic states in substance dependent individuals when pondering decisions with negative future consequences. *Neuropsychologia, 40,* 1675–1689.

Bechara, A., Damasio, A. R., Damasio, H., & Anderson, S. W. (1994). Insensitivity to future consequences following damage to human prefrontal cortex. *Cognition, 50,* 7–15.

Bechara, A., Damasio, H., Tranel, D., & Damasio, A. R. (1997). Deciding advantageously before knowing the advantageous strategy. *Science, 275,* 1293–1295.

Bechara, A., Dolan, S., Denburg, N., Hindes, A., Anderson, S. W., & Nathan, P. E. (2001). Decision-making deficits, linked to a dysfunctional ventromedial prefrontal cortex, revealed in alcohol and stimulant abusers. *Neuropsychologia, 39,* 376–389.

Bechara, A., Dolan, S., & Hindes. A. (2002). Decision-making and addiction (part II): Myopia for the future or hypersensitivity to reward? *Neuropsychologia, 40,* 1690–1705.

Bechara, A., Tranel, D., & Damasio, H. (2000). Characterization of the decision-making deficit of patients with ventromedial prefrontal cortex lesions. *Brain, 123,* 2189–2202.

Beckham, J. C., Feldman, M. E., Kirby, A. G., Hertzberg, M. A., & Moore, S. D. (1997). Interpersonal violence and its correlates in Vietnam veterans with chronic posttraumatic stress disorder. *Journal of Clinical Psychology, 53,* 859–869.

Beckham, J. C., Roodman, A. A., Barefoot, J. C., Haney, T. L., Helms, M. J., Fairbank, J. A., Hertzberg, M. A., & Kudler, H. S. (1996). Interpersonal and self-reported hostility among combat veterans with and without posttraumatic stress disorder. *Journal of Traumatic Stress, 9,* 335–342.

Beebe, B. (2000). Coconstructing mother-infant distress: The microsychrony of maternal impingement and infant avoidance in the face-to-face encounter. *Psychoanalytic Inquiry, 20,* 412–440.

Beebe, B., & Lachmann, F. M. (1988a). Mother-infant mutual influence and precursors of psychic structure. In A. Goldberg (Ed.), *Progress in self psychology* (Vol. 3, 3–25). Hillsdale, NJ: Analytic Press.

Beebe, B., & Lachmann, F. M. (1988b). The contribution of mother-infant mutual influence to the origins of self-and object relationships. *Psychoanalytic Psychology, 5,* 305–337.

Beebe, B., & Lachmann, F. M. (1994). Representations and internalization in infancy: Three principles of salience. *Psychoanalytic Psychology, 11,* 127–165.

Beeman, M., & Chiarello, C. (Eds.). (1998). *Right hemisphere language comprehension: Perspectives from cognitive neuroscience.* Mahwah, NJ: Erlbaum.

Beers, S. R., & De Bellis, M. D. (2002). Neuropsychological function in children with maltreatment-related posttraumatic stress disorder. *American Journal of Psychiatry, 159,* 483–486.

Benedikt, R., & Kolb, L. (1986). Preliminary findings on chronic pain and posttraumatic stress disorder. *American Journal of Psychiatry, 143,* 908–910.

Benes, F. M. (1994). Developmental changes in stress adaptation in relation to psychopathology. *Development and Psychopathology, 6,* 723–739.

Benowitz, L. I., Bear, D. M., Rosenthal, R., Mesulam, M-M., Zaidel, E., & Sperry, R. W. (1983). Hemispheric specialization in nonverbal communication. *Cortex, 19,* 5–11.

Ben-Shachar, D., Zuk, R., & Glinka, Y. (1994). Dopamine neurotoxicity: Inhibition of mitochondrial respiration. *Journal of Neurochemistry, 64,* 718–723.

Bergman, A. (1999). *Ours, yours, mine: Mutuality and the emergence of the separate self.* Northvale, NJ: Analytic Press.

Berkowitz, L. (1990). On the formation and regulation of anger and aggression. *American Psychologist, 45,* 494–503.

Bernardo, J. (1996). Maternal effects in animal ecology. *American Zoologist, 36,* 83–105.

Bernier, P. J., & Parent, A. (1997). The anti-apoptosis bcl-2 proto-oncogene is preferentially expressed in limbic structures of the primate brain. *Neuroscience, 82,* 635–640.

Berntman, L., Dahlgren, N., & Siesjo, B. K. (1978). Influence of intravenously administered catecholamines on cerebral oxygen consumption and blood flow in the rat. *Acta Physiologica Scandinavica, 104,* 101–108.

Berntson, G. G., Cacioppo, J. T., & Quigley, K. S. (1991). Autonomic determinism:

The modes of autonomic control, the doctrine of autonomic space, and the laws of autonomic constraint. *Psychological Review, 98,* 459–487.

Berretta, S., Robertson, H. A., & Graybiel, A. M. (1992). Dopamine and glutamate agonists stimulate neuron-specific expression of Fos-like protein in the striatum. *Journal of Neurophysiology, 68,* 767–777.

Berridge, K. C. (2000). Measuring hedonic impact in animals and infants: Microstructure of affective taste reactivity patterns. *Neuroscience and Biobehavioral Reviews, 24,* 173–198.

Berridge, K. C., & Robinson, T. E. (1998). What is the role of dopamine in reward: Hedonic impact, reward learning, or incentive salience? *Brain Research Reviews, 28,* 309–369.

Berthier, M., Starkstein, S., & Leiguarda, R. (1987). Behavioral effects of damage to the right insula and surrounding regions. *Cortex, 23,* 673–678.

Berthier, M. L., Posada, A., & Puentes, C. (2001), Dissociative flashbacks after right frontal injury in a Vietnam veteran with combat-related posttraumatic stress disorder. *Journal of Neuropsychiatry and Clinical Neuroscience, 13,* 101–105.

Bertolucci-D'Angio, M., Serrano, A., Driscoll, P., & Scatton, B. (1990). Involvement of mesocorticolimbic dopaminergic systems in emotional states. *Progress in Brain Research, 85,* 405–417.

Bertoni, J. M., & Siegel, G. J. (1978). Development of (Na$^+$ + K$^+$)-ATPase in rat cerebrum: Correlation with Na$^+$-dependent phosphorlyation and K$^+$-paranitrophenyl-phosphatase. *Journal of Neurochemistry, 31,* 1501–1511.

Besson, C., & Louilot, A. (1995). Asymmetrical involvement of mesolimbic dopaminergic neurons in affective perception. *Neuroscience, 68,* 963–968.

Best, C. T., & Queen, H. F. (1989). Baby, it's in your smile: Right hemiface bias in infant emotional expressions. *Developmental Psychology, 25,* 264–276.

Best, M., Williams, J. M., & Coccaro, E. F. (2002). Evidence for a dysfunctional prefrontal circuit in patients with an impulsive aggressive disorder. *Proceedings of the National Academy of Sciences of the United States of America, 99,* 8448–8453.

Bever, T. G. (1983). Cerebral lateralization, cognitive asymmetry, and human consciousness. In E. Perecman (Ed.), *Cognitive processing in the right hemisphere* (pp. 19–39). New York: Academic Press.

Bigler, E. D. (2001). Frontal lobe pathology and antisocial personality disorder. *Archives of General Psychiatry, 58,* 609–611.

Bion, W. R. (1962). *Learning from experience.* London: Heinemann.

Bittigau, P., Sifringer, M., Pohl, D., Stadhaus, D., Ishimaru, M., Shimizu, H., Ikeda, M., Lang, D., Speer, A., Olney, J. W., & Ikonomidou, C. (1999). Apoptotic neurodegeneration following trauma is markedly enhanced in the immature brain. *Annals of Neurology, 45,* 724–735.

Biver, F., Goldman, S., Delvenne, V., Luxen, A., De Maertaer, V., Hubain, P., Mendlewicz, J., & Lotstra, F. (1994). Frontal and parietal metabolic disturbances in unipolar depression. *Biological Psychiatry, 36,* 3811–388.

Biver, F., Wikler, D., Lotstra, F., Damhaut, P., Goldman, S., & Mendlewicz, J. (1997). Serotonin 5-HT$_2$ receptor imaging in major depression: Focal changes in orbito-insular cortex. *British Journal of Psychiatry, 171,* 444–448.

Blair, R. J. R. (1995). A cognitive developmental approach to morality: Investigating the psychopath. *Cognition, 57,* 1–29.

Blair, R. J. R. (1999). Responsiveness to distress cues in the child with psychopathic tendencies. *Personality and Individual Differences, 27,* 135–145.

Blair, R. J. R. (2001). Neurocognitive models of aggression, the antisocial personality disorders, and psychopathy. *Journal of Neurology, Neurosurgery, and Psychiatry, 71,* 727–731.

Blair, R. J. R., & Cipolotti, L. (2000). Impaired social response reversal: A case of acquired sociopathy. *Brain, 123*, 1122–1141.

Blair, R. J. R., Colledge, E., & Mitchell, D. G. V. (2001). Somatic markers and response reveral: Is there orbitofrontal cortex dysfunction in boys with psychopathic tendencies? *Journal of Abnormal Child Psychology, 29*, 499–511.

Blair, R. J. R., Colledge, E., Murray, L., & Mitchell, D. G. V. (2001). A selective impairment in the processing of sad and fearful expressions in children with psychopathic tendencies. *Journal of Abnormal Child Psychology, 29*, 491–498.

Blair, R. J. R., Mitchell, D. G. V., Richell, R. A., Kelly, S., Leonard, A., Newman, C., & Scott, S. K. (2002). Turning a deaf ear to fear: Impaired recognition of vocal affect on psychopathic individuals. *Journal of Abnormal Psychology, 111*, 682–686.

Blair, R. J. R., Morris, J. S., Frith, C. D., Perrett, D. I. & Dolan, R. J. (1999). Dissociable neural responses to facial expressions of sadness and anger. *Brain, 122*, 883–893.

Blatt, S. J., Quinlan, D. M., & Chevron, E. (1990). Empirical investigations of a psychoanalytic theory of depression. In J. Masling (Ed.), *Empirical studies of psychoanalytic theories* (Vol. 3, pp. 89–147). Hillsdale, NJ: Analytic Press.

Bloch, H. (1998, April). *Do tactual qualities of objects influence early hand-mouth coordination?* Paper presented at the International Conference on Infant Studies, Atlanta, GA.

Blonder, L. X., Bowers, D., & Heilman, K. M. (1991). The role of the right hemisphere in emotional communication. *Brain, 114*, 1115–1127.

Blonder, L. X., Burns, A. F., Bowers, D., Moore, R. W., & Heilman, K. M. (1995). Spontaneous gestures following right hemisphere infarct. *Neuropsychologia, 33*, 203–213.

Blood, A. J., Zatorre, R. J., Bermudez, P., & Evans, A. C. (1999). Emotional responses to pleasant and unpleasant music correlate with activity in paralimbic brain regions. *Nature Neuroscience, 2*, 382–387.

Blos, P. (1984). Sons and fathers. *Psychoanalytic Study of the Child, 32*, 301–324.

Blumberg, H. P., Stern, E., Ricketts, S., Martinez, D., de Asis, J., White, T., Epstein, J., Isenberg, N., McBride, A., Kemperman, I., Emmerich, S., Dhawan, V., Eidelberg, D., Kocis, J. H., & Silbersweig, D. A. (1999). Rostral and orbital prefrontal cortex dysfunction in the manic state of bipolar disorder. *American Journal of Psychiatry, 156*, 1986–1988.

Boris, N. W., & Zeanah, C. H. (1999). Disturbances amd disorders of attachment in infancy: An overview. *Infant Mental Health Journal, 20*, 1–9.

Borod, J. (2000). *The neuropsychology of emotion*. New York: Oxford University Press.

Borod, J., Cicero, B. A., Obler, L. K., Welkowitz, J., Erhan, H. M., Santschi, C., Grunwald, I. S., Agosti, R. M., & Whalen, J. R. (1998). Right hemisphere emotional perception: Evidence across multiple channels. *Neuropsychology, 12*, 446–458.

Borod, J., Haywood, C. S., & Koff, E. (1997). Neuropsychological aspects of facial asymmetry during emotional expression: A review of the adult literature. *Neuopsychology Review, 7*, 41–60.

Bouwmeester, H., Smits, K., & van Ree, J. (2002). Neonatal development of projections to the basolateral amygdala from prefrontal and thalamic structures in the rat. *Journal of Comparative Neurology, 450*, 241–255.

Bouwmeester, H., Wolterink, G., & van Ree, J. (2002). Neonatal development of projections from the basolateral amygdala to prefrontal, striatal, and thalamic structures in the rat. *Journal of Comparative Neurology, 442*, 239–249.

Bowers, D., Bauer, R. M., & Heilman, K. M. (1993). The nonverbal affect lexicon: Theoretical perspectives from neuropsychological studies of affect perception. *Neuropsychology, 7*, 433–444.

Bowlby, J. (1944) Forty-four juvenile thieves: their characters and home life. *International Journal of Psychoanalysis, 25*, 1–57 and 207–228.

Bowlby, J. (1969). *Attachment and loss: Vol 1. Attachment.* New York: Basic.

Bowlby, J. (1973). *Attachment and loss: Vol. 2. Separation.* New York: Basic.

Bowlby, J. (1978). Attachment theory and its therapeutic implications. In S. C. Feinstein & P. L. Giovacchini (Eds.), *Adolescent psychiatry: Developmental and clinical studies* (pp. 5–33). Chicago: University of Chicago Press.

Bowlby, J. (1981). *Attachment and loss: Vol. 3. Loss, sadness, and depression.* New York: Basic.

Bowlby, J. (1988). *A secure base* (2nd ed.). New York: Basic.

Bowling, A. C., Mutisya, E. M., Walker, L. C., Price, D. L., Cork, L. C., & Beal, M. F. (1993). Age-dependent impairment of mitochondrial function in primate brain. *Journal of Neurochemistry, 60,* 1964–1967.

Bozarth, M. A., & Wise, R. A. (1981). Intracranial self-administration of morphine into the ventral tegmental area of rats. *Life Sciences, 28,* 551–555.

Bradley, M., Cuthbert, B. N., & Lang, P. J. (1996). Lateralized startle probes in the study of emotion. *Psychophysiology, 33,* 156–161.

Bradley, S. (2000). *Affect regulation and the development of psychopathology.* New York: Guilford.

Bradshaw, J. L., & Nettleton, N. C. (1983). *Human cerebral asymmetry.* Englewood Cliffs, NJ: Prentice Hall.

Braeutigam, S., Bailey, A. J., & Swithenby, S. J. (2001). Task-dependent early latency (30–60ms) visual processing of human faces and other objects. *NeuroReport, 12,* 1531–1536.

Brake, W. G., Sullivan, R. M., & Gratton, A. (2000). Perinatal distress leads to lateralized medial prefrontal cortical dopamine hypofunction in adult rats. *Journal of Neuroscience, 20,* 5538–5543.

Braun, A. R., Balkin, T. J., Wesensten, N. J., Carson, R. E., Varga, M., Baldwin, P., Selbie, S., Belensky, G., & Herscovitch, P. (1997). Regional cerebral blood flow throughout the sleep-wake cycle. An $H_2^{15}O$ PET study. *Science, 279,* 91–95.

Braun, C. M. J., Archambault, M-A., Daigneault, S., & Larocque, C. (2000). Right body performance decrement in congenitally dyslexic children and left body side performance decrement in congenitally hyperactive children. *Neuropsychiatry, Neuropsychology, and Behavioral Neurology, 13,* 89–100.

Braun, K., & Poeggel, G. (2001). Recognition of mother's voice evokes metabolic activation in the medial prefrontal cortex and lateral thalamus of *octodon degus* pups. *Neuroscience, 103,* 861–864.

Brazelton, T. B. (2000). In response to Louis Sander's challenging paper. *Infant Mental Health Journal, 21,* 52–62.

Brazelton, T. B., & Cramer, B. G. (1990). *The earliest relationship.* Reading, MA: Addison-Wesley.

Brazzelli, M., Colombo, N., Della Sala, S., & Spinnler, H. (1994). Spared and impaired cognitive abilities after bilateral frontal damage. *Cortex, 30,* 27–51.

Bremner, J. D. (1999). Acute and chronic responses to psychological trauma: where do we go from here? *American Journal of Psychiatry, 156,* 349–351.

Bremner, J. D., & Brett, E. (1997). Trauma related dissociative states and long-term psychopathology in posttraumatic stress disorder. *Journal of Traumatic Stress, 10,* 37–50.

Bremner, J. D., Innis, R. B., Ng, C. K., Staib, L. H., Salomon, R. M., Bronen, R. A., Duncan, J., Southwick, S. M., Krystal, J. H., Rich, D., Zubal, G., Dey, H., Soufer, R., & Charney, D. S. (1997). Positron emission tomography measurement of cerebral metabolic correlates of yohimbe administration in combat-related posttraumatic stress disorder. *Archives of General Psychiatry, 54,* 246–254.

Bremner, J. D., Southwick, S., Brett, E., Fontana, A., Rosenheck, R., & Charney, D. S. (1992). Dissociation and posttraumatic stress disorder in Vietnam combat veterans. *American Journal of Psychiatry, 149,* 328–332.

Bremner, J. D., Staib, L. H., Kaloupek, D., Southwick, S. M., Soufer, R., & Charney, D. S. (1999). Neural correlates of exposure to traumatic pictures and sound in combat veterans with and without posttraumatic stress disorder: A positron emission tomography study. *Biological Psychiatry, 45,* 806–818.

Brent, L., & Resch, R. C. (1987). A paradigm of infant-mother reciprocity: A reexamination of "emotional refueling." *Psychoanalytic Psychology, 4,* 15–31.

Bretherton, I. (1985). Attachment theory: Retrospect and prospect. *Monographs of the Society for Research in Child Development, 50,* 3–35.

Bretherton, I., McNew, S., & Beeghly, M. (1981). Early person knowledge in gestural and verbal communication: When do infants acquire a "theory of mind"? In M. Lamb & L. Sherrod (Eds.), *Infant social cognition* (pp. 335–373). Hillsdale, NJ: Erlbaum.

Bretherton, I., & Munholland, K. A. (1999). Internal working models in attachment relationships: A construct revisited. In J. Cassidy & P. R. Shaver (Eds.), *Handbook of attachment: Theory, research, and clinical applications* (pp. 89–111). New York: Guilford.

Breuer, J., & Freud, S. (1955). Studies on hysteria. In J. Strachey (Ed. & Trans.), *The standard edition of the complete psychological works of Sigmund Freud: Vol. 2. Studies on hysteria* (pp. 3–305). New York: W. W. Norton. (Original work published 1893–1895)

Broadbent, D. E. (1977). The hidden preattentive process. *American Psychologist, 32,* 109–118.

Brodsky, B. S., Cloitre, M., & Dulit, R. A. (1995). Relationship of dissociation to self-mutilation and childhood abuse in borderline personality disorder. *American Journal of Psychiatry, 152,* 1788–1792.

Bromberg, P. (1991). On knowing one's patient inside out: The aesthetics of unconscious communication. *Psychoanalytic Dialogues, 1,* 399–422.

Brothers, L. (1990). The social brain: A project for integrating primate behavior and neurophysiology in a new domain. *Concepts in Neuroscience, 1,* 27–51.

Brothers, L. (1995). Neurophysiology of the perception of intention by primates. In M. S. Gazzaniga (Ed.), *The cognitive neurosciences* (pp. 1107–1115). Cambridge, MA: MIT Press.

Brothers, L. (1997). *Friday's footprint: How society shapes the human mind.* New York: Oxford University Press.

Brower, M. C., & Price, B. H. (2000). Epilepsy and violence: When is the brain to blame? *Epilepsy & Behavior, 1,* 145–149.

Brower, M. C., & Price, B. H. (2001). Neuropsychiatry of frontal lobe dysfunction in violent and criminal behaviour: A critical review. *Journal of Neurology, Neurosurgery, and Psychiatry, 71,* 720–726.

Brown, M. R., Fisher, L. A., Rivier, J., Spiess, J., Rivier, C., & Vale, W. (1982). Corticotropin-releasing factor: Effects on the sympathetic nervous system and oxygen consumption. *Life Sciences, 30,* 207–219.

Brown, M. R., Fisher, L. A., Spiess, J., Rivier, C., & Vale, W. (1982). Corticotropin-releasing factor: Actions on the sympathetic nervous system and metabolism. *Endocrinology, 111,* 928–931.

Brown, R., & Kulik, J. (1977). Flashbulb memories. *Cognition, 5,* 73–79.

Brownstein, M. J. (1989). Neuropeptides. In G. Siegel, B. Agranoff, R. W. Albers, & P. Molinoff (Eds.), *Basic neurochemistry* (4th ed., pp. 287–309). New York: Raven.

Bruer, J. T. (1999). *The myth of the first three years: A new understanding of early brain development and lifelong learning.* New York: Free Press.

Brunson, K. L., Eghbal-Ahmadi, M., Bender, R., Chen, Y., & Baram, T. Z. (2001). Long-term, progressive hippocampal cell loss and dysfunction induced by early-life administration of corticotropin-releasing hormone reproduce the effects of early-life status. *Proceedings of the National Academy of Sciences of the Unisted States of American, 98,* 8856–8861.

Buck, R. (1993). Spontaneous communication and the foundation of the interpersonal self. In U. Neisser (Ed.), *The perceived self: Ecological and interpersonal sources of self-knowledge* (pp. 216–236). New York: Cambridge University Press.

Buck, R. (1994). The neuropsychology of communication: Spontaneous and symbolic aspects. *Journal of Pragmatics, 22*, 265–278.

Burgoyne, R. D., Pearce, I. A., & Cambray-Deakin, M. A. (1988). N-Methyl-D-aspartate raises cytosolic calcium concentration in rat cerebellar granule cells in culture. *Neuroscience Letters, 91*, 47–52.

Burstein, R., & Potrebic, S. (1993). Retrograde labeling of neurons in the spinal cord that project directly to the amygdala or the orbital cortex in the rat. *Journal of Comparative Neurology, 335*, 335–485.

Burek, M. J., & Oppenheim, R. W. (1996). Programmed cell death in the developing nervous system. *Brain Pathology, 6*, 427–446.

Butler, P. D., Weiss, J. M., Stout, J. C., & Nemeroff, C. B. (1990). Corticotropin-releasing factor produces fear-enhancing and behavioral activating effects following infusion into the locus coeruleus. *Journal of Neuroscience, 10*, 176–183.

Butter, C. M., Snyder, D. R., & McDonald, J. A. (1970). Effects of orbital frontal lesions on aversive and aggressive behavior in rhesus monkeys. *Journal of Comparative and Physiological Psychology, 72*, 132–144.

Butterworth, G. E. (1991). The ontogeny and phylogeny of joint visual attention. In A. Whiten (Ed.), *Natural theories of mind* (pp. 223–232). Oxford: Basil Blackwell.

Butterworth, G., & Hopkins, B. (1988). Hand-mouth coordination in the newborn baby. *British Journal of Psychology, 6*, 303–314.

Cabib, S., Puglisi-Allegra, S., & D'Amato, F. R. (1993). Effects of postnatal stress on dopamine mesolimbic system responses to aversive experiences in adult life. *Brain Research, 604*, 232–239.

Cacioppo, J. T., & Berntson, G. G. (1992). Social psychological contributions to the decade of the brain: Doctrine of multilevel analysis. *American Psychologist, 47*, 1019–1028.

Cacioppo, J. T., & Berntson, G. G. (1994). Relationship between attitudes and evaluative space: A critical review, with emphasis on the separability of positive and negative states. *Psychological Bulletin, 115*, 401–423.

Cahil, L., Prins, B., Weber, M., & McGaugh, J. L. (1994). β-adrenergic activation and memory for emotional events. *Nature, 371*, 702–704.

Cairns, R. B., & Stoff, D. M. (1996). Conclusion: a synthesis of studies on the biology of aggression and violence. In D. M. Stoff & R. B. Cairns, *Aggression and violence: Genetic, neurobiological, and biosocial perspectives* (pp. 337–351). Mahwah, NJ: Erlbaum.

Caldji, C., Diorio, J., & Meaney, J. (2000). Variations in maternal care in infancy regulate the development of stress reactivity. *Biological Psychiatry, 48*, 1164–1174.

Caldji, C., Tannenbaum, B., Sharma, S., Francis, D., Plotsky, P. M., & Meaney, M. J. (1998). Maternal care during infancy regulates the development of neural systems mediating the expression of fearfulness in the rat. *Proceedings of the National Academy of Sciences of the United States of America, 95*, 5335–5340.

Calhoun, P. S., Beckham, J. C., & Bosworth, H. B. (2002). Caregiver burden and psychological distress in partners of veterans with chronic posttraumatic stress disorder. *Journal of Traumatic Stress, 15*, 205–212.

Calkins, S. D., & Fox, N. A. (1994). Individual differences in the biological aspects of temperament. In J. E. Bates & T. D. Wachs (Eds.), *Temperament: Individual differences at the interface of biology and behavior* (pp. 199–217). Washington, DC: American Psychological Association.

Campbell, P. S., Zarrow, M. X., & Denenberg, V. H. (1973). The effect of infantile stimulation upon hypothalamic CRF levels following adrenalectomy in the adult rat. *Proceedings of the Society for Experimental Biology and Medicine, 142,* 781–783.

Camras, L., Grow, G., & Ribordy, S. (1983). Recognition of emotional expression by abused children. *Journal of Clinical Child Psychology, 12,* 325–328.

Canli, T. (1999). Hemispheric asymmetry in the experience of emotion: A perspective from functional imaging. *The Neuroscientist, 5,* 201–207.

Caplan, R., Chugani, H. T., Messa, C., Guthrie, D., Sigman, M., De Traversay, J., & Mundy, P. (1993). Hemispherectomy for intractible seizures: Presurgical cerebral glucose metabolism and post-surgical non-verbal communication. *Developmental Medicine and Child Neurology, 35,* 582–592.

Carlson, M., Earls, F., & Todd, R. D. (1988). The importance of regressive changes in the development of the nervous system: Towards a neurobiological theory of child development. *Psychiatric Development, 1,* 1–22.

Carlson, V., Cicchetti, D., Barnett, D., & Braunwald, K. (1989). Disorganized/disoriented attachment relationships in maltreated infants. *Developmental Psychology, 25,* 525–531.

Carlsson, K., C., Petrovic, P., Skare, S., Petersson, K. M., & Ingvar, M. (2000). Tickling expectations: Neural processing in anticipation of a sensory stimulus. *Journal of Cognitive Neuroscience, 12,* 691–703.

Carmichael, S. T., & Price, J. L. (1995). Limbic connections of the orbital and medial prefrontal cortex in macaque monkeys. *Journal of Comparative Neurology, 363,* 615–641.

Carmon, A., & Nachson, I. (1973). Ear asymmetry in perception of emotional nonverbal stimuli. *Acta Psychologica, 37,* 351–357.

Carmon, A. J., & Benton, A. L. (1969). Tactile perception of direction and number in patients with unilateral cerebral disease. *Neurology, 19,* 525–532.

Carrey, N. J., Butter, H. J., Pessinger, M. A., & Bialek, R. J. (1995). Physiological and cognitive correlates of child abuse. *Journal of the American Academy of Child and Adolescent Psychiatry, 34,* 1067–1075.

Carrion, V. G., Weems, C. F., Eliez, S., Patwardhan, A., Brown, W., Ray, R. D., & Reiss, A. L. (2001). Attenuation of frontal asymmetry in pediatric posttraumatic stress disorder. *Biological Psychiatry, 50,* 943–951.

Carrion, V. G., Weems, C. F., Ray, R. D., Glaser, B., Hessl, D., & Reiss, A. L. (2002). Diurnal salivary cortisol in pediatric posttraumatic stress disorder. *Biological Psychiatry, 51,* 575–582.

Carroll, E. M., Foy, D. W., Cannon, B. J., & Zwier, G. (1991). Assessment issues involving families of trauma victims. *Journal of Traumatic Stress, 4,* 25–40.

Carter, C. S,. Krener, P., Chaderjian, M., Norhtcutt, C., & Wolfe, V. (1995). Asymmetrical visual-spatial attentional performance in ADHD: Evidence for a right hemispheric deficit. *Biological Psychiatry, 37,* 789–797.

Casey, B. J., Castellanos, F. X., Giedd, J. N., Marsh, W. L., Hamburger, S. D., Schubert, A. B., Vauss, Y. C., Vaituzis, A. C., Dickstein, D. P., Sarfatti, S. E., & Rapoport, J. L. (1997). Implication of right frontostriatal circuitry in response inhibition and attention-deficit/hyperactivity disorders. *Journal of the American Academy of Child and Adolescent Psychiatry, 36,* 374–383.

Casey, B. J., Trainor, R., Giedd, J., Vauss, Y., Vaituzis, C. K., Hamburger, S., Kozuch, P., & Rapoport, J. L. (1997). The role of the anterior cingulate in automatic and controlled processes: A developmental neuroanatomical study. *Developmental Psychobiology, 30,* 61–69.

Casolini, P., Piazza, P. V., Kabbaj, M., Leprat, F., Angelucci, L., Simon, H., Le Moal, M., & Maccari, S. (1993). The mesolimbic dopaminergic system exerts an inhibitory influence on brain corticosteroid receptor affinities. *Neuroscience, 55,* 429–434.

Caspi, A., Moffitt, T. E., Newman, D. L., & Silva, P. A. (1996). Behavioral observations at age 3 years predict adult psychiatric disorders. *Archives of General Psychiatry*, 53, 1033–1039.

Cassidy, J. (1994). Emotion regulation: Influences of attachment relationships. *Monographs of the Society for Research in Child Development*, 59, 228–249.

Cassidy, J., & Shaver, P. R. (1999). *Handbook of attachment: Theory, research, and clinical applications*. New York: Guilford.

Castellanos, F. X., Giedd, J. N., Marsh, W. L., Hamburger, S. D., Vaituzis, A. C., Dickstein, D. P., Sarfatti, S. E., Vauss, Y. C., Snell, J. W., Lange, N., Kaysen, D., Krain, A. L., Ritchie, G. F., Rajapaske, J. C., & Rapaport, J. L. (1996). Quantitative brain magnetic resonance imaging in attention-deficit hyperactivity disorder. *Archives of General Psychiatry*, 53, 607–616.

Castro-Caldas, A., Petersson, K. M., Reis, A., Stone-Elander, S., & Ingvar, M. (1998). The illiterate brain. Learning to read and write during childhood influences the functional organization of the adult brain. *Brain*, 121, 1053–1063.

Causey, D. L., Robertson, J. M., & Elam, S. M. (1998). Characteristics of toddlers and preschoolers exhibiting severe psychiatric disturbance. *Child Psychiatry and Human Development*, 29, 33–48.

Cavada, C., Company, T., Tejedor, J., Cruz-Rizzolo, R. J., & Reinoso-Suarez-Suarez, F. (2000). The anatomical connections of the macaque monkey orbitofrontal cortex: A review. *Cerebral Cortex*, 10, 220–242.

Cavada, C., & Schultz, W. (2000). The mysterious orbitofrontal cortex. Foreword. *Cerebral Cortex*, 10, 205.

Cernoch, J. M., & Porter, R. H. (1985). Recognition of maternal axillary odors by infants. *Child Development*, 56, 1593–1598.

Chambers, R. A., Bremner, J. D., Moghaddam, B., Southwick, S. M., Charney, D. S., & Krystal, J. H. (1999). Glutamate and post-traumatic stress disorder: Toward a psychobiology of dissociation. *Seminars in Clinical Neuropsychiatry*, 4, 274–281.

Champoux, M., Byrne, E., DeLizio, R., & Suomi, S. J. (1992). Motherless mothers revisited: Rhesus maternal behavior and rearing history. *Primates*, 33, 251–255.

Changeux, J. P., & Dehaene, S. (1989). Neuronal models of cognitive function. *Cognition*, 33, 63–109.

Chapple, E. D. (1970). Experimental production of transients in human interaction. *Nature*, 228, 630–633.

Chaparro-Huerta, V., Rivera-Cervantes, M. C., Torres-Mendoza, B. M., & Beas-Zárate, C. (2002). Neuronal death and tumor necrosis factor-α response to glutamate-induced excitotoxicity in the cerebral cortex of neonatal rats. *Neuroscience Letters*, 333, 95–98.

Charney, D. S., Deutch, A. Y., Southwick, S. M., & Krystal, J. H. (1995). Neural circuits and mechanisms of post-traumatic stress disorder. In M. J. Friedman & D. S. Charney (Eds.), *Neurobiological and clinical consequences of stress: From normal adaptation to post-traumatic stress disorder* (pp. 291–314). Philadelphia: Lippincott Williams & Wilkins.

Chechik, G., Meilijson, I., & Ruppin, E. (1999). Neuronal regulation: A mechanism for synaptic pruning during brain maturation. *Neural Computation*, 11, 2061–2080.

Chemtub, C. M., Novaco, R. W., Hamada, R. S., Gross, D. M., & Smith, G. (1997). Anger regulation deficits in combat-related posttraumatic stress disorder. *Journal of Traumatic Stress*, 10, 17–36.

Cheng, Z., & Powley, T. L. (2000). Nucleus ambiguus projections to cardiac ganglia of rat atria: An anterograde tracing study. *Journal of Comparative Neurology*, 424, 588–606.

Cheng, Z., Powley, T. L., Schwaber, J. S., & Doyle, F. J. (1999). Projections of the dorsal motor nucleus of the vagus to cardiac ganglia of rat atria: An anterograde tracing study. *Journal of Comparative Neurology, 410,* 320–341.

Chi, J. G., Dooling, E. C., & Gilles, F. H. (1977). Gyral development of the human brain. *Annals of Neurology, 1,* 86–93.

Chibnall, J. T., & Duckro, P. N. (1994). Post-traumatic stress disorder in chronic post-traumatic headache patients. *Headache, 34,* 257–361.

Chiron, Jambaque, I., Nabbout, R., Lounes, R., Syrota, A., & Dulac, O. (1997). The right brain hemisphere is dominant in human infants. *Brain, 120,* 1057–1065.

Choi, D. W. (1992). Excitotoxic cell death. *Journal of Neurobiology, 23,* 1261–1276.

Chrousos, G. P. (1998). Stressors, stress, and neuroendocrine integration of the adaptive response. *Annals of the New York Academy of Sciences, 851,* 311–335.

Chu, J. A. (2001). A decline in the abuse of children? *Journal of Trauma and Dissociation, 2,* 1–4.

Chu, J. A., & Dill, D. L. (1990). Dissociative symptoms in relation to childhood physical and sexual abuse. *American Journal of Psychiatry, 147,* 887–892.

Chugani, H. T. (1996). Neuroimaging of developmental nonlinearity and developmental pathologies. In R. W. Thatcher, G. Reid Lyon, J. Rumsey, & N. Krasnegor (Eds.), *Developmental neuroimaging: Mapping the development of brain and behavior* (pp.187–195). San Diego: Academic Press.

Cicchetti, D. (1994). Integrating developmental risk factors: Perspectives from developmental psychopathology. In C. A. Nelson (Ed.), *Minnesota symposium on child psychology: Vol. 27. Threats to optimal development* (pp. 285–325). Hillsdale, NJ: Erlbaum.

Cicchetti, D., Ganiban, J., & Barnett, D. (1991). Contributions from the study of high-risk populations to understanding the development of emotion regulation. In J. Garber & K. A. Dodge (Eds.), *The development of emotion regulation and dysregulation* (pp. 15–48). Cambridge, U.K.: Cambridge University Press.

Cicchetti, D., & Toth, S. L. (1991). A developmental perspective on internalizing and externalizing disorders. In D. Cicchetti & S. L. Toth (Eds.), *Internalizing and externalizing expressions of dysfunction: Rochester symposium on developmental psychopathology* (Vol. 2, pp. 1–19). Hillsdale, NJ: Erlbaum.

Cicchetti, D., & Tucker, D. (1994). Development and self-regulatory structures of the mind. *Development and Psychopathology, 6,* 533–549.

Cicero, B. A., Borod, J. C., Santschi, C., Erhan, H. M., Obler, L. K., Agosti, R. M., Welkowitz, J., & Grunwald, I. S. (1999). Emotional versus nonemotional lexical perception in patients with right and left brain damage. *Neuropsychiatry, Neuropsychology, and Behavioral Neurology, 12,* 255–264.

Ciompi, L. (1991). Affects as central organising and integrating factors. A new psychosocial/biological model of the psyche. *British Journal of Psychiatry, 159,* 97–105.

Clarke, A. S., Hedeker, D. R., Ebert, M. H., Schmidt, D. E., McKinney, W. T., & Kraemer, G. W. (1996). Rearing experience and biogenic amine activity in infant rhesus monkeys. *Biological Psychiatry, 40,* 338–352.

Clarke, A. S., Kammerer, C., George, K., et al. (1995). Evidence of heritability of norepinephrine, HVA, and 5-HIAA values in cerebrospinal fluid of rhesus monkeys. *Biological Psychiatry, 38,* 572–577.

Classen, C., Koopman, C., & Spiegel, D. (1993). Trauma and dissociation. *Bulletin of the Menninger Clinic, 57,* 178–194.

Coe, C. L., Wiener, S. G., Rosenberg, L. T., & Levine, S. (1985). Endocrine and immune responses to separation and maternal loss in nonhuman primates. In M. Reite & T. Field (Eds.), *The psychobiology of attachment and separation* (pp. 163–199). Orlando, FL: Academic Press.

Coghill, R. C., Gilron, I., & Iadorola, M. J. (2001) Hemispheric lateralization of somatosensory processing. *Journal of Neurophysiology, 85,* 2602–2612.

Cohen, M. J., Branch, W. B., & Hynd, G. W. (1994). Receptive prosody in children with left or right hemisphere dysfunction. *Brain & Language, 47,* 171–181.

Cohen, N. J., Loj Kasek, M., Muir, E., Muir, R., & Parker, C. J. (2002). Six-month follow-up of two mother-infant psychotherapies: convergence of therapeutic outcomes. *Infant Mental Health Journal, 23,* 361–380.

Cohn, J. F., & Tronick, E. Z. (1987). Mother-infant face-to-face interaction: The sequence of dyadic states at 3, 6, and 9 months. *Developmental Psychology, 23,* 68–77.

Cole, J. (1998). *About face.* Cambridge, MA: MIT Press.

Cole, P. M., Michel, M. K., & Teti, L. O. (1994). The development of emotion regulation and dysregulation: A clinical perspective. *Monographs of the Society for Research in Child Development, 59,* 73–100.

Colman-Mensches, K., & McGaugh, J. L. (1995). Differential involvement of the right and left amygdalae in expression of memory for aversively motivated training. *Brain Research, 670,* 75–81.

Colombani, P. M., Buck, J. R., Dudgeon, D. L., Miller, D., & Hiller, J. A. (1985). One year experience in a regional pediatric trauma center. *Journal of Pediatric Surgery, 20,* 8–13.

Colpaert, F. C. (1975). The ventromedial hypothalamus and the control of avoidance behavior and aggression: Fear hypothesis versus response-suppression theory of limbic system function. *Behavioral Biology, 15,* 27–44.

Connally, K., & Kvalsvig, J. D. (1993). Infection, nutrition and cognitive performance in children. *Parasitology, 107,* S187–S200.

Connely, K. J., & Prechtl, H. F. R. (1981). *Maturation and development: Biological and psychological perspectives.* Philidelphia: Lippincott.

Cooper, S.J. (1975). Anaesthetisation of prefrontal cortex and response to noxious stimulation. *Nature, 254,* 439–440.

Coplan, J. D., Andrews, M. W., Rosenblum, L. A., Owens, M. J., Gorman, J. M., & Nemeroff, C. B. (1996). Increased cerebrospinal fluid CRF concentrations in adult non-human primates previously exposed to adverse experiences as infants. *Proceedings of the National Academy of Sciences of the United States of America, 93,* 1619–1623.

Coplan, J. D., Trost, R. C., Owens, M. J., Cooper, T. B., Gorman, J. M., Nemeroff, C. B., & Rosenblum, L. A. (1998). Cerebrospinal fluid concentrations of somatostatin and biogenic amines in grown primates reared by mothers exposed to manipulated foraging conditions. *Archives of General Psychiatry, 55,* 473–477.

Cornford, M. E., Philippart, M., Jacobs, B., & Scheibel, A. B., & Vintners, H. V. (1994). Neuropathology of Rett syndrome: Case report with neuronal and mitochondrial abnormalities in the brain. *Journal of Child Neurology, 9,* 424–431.

Corodimas, K. P., LeDoux, J. E., Gold, P. W., & Schulkin, J. (1994). Corticosterone potentiation of learned fear. *Annals of the New York Academy of Sciences, 746,* 392–393.

Corrigan, F. M., Davidson, A., & Heard, H. (2000). The role of dysregulated amygdalic emotion in borderline personality disorder. *Medical Hypotheses, 54,* 574–579.

Coule, J. T., Frith, C. D., Frackowiak, R. S. J., & Grasby, P. M. (1996). A fronto-parietal network for rapid visual information processing: A PET study of sustained attention and working memory. *Neuropsychologia, 34,* 1085–1095.

Craig, A. D. (2002). How do you feel? Interoception: The sense of the physiological condition of the body. *Nature Neuroscience, 3,* 655–666.

Craig, A. D., Chen, K., Bandy, D., & Reiman, E. M. (2000). Thermosensory activation of insular cortex. *Nature Neuroscience, 3,* 184–190.

Cratty, M. S., Ward, H. E., Johnson, E. A., Azzaro, A. J., & Birkle, D. L. (1995). Prenatal stress increases corticotropin-releasing factor (CRF) content and release in rat amygdala minces. *Brain Research, 675,* 675–302.

Critchley, H., Daly, E., Philips, M., Brammer, M., Bullmore, E., Williams, S., Van Amelsvoort, T., Robertson, D., David, A., & Murphy, D. (2000). Explicit and implicit neural mechanisms for processing of social information from facial expressions: A functional magnetic resonance imaging study. *Human Brain Mapping, 9,* 93–105.

Critchley, H. D., Elliott, R., Mathias, C. J., & Dolan, R. J. (2000). Neual activity relating to generation and representation of galvanic skin conductance responses: A functional magnetic resonance imaging study. *Journal of Neuroscience, 20,* 3033–3040.

Critchley, H. D., Melmed, R. N., Featherstone, E., Mathias, C. J., & Dolan, R. J. (2001). Brain activity during biofeedback relaxation: A functional neuroimaging investigation. *Brain, 124,* 1003–1012.

Crittenden, P. M. (1995). Attachment and psychopathology. In S. Goldberg, R. Muir, & J. Kerr (Eds.), *Attachment theory: Social, developmental, and clinical perspectives* (pp. 367–406). Mahwah, NJ: Analytic Press.

Crittenden, P. M., & Ainsworth, M. D. S. (1989). Child maltreatment and attachment theory. In D. Cicchetti & V. Carlson (Eds.), *Child maltreatment: Theory and research on the causes and consequences of child abuse and neglect* (pp. 432–463). New York: Cambridge University Press.

Crittenden, P. M., & DiLalla, D. L. (1988). Compulsive compliance: the development of an inhibitory coping strategy in infancy. *Journal of Abnormal and Child Psychology, 16,* 585–599.

Crowell, D. H., Jones, R. H., Kapuniai, L. E., & Nakagawa, J. K. (1973). Unilateral cortical activity in newborn humans: An early index of cerebral dominance? *Science, 180,* 205–208.

Crowell, J. A., & Feldman, S. S. (1991). Mothers' working models of attachment relationships and mother and child behavior during separation and reunion. *Developmental Psychology, 27,* 597–605.

Crucian, G. P., Hughes, J. D., Barrett, A. M., Williamson, D. J. G., Bauer, R. M., Bowres, D., & Heilman, K. M. (2000). Emotional and physiological responses to false feedback. *Cortex, 36,* 623–647.

Crume, T. L., DiGuiseppi, C., Byers, T., Sirotnak, A. P., & Garrett, C. J. (2002). Under ascertainment of child maltreatment fatalities by death certificates, 1990–1998. *Pediatrics, 110,* e18.

Cummings, J. L. (1997). Neuropsychiatric manifestations of right hemisphere lesions. *Brain and Language, 57,* 22–37.

Cummins, C. J., Loreck, D. J., & McCandless, D. W. (1985). Ancillary pathways of energy metabolism in mammalian brain: The pentose phosphate pathway and galactose metabolism. In R. C. Wiggins, D. W. McCandless, & S. J. Enna (Eds.), *Developmental Neurochemistry* (pp. 160–179). Austin: University of Texas Press.

Cutting, J. (1992). The role of right hemisphere dysfunction in psychiatric disorders. *British Journal of Psychiatry, 160,* 583–588.

Cutting, J. (1994). Evidence for right hemispheric dysfunction in schizophrenia. In A. S. David & J. S. Cutting (Eds.), *The neuropsychology of schizophrenia* (pp. 231–242). Hove, U.K.: Erlbaum.

Damasio, A. R. (1994). *Descartes' error.* New York: Grosset/Putnam.

Damasio, A. R. (1995). Toward a neurobiology of emotion and feeling: Operational concepts and hypotheses. *The Neuroscientist, 1,* 19–25.

Damasio, A. R. (1998). Emotion in the perspective of an integrated nervous system. *Brain Research Reviews, 26,* 83–86.

Damasio, A. R. (2000). A neural basis for sociopathy. *Archives of General Psychiatry, 57,* 128–129.

Damasio, A. R., Grabowski, T. J., Bechara, A., Damasio, H., Ponto, L. L. B., Parvizi, J., & Hichwa, R. D. (2000). Subcortical and cortical brain activity during the feeling of self-generated emotions. *Nature Neuroscience, 3,* 1049–1056.

Damasio, A. R., Tranel, D., & Damasio, H. (1990). Individuals with sociopathic behavior caused by frontal damage fail to respond autonomically to social stimuli. *Behavioral Brain Research, 41,* 81–94.

Darwin, C. (1965). *The expression of emotions in man and animals.* Chicago: University of Chicago Press. (Original work published 1872)

Davidson, J. R. T., & Foa, E. (1993). *Post traumatic stress disorder: DSM-IV and beyond.* Washington, DC: American Psychiatric Press.

Davidson, R. J., Ekman, P., Friesen, W. V., Saron, C. D., & Senulis, J. A. (1990). Approach-withdrawal and cerebral asymmetry: Emotional expression and brain physiology I. *Journal of Personality and Social Psychology, 58,* 330–341.

Davidson, R. J., & Fox, N. A. (1989). Frontal brain asymmetry predicts infants' response to maternal separation. *Journal of Abnormal Psychology, 98,* 127–131.

Davidson, R. J., & Hugdahl, K. (1995). *Brain asymmetry.* Cambridge, MA: MIT Press.

Davidson, R. J., Marshall, J. R., Tomarken, A. J., & Henriques, J. B. (2000). While a phobic waits: Regional brain electrical and autonomic activity in social phobics during anticipation of public speaking. *Biological Psychiatry, 47,* 85–95.

Davidson, R. J., Putnam, K. M., & Larson, C. L. (2000). Dysfunction in the neural circuitry of emotion regulation—A possible prelude to violence. *Science, 289,* 591–594.

Davidson, R. J., & Slatger, H. A. (2000). Probing emotion in the developing brain: functional neuroimaging in the assessment of the neural substrates of emotion in normal and disordered children and adolescents. *Mental Retardation and Developmental Disabilities Research Reviews, 6,* 166–170.

Davies, J. M., & Frawley, M. G. (1994). *Treating the adult survivor of childhood sexual abuse: A psychoanalytic perspective.* New York: Basic.

Davis, M. (1989). The role of the amygdala and its efferent projections in fear and anxiety. In P. Tyrer (Ed.), *Psychopharmacology of anxiety* (pp. 52–79). Oxford: Oxford University Press.

Dawson, G. (1994). Development of emotional expression and emotion regulation in infancy. In G. Dawson & K. W. Fischer (Eds.), *Human behavior and the developing brain* (pp. 346–379). New York: Guilford.

Dawson, G., Panagiotides, H., Grofer Klinger, L., & Hill, D. (1992). The role of frontal lobe functioning in the development of infant self-regulatory behavior. *Brain & Cognition, 20,* 152–175.

Day, R., & Wong, S. (1996). Anomalous perceptual asymmetries for negative emotional stimuli in the psychopath. *Journal of Abnormal Psychology, 105,* 648–652.

De Bellis, M. D. (2001). Developmental traumatology: The psychobiological development of maltreated children and its implications for research, treatment, and policy. *Development and Psychopathology, 13,* 539–564.

De Bellis, M. D. (2002). Developmental traumatology: A contributory mechanism for alcohol and substance use disorders. *Psychoneuroendocrinology, 27,* 155–170.

De Bellis, M. D., Casey, B. J., Dahl, R. E., Birmaher, B., Williamson, D. E., Thomas, K. M., Axelson, D. A., Frustaci, K., Boring, A. M., Hall, J., & Ryan, N. D. (2000). A pilot study of amygdala volume in pediatric generalized anxiety disorder. *Biological Psychiatry, 48,* 51–57.

De Bellis, M. D., Keshavan, M. S., Clark, D. B., Casey, B. J., Giedd, J. N., Boring, A. M., Frustaci, K., & Ryan, N. D. (1999). Developmental traumatology Part II: Brain development. *Biological Psychiatry, 45,* 1271–1284.

De Bellis, M. D., Keshavan, M. S., Frustaci, K., Shifflett, H., Iyengar, S., Beers, S. R., & Hall, J. (2002a). Superior temporal gyrus volumes in maltreated children and adolescents with PTSD. *Biological Psychiatry, 51,* 544–552.

De Bellis, M. D., Keshavan, M. S., Shifflett, H., Iyengar, S., Beers, S. R., Hall, J., & Mortiz, G. (2002b). Brain structures in pediatric maltreatment-related posttraumatic stress disorder: A sociodemographically matched study. *Biological Psychiatry, 52,* 1066–1078.

De Bellis, M. D., Keshaven, M. S., Spencer, S., & Hall, J. (2000). N-acetylaspartate concentration in anterior cingulate with PTSD. *American Journal of Psychiatry, 157,* 1175–1177.

de Bruin, J. P. C. (1990). Social behaviour and the prefrontal cortex. *Progress in Brain Research, 85,* 485–500.

de Guise, E., del Pesce, M., Foschi, N., Quattrini, A., Papo, I., & Lassonde, M. (1999). Callosal and cortical contribution to procedural learning. *Brain, 122,* 1049–1062.

De Haan, E. H. F., Young, A. W., & Newcombe, F. (1987). Face recognition without awareness. *Cognitive Neuropsychology, 4,* 385–415.

de Haan, M., Nelson, C. A., Gunnar, M. R., & Tout, K. A. (1998). Hemispheric differences in brain activity related to the recognition of emotional expressions by 5-year-old children. *Developmental Neuropsychology, 14,* 495–518.

de Oliveira, L., Hoffmann, A., & Menescal-de-Oliveira, L. (1997). The lateral hypothalamus in the modulation of tonic immobility in guinea pigs. *NeuroReport, 8,* 3489–3493.

de Schonen, S., Deruelle, C., Mancini, J., & Pascalis, O. (1993). Hemispheric differences in face processing and brain maturation. In B. de Boysson-Bardies, S. de Schonen, P. Jusczyk, P. McNeilage, & J. Morton (Eds.), *Developmental neurocognition: Speech and face processing in the first year of life* (pp. 149–163). Dordrecht, Netherlands: Kluwer Academic Publishing.

de Schonen, S., Gil de Diaz, M., & Mathivet, E. (1986). Hemispheric asymmetry in face processing in infancy. In H. D. Ellis, M. A. Jeeves, F. Newcombe, & A. W. Young (Eds.), *Aspects of face processing* (pp. 199–209). Dordrecht, Netherlands: Nijhoff.

DeCasper, A., & Fifer, W. (1980). Of human bonding: Newborns prefer their mothers' voices. *Science, 208,* 1174–1176.

Deckel, A. W., Hesselbroock, V., & Bauer, L. (1996). Antisocial personality disorder, childhood delinquency, and frontal brain functioning: EEG and neuropsychological findings. *Journal of Clinical Psychology, 52,* 1–12.

Deecke, L., Kornhuber, M., Long, M., & Schreiber, H. (1985). Timing function of the frontal cortex in sequential motor and learning tasks. *Human Neurobiology, 4,* 143–154.

DeKosky, S. T., Nonneman, A. J., & Scheff, S. W. (1982). Morphologic and behavioral effects of perinatal glucocorticoid administration. *Physiology and Behavior, 29,* 895–900.

Deldin, P. J., Keller, J., Gergen, J. A., & Miller, G. A. (2000). Right-posterior face processing anomaly in depression. *Journal of Abnormal Psychology, 109,* 116–121.

DeLong, G. R. (2002). Mid-gestation right basal ganglia lesion. Clinical observations in two childen. *Neurology, 59,* 54–58.

Demaree, H. A., & Harrison, D. W. (1997). Physiological and neuropsychological correlates of hostility. *Neuropsychologia, 35,* 1405–1411.

Demos, V. (1991). Resiliency in infancy. In T. F. Dugan & R. Coles (Eds.), *The child in our times: Studies in the development of resiliency* (pp. 3–17). New York: Brunner/Mazel.

Demos, V., & Kaplan, S. (1986). Motivation and affect reconsidered: Affect biographies of two infants. *Psychoanalysis and Contemporary Thought, 9,* 147–221.

Denenberg, V. H., Garbanti, J., Sherman, G., Yutzey, D. A., & Kaplan, R. (1978). Infantile stimulation induces brain lateralization in rats. *Science, 201,* 1150–1152.

Denton, D., Shade, R., Zamarippa, F., Egan, G., Blair-West, J., McKinley, M., Lancaster, J., & Fox, P. (1999). Neuroimaging of genesis and satiation of thirst and an interoceptor-driven theory of origins of primary consciousness. *Proceedings of the National Academy of Sciences of the United States of America, 96,* 5304–5309.

Derryberry, D., & Tucker, D. M. (1992). Neural mechanisms of emotion. *Journal of Clinical and Consulting Psychology, 60,* 329–338.

Deruelle, C., & de Schonen, S. (1998). Do the right and left hemispheres attend to the same visuospatial information within a face in infancy? *Developmental Neuropsychology, 14,* 535–554.

Deutch, A. Y. (1992). The regulation of subcortical dopamine systems by the prefrontal cortex: Interactions of central dopamine systems and the pathogenesis of schizophrenia. *Journal of Neural Transmission, 36*(Suppl.), 61–89.

Deutsch, A. Y., Goldstein, M., & Roth, R. H. (1986). Activation of the locus coeruleus induced by selective stimulation of the ventral tegmental area. *Brain Research, 363,* 307–314.

Deutch, A. Y., Lee, M. C., Gilham, M. H., Cameron, D. A., Goldstein, M., & Iadarola, M. J. (1991). Stress selectively increases Fos protein in dopamine neurons innervating the prefrontal cortex. *Cerebral Cortex, 1,* 273–292.

Deutch, A. Y., & Young, C. D. (1995). A model of the stress-induced activation of prefrontal cortical dopamine systems: Coping and the development of post-traumatic stress disorder. In M. J. Friedman & D. S. Charney (Eds.), *Neurobiological and clinical consequences of stress: From normal adaptation to post-traumatic stress disorder* (pp. 163–175). Philadelphia: Lippincott Williams & Wilkins.

Devinsky, O. (2000). Right cerebral hemisphere dominance for a sense of corporeal and emotional self. *Epilepsy & Behavior, 1,* 60–73.

Devinsky, O., Morrell, M. J., & Vogt, B. A. (1995). Contributions of anterior cingulate cortex to behaviour. *Brain, 118,* 279–306.

Dewarja, R., & Sasaki, Y. (1990). A right to left callosal transfer defict of nonlinguistic information in alexithymia. *Psychotherapy and Psychosomatics, 54,* 201–207.

Diamond, A., & Doar, B. (1989). The performance of human infants on a measure of frontal cortex function, the delayed response task. *Developmental Psychobiology, 22,* 271–294.

Diamond, M. C., Krech, D., & Rosenzweig, M. R. (1963). The effects of an enriched environment on the histology of the rat cerebral cortex. *Journal of Comparative Neurology, 123,* 111–120.

Diamond, S., Balvin, R., & Diamond, F. (1963). *Inhibition and choice.* New York: Harper & Row.

Dias, R., Robbins, T. W., & Roberts, A. C. (1996). Dissociation in prefrontal cortex of affective and attentional shifts. *Nature, 380,* 69–72.

Dimberg, U., & Petterson, M. (2000). Facial reactions to happy and angry facial expressions: Evidence for right hemisphere dominance. *Psychophysiology, 37,* 693–696.

Dinn, W. M., & Harris, C. L. (2000). Neurocognitive function in antisocial personality disorder. *Psychiatry Research, 97,* 173–190.

Diorio, D., Viau, V., & Meaney, M. J. (1993). The role of the medial prefrontal cortex (cingulate gyrus) in the regulation of hypothalamic-pituitary-adrenal responses to stress. *Journal of Neuroscience, 13,* 3839–3847.

Dix, T. (1991). The affective organization of parenting: Adaptive and maladaptive processes. *Psychologial Bulletin, 110,* 3–25.

Dixon, A. K. (1998). Ethological strategies for defense in animals and humans: Their role in some psychiatric disorders. *British Journal of Medical Psychology, 71,* 417–445.

Dobbing, J. (1997). *Developing brain and behavior: The role of lipids in infant formula.* San Diego: Academic Press.

Dobbing, J., & Sands, J. (1973). Quantitative growth and development of human brain. *Archives of Diseases of Childhood, 48,* 757–767.

Dobbing, J., & Smart, J. L. (1974). Vulnerability of developing brain and behavior. *British Medical Bulletin, 30,* 164–168.

Dodge, K. A., Lochman, J. E., Harnish, J. D., & Bates, J. E. (1997). Reactive and proactive aggression in school children and psychiatrically impaired chronically assaultive youth. *Journal of Abnormal Psychology, 106,* 37–51.

Dodge, K. A., & Somberg, D. R. (1987). Hostile attributional biases among aggressive boys are exacerbated under conditions of threat to the self. *Child Development, 58,* 213–224.

Dolan, M., Deakin, W. J. F., Roberts, N., & Anderson, I. (2002). Serotonergic and cognitive impairment in impulsive aggressive personality disordered offenders: Are there implications for treatment? *Psychological Medicine, 32,* 105–117.

Dolan, M., & Park, J. (2002). The neuropsychology of antisocial personality disorder. *Psychological Medicine, 32,* 417–427.

Dolan, R. J. (1999). On the neurology of morals. *Nature Neuroscience, 2,* 927–929.

Dolan, R. J., & Grasby, P. M. (1994). Exploring the functional role of monoaminergic neurotransmission: A method for exploring neurotransmitter dysfunction in psychiatric disorders. *British Journal of Psychiatry, 164,* 575–580.

Donovan, W. L., Leavitt, L. A., & Balling, J. D. (1978). Maternal physiological response to infant signals. *Psychophysiology, 15,* 68–74.

Dostrovsky, J. O., Hutchison, W. D., Davis, K. D., & Lozano, A. (1995). Potential role of orbital and cingulate cortices in nociception. In J. M. Beeson, G. Guilbaud, & H. Ollat (Eds.), *Forebrain areas involved in pain processing* (pp. 171–181). Paris: John Libbey Eurotext.

Dougherty, D. M., Bjork, J. M., Huckabee, H. C. G., Moeller, F. G., & Swann, A. C. (1999). Laboratory measures of aggression and impulsivity in women with borderline personality disorder. *Psychiatry Research, 85,* 315–326.

Dowling, A. L. S., Martz, G. U., Leonard, J. L., & Zoeller, R. T. (2000). Acute changes in maternal thyroid hormone induce rapid and transient changes in gene expression in fetal rat brain. *Journal of Neuroscience, 20,* 2255–2265.

Dozier, M., & Kobak, R. R. (1992). Psychophysiology in attachment interviews: Converging evidence for deactivating strategies. *Child Development, 63,* 1473–1480.

Draijer, N., & Langeland, W. (1999). Childhood trauma and perceived parental dysfunction in the etiology of dissociative symptoms in psychiatric patients. *American Journal of Psychiatry, 156,* 379–385.

Durig, J., & Hornung, J.-P. (2000). Neonatal serotonin depletion affects developing and mature mouse cortical neurons. *NeuroReport, 11,* 833–837.

Ebbesson, S. O. E. (1980). The parcellation theory and its relation to interspecific variability in brain organization, evolutionary and ontogenetic development, and neuronal plasticity. *Cell and Tissue Research, 213,* 179–212.

Eckenrode, J., Ganzel, B., Henderson, C. R., Jr., Smith, E., Olds, D. L., Powers, J., Cole, R., Kitzman, H., & Sidora, K. (2000). Preventing child abuse and neglect with a program of nurse home visitation: The limiting effects of domestic violence. *Journal of the Amercian Medical Association, 284,* 1385–1391.

Edelman, G. (1989). *The remembered present: A biological theory of consciousness.* New York: Basic.

Egger, M. D., & Flynn, J. P. (1967). Further studies on the effects of amygdaloid stimulation and ablation on hypothalamically elicited attack behavior in cats. *Progress in Brain Research, 27,* 165–182.

Eisenberg, L. (1995). The social construction of the human brain. *American Journal of Psychiatry, 152,* 1563–1575.

El-Khodor, B. F., & Boksa, P. (2002). Birth insult and stress interact to alter dopamine transporter binding in rat brain. *NeuroReport, 13,* 201–206.

Elliott, D. (1997). Traumatic events: Prevalence and delayed recall in the general population. *Journal of Consulting and Clinical Psychology, 65,* 811–820.

Elliott, R., Dolan, R. J., & Frith, C. D. (2000). Dissociable functions in the medial and lateral orbitofrontal cortex: Evidence from human neuroimaging studies. *Cerebral Cortex, 10,* 308–317.

Elliott, R., Frith, C. D., & Dolan, R. J. (1997). Differential neural response to positive and negative feedback in planning and guessing tasks. *Neuropsychologia, 35,* 1395–1404.

Emde, R. N. (1983). The pre-representational self and its affective core. *Psychoanalytic Study of the Child, 38,* 165–192.

Emde, R. N. (1988). Development terminable and interminable: I. Innate and motivational factors from infancy. *International Journal of Psycho-Analysis, 69,* 23–42.

Emde, R. N. (1990). Mobilizing fundamental modes of development: Empathic availability and therapeutic action. *Journal of the American Psychoanalytic Association, 38,* 881–913.

Emery, N. J. (2000). The eyes have it: The neuroethology, function and evolution of social gaze. *Neuroscience and Biobehavioral Reviews, 24,* 581–604.

Eppinger, H. & Hess, L. (1915). Vagotonia: A clinical study in vegetative neurology. *Journal of Nervous and Mental Disease, 20,* 1–93.

Epstein, H. T. (2001). An outline of the role of brain in human cognitive development. *Brain and Cognition, 45,* 44–51.

Epstein, J. N., Conners, C. K., Erhardt, D., March, J. S., & Swanson, J. M. (1997). Asymmetrical hemispheric control of visual-spatial attention in adults with attention deficit hyperactivity disorder. *Neuropsychology, 11,* 467–473.

Erciyas, A. H., Topalkara, K., Topaktas, S., Akyuz, A., & Dener, S. (1999). Suppression of cardiac paraympathetic functions in patients with right hemispheric stroke. *European Journal of Neurology, 6,* 685–690.

Erecinska, M., Nelson, D., & Silver, I. A. (1996). Metabolic and energetic properties of isolated nerve ending particles (synaptosomes). *Biochimica et Biophysica Acta, 1277,* 13–34.

Erecinska, M., & Silver, I. A. (1989). ATP and brain function. *Journal of Cerebral Blood Flow and Metabolism, 9,* 2–19.

Erikson, E. (1950). *Childhood and society.* New York: W. W. Norton.

Erikson, M. F., Egeland, B., & Pianta, R. (1989). The effects of maltreatment on the development of young children. In D. Cicchetti, & V. Carlson (Eds.), *Child maltreatment: Theory and research on the causes and consequences of child abuse and neglect* (pp. 647–684). New York: Cambridge University Press.

Ernst, M., Zametkin, A. J., Matochik, J. A., Pascualvaca, D., Jons, P. H., & Cohen, R. M. (1999). High midbrain [^{18}F] DOPA accumulation in children with attention deficit hyperactivity disorder. *American Journal of Psychiatry, 156,* 1209–1215.

Erzurumlu, R. S., & Killackey, H. P. (1982). Critical and sensitive periods in neurobiology. *Current Topics in Developmental Biology, 17,* 207–240.

Eslinger, P. J. (1999). Orbital frontal cortex: historical and contemporary views about its behavioral and physiological significance. An introduction to special topic papers: Part I. *Neurocase, 5,* 225–229.

Espinosa, M., Beckwith, L., Howard, J., Tyler, R., & Swanson, K. (2001). Maternal psychopathology and attachment in toddlers of heavy cocaine-using mothers. *Infant Mental Health Journal, 22,* 316–333.

Espy, K. A., Kaufmann, P. M., & Glisky, M. L. (1999). Neuopsychological function in toddlers exposed to cocaine in utero: A preliminary study. *Developmental Neuropsychology, 15,* 447–460.

Essex, M. J., Klein, M. H., Cho, E., & Kalin, N. H. (2002). Maternal stress beginning in infancy may sensitize children to later stress exposure: Effects on cortisol and behavior. *Biological Psychiatry, 52,* 776–784.

Etcoff, N. L. (1984). Selective attention to facial identity and facial emotion. *Neuropsychologia, 22,* 281–295.

Euler, U. S. von, & Folkow, B. (1958). The effect of stimulation of autonomic areas in the cerebral cortex upon the adrenaline and noradrenaline secretion from the adrenal gland in the cat. *Acta Physiologica Scandinavica, 42,* 313–320.

Fagen, R. (1977). Selection for optimal age-dependent schedules of play behavior. *American Naturalist, 111,* 395–414.

Falk, D., Hildebolt, C., Cheverud, J., Vannier, M., Helmkamp, R. C., & Konigsberg, L. (1990). Cortical asymmetries in frontal lobes of Rhesus monkeys (*Macaca mulatta*). *Brain Research, 512,* 40–45.

Famularo, R., Kinscherff, R., & Fenton, T. (1992a). Posttraumatic stress disorder among children clinically diagnosed as borderline personality disorder. *Journal of Nervous and Mental Disease, 179,* 428–431.

Famularo, R., Kinscherff, R., & Fenton, T. (1992b). Psychiatric diagnoses of abusive mothers: A preliminary report. *Journal of Nervous and Mental Disease, 180,* 658–661.

Fanselow, M. S. (1986). Conditioned fear-induced opiate analgesia: A compelling motivational state theory of stress analgesia. In D. D. Kelly (Ed.), *Stress-induced analgesia* (pp. 40–54). New York: New York Academy of Sciences.

Farber, J. L. (1981). The role of calcium in cell death. *Life Sciences, 29,* 1289–1295.

Feeny, N. C., Zoellner, L. A., & Foa, E. B. (2000). Anger, dissociation, and posttraumatic stress disorder among female assault victims. *Journal of Traumatic Stress, 13,* 89–100.

Feinman, S. (1982). Social referencing in infancy. *Merrill-Palmer Quarterly, 28,* 445–470.

Feldman, R., Greenbaum, C. W., & Yirmiya, N. (1999). Mother-infant affect synchrony as an antecedent of the emergence of self-control. *Developmental Psychology, 35,* 223–231.

Feldman, R., Greenbaum, C. W., Yirmiya, N., & Mayes, L. C. (1996). Relations between cyclicity and regulation in mother-infant interaction at 3 and 9 months and cognition at 2 years. *Journal of Applied Developmental Psychology, 17,* 347–365.

Felitti, V. J., Anda, R. F., Nordenberg, D., Williamson, D. F., Spitz, A. M., Edwards, V., Koss, M. P., & Marks, J. S. (1998). Relationship of childhood abuse and household dysfunction to many of the leading causes of death in adults. The adverse childhood experiences (ACE) study. *American Journal of Preventive Medicine, 14,* 245–258.

Fergusson, D. M., Woodward, L. J., & Horwood, L. J. (1998). Maternal smoking during pregnancy and psychiatric adjustment in late adolescence. *Archives of General Psychiatry, 55,* 721–727.

Fernald, A. (1989). Intonation and communicative interest in mother's speech to infants: Is the melody the message? *Child Development, 60,* 1497–1510.

Fernald, A. (1992). Human maternal vocalizations to infants as biologically relevant signals: An evolutionary perspective. In J. Barkow, L. Cosmides, & J. Tooby (Eds.), *The adapted mind* (pp. 391–428). Oxford: Oxford University Press.

Ferrie, J. C., Barantin, L., Saliba, E., Akoka, S., Tranquart, F., Sirinelli, D., & Pourcelot, L. (1999). MR assessment of the brain maturation during the perinatal period: Quantitative T_2 MR study in premature newborns. *Magnetic Resonance Imaging, 17,* 1275–1288.

Field, T. (1985). Attachment as psychobiological attunement: Being on the same wavelength. In M. Reite & T. Field (Eds.), *The psychobiology of attachment and separation* (pp. 415–454). Orlando, FL: Academic Press.

Field, T., Diego, M., Hernandez-Reif, M., Schanberg, S., & Kuhn, C. (2002). Relative right versus left frontal EEG in neonates. *Developmental Psychobiology, 41,* 147–155.

Field, T., & Fogel, A. (1982). *Emotion and early interaction.* Hillsdale, NJ: Erlbaum.

Field, T., Fox, N. A., Pickens, J., & Nawrocki, T. (1995). Relative right frontal EEG activation in 3- to 6-month-old infants of "depressed" mothers. *Developmental Psychology, 31,* 358–363.

Field, T., Pickens, J., Fox, N. A., Nawrocki, T., & Gonzalez, J. (1995). Vagal tone in infants of depressed mothers. *Development and Psychopathology, 7,* 227–231.

Field, T. M. (1977). Effects of early separation, interactive deficits and experimental manipulations on infant-mother face-to-face interactions. *Child Development, 48,* 763–771.

Filley, C. M., Price, B. H., Nell, V., Antoinette, T., Morgan, A. S., Bresnahan, J. F., Pincus, J. H., Gelbort, M. M., Weisberg, M., & Kelly, J. P. (2001). Toward an understanding of violence: Neurobiobehvioral conference consensus statement. *Neuropsychiatry, Neuropsychology, and Behavioral Neurology, 14,* 1–14.

Filloux, F., & Townsend, J. J. (1993). Pre- and postsynaptic neurotoxic effects of dopamine demonstrated by intrastriatal injection. *Experimental Neurology, 119,* 79–88.

Fink, G. R., Halligan, P. W., Marshall, J. C., Frith, C. D., Frackowiak, R. S. J., & Dolan, R. J. (1996). Where in the brain does visual attention select the forest from the trees? *Nature, 382,* 626–628.

Fink, G. R., Markowitsch, H. J., Reinkemeier, M., Bruckbauer, T., Kessler, J., & Heiss, W.-D. (1996). Cerebral representation of one's own past: Neural networks involved in autobiographical memory. *Journal of Neuroscience, 16,* 4275–4282.

Fischer, H., Andersson, J. L. R., Furmark, T. Wik, G., & Fredrikson, M. (2002). Right-sided human prefrontal brain activation during acquisition of conditioned fear. *Emotion, 2,* 233–241.

Fischer, K. W., & Rose, S. P. (1994). Dynamic development of coordination of components in brain and behavior: A framework for theory and research. In G. Dawson & K. W. Fischer (Eds.), *Human behavior and the developing brain* (pp. 3–66). New York: Guilford.

Fish, B., Marcus, J., Hans, S. L., Auerbach, J. G., & Perdue, S. (1992). Infants at risk for schizophrenia: Sequelae of a genetic neurointegrative defect. *Archives of General Psychiatry, 49,* 221–235.

Fisher, R. S., & Almli, C. R. (1984). Postnatal development of sensory influences on labeled hypothalamic neurons of the rat. *Developmental Brain Research, 12,* 55–75.

Fitzgerald, L. W., Keller, R. W., Glick. S. D., & Carlson, J. N. (1989). The effects of stressor controllability on regional changes in mesocorticolimbic dopamine activity. *Society of Neuroscience Abstracts, 15,* 1316.

Fleming, A. S., O'Day, D. H., & Kraemer, G. W. (1999). Neurobiology of mother-infant interactions: experience and central nervous system plasticity across development and generations. *Neuroscience and Biobehavioral Reviews, 23,* 673–685.

Flicker, C., McCarley, R. W., & Hobson, J. A. (1981). Aminergic neurons: State control and plasticity in three model systems. *Cellular and Molecular Neurobiology, 1,* 123–166.

Fogel, A. (1982). Affect dynamics in early infancy: affective tolerance. In T. Field & A. Fogel (Eds.), *Emotion and early interaction.* Hillsdale, NJ: Erlbaum.

Fogel, A. (in press). Remembering infancy: accessing our earliest experiences. In G. Bremner & A. Slater (Eds.), *Theories of infant development.* Cambridge, U.K.: Blackwell.

Fogel, A., & Branco, A. U. (1997). Metacommunication as a source of indeterminism in relationship development. In A. Fogel, M. C. D. P. Lyra, & J. Valsinger (Eds.), *Dynamics and indeterminism in developmental and social processes* (pp. 65–92). Mahwah, NJ: Erlbaum.

Folkman, S., & Lazarus, R. S. (1980). An analysis of coping in a middle-aged community sample. *Journal of Health and Social Behavior, 21,* 219–239.

Fonagy, P., Leigh, T., Steele, M., Steele, H., Kennedy, R., Matoon, G., Target, M., & Garber, A. (1996). The relation of attachment status, psychiatric classification, and response to psychotherapy. *Journal of Consulting and Clinical Psychology, 64,* 22–31.

Fonagy, P., & Target, M. (1997). Attachment and reflective function: Their role in self-organization. *Development and Psychopathology, 9,* 679–700.

Fonagy, P., & Target, M. (2002). Early intervention and development of self-regulation. *Psychoanalytic Inquiry, 22,* 307–335.

Fonberg, E. (1986). Amygdala, emotions, motivation, and depressive states. In R. Plutchik & H. Kellerman (Eds.), *Emotion: Theory, research, and experience: Vol. 3. Biological foundations of emotion* (pp. 301–331). New York: Academic Press.

Foote, S. L. (1987). Extrathalamic modulation of cortical function. *Annual Review of Neuroscience, 10,* 67–95.

Foote, S. L. & Morrison, S. H. (1991). Development of the noradrenergic, serotonergic, and dopaminergic innervation of the cortex. *Current Topics in Developmental Biology, 21,* 391–423.

Fornai, F., Vaglini, F., Maggio, R., Bonuccelli, U., & Corsini, G. U. (1997). Species differences in the role of excitatory amino acids in experimental Parkinsonism. *Neuroscience and Biobehavioral Reviews, 21,* 401–415.

Fornazarrari, L., Farenik, K., Smith, I., Heasman, G. A., & Ischise, M. I. (1992). Violent visual hallucinations and aggression in frontal lobe dysfunction: Clinical manifestations of deep orbitofrontal foci. *Journal of Neuropsychiatry and Clinical Neuroscience, 4,* 42–44.

Fox, N. A. (1991). If it's not left, it's right: Electroencephalography asymmetry and the development of emotion. *American Psychologist, 46,* 863–872.

Fox, N. A., Calkins, S. D., & Bell, M. A. (1994). Neural plasticity and development in the first two years of life: Evidence from cognitive and socioemotional domains of research. *Development and Psychopathology, 6,* 677–696.

Fox, N. A., & Davidson, R. J. (1988). Patterns of brain electrical activity during facial signs of emotion in 10-month-old infants. *Developmental Psychology, 24,* 230–236.

Fox, N. A., Schmidt, L. A., Calkins, S. D., Rubin, K. H., & Coplan, R. J. (1996). The role of frontal activation in the regulation and dysregulation of social behavior during the preschool years. *Development and Psychopathology, 8,* 89–102.

Fraiberg, S. (1969). Libidinal object constancy and mental representation. *Psychoanalytic Study of the Child, 24,* 9–47.

Fraiberg, S., Adelson, E., & Shapiro, V. (1975). Ghosts in the nursery: A psychoanalytic approach to the problem of impaired infant-mother relationships. *Journal of the American Academy of Child Psychiatry, 14,* 387–422.

Francis, D. D., Diorio, J., Liu, D., & Meaney, M. J. (1999). Nongenomic transmission across generations of maternal behavior and stress responses in the rat. *Science, 286,* 1155–1158.

Francis, D. D., & Meaney, M. J. (1999). Maternal care and the development of stress responses. *Current Opinion in Neurobiology, 9,* 128–134.

Francis, S., Rolls, E. T., Bowtell, R., McGlone, F., O'Doherty, J., Browning, A., Clare, S., & Smith, E. (1999). The representation of pleasant touch in the brain and its relationship with taste and olfactory areas. *Cognitive Neuroscience, 10,* 453–459.

Franklin, T. R., Acton, P. D., Maldjian, J. A., Gray, J. D., Croft, J. R., Dackis, C. A., O'Brien, C. P., & Childress, A. R. (2002). Decreased gray matter concentration in insular, orbitofrontal, cingulate, and temporal cortices of cocaine patients. *Biological Psychiatry, 51,* 134–142.

Frederikson, M., Wik, G., Annas, P., Ericson, K., & Stone-Elander, S. (1995). Functional neuroanatomy of visually elicited simple phobic fear: Additional data and theoretical analysis. *Psychophysiology, 32,* 43–48.

Freeman, A. S., Meltzer, L. T., & Bunney, B. S. (1985). Firing properties of substantia nigra dopaminergic neurons in freely moving rats. *Life Sciences, 36,* 1983–1994.

Freeman, T. W., & Kimbrell, T. (2001). A "cure" for chronic combat-related posttraumatic stress disorder secondary to a right frontal lobe infarct: A case report. *Journal of Neuropsychiatry and Clinical Neuroscience, 13,* 106–109.

Freud, A. (1968). Notes on the connection between the states of negativism and psychic surrender. In *The writings of Anna Freud* (Vol. 4, pp. 256–259). New York: International Universities Press. (Original work published 1951)

Freud, A. (1969). Comments on psychic trauma. In *The writings of Anna Freud* (Vol. 5, pp. 221–241). New York: International Universities Press. (Original work published 1967)

Freud, S. (1953). The interpretation of dreams. In J. Strachey (Ed. & Trans.), *The standard edition of the complete psychological works of Sigmund Freud* (Vols. 4 & 5). London: Hogarth Press. (Original work published 1900)

Freud, S. (1955). Beyond the pleasure principle. In J. Strachey (Ed. & Trans.), *The standard edition of the complete psychological works of Sigmund Freud* (Vol. 18, pp. 7–64). London: Hogarth Press. (Original work published 1920)

Freud, S. (1957). The unconscious. In J. Strachey (Ed. & Trans.), *The standard edition of the complete psychological works of Sigmund Freud* (Vol. 14, pp. 159–209). London: Hogarth Press. (Original work published 1915)

Freud, S. (1959a). An autobiographical study. In J. Strachey (Ed. & Trans.), *The standard edition of the complete psychological works of Sigmund Freud* (Vol. 20, pp. 7–71). London: Hogarth Press. (Original work published 1925)

Freud, S. (1959b). Inhibition, symptoms, and anxiety. In J. Strachey (Ed. & Trans.), *The standard edition of the complete psychological works of Sigmund Freud* (Vol. 20, pp. 77–175). London: Hogarth Press. (Original work published 1926)

Freud, S. (1964). An outline of psycho-analysis. In J. Strachey (Ed. & Trans.), *The standard edition of the complete psychological works of Sigmund Freud* (Vol. 23, pp. 141–291). London: Hogarth Press. (Original work published 1940)

Freud, S. (1966). Project for a scientific psychology. In J. Strachey (Ed. & Trans.), *The standard edition of the complete psychological works of Sigmund Freud* (Vol. 1, pp. 283–392). London: Hogarth Press. (Original work published 1895)

Frey, S., & Petrides, M. (2000). Orbitofrontal cortex: a key prefrontal region for encoding information. *Proceedings of the National Academy of Sciences of the United States of America, 97,* 8723–8727.

Freyd, J. J. (1987). Dynamic mental representations. *Psychological Reviews, 94,* 427–438.

Freyd, J. J. (1996). *Betrayal trauma theory: The logic of forgetting childhood abuse.* Cambridge, MA: Harvard University Press.

Friede, E., & Weinstock, M. (1988). Prenatal stress increases anxiety related behavior and alters cerebral lateralization of dopamine activity. *Life Sciences, 42,* 1059–1065.

Friedman, B. H., & Thayer, J. F. (1998). Autonomic balance revisited: Panic anxiety and heart rate variability. *Journal of Psychosomatic Research, 44,* 133–151.

Frijda, N. H. (1988). The laws of emotion. *American Psychologist, 43,* 349–358.

Frodi, A. M., & Lamb, M. E. (1980). Child abusers' responses to infant smiles and cries. *Child Development, 51,* 238–241.

Funayama, F. S., Grillon, C., Davis, M., & Phelps, E. A. (2001). A double dissociation in the affective modulation of startle in humans: Effects of unilateral temporal lobectomy. *Journal of Cognitive Neuroscience, 13,* 721–729.

Funnell, M. G., Corballis, P. M., & Gazzaniga. M. S. (2001). Hemispheric processing asymmetries: Implications for memory. *Brain and Cognition, 46,* 135–139.

Fuster, J. M. (1985). The prefrontal cortex and temporal integration. In A. Peters & E. G. Jones (Eds.), *Cerebral cortex: Vol. 4. Association and auditory cortices* (pp. 151–171). New York: Plenum.

Gabbard, G. O. (1994). Mind and brain in psychiatric treatment. *Bulletin of the Menninger Clinic, 58,* 427–446.

Gabrieli, J. D. D., Poldrack, R. A., & Desmond, J. E. (1998). The role of the left prefrontal cortex in language and memory. *Proceedings of the National Academy of Sciences of the United States of America, 95,* 906–913.

Gaensbauer, T. J. (1982). Regulation of emotional expression in infants from two contrasting caretaking environments. *Journal of the American Academy of Child Psychiatry, 21,* 163–171.

Gaensbauer, T. J. (2002). Representations of trauma in infancy: clinical and theoretical implications for the understanding of early memory. *Infant Mental Health Journal, 23,* 259–277.

Gaensbauer, T. S., & Hiatt, S. (1984). Facial communication of emotion in early infancy. In N. Fox & R. Davidson (Eds.), *The psychobiology of affective development* (pp. 207–230). Hillsdale, NJ: Erlbaum.

Gaensbauer, T. J., & Mrazek, D. (1981). Differences in the patterning of affective expression in infants. *Journal of the American Academy of Child Psychiatry, 20,* 673–691.

Gaensbauer, T. J., & Sands, K. (1979). Distorted affective communications in abused/neglected infants and their potential impact on caretakers. *Journal of the American Academy of Child Psychiatry, 18,* 238–250.

Gaensbauer, T. J., & Siegel, C. H. (1995). Therapeutic approaches to posttraumatic stress disorder in infants and toddlers. *Infant Mental Health Journal, 16,* 292–305.

Gainotti, G. (2000). Neuropsychological theories of emotion. In J. Borod (Ed.), *The neuropsychology of emotion* (pp. 214–236). New York: Oxford University Press.

Galderisi, S., Bucci, P., Mucci, A., Bernardo, A., Koenig, T., & Maj, M. (2001). Brain electrical microstates in subjects with panic disorder. *Psychophysiology, 54,* 427–435.

Galin, D. (1974). Lateral specialization and psychiatric issues: Speculations on development and the evolution of consciousness. *Annals of the New York Academy of Sciences, 299,* 397–411.

Galletly, C., Clark, C. R., McFarlane, A. C., & Weber, D. L. (2001). Working memory in posttraumatic stress disorder—an event-related potential study. *Journal of Traumatic Stress, 14,* 295–309.

Galton, V. A. (1965). Thyroid hormone-catecholamine relationships. *Endocrinology, 77,* 278–284.

Garavan, H., Pendergrass, J. C., Ross, T. J., Stein, E. A., & Risinger, R. C. (2001). Amygdala response to both positively and negatively valenced stimuli. *NeuroReport, 12,* 2779–2783.

Garavan, H., Ross, T. J., & Stein, E. A. (1999). Right hemisphere dominance of inhibitory control: An event-related functional MRI study. *Proceedings of the National Academy of Sciences of the United States of America, 96,* 8301–8306.

Gardner, H. (1983). *Frames of mind: The theory of multiple intelligences.* New York: Basic.

Gariano, R. F., & Groves, P. M. (1988). Burst firing induced in midbrain dopamine neurons by stimulation of the medial prefrontal and anterior cingulate cortices. *Brain Research, 462,* 194–198.

Garthwaite, G., & Garthwaite, J. (1986). Amino acid toxicity: Intracellular sites of calcium accumulation associated with the onset of irreversible damage to rat cerebellar neurones in vitro. *Neuroscience Letters, 71,* 53–58.

Gedo, J. E. (1999). *The evolution of psychoanalysis: Contemporary theory and practice.* New York: Other Press.

Gedo, J. E., & Wilson, A. (1993). *Hierarchical concepts in psychoanalysis: Theory, research, and clinical practice.* New York: Guilford.

Geisser, M. E., Roth, S. R., Bachman, J. E., & Eckert, T. A. (1996). The relationship between symptoms of post-traumatic stress disorder and pain, affective disturbance and disability among patients with accident and non-accident related pain. *Pain Augmentation, 66,* 207–214.

Gellhorn, E. (1967). The tuning of the nervous system: Physiological foundations and implications for behavior. *Perspectives in Biological Medicine, 10,* 559–591.

Gellhorn, E. (1970). The emotions and the ergotropic and trophotropic systems. *Psychologische Forschung, 34,* 48–94.

Gennarelli, T. A. (1994). Animal models of human head injury. *Journal of Neurotrauma, 1,* 357–368.

George, C., & Solomon, J. (1996). Representational models of relationships: Links between caregiving and attachment. *Infant Mental Health Journal, 17,* 198–216.

George, M. S., Parekh, P. I., Rosinsky, N., Ketter, T. A., Kimbrell, T. A., Heilman, K. M., Herscovitch, P., & Post, R. M. (1996). Understanding emotional prosody activates right hemispheric regions. *Archives of Neurology, 53,* 665–670.

George, M. S., Sackheim, H. A., Rush, A. J., Marangell, L. B., Nahas, Z., Hasain, M. M., Lisanby, S., Burt, T., Goldman, J., & Ballenger, J. C. (2000). Vagus nerve stimulation: A new tool for brain reserach and therapy. *Biological Psychiatry, 47,* 287–295. New York: Elsevier.

George, N., Dolan, R. J., Fink, G., Baylis, G. C., Russell, C., & Driver. J. (1999). Human fusiform gyrus extracts shape-from-shading to recognize familiar faces. *Nature Neuroscience, 2,* 574–580.

Geracioti, T. D., Baker, D. G., Ekhator, N. N., West, S. A., Hill, K. K., Bruce, A. B., Scmidt, D., Rounds-Kugler, R. N., Yehuda, R., Keck, P. E., & Kasckow, J. W. (2001). CSF norepinephrine concentrations in posttraumatic stress disorder. *American Journal of Psychiatry, 158,* 1227–1330.

Gergely, G., Nadasdy, Z., Csibra, G., & Biro, S. (1995). Taking the intentional stance at 12 months of age. *Cognition, 56,* 165–193.

Gerschenson, L. E., & Rotello, R. J. (1992). Apoptosis: A different type of cell death. *Federation of American Societies for Experimental Biology Journal, 6,* 2450–2455.

Geschwind, N., & Galaburda, A. M. (1987). *Cerebral lateralization: Biological mechanisms, associations, and pathology.* Boston: MIT Press.

Gibbons, A. (1998). Solving the brain's energy crisis. *Science, 280,* 1345–1347.

Gibson, K. R. (1996). The biocultural human brain, seasonal migrations, and the emergence of the upper paleolithic. In P. Mellars & K. R. Gibson (Eds.), *Modeling the human mind* (pp. 33–36). Cambridge, England: McDonald Institute for Archeological Research.

Gilbert, P. (1992). *Depression: The evolution of powerlessness.* New York: Guilford.

Gitelman, D. R., Alpert, N. M., Kosslyn, S., Daffner, K., Scinto, L., Thompson, W., Giulivi, C., Boveris, A., & Cadenas, E. (1995). Hydroxyl radical generation during mitochondrial electron transfer and the formation of 8-hydroxy desoxyguanosine in mitochondrial DNA. *Archives of Biochemistry and Biophysics, 316,* 909–916.

Glaser, D. (2000). Child abuse and neglect and the brain—A review. *Journal of Child Psychology and Psychiatry, 41,* 97–116.

Gleick, J. (1987). *Chaos, making a new science.* New York: Viking Penguin.

Glover, D. A., & Poland, R. E. (2002). Urinary cortisol and catecholamines in mothers of child cancer survivors with and without PTSD. *Psychoneuroendocrinology, 27,* 805–819.

Glover, V. (1997). Maternal stress or anxiety in pregnancy and emotional development of the child. *British Journal of Psychiatry, 171,* 105–106.

Glynn, L. M., Wadhwa, P. D., & Sandman, C. A. (2000). The influence of corticotropin-releasing hormone on human fetal development and parturition. *Journal of Prenatal and Perinatal Psychology and Health, 14,* 243–256.

Goerner, S. (1995). Chaos, evolution, and deep ecology. In R. Robertson & A.

Combs (Eds.), *Chaos theory in psychology and the life sciences* (pp. 17–38). Mahwah, NJ: Erlbaum.

Goldberg, E. & Bilder, R. M. (1987). The frontal lobes and hierarchical organization of cognitive control. In E. Perecman (Ed.), *The frontal lobes revisited* (pp. 159–187). Hillsdale, NJ: Erlbaum.

Goldberg, S., Muir, R., & Kerr, J. (1995). *Attachment theory: Social, developmental, and clinical perspectives.* Mahwah, NJ: Analytic Press.

Goldberger, A. L., Rigney, D. R., & West, B. J. (1990). Chaos and fractals in human physiology. *Scientific American, 262*(2), 43–49.

Goldenberg, G., Podreka, I., Uhl, F., Steiner, M., Willmes, K., & Deecke, L. (1989). Cerebral correlates of imagining colours, faces and a map: I. SPECT of regional cerebral blood flow. *Neuropsychologia, 27,* 1315–1328.

Goldin-Meadow, S. (2000). Beyond words: The importance of gesture to researchers and learners. *Child Development, 71,* 231–239.

Goldman-Rakic, P. S. (1987). Circuitry of the primate prefontal cortex and regulation of behavior by representational memory. In F. Plum & V. Mountcastle (Eds.), *Handbook of physiology* (Vol. 5, pp. 373–418). Bethesda, MD: American Physiological Society.

Goldman-Rakic, P. S., Muly, E. C., & Williams, G. V. (2000). D1 receptors in prefrontal cells and circuits. *Brain Research Reviews, 31,* 295–301.

Goldsmith, H. H. & Campos, J. J. (1982). Toward a theory of infant temperament. In R. N. Emde & R. J. Harmon (Eds.), *The development of attachment and affiliative systems* (pp. 161–193). New York: Plenum.

Goldstein, R. Z., Volkow, N. D., Wang, G-J., Fowler, J. S., & Rajaram, S. (2001). Addiction changes in orbitofrontal gyrus function: Involvement in response inhibition. *NeuroReport, 12,* 2595–2599.

Golynkina, K., & Ryle, A. (1999). The identification and characteristics of the partially dissociated states of patients with borderline personality disorder. *British Journal of Medical Psychology, 72,* 429–435.

Gomez-Pinilla, F., Choi, J., & Ryba, E. A. (1999). Visual input regulates the expression of basic fibroblast growth factor and its receptor. *Neuroscience, 88,* 1051–1058.

Gonon, F.G. (1988). Nonlinear relationship between impulse flow and dopamine release by midbrain dopaminergic neurons as studied by in vivo electochemistry. *Neuroscience, 24,* 19–28.

González-García, M., García, I., Ding, L., O'Shea, S., Boise, L. H., Thompson, C. B., & Núñez, G. (1995). Bcl-x is expressed in embryonic and postnatal neural tissues and functions to prevent neuronal cell death. *Proceeding of the National Academy of Science USA, 92,* 4304–4308.

Goodwin, R. D., & Hamilton, S. P. (2002). The early-onset fearful panic attack as a predictor of severe psychoapthology. *Psychiatry Research, 109,* 71–79.

Gopnik, A., Meltzoff, A. N., & Kuhl, P. K. (1999). *The scientist in the crib: Minds, brains, and how children learn.* New York: Morrow.

Gordon, H. W. (2002). Early environmental stress and biological vulnerability to drug abuse. *Psychoneuroendocrinology, 27,* 115–126.

Gould, E., Wooley, C. S., & McEwen, B. S. (1991). Adrenal steroids regulate postnatal development of the rat dentate gyrus: I. Effects of glucocorticoids on cell death. *Journal of Comparative Neurology, 313,* 479–485.

Goyer, P. F., Konicki, P. E., & Schulz, S. C. (1994). Brain imaging in personality disorders. In K. R. Silk (Ed.), *Biological and neurobehavioral studies of borderline personality disorder* (pp. 109–125). Washington, DC: American Psychiatric Press.

Grace, J., & Malloy, P. (1992). Neuropsychiatric aspects of right hemispheric learning disability. *Neuropsychiatry, Neuropsychology, and Behavioral Neurology, 5,* 194–204.

Grafman, J., Schwab, K., Warden, D., Pridgen, A., Brown, H. R., & Salazar, A. M. (1996). Frontal lobe injuries, violence, and aggression: A report of the Vietnam head injury study. *Neurology, 46,* 1231–1238.

Graham, J. E., Lobel, M., & Stein DeLuca, R. (2002). Anger after childbirth: an overlooked reaction to postpartum stressors. *Psychology of Women Quarterly, 26,* 222–233.

Graham, Y. P., Heim, C., Goodman, S. H., Miller, A. H., & Nemeroff, C. B. (1999). The effects of neonatal stress on brain development: Implications for psychopathology. *Development and Psychopathology, 11,* 545–565.

Gray, J. A. (1990). Brain systems that mediate both emotion and cognition. *Cognition and Emotion, 4,* 269–288.

Greenough, W. T., & Black, J. E. (1992). Induction of brain structure by experience: Substates for cognitive development. In M. R. Gunnar & C. A. Nelson (Eds.), *Minnesota symposium on child psychology: Vol. 24. Developmental behavioral neuroscience* (pp. 155–200). Hillsdale, NJ: Erlbaum.

Greenough, W. T., Black, J., & Wallace, C. (1987). Experience and brain development. *Child Development, 58,* 539–559.

Greenspan, S. I. (1979). *Intelligence and adaptation.* New York: International Universities Press.

Greenspan, S. I. (1981). *Psychopathology and adaptation in infancy and early childhood.* New York: International Universities Press.

Griffin, M. G., Resick, P. A., & Mechanic, M. B. (1997). Objective assessment of peritraumatic dissociation: Psychophysiological indicators. *American Journal of Psychiatry, 154,* 1081–1088.

Grings, W. W., & Dawson, M. E. (1978). *Emotions and bodily responses.* New York: Academic Press.

Grossman, E., Donnelly, M., Price, R., Pickens, D., Morgan, V., Neighbor, G., & Blake, R. (2000). Brain areas involved in perception of biological motion. *Journal of Cognitive Neuroscience, 12,* 711–720.

Grossmann, K. E., Grossmann, K., & Zimmermann, P. (1999). A wider view of attachment and exploration. Stability and change during the years of immaturity. In J. Cassidy & P. R. Shaver (Eds.), *Handbook of attachment: theory, research and clinical applications* (pp. 760–786). New York: Guilford.

Gross-Tsur, V., Shalev, R. S., Manor, O., & Amir, N. (1995). Developmental right-hemisphere syndrome: Clinical spectrum of the nonverbal learning disability. *Journal of Learning Disabilities, 28,* 80–86.

Grotstein, J. S. (1986). The psychology of powerlessness: Disorders of self-regulation and interactional regulation as a newer paradigm for psychopathology. *Psychoanalytic Inquiry, 6,* 93–118.

Grotstein, J. S. (1990). Nothingness, meaninglessness, chaos, and the "black hole": I. The importance of nothingness, meaninglessness, and chaos in psychoanalysis. *Contemporary Psychoanalysis, 26,* 257–290.

Grunau, R. V. E., Whitfield, M. F., Petrie, J. H., & Fryer, E. L. (1994). Early pain experience, child and family factors, as precursors of somatization: A prospective study of extremely premature and full-term children. *Pain, 56,* 353–359.

Guedeney, A., & Fermanian, J. (2001). A validity and reliability study of assessment and screening for sustained withdrawal in infancy: The alarm distress scale. *Infant Mental Health Journal, 22,* 559–575.

Guilarte, T. R. (1998). The N-methyl-D-aspartate receptor: Physiology and neurotoxicology in the developing brain. In W. Slikker & L. W. Chang (Eds.), *Handbook of developmental neurotoxicology* (pp. 285–304). San Diego: Academic Press.

Gunnar, M. R., & Donzella, B. (2002). Social regulation of the cortisol levels in early human development. *Psychoneuroendocrinology, 27,* 199–220.

Gunnar, M. R., & Vazquz, D. M. (2001). Low cortisol and a flattening of expected daytime rhythm: potential indices of risk in human development. *Development and Psychopathology, 13*, 515–538.

Gurvits, I. G., Koenigsberg, H. W., & Siever, L. J. (2000). Neurotransmitter dysfunction in patients with borderline personality disorder. *Psychiatric Clinics of North America, 23*, 27–40.

Gurvits, T. V., Gilbertson, M. W., Lasko, N. B., Tarhan, A. S., Simeon, D., Macklin, M. L., Orr, S. P., & Pitman, R. K. (2000). Neurologic soft signs in chronic posttraumatic stress disorder. *Archives of General Psychiatry, 57*, 181–186.

Gyulai, F., Firestone, L. L., Mintun, M. A., & Winter, P. M. (1997). In vivo imaging of nitrous oxide-induced changes in cerebral activation during noxious heat stimuli. *Anesthesiology, 86*, 538–548.

Haber, S. N., Kunishio, K., Mizobuchi, M., & Lynd-Balta, E. (1995). The orbital and medial prefrontal circuit through the primate basal ganglia. *Journal of Neuroscience, 15*, 4851–4867.

Halgren, E. (1992). Emotional neurophysiology of the amygdala within the context of human cognition. In J. P. Aggleton (Ed.), *The amygdala: neurobiological aspects of emotion, memory, and mental dysfunction* (pp. 191–228). New York: Wiley-Liss.

Hall, R. E., & Marr, H. B. (1975). Influence of electrical stimulation of posterior orbital cortex upon plasma cortisol levels in unanesthetized sub-human primate. *Brain Research, 93*, 367–371.

Halliday, G., & Tork, I. (1986). Comparative anatomy of the ventromedial mesencephalic tegmentum in the rat, cat, monkey and human. *Journal of Comparative Neurology, 252*, 423–445.

Halliday, G. M., Li, Y. W., Joh, T. H., Cotton, R. G. H., Howe, P. R. C., Geffen, L. B., & Blessing, W. W. (1988). Distribution of monoamine-synthesizing neurons in the human medulla oblongata. *Journal of Comparative Neurology, 273*, 301–317.

Hamann, S. B., Ely, T. D., Grafon, S. T., & Kilts, C. D. (1999). Amygdala activity related to enhanced memory for pleasant and aversive stimuli. *Nature Neuroscience, 2*, 289–293.

Hamner, M. B., Lorberbaum, J. P., & George, M. S. (1999). Potential role of the anterior cingulate cortex in PTSD: Review and hypothesis. *Depression and Anxiety, 9*, 1–14.

Haracz, J. L. (1985). Neural plasticity in schizophrenia. *Schizophrenia Bulletin, 11*, 191–229.

Hare, R. D. (1993). *Without conscience: The disturbing world of the psychopaths among us.* New York: Simon & Schuster.

Hari, R., Portin, K., Kettenmann, B., Jousmaki, V., & Kobal, G. (1997). Right-hemisphere preponderance of responses to painful CO_2 stimulation of the human nasal mucosa. *Pain, 72*, 145–151.

Hariri, A. R., Bookheimer, S. Y., & Mazziotta, J. C. (2000). Modulating emotional responses: Effects of a neocortical network on the limbic system. *NeuroReport, 11*, 43–48.

Harkness, K. L., & Tucker, D. M. (2000). Motivation of neural plasticity: Neural mechanisms in the self-organization of depression. In M. D. Lewis & I. Granic (Eds.), *Emotion, development, and self-organization* (pp. 186–208). New York: Cambridge University Press.

Harlow, H. F. (1958). The nature of love. *American Psychologist, 13*, 673–685.

Harold, F. M. (1986). *The vital force: A study of bioenergetics.* New York: W. H. Freeman.

Harrington, A. (1985). Nineteenth-century ideas on hemisphere differences and "duality of mind." *Behavioral and Brain Sciences, 8*, 617–634.

Harris, L. J., Almergi, J. B., & Kirsch, E. A. (2000). Side preference in adults for

holding infants: Contributions of sex and handedness in a test of imagination. *Brain &*
Cognition, 43, 246–252.

Hart, S. N., & Brassard, M. R. (1987). A major threat to children's mental health.
American Psychologist, 42, 160–165.

Hartmann, H. (1939). *Ego psychology and the problem of adaptation.* New York:
International Universities Press.

Hatalski, C. G., & Baram, T. Z. (1997). Stress-induced transcriptional regulation
in the developing rat brain involves increased cyclic adenosine 3:5'-monophosphate-
regulatory element binding activity. *Molecular Endocrinology, 11,* 2016–2024.

Hauser, K. F., McLaughlin, P. J., & Zagon, I. S. (1989). Endogenous opioid systems
and the regulation of dendritic growth and spine formation. *Journal of Comparative
Neurology, 281,* 13–22.

Heilman, K. M., Schwartz, H., & Watson, R. T. (1977). Hypoarousal in patients
with the neglect syndrome and emotional indifference. *Neurology, 38,* 229–232.

Heilman, K. M., & Van Den Abell, T. (1979). Right hemispheric dominance for
mediating cerebral activation. *Neuropsychologia, 17,* 315–321.

Heim, C., & Nemeroff, C. B. (1999). The impact of early adverse experiences on
brain systems involved in the pathophysiology of anxiety and affective disorders. *Biological Psychiatry, 46,* 1509–1522.

Heim, C., & Nemeroff, C. B. (2001). The role of childhood trauma in the neurobiology of mood and anxiety disorders: Preclinical and clinical studies. *Biological Psychiatry,
49,* 1023–1039.

Heller, W. (1993). Neuropsychological mechanisms of individual differences in
emotion, personality, and arousal. *Neuropsychology, 7,* 476–489.

Heller, W., Etienne, M. A., & Miller, G. A. (1995). Patterns of perceptual asymmetry
in depression and anxiety: Implications for neuropsychological models of emotion and
psychopathology. *Journal of Abnormal Psychology, 104,* 327–333.

Hellige, J. B. (1990). Hemispheric asymmetry. *Annual Review of Psychology, 41,*
55–80.

Helmeke, C., Ovtscharoff, W. Jr., Poeggel, G., & Braun, K. (2001). Juvenile emotional experience alters synaptic inputs on pyramidal neurons in anterior cingulate cortex. *Cerebral Cortex, 11,* 717–727.

Helmeke, C., Poeggel, G., & Braun, K. (2001). Differential emotional experience
induces elevated spine densities on basal dendrites of pyramidal neurons in the anterior
cingulate of *Octodon degus. Neuroscience, 104,* 927–931.

Helmuth, L. (2000). Has America's tide of violence receded for good? *Science, 289,*
582–585.

Hennessy, M. B. (1997). Hypothalamic-pituitary-adrenal responses to brief social separation. *Neuroscience & Biobehavioral Reviews, 21,* 11–29.

Henry, J. P. (1993). Psychological and physiological responses to stress: The right
hemisphere and the hypothalamo-pituitary-adrenal axis, an inquiry into problems of
human bonding. *Integrative Physiological and Behavioral Science, 28,* 369–387.

Henry, J. P., Haviland, M. G., Cummings, M. A., Anderson, D. L., MacMurray,
F. P., McGhee, W. H., & Hubbard, R. W. (1992). Shared neuroendocrine patterns of
post-traumatic stress disorder and alexithymia. *Psychosomatic Medicine, 54,* 407–415.

Henry, J. P., & Wang, S. (1998). Effects of early stress on adult affiliative behavior.
Psychoneuroendocrinology, 23, 863–875.

Herman, J., Perry, J., & van der Kolk, B. A. (1989). Childhood trauma in borderline
personality disorder. *American Journal of Psychiatry, 146,* 490–495.

Herman, J. L., & van der Kolk, B. A. (1987). Traumatic antecedents of borderline
personality disorder. In B.A. van der Kolk (Ed.), *Psychological trauma* (pp. 111–126).
Washington, DC: American Psychiatric Press.

Hernandez-Reif, M., Field, T., Del Pino, N., & Diego, M. (2000). Less exploring by mouth occurs in newborns of depressed mothers. *Infant Mental Health Journal, 21,* 204–210.

Herpetz, S., Dietrich, T. M., Wenning, B., Krings, T., Erberich, S. G., Wilmes, K., Thron, A., & Sass, H. (2001). Evidence of abnormal amygdala functioning in borderline personality disorder: A functional MRI study. *Biological Psychiatry, 50,* 292–298.

Hertsgaard, L., Gunnar, M., Erickson, M. F., & Nachmias, M. (1995). Adrenocortical responses to the strange situation in infants with disorganized/disoriented attachment relationships. *Child Development, 66,* 1100–1106.

Herzog, J. M. (1980). Sleep disturbance and father hunger in 18- to 28-month-old boys: The Erlkonig syndrome. *Psychoanalytic Study of the Child, 35,* 219–233.

Herzog, J. M. (2001). *Father hunger: Explorations with adults and children.* Hillsdale, NJ: Analytic Press.

Hess, E. H. (1975). The role of pupil size in communication. *Scientific American, 233,* 110–119.

Hesse, E., (1999). The Adult Attachment Interview. Historical and current perspectives. In J. Cassidy & P. R. Shaver (Eds.), *Handbook of attachment: Theory, research, and clinical applications* (pp. 395–433). New York: Guilford.

Hesse, E., & Main, M. M. (1999). Second-generation effects of unresolved trauma in nonmaltreating parents: Dissociated, frightened, and threatening parental behavior. *Psychoanalytic Inquiry, 19,* 481–540.

Hesse, E., & Main, M. (2000). Disorganized infant, child and adult attachment: Collapse in behavioral and attentional strategies. *Journal of the American Psychoanalytic Association, 48,* 1097–1028.

Hevner, R. F., Duff, R. S., & Wong-Riley, M. T. T. (1992). Coordination of ATP production and consumption in brain: Parallel regulation of cytochrome oxidase and $Na^+,+ K^+$-ATPase. *Neuroscience Letters, 138,* 188–192.

Hevner, R. F., & Wong-Riley, M. T. T. (1993). Mitochondrial and nuclear gene expression for cytochrome oxidase subunits are disproportionately regulated by functional activity in neurons. *Journal of Neuroscience, 13,* 1805–1819.

Higley, J. D., Suomi, S. J., & Linnoila, M. (1991). CSF monoamine metabolite concentrations vary according according to age, rearing and sex, and are influenced by the stressor of social separation in rhesus monkeys. *Psychopharmacology, 103,* 551–556.

Hildyard, K. L., & Wolfe, D. A. (2002). Child neglect: Developmental issues and outcomes. *Child Abuse & Neglect, 26,* 679–695.

Hill, S. Y., de Bellis, M. D., & Keshavan, M. S., Lowers, L., Shen, S., Hall, J., & Pitts, T. (2001). Right amygdala volume in adolescent and young adult offspring from families at high risk for developing alcoholism. *Biological Psychiatry, 49,* 894–905.

Hilz, H. W., Tarnowski, W., & Arend, P. (1963). Glucose polymerisation and cortisol. *Biochemical and Biophysical Research Communications, 10,* 492–502.

Hinde, R. (1990). Causes of social development from the perspective of an integrated developmental science. In G. Butterworth & P. Bryant (Eds.), *Causes of development* (pp. 161–185). Hillsdale, NJ: Erlbaum.

Hinshaw-Fuselier, S., Boris, N. W., & Zeanah, C. H. (1999). Reactive attachment disorder in maltreated twins. *Infant Mental Health Journal, 20,* 42–59.

Hobson, R. P. (1993). Through feeling and sight to self and symbol. In U. Neisser (Ed.), *The perceived self: Ecological and interpersonal sources of self-knowledge* (pp. 254–279). New York: Cambridge University Press.

Hockenberry, D., Nunez, G., Milliman, C., Schreiber, R. D., & Korsmeyer, S. J. (1990). Bcl-2 is an inner mitochondrial membrane protein that blocks programmed cell death. *Nature, 348,* 334–336.

Hofer, M. A. (1984). Relationships as regulators: A psychobiologic perspective on bereavement. *Psychosomatic Medicine, 46,* 183–197.

Hofer, M. A. (1990). Early symbiotic processes: Hard evidence from a soft place. In R. A. Glick & S. Bone (Eds.), *Pleasure beyond the pleasure principle* (pp. 55–78). New Haven, CT: Yale University Press.

Hofer, M. A. (1994). Hidden regulators in attachment, separation, and loss. *Monographs of the Society for Research in Child Development, 59,* 192–207.

Hoffman, R. E., & Dobscha, S. K. (1989). Cortical pruning and the development of schizophrenia: A computer model. *Schizophrenia Bulletin, 15,* 477–490.

Hoffmann, R. F. (1978). Developmental changes in human infant visual-evoked potentials to patterned stimuli recorded at different scalp locations. *Child Development, 49,* 110–118.

Hollrigel, G. S., Chen, K., Baram, T. Z., & Soltesz, I. (1998). The pro-convulsant actions of corticotropin-releasing hormone in the hippocampus of infant rats. *Neuroscience, 84,* 71–79.

Holmes, J. (1993). *John Bowlby and attachment theory.* London: Routledge.

Holowka, S., & Petitto, L. A. (2002). Left hemisphere cerebral specialization for babies while babbling. *Science, 297,* 1515.

Hommer, D., Andreasen, P., Rio, D., Williams, W., Ruttimann, U., Momenan, R., Zametkin, A., Rawlinngs, R., & Linnoila, M. (1997). Effects of *m-* chlorophenylpiperazine on regional brain glucose utilization: A positron emission tomographic comparison of alcoholic and control subjects. *Journal of Neuroscience, 17,* 2796–2806.

Hopkins, B., & Butterworth, G. (1990). Concepts of causality in explanations of development. In G. Butterworth & P. Bryant (Eds.), *Causes of development* (pp. 3–32). Hillsdale, NJ: Erlbaum.

Horn, G., & McCabe, B. J. (1984). Predispositions and preferences. Effects on imprinting of lesions to the chick brain. *Animal Behavior, 32,* 288–292.

Hornik, R., Risenhoover, N., & Gunnar, M. (1987). The effects of maternal positive, neutral, and negative affective communications on infant responses to new toys. *Child Development, 58,* 937–944.

Horowitz, M.J. (1992). Formulation of states of mind in psychotherapy. In N. G. Hamilton (Ed.), *From inner sources: New directions in object relations psychotherapy* (pp. 75–83). Northvale, NJ: Jason Aronson.

Horton, P. C. (1985). Personality disorder. *Archives of Neurology, 42,* 840.

Horton, P. C. (1995). The comforting substrate and the right brain. *Bulletin of the Menninger Clinic, 59,* 480–486.

Horvitz, J. C., Stewart, T., & Jacobs, B. L. (1997). Burst activity of ventral tegmental dopamine neurons is elicited by sensory stimuli in the awake cat. *Brain Research, 759,* 251–258.

Houstek, J., Kopecky, J., Baudysova, M., Janikova, D., Pavelka, S., & Klement, P. (1990). Differentiation of brown adipose tissue and biogenesis of thermogenic mitochondria in situ and in cell culture. *Biochimica et Biophysica Acta, 1018,* 243–247.

Hsieh, J.-C., Backdahl, M., Hagermark, O., Stone-Elander, S., Rosenquist, G., & Ingvar, M. (1995). Traumatic nociceptive pain activates the hypothalamus and the periaqueductal gray: A positron emission tomography study. *Pain, 64,* 303–314.

Hsieh, J.-C., Belfrage, M., Stone-Elander, S., Hansson, P., & Ingvar, M. (1995). Central representation of chronic ongoing neuropathic pain studied by positron emission tomography. *Pain, 63,* 225–236.

Huang, Q., Zhou, D., Chase, K., Gusella, J. F., Aronin, N., & DiFiglia, M. (1992). Immunohistochemical localization of the D1 dopamine receptor in rat brain reveals its axonal transport, pre- and postsynaptic localization, and prevalence in the basal ganglia, limbic system, and thalamic reticular nucleus. *Proceedings of the National Academy of Sciences of the United States of America, 89,* 11988–11992.

Huang, R., Peng, L., Chen, Y., Hajek, I., Zhao, Z., & Hertz, L. (1994). Signalling effect of monoamines and of elevated potassium concentrations on brain energy metabolism at the cellular level. *Developmental Neuroscience, 16,* 337–351.

Huang, Z.J., Kirkwood, A., Pizzorusso, T., Porciatti, V., Morales, B., Bear, M. F., Maffei, L., & Tonegawa, S. (1999). BDNF regulates the maturation of inhibition and the critical period of plasticity in mouse visual cortex. *Cell, 98,* 739–755.

Hubbard, J. A., Smithmyer, C. M., Ramsden, S. R., Parker, E. H., Flanagan, K. D., Dearing, K. F., Relyea, N., & Simons, R. F. (2002). Observational, physiological, and self-report measures of children's anger: Relations to reactive versus proactive aggression. *Child Development, 73,* 1101–1118.

Hudspeth, W. J., & Pribram, K. H. (1992). Psychophysiological indices of cerebral maturation. *International Journal of Psychophysiology, 12,* 19–29.

Hugdahl, K. (1995). Classical conditioning and implicit learning: The right hemisphere hypothesis. In R. J. Davidson & K. Hugdahl (Eds.), *Brain asymmetry* (pp. 235–267). Cambridge, MA: MIT Press.

Hugdahl, K., Berardi, A., Thompson, W. L., Kosslyn, S. M., Macy, R., Baker, D. P., Alpert, N. M., & LeDoux, J. E. (1995). Brain mechanisms in human classical conditioning: A PET blood flow study. *NeuroReport, 6,* 1723–1728.

Hugdahl, K., Iversen, P. M., & Ness, H-M. (1989). Hemispheric differences in recognition of facial expressions: A VHF-study of negative, positive, and neutral emotions. *Journal of Neuroscience, 45,* 205–213.

Hunter, R. S., Kilstom, N., Kraybill, E. N., & Loda, F. (1978). Antecedents of child abuse and neglect in premature infants: A prospective study in a premature nursery. *Pediatrics, 61,* 629–635.

Huppi, P. S., Schuknecht, B., Boesch, C., Bossi, E., Felblinger, J., Fusch, C., & Herschkowitz, N. (1996). Structural and neurobehvioral delay in postnatal brain development of preterm infants. *Pediatric Research, 39,* 895–901.

Hurvich, M. (1989). Traumatic moment, basic dangers and annihilation anxiety. *Psychoanalytic Review, 6,* 309–323.

Hutcheon, B., & Yarom, Y. (2000). Resonance, oscillation and the intrinsic frequency preferences of neurons. *Trends in Neuroscience, 23,* 216–222.

Hutchison, W. D., Harfa, L., & Dostrovsky, J. O. (1996). Ventrolateral orbital cortex and periaqueductal gray stimulation-induced effects on on- and off-cells in the rostral ventomedial medulla in the rat. *Neuroscience, 70,* 391–407.

Huttenlocher, P. R. (1979). Synaptic density in human frontal cortex — developmental changes and effects of aging. *Brain Research, 163,* 195–205.

Huttenlocher, P. R. (1984). Synapse elimination and plascticity in developing human cerebral cortex. *American Journal of Mental Deficiency, 88,* 488–496.

Hyman, C., Hofer, M., Barde, Y-A., Juhasz, M., Yancopoulos, R. M., Squinto, S. P., & Lindsay, R. M. (1991). BDNF is a neurotrophic factor for dopaminergic neurons of the substantia nigra. *Nature, 350,* 230–232.

Iberal, A. S., & McCulloch, W. S. (1969). The organizing principle of complex living systems. *Journal of Basic Engineering, 91,* 290–294.

Irwin, H. J. (1994). Proneness to dissociation and traumatic childhood events. *Journal of Nervous and Mental Disease, 182,* 456–460.

Isenberg, N., Silbersweig, D., Engelien, A., Emmerich, S., Malavade, K., Beattie, B., & Leon, A. C. (1999). Linguistic threat activates the human amygdala. *Proceedings of the National Academy of Sciences of the United States of America, 96,* 10456–10459.

Itil, T. M., Hsu, W., Saletu, B., & Mednick, S. A. (1974). Computer EEG and auditory evoked potential investigations in children at high risk for schizophrenia. *American Journal of Psychiatry, 131,* 892–900.

Iversen, S. D. (1977). Brain dopamine systems and behavior. In L.L. Iversen, S. D.

Iversen, & S. H. Snyder (Eds.), *Drugs, neurotransmitters and behavior: Vol. 8. Handbook of psychopharmacology* (pp. 333–383). New York: Plenum.

Izard, C. E. (1991). *The psychology of emotions.* New York: Plenum.

Izard, C. E., Hembree, E. A., & Huebner, R. R. (1987). Infants' emotion expressions to acute pain: Developmental change and stability of individual differences. *Developmental Psychology, 23,* 105–113.

Izard, C. E., Porges, S. W., Simons, R. F., Haynes, O. M., Hyde, C., Parisi, M., & Cohen, B. (1991). Infant cardiac activity: Developmental changes and relations with attachment. *Developmental Psychology, 27,* 432–439.

Jackson, E. A. (1991). Controls of dynamic flows with attractors. *Physical Review A, 44,* 4839–4853.

Jackson, J. H. (1931). *Selected writings of J.H. Jackson: Vol. I.* London: Hodder and Soughton.

Jacobson, S. W., Jacobson, J. L., Sokol, R. J., Martier, S. S., & Chiodo, L. M. (1996). New evidence for neuobehavioral effects of in utero cocaine exposure. *Journal of Pediatrics, 129,* 581–590.

Jamme, I., Petit, E., Divoux, D., Gerbi, A., Maixent, J.-M., & Nouvelet, A. (1995). Modulation of mouse cerebral Na$^+$,K$^+$-ATPase activity by oxygen free radicals. *Neuro-Report, 7,* 333–337.

Janet, P. (1911). *L'etat mental des hystériques* (2nd ed.). Paris: Alcan.

Janet, P. (1924). *The major symptoms of hysteria* (2nd ed.). New York: Macmillan.

Janet, P. (1973). *L'Automatisme psychologique* (Psychological Automatism). Société Pierre Janet. Paris. (Original work published in 1889)

Jessimer, M., & Markham, R. (1997). Alexithymia: A right hemisphere dysfunction specific to recognition of certain facial expression? *Brain and Cognition, 34,* 276–258.

Johnsen, B. H., & Hugdahl, K. (1991). Hemispheric asymmetry in conditioning to facial emotional expressions. *Psychophysiology, 28,* 154–162.

Johnsen, B. H., & Hugdahl, K. (1993). Right hemisphere representation of autonomic conditioning to facial emotional expressions. *Psychophysiology, 28,* 154–162.

Johnson, J. G., Cohen, P., Brown, J., Smailes, E. M., & Bernstein, D. P. (1999). Childhood maltreatment increases risk for personality disorders during early development. *Archives of General Psychiatry, 56,* 600–605.

Johnson, J. G., Cohen, P., Kasen, S., Smailes, E., & Brook, J. S. (2001). Association of maladaptive parental behavior with psychiatric disorder among parents and their offspring. *Archives of General Psychiatry, 58,* 453–460.

Johnston, D., Magee, J. C., Colbert, C. M., & Christie, B. R. (1996). Active properties of neuronal dendrites. *Annual Review of Neuroscience, 19,* 165–186.

Johnston, M. V. (2001). Excitotoxicity in neonatal hypoxia. *Mental Retardation and Developmental Disabilities Research Reviews, 7,* 229–234.

Jones, A., Field, T., Fox, N. A., Lundy, B., & Davalos, M. (1997). EEG activation in one-month-old infants of depressed mothers. *Development and Psychopathology, 9,* 491–505.

Jones, N. A., Field, T., & Davalos, M. (2000). Right frontal EEG asymmetry and lack of empathy in preschool children of depressed mothers. *Child Psychiatry and Human Development, 30,* 189–204.

Jones, T., & Greenough, W. T. (1996). Ultrastructural evidence for increased contact between astrocytes and synapses in rats reared in a complex environment. *Neurobiology of Learning and Memory, 65,* 4556.

Joseph, R. (1982). The neuropsychology of development: Hemispheric laterality, limbic language, and the origin of thought. *Journal of Clinical Psychology, 38,* 4–33.

Joseph, R. (1992a). *The right brain and the unconscious: discovering the stranger within.* New York: Plenum.

Joseph, R. (1992b). The limbic system: Emotion, laterality, and unconscious mind. *Psychoanalytic Review, 79,* 405–456.

Joseph, R. (1996). *Neuropsychiatry, neuropsychology, and clinical neuroscience* (2nd ed.). Baltimore: Williams & Wilkins.

Kagan, J. (1994). *Galen's prophecy: Temperament in human nature.* New York: Basic.

Kagan, J., Reznick, J. S., & Snidman, N. (1987). The physiology and psychology of behavioral inhibition in children. *Child Development, 58,* 1459–1473.

Kalin, N. H. (1993). The neurobiology of fear. *Scientific American, 268*(5), 54–60.

Kalin, N. H., Larson, C., Shelton, C. E., & Davidson, R. J. (1998). Asymmetric frontal brain activity, cortisol, and behavior associated with fearful temperament in rhesus monkeys. *Behavioral Neuroscience, 112,* 286–292.

Kalin, N. H., Shelton, S. E., & Lynn, D. E. (1995). Opiate systems in mother and infant primates coordinate intimate contact during reunion. *Psychoneuroendocrinology, 20,* 735–742.

Kalin, N. H., Shelton, S. E., Rickman, M., & Davidson, R. J. (1998). Individual differences in freezing and cortisol in infant and mother rhesus monkeys. *Behavioral Neuroscience, 112,* 251–254.

Kalogeras, K. T., Nieman, L. K., Friedman, T. C., Doppman, J. L., Cutler, G. B. Jr., Chrousos, G. P., Wilder, R. L., Gold, P. W., & Yanovski, J. A. (1996). Inferior petrosal sinus sampling in healthy human subjects reveals a unilateral corticotropin-releasing hormone-induced arginine vasopressin release associated with ipsilateral adrenocorticotropin secretion. *Journal of Clinical Investigation, 97,* 2045–2050.

Kalsbeek, A., Buijs, R. M., Hofman, M. A., Matthijssen, M. A. H., Pool, C. W., & Uylings, H. B. M. (1987). Effects of neonatal thermal lesioning of the mesocortical dopaminergic projection on the development of the rat prefrontal cortex. *Developmental Brain Research, 32,* 123–132.

Kandel, E. R. (1999). Biology and the future of psychoanalysis: A new intellectual framework for psychiatry revisited. *American Journal of Psychiatry, 156,* 505–524.

Kaplan-Solms, K., & Solms, M., (1996), Psychoanalytic observations on a case of frontal-limbic disease. *Journal of Clinical Psychoanalysis, 5,* 405–438.

Karmiloff-Smith, A. (1998). Development itself is the key to understanding developmental disorders. *Trends in Cognitive Sciences, 2,* 389–398.

Karr-Morse, R., & Wiley, M. S. (1997). *Ghosts from the nursery: Tracing the roots of violence.* New York: Atlantic Monthly Press.

Kathol, R. G., Jaeckle, R. S., Lopez, J. F., & Meller, W. H. (1989). Pathophysiology of HPA axis abnormalities in patients with major depression: An update. *American Journal of Psychiatry, 146,* 311–317.

Katsuri, S., Amtey, S., & Beall, P. (1984). *NMR data handbook for biomedical applications.* New York: Pergamon Press.

Katz, L. C. (1999). What's critical for the critical period in visual cortex? *Cell, 99,* 673–676.

Kaufman, I. C., & Rosenblum, L. A. (1967). The reaction to separation in infant monkeys: Anaclitic depression and conservation-withdrawal. *Psychosomatic Medicine, 40,* 649–675.

Kaufman, I. C., & Rosenblum, L. A. (1969). Effects of separation from mother on the emotional behavior of infant monkeys. *Annals of the New York Academy of Sciences, 159,* 681–695.

Kaufman, J., Plotsky, P. M., Nemeroff, C. B., & Charney, O. S. (2000). Effects of early adverse experiences on brain structure and function: clinical implications. *Biological Psychiatry, 48,* 778–790.

Kaufman, J., & Zigler, E. (1989). The intergenerational transmission of child abuse. In D. Cicchetti & V. Carlson (Eds.), *Child maltreatment: Theory and research on the causes and consequences of child abuse and neglect* (pp. 129–150). New York: Cambridge University Press.

Kaufmann, S. A. (1993). *The origins of order: Self-organization and selection in evolution.* New York: Oxford University Press.

Kaufmann, S. H., & Hengartner, M. O. (2001). Programmed cell death: alive and well in the new millennium. *Trends in Cell Biology, 11,* 526–534.

Kawasaki, H., Adolphs, R., Kaufman, O., Damasio, H., Damasio, A. R., Granner, M., Bakken, H., Hori, T., & Howard, M. A. (2001). Single-neuron responses to emotional visual stimuli recorded in human ventral prefrontal cortex. *Nature Neuroscience, 4,* 15–16.

Kazdin, A. E., Siegel, T. C., & Bass, D. (1990). Drawing upon clinical practice to inform research on child and adolescent psychotherapy: A survey of practitioners. *Professional Psychology: Research and Practice, 21,* 189–198.

Keenan, J. P., McCutcheon, B., Freund, S., Gallup, G. C. Jr., Sanders, G., & Pascual-Leone, A. (1999). Left hand advantage in a self-face recognition task. *Neuropsychologia, 37,* 1421–1425.

Keenan, J. P., Nelson, A., O'Connor, M., & Pascual-Leone, A. (2001). Self-recognition and the right hemisphere. *Nature, 409,* 305.

Keenan, J. P., Wheeler, M. A., Gallup, G. G. Jr., & Pascual-Leone, A. (2000). Self-recognition and the right prefrontal cortex. *Trends in Cognitive Science, 4,* 338–344.

Kehoe, P., Shoemaker, W. J., Triano, L., Hoffman, J., & Arons, C. (1996). Repeated isolation in the neonatal rat produces alterations in behavior and ventral striatal dopamine release in the juvenile after amphetamine challenge. *Behavioral Neuroscience, 110,* 1435–1444.

Keil, A., Bradley, M. M., Hauk, O., Rockstroh, B., Elbert, T., & Lang, P. J. (2002). Large-scale neural correlates of affective picture processing. *Psychophysiology, 39,* 641–649.

Keil, A., Müller, M. M., Gruber, T., Wienbruch, C., Stolarova, M., & Elbert, T. (2001). Effects of emotional arousal in the cerebral hemispheres: A study of oscillatory brain activity and event-related potentials. *Clinical Neurophysiology, 112,* 2057–2068.

Kendler, K. S., & Eaves, L. S. (1986). Models for the joint effect of genotype and environment on liability to psychiatric illness. *American Journal of Psychiatry, 143,* 279–289.

Kennard, M. A. (1955). The cingulate gyrus in relation to consciousness. *Journal of Nervous and Mental Disease, 121,* 34–39.

Kennedy, C., Grave, G. D., Jehle, J. W., & Sokoloff, L. (1972). Changes in blood flow in the component structures of the dog brain during postnatal maturation. *Journal of Neurochemistry, 19,* 2423–2433.

Kennedy, C., & Sokoloff, L. (1957). An adaptation of the nitrous oxide method to the study of the cerebral circulation in children: Normal values for cerebral blood flow and cerebral metabolic rate in childhood. *Journal of Clinical Investigation, 36,* 1130–1137.

Kernberg, O. (1975). *Borderline conditions and pathological narcissism.* New York: Jason Aronson.

Kernberg, O. (1988). Developer of an object relations psychoanalytic therapy for borderline personality disorder (by L. K. McGinn). *American Journal of Psychotherapy, 52*(2).

Keshavan, M. S., Anderson, S., & Pettegrew, J. W. (1994). Is schizophrenia due to excessive synaptic pruning in the prefrontal cortex? The Feinberg hypothesis revisited. *Journal of Psychiatric Research, 28,* 239–265.

Kessler, D. C., Sonnega, A., Bromet, E., Hughes, M., & Nelson, C. B. (1995). Posttraumatic stress disorder in the National Comorbidity Survey. *Archives of General Psychiatry, 52,* 1048–1060.

Kestenberg, J. (1985). The flow of empathy and trust between mother and child. In E.J. Anthony & G. H. Pollack (Eds.), *Parental influences in health and disease* (pp. 137–163). Boston: Little Brown.

Kiersky, S., & Beebe, B. (1994). The reconstruction of early nonverbal relatedness in the treatment of difficult patients: A special form of empathy. *Psychoanalytic Dialogues, 4,* 389–408.

Kim, J. J., Andreasen, N. C., O'Leary, D. S., Wiser, A. K., Boles Ponto, L. L., Watkins, G. L., & Hichwa, R. D. (1999). Direct comparison of the neural substrates of recognition memory for words and faces. *Brain, 122,* 1069–1083.

Kimberg, D. V., Loud, A. V., & Wiener. (1968). Cortisone-induced alterations in mitochondrial function and structure. *Journal of Cell Biology, 37,* 63–76.

King, R. (1985). Motivational diversity and mesolimbic dopamine: An hypothesis concerning temperament. In R. Plutchik & H. Kellerman (Eds.), *Emotion.* Vol. 3. *Theory, research and experience* (pp. 363–380). New York: Academic Press.

King, V., Corwin, J. V., & Reep, R. L. (1989). Production and characterization of neglect in rats with unilateral lesions of ventrolateral orbital cortex. *Experimental Neurology, 105,* 287–299.

Kingstone, A., Friesen, C. K., & Gazzaniga, M. S. (2000). Reflexive joint attention depends on lateral and cortical connections. *Psychologiocal Science, 11,* 159–166.

Kinney, D. K., Steingard, R. J., Renshaw, P. F., & Yurgelun-Todd, D. A. (2000). Perinatal complications and abnormal proton metabolite concentrations in frontal cortex of adolescents seen on magnetic resonance spectroscopy. *Neuropsychiatry, Neuropsychology, and Behavioral Neurology, 13,* 8–12.

Kinney, H. C., Brody, B. A., Kloman, A. S., & Gilles, F. H. (1988). Sequence of central nervous system myelination in human infancy: II. Patterns of myelination in autopsied infants. *Journal of Neuropathology and Experimental Neurology, 47,* 217–234.

Kinsbourne, M., & Bemporad, B. (1984). Lateralization of emotion: A model and the evidence. In N. A. Fox & R. J. Davidson (Eds.), *The psychobiology of affective development* (pp. 259–291). Hillsdale, NJ: Erlbaum.

Kinsley, C. H., Madonia, L., Gifford, G. W., Tureski, K., Griffin, G. R., Lowry, C., Williams, J., Collins, J., McLearie, H., & Lambert, K. G. (1999). Motherhood improves learning and memory. *Nature, 402,* 137.

Kircher, T. T. J., Senior, C., Phillips, M. L., Rabe-Hesketh, S., Benson, P. J., Bullmore, E. T., Brammer, M., Simmons, A., Bartels, M., & David, A. S. (2001). Recognizing one's own face. *Cognition, 78,* B1–B15.

Kirschbaum, C., Wolf, O. T., May, M., Wippich, W., & Hellhammer, D. H., (1996). Stress- and treatment-induced elevations of cortisol levels associated with impaired declarative memory in healthy adults. *Life Sciences, 58,* 1475–1483.

Kita, H., & Oomura, Y. (1981). Reciprocal connections between the lateral hypothalamus and the frontal cortex in the rat. *Brain Research, 213,* 1–16.

Kling, A., & Steklis, H. D. (1976). A neural substrate for affiliative behavior in nonhuman primates. *Brain, Behavior, and Evolution, 13,* 216–238.

Knapp, A. G., Schmidt, K. F., & Dowling, J. E. (1990). Dopamine modulates the kinetics of ion channels gated by excitatory amino acids in retinal horizontal cells. *Proceedings of the National Academy of Sciences of the United States of America, 87,* 767–771.

Kobak, R. R., & Sceery, A. (1988). Attachment in late adolescence: Working models, affect regulation, and representations of self and others. *Child Development, 59,* 135–146.

Koch, K. L., Summy-Long, J., Bingaman, S., Sperry, N., & Stern, R. M. (1990). Vasopressin and oxytocin responses to illusory self-motion and nausea in man. *Journal of Clinical and Endocrinological Metabolism, 71,* 1269–1275.

Koenen, K. C., Driver, K. L., Oscar-Berman, M., Wolfe, J., Folsom, S., Huang,

M. T., & Schlessinger, L. (2001). Measures of prefrontal system dysfunction in posttraumatic stress disorder. *Brain and Cognition, 45,* 64–78.

Koenigsberg, H. W., Harvey, P. D., Mitropoulou, V., Schmeidler, J., New, A. S., Goodman, M., Silverman, J. M., Serby, M., Schopick, F., & Siever, L. J. (2002). Characterizing affective instability in borderline personality disorder. *American Journal of Psychiatry, 159,* 784–788.

Koizumi. K., Terui, N., Kollai, M., & Brooks, C. M. (1982). Functional significance of coactivation of vagal and sympathetic cardiac nerves. *Proceedings of the National Academy of Sciences of the United States of America, 79,* 2116–2120.

Kolb, B. (1984). Functions of the frontal cortex in the rat: A comparative review. *Brain Research Reviews, 8,* 65–98.

Kolb, B., & Whishaw, I. Q. (1996). *Fundamentals of human neuropsychology* (3rd ed). New York: W. H. Freeman.

Kolb, B., & Whishaw, I. Q. (1998). Brain plasticity and behavior. *Annual Review of Psychology, 49,* 43–64.

Kolb, L. C., & Multipassi, L. R. (1982). The conditioned emotional response: a subclass of the chronic and delayed posttraumatic stress disorder. *Psychiatric Annals, 12,* 979–987.

Koolhaas, J. M., Korte, S. M., De Boer, S. F., Van derr Vegt, B. J., Van Reenen, C. G., Hopster, H., De Jong, I. C., Ruis, M. A. W., & Blokhuis, H. J. (1999). Coping styles in animals: Current status in behavior and stress-physiology. *Neuroscience and Biobehavioral Reviews, 23,* 925–935.

Koopman, C., Classen, C., & Spiegel, D. (1994). Predictors of posttraumatic stress symptoms among survivors of the Oakland/Berkeley, California firestorm. *American Journal of Psychiatry, 151,* 888–894.

Kop, W. J., Appels, P. W. M., Mendes de Leon, C. F., de Swart, H. B., & Bär, F. W. (1994). Vital exhaustion predicts new cardiac events after successful coronary angioplasty. *Psychosomatic Medicine, 56,* 281–287.

Korfman, O. (2002). The role of prenatal stress in the etiology of developmental behavioural disorders. *Neuroscience and Biobehavioral Reviews, 26,* 457–470.

Korsmeyer, S. J., Shutter, J. R., Veis, D. J., Merry, D. E., & Oltvai, Z. N. (1993). Bcl-2/Bax: A rheostat that regulates an anti-oxidant pathway and cell death. *Seminars in Cancer Biology, 4,* 327–332.

Korte, S. M. (2001). Corticosteroids in relation to fear, anxiety and psychopathology. *Neuroscience and Biobehavioral Reviews, 25,* 117–142.

Kosson, D. S., Suchy, Y., Mayer, A. R., & Libby, J. (in press). Facial affect recognition in criminal psychopaths. *Emotion.*

Kostovic, I. (1990). Structural and histochemical reorganization of the human prefrontal cortex during perinatal and postnatal life. *Progress Brain Research, 85,* 223–239.

Kotler, T., Buzwell, S., Romeo, Y., & Bowland, J. (1994). Avoidant attachment as a risk for health. *British Journal of Medical Psychology, 67,* 237–245.

Kraemer, G. W. (1992). A psychobiological theory of attachment. *Behavioral and Brain Sciences, 15,* 493–541.

Kraemer, G. W., & Clarke, A. S. (1996). Social attachment, brain function, and aggression. *Annals of the New York Academy of Sciences, 794,* 121–135.

Kraemer, G. W., Ebert, M. H., Schmidt, D. E., & Mckinney, W. T. (1991). Strangers in a strange land: A psychobiological study of infant monkeys before and after separation from real or inanimate mothers. *Child Development, 62,* 548–566.

Krikorian, R., & Layton, B. S. (1998). Implicit memory in posttraumatic stress disorder with amnesia for the traumatic event. *Journal of Neuropsychiatry and Clinical Neuroscience, 10,* 359–362.

Krimer, L. S., Mully, C. III, Williams, G. V., & Goldman-Rakic, P. S. (1998). Dopaminergic regulation of cortical microcirculation. *Nature Neuroscience, 1,* 286–289.

Kroemer, G., Zamzami, N., & Susin, S. A. (1997). Mitochondrial control of apoptosis. *Immunology Today, 18,* 44–51.

Kruk, M. R., Van der Poel, A. M., & De Vos-Frerichs, T. P. (1979). The induction of aggressive behavior by electrical stimulation in the hypothalamus of male rats. *Behaviour, 70,* 292–321.

Krystal, H. (1988). *Integration and self-healing: Affect-trauma-alexithymia.* Hillsdale, NJ: Analytic Press.

Krystal, H. (1997). Desomatization and the consequences of infantile psychic trauma. *Psychoanalytic Inquiry, 17,* 126–150.

Kuhn, C. M., & Schanberg, S. M. (1998). Responses to maternal separation: mechanisms and mediators. *International Journal of Developmental Neuroscience, 16,* 261–270.

Kupfermen, I. (1985). Hypothalamus and limbic system I: Peptidergic neurons, homeostasis, and emotional behavior. In E. R. Kandel & J. H. Schwartz (Eds.), *Principles of neuroscience* (2nd ed., pp. 446–447). New York: Elsevier.

Kusnecov, A. W., Liang, R., & Shurin, G. (1999). T-lymphocyte activation increases hypothalamic and amygdaloid expression of CRH mRNA and emotional reactivity to novelty. *Journal of Neuroscience, 19,* 4533–4543.

Kvetnansky, R., Dobrakovova, M., Jezova, D., Oprsalova, Z., Lichardus, B., & Makara, G. (1989). Hypothalamic regulation of plasma catecholamine levels during stress: Effect of vasopressin and CRF. In G. R. Van Loon, R. Kvetnansky, R. McCarty, & J. Axelrod (Eds.), *Stress: Neurochemical and humoral mechanisms* (pp. 549–570). New York: Gordon and Breach Science.

Kvetnansky, R., Jezova, D., Oprsalova, Z., Foldes, O., Michjlovskij, N., Dobrakovova, M., Lichardus, B., & Makara, G. B. (1990). Regulation of the sympathetic nervous system by circulating vasopressin. J. C. Porter & D. Jezova (Eds.), *Circulating regulatory factors and neuroendocrine function* (pp. 113–134). New York: Plenum.

La Bar, K. S., Gatenby, J. C., Gore, J. C., LeDoux, J. E., & Phelps, E. A. (1998). Human amygdala activation during conditioned fear acquisition and extinction: A mixed-trial fMRI study. *Neuron, 20,* 937–945.

Ladd, C. O., Owens, M. J., & Nemeroff, C. B. (1996). Persistent changes in corticotropin-releasing factor neuronal systems induced by maternal deprivation. *Endocrinology, 137,* 1212–1218.

Lafon-Cazal, M., Pietri, S., Culcasi, M., & Bockaert, J. (1993). NMDA-dependent superoxide production and neurotoxicity. *Nature, 364,* 535–537.

Lakatos, K., Toth, I., Nemoda, Z., Ney, K., Sasvari-Szekely, M., & Gervai, J. (2000). Dopamine D4 receptor (DRD4) polymorphism is associated with attachment disorganization in infants. *Molecular Psychiatry, 5,* 633–637.

Laming, P. R., Kimelberg, H., Robinson, S., Salm, A., Hawrylak, N., Muller, C., Roots, B., & Ng., K. (2000). Neuronal-glial interactions and behavior. *Neuroscience and Biobehavioral Reviews, 24,* 295–340.

Lane, R. D., Ahern, G. L., Schwartz, G. E., & Kasgniak, A. W. (1997). Is alexithymia the emotional equivalent of blindsight? *Biological Psychiatry, 42,* 834–844.

Lane, R. D., Chua, P. M-L., & Dolan, R. J. (1999). Common effects of emotional valence, arousal and attention on neural activation during visual processing of pictures. *Neuropsychologia, 37,* 989–997.

Lane, R. D., & Jennings, J. R. (1995). Hemispheric asymmetry, autonomic asymmetry, and the problem of sudden cardiac death. In R. J. Davidson & K. Hugdahl (Eds.), *Brain asymmetry* (pp. 271–304). Cambridge, MA: MIT Press.

Lane, R. D., Kivley, L. S., Du Bois, M. A., Shamasundara, P., & Schwartz, G. E.

(1995). Levels of emotional awareness and the degree of right hemispheric dominance in the perception of facial emotion. *Neuropsychologia, 33,* 525–538.

Lang, S., af Klinteberg, B., & Alm, P-O. (2002). Adult psychopathology and violent behavior in males with early neglect and abuse. *Acta Psychiatrica Scandinavica, 106,* (s412), 93–100.

Lanius, R. A., Williamson, P. C., Boksman, K., Densmore, M., Gupta, M., Neufeld, R. W. J., Gati, J. S., & Menon, R. S. (2002). Brain activation during script-driven imagery induced dissociative responses in PTSD: A functional magnetic resonance imaging investigation. *Biological Psychiatry, 52,* 305–311.

Lanius, R. A., Williamson, P. C., Densmore, M., Boksman, K., Gupta, M. A., Neufeld, R. W., Gati, J. S., & Menon. R. S. (2001). Neural correlates of traumatic memories in posttraumatic stress disorder: A functional MRI investigation. *American Journal of Psychiatry, 158,* 1920–1922.

Lansky, M. R. (1995). *Posttraumatic nightmares: Psychodynamic explorations.* New York: Analytic Press.

Lapierre, D., Braun, C. M. J., & Hodgins, S. (1995). Ventral frontal deficits in psychopathy: Neuropsychological test findings. *Neuropsychologia, 33,* 139–151.

Lauder, J. M., & Krebs, H. (1986). Do neurotransmitters, neurohumors, and hormones specify critical periods? In W. T. Greenough & J. M. Juraska (Eds.), *Developmental neuropsychobiology* (pp. 119–174). Orlando, FL: Academic Press.

Laureys, S., Faymonville, M-E., Degueldre, C., Del Fiore, G., Damas, P., Lambermont, B., Janssens, N., Aerts, J., Franck, G., Luxen, A., Moonen, G., Lamy, M., & Maquet, P. (2000). Auditory processing in the vegetative state. *Brain, 123,* 1589–1601.

Layton, B., & Krikorian, R. (2002). Memory mechanisms in posttraumatic stress disorder. *Journal of Neuropsychiatry and Clinical Neuroscience, 14,* 254–261.

Lazarus, R. S. (1991a). Progress on a cognitive-motivational-relational theory of emotion. *American Psychologist, 46,* 819–834.

Lazarus, R. S. (1991b). Cognition and motivation in emotion. *American Psychologist, 46,* 352–367.

Lazarus, R. S., & Smith, C. A. (1988). Knowledge and appraisal in the cognition-emotion relationship. *Cognition and Emotion, 2,* 281–300.

Le Moal, M., & Simon, H. (1991). Mesocorticolimbic dopaminergic network: Functional and regulatory roles. *Physiological Reviews, 71,* 155–234.

LeDoux, J. E. (1989). Cognitive-emotional interactions in the brain. *Cognition and Emotion, 3,* 267–289.

LeDoux, J. E. (1996). *The emotional brain.* New York: Simon and Schuster.

LeDoux, J. E. (2002). *Synaptic self: How our brains become who we are.* New York: Viking.

Lee, D. H., Severin, K., Yokobayashi, Y., & Reza Ghadiri, M. (1997). Emergence of symbiosis in peptide self-replication through a hypercyclic network. *Nature, 390,* 591–594.

Lehtonen, J. (1994). From dualism to psychobiological interaction. A comment on the study by Tenari and his co-workers, *British Journal of Psychiatry, 164,* 27–28.

Lester, B. M., Hoffman, J., & Brazelton, T. B. (1985). The rhythmic structure of mother-infant interaction in term and preterm infants. *Child Development, 56,* 15–27.

Leung, E. H. L., & Rheingold, H. L. (1981). Development of pointing as a social gesture. *Developmental Psychology, 17,* 215–220.

Leventhal, H. (1984). A perceptual-motor theory of emotion. *Advances in Experimental Social Psychology, 17,* 117–182.

Levin, B. E., & Routh, V. H. (1996). Role of the brain in energy balance and obesity. *American Journal of Physiology, 40,* R491-R500.

Levine, S. (1994). The ontogeny of the hypothalamic-pituitary-adrenal axis: The influence of maternal factors. *Annals of the New York Academy of Sciences, 746,* 275–288.

Levitsky, D. A., & Strupp, B. J. (1995). Malnutrition and the brain: Changing concepts, changing concerns. *Journal of Nutrition, 125,* 2212S–2220S.

Levitt, P., Rakic, P., & Goldman-Rakic, P. (1984). Region-specific distribution of catecholamine afferents in primate cerebral cortex: A flourescence histochemical analysis. *Journal of Comparative Neurology, 227,* 23–36.

Lewis, H. B. (1980). "Narcissistic personality" or "shame-prone superego mode." *Comprehensive Psychotherapy, 1,* 59–80.

Lewis, J. M. (2000). Repairing the bond in important relationships: A dynamic for personality maturation. *American Journal of Psychiatry, 157,* 1375–1378.

Lewis, M., & Miller, S. M. (1990). *Handbook of developmental psychopathology.* New York: Plenum.

Lewis, M. D. (1995). Cognition-emotion feedback and the self-organization of developmental paths. *Human Development, 38,* 71–102.

Lewis, M. D. (1996). Self-organizing appraisals. *Cognition and Emotion, 10,* 1–25.

Lewis, M. D. (1999). A new dynamic systems method for the analysis of early socioemotional development. *Developmental Science, 2,* 457–475.

Lewis, M. D. (2000). The promise of dynamic systems approaches for an integrated account of human develpment. *Child Development, 71,* 1–23.

Lewis, M. H., Gluck, J. P., Beauchamp, A. J., Keresztury, M. F., & Mailman, R. B. (1990). Long-term effects of early social isolation in *Macaca mulatta*: Changes in dopamine receptor function following apomorphine challenge. *Brain Research, 513,* 67–73.

Liberzon, I., Zubieta, J. K., Fig, L. M., Phan, K. L., Koeppe, R. A., & Taylor, S. F. (2002). μ-opioid receptors and limbic responses to aversive emotional stimuli. *Proceedings of the National Academy of Sciences of the United States of America, 99,* 7084–7089.

Lieberman, A. F. (1997). Toddler's internalization of maternal attributions as a factor in quality of attachment. In L. Atkinson & K. J. Zucker (Eds.), *Attachment and psychopathology* (pp. 277–291). New York: Guilford.

Lieberman, A. F., & Zeanah, C. H. (1999). Contributions of attachment theory to infant-parent psychotherapy and other interventions with infants and young children. In J. Cassidy & P. Shaver (Eds.), *Handbook of attachment theory and research* (pp. 555–574). New York: Guilford.

Lieberman, A. S. (1996). Aggression and sexuality in relation to toddler attachment: Implications for the caregiving system. *Infant Mental Health Journal, 17,* 276–292.

Lieberman, M. D. (2000). Intuition: A social cognitive neuroscience approach. *Psychological Bulletin, 126,* 109–137.

Liebeskind, J. C. (1991). Pain can kill. *Pain, 44,* 3–4.

Lindberg, L., Asberg, M., & Sunquist-Stensman, M. (1984). 5-hydroxyindoleacetic acid levels in attempted suicides who have killed their children [Letter to the editor]. *Lancet 2,* 928.

Liotti, G. (1992). Disorganized/disoriented attachment in the etiology of the dissociative disorders. *Dissociation, 4,* 196–204.

Liotti, G. (1999). Understanding the dissociative processs: The contribution of attachment theory. *Psychoanalytic Inquiry, 19,* 757–783.

Liotti, M., & Tucker, D. M. (1992). Right hemisphere sensitivity to arousal and depression. *Brain and Cognition, 18,* 138–151.

Lipska, B. K., & Weinberger, D. R. (1995). Genetic variation in vulnerability to the behavioral effects of neonatal hippocampal damage in rats. *Proceedings of the National Academy of Sciences of the United States of America, 92,* 8906–8910.

Lipton, P., & Whittingham, T. S. (1982). Reduced ATP concentration as a basis for synaptic transmission failure during hypoxia in the in vitro guinea-pig hippocampus. *Journal of Physiology*, 325, 51–65.

Lipton, P. A., Alvarez, P., & Eichenbaum, H. (1999). Crossmodal associative memory representations in rodent orbitofrontal cortex. *Neuron*, 22, 349–359.

Litz, B. T., Orsillo, S. M., Kaloupek, D., & Weathers, F. (2000). Emotional processing in posttraumatic stress disorders. *Journal of Abnormal Psychology*, 109, 26–39.

Liu, D., Diorio, J., Day, J. C., Francis, D. D., & Meaney, M. J. (2000). Maternal care, hippocampal synaptogenesis and cognitive development in rats. *Nature Neuroscience*, 3, 799–806.

Liu, J., Wang, X., Shigenaga, M. K., Yeo, H. C., Mori, A., & Ames, B. N. (1996). Immobilization stress causes oxidative damage to lipid, protein, and DNA in the brain of rats. *The Federation of American Societies for Experimental Biology Journal*, 10, 1532–1538.

Locke, J. L. (1997). A theory of neurolinguistic development. *Brain and Cognition*, 58, 265–326.

Loeber, R., & Farrington, D. P. (2000). Young children who commit crime: Epidemiology, developmental origins, risk factors, early interventions, and policy implications. *Development and Psychopathology*, 12, 737–762.

Lohr, J. B. (1991). Oxygen radicals and neuropsychiatric illness: Some speculations. *Archives of General Psychiatry*, 48, 1097–1106.

London, E. D., Ernst, M., Grant, S., Bonson, K., & Weinstein, A. (2000). Orbitofrontal cortex and human drug abuse: Functional imaging. *Cerebral Cortex*, 10, 334–342.

Lonstein, J. S., & Stern, J. M. (1997). Role of the midbrain periaqueductal gray in maternal nurturance and aggression: c-fos and electrolytic lesion studies in lactating rats. *Journal of Neuroscience*, 17, 3364–3378.

Lorberbaum, J. P., Newman, J. D., Dubno, J. R., Horwitz, A. R., Nahas, Z., Teneback, C., Johnson, M. R., Lydiard, R. B., Ballenger, J. C., & George, M. S. (n.d.). *Feasibility of using fMRI to study mothers: Responding to infant cries* Retrieved January 30, 2003, from http:www.musc.edu/psychiatry/fnrd/babycry.htm

Lorberbaum, J. P., Newman, J. D., Horwitz, A. R., Dubno, J. R., Lydiard, R. B., Hamner, M. B., Bohning, D. E., & George, M. S. (2002), A potential role for thalamocingulate circuitry in human maternal behavior. *Biological Psychiatry*, 51, 431–445.

Luecken, L. J. (1998). Childhood attachment and loss experiences affect adult cardiovascular and cortisol function. *Psychosomatic Medicine*, 60, 765–772.

Luntz, B. K., & Widom, C. S. (1994). Antisocial personality disorder in abused and neglected children grown up. *American Journal of Psychiatry*, 151, 670–674.

Luria, A. R. (1973). *The working brain*. New York: Basic.

Luria, A. R. (1980). *Higher cortical functions in man* (2nd ed). New York: Basic.

Luu, P., & Tucker, D. M. (1996). Self-regulation and cortical development: Implications for functional studies of the brain. In R. W. Thatcher, G. R. Lyon, J. Rumsey, & N. Krasnegor (Eds.), *Developmental neuroimaging: Mapping the development of brain and behavior* (pp. 297–305). San Diego: Academic Press.

Lydic, R. (1987). State-dependent aspects of regulatory physiology. *The Federation of American Societies for Experimental Biology Journal*, 1, 6–15.

Lynch, G. (1986). *Synapses, circuits, and the beginnings of memory*. Cambridge, MA: MIT Press.

Lyons-Ruth, K., Alpern, L., & Repacholi, B. (1993). Disorganized infant attachment classification and maternal psychosocial problems as predictors of hostile-aggressive behavior in the preschool classroom. *Child Development*, 64, 572–585.

Lyons-Ruth, K., & Jacobvitz, D. (1999). Attachment disorganization. Unresolved loss, relational violence, and lapses in behavioral and attentional strategies. In J. Cassidy & P. R. Shaver (Eds.), *Handbook of attachment: Theory, research, and clinical applications* (pp. 520–554). New York: Guilford.

Lyons-Ruth, K., Repacholi, B., McLeod, S., & Silva, E. (1991). Disorganized attachment behavior in infancy: Short-term stability, maternal and infant correlates, and risk-related subtypes. *Development and Psychopathology, 3*, 377–396.

Maas, J. W., & Katz, M. M. (1992). Neurobiology and psychopathological states: Are we looking in the right place? *Biological Psychiatry, 31*, 757–758.

Maccoby, E. (1966). *The development of sex differences.* Stanford, CA: Stanford University Press.

MacFarlane, A. (1977). *The psychology of childbirth.* Cambridge, MA: Harvard University Press.

MacLean, P. D. (1985). Evolutionary psychiatry and the triune brain. *Psychological Medicine, 15*, 219–221.

MacLean, P. D. (1987). The midline frontolimbic cortex and the evolution of crying and laughter. In E. Perecman (Ed.), *The frontal lobes revisited* (pp. 121–140). Hillsdale, NJ: Erlbaum.

MacLean, P. D. (1990). *The evolution of the triune brain.* New York: Plenum.

MacLean, P. D. (1993). Perspectives on cingulate cortex in the limbic system. In B. A. Vogt & M. Gabriel (Eds.), *Neurobiology of cingulate cortex and limbic thalamus* (pp. 1–15). Boston: Birkhauser.

MacLean, P. D., & Newman, J. D. (1988). Role of midline frontolimbic cortex in production of the isolation call of squirrel monkeys. *Brain Research, 450*, 111–123.

Maestripieri, D. (1999). The biology of human parenting: Insights from nonhuman primates. *Neuroscience and Biobehavioral Reviews, 23*, 411–422.

Mahler, M., Pine, F., & Bergman, A. (1975). *The psychological birth of the human infant.* New York: Basic.

Mahler, M. S. (1958). Autism and symbiosis: Two extreme disturbances of identity. *International Journal of Psycho-Analysis, 39*, 77–83.

Main, M. (1991). Discourse, prediction, and recent studies in attachment: Implications for psychoanalysis. *Journal of the American Psychoanalytic Association, 41* (Suppl.), 209–244.

Main, M. (1995). Recent studies in attachment: Overview, with selected implications for clinical work. In S. Goldberg, R. Muir, & J. Kerr (Eds.), *Attachment theory: Social, developmental, and clinical perspectives* (pp. 407–474). New York: Analytic Press.

Main, M. (1996). Introduction to the special section on attachment and psychopathology: 2. Overview of the field of attachment. *Journal of Consulting and Clinical Psychology, 64*, 237–243.

Main, M. (1999). Epilogue. Attachment theory: Eighteen points with suggestions for future studies. In J. Cassidy & P. R. Shaver (Eds.), *Handbook of attachment: Theory, research, and clinical applications* (pp. 845–887). New York: Guilford.

Main, M., Kaplan, N., & Cassidy, J. (1985). Security in infancy, childhood and adulthood: A move to the level of representation. *Monographs of the Society for Research in Child Development, 50*, 66–104.

Main, M., & Morgan, H. (1996). Disorganization and disorientation in infant strange situation: Phenotypic resemblance to dissociative states. In L. K. Michelson & W. J. Ray (Eds.), *Handbook of dissociation: Theoretical, empirical, and clinical perspectives* (pp. 107–138). New York: Plenum.

Main, M., & Solomon, J. (1986). Discovery of an insecure-disorganized/disoriented attachment pattern. In T. B. Brazelton & M. W. Yogman (Eds.), *Affective development in infancy* (pp. 95–124). Norwood, NJ: Ablex.

Main, M., & Stadtman, J. (1981). Infant response to rejection of physical contact by the mother: Aggression, avoidance and conflict. *Journal of the American Academy of Child Psychiatry, 20*, 292–307.

Main, M., & Weston, D. R. (1981). The quality of the toddler's relationship to mother and to father: Related to conflict behavior and the readiness to establish new relationships. *Child Development, 52*, 932–940.

Main, M., & Weston, D. R. (1982). Avoidance of the attachment figure in infancy: Descriptions and interpretations. In C. M. Parkes & Journal of Stevenson-Hinde (Eds.), *The place of attachment in human behavior* (pp. 31–59). New York: Basic.

Majewska, M. D., Harrison, N. L., Schwartz, R. D., Barker, J. L., & Paul, S. M. (1986). Steroid hormone metabolites are barbiturate-like modulators of the GABA receptor. *Science, 232,* 1004–1007.

Malarkey, W. B., Lipkus, I. M., & Cacioppo, J. T. (1995). The dissociation of catecholamine and hypothalamic-pituitary-adrenal responses to daily stressors using dexamethasone. *Journal of Clinical Endocrinology and Metabolism, 80,* 2458–2463.

Malatesta, C. Z., Culver, C., Tesman, J. R., & Shepard, B. (1989). The development of emotion expression during the first two years of life. *Monographs of the Society for Research in Child Development, 54,* 1–103.

Malatesta-Magai, C. (1991). Emotional Socialization: Its role in personality and developmental psychopathology. In D. Cicchetti & S. L. Toth (Eds.), *Internalizing and externalizing expressions of dysfunction: Rochester symposium on developmental psychopatholgy* (Vol. 2, pp. 203–224). Hillsdale, NJ: Erlbaum.

Malizia, A. L., Cunningham, V. J., Bell, C. J., Liddle, P. F., Jones, T., & Nutt, D. J. (1998). Decreased brain GABA_A-benzodiazepine receptor binding in panic disorder: Preliminary results from a quantitative PET study. *Archives of General Psychiatry, 55,* 715–720.

Malkova, L., Mishkin, M., Suomi, S. J., & Bachevalier, J. (1997). Socioemotional behavior in adult rhesus monkeys after early versus late lesions of the medial temporal lobe. *Annals of the New York Academy of Sciences, 807,* 538–540.

Mallet, J. (1996). Catecholamines: From gene regulation to neuropsychiatric disorders. *Trends in Neurosciences, 19,* 191–196.

Mamelak, M. (2000). The motor vehicle collision injury syndrome. *Neuropsychiatry, Neuropsychology, and Behavioral Neurology, 13,* 125–135.

Manning, J. T., Trivers, R. L., Thornhill, R., Singh, D., Denman, J., Eklo, M. H., & Anderton, R. H. (1997). Ear asymmetry and left-side cradling. *Evolution and Human Behavior, 18,* 327–340.

Manoach, D. S., Sandson, T. A., Mesulam, M. M., Price, B. H., & Weintraub, S. (1993). The developmental social-emotional processing disorder is associated with right-hemispheric electrophysiological abnormalities [Abstract]. *Journal of Clinical and Experimental Neuropsychology, 14,* 56.

Manoach, D. S., Weintraub, S., Daffner, K. R., & Scinto, L. F. M. (1997). Deficient antisaccades in the social-emotional processing disorder. *NeuroReport, 8,* 901–905.

Maquet, P., Peters, J. M., Aerts, J., Delfiore, G., degueldre, C., Luxen, A., & Frank, G. (1996). Functional neuroanatomy of human rapid-eye movement sleep and dreaming. *Nature, 383,* 163–166.

Marchbanks, R. M., Mulcrone, J., & Whatley, S. A. (1995). Aspects of oxidative metabolism in schizophrenia. *British Journal of Psychiatry, 167,* 293–298.

Marder, E. E., Hooper, S. L., & Eisen, J. S. (1987). Multiple neurotransmitters provide a mechanism for the production of multiple outputs from a single neuronal circuit. In G. M. Edelman, W. E. Gall, & W. M. Cowan (Eds.), *Synaptic function* (pp. 305–327). New York: Wiley.

Margolis, R. L., Chuang, D. M., & Post, R. M. (1994). Programmed cell death: Implications for neuropsychiatric disorders. *Biological Psychiatry, 35,* 946–956.

Marín-Padilla, M., Parisi, J. E., Armstrong, D. L., Sargent, S. K., & Kaplan, J. A. (2002). Shaken infant syndrome: Developmental neuropathology, progressive cortical dysplasia, and epilepsy. *Acta Neuropathologica, 103,* 321–332.

Markowitsch, H. J., Kessler, J., Weber-Luxenburger, G., Van der Ven, C., Albers, M., & Heiss, W-D. (2000). Neuroimaging and behavioral correlates of recovery from mnestic block syndrome and other cognitive deteriorations. *Neuropsychiatry, Neuropsychology, and Behavioral Neurology, 13,* 60–66.

Marks, G. A., Shaffery, J. P., Oksenberg, A., Speciale, S. G., & Roffwarg, H. P. (1995). A functional role for REM sleep in brain maturation. *Behavioral Brain Research, 69,* 1–11.

Martin, E., Kikinis, R., Zuerrer, M., Boesch, Ch., Briner, J., Kewitz, G., & Kaelin, P. (1988). Developmental stages of human brain: An MR study. *Journal of Computer Assisted Tomography, 12,* 917–922.

Martin, J. H. (1989). *Neuroanatomy: Text and atlas.* New York: McGraw-Hill.

Martin, L. J., Spicer, D. M., Lewis, M. H., Gluck, J. P., & Cork, L. C. (1991). Social deprivation of infant rhesus monkeys alters the chemoarchitecture of the brain: 1. Subcortical regions. *Journal of Neuroscience, 11,* 3344–3358.

Mason, J. W., Kosten, T. R., Southwick, S., & Giller, E. L. (1990). The use of psychoendocrine strategies in posttraumatic stress disorder. *Journal of Applied Social Psychology, 20,* 1822–1846.

Mason, J. W., Wang, S., Yehuda, R., Riney, S., Charney, D. S., & Southwick, S. M. (2001). Psychogenic lowering of urinary cortisol levels linked to increased emotional numbing and a shame-depressive syndrome in combat-related posttraumatic stress disorder. *Psychosomatic Medicine, 63,* 387–401.

Masur, E. F. (1983). Gestural development, dual-directional signaling, and the transition to words. *Journal of Psycholinguistic Research, 12,* 93–109.

Matthes, H. W. D., Maldonado, R., Simonín, F., Valverde, O., Slowe, S., Kitchen, I., Befort, K., Dierich, A., LeMur, M., Dolle, P., Tzavara, E., Hannoune, J., Roques, B. P., & Kieffer, B. L. (1996). Loss of morphine-induced analgesia, reward effect, and withdrawal symptoms in mice lacking the μ-opioid-receptor gene. *Nature, 383,* 819–823.

Matsuzawa, J., Matsui, M., Konishi, T., Noguchi, K., Gur, R. C., Bilker, W., & Miyawaki, T. (2001). Age-related changes of brain gray and white matter in healthy infants and children. *Cerebral Cortex, 11,* 335–342.

Mattingly, J. B. (1999). Right hemisphere contributions to attention and intention. *Journal of Neurology, Neurosurgery, and Psychiatry, 6,* 5.

Mattson, M. P., & Duan, W. (1999). "Apoptotic" biochemical cascades in synaptic compartments: Roles in adaptive plasticity and neurodegenerative disorders. *Journal of Neuroscience Research, 58,* 152–166.

Maunder, R. G., & Hunter, J. J. (2001). Attachment and psychosomatic medicine: Developmental contributions to stress and disease. *Psychosomatic Medicine, 63,* 556–567.

Mayberg, H. S., Lewis, P. J., Regenold, W., & Wagner, H. N. Jr. (1994). Paralimbic hypoperfusion in unipolar depression. *Journal of Nuclear Medicine, 35,* 929–934.

Mayer, P., Ammon, S., Braun, H., Tischmeyer, H., Riechert, U., Kahl, E., & Höllt, V. (2002). Gene expression profile after intense second messenger activation in cortical primary neurones. *Journal of Neurochemistry, 82,* 1077–1086.

Mayseless, O. (1998). Maternal caregiving strategy—a distinction between the ambivalent and the disorganized profile. *Infant Mental Health Journal, 19,* 20–33.

McCabe, P. M., & Schneiderman, N. (1985). Psychphysiologic reactions to stress. In N. Schneiderman & J. T. Tapp (Eds.), *Behavioral medicine: The biophysical approach* (pp. 99–131). Hillsdale, NJ: Erlbaum.

McCauley, J., Kern, D., Kolodner, K., Dill, L., Schroeder, A., DeChant, H., Ryden, J., Derogatis, L., & Bass, L. (1997). Clinical characteristics of women with a history of childhood abuse. *Journal of the American Medical Association, 277,* 1362–1368.

McDonald, J. W., Silverstein, F. S., & Johnston, M. V. (1988). Neurotoxicity of N-methyl-D-aspartate is markedly enhanced in developing rat central nervous system. *Brain Research, 459,* 200–203.

McDonald, P. W., & Prkachin, K. M. (1990). The expression and perception of facial emotion in alexithymia: A pilot study. *Psychosomatic Medicine, 52,* 199–210.

McEwen, B. S. (2000). The neurobiology of stress: From serendipity to clinical relevance. *Brain Research, 886,* 172–189.

McEwen, B. S., & Stellar, E. (1993). Stress and the individual: Mechanisms leading to disease. *Archives of Internal Medicine, 153,* 2093–2101.

McFarlane, A. C. (2000). Traumatic stress in the 21st century. *Australian and New Zealand Journal of Psychiatry, 34,* 896–902.

McFarlane, A. C., & Yehuda, R. (2000). Clinical treatment of posttraumatic stress disorder: Conceptual challenges raised by recent research. *Australian and New Zealand Journal of Psychiatry, 34,* 940–953.

McGregor, I. S., & Atrens, D. M. (1991). Prefrontal cortex self-stimulation and energy balance. *Behavorial Neuroscience, 105,* 870–883.

McGuiness, D., Pribram, K. H., & Pirnazar, M. (1990). Upstaging the stage model. In C.N. Alexander & E. Langer (Eds.), *Higher stages of human development* (pp. 97–113). New York: Oxford University Press.

McGuire, P. K., Bench, C. J., Frith, C. D., Marks, I. M., Frackowiak, R. S. J., & Dolan, R. J. (1994). Functional anatomy of obsessive-compulsive phenomena. *British Journal of Psychiatry, 164,* 459–468.

McIntosh, T. K., Vink, R., Noble, L., Yamakami, I., Frenyak, S., & Faden, A. L. (1989). Traumatic brain injury in the rat: Characterization of a lateral fluid-percussion model. *Neuroscience, 28,* 233–244.

McLaughlin, B. A., Nelson, D., Erecinska, M., & Chesselet, M.-F. (1998). Toxicity of dopamine to striatal neurons in vitro and potentiation of cell death by a mitochondrial inhibitor. *Journal of Neurochemistry, 70,* 2406–2415.

McNally, R. J., & Amir, N. (1996). Perceptual implicit memory for trauma-related information in post-traumatic stress disorder. *Cognition and Emotion, 10,* 551–556.

Meares, R. (1993). *The metaphor of play: Disruption and restoration in the borderline experience.* Northvale, NJ: Jason Aronson.

Meares, R. (1999). The contribution of Hughlings Jackson to an understanding of dissociation. *American Journal of Psychiatry, 156,* 1850–1855.

Meerlo, P., Horvath, K. M., Luiten, P. G. M., Angelucci, L., Catalani, A., & Koolhaas, J. M. (2001). Increased maternal corticosterone levels in rats: Effects on brain 5-HT1A receptors and behavioral coping with stress in adult offspring. *Behavioral Neuroscience, 115,* 1111–1117.

Mega, M. S., & Cummings, J. L. (1994). Frontal-subcortical circuits and neuropsychiatric disorders. *Journal of Neuropsychiatric and Clinical Neuroscience , 6,* 358–370.

Meltzoff, A. N. (1995a). Understanding the intentions of others: Re-enactment of intended acts by 18-month-old chidren. *Developmental Psychology, 31,* 838–850.

Meltzoff, A. N. (1995b). What infant memory tells us about infantile amnesia: Long-term recall and deferred imitation. *Journal of Experimental Child Psychology, 59,* 497–515.

Melzack, R., & Wall, P. D. (1996). *The challenge of pain.* Harmondsworth, U.K.: Penguin.

Mender, D. M. (1994). *The myth of neuropsychiatry: A look at paradoxes, physics, and the human brain.* New York: Plenum.

Mendez, M. A., & Adair, L. S. (1999). Severity and timing of stunting in the first two years of life affect performance on cognitive tests in late childhood. *Journal of Nutrition, 129,* 1555–1562.

Mesulam, M. M. (1996). Functional imaging of human right hemisphere activation for exploratory movements. *Annals of Neurology, 39,* 174–179.

Mesulam, M. M. (1998). From sensation to cognition. *Brain, 121,* 1013–1052.

Mesulam, M. M., & Geschwind, N. (1978). On the possible role of neocortex and its limbic connections in the process of attention in schizophrenia: Clinical cases of inattention in man and experimental anatomy in monkey. *Journal of Psychiatric Research, 14*, 249–259.

Mesulam, M. M., & Mufson, E. J. (1982). Insula of the Old World monkey: I. Architectonics in the insulo-orbito-temporal component of the paralimbic brain. *Journal of Comparative Neurology, 212*, 1–22.

Metcalfe, J., & Jacobs, W. (1998). Emotional memory: the effects of stress on "cool" and "hot" memory systems. *Psychology of Learning and Motivation, 38*, 187–222.

Mezzacappa, E. S., Kelsey, R. M., Katkin, E. S., & Sloan, R. P. (2001). Vagal rebound and recovery from psychological stress. *Psychosomatic Medicine, 63*, 650–657.

Michel, G. F., & Moore, C. L. (1995). *Developmental psychobiology.* Cambridge, MA: MIT Press.

Mikulincer, M., Gillath, O., Halevy, V., Avihou, V., Avidan, S., & Eshkoli, N. (2001). Attachment theory and reaction to others' needs: Evidence that activation of the sense of attachment security promotes empathic responses. *Journal of Personality and Social Psychology, 81*, 1205–1224.

Mikulincer, M., & Orbach, I. (1995). Attachment styles and repressive defensiveness: The accessibility and architecture of affective memories. *Journal of Personality and Social Psychology, 68*, 917–925.

Miller, B. L., Darby, A., Benson, D. F., Cummings, J. L., & Miller, M. H. (1997). Aggressive, socially disruptive and antisocial behaviour associated with fronto-temporal dementias. *British Journal of Psychiatry, 170*, 150–155.

Miller, L. (1986). Some comments on cerebral hemsipheric models of consciousness. *Psychoanalytic Review, 73*, 129–144.

Milner, B., & Taylor, L. (1972). Right hemisphere superiority in tactile pattern recognition after cerebral commissurotomy: Evidence for nonverbal memory. *Neuropsychologia, 10*, 10–15.

Min, S. K., & Lee, B. O. (1997). Laterality in somatization. *Psychosomatic Medicine, 59*, 236–240.

Mirenowicz, J., & Schultz, W. (1996). Preferential activation of midbrain dopamine neurons by appetitive rather than aversive stimuli. *Nature, 379*, 449–451.

Mitchell, D. G. V., Colledge, E., Leonard, A., & Blair, R. J. R. (2002). Risky decisions and response reversal: Is there evidence of orbitofrontal cortex dysfunction in psychopathic individuals? *Neuropsychologia, 40*, 2013–2022.

Mizuno, N., Sauerland, E. K., & Clemente, C. D. (1968). Projections from the orbital gyrus in the cat: I. To brain stem structures. *Journal of Comparative Neurology, 133*, 463–476.

Mjaatvedt, A. E., & Wong-Riley, M. T. T. (1988). Relationship between synaptogenesis and cytochrome oxidase activity in Purkinje cells of the developing rat cerebellum. *Journal of Comparative Neurology, 277*, 155–182.

Mogenson, G. J., Jones, D. L., & Yim, C. Y. (1980). From motivation to action: Functional interface between the limbic system and the motor system. *Progress in Neurobiology, 14*, 69–97.

Mogg, K., Bradley, B. P., Williams, R., & Mathews, A. (1993). Subliminal processing of emotional information in anxiety and depression. *Journal of Abnormal Psychology, 102*, 304–311.

Moghaddam, B. (1993). Stress preferentially increases extraneuronal levels of excitatory amino acids in the prefrontal cortex: Comparison to hippocampus and basal ganglia. *Journal of Neurochemistry, 60*, 1650–1657.

Moghaddam, B., Bolinao, M. L., Stein-Behrens, B., & Sapolsky, R. (1994). Glucocorticoids mediate the stress-induced extracellular accumulation of glutamate. *Brain Research, 655*, 251–254.

Moleman, N., van der Hart, O., & van der Kolk, B. A. (1992). The partus stress reaction: A neglected etiological factor in postpartum psychiatric disorders. *Journal of Nervous and Mental Disease, 180,* 271–2272.

Moller, A. P., & Swaddle, J. P. (1997). *Asymmetry, developmental stability, and evolution.* Oxford, U.K.: University Press.

Mollon, P. (1996). *Muliple selves, multiple voices: Working with trauma, violation and dissociation.* Chichester, U.K.: Wiley.

Mollon, P. (2001). *Releasing the self: The healing legacy of Heinz Kohut.* Philadelphia, PA: Whurr.

Morange-Majoux, F., Cougnot, P., & Bloch, H. (1997). Hand tactual exploration of infants from 4 to 6 months. *Early Development and Parenting, 6,* 127–135.

Morgan, C. A. III, Wang, S., Rasmusson, A., Hazlett, G., Anderson, G., & Charney, D. S. (2001). Relationship among plasma cortisol, catecholamines, neuropeptide Y, and human performance during exposure to uncontrollable stress. *Psychosomatic Medicine, 63,* 412–422.

Morgan, C. A., Grillon, C., Lubin, H., & Southwick, S. M. (1997). Startle reflex abnormalities in women with sexual assault-related posttraumatic stress disorder. *American Journal of Psychiatry, 154,* 1076–1080.

Morgan, M. A., & LeDoux, J. E. (1995). Differential contribution of dorsal and ventral medial prefrontal cortex to the acquisition and extinction of conditioned fear in rats. *Behavioral Neuroscience, 109,* 681–688.

Morgan, M. A., Romanski, L. M., & LeDoux, J. E. (1993). Extinction of emotional learning: Contribution of medial prefrontal cortex. *Neuroscience Letters, 163,* 109–113.

Morris, G., Seidler, F. J., & Slotkin, T. A. (1983). Stimulation of ornithine decarboxylase by histamine or norepinephrine in brain regions of the developing rat: Evidence for biogenic amines as trophic agents in neonatal development. *Life Sciences, 32,* 1565–1571.

Morris, J. S., Ohman, A., & Dolan, R. J. (1998). Conscious and unconscious emotional learning in the human amygdala. *Nature, 393,* 467–470.

Morris, J. S., Ohman, A., & Dolan, R. J. (1999). A subcortical pathway to the right amygdala mediating "unseen" fear. *Proceedings of the National Academy of Sciences of the United States of America, 96,* 1680–1685.

Morris, J. S., Robinson, R. G., Raphael, B., & Hopwood, M. J. (1996). Lesion location and poststroke depression. *Journal of Neuropsychiatry and Clinical Neurosciences, 8,* 399–403.

Mrzljak, L., Uylings, H. B. M., van Eden, C. G., & Judas, M. (1990). Neuronal development in human prefrontal cortex in prenatal and postnatal stages. *Progress in Brain Research, 85,* 185–222.

Muller, M. M., Keil, A., Gruber, T., & Elbert, T. (1999). Processing of affective pictures modulates right-hemispheric gamma band EEG activity. *Clinical Neurophysiology, 110,* 1913–1920.

Multi-Society Task Force on Persistent Vegetative State. (1994). Medical aspect of the persistent vegetative state. *New England Journal of Medicine, 330,* 1499–1508.

Murphy, C. M. (1978). Pointing in the context of a shared activity. *Child Development, 49,* 371–380.

Mussen, P. H., Conger, J. J., & Kagan, J. (1969). *Child development and personality.* New York: Harper & Row.

Nachmias, M., Gunnar, M. R., Mangelsdorf, S., Parritz, R., & Buss, K. (1996). Behavioral inhibition and stress reactivity: moderating role of attachment security. *Child Development, 67,* 508–522.

Nair, H. P., Berndt, J. D., Barrett, D., & Gonzalez-Lima, F. (2001). Maturation of extinction behavior in infant rats: Large-scale regional interactions with medial prefrontal cortex, orbitofrontal cortex, and anterior cingulate. *Journal of Neuroscience, 21*, 4400–4407.

Nakamura, K., Kawashima, R., Sato, N., Nakamura, A., Sugiura, M., Kato, T., Hatano, K., Ito, K., Fukuda, H., Schorman, T., & Zilles, K. (2000). Functional delineation of the human occipito-temporal areas related to face and scene processing: A PET study. *Brain, 123*, 1903–1912.

Nakamura, K., Kawashima, R., Sugiura, M., Kato, T., Nakamura, A., Hatano, K., Nagumo, S., Kubota, K., Fukuda, H., & Kojima, S. (1999). Acivation of the right inferior frontal cortex during assessment of facial emotion. *Journal of Neurophysiology, 82*, 1610–1614.

Narrow, W. E., Rae, D. S., Robins, L. N., & Reiger, D. A. (2002). Revised prevalence estimates of mental disorders in the United States. *Archives of General Psychiatry, 59*, 115–123.

Nass, R., & Koch, D. (1991). Innate specialization for emotion: Temperament differences in children with left versus right brain brain damage. In N. Amir, I. Rapin, & D. Branski (Eds.), *Pediatric neurology: Behavior and cognition of the child with brain dysfunction*, (Vol. I, pp. 1–17). Basel, Switzerland: Karger.

Natale, M., Gur, R. E., & Gur, R. C. (1983). Hemispheric asymmetries in processing emotional expressions. *Neuropsychologia, 21*, 555–565.

National Center on Child Abuse and Neglect. (1981). *Executive summary: National study of the incidence and severity of child abuse and neglect* (DHHS Publication No. OHDS 81-30329). Washington, DC: U.S. Government Printing Office.

Nauta, W. J. H. (1964). Some efferent connections of the prefrontal cortex in the monkey. In J. M. Warren & K. Akert (Eds.), *The frontal granular cortex and behavior* (pp. 397–407). New York: McGraw Hill.

Nauta, W. J. H., & Domesick, V. B. (1982). Neural associations of the limbic system. In A. L. Beckman (Ed.), *The neural basis of behavior* (pp. 175–206). New York: SP Medical and Scientific Books.

Nayak, M. B., & Milner, J. S. (1998). Neuropsychological functioning: Comparison of mothers at high- and low-risk for child physical abuse. *Child Abuse & Neglect, 22*, 687–703.

Neafsey, E. J. (1990). Prefrontal cortical control of the autonomic nervous system: Anatomical and physiological observations. *Progress in Brain Research, 85*, 147–166.

Nelson, C. A. (1987). The recognition of facial expressions in the first two years of life: Mechanisms of development. *Child Development, 58*, 889–909.

Nelson, C. A. (1994). Neural bases of infant temperament. In J. E. Bates & T. D. Wachs (Eds.), *Temperament: Individual differences at the interface of biology and behavior* (pp. 47–82). Washington, DC: American Psychological Association.

Nelson, E. E., & Panksepp, J. (1998). Brain substrates of infant-mother attachment: Contributions of opioids, oxytocin, and norepinephrine. *Neuroscience & Biobehavioral Reviews, 22*, 437–452.

Nemiah, J. C., & Sifneos, P. E. (1970), Affect and fantasy in patients with psychosomatic disorders. In O. W. Hill (Ed.), *Modern trends in psychosomatic medicine* (Vol. 2, pp. 26–34). London: Buttersworth.

Neve, R. L., & Bear, M. F. (1989). Visual experience regulates gene expression in the developing striate cortex. *Proceedings of the National Academy of Sciences of the United States of America, 86*, 4781- 4784.

Niedenthal, P. M. (1990). Implicit perception of affective information. *Journal of Experimental Social Psychology, 26*, 505–527.

Nieuwenhuys, R., Voogd, J., & van Huijzen, Chr. (1981). *The human central nervous system: A synopsis and atlas* (2nd ed., rev.). New York: Springer-Verlag.

Nijenhuis, E. R. S. (2000). Somatoform dissociation: major symptoms of dissociative disorders. *Journal of Trauma & Dissociation, 1*, 7–32.

Nijenhuis, E. R. S., Vanderlinden, J., & Spinhoven, P. (1998). Animal defensive reactions as a model for trauma-induced dissociative reactions. _Journal of Traumatic Stress, 11_, 242–260.

Nobre, A. C., Coull, J. T., Frith, C. D., & Mesulam, M.-M. (1999). Orbitofrontal cortex is activated during breaches of expectation in tasks of visual attention. _Nature Neuroscience, 2_, 11–12.

Norman, R. M. G., Malla, A. K., Morrison-Stewart, S. L., Helmes, E., Williamson, P. C., Thomas, J., & Cortese, L. (1997). Neuropsychological correlates of syndromes in schizophrenia. _British Journal of Psychiatry, 170_, 134–139.

Northoff, G., Richter, A., Gessner, M., Schlagenhauf, F., Fell, J., Baumgart, F., Kaulisch, T., Kotter, R., Stephan, K. E., Leschinger, A., Hagner, T., Bargel, B., Witzel, T., Hinrichs, H., Bogerts, B., Scheich, H., & Heinze, H-J. (2000). Functional dissociation between medial and lateral prefrontal cortical spatiotemporal activation in negative and positive emotions: A combined fMRI/MEG study. _Cerebral Cortex, 10_, 93–107.

Novelli, A., Reilly, J. A., Lysko, P. G., & Henneberry, R. C. (1988). Glutamate becomes neurotoxic via the N-methyl-D-aspartate receptor when intracellular energy levels are reduced. _Brain Research, 451_, 205–212.

Nunez, J. (1984). Effects of thyroid hormones during brain differentiation. _Molecular and Cellular Endocrinology, 37_, 125–132.

O'Connor, M. J., Sigman, M., & Brill, N. (1987). Disorganization of attachment in relation to maternal alcohol consumption. _Journal of Consulting and Clinical Psychology, 55_, 831–836.

O'Dowd, B. S., Barrington, J., Ng, K. T., Hertz, E., & Hertz, L. (1994). Glycogenolytic response to primary chick and mouse cultures of astrocytes to noradrenaline across development. _Developmental Brain Research, 88_, 220–223.

O'Hagan, K. P. (1995). Emotional and psychological abuse-problems of definition. _Child Abuse & Neglect, 19_, 449–461.

Oatley, K., & Jenkins, J. M. (1992). Human emotions: Function and dysfunction. _Annual Review of Psychology, 43_, 55–85.

Offen, D., Ziv, I., Sternin, H., Melamed, E., & Hochman, A. (1996). Prevention of dopamine-induced cell death by thiol antioxidants: Possible implications for treatment of Parkinson's disease. _Experimental Neurology, 141_, 32–39.

Ogawa, J. R., Sroufe, L. A., Weinfield, N. S., Carlson, E. A., & Egeland, B. (1997). Development and the fragmented self: Longitudinal study of dissociative symptomatology in a nonclinical sample. _Development and Psychopathology, 9_, 855–879.

Ohman, A. (1986). Face the beast and fear the face: Animal and social fears as prototypes for evolutionary analyses of emotion. _Psychophysiology, 23_, 123–145.

Ohta, M., & Oomura, Y. (1979). Inhibitory pathway from the frontal cortex to the hypothalamic ventromedial nucleus in the rat. _Brain Research Bulletin, 4_, 231–238.

Oltvai, Z. N., & Korsmeyer, S. J. (1994). Checkpoints of dueling dimers foil death wishes. _Cell, 79_, 189–192.

Oltvai, Z. N., Milliman, C. L., & Korsmeyer, S. J. (1993). Bcl-2 heterodimerizes in vivo with a conserved homolog, Bax, that accelerates programmed cell death. _Cell, 74_, 609–619.

Ongur, D., An, X., & Price, J. L. (1998). Prefrontal cortical connections to the hypothalamus in macaque monkeys. _Journal of Comparative Neurology, 401_, 480–505.

Oquendo, M. A., & Mann, J. J. (2000). The biology of impulsivity and suicidality. _The Psychiatric Clinics of North America, 23_, 11–25.

Orchinik, M., Murray, T. F., & Moore, F. L. (1994). Steroid modulation of GABA receptors in an amphibian brain. _Brain Research, 646_, 258–266.

Orlinsky, D. E., & Howard, K. I. (1986). Process and outcome in psychotherapy. In S. L. Garfield & A. E. Bergin (Eds.), _Handbook of psychotherapy and behavior change_ (3rd ed., pp. 311–381). New York: John Wiley.

Ornstein, R. (1997). *The right mind: Making sense of the hemispheres.* New York: Harcourt Brace.

Osofsky, J. D., Cohen, G., & Drell, M. (1995). The effects of trauma on young children: A case of 2-year-old twins. *International Journal of Psycho-Analysis, 76,* 595–607.

Osterheld-Haas, M. C., Van der loos, H., & Hornung, J.-P. (1994). Monoaminergic afferents to cortex modulate structural plasticity in the barrelfield of the mouse. *Developmental Brain Research, 77,* 189–202.

Ostrowsky, K., Magnin, M., Ryvlin, P., Isnard, J., Guenot, M., & Mauguière, F. (2002). Representation of pain and somatic sensation in the human insula: A study of responses to direct electrical cortical stimulation. *Cerebral Cortex, 12,* 376–385.

Otto, M. W., Yeo, R. A., & Dougher, M. J. (1987). Right hemisphere involvement in depression: Toward a neuropsychological theory of negative affective experience. *Biological Psychiatry, 22,* 1201–1215.

Overman, W. H., Bachevalier, J., Schuhmann, E., & Ryan, P. (1996). Cognitive gender differences in very young children parallel biologically based cognitive gender differences in monkeys. *Behavioral Neuroscience, 110,* 673–684.

Overton, P. G., & Clark, D. (1997). Burst firing in midbrain dopaminergic neurons. *Brain Research Reviews, 25,* 312–334.

Ovtscharoff, W. Jr., & Braun, K. (2001). Maternal separation and social isolation modulate the postnatal development of synaptic composition in the infralimbic cortex of *octodon degus. Neuroscience, 104,* 33–40.

Oxford English Dictionary, New Shorter Edition (1993). Oxford, UK: Clarendon Press.

Ozonoff, S., & Miller, J. N. (1996). An exploration of right-hemisphere contributions to the pragmatic impairments of autism. *Brain and Language, 52,* 411–434.

Pandya, D. N., & Barnes, C. L. (1987). Architecture and connections of the frontal lobes. In E. Perecman (Ed.), *The frontal lobes revisited* (pp. 41–72). Hillsdale, NJ: Erlbaum.

Pandya, D. N., & Yeterian, E. H. (1985). Architecture and connections of cortical association areas. In A. Peters & E. G. Jones (Eds.), *Cerebral cortex: Vol. 4. Association and auditory cortices* (pp. 3–61). New York: Plenum.

Panksepp, J. (1998). *Affective neuroscience: The foundations of human and animal emotions.* New York: Oxford University Press.

Panksepp, J. (2000). The long-term psychobiological consequences of infant emotions: Prescriptions for the 21st century. *Infant Mental Health Journal, 22,* 132–173.

Papousek, H., & Papousek, M. (1975). *Parent-infant interaction.* New York: Associated Science.

Papousek, H., & Papousek, M. (1997). Fragile aspects of early social integration. In L. Murray & P. J. Cooper (Eds.), *Postpartum depression and child development* (pp. 35–53). New York: Guilford.

Papousek, H., Papousek, M., Suomi, S. J., & Rahn, C. W. (1991). Preverbal communication and attachment: Comparative views. In J. L. Gewirtz & W. M. Kurtines (Eds.), *Intersections with attachment* (pp. 97–122). Hillsdale, NJ: Erlbaum.

Papousek, I., & Schulter, G. (2001). Associations between EEG asymmetrics and electrodermal lability in low vs. high depressive and anxious normal individuals. *International Journal of Psychophysiology, 41,* 105–117.

Papousek, M., & von Hofacker, N. (1998). Persistent crying in early infancy: A nontrivial condition of risk for the developing mother-infant relationship. *Child: Care, Health and Development, 24,* 395–424.

Paradiso, S., Chemerinski, E., Yazici, K. M., Tartaro, A., & Robinson, R. G. (1999). Frontal lobe syndrome reassessed: Comparison of patients with lateral or medial frontal brain damage. *Journal of Neurology, Neurosurgery, and Psychiatry, 67,* 664–667.

Parens, H. (1987). *Aggression in our children*. Northvale, NJ: Jason Aronson.

Paris, J. (1995). Memories of abuse in borderline patients: True or false? *Harvard Review of Psychiatry, 3,* 10–17.

Park, J. S., Bateman, M. C., & Goldberg, M. P. (1996). Rapid alterations in dendrite morphology during sublethal hypoxia or glutamate receptor activation. *Neurobiology of Disease, 3,* 215–227.

Parsadanian, A. Sh., Cheng, Y., Keller-Peck, C. R., Holtzman, D. M., & Snider, W. D. (1998). Bcl-x$_L$ is an antiapoptotic regulator for postnatal CNS neurons. *Journal of Neuroscience, 18,* 1009–1019.

Paus, T., Petrides, M., Evans, A. C., & Meyer, E. (1993). Role of the human anterior cingulate cortex in the control of oculomotor, manual, and speech responses: A positron emission tomography study. *Journal of Neurophysiology, 70,* 453–469.

Pazdernik, T., Cross, R., & Nelson, S. (1994). Is there an energy conservation "system" in brain that protects against the consequences of energy depletion? *Neurochemistry Research, 19,* 1393–1400.

Penman, R., Meares, R., & Milgrom-Friedman, J. (1983). Synchrony in mother-infant interaction: A possible neurophysiological base. *British Journal of Medical Psychology, 56,* 1–7.

Peper, M., & Karcher, S. (2001). Differential conditioning to facial emotional expressions: Effects of hemispheric asymmetries and CS identification. *Psychophysiology, 38,* 936–950.

Perry, B. D., Pollard, R. A., Blakley, T. L., Baker, W. L., & Vigilante, D. (1995). Childhood trauma, the neurobiology of adaptation, and "use-dependent" development of the brain: How states become traits. *Infant Mental Health Journal, 16,* 271–291.

Perry, R. J., Rosen, H. R., Kramer, J. H., Beer, J. S., Levenson, R. L., & Miller, B. L. (2001). Hemispheric dominance for emotions, empathy, and social behavior: Evidence from right and left handers with frontotemporal dementia. *Neurocase, 7,* 145–160.

Perry, S., Cella, D., Falkenberg, J., Heidrich, G., & Gaudwin, C. (1987). Pain perception in burn patients with stress disorders. *Journal of Pain and Symptom Management, 2,* 29–33.

Persinger, M. A., & Makarec, M. (1991). Greater right hemisphericity is associated with lower self-esteem in adults. *Perceptual and Motor Skills, 73,* 1244–1246.

Petrovic, P., Petersson, K. M., Ghatan, P. H., Stone-Elander, S., & Ingvar, M. (2000). Pain-related cerebral activation is altered by a distracting cognitive task. *Pain, 85,* 19–30.

Petrovich, S. B. & Gewirtz, J. L. (1985). The attachment learning process and its relation to cultural and biological evolution: Proximate and ultimate considerations. In M. Reite & T. Field (Eds.), *The psychobiology of attachment and separation* (pp. 259–291). Orlando, FL: Academic Press.

Phelps, E. A., O'Connor, K. J., Gatenby, J. C., Gore, J. C., Grillon, C., & Davis, M. (2001). Activation of the left amygdala to a cognitive representation of fear. *Nature Neuroscience, 4,* 437–441.

Phelps, J. L., Belsky, J., & Crnic, K. (1998). Earned security, daily stress, and parenting: A comparison of five alternative models. *Development and Psychopathology, 10,* 21–38.

Phillips, M. L., Young, A. W., Scott, S. K., Calder, A. J., Andrew, V., Giampietro, S. C. R., Williams, E. T., Bullmore, M., Brammer, M., & Gray, J. A. (1998). Neural responses to facial and vocal expressions of fear and disgust. *Proceedings of the Royal Society of London, B, 265,* 1809–1817.

Pietrini, P., Guazzelli, M., Basso, G., Jaffe, K., & Grafman, J. (2000). Neural correlates of imaginal aggressive behavior assessed by positron emission tomography in healthy subjects. *American Journal of Psychiatry, 157,* 1772–1781.

Pipp, S. (1993). Infant's knowledge of self, other, and relationship. In U. Neisser (Ed.), *The perceived self* (pp. 185–204). New York: Cambridge University Press.

Pipp, S., & Harmon, R. J. (1987). Attachment as regulation: A commentary. *Child Devopment, 58,* 648–652.

Pitett, R. D., Maffei, F., Chang, K., Hickey, R., Berger, R., & Pierce, M. C. (2002). Prevalence of retinal hemorrhages and child abuse in children who present with an apparent life-threatening event. *Pediatrics, 110,* 557–562.

Pizzagalli, D. A., Lehmann, D., Hendrick, A. M., Regard, M., Pascual-Marqui, R. D., & Davidson, R. J. (2002). Affective judgments of faces modulate early activity (~160 ms) within the fusiform gyri. *NeuroImage, 16,* 663–677.

Pizzagalli, D., Regard, M., & Lehmann, D. (1999). Rapid emotional face processing in the human right and left brain hemispheres: An ERP study. *NeuroReport, 10,* 2691–2698.

Pliszka, S. R., Liotti, M., & Woldorff, M. G. (2000). Inhibitory control in children with attention deficit/hyperactivity disorder: Event-related potentials identify the processing component and timing of an impaired right-frontal response inhibition mechanism. *Biological Psychiatry, 48,* 238–246.

Plomin, R. (1983). Developmental behavioral genetics. *Child Development, 54,* 252–259.

Plomin, R., Rende, R., & Rutter, M. (1991). Quantitative genetics and developmental psychopathology. In D. Cicchetti & S. L. Toth (Eds.), *Internalizing and externalizing expressions of dysfunction: Rochester symposium on developmental psychopatholgy* (Vol. 2, pp. 155–202). Mahwah, NJ: Erlbaum.

Poeggel, G., & Braun, K. (1996). Early auditory filial learning in degus (*octodon degus*): behavioral and autoradiographic studies. *Brain Research, 743,* 162–170.

Poeggel, G., Lange, E., Hase, C., Metzger, M., Gulyaeva, N., & Braun, K. (1999). Maternal separation and early social deprivation in *octodon degus*: quantitative changes of nicotinamide adenine dinucleotide phosphate-diasporase-reactive neurons in the prefrontal cortex and nucleus accumbens. *Neuroscience, 94,* 497–504.

Polan, H. J., & Hofer, M. A. (1999). Psychobiological origins of infant attachment and separation responses. In J. Cassidy & P. R. Shaver (Eds.), *Handbook of attachment: Theory, research, and clinical applications* (pp. 162–180). New York: Guilford.

Pollak, S. D., Cicchetti, D., Hornung, K., & Reed, A. (2000). Recognizing emotion in faces: Developmental effects of child abuse and neglect. *Developmental Psychology, 36,* 679–688.

Pontius, A. A., & Ruttiger, K. F. (1976). Frontal lobe system maturational lag in juvenile delinquents shown the narratives test. *Adolescence, 11,* 509–518.

Porges, S. W. (1991). Vagal tone: A mediator of affect. In J. A. Garber & K. A. Dodge (Eds.), *The development of affect regulation and dysregulation* (pp. 111–128). New York: Cambridge University Press.

Porges, S. W. (1995). Orienting in a defensive world: Mammalian modifications of our evolutionary heritage: A polyvagal theory. *Psychophysiology, 32,* 301–318.

Porges, S. W. (1997). Emotion: An evolutionary by-product of the neural regulation of the autonomic nervous system. *Annals of the New York Academy of Sciences, 807,* 62–77.

Porges, S. W. (2001). The polyvagal theory: Phylogenetic substrates of a social nervous system. *International Journal of Psychophysiology, 42,* 29–52.

Porges, S. W., Doussard-Roosevelt, J. A., & Maiti, A. K. (1994). Vagal tone and the physiological regulation of emotion. *Monographs of the Society for Research in Child Development, 59,* 167–186.

Porter, R., Cernoch, J., & McLaughlin, F. (1983). Maternal recognition of neonates through olfactory cues. *Physiology and Behavior, 30,* 151–154.

Porter, R. H., & Winberg, J. (1999). Unique salience of maternal breast odors for newborn infants. *Neuroscience and Biobehavioral Reviews, 23,* 439–449.

Portera-Cailliau, C., Price, D. L., & Martin, L. J. (1997). Excitotoxic neuronal death in the immature brain is an apoptosis-necrosis morphological continuum. *Journal of Comparative Neurology, 378,* 70–87.

Posner, M .I., & Petersen, S. E. (1990). The attention system of the human brain. *Annual Review of Neuroscience, 13,* 182–196.

Post, R., & Weiss, S. (1997). Emergent properties of neural systems: How focal molecular neurobiological alterations can affect behavior. *Development and Psychopathology, 9,* 907–929.

Post, R. M., Weiss, R. B., Smith, M., & McCann, U. (1997). Kindling versus quenching: Implications for the evolution and treatment of posttraumatic stress disorder. *Annals of the New York Academy of Sciences, 821,* 285–295.

Post, R. M., Weiss, S. R. B., & Leverich, G. S. (1994). Recurrent affective disorder: Roots in developmental neurobiology and illness progression based on changes in gene expression. *Development and Psychopathology, 6,* 781–813.

Povinelli, D., & Preuss, T. M. (1995). Theory of mind: evolutionary history of a cognitive specialization. *Trends in Neuroscience, 18,* 418–424.

Powles, W. E. (1992). *Human development and homeostasis.* Madison, CT: International Universities Press.

Preisler, G. M. (1995). The development of communication in blind and in deaf infants — similarities and differences. *Child: Care, Health, and Development, 21,* 79–110.

Pribram, K. H. (1981). Emotions. In S. B. Filskov & T. J. Boll (Eds.), *Handbook of clinical neuropsychology* (pp. 102–134). New York: Wiley.

Pribram, K. H. (1987). The subdivisions of the frontal cortex revisited. In E. Perecman (Ed.), *The frontal lobes revisited* (pp. 11–39). Hillsdale, NJ: Erlbaum.

Pribram, K. H. (1991). *Brain and perception: Holonomy and structure in figural processing.* Hillsdale, NJ: Erlbaum.

Price, D. D. (2000). Psychological and neural mechanisms of the affective dimension of pain. *Science, 288,* 1769–1772.

Price, J. L., Carmichael, S. T., & Drevets, W. C. (1996). Networks related to the orbital and medial prefrontal cortex; a substrate for emotional behavior? *Progress in Brain Research, 107,* 523–536.

Prigogine, I., & Stengers, I. (1984). *Order out of chaos.* New York: Bantam.

Prins, A., Kaloupek, D. G., & Keane, T. M. (1995). Psychophysiological evidence for autonomic arousal and startle in traumatized adult populations. In M. J. Friedman, D. S. Charney, & A. Y. Deutsch (Eds.), *Neurobiological and clinical consequences of stress: From normal adaptation to post-traumatic stress disorders* (pp. 291–314). Philadelphia: Lippincott-Raven.

Pruessner J., Hellhammer, D. H., & Kirschbaum, C. (1999). Burnout, perceived stress and salivary cortisol upon wakening. *Psychosomatic Medicine, 61,* 197–204.

Pryce, C. R. (1992). A comparative systems model of the regulation of maternal motivation in mammals. *Animal Behavior, 43,* 417–441.

Pryce, C. R. (1995). Determinants of motherhood in human and nonhuman primates. A biosocial model. In C. R. Pryce, R. D. Martin, & D. Skuse (Eds.), *Motherhood in human and nonhuman primates* (pp. 1–15). Basel, Switzerland: Karger.

Purves, D., & LaMantia, A.-S. (1990). Construction of modular circuits in the mammalian brain. *Cold Spring Harbor Symposia on Quantitative Biolology, LV,* 445–452.

Putnam, F. W. (1989). *Diagnosis and treatment of multiple personality disorder.* New York: Guilford.

Putnam, F. W. (1995). Development of dissociative disorders. In D. Cicchetti &

D. J. Cohen (Eds.), *Developmental psychopathology: Vol. 2 Risk, disorder, and adaptation* (pp. 581–608). New York: Wiley.

Putnam, F. W. (1997). *Dissociation in children and adolescents: A developmental perspective*. New York: Guilford.

Pynoos, R. S. (1993). Traumatic stress and developmental psychopathology in children and adolescents. In J. M. Oldham, M. B. Riba, & A. Tasman (Eds.), *Review of psychiatry* (pp. 239–272). Washington, DC: American Psychiatric Press.

Pysh, J. J. (1970). Mitochondrial changes in rat inferior colliculus during postnatal development: An electron microscopic study. *Brain Research, 18*, 325–342.

Rabinowicz, T. (1979). The differentiate maturation of the human cerebral cortex. In F. Falkner & J. M. Tanner (Eds.), *Human growth: Vol. 3. Neurobiology and nutrition* (pp. 97–123). New York: Plenum.

Raff, M. C. (1992). Social controls on cell survival and cell death. *Nature, 356,* 397–400.

Raine, A. (2002). Biosocial studies of antisocial and violent behavior in children and adults: A review. *Journal of Abnormal Child Psychology, 30,* 311–326.

Raine, A., Brennan, P., & Mednick, S. A. (1994). Birth complications combined with early maternal rejection at age 1 year predispose to violent crime at age 18 years. *Archives of General Psychiatry, 51,* 984–988.

Raine, A., Lencz, T., Bihrle, S., LaCasse, L., & Colletti, P. (2000). Reduced prefrontal gray matter volume and reduced autonomic activity in antisocial personality disorder. *Archives of General Psychiatry, 57,* 119–127.

Raine, A., Meloy, J. R., Bihrle, S., Stoddard, J., Lacasse, L., & Buchsbaum, M. S. (1998). Reduced prefrontal and increased subcortical brain functioning assessed using positron emission tomography in predatory and affective muderers. *Behavioral Sciences and the Law, 16,* 319–332.

Raine, A., Park, S., Lencz, T., Bihrle, S., Lacasse, L., Widom, C. S., Louai, A.-D., & Singh, M. (2001). Reduced right hemisphere activation in severely abused violent offenders during a working memory task: An fMRI study. *Aggressive Behavior, 27,* 111–129.

Raine, A., Reynolds, C., Venables, P. H., Mednick, S. A., & Farrington, D. P. (1998). Fearlessness, stimulation-seeking, and large body size at 3 years as early predispositions to childhood aggression at age 11 years. *Archives of General Psychiatry, 55,* 745–751.

Raine, A., Stoddard, J., Bihrle, S., & Buchsbaum, M. (1998). Prefrontal glucose deficits in murderers lacking psychosocial deprivation. *Neuropsychiatry, Neuropsychology, and Behavioral Neurology, 11,* 1–7.

Raine, A., Venables, P. H., & Mednick, S. A. (1997). Low resting heart rate at age 3 years predisposes to aggression at age 11 years: Evidence from the Mauritius Child Health Project. *Journal of the American Academy of Child and Adolescent Psychiatry, 36,* 1457–1464.

Rakic, P., Bourgeois, J-P., & Goldman-Rakic, P. S. (1994). Synaptic development of the cerebral cortex: Implications for learning, memory, and mental illness. *Progress in Brain Research, 102,* 227–243.

Raleigh, M. J., & Brammer, G. L. (1993). Individual differences in serotonin-2 receptors and social behavior in monkeys. *Society for Neuroscience Abstracts, 19,* 592.

Raleigh, M. J., & Steklis, H. D. (1981). Effects of orbitofrontal and temporal neocortical lesions on the affiliative behavior of vervet monkeys (*Cercopithecus aethiops sabaeus*). *Experimental Neurology, 73,* 378–389.

Raleigh, M. J., Steklis, H. D., Ervin, F. R., Kling, A. S., & McGuire, M. J. (1979). The effecs of orbital frontal lesions on the aggressive behavior of vervet monkeys (*Cercopitheous aethiops sabaeus*). *Experimental Neurology, 66,* 158–168.

Ramus, F., Hauser, M. D., Miller, C., Morris, D., & Mehler, J. (2000). Language discrimination by human newborns and by cotton-top tamarin monkeys. *Science, 288,* 349–351.

Rapoport, S. (2000). The development of neurodevelopmental psychiatry. *American Journal of Psychiatry, 157,* 159–161.

Rauch, S. C., Savage, C. R., Alpert, N. M., Miguel, E. C., Baer, L., Breiter, H. C., Fischman, A. J., Manzo, P. A., Moretti, C., & Jenike, M. A. (1995). A positron emission tomographic study of simple phobic symptom provocation. *Archives of General Psychiatry, 52,* 20–28.

Rauch, S. L., Jenike, M. A., Alpert, N. M., Baer, L., Breiter, H. C. R., Savage, C. R., & Fischman, A. J. (1994). Regional cerebral blood flow measured during symptom provocation in obsessive-compulsive disorder using oxygen 15-labeled carbon dioxide and positron emission tomography. *Archives of General Psychiatry, 51,* 62–70.

Rauch, S. L., van der Kolk, B. A., Fisler, R. E., Alpert, N. M., Orr, S. P., Savage, C. R., Fischman, A. J., Jenike, M. A., & Pitman, R. K. (1996). A symptom provocation study of posttraumatic stress disorder using positron emission tomography and script-driven imagery. *Archives of General Psychiatry, 53,* 380–387.

Rauch, S. L., Whalen, P. J., Shin, L. M., McInerney, S. C., Macklin, M. L., Lasko, N. B., Orr, S. P., & Pitman, R. K. (2000). Exaggerated amygdala response to masked facial stimuli in posttraumatic stress disorder: A functional MRI study. *Biological Psychiatry, 47,* 769–776.

Reid, S. (1999). Autism and trauma: Autistic post-traumatic developmental disorder. In A. Alvarez & S. Reid (Eds.), *Autism and personality: Findings from the Tavistock autism workshop* (pp. 93–109). London: Routledge.

Reilly, J. S., Stiles, J., Larsen, J., & Trauner, D. (1995). Affective expression in infants with focal brain damage. *Neuropsychologia, 33,* 83–99.

Reiss, A. J., & Roth, J. A. (1993). *Understanding and preventing violence.* Washington, DC: National Academy of Sciences.

Reite, M., & Capitanio, J. P. (1985). On the nature of social separation and attachment. In M. Reite & T. Field. (Ed.), *The psychobiology of attachment and separation* (pp. 223–255). Orlando, FL: Academic Press.

Reshetniak, V. K., & Kukushkin, M. L. (1989). Effects of removal of orbitofrontal cortex and the development of reflex analgesia. *Bulletin of Experimental Biology and Medicine, 108,* 14–16.

Reynolds, M., & Brewin, C. R. (1998). Intrusive cognitions, coping strategies, and emotional responses in depression, post-traumatic stress disorder and a non-clinical population. *Behavior Research and Therapy, 36,* 135–147.

Ricciardelli, P., Ro, T., & Driver, J. (2002). A left visual field advantage in perception of gaze direction. *Neuropsychologia, 40,* 769–777.

Riecker, A., Ackermann, H., Wildgruber, D., Dogil, G., & Grodd, W. (2000). Opposite hemispheric lateralization effects during speaking and singing at motor cortex, insula and cerebellum. *NeuroReport, 11,* 1997–2000.

Rinaman, L., Levitt, P., & Card, J. P. (2000). Progressive postnatal assembly of limbic-autonomic circuits revealed by central transneuronal transport of pseudorabies virus. *Journal of Neuroscience, 20,* 2731–2741.

Robbins, T. W. & Everitt, B. J. (1982). Functional studies of the central catecholamines. *International Review of Neurobiology, 23,* 303–365.

Robbins, T. W., & Everitt, B. J. (1996). Neurobehavioral mechanisms of reward and motivation. *Current Opinions in Neurobiology, 6,* 228–236.

Roberts, A. C., & Wallis, J. D. (2000). Inhibitory control and affective processing in the prefrontal cortex: Neuropsychological studies in the common marmoset. *Cerebral Cortex, 10,* 252–262.

Roca, V., & Freeman, T. W. (2002). Psychosensory symptoms in combat veterans with posttraumatic stress disorder. *Journal of Neuropsychiatry and Clinical Neuroscience, 14*, 185–189.

Rochat, P. (1983). Oral touch in young infants: Responses to variations of nipple characteristics in the first months of life. *International Journal of Behavioral Development, 6*, 123–133.

Rogeness, G. A., & McClure, E. B. (1996). Development and neurotransmitter-environmental interactions. *Development and Psychopathology, 8*, 183–199.

Rolls, E. T. (1986). Neural systems involved in emotion in primates. In R. Plutchik & H. Kellerman (Eds.), *Emotion: Theory, research, and practice Vol. 3* (pp. 125–143). Orlando: Academic Press.

Rolls, E. T. (1996). The orbitofrontal cortex. *Philosophical Transactions of the Royal Society of London B, 351*, 1433–1444.

Rolls, E. T. (2000). The orbitofrontal cortex and reward. *Cerebral Cortex, 10*, 284–294.

Rolls, E. T., Hornak, J., Wade, D., & McGrath, J. (1994). Emotion-related learning in patients with social and emotional changes associated with frontal lobe damage. *Journal of Neurology, Neurosurgery, and Psychiatry, 57*, 1518–1524.

Romanski, L. M., Tian, B., Fritz, J., Mishkin, M., Goldman-Rakic, P. S., & Rauschecker, J. P. (1999). Dual streams of auditory afferents target multiple domains in the primate prefrontal cortex. *Nature Neuroscience, 2*, 1131–1136.

Roozendaal, B., Koolhaas, J. M., & Bohus, B. (1997). The role of the central amygdala in stress and adaptation. *Acta Physiologica Scandinavica, 640* (Suppl.), 51–54.

Rosenblum, L. A. (1987). Influences of environmental demand on maternal behavior and infant development. In N. A. Krasnegor, E. M. Blass, M. A. Hofer, & W. P. Smotherman (Eds.), *Perinatal development: A psychobiological perspective* (pp. 377–395). Orlando, FL: Academic Press.

Rosenblum, L. A., Coplan, J. D., Friedman, S., Basoff, T., Gorman, J. M., & Andrews, M. W. (1994). Adverse early experiences affect noradrenergic and serotonergic functioning in adult primates. *Biological Psychiatry, 35*, 221–227.

Ross, E. D. (1983). Right-hemisphere lesions in disorders of affective language. In A. Kertesz (Ed.), *Localization in neuropsychology* (pp. 493–508). New York: Academic Press.

Ross, E. D., Homan, R. W., & Buck, R. (1994). Differential hemispheric lateralization of primary and social emotions: Implications for developing a comprehensive neurology for emotions, repression, and the subconscious. *Neuropsychiatry, Neuropsychology, and Behavioral Neurology, 7*, 1–19.

Rotenberg, V. S. (1995). Right hemisphere insufficiency and illness in the context of search activity concept. *Dynamic Psychiatry, 150/151*, 54–63.

Rothbart, M. K., Derryberry, D., & Posner, M. I. (1994). A psychobiological approach to the development of temperament. In J. E. Bates & T. D. Wachs (Eds.), *Temperament; Individual differences at the interface of biology and behavior* (pp. 83–116). Washington, DC: American Psychological Association.

Rothbart, M. K., Taylor, S. B., & Tucker, D. M. (1989). Right-sided facial asymmetry in infant emotional expression. *Neuropsychologia, 27*, 675–687.

Rourke, B. P., Young, G. C., & Leenaars, A. A. (1989). A childhood learning disability that predisposes those affected to adolescent and adult depression and suicide risk. *Journal of Learning Disabilities, 22*, 169–175.

Roy, A. (2002). Urinary free cortisol and childhood trauma in cocaine dependent adults. *Journal of Psychiatric Research, 36*, 173–177.

Ruby, P., & Decety, J. (2001). Effect of subjective perspective taking during stimulation of action: A PET investigation of agency. *Nature Neuroscience, 4*, 546–550.

Ruch, T. C., & Shenkin, H. A. (1943). The relation of area 13 on orbital surface of frontal lobes to hyperactivity and hyperphagia in monkeys. *Journal of Neurophysiology,* 6, 349–360.

Ruda, M. A., Ling, Q-D., Hohmann, A. G., Peng, Y. B., & Tachibana, T. (2000). Altered nociceptive neuronal circuits after neonatal peripheral inflammation. *Science,* 289, 628–630.

Rueckert, L., & Grafman, J. (1996). Sustained attention deficts in patients with right frontal lesions. *Neuropsychologia, 10,* 953–963.

Russ, M. J., Roth, S. D., Lerman, A., Kakuma, T., Harrison, K., Shindledecker, R. D., Hull, J., & Mattis, S. (1992). Pain perception in self-injurious patients with borderline personality disorder. *Biological Psychiatry, 32,* 501–511.

Russell, M. J. (1976). Human olfactory communication. *Science, 260,* 520–521.

Rutter, M. (1987). Temperament, personality and personality disorder. *British Journal of Psychiatry, 150,* 443–458.

Rutter, M. (1995). Relationships between mental disorders in childhood and adulthood. *Acta Psychiatrica Scandinavica, 91,* 73–85.

Ryan, R. M., Kuhl, J., & Deci, E. L. (1997). Nature and autonomy: An organizational view of social and neurobiological aspects of self-regulation in behavior and development. *Development and Psychopathology, 9,* 701–728.

Sabban, E. L., & Kvetnansky, R. (2001). Stress-triggered activation of gene expression in catecholaminergic systems: Dynamics of transcriptional events. *Trends in Neuroscience, 24,* 91–98.

Sahar, T., Shalev, A. Y., & Porges, S. W. (2001). Vagal modulation of responses to mental challenge in posttraumatic stress disorder. *Biological Psychiatry, 49,* 637–643.

Salansky, N., Fedotchev, A., & Bondar, A. (1998). Responses of the nervous system to low frequency stimulation and EEG rhythms: Clinical implications. *Neuroscience and Biobehavioral Reviews, 22,* 395–409.

Salovey, P., & Mayer, J. D. (1989/1990). Emotional intelligence. *Imagination, cognition, and personalty, 9,* 185–211.

Salovey, P., Rothman, A. J., Detweiler, J. B., & Steward, W. T. (2000). Emotional states and physical health. *American Psychologist, 55,* 110–121.

Sander, L. (1988). The event-structure of regulation in the neonate-caregiver system as a biological background of early organization of psychic ctruture. In A. Goldberg (Ed.), *Frontiers in self psychology* (pp. 64–77). Hillsdale, NJ: Erlbaum.

Sander, L. (1991). *Recognition process: Specificity and organization in early human development.* Paper presented at University of Massachussetts conference, "The psychic Life of the Infant," Amherst, MA.

Sander, L. (1997). Paradox and resolution: From the beginning. In J. Noshpitz, S. Greenspan, S. Weider, & J. Osofsky (Eds.), *Handbook of child and adolescent psychiatry* (Vol. 1, pp. 153–159). New York: Wiley.

Sander, L. (2000). Where are we going in the field of infant mental health? *Infant Mental Health Journal, 21,* 5–20.

Sandman, C. A., Wadha, P. D., Dunkel-Schetter, Chicz-DeMet, A., Belman, J., Porto, M., Murata, Y., Garite, T. J., & Crinella, F. M. (1994). Psychobiological influences of stress and HPA regulation on the human fetus and infant birth outcomes. *Annals of the New York Academy of Sciences, 739,* 198–209.

Savage, C. R., Deckersbach, T., Heckers, S., Wagner, A. D., Schacter, D. L., Alpert, N. M., Fischman, A. J., & Rauch, S. L. (2001). Prefrontal regions supporting spontaneous and directed application of verbal learning strategies: Evidence from PET. *Brain, 124,* 219–231.

Savarese, V. W., Suvak, M. K., King, L. A., & King, D. W. (2001). Relationships among alcohol use, hyperarousal, and marital abuse and violence in Vietnam veterans. *Journal of Traumatic Stress, 14,* 717–732.

Saxby, G. P., & Bryden, M. P. (1985). Left visual-field advantage in children for processing visual emotional stimuli. *Developmental Psychology, 21,* 253–261.

Scaer, R. C. (2001). *Trauma, dissociation, and disease: The body bears the burden.* New York: Haworth.

Scaife, M., & Bruner, J. S. (1975). The capacity for joint visual attention in the infant. *Nature, 253,* 265–266.

Scalaidhe, S. P., Wilson, F. A. W., & Goldman-Rakic, P. S. (1997). Areal segregation of face-processing neurons in prefrontal cortex. *Science, 278,* 1135–1138.

Schaffer, H. R., & Emerson, P. E. (1964). The development of social attachments in infancy. *Monographs of the Society for Research in Child Development, 29,* (3, No. 94): 1–77.

Scheeringa, M. S., & Zeanah, C. H. (2001). A relational perspective on PTSD in early childhood. *Journal of Traumatic Stress, 14,* 799–815.

Scherer, K. R. (1986). Vocal affect expression: A review and a model for future research. *Psychological Bulletin, 99,* 143–165.

Scherer, K. R. (1994). Affect bursts. In S. H. M. van Goozen, N. E. van de Poll, & J. A. Sergeant (Eds.), *Emotions: Essays on emotion theory* (pp. 161–193). Mahwah, NJ: Erlbaum.

Schiffer, F., Teicher, M. H., & Papanicolaou, A. C. (1995). Evoked potential evidence for right brain activity during recall of traumatic memories. *Journal of Neuropsychiatry, 7,* 169–175.

Schinder, A. F., Olson, E. C., Spitzer, N. C., & Montal, M. (1996). Mitochondrial dysfunction is a primary event in glutamate toxicity. *Journal of Neuroscience, 16,* 6125–6133.

Schlussman, S. D., Nyberg, F., & Kreck, M. J. (2002). The effects of drug abuse on the stress responsive hypothalamic-pituitary-adrenal axis and the dopaminergic and endogenous opioid systems. *Acta Psychiatrica Scandinavica, 106,* 121–124.

Schmahl, C. G., Elzinga, B. M., & Bremner, J. D. (2002). Individual differences in psychophysiological reactivity in adults with childhood abuse. *Clinical Psychology and Psychotherapy, 9,* 271–276.

Schmidt, J. J., Hartje, W., & Wilmes, K. (1997). Hemispheric asymmetry in the recognition of emotional attitude conveyed by facial expression, prosody and propositional speech. *Cortex, 33,* 65–81.

Schmidt, S., Nachtigall, C., Wuethrich-Martone, O., & Strauss, B. (2002). Attachment and coping with chronic disease. *Journal of Psychosomatic Research, 53,* 763–773.

Schneider, F., Gur, R. E., Alavi, A., Seligman, M. E., Mozley, L. H., Smit, R. V., Mozley, P. D., & Gur, R. C. (1996). Cerebral blood flow changes in limbic regions induced by unsolvable anagram tasks. *American Journal of Psychiatry, 153,* 206–212.

Schneider, M. L., Clarke, S., Kraemer, G. W., Roughton, E. C., Lubach, G. R., Rimm-Kaufman, S., Schmidt, D., & Ebert, M. (1998). Prenatal stress alters biogenic amine levels in primates. *Development and Psychopathology, 10,* 427–440.

Schnider, A., & Ptak, R. (1999). Spontaneous confabulators fail to suppress currently irrelevant memory traces. *Nature Neuroscience, 2,* 677–681.

Schnider, A., Treyer, V., & Buck, A. (2000). Selection of currently relevant memories by the human posterior medial orbitofrontal cortex. *Journal of Neuroscience, 20,* 5880–5884.

Schnurr, P. P., & Friedman, M. J. (1997). An overview of research findings on the nature of posttraumatic stress disorder. *In Session: Psychotherapy in Practice, 3,* 11–25.

Schoenbaum, G., Chiba, A. A., & Gallagher, M. (2000). Changes in functional connectivity in orbitofrontal cortex and basolateral amygdala during learning and reversal training. *Journal of Neuroscience, 20,* 5179–5189.

Schore, A. N. (1991). Early superego development: The emergence of shame and narcissistic affect regulation in the practicing period. *Psychoanalysis and Contemporary Thought, 14*, 187–250.

Schore, A. N. (1994). *Affect regulation and the origin of the self: The neurobiology of emotional development.* Hillsdale, NJ: Erlbaum.

Schore, A. N. (1995, April). *One hundred years after* Freud's Project for a Scientific Psychology—*Is the time right for a rapprochement between psychoanalysis and neurobiology?* Keynote address, American Psychological Association, Division of Psychoanalysis (39), Santa Monica, CA.

Schore, A. N. (1996). The experience-dependent maturation of a regulatory system in the orbital prefrontal cortex and the origin of developmental psychopathology. *Development and Psychopathology, 8*, 59–87. New York: Cambridge University Press.

Schore, A. N. (1997a). The early organization of the nonlinear right brain and the development of a predisposition to psychiatric disorders. *Development and Psychopathology, 9*, 595–631. New York: Cambridge University Press.

Schore, A. N. (1997b). A century after Freud's Project: Is a rapprochement between psychoanalysis and neurobiology at hand? *Journal of the American Psychoanalytic Association, 45*, 841–867.

Schore, A. N. (1997c). Interdisciplinary developmental research as a source of clinical models. In M. Moskowitz, C. Monk, C. Kaye, & S. Ellman (Eds.), *The neurobiological and developmental basis for psychotherapeutic intervention* (pp. 1–71). Northvale, NJ: Aronson.

Schore, A. N. (1997d, October). *The relevance of recent research on the infant brain to clinical psychiatry.* Grand rounds presentation to the Department of Psychiatry, Columbia University School of Medicine, New York.

Schore, A. N. (1998a). The experience-dependent maturation of an evaluative system in the cortex. In K. Pribram (Ed.), *Brain and values: Is a biological science of values possible?* (pp. 337–358). Mahwah, NJ: Erlbaum.

Schore, A. N. (1998b). Early shame experiences and infant brain development. In P. Gilbert & B. Andrews (Eds.), *Shame: interpersonal behavior, psychopathology, and culture* (pp. 57–77). New York: Oxford University Press.

Schore, A. N. (1998c, July). *Affect regulation: A fundamental process of psychobiological development, brain organization, and psychotherapy.* Paper presented at the Tavistock Clinic, London.

Schore, A. N. (1998d, September). *Parent-infant communications and the neurobiology of emotional development.* Paper presented at the symposium of the Erikson Institute's Faculty Development Project on the Brain and the University of Chicago's Early Childhood Initiative, "The Developing Child: Brain and Behavior," Loyola University, Chicago, IL.

Schore, A. N. (1998e, October). *The relevance of recent research on the infant brain to pediatrics.* Paper presented at the annual meeting of the American Academy of Pediatrics, Scientific Section on Developmental and Behavioral Pediatrics, San Francisco, CA.

Schore, A. N. (1998f, October). *The right brain as a neurobiological substrate of Freud's dynamic unconscious.* Keynote address, Conference, "Freud at the Millennium," Georgetown University. Washington, DC.

Schore, A. N. (1998g, February). *Early trauma and the development of the right brain.* Paper presented at the UCLA conference, "Understanding and Treating Trauma: Developmental and Neurobiological Approaches," Los Angeles, CA.

Schore, A. N. (1998h, October). *The relevance of recent research on the infant brain to clinical psychiatry.* Keynote address at the 11th annual conference of the Royal Australian and New Zealand College of Psychiatrists, Sydney, Australia.

Schore, A. N. (1998i, November). *Early trauma and the development of the right brain.* Keynote address, C.M. Hincks Institute Conference on "Traumatized Parents and Infants: The Long Shadow of Early Childhood Trauma," University of Toronto, Canada.

Schore, A. N. (1999a). Commentary on emotions: Neuro-psychoanalytic views. *Neuro-Psychoanalysis, 1*, 49–55.

Schore, A. N. (1999b, December). *Parent-infant communications and the neurobiology of emotional development*. Workshop presented at the Zero to Three 14th Annual Training Conference, Anaheim, CA.

Schore, A. N. (1999c, March). *The development of a predisposition to violence: The critical roles of attachment disorders and the maturation of the right brain*. Invited address presented at the Children's Institute International Conference, "Understanding the Roots of Violence: Kids Who Kill," Los Angeles, CA.

Schore, A. N. (1999d, October). The enduring effects of early trauma on the right brain. In *Attachment, trauma, and the developing mind*. Symposium conducted at the annual meeting of the American Academy of Child and Adolescent Psychiatry, Chicago, IL.

Schore, A. N. (1999e, May). *Practical implications of brain research as it relates to infant/toddler development*. Paper presented at the Rand/UCLA Child and Adolescent Health Policy Seminar. Rand Corporation, Santa Monica, CA.

Schore, A. N. (1999f, December). *Psychoanalysis and the development of the right brain*. Invited address presented at the first North American International Psychoanalytic Association Regional Research Conference, "Neuroscience, Development & Psychoanalysis." New York, NY.

Schore, A. N. (1999g, April). *Early trauma and the development of the right brain*. Invited address presented at the Boston University School of Medicine conference, "Psychological Trauma: Maturational Processes and Therapeutic Interventions," Boston, MA.

Schore, A. N. (1999h). *The right brain, the right mind, and psychoanalysis* Retrieved, January 30, 2003, from http:www.neuro-psa.com/schore.htm

Schore, A. N. (2000a). Foreword. In Bowlby, J., *Attachment and Loss: Vol. 1. Attachment* (Reissue). New York: Basic.

Schore, A. N. (2000b). The self-organization of the right brain and the neurobiology of emotional development. In M. D. Lewis & I. Granic (Eds.), *Emotion, development, and self-organization* (pp. 155–185). New York: Cambridge University Press.

Schore, A. N. (2000c). Attachment and the regulation of the right brain. *Attachment & Human Development, 2*, 23–47. New York: Taylor & Francis.

Schore, A. N. (2000d). Parent-infant communication and the neurobiology of emotional development. In Lamb-Parker, F., Hagen, J., & Robinson, R. (Eds.), *Proceedings of Head Start's Fifth National Reseach Conference, "Developmental and Contextual Transitions of Children and Families: Implications for Research, Policy, and Practice,"* (pp. 49–73). Washington, DC: Department of Health and Human Services.

Schore, A. N. (2000e, March). *Early relational trauma and the development of the right brain*. Paper presented to the Anna Freud Centre, London.

Schore, A. N. (2000f, November). *Healthy childhood and the development of the human brain*. Keynote address, Luxembourg and World Health Organization, Healthy Children Foundation Conference, Luxembourg.

Schore, A. N. (2001a). The effects of a secure attachment relationship on right brain development, affect regulation, and infant mental health. *Infant Mental Health Journal, 22*, 201–269.

Schore, A. N. (2001b). The right brain as the neurobiological substratum of Freud's dynamic unconscious. In D. Scharff (Ed.), *Freud at the millennium: The evolution and application of psychoanalysis* (pp. 61–88). New York: Other Press.

Schore, A. N. (2001c). The effects of relational trauma on right brain development, affect regulation, and infant mental health. *Infant Mental Health Journal, 22*, 201–269.

Schore, A. N. (2001d). The Seventh Annual John Bowlby Memorial Lecture,

"Minds in the making: Attachment, the self-organizing brain, and developmentally oriented psychoanalytic psychotherapy." *British Journal of Psychotherapy, 17,* 299–328.

Schore, A. N. (2001e, March). Early relational trauma and the development of the right brain. Keynote address, Joint Annual Conference, Australian Centre for Posttraumatic Mental Health and The Australasian Society for Traumatic Stress Studies, Canberra, Australia.

Schore, A. N. (2001f, January). *The development of a predisposition to violence: The critical roles of attachment disorders and the maturation of the right brain.* Plenary address, Caring Foundation and Safe Start Conference, New Orleans, LA.

Schore, A. N. (2001g, June). *Regulation of the right brain: A fundamental mechanism of attachment, trauma, dissociation, and psychotherapy, Parts 1 & 2.* Paper presented at the University College of London Attachment Research Unit and the Clinic for the Study of Dissociative Disorders conference, "Attachment, Trauma, and Dissociation: Developmental, Neuropsychological, Clinical, and Forensic Considerations," London.

Schore, A. N. (2002a). Clinical implications of a psychoneurobiological model of projective identification. In S. Alhanati (Ed.), *Primitive mental states: Vol. Ill. Pre- and peri-natal influences on personality development* (pp. 1–65). London: Karnac.

Schore, A. N. (2002b). Dysregulation of the right brain: A fundamental mechanism of traumatic attachment and the psychopathogenesis of posttraumatic stress disorder. *Australian & New Zealand Journal of Psychiatry, 36,* 9–30.

Schore, A. N. (2002c). Neurobiology and psychoanalysis: Convergent findings on the subject of projective identification. In J. Edwards (Ed.), *Being alive: Building on the work of Anne Alvarez* (pp. 57–74). London: Brunner-Routledge.

Schore, A. N. (in press). Early relational trauma, disorganized attachment, and the development of a predisposition to violence. In M. Solomon & D. Siegel (Eds.). *Healing trauma: attachment, trauma, the brain, and the mind.* New York: W. W. Norton.

Schuengel, C., Bakersmans-Kranenburg, M. J., & Van Ijzendoorn, M. H. (1999). Frightening maternal behavior linking unresolved loss and disorganized infant attachment. *Journal of Consulting and Clinical Psychology, 67,* 54–63.

Schuff, N., Marmar, C. R., Weiss, D. S., Neylan, T. C., Schoenfield, F., Fein, G., & Weiner, M. W. (1997). Reduced hippocampal volume and n-acetyl aspartate in posttraumatic stress disorder. *Annals of the New York Academy of Sciences, 821,* 516–520.

Schulkin, J., Gold, P. W., & McEwen, B. (1998). Induction of corticotropin-releasing factor hormone gene expression by glucocorticoids: Implication for understanding the states of fear and anxiety and allostatic load. *Psychoneuroendocrinology, 23,* 219–243.

Schwaber, J. S., Kapp, B. S., Higgins, G. A., & Rapp, P. R. (1982). Amygdaloid and basal forebrain direct connections with the nucleus of the solitary tract and the dorsal motor nucleus. *Journal of Neuroscience, 2,* 1424–1438.

Schwalbe, M. L. (1991). The autogenesis of the self. *Journal of the Theory of Social Behavior, 21,* 269–295.

Schwartz, A. (1990). On narcissism: An (other) introduction. In R. A. Glick & S. Bone (Eds.), *Pleasure beyond the pleasure principle* (pp. 111–137). New Haven, CT: Yale University Press.

Segal, M., Korkotian, E., & Murphy, D. D. (2000). Dendritic spine formation and pruning: common cellular mechanisms? *Trends in Neuroscience, 23,* 53–57.

Seidman, L. J., Oscar-Berman, M., Kalinowski, A. G., Ajilore, O., Kreman, W. S., Faraone, S. V., & Tsuang, M. J. (1995). Experimental and clinical neuropsychological measures of prefrontal dysfunction in schizophrenia. *Neuropsychology, 9,* 481–490.

Seligman, S., & Shahmoon-Shanok, R. (1995). Subjectivity, complexity, and the social world: Erikson's identity concept and contemporary relational theories. *Psychoanalytic Dialogues, 5,* 537–565.

Selye, H. (1956). *The stress of life.* New York: McGraw Hill.

Semple, W. E., Goyer, P., McCormick, R., Morris, E., Compton, B., Donvan, B., Berridge, M., Miraldi, F., & Schulz, S. C. (1992). Increased orbital frontal cortex blood flow and hippocampal abnormality in PTSD: A pilot PET study. *Biological Psychiatry, 31*, 129A.

Semrud-Clikeman, M., & Hynd, G. W. (1990). Right hemisphere dysfunction in nonverbal learning disabilities: Social, academic, and adaptive functioning in adults and children. *Psychological Bulletin, 107*, 196–209.

Sergent, J., Ohta, S., & MacDonald, B. (1992). Functional neuroanatomy of face and object processing. *Brain, 115*, 15–36.

Sesack, S. R., & Pickel, V. M. (1992). Prefrontal cortical efferents in the rat synapse on unlabeled neuronal targets of catecholamine terminals in the nucleus accumbens septi and on dopamine neurons in the ventral tegmental area. *Journal of Comparative Neurology, 320*, 145–160.

Sgoifo, A., Koolhaas, J., De Boer, S., Musso, E., Stilli, D., Buwalda, B., & Meerlo, P. (1999). Social stress, autonomic neural activation, and cardiac activity in rats. *Neuroscience and Biobehavioral Reviews, 23*, 915–923.

Shalev, A. Y., Peri, T., Canetti, L., & Schreiber, S. (1996). Predictors of PTSD in injured trauma survivors: A prospective study. *American Journal of Psychiatry, 153*, 219–225.

Shalev, A. Y., Sahar, T., Freedman, S., Peri, T., Glick, N., Brandes, D., Orr, S., & Pitman, R. K. (1998). A prospective study of heart rate response following trauma and the subsequent development of posttraumatic stress disorder. *Archives of General Psychiatry, 55*, 553–559.

Shammi, P., & Stuss, D. T. (1999). Humour appreciation: A role of the right frontal lobe. *Brain, 122*, 657–666.

Shapiro, D., Jamner, L. D., & Spence, S. (1997). Cerebral laterality, repressive coping, autonomic arousal, and human bonding. *Acta Physiologica Scandinavica, 640* (Suppl.), 60–64.

Shea, M. T., Zlotnick, C., & Weisberg, R. B. (1999). Commonality and specificity of personality disorder profiles in subjects with trauma histories. *Journal of Personality Disorders, 13*, 199–210.

Shearer, S. L., Peters, C. P., Quaytman, M. S., & Ogden, R. L. (1990). Frequency and correlates of childhood sexual and physical abuse histories in adult female borderline patients. *American Journal of Psychiatry, 14*, 214–216.

Shimazu, T. (1971). Regulation of glycogen metabolism in liver by the autonomic nervous system: IV. Activation of glycogen synthetase by vagal stimulation. *Biochimica Biophysica Acta, 252*, 28–38.

Shimazu, T., & Amakawa, A. (1968). Regulation of glycogen metabolism in liver by the autonomic nervous system: II. Neural control of glycogenolytic enzymes. *Biochimica Biophysica Acta, 165*, 335–348.

Shin, L. M., Kosslyn, S. M., McNally, R. J., Alpert, N. M., Thompson, W. L., Rauch, S. L., Macklin, M. L., & Pitman, R. K. (1997). Visual imagery and perception in posttraumatic stress disorder: A positron emission tomographic investigation. *Archives of General Psychiatry, 54*, 233–241.

Shin, L. M., McNally, R. J., Kosslyn, S. M., Thompson, W. L., Rauch, S. L., Alpert, N. M., Metzger, L. J., Lasko, N. B., Orr, S. P., & Pitman, R. K. (1999). Regional cerebral blood flow during script-driven imagery in childhood sexual abuse-related PTSD: A PET investigation. *American Journal of Psychiatry, 156*, 575–584.

Shin, L. M., Whalen, P. J., Pitman, R. K., Bush, G., Macklin, M. L., Lasko, N. B., Orr, S. P., McInerney, S. C., & Rauch, S. L. (2001). An fMRI study of anterior cingulate function in posttraumatic stress disorder. *Biological Psychiatry, 50*, 932–942.

Shinbrot, T., Grebogi, C., Ott, E., & Yorke, J. A. (1993). Using small perturbations to control chaos. *Nature, 363*, 411–417.

Shoffner, J. M. (1996). Maternal inheritance and the evaluation of oxidative phosphorylation diseases. *Lancet, 348,* 1283–1288.

Siegel, A., Roeling, T. A. P., Gregg, T. R., & Kruk, M. R. (1999). Neuropharmacology of brain-stimulation-evoked aggression. *Neuroscience and Biobehavioral Reviews, 23,* 359–389.

Siegel, D. J. (1999). *The developing mind: Toward a neurobiology of interpersonal experience.* New York: Guilford.

Siever, L. J., & Trestman, R. L. (1993). The serotonin system and aggressive personality disorders. *Integrative Clinical Psychopharmacology, 8* (Suppl. 2), 33–39.

Silverman, R. C., & Lieberman, A. F. (1999). Negative maternal attributions, projective identification, and the intergenerational transmission of violent relational patterns. *Psychoanalytic Dialogues, 9,* 161–186.

Simantov, R., Blinder, E., Ratovitski, T., Tauber, M., Gabbay, M., & Porat, S. (1996). Dopamine-induced apoptosis in human neuronal cells: Inhibition by nucleic acids antisense to the dopamine transporter. *Neuroscience, 74,* 39–50.

Simonetti, S., Chen, X., DiMauro, S., & Schon, E. A. (1992). Accumulation of deletions in human mitochondrial DNA during normal aging: Analysis by quantitative PCR. *Biochimica et Biophysica Acta, 1180,* 113–122.

Simons, J. S., Graham, K. S., Owen, A. M., Patterson, K., & Hodges, J. R. (2001). Perceptual and semantic components of memory for objects and faces: A PET study. *Journal of Cognitive Neuroscience, 13,* 430–443.

Singer, W. (1986). Neuronal activity as a shaping factor in postnatal development of visual cortex. In W. T. Greenough & J. M. Juraska (Eds.), *Developmental neuropsychobiology* (pp. 271–293). Orlando, FL: Academic Press.

Sirevaag, A. M., & Greenough, W. T. (1987). Differential rearing effects on rat visual cortex synapses. III. Neuronal and glial nuclei, boutons, dendrites, and capillaries. *Brain Research, 424,* 320–332.

Sirven, J. I., & Glosser, D. S. (1998). Psychogenic nonepileptic seizures: Theoretic and clinical considerations. *Neuropsychiatry, Neuropsyhology, and Behavioral Neurology, 11,* 225–235.

Skinner, J. E., Molnar, M., Vybiral, T., & Mitra, M. (1992). Application of chaos theory to biology and medicine. *Integrative Physiology and Behavioral Science, 27,* 43–57.

Slade, A. (1987). The quality of attachment and symbolic play. *Developmental Psychology, 23,* 78–85.

Slade, A. (1994). Making meaning and making believe: Their role in the clinical processs. In A. Slade & D. Wolf (Eds.), *Children at play: Clinical and developmental approaches to meaning and representation* (pp. 81–110). New York: Oxford University Press.

Slotnick, B. M. (1967). Disturbances of maternal behavior in the rat following lesions of the cingulate cortex. *Behaviour, 24,* 204–236.

Small, D. N., Zald, D. H., Jones-Gotman, M., Zatorre, R. J., Pardo, J. V., Frey, S., & Petrides, M. (1999). Human cortical gustatory areas: A review of functional neuroimaging data. *NeuroReport, 10,* 7–14.

Smiley, J. F., Levey, A. I., Ciliax, B. J., & Goldman-Rakic. (1994). D1 dopamine receptor immunoreactivity in human and monkey cerebral cortex: Predominant and extrasynaptic localization in dendritic spines. *Proceedings of the National Academy of Sciences of the United States of America, 91,* 5720–5724.

Smith, C. G. (1981). *Serial dissection of the human brain.* Baltimore-Munich: Urban & Schwarzenberg.

Smith, M. Y., Egert, S., Winkel, G., & Jacobson, J. (2002). The impact of PTSD on pain experience in persons with HIV/AIDS. *Pain, 98,* 9–17.

Snow, D. (2000). The emotional basis of linguistic and nonlinguistic intonation: Implications for hemispheric specialization. *Developmental Neuropsychology, 17,* 1–28.

Solomon, J., & George, C. (1999). *Attachment disorganization.* New York: Guilford Press.

Southall, D. P., Plunkett, M. C. B., Banks, M. W., Falkov, A. F., & Samuels, M. P. (1997). Covert videorecordings of life-threatening child abuse: Lessons for child protection. *Pediatrics, 100,* 735–760.

Southwick, S. M., Krystal, J. H., Morgan, A., Johnson, D., Nagy, L. M., Nicolaou, A., Heninger, G. R., & Charney, D. S. (1993). Abnormal noradrenergic function in posttraumatic stress disorder. *Archives of General Psychiatry, 50,* 266–274.

Sowell, E. R., & Jernigan, T. L. (1998). Further MRI evidence of late brain maturation: Limbic volume increases and changing asymmetries during childhood and adolescence. *Developmental Neuropsychology, 14,* 599–617.

Spangler, G., & Grossmann, K. (1999). Individual and physiological correlates of attachment disorganization in infancy. In J. Solomon & C. George (Eds.), *Attachment disorganization* (pp. 95–124). New York: Guilford.

Spangler, G., & Grossmann, K. E. (1993). Biobehavioral organization in securely and insecurely attached infants. *Child Development, 64,* 1439–1450.

Spangler, G., Schieche, M., Ilg, U., Maier, U., & Ackerman, C. (1994). Maternal sensitivity as an organizer for biobehavioral regulation in infancy. *Developmental Psychobiology, 27,* 425–437.

Spear, L. P. (2000). The adolescent brain and age-related behavioral manifestations. *Neuroscience and Biobehavioral Reviews, 24,* 417–463.

Spence, S., Shapiro, D., & Zaidel, E. (1996). The role of the right hemisphere in the physiological and cognitive components of emotional processing. *Psychophysiology, 33,* 112–122.

Spencer, J. P. E., Jenner, A., Aruoma, O. I., Evans, P. J., Kaur, H., Dexter, D. T., Leesa, A. J., Marsden, D. C., & Halliwell, B. (1994). Intense oxidative DNA damage promoted by L-DOPA and its metabolites: Implications for neurodegenerative disease. *Federation of European Biochemical Societies, 353,* 246–250.

Spivak, B., Segal, M., Mester, R., & Weizman, A. (1998). Lateral preference in posttraumatic stress disorder. *Psychological Medicine, 28,* 229–232.

Sroufe, L. A. (1989). Relationships, self, and individual adaptation. In A. J. Sameroff & R. N. Emde (Eds.), *Relationship disturbances in early childhood* (pp. 70–94). New York: Basic.

Sroufe, L. A. (1996). *Emotional development: The organization of emotional life in the early years.* New York: Cambridge University Press.

Starkstein, S. E., Boston, J. D., & Robinson, R. F. (1988). Mechanisms of mania after brain injury: 12 case reports and review of the literature. *Journal of Nervous and Mental Disease, 176,* 87–100.

Starkstein, S. E., Federoff, P., Berthier, M. L., & Robinson, R. G. (1991). Manic-depressive and pure manic states after brain lesions. *Biological Psychiatry, 29,* 149–158.

Starkstein, S. E., & Robinson, R. G. (1997). Mechanism of disinhibition after brain lesions. *Journal of Nervous and Mental Disease, 185,* 108–114.

Steklis, H. D., & Kling, A. (1985). Neurobiology of affiliative behavior in nonhuman primates. In M. Reite & T. Field (Ed.), *The psychobiology of attachment and separation* (pp. 93–134). Orlando, FL: Academic Press.

Stern, D. N. (1983a). The early differentiation of self and other. In S. Kaplan & J. D. Lichtenberg (Eds.), *Reflections on self psychology.* Hillsdale, NJ: Analytic Press.

Stern, D. N. (1983b). Early transmission of affect: Some research issues. In J. Call, E. Galenson, & R. Tyson (Eds.), *Frontiers of infant psychiatry* (pp. 52–69). New York: Basic.

Stern, D. N. (1985). *The interpersonal world of the infant.* New York: Basic.

Stern, D. N. (1990). Joy and satisfaction in infancy. In R. A. Glick & S. Bone (Eds.), *Pleasure beyond the pleasure principle* (pp. 13–25). New Haven, CT: Yale University Press.

Stoddard-Apter, S. L., Levin, B., & Siegel, A. (1983). A sympathoadrenal and cardiovascular correlate of aggressive behavior in the awake cat. *Journal of the Autonomic Nervous System, 8,* 343–360.

Stone, V. E., Baron-Cohen, S., & Knight, R. T. (1998). Frontal lobe contributions to theory of mind. *Journal of Cognitive Neuroscience, 10,* 640–656.

Strauss, M. S. (1979). Abstraction of prototypical information by adults and 10 month old infants. *Journal of Experimental Psychology: Human Learning and Memory, 5,* 618–632.

Streeck-Fischer, A., & van der Kolk, B. A. (2000). Down will come baby, cradle and all: Diagnostic and therapeutic implications of chronic trauma on child development. *Australian and New Zealand Journal of Psychiatry, 34,* 903–918.

Streissguth, A. P., Sampson, P. D., Carmichael Olson, H., Bookstein, F. L., Barr, H. M., Scott, M., Feldman, J., & Mirsky, A. F. (1994). Maternal drinking during pregnancy: Attention and short-term memory in 14-year-old offspring—A longitudinal perspective study. *Alcoholism: Clinical and Experimental Research, 18,* 202–218.

Strome, E. M., Wheler, G. H. T., Higley, J. D., Loriqux, D. L., Suomi, S. J., & Doudet, D. J. (2002). Intracebroventricular corticotropin-releasing factor increases limbic glucose metabolism and has social-context dependent behavioral effects in nonhuman primates. *Proceedings of the National Academy of Sciences of the United States of America, 99,* 15749–15754.

Sturm, W., de Simone, A., Krause, B. J., Specht, K., Hesselmann, V., Radermacher, I., Herzog, H., Tellann, L., Müller-Gärtner, H.-W., & Willmes, K. (1999). Functional anatomy of intrinsic alertness: Evidence for a fronto-parietal-thalamic-brainstem network in the right hemisphere. *Neuropsychologia, 37,* 797–805.

Stuss, D. T., & Alexander, M. P. (1999). Affectively burnt in: A proposed role of the right frontal lobe. In E. Tulving (Ed.). *Memory, consciousness, and the brain: the Talin Conference* (pp. 215–227). Philadelphia: Psychology Press.

Stuss, D. T., Gow, C. A., & Hetherington, C. R. (1992). "No longer Gage": Frontal lobe dysfunction and emotional changes. *Journal of Consulting and Clinical Psychology, 60,* 349–359.

Stuss, D. T., Kaplan, E. F., Benson, D. F., Weir, W. S., Chiulli, S., & Sarazin, F. F. (1982). Evidence for the involvement of orbitofrontal cortex in memory functions: An interference effect. *Journal of Comparative Physiological Psychology, 96,* 913–925.

Stuss, D. T., & Levine, B. (2002). Adult clinical neuropsychology: Lessons from studies of the frontal lobes. *Annual Review of Psychology, 53,* 401–433.

Suberi, M., & McKeever, W. F. (1977). Differential right hemispheric memory storage of emotional and non-emotional faces. *Neuropsychologia, 15,* 757–768.

Suchecki, D., Nelson, D. Y., Van Oers, H., & Levine, S. (1995). Activation and exhibition of the hypothalamic-pituitary-adrenal axis of the neonatal rat: effects of maternal deprivation. *Psychoneuroendocrinology, 20,* 169–182.

Sullivan, R. M., Landers, M., Yeaman, B., & Wilson, D. A. (2000). Good memories of bad events in infancy. *Nature, 407,* 38–39.

Sullivan, R. M., & Gratton, A. (1999). Lateralized effects of medial prefrontal cortex lesions on neuroendocrine and autonomic stress responses in rats. *Journal of Neuroscience, 19,* 2834–2840.

Sullivan, R. M., & Gratton, A. (2002). Prefrontal cortical regulation of hypothalamic-pituitary-adrenal function of the rat and implications for psychopathology: Side matters. *Psychoneuroendocrinology, 27,* 99–114.

Sullivan, R. M., & Szechtman, H. (1995). Asymmetrical influence of mesocortical dopamine depletion on stress ulcer development and subcortical dopamine systems in rats: Implications for psychopathology. *Neuroscience, 65,* 757–766.

Suomi, S. J. (1995). Influence of attachment theory on ethological studies of biobehavioral development in nonhuman primates. In S. Goldberg, R. Muir, & J. Kerr (Eds.), *Attachment theory: Social, developmental and clinical perspectives* (pp. 185–201). Hillsdale, NJ: Analytic Press.

Sutker, P. B., Vasterling, J. J., Brailey, K., & Allain, A. N. Jr. (1995). Memory, attention, and executive deficits in POW survivors: Contributing biological and psychological factors. *Neuropsychology, 9,* 118–125.

Svensson, T. H. (1987). Peripheral, autonomic regulation of locus coeruleus noradrenergic neurons in brain: Putative implications for psychiatry and psychopharmacology. *Psychopharmacology, 92,* 1–7.

Sweet, S. D., McGrath, P. J., & Symons, D. (1999). The roles of child reactivity and parenting context in infant pain responses. *Pain, 80,* 655–661.

Szatkowska, I., Grabowska, A., & Szymanska, O. (2001). Evidence for the involvement of the ventromedial prefrontal cortex in a short-term storage of visual images. *NeuroReport, 12,* 1187–1190.

Talamini, L. M., Koch, T., Luiten, P. G. M., Koolhaas, J. M., & Korf, J. (1999). Interruptions of early cortical development affect limbic association areas and social behavior in rats; possible relevance for neurodevelopmental disorders. *Brain Research, 847,* 105–120.

Tan, S., Sagara, Y., Liu, Y., Maher, P., & Schubert, D. (1998). The regulation of reactive oxygen species production during programmed cell death. *Journal of Cell Biology, 141,* 1423–1432.

Tanaka, M., Tsuda, A., Tokoo, H., Yoshida, M., Ida, Y., & Nishimura, H. (1990). Involvement of the brain noradrenaline system in emotional changes caused by stress in rats. *Annals of the New York Academy of Sciences, 597,* 159–174.

Taylor, G. (1987). *Psychosomatic medicine and contemporary psychoanalysis.* Madison, CT: International Universities Press.

Taylor, G. (2000). Recent developments in alexithymia theory and research. *Canadian Journal of Psychiatry, 45,* 134–142.

Taylor, G. J., Bagby, R. M., & Parker, J. D. (1997). *Disorders of affect regulation: Alexithymia in medical and psychiatric illness.* Cambridge, U.K.: Cambridge University Press.

Taylor, G. J., Parker, J. D. A., & Bagby, R. M. (1999). Emotional intelligence and the emotional brain: Points of convergence and implications for psychoanalysis. *Journal of the American Academy of Psychoanalysis, 27,* 339–354.

Teasdale, J. D., Howard, R. J., Cox, S. G., Ha, Y., Brammer, M. J., Williams, S. C. R., & Checkley, S. A. (1999). Functional MRI Study of the cognitive generation of affect. *American Journal of Psychiatry, 156,* 209–215.

Teicher, M. H., Glod, C. A., Surrey, J., & Swett, C. Jr. (1993). Early childhood abuse and limbic system ratings in adult psychiatric conditions. *Journal of Neuropsychiatry and Clinical Neuroscience, 5,* 301–306.

Teicher, M. H., Ito, Y., & Glod, C. A. (1996). Neurophysiological mechanisms of stress response in children. In C. R. Pfeffer (Ed.), *Severe stress and mental disturbances in children* (pp. 59–84). Washington, DC: American Psychiatric Press.

Teicher, M. H., Ito, Y., Glod C. A., Andersen, S. L., Dumont, N., & Ackerman, E. (1997). Preliminary evidence for abnormal cortical development in physically and sexually abused children using EEG coherence and MRI. *Annals of the New York Academy of Sciences, 821,* 160–175.

Tekin, S., & Cummings, J. L. (2002). Frontal-subcortical neuronal circuits and clinical neuropsychiatry. An update. *Journal of Psychosomatic Research, 53,* 647–654.

Terman, G., Shavit, Y., Lewis, J., & Liebeskind, J. (1984). Intrinsic mechanisms of pain inhibition: activation by stress. *Science, 226,* 1270–1277.

Terr, L. C. (1988). What happened to early memories of trauma? *Journal of the American Academy of Child and Adolescent Psychiatry, 1,* 96–104.

Thatcher, R. W. (1994). Cyclical cortical reorganization: Origins of human cognitive development. In G. Dawson & K. W. Fischer (Eds.), *Human behavior and the developing brain* (pp. 232–266). New York: Guilford.

Thatcher, R. W. (1997). Neuroimaging of cyclic cortical reorganization during human development. In R. W. Thatcher, G. Reid Lyon, J. Rumsey, & N. Krasnegor (Eds.), *Developmental neuroimaging: Mapping the development of brain and behavior* (pp. 91–106). San Diego, CA: Academic Press.

Thelen, E. (1989). Self-organization in developmental processes: Can systems approaches work? In M. Gunnar & E. Thelen (Eds.), *Systems and development: The Minnesota symposium in child psychology* (Vol. 22, pp. 77–117). Hillsdale, NJ: Erlbaum.

Thelen, E. (1995). Motor development: A new synthesis. *American Psychologist, 50,* 79–95.

Thomas, A., & Chess, S. (1982). The reality of difficult temperament, *Merrill-Palmer Quarterly, 28,* 1–20.

Thomas, D. G., Whitaker, E., Crow, C. D., Little, V., Love, L., Lykins, M. S., & Lettermman, M. (1997). Event-related potential variability as a measure of information storage in infant development. *Developmental Neuropsychology, 13,* 205–232.

Thompson, R. A. (1990). Emotion and self-regulation. *Nebraska symposium on motivation* (pp. 367–467). Lincoln: University of Nebraska Press.

Thompson, R. A. (2000). The legacy of early attachments. *Child Development, 71,* 145–152.

Thorpe, S. J., Rolls, E. T., & Maddison, S. (1983). The orbitofrontal cortex: Neuronal activity in the behaving monkey. *Experimental Brain Research, 49,* 93–115.

Tiihonen, J., Kuikka, J., Viinamaki, H., Lehtonen, J., & Partanen, J. (1995). Altered cerebral blood flow during hysterical paresthesia. *Biological Psychiatry, 37,* 134–135.

Timms, R. J. (1977). Cortical inhibition and facilitation of defense reaction. *Journal of Physiology, 266,* 98P-99P.

Toates, F. (1998). The interaction of cognitive and stimulus-response processes in the control of behaviour. *Neuroscience and Biobehavioral Reviews, 22,* 59–83.

Tomasello, M. (1993). On the interpersonal origins of self-concept. In U. Neisser (Ed.), *The perceived self: Ecological and interpersonal sources of self-knowledge* (pp. 174–184). New York: Cambridge University Press.

Tomasello, M., & Camaioni, L. (1997). A comparison of the gestural communication of apes and human infants. *Human Development, 40,* 7–24.

Tomkins, S. (1963). *Affect/imagery/consciousness: Vol. 2. The negative affects.* New York: Springer.

Tomkins, S. (1984). Afffect theory. In P. Ekman (Ed.), *Approaches to emotion* (pp. 163–195). Hillsdale, NJ: Erlbaum.

Toth, S. C., & Cicchetti, D. (1998). Remembering, forgetting, and the effects of trauma on memory: A developmental psychopathologic perspective. *Developmental Psychopathology, 10,* 580–605.

Trad, P. V. (1986). *Infant depression.* New York: Springer-Verlag.

Tranel, D. (1994). "Acquired sociopathy": The development of sociopathic behavior following focal brain damage. In D. C. Fowles, P. Sutker, & S. H. Goodman (Eds.), *Progress in experimental personality and psychopathology research* (Vol. 17, pp. 285–311). New York: Springer-Verlag.

Travers, J. B., Dinardo, L. A., & Karimnamazi, H. (1997). Motor and premotor mechanism of licking. *Neuroscience and Biobehavioral Reviews, 21,* 631–647.

Tremblay, L., & Schultz, W. (1999). Relative reward preference in primate orbitofrontal cortex. *Nature, 398,* 704–708.

Trendelenburg, U. (1963). Supersensitivity and subsensitivity to sympathomimetic amines. *Pharmacological Reviews, 15,* 225–276.

Trevarthen, C. (1990). Growth and education of the hemispheres. In C. Trevarthen (Ed.), *Brain circuits and functions of the mind* (pp. 334–363). Cambridge, England: Cambridge University Press.

Trevarthen, C. (1993). The self born in intersubjectivity: The psychology of an infant communicating. In U. Neisser (Ed.), *The perceived self: Ecological and interpersonal sources of self-knowledge* (pp. 121–173). New York: Cambridge University Press.

Trevarthen, C. (1996). Lateral asymmetries in infancy: Implications for the development of the hemispheres. *Neuroscience and Biobehavioral Reviews, 20,* 571–586.

Trevarthen, C. (2001). Intrinsic motives for companionship in understanding: Their origin, development and significance for infant mental health. *Infant Mental Health Journal, 22,* 95–131.

Trevarthen, C., & Aitken, K. J. (1994). Brain development, infant communication, and empathy disorders: Intrinsic factors in child mental health. *Development and Psychopathology, 6,* 597–633.

Trevarthen, C., Aitken, K., Papoudia, D., & Robarts, J. (1998). *Children with autism, Second edition: Diagnosis and interventions to meet their needs.* London: Jessica Kingsley.

Trickett, P. K., & McBride-Chang, C. (1995). The developmental impact of different forms of child abuse and neglect. *Developmental Review, 15,* 311–337.

Tronick, E. Z. (1989). Emotions and emotional communication in infants. *American Psychologist, 44,* 112–119.

Tronick, E. Z., Bruschweilwe-Stern, N., Harrison, A. M., Lyons-Ruth, K. Morgan, A. C., Nahum, J. P., Sander, L., & Stern, D. N. (1998). Dyadically expanded states of consciousness and the process of therapeutic change. *Infant Mental Health Journal, 19,* 290–299.

Tronick, E. Z., Cohn, J., & Shea, E. (1986). The transfer of affect between mothers and infants. In T. B. Brazelton & M. W. Yogman (Eds.), *Affective development in infancy* (pp. 11–25). Norwood, NJ: Ablex.

Tronick, E. Z., Ricks, M., & Cohn, J. F. (1982). Maternal and infant affective exchange: Patterns of adaptation. In T. Field & A. Fogel (Eds.), *Emotion and early interaction.* Hillsdale, NJ: Erlbaum.

Tronick, E. Z., & Weinberg, M. K. (1997). Depressed mothers and infants: Failure to form dyadic states of consciousness. In L. Murray & P. J. Cooper (Eds.), *Postpartum depression in child development* (pp. 54–81). New York: Guilford.

Tucker, D. M. (1981). Lateral brain function, emotion, and conceptualization. *Psychological Bulletin, 89,* 19–46.

Tucker, D. M. (1992). Developing emotions and cortical networks. In M .R. Gunnar & C. A. Nelson (Eds.), *Minnesota symposium on child psychology: Vol. 24. Developmental behavioral neuroscience* (pp. 75–128). Hillsdale, NJ: Erlbaum.

Tucker, D. M., & Derryberry, D. (1994). Motivating the focus of attention. In P. M. Niedenthal & S. Kitayama, S. (Eds.), *The heart's eye: Emotional influences in perception and attention* (pp. 167–196). San Diego, CA: Academic Press.

Tucker, D. M., Luu, P., & Pribram, K. H. (1995). Social and emotional self-regulation. *Annals of the New York Academy of Sciences, 769,* 213–239.

Tulving, E. (1985). Memory and consciousness. *Canadian Psychologist, 26,* 1–12.

Tustin, F. (1981). Psychological birth and psychological catastrophe. In J. S.

Grotstein (Ed.), *Do I dare disturb the universe: A memorial to W.R. Bion* (pp. 181–196). London: Karnac.

Tzourio-Mazoyer, N., De Schonen, S., Crivello, F., Reutter, B., Aujard, Y., & Mazoyer, B. (2002). Neural correlates of woman face processing by 2-month-old infants. *Neuroimage, 15,* 454–461.

Uchino, B. N., Cacioppo, J. T., & Kiecolt-Glaser, J. K. (1996). The relationship between social support and physiological processes: A review with emphasis on underlying mechanisms and implications for health. *Psychological Bulletin, 119,* 488–513.

Uddo, M., Vasterling, J. J., Brailey, K., & Sutker, P. B. (1993). Memory and attention in combat-related post-traumatic stress disorder (PTSD). *Journal of Psychopathology and Behavioral Assessment, 15,* 43–52.

Ungerleider, L. G., & Haxby, J. V. (1994). "What" and "where" in the human brain. *Current Opinions in Neurobiology, 4,* 157–165.

Utsunomiya, H., Takano, K., Okazaki, M., & Mitsudome, A. (1999). Development of the temporal lobe in infants and children: Analysis by MR-based volumetry. *American Journal of Neuroradiology, 20,* 717–723.

Uvnas-Moberg, K. (1997). Oxytocin linked antistress effects—the relaxation and growth response. *Acta Physiologica Scandinavica, Supplement, 640,* 38–42.

Valent, P. (1998). *From survival to fulfillment: A framework for the life-trauma dialectic.* Philadelphia, PA: Brunner/Mazel.

van den Boom, D. C., & Gravenhorst, J. B. (1995). Prenatal and perinatal correlates of neonatal irritability. *Infant Behavior and Development, 18,* 117–121.

van der Hart, O., & Nijenhuis, E. (1995). Amnesia for traumatic experiences. *Hypnosis, 4,* 417–453.

van der Kolk, B., Hostetler, A., Heron, N., & Fisler, R. (1994). Trauma and the development of borderline personality disorder. *Psychiatric Clinics of North America, 17,* 715–730.

van der Kolk, B. A. (1987). *Psychological trauma.* Washington, DC: American Psychiatric Press.

van der Kolk, B. A. (1996). The body keeps the score: Approaches to the psychobiology of posttraumatic stress disorder. In B. A. van der Kolk, A. C. McFarlane, & L. Weisaeth (Eds.), *Traumatic stress: The effects of overwhelming experience on mind, body, and society* (pp. 214–241). New York: Guilford.

van der Kolk, B. A., & Fisler, R. E. (1994). Childhood abuse and neglect and loss of self-regulation. *Bulletin of the Menninger Clinic, 58,* 145–168.

van der kolk, B. A., & McFarlane, A. C. (1996). The black hole of trauma. In B. A. van der Kolk, A. C. McFarlane, & L. Weisaeth (Eds.), *Traumatic stress: The effects of overwhelming experience on mind, body, and society* (pp. 3–23). New York: Guilford.

van der Kolk, B. A., McFarlane, A. C., & Weisaeth, L. (1996). *Traumatic stress: The effects of overwhelming experience on mind, body, and society.* New York: Guilford.

van der Kolk, B. A., Perry, J. C., & Herman, J. L. (1991). Childhood origins of self-destructive behavior. *American Journal of Psychiatry, 148,* 1665–1671.

Van der Krogt, J. A., & Belfroid, R. D. M. (1980). Characterization and localization of catecholamine-susceptible Na-K ATPase activity of rat striatum: Studies using catecholamine receptor (ant)agonists and lesion techniques. *Biochemical Pharmacology, 29,* 857–868.

van Hoesen, G. W., Parvizi, J., & Chu, C.-C. (2000). Orbitofrontal cortex pathology and Alzheimer's disease. *Cerebral Cortex, 10,* 243–251.

van Honk, J., Hermans, E. J., Putnam, P., Montagne, B., Schutter, D. J. L. G. (2002). Defective somatic markers in sub-clinical psychopathy. *NeuroReport, 13,* 1025–1027.

van IJzendoorn, M. H., Juffer, F., & Duyvesteyn, M. G. F. (1995). Breaking the intergenerational cycle of insecure attachment: A review of the effects of attachment-based interventions on maternal sensitivity and infant security. *Journal of Child Psychology and Psychiatry, 36,* 225–248.

van IJzendoorn, M. H., Schuengel, C., & Bakermans-Kranenburg, M. J. (1999).

Disorganized attachment in early childhood: Meta-analysis of precursors, concomitants, and sequelae. *Development and Psychopathology, 11*, 225–249.

Van Kleek, M. H. (1989). Hemispheric differences in global versus local processing of hierarchical visual stimuli by normal subjects: New data and a meta-analysis of previous studies. *Neuropsychologia, 27*, 1165–1178.

Van Lancker, D. (1991). Personal relevance and the human right hemisphere. *Brain and Cognition, 17*, 64–92.

Van Lancker, D. (1997). Rags to riches: Our increasing appreciation of cognitive and communicative abilities of the human right cerebral hemisphere. *Brain and Language, 57*, 1–11.

Van Lancker, D., & Cummings, J. L. (1999). Expletives: Neurolingusitic and neurobehavioral perspectives on swearing. *Brain Research Reviews, 31*, 83–104.

van Pelt, J., Corner, M. A., Uylings, H. B. M., Lopes da Silva, F. H. (Eds.). (1994). *Progress in Brain Research: Vol. 102. The self-organizing brain: From growth cones to functional networks.* Amsterdam: Elsevier.

Van Toller, S., & Kendal-Reed, M. (1995). A possible protocognitive role for odor in human infant development. *Brain and Cognition, 29*, 275–293.

van Vreeswijk, C., & Sompolinsky, H. (1996). Chaos in neuronal networks with balanced excitatory and inhibitory activity. *Science, 274*, 1724–1726.

Vasterling, J. J., Brailey, K., & Sutker, P. B. (2000). Olfactory identification in combat-related posttraumatic stress disorder. *Journal of Traumatic Stress, 13*, 241–253.

Vaughn, C. E., & Leff, J. P. (1976). The influence of family and social factors on the course of psychiatric illness. *British Journal of Psychiatry, 129*, 125–137.

Vayssiere, J.-L., Petit, P. Y., Risler, Y., & Mignotte, B. (1994). Commitment to apoptosis in mitochondrial biogenesis and activity in cell lines conditionally immortalized with simian virus 40. *Proceedings of the National Academy of Sciences of the United States of America, 87*, 767–771.

Vercesi, A., & Hoffmann, M. F. (1993). Generation of reactive oxygen metabolites and oxidative damage in mitochondria: Role of calcium. In L. H. Lash & D. P. Jones (Eds.), *Mitochondrial dysfunction* (pp. 256–265). San Diego, CA: Academic Press.

Vermetten, E. & Bremner, J. D. (2002). Circuits and systems in stress. II. Applications to neurobiology and treatment in posttraumatic stress disorder. *Depression and Anxiety, 16*, 14–38.

Verny, T. R. (2002). *Tomorrow's baby.* New York: Simon & Schuster.

Vianna, D. M. L., Graeff, F. G., Brandao, M. L., & Landeira-Fernandez, J. (2001). Defensive freezing evoked by electrical stimulation of the periaqueductal gray: Comparison between dorsolateral and ventrolateral regions. *NeuroReport, 12*, 4109–4112.

Virkkunen, M. (1985). Urinary free cortisol secretion in habitually violent offenders. *Acta Psychiatrica Scandinavica, 72*, 40–44.

Vitz, P. C. (1990). The use of stories in moral development. *American Psychologist, 45*, 709–720.

Voeller, K. K. S. (1986). Right-hemisphere deficit syndrome in children. *American Journal of Psychiatry, 143*, 1004–1009.

Voigt, T., Baier, H., & de Lima, A. D. (1997). Synchronization of neuronal activity promotes survival of individual rat neocortical neurons in early development. *European Journal of Neuroscience, 9*, 990–999.

Volavka, J. (1999). The neurobiology of violence: An update. *Journal of Neuropsychiatry and Clinical Neuroscience, 11*, 307–314.

Volkow, N. D., & Fowler, J. S. (2000). Addiction, a disease of compulsion and drive: Involvement of the orbitofrontal cortex. *Cerebral Cortex, 10*, 318–325.

Volkow, N. D., Fowler, J. S., Wolf, A. P., et al. (1991). Changes in brain glucose metabolism in cocaine dependence and withdrawal. *American Journal of Psychiatry, 148*, 621–626.

Volkow, N. D., Wang, G.-J., Fowler, J. S., Hitzemann, R., Angrist, B., Gatley, S. J., Logan, J., Ding, Y.-S., & Pappas, N. (1999). Association of methylphenidate-induced craving with changes in right striato-orbitofrontal metabolism in cocaine abusers: implications in addiction. *American Journal of Psychiatry, 156,* 19–26.

Volkow, N. D., Wang, G-J., Overall, J. E., Hitzmann, R., Fowler, J. S., Pappas, N., Frecska, E., & Piscani, K. (1997). Regional brain alcoholic response to lorazepam in alcoholics during early and late alcohol detoxification. *Alcoholism: Clinical and Experimental research, 21,* 1278–1284.

von Bertalanffy, L. (1974). General systems theory and psychiatry. In S. Arieti (Ed.), *American Handbook of psychiatry* (Vol. 1, pp. 1095–1117). New York: Basic.

Vyas, A., Mitra, R., Shankaranarayana Rao, B. S., & Chattarji, S. (2002). Chronic stress induces contrasting pattern of dendritic remodeling in hippocampal and amygdaloid neurons. *Journal of Neuroscience, 22,* 6810–6818.

Vygotsky, L. S. (1978). *Mind in society.* Cambridge, MA: Harvard University Press.

Wagner, A. D., Poldrack, R. A., Eldridge, L. L., Desmond, J. E., Glover, G. H., & Gabrieli, J. D. E. (1998). Material-specific lateralization of prefrontal activation during episodic encoding and retrieval. *NeuroReport, 9,* 3711–3717.

Walden, T. A., & Ogan, T. A. (1988). The development of social referencing. *Child Development, 59,* 1230–1240.

Walker, E., Grimes, K., Davis, D., & Smith, A. (1993). Childhood precursors of schizophrenia: Facial expressions of emotion. *American Journal of Psychiatry, 150,* 1654–1660.

Walker, E. F. (1994). Developmentally moderated expressions of the neuropathology underlying schizophrenia. *Schizophrenia Bulletin, 20,* 453–480.

Waller, G., Hamilton, K., Elliott, P., Lewendon, J., Stopa, L., Waters, A., Kennedy, F., Lee, G., Pearson, D., Kennerley, H., Hargreaves, I., Bashford, V., & Chalkley, J. (2000). Somatoform dissociation, psychological dissociation, and specific forms of trauma. *Journal of Trauma and Dissociation, 1,* 81–98.

Walton, G., Bower, N., & Bower, T. (1992). Recognition of familiar faces by newborns. *Infant Behavior and Development, 15,* 265–269.

Walton, M. R., & Dragunow, M. (2000). Is CREB a key to neuronal survival? *Trends in Neuroscience, 23,* 48–53.

Wang, G. F., Volkow, N. D., Fowler, J. S., Cervany, P., Hitzemann, R. J., Pappas, N. R., Wong, C. T., & Felder, C. (1999). Regional brain metabolic activation during craving elicited by recall of previous drug experiences. *Life Sciences, 64,* 775–784.

Wang, L., & Pitts, D. K. (1994). Postnatal development of mesoaccumbens dopamine neurons in the rat: Electrophysiological studies. *Developmental Brain Research, 79,* 19–28.

Wang, S. (1997). Traumatic stress and attachment. *Acta Physiologica Scandinavica, 640* (Suppl.), 164–169.

Wang, S., Wilson, J. P., & Mason, J. W. (1996). Stages of decompensation in combat-related posttraumatic tress disorder: A new conceptual model. *Integrative Physiological and Behavioral Science, 31,* 237–253.

Wang, W., Dow, K. E., & Fraser, D. D. (2001). Elevated corticotropin releasing hormone/corticotropin relasing hormone-R1 expression in postmortem brain obtained from children with generalized epilepsy. *Annals of Neurology, 50,* 404–409.

Watanabe, S., Miki, K., & Kakigi, R. (2002). Gaze direction affects face perception in humans. *Neuroscience Letters, 325,* 163–166.

Watson, C. (1977). *Basic human neuroanatomy: An introductory atlas* (2nd ed.). Boston: Little, Brown.

Watt, D. F. (1990). Higher cortical functions and the ego: Explorations of the boundary between behavioral neurology, neuropsychology, and psychoanalysis. *Psychoanalytic Psychology, 7,* 487–527.

Weaver, I. C. G., Grant, R. J., & Meaney, M. J. (2002). Maternal behavior regulates long-term hippocampal expression of BAX and apoptosis in the offspring. *Journal of Neurochemistry, 82,* 998–1002.

Weil, J. L. (1992). *Early deprivation of empathic care.* Madison CT: International Universities Press.

Weinberg, I. (2000). The prisoners of despair: Right hemisphere deficiency and suicide. *Neuroscience and Biobehavioral Reviews, 24,* 799–815.

Weinberg, M. K., Tronick, E. Z., Cohn, J. F., & Olson, K. L. (1999). Gender differences in emotional expressivity and self-regulation during infancy. *Developmental Psychology, 35,* 175–188.

Weinberger, D. R., & Lipska, B. K. (1995). Cortical maldevelopment, anti-psychotic drugs, and schizophrenia: A search for common ground. *Schizophrenia Research, 16,* 87–110.

Weinfeld, N. S., Sroufe, L. A., Egeland, B., & Carlson, E. A. (1999). The nature of individual differences in infant-caregiver attachment. In J. Cassidy & P. R. Shaver (Eds.), *Handbook of attachment: Theory, research, and clinical applications* (pp. 68–88). New York: Guilford.

Weinstock, M. (1997). Does prenatal stress impair coping and regulation of hypothalamic-pituitary-adrenal axis? *Neuroscience and Biobehavioral Reviews, 21,* 1–10.

Weintraub, S., & Mesulam, M. M. (1983). Developmental learning disabilities of the right hemisphere: Emotional, interpersonal, and cognitive components. *Archives of Neurology, 40,* 463–468.

Weiss, S. J., Wilson, P., St. Jonn Seed, M., & Paul, S. J. (2001). Early tactile experience of low birth weight children: Links to later mental health and social adaptation. *Infant and Child Development, 10,* 93–115.

Werner, H. (1948). *Comparative psychology of normal development.* New York: International Universities Press.

Westen, D. (1997). Towards a clinically and empirically sound theory of motivation. *International Journal of Psychoanalysis, 78,* 521–548.

Wexler, B. E., Warrenburg, S., Schwartz, G. E. & Janer, L. D. (1992). EEG and EMG responses to emotion-evoking stimuli processed without conscious awareness. *Neuropsychologia, 30,* 1065–1079.

Whalen, P. J., Rauch, S. L., Etcoff, N., McInerney, S. C., Lee, M. B., & Jenike, M. A. (1998). Masked presentations of emotional facial expressions modulate amygdala activity without explicit knowledge. *Journal of Neuroscience, 18,* 411–418.

Wheeler, M. A., Stuss, D. T., & Tulving, E. (1997). Toward a theory of episodic memory: The frontal lobes and autonoetic consciousness. *Psychological Bulletin, 121,* 331–354.

Wheeler, R. E., Davidson, R. J., & Tomarken, A. J. (1993). Frontal brain asymmetry and emotional reactivity: A biological substrate of affective style. *Psychophysiology, 30,* 82–89.

White, L. E., Lucas, G., Richards, A., & Purves, D. (1994). Cerebral asymmetry and handedness. *Nature, 368,* 197–198.

Wicker, B., Michel, F., Henaff, M. A., & Decety, J. (1998). Brain regions involved in the perception of gaze: a PET study. *Neuroimage, 8,* 221–227.

Wiedemann, G., Pauli, P., Dengler, W., Lutzenberger, W., Birbaumer, N., & Buchkremer, G. (1999). Frontal brain asymmetry as a biological substrate of emotions in patients with panic disorders. *Archives of General Psychiatry, 56,* 78–84.

Williams, G. V., & Goldman-Rakic, P. S. (1995). Modulation of memory fields by dopamine D1 receptors in prefrontal cortex. *Nature, 376,* 572–575.

Williams, M. T., Hennessey, M. B., & Davis, H. N. (1995). CRH administered to pregnant rats alters offspring behavior and morphology. *Pharmacology, Biochemistry & Behavior, 52,* 161–167.

Wilson, A., Passik, S. D., & Faude, J. P. (1990). Self-regulation and its failures. In J.

Masling (Ed.), *Empirical studies of psychoanalytic theory* (Vol. 3. pp. 149–213). Hillsdale, NJ: Analytic Press.

Wilson, C. L., Isokawa, M., Babb, T. L., Crandal, P. H., Levesque, M. F., & Engel, J. (1991). Functional connections in the human temporal lobe: Part II. Evidence for loss of a functional linkage between contralateral limbic structures. *Experimental Brain Research, 85*, 174–187.

Winick, M., Rosso, P., & Waterlow, J. (1970). Cellular growth of the cerebrum, cerebellum and brain stem in normal and marasmic children. *Experimental Neurology, 26*, 393–400.

Winn, P. (1994). Schizophrenia research moves to the prefrontal cortex. *Trends in Neurosciences, 17*, 265–268.

Winnicott, D. W. (1958). The capacity to be alone. *International Journal of Psycho-Analysis, 39*, 416–420.

Winnicott, D. W. (1960). The theory of the parent-infant relationship. In *The maturational process and the facilitating environment* (pp. 37–55). New York: International Universities Press.

Winnicott, D. W. (1971a). Mirror-role of mother and family in child development. In *Playing and reality*. New York: Basic.

Winnicott, D. (1971b). *Playing and reality*. New York: Basic.

Winnicott, D. W. (1986). *Home is where we start from*. New York: W. W. Norton.

Winston, J. S., Strange, B. A., O'Doherty, J. O., & Dolan, R. J. (2002). Automatic and intentional brain responses during evaluation of trustworthiness of faces. *Nature Neuroscience, 5*, 277–283.

Wise, R. A., & Rompre, P.-P. (1989). Brain dopamine and reward. *Annual Review of Psychology, 40*, 191–225.

Wittling, W. (1997). The right hemisphere and the human stress response. *Acta Physiologica Scandinavica, 640* (Suppl.), 55–59.

Wittling, W., Block, A., Schweiger, E., & Genzel, S. (1998). Hemisphere asymmetry in sympathetic control of the human myocardium. *Brain and Cognition, 38*, 17–35.

Wittling, W., & Pfluger, M. (1990). Neuroendocrine hemisphere asymmetries: Salivary cortisol secretion during lateralized viewing of emotion-related and neutral films. *Brain and Cognition, 14*, 243–265.

Wittling, W., & Roschmann, R. (1993). Emotion-related hemisphere asymmetry: Subjective emotional responses to laterally presented films. *Cortex, 29*, 431–448.

Wittling, W., & Schweiger, E. (1993). Neuroendocrine brain asymmetry and physical complaints. *Neuropsychologia, 31*, 591–608.

Wolf, S. (1995). Psychosocial forces and neural mechanisms in disease: Defining the question and collecting the evidence. *Integrative Physiological and Behavioral Science, 30*, 85–94

Wong-Riley, M. T. T. (1979). Changes in the visual system of monocularly sutured or enucleated cats demonstrable with cytochrome oxidase histochemistry. *Brain Research, 171*, 11–28.

Wong-Riley, M. T. T. (1989). Cytochrome oxidase: An endogenous metabolic marker for neuronal activity. *Trends in Neurosciences, 12*, 94–101.

Wright, C. I., Fisher, H., Whalen, P. J., McInerney, S. C., Shin, L. M., & Rauch, S. L. (2001). Differential prefrontal cortex and amygdala habituation to repeatedly presented emotional stimuli. *NeuroReport, 12*, 379–383.

Wright, K. (1991). *Vision and separation: Between mother and baby*. Northvale, NJ: Jason Aronson.

Wyllie, A. (1997). Apoptosis—clues in the p53 murder mystery. *Nature, 389*, 237–238.

Wyllie, A. H. (1980). Glucocorticoid-induced thymocyte apoptosis is associated with endogenous endonuclease activation. *Nature, 284*, 555–556.

Yakovlev, P. I., & Lecours, A. R. (1967). The myelogenetic cycles of regional maturation of the brain. In A. Minkow (Ed.), *Regional development of the brain in early life.* Oxford, UK: Blackwell.

Yamada, H., Sadato, N., Konishi, Y., Kimura, K., Tanaka, M., Yonekura, Y., & Ishii, Y. (1997). A rapid brain metabolic change in infants detected by fMRI. *NeuroReport, 8,* 3775–3778.

Yamada, H., Sadato, N., Konishi, Y., Muramoto, S., Kimura, K., Tanaka, M., Yonekura, Y., Ishii, Y., & Itoh, H. (2000). A milestone for normal development of the infantile brain detected by functional MRI. *Neurology, 55,* 218–223.

Yasui, Y., Itoh, K., Kaneko, T., Shigemoto, R., & Mizuno, N. (1991). Topographical projections from the cerebral cortex to the nucleus of the solitary tract in the cat. *Experimental Brain Research, 85,* 75–84.

Yehuda, R. (1999a). Linking the neuroendocrinology of post-traumatic stress disorder with recent neuroanatomic findings. *Seminars in Clinical Neuropsychiatry, 4,* 256–265.

Yehuda, R. (1999b). Managing anger and aggression in patients with posttraumatic stress disorder. *Journal of Traumatic Stress, 12,* 501–517.

Yehuda, R., Halligan, S. L., & Grossman, R. (2001). Childhood trauma and risk for PTSD: Relationship to intergenerational effects of trauma, parental PTSD, and cortisol excretion. *Development and Psychopathology, 13,* 733–753.

Yehuda, R., McFarlane, A. C., & Shalev, A. Y. (1998). Predicting the development of posttraumatic stress disorder from the acute response to a traumatic event. *Biological Psychiatry, 44,* 1305–1313.

Yeo, R. A., Gangestad, S. W., Thoma, R. A., Shaw, P., & Repa, K. (1997). Developmental instability and cerebral lateralization. *Neuropsychology, 11,* 552–561.

Yeo, R. A., Hill, D., Campbell, R., Vigil, J., & Brooks, W. M. (2000). Developmental instability and working memory in children: A magnetic resonance spectroscopy investigation. *Developmental Neuropsychology, 17,* 143–159.

Yeo, R. A., Hodde-Vargas, J., Hendren, R. L., Vargas, L. A., Brooks, W. M., Ford, C. C., Gangestad, S. W., & Hart, B. L. (1997). Brain abnormalities in schizophrenia-spectrum children: Implications for the etiology of adult schizophrenia. *Psychiatry Research, Neuroimaging, 76,* 1–13.

Yoon, B-U., Morillo, C. A., Cechetto, D. F., & Hachinski, V. (1997). Cerebral hemispheric lateralization in cardiac autonomic control. *Archives of Neurology, 54,* 741–744.

Yoshida, M., Yokoo, H., Tanaka, T., Mizoguchi, K., Emoto, H., Ishii, H., & Tanaka, M. (1993). Facilitory modulation of mesolimbic dopamine neuronal activity by mu-opioid agonist and nicotine as examined with in vivo microdyalysis. *Brain Research, 624,* 277–280.

Yoshino, A., Hovda, D. A., Kawamata, T., Katayama, Y., & Becker, D. P. (1991). Dynamic changes in local cerebral glucose utilization following cerebral concussion in rats: Evidence of a hyper- and subsequent hypometabolic state. *Brain Research, 561,* 106–119.

Young, J. B., Rosa, R. M., & Landsberg, L. (1984). Dissociation of sympathetic nervous system and adrenal medullary responses. *American Journal of Physiology, 247,* E35-E40.

Yurgelun-Todd, D. (1998, June). *Brain and psyche: The neurobiology of the self.* Paper presented at the "Brain and Psyche" seminar at the Whitehead Institute for Biomedical Research, Cambridge, MA.

Yuste, R., & Katz, L. C. (1991). Control of postsynaptic Ca^{2+} influx in developing neocortex by excitatory and inhibitory neurotransmitters. *Neuron, 6,* 333–344.

Zahrt, J., Taylor, J. R., Mathew, R. G., & Arnsten, A. M. (1997). Supranormal stimulation of D_1 dopamine receptors in the rodent prefrontal cortex impairs spatial working memory performance. *Journal of Neuroscience, 17,* 8528–8535.

Zaidel, D. W., Esiri, M. M., & Beardsworth, E. D. (1998). Observations on the relationship between verbal explicit and implicit memory and density of neurons in the hippocampus. *Neuropsychologia, 36,* 1049–1062.

Zajonc, R. B. (1984). On primacy of affect. In K. R. Scherer & P. Ekman (Eds.), *Approaches to emotion* (pp. 259–270). Hillsdale, NJ: Erlbaum.

Zald, D. H., & Kim, S. W. (1996). Anatomy and function of the orbital frontal cortex: II. Function and relevance to obsessive-compulsive disorder. *Journal of Neuropsychiatry, 8,* 249–261.

Zald, D. H., Lee, J. T., Fluegel, K. W., & Pardo, J. V. (1998). Aversive gustatory stimulation activates limbic circuits in humans. *Brain, 121,* 1143–1154.

Zamzimi, N., Marchetti, P., Castedo, M., Decaudin, D., Macho, A., Hirsch, T., Susin, S. A., Petit, P. Y., Mignotte, B., & Kroemer, G. (1995). Sequential reduction of mitochondrial transmembrane potential and generation of reactive oxygen species in early programmed cell death. *Journal of Experimental Medicine, 182,* 367–377.

Zanarini, M. C., Frankenburg, F. R., Dubo, E. D., Sickel, A. E., Trikha, A., Levin, A., & Reynolds, V. (1998). Axis I comorbidity of borderline personality disorder. *American Journal of Psychiatry, 155,* 1733–1739.

Zanarini, M. C., Ruser, T., Frankenburg, F. R., & Hennen, J. (2000). The dissociative experiences of borderline patients. *Comprehensive Psychiatry, 41,* 223–227.

Zanarini, M. C., Williams, A. A., Lewis, R. E., Reich, R. B., Vera, S. C., Marino, M. F., Levin, A., Yong, L., & Frankenburg, F. R. (1997). Reported pathological childhood experiences associated with the development of borderline personality disorder. *American Journal of Psychiatry, 154,* 1101–1106.

Zhang, L.-X., Levine, S., Dent, G., Zhan, Y., Xing, G., Okimoto, D., Gordon, M. K., Post, R. M., & Smith, M. A. (2002). Maternal deprivation increases cell death in the infant rat brain. *Developmental Brain Research, 133,* 1–11.

Zhang, L.-X., Xing, G. Q., Levine, S., Post, R. M., & Smith, M. A. (1997). Maternal deprivation induces neuronal death. *Society for Neuroscience Abstracts, 23,* 1113.

Zhang, Y-U., Tang, J-S., Yuan, B., & Jia, H. (1997). Inhibitory effects of electrically evoked activation of ventrolateral orbital cortex on the tail-flick reflex are mediated by periaqueductal gray in rats. *Pain, 72,* 127–135.

Zhou, Q.-Y., Qualfe, C. J., & Palmiter, R. D. (1995). Targeted disruption of the tyrosine hydroxylase gene reveals that catecholamines are required for mouse fetal development. *Nature, 374,* 640–646.

Zlotnick, C., Warshaw, M., Shea, M. T., Allsworth, J., Pearlstein, T., & Keller, M. B. (1999). Chronicity in posttraumatic stress disorder (PTSD) and predictors of course of comorbid PTSD in patients with anxiety disorders. *Journal of Traumatic Stress, 12,* 89–100.

Zubieta, J-K., Smith, Y. R., Bueller, J. A., Yu, Y., Kilbourn, M. R., Jewett, D. M., Meyer, C. R., Koeppe, R. A., & Stohler, C. S. (2002). μ-opioid receptor-mediated antinociceptive responses differ in men and women. *Journal of Neuroscience, 22,* 5100–5107.

Index

abuse
  and adult morbidity, 265
  and affect, 300–301
  and brain development, 119, 180–84
  by caregiver, 183, 231–32
  of caregiver, 286
  chronic, 269
  and dissociation, 220
  emotional, 181
  and facial expressions, 119, 225
  incidence of, 185
  neurophysiology, 254
  physical, 268, 297, 298, 301
  prenatal, 119
  and PTSD, 211
  screening for, 304
  sexual, 231, 261
  see also neglect; trauma
ACTH
  and gaze, 81
  and orbitofrontal cortex, 15
  and stress, 21
  and trauma, 202
action selection, 63
activity levels, 28
adaptive ability
  and abuse, 187
  Bowlby's view, 134
  and chaos, 94
  chronology, xvii, 105
  and dyadic relationship, 30–32
  in infants, 138–44
  lack of, 125
  and limbic system, 61, 151–53
  and orbital frontal cortex, 60
  and psychopathology, 30–32, 122–23
  and stress, 22, 30–32
  see also evaluative ability
addictions, 35, 302
adenosine triphosphate, 99–100, 117
adolescence
  and attachment, 173–74
  brain reorganization, 297–98

parcellation in, 173, 230, 297–98
  and perinatal trauma, 202–3
  personality disorder predictors, 302
  and Type D, 202–3, 297–98
Adolphs, R., 169, 293
adrenaline, 81, 247, 282
adulthood, 172
affect
  and abuse versus neglect, 301
  brain sites, 84, 272
  high- versus low-arousal, 111
  and infant trauma, 262–63
  lack of, 28
  nonverbal, 82
  and objects, 45–46
  tolerance of, 24
  see also negative affect; positive affect
affect regulation
  in adults, 125
  and attachment interruption, 18
  brain sites, 272
  and positive affect, 78, 143–44
  in toddlers, 24
affect synchrony
  with caregiver, 75, 138–46, 158, 241–42,
    273–75
  with peers, 173
aggression
  brain sites, 224, 257, 272–73, 278–81
  of caregiver, 251, 294
  dysregulation of, 210–12
  dysregulation psychopathogenesis, 288–91
  and eleven-year-olds, 296
  and fathers, 275–76
  predisposing factors, 295–96
  in preschoolers, 296
  regulation of, 281
  and relational trauma, 267–68, 284
  socialization of, 29
  in toddlers, 296
  and Type D, 284–91
  types, 292–93
  see also rage; violence

Ainsworth, M., 54, 60, 78
alcohol dependence, 302
alexithymia, 228–29
Allen, J. G., 220, 260
Allen, J. P., 173
amines, *see* bioamines
amnesia, 219, 258
amygdala
    and adolescence, 173–74, 297
    and aggression, 292
    and BPD, 211
    chronology, 104, 155–57
    and decisions, 163
    and dissociation, 214–15
    and facial expressions, 257, 294
    imaging study, 165
    and maternal depression, 124
    and pain, 218–19
    and PTSD, 208, 256–58
    and rage, 211, 291–95
    right, 257–58, 294
    and sensory stimuli, 155–57
    and stress, 256–57
    and trauma, 199–202, 208, 223
Anders, T. F., 137
Anderson, S. W., 203–4, 298
anger
    facial expression, 210, 225, 297, 300
    in insecure-avoidant toddler, 27
    perception of, 60
    in personality disorder, 267
    and postpartum depression, 304
    rage, 211–12, 267–68
    unregulated, 29
anhedonia, 207
anterior cingulate
    and attention, 258
    development, 104, 158–59
    and faces, 104
    and pain, 218
    and separation anxiety, 158–59
    and trauma, 202
    see also limbic system
antisocial personality disorder, 267, 268, 273,
    302
anxiety, 158–59, 197, 211, 294
anxiety disorders, 202
apoptosis
    and psychopathology, 117–18, 288–89
    and stress, 117
    and trauma, 190, 206–7, 253–54
    see also parcellation
appetitive-aversive stimuli, 162, 163
appraisal, *see* evaluative ability
approach behavior, 162
arousal
    and attachment, 77–78
    and brain growth, 91

and caregiver–infant dyad, 76–77, 141–42,
    282
and catecholamines, 100–101
and energy state, 96
ergotropic/trophotropic balance, 22
excessive, 28–29 (*see also* hyperarousal)
in infancy, 10, 34, 143
inhibition of, 21
optimal, 26
and parcellation, 255–56
and right hemisphere, 111, 162, 224
in toddlers, 12, 18–20
astrocytes, 206, 230
attachment
    and affective state, 10
    and affect regulation strategies, 23
    and arousal, 77–78
    Bowlby's views, 56–59, 112, 133–34
    brain sites, 44, 61–62, 74, 108, 168, 243–
        46
    capacity evaluation, 67
    chronology, 62
    and communication, 75–78, 276–77
    and coping, 65–66, 74, 190
    definition, 242
    disorganized/disoriented (*see* Type D)
    (dis)organized-insecure, 207, 230–31, 247
    disruption-repair, 20, 21, 26, 30–31, 65, 143
    disruptions, 116–17, 190, 211
        repair of, 20, 21; 26, 65, 143
    and dissociation, 212–13
    duration of, 23
    and energy, 95–97
    and environment, 112
    insecure-avoidant, 26–28, 120, 231
    insecure-resistant, 28–29, 119–20
    with neo-toddlers, 44–46
    neurobiology, 42, 59–64, 78–82, 241–43,
        276–78
    and positive affect, 78
    psychobiology, 78–82
    and psychotherapy, 69
    research directions, 66–70
    secure, 241–43, 273–78
    shame as, 17–18
    social referencing, 44–46
    and synchrony, 143
    and systems theory, 95–97
    traumatic, 180–84, 240–41 (*see also* rela-
        tional trauma)
attachment theory
    brain effect, 172
    and limbic system, 74
    and psychopathology, 30, 66, 85, 133,
        179–80
    and regulation, 64–66
    as regulatory theory, 134–35
    and violence, 270

attachment transactions
    and limbic system, 150–61
    resonance, 76, 141
    as template, 80
attention, 67–68, 160, 258
attention disorders, 68, 227
auditory signals, 9, 42–43, 60, 78
autism
    and cytochrome oxidase, 113
    and orbitofrontal cortex, 35
    and parcellation, 118
    and right hemisphere, 123
    and trauma, 202
autonomic nervous system (ANS)
    and attachment, 81–82, 243–46, 277
    and communication, 157
    and decompensation, 263
    and dissociation, 213–14
    and emotion states, 136
    and insecure-resistant attachments, 119–20
    and orbitofrontal areas, 61, 105–6, 164
    oxygen demands, 109
    and PTSD, 263
    and right brain, 25, 82–83, 168, 243–46
    and socioemotional stimulation, 28
    and stress, 116–17
    and systems theory, 97
    and unpredictable caregiver, 29
    see also parasympathetic nervous system;
        sympathetic nervous system
avoidance, of mother, 27–28

Bargh, J. A., 67, 83, 170
Barnett, D., 295
Baron-Cohen, S., 176
Bear, D. M., 51
Bechara, A., 298
Beebe, B., 8, 31, 38–39, 188, 247, 248, 282
behavior
    approach, 162
    hostile-aggressive, 210
    inflexible, 209–10
    instinctual, 61
    intergenerational transmission, 66, 195, 254
    of maltreated infants, 193–94, 250–51
    and orbitofrontal cortex, 63
    self-destructive, 219
    threatening, 285
    of Type D children, 229–30, 250, 284–85
        of parents of, 195, 251, 285
    see also coping; reunion behavior
Benes, F. M., 33, 117
Berntson, G. G., 214
biases, 63
bioamines
    and dendrites, 103
    and neurotransmitters, 106
    and prenatal stress, 190

and psychopathology, 113, 123–24
    role of, 98–100
birth, 68, 202–3
Blair, R. J. R., 297, 300, 301
blood flow, 100–101
body image, 202
bond formation, 10
borderline personality disorder (BPD), 35, 211,
        267, 298–303
Bowlby, J., xv, 9, 13, 29, 30, 42, 54–59, 61,
        62, 63, 64, 65, 66, 68, 70, 112, 133,
        134, 137, 150, 155, 157, 159, 162, 178,
        179, 189, 191, 235, 236, 240, 243, 248,
        252, 262, 270, 271, 278
BPD, *see* borderline personality disorder
brain
    and arousal, 91
    of caregiver, 80, 122, 149, 276
    fetal, 182, 291–92, 304
    growth, 91, 112–13
    growth spurts, 69, 112–13, 131
    hierarchical, 153–55
    metabolism, 90–91, 97–103
    and post-toddler crises, 172–73
    triune, 155
    and withdrawal, 28
    see also orbitofrontal cortex; right brain
brain-derived neurotrophic factor (BDNF), 148
brain development
    chronology
        eight weeks, 139, 157, 276
        fetus, 182
        five months, 276
        neonates, 112–13, 183
        10 to 12 months, 13–16, 278
        two years, 237, 271
    critical periods, 102
    and dyadic relationship, 9–11, 12–13, 34,
        42–44
    and energy, 91, 97–104, 131
    and environment, 14, 95, 97–98, 132–33
    and gender, 68
    and gene expression, 112
    metabolism, 100–104
    and play, 104, 148, 158
    of prefrontal cortex, 14
    regressive events, 103–4
    right brain, 69, 89–90, 126, 229
    self-organization, xv, 5–6
    and stress, 21
    and trauma, 119, 180–84, 252–59, 270–73,
        289–90
    weight change, 72
brain stem, 50(fig.), 109, 136, 163
    see also medulla oblongata
Bramsen, 187
Brazelton, T. B., 131, 151–52, 157, 159, 161,
        266, 272, 304

Brent, L., 12
Breuer, J., 221, 228
Broadbent, D. E., 51–52
Bromberg, P., 226
Brothers, L., 161, 176
Brower, M. C., 293
Buck, R., 144–45, 150, 276

Cairns, R. B., 133, 270
calcium, 190–91
Caldji, C., 277
calming, 163
cAMP, 136
Caplan, R., 160
cardiovascular system, 253–54, 260–61, 284,
    301
caregiver
    abusive, 183, 194–96, 231–32 (*see also*
        abuse; relational trauma)
    in abusive relationship, 286
    avoidance of, 27–28
    brain of, 80, 122, 149, 276
    depressed, 31, 124, 196–97, 223–24
    experiences of, 66
    face of, 38–42, 225–26, 251 (*see also* faces)
    good-enough, 19, 142–43, 221, 242, 246,
        275
    inaccessible, 26–28
    intrusive, 28–29
    (mis)attuned, 77
    and nucleic acids, 112–14
    predictable, 28–29, 78
    rejecting, 31
    right hemisphere of, 122
caregiver–infant dyad
    and adaptive capacity, 30–32
    and adolescence, 174
    affect synchrony, 75, 138–46, 158, 273–75
    and appraisal system, 37
    and arousal, 76–77, 141–42, 282
    Bowlby's view, 55, 56–57
    contingent responsivity, 39, 75–76, 96, 140
        (*see also* affect synchrony)
    and corticosteroids, 116
    duration, 23
    and gene expression, 112–13
    and hormones, 253
    in infancy, 7–11, 112–13
    (in)securely attached, 26–29
    monitoring, xv–xvi
    and neo-toddler, 11–13, 44–46
    physical effects, 5–6
    and right brain, 80–81, 144–50
    storage of, 280
    and stress, 31
    and systems theory, 95–96
    and toddlers, 16–20, 44–46 (*see also* com-
        munication)

Carlson, M., 118
catecholamines
    and arousal, 100–101
    and brain metabolism, 99–100
    and caregiver, 112
    and gene expression, 114
    maternally induced, 10
    regulation of, 279
    and stress, 114–15, 117, 118–19, 247–48
    and sympathetic nervous system, 34
    see also specific catecholamines
Causey, D. L., 187
Changeux, J. P., 103
chaotic systems, 94, 104–8, 120
children, older, 261, 296
Chiron, J. I., 62
Chu, J. A., 269
Cicchetti, D., 5, 72–73, 97, 105, 130, 132,
    179, 228, 238
cingulate, *see* anterior cingulate
Ciompi, L., 108
cognitive-emotional interaction, 63
Cole, J., 150
communication
    and autonomic nervous system, 157
    facial expressions, 133, 142
    infant-caregiver, 75–78
    and limbic system, 276–77
    of nonverbal affect, 82, 110
    olfactory, 155–56
    physical effects, 80–81
    protoconversation, 42, 43(fig.), 158
    and right brain, 171
    spontaneous-emotional, 144–45
    state-sharing, 96
contingent responsivity, 39, 75–76, 96, 140
coping
    and abuse, 185, 187
    in adolescence, 173–74
    and attachment theory, 65–66, 74, 190
    Bowlby's view, 134
    brain sites, 162, 168, 172
    deficit continuum, 192
    and dissociation, 198–99
    and insecure-avoidance, 231
    maternal role, 277–78
    with pain, 218–19
    and parasympathetic system, 18, 109–10
    problem- *versus* emotion-focus, 109–10
    and psychopathology, 85
    and right brain, 74, 83, 172, 235–36, 280
    and security, xvii
    and trauma, 192, 202, 204–5
    see also dissociation
corpus callosum, 228
cortical-subcortical circuits, 104–5
corticosteroids
    and apoptosis, 289

and caregiver–infant dyad, 116
in infancy, 33
and limbic system, 33
and orbitofrontal cortex, 21
regulation of, 279
and shame, 18, 21, 116–17
in toddlers, 116–17, 118–19
and trauma, 191
corticotropin releasing factor (CRF)
and fetal brain, 182, 291–92
and hyperarousal, 21
and maternal face, 10
and mutual gaze, 81
and repair, 19–20, 21–22
and SAM axis, 135
and seizures, 290
and shame, 18, 21
and trauma, 188, 198, 253
cortisol
and stress, 135–36
and trauma, 205, 253–54
and Type D, 118–19, 192
cradling, 81, 156–57
critical periods
and corticosteroids, 116
at eight weeks, 139, 157
and genetics, 112–15
and imprinting, 100–104
and intervention, 232–33, 265, 304
and right brain, 172
trauma in, 199–207
Crittenden, P. M., 137–38
culture, 83–84, 84–85
cutting, 219
cytochrome oxidase, 99–101, 113

Damasio, A. R., 53, 81, 97, 106, 129, 143,
    167, 202
danger, 272
Darwin, C., 54–55, 59, 133, 216
Davidson, R. J., xv, 210
Davies, J. M., 186, 246
Dawson, G., 25
De Bellis, M. D., 184
decompensation, 262–63
delayed response function, 15–16
dendrites, 99–100, 103, 205–6
deoxyribonucleic acid (DNA), 191
depression
in caregiver, 31, 124, 196–97, 223–24
and orbitofronal cortex, 35
postpartum, 304
and right hemisphere, 123
and trauma, 207
disorganization/disorientation, *see* Type D
dissociation
description, 215, 220, 226, 248–49
gender factors, 254–55

initial *versus* later, 248–49
and limbic system, 218–19, 253
neurobiology, 212–16, 283–84
and parasympathetic system, 118–19,
    213–15
and parcellation, 213
postpartum, 196–97
psychopathology, 216–22
and PTSD, 191–92, 239–40, 260–61
and right brain, 239–40
signs of, 188–89
and trauma, 188–89, 260
and Type D, 118–19, 198–99, 285, 286
Dodge, K. A., 297
dopamine
and aggression, 290
and apoptosis, 117
and attention, 227
and caregiver, 41, 147
and dendrites, 100
and dissociation, 219–20
and frontal areas, 13–14, 162, 163–64
and gene expression, 114
in infancy, 10
and infant distress, 247, 282
and memory, 162–63
midbrain, 162
and mother's face, 81
in neonates, 114–15
and nonlinearity, 106–7
and prenatal stress, 123–24
rate-limiting enzyme, 113
and social experience, 33–34
and stress, 110, 114–15, 291
and toddlers, 13–14, 19–20
and trauma, 191, 205
and Type D, 230
drug dependence, 35, 302
dyslexia, 227

Eckenrode, J., 232
Edelman, G., 80, 159
Eisenberg, L., 37, 185
Emde, R. N, 13, 23, 25, 32, 79, 137, 187, 232
emotional deficits, 33
emotional information, 110
emotion biases, 25, 28, 29, 52
empathy
brain sites, 23–24, 175, 280
and intelligence, 176–77
and prefrontal damage, 202
and psychotherapy, 69–70
and right hemisphere, 35
and trauma, 119, 199
endorphins
and corticosteroids, 18
and dopamine, 148
and mother's face, 81

endorphins (*continued*)
    and repair, 19–20, 21–22
    and right cortex, 15
    and shame, 21
energy
    and arousal, 96
    and attachment dynamic, 95–97
    and brain development, 91, 97–104, 131
    and critical periods, 100–104
    and dissociation, 215
    and dyadic relationship, 12, 64, 80, 148–49
    and emotion, 146–47
    and environment, 106
    and evaluative systems, 49, 53
    and imprinting, 100–104
    and psychology, 95
    and psychopathology, 113, 117
    and resonance, 141
    and shame, 18
    and systems theory, 90–91, 92–93, 94–96, 100
    see also metabolism
environment
    appraisal of, 23, 36 (*see also* evaluative ability)
    and attachment, 112
    and brain development, 14, 95, 97–98, 132–33
    and energy states, 106
    and genes, 14, 33, 114–15, 295–96
    growth-inhibiting, 32–33, 121–22
    and infant memory, 107–8
    and systems theory, 92–95
enzymes, 112–13
Epstein, H. T., 277
evaluative ability
    brain sites, 23, 46–53, 63, 111, 167
    and caregiver–infant dyad, 37
    and coping resources, 60
    and danger, 297
    emotional biases, 52
    and facial expressions, 82
    and late first year, 44–46
    and pleasure, 61
    see also environment, appraisal of
excitation–inhibition balance, 25
excitement, tolerance of, 34
    see also arousal
executive control function, 50, 61, 110
expectations
    of being tickled, 158
    and energy states, 106
    and security, 62, 83, 245
eyes, 75

faces
    and adolescents, 173–74
    and amygdala, 257, 294

angry, 60, 210, 225, 297, 300
    and anterior cingulate, 158
    and appraisal, 38–42, 82
    of caregiver, 38–42, 225–26, 251
    and early abuse, 119
    expressing fear, 251, 285, 294, 300
    frightening, 208
    and gene-environment, 112
    and insecure-avoidance, 27
    and late infancy, 104–5
    left side, 43
    memory of, 15–16, 225–26
    mirroring, 7–8, 38–42
    and personality disorders, 300
    preattentive analysis, 51–52
    and right brain, 61, 79, 108–10, 147
    sad, 60, 297, 300
    and shame, 18
    and stress, 81
    threatening, 251, 257, 285, 294
    see also gaze
fathers, 68, 275–76, 286–87
fear
    and arousal, 188
    and attachment, 195
    extinction of, 209–10
    facial expression, 251, 285, 294, 300
    physical effects, 198, 205
fear–freeze states, *see* freeze response
Feldman, R., 64, 139, 140, 145
fetal abuse, 181, 182
fetal brain, 182, 291–92, 304
fetal stress, 190
Field, T., 12, 29, 305
Fischer, K. W., 152
Fisher, R. S., 211
Fogel, A., 8, 139, 157–58
Fonagy, P., 63, 220, 226
Foote, S. L., 199
Fornai, F., 206
Fraiberg, S., 197
free radicals, 117
freeze response
    and amygdala, 294
    description, 216–17
    physical effects, 213–14
    and temperament, 213–14
    and Type D infant, 210, 223
    and vasopressin, 247–48
Freud, A., 198
Freud, S., 54–55, 58, 133, 167, 184, 197–98, 221, 228, 268
Freyd, J. J., 246–47
functional deficits
    intergenerational, 122, 195, 254
    and orbitofronal defect, 209–10
    pain response, 264
    and PTSD, 261–62

representational, 226–27
social and emotional, 33, 113
stress-coping, 66, 85, 122, 192 (*see also* coping)
stress-related, 237–38
fusiform gyri, 294, 300

Gaensbauer, T. J., 186
gamma-aminobutyric acid (GABA), 102–3, 189
Gardner, H., 176–77
gaze
and appraisal, 38–42
as communication, 75, 139
and hormones, 81
and joint attention, 160
mutual, 38–42
and neo-toddlers, 44–46
and neurotransmitters, 81
and three-month-olds, 158
see also faces
gaze aversion, 27–28, 29, 39
gaze transactions, 7–10, 38–42
Gedo, J. E., 151
gender
and brain maturation, 68
and cradling, 81
and fathers, 81, 275–76
and limbic system, 120
mothers and sons, 286
and trauma, 254–55
genes
and apoptosis, 289
and brain growth, 112
in critical periods, 100–104
and environment, 14, 33, 114–15, 295–96
for limbic system, 112
mitochondrial, 113–14
mutations, 113–14
and oxygen, 114
and trauma, 204
glial cells, 206
glucocorticoids
and HPA axis, 135
and limbic system, 33
and trauma, 190, 202
glutamate, 117, 205, 282
glycogenolysis, 99
Goldberg, E., 32
Gomez-Pinilla, F., 132
Greenspan, S. I., 32–33
Grunau, R. V. E., 218
gut feelings, 164–65

hands, 156
happiness, 163, 167
Hariri, A. R., 69, 210, 231–32
Harkness, K. L., 188

Harlow, H. F., 156
Harold, F. M., 95
Hartmann, H., 151
Head Start, 74
health
mental, 169–77, 184–87
physical, 175–76
Hebbian cell assemblies, 102
Heim, C., 198
helplessness, 28, 198, 248
Henry, J. P., 214, 264–65
Herman, J. L., 299
Hernandez-Reif, M., 156
Herzog, J. M., 275, 276, 286–87
Hesse, E., 251
hexose monophosphate shunt, 99, 112
Hinde, R., 6, 61, 151
hippocampus, 258
Hofer, M., 11, 41–42, 107, 112, 149–50
Hopkins, B., 187
hormones
and caregiver-infant dyad, 253
and fetal brain, 182
and gaze, 81
and parcellation, 34
and psychopathology, 33, 34
thyroid, 247–48
see also corticosteroids
Horowitz, M. J., 267–68
HPA axis, *see* hypothalamo-pituitary-adrenocortical axis
Hudspeth, W. J., 102, 103
Hughlings-Jackson, J., 153–54, 155
Hurvich, M., 198
hyperarousal
alternating, 34, 191–92
and caretaker state, 285–86
gender factors, 254–55
and parcellation, 34, 255–56
and personality disorders, 299–300
physical effects, 188, 247–49, 282–84
and PTSD, 191–92, 247–49
hyperexcitation, 197
hypoarousal, 34, 207
see also dissociation
hypothalamo-pituitary-adrenocortical (HPA) axis
and addiction, 302
and fetus, 182
and later pathology, 119
and parcellation, 256
and PTSD, 258
and stress, 135
and trauma, 256
and Type D, 192–93
hypothalamus
and adolescence, 173, 297
and aggression, 280, 292

hypothalamus (*continued*)
  and amygdala, 157
  and happiness, 167
  lateralization, 82–83, 166–67
  in limbic system, 163
  neuroanatomy, 105
  and psychopathology, 34
  and PTSD, 208–9, 212
  and rage, 211, 292–93
  and right brain, 167
  and self-regulation, 279
  and trauma, 255
  and Type D, 230–31, 283
hysterical paresthesia, 228

imaging studies
  of adolescents, 173–74
  of amygdala, 165, 173–74
  antisocial personality disorder, 273
  of brain development, 237
  depressed mother effect, 223–24
  of eight-week old, 139
  of facial recognition, 173–74
  happiness and sadness, 163, 167
  of hypothalamus, 166–67
  of orbitofrontal areas, 163, 276
  and pain, 218
  recommendation, xv
  of right brain, 80, 125–26, 166–67, 231–32
  of sadness, 163
  and schizophrenia, 124
  of trauma effect, 125–26, 199–200, 203, 219
  and violence, 211–12, 224
immune response, 175–76
imprinting
  and attachment, 80, 277, 280
  brain site, 22
  and catecholamines, 100–101
  of defenses, 294
  and dopamine, 13–14
  energy-dependence, 100–104
  and limbic learning, 61
  neurobiology, 9, 42
  and opiates, 13–14
  and PTSD, 208
  of relationships, 22
  of trauma, 194–95, 225, 238–39
infants
  affect regulation, 24
  brain growth, 112–13, 131
  critical periods, 100–104 (*see also* critical periods)
  dissociation in, 212–16, 217, 221–22 (*see also* dissociation)
  and environment, 32–33 (*see also* environment)
  face-to-face interaction, 75
  maltreated, 192–99, 250–51, 268, 284–88 (*see also* trauma)

  mental health, 138–44, 184–87
  mutual gaze, 7–10 (*see also* gaze)
  and self, 24, 149 (*see also* self)
  and stress, 116–17, 183 (*see also* stress)
  temperament, 25
  see also neonates
information
  emotional, 110
  self-related, 243–44
inhibition, 21, 61
insecure-avoidance
  and coping, 231
  neurobiology, 27–28, 120
  origins, 26–27
insecure-resistance, 28–29, 119–20
instinctual behavior, 61
insula, 159, 200, 202
intelligence, 176–77
interaction representations, 22–23
interest, 8–9
intergenerational transmission, 66, 122, 195, 254
iteration, 96
Izard, C. E., 28

Jackson, E. A., 94
Jackson, J. H., 263
Janet, P., 187, 221, 228, 240
joint attention, 160
Joseph, R., 23, 27, 33
joy, 34
  see also anhedonia

Kalin, N. H., 148, 213–14
Kalogeras, K. T., 157
Karr-Morse, R., 184, 266, 306
Kehoe, P., 138, 235–36
Kennedy, C., 102
Kernberg, O., 299
Kestenberg, J., 197
Kiersky, S., 226
Kling, A., 202
Kolb, B., 206
Kraemer, G. W., 278
Krystal, H., 24, 198, 216, 262

Lane, R. D., 174, 217
language, 170–71, 228
laughing, 104, 158
Lazarus, R. S., 51
learning
  cultural, 83–84, 170
  emotion-related, 69
  implicit *versus* explicit, 168, 170
  and orbitofrontal cortex, 69, 170, 208
LeDoux, J. E., 23, 52, 243
left brain, 62, 228
Lester, B. M., 75, 140
Leventhal, H., 44

Lewis, M. D., 95, 146–47
Lieberman, A. S., 81, 166, 286
life cycle, 172–75
limbic system, 152(fig.), 200(fig.), 201(fig.)
  and abuse, 186
  and adaptivity, 61
  and adolescence, 173
  anterior, 152
  and attachment
    and attachment theory, 60, 74
    and genetics, 68, 112
    hierarchical organization, 151–60
    of insecure-avoidance, 120
    insecure-organized, 230–31
    of insecure-resistance, 119–20
    and right brain, 137
    secure, 277
  components, 151–53, 152(fig.)
  critical period, 104, 136–37
  and dissociation, 218–19, 253
  and gender, 120
  in infancy, 33
  lateral tegmental, 105, 109
  maturation, 60
  metabolism, 290
  and mirroring, 34
  and motivation, 105
  ontogeny, 155
  and PTSD, 259, 262–65
  and rage, 211
  right, 145, 154(fig.), 201(fig.), 262–65, 289
  as social editor, 161, 175
  in toddlers, 52–53
  and trauma, 189–91, 198, 199–202, 206–7,
      255–56
  ventral tegmental, 34, 105, 110, 162, 205
  see also rostral limbic system
limit setting, 29
Locke, J. L., 171
Luu, P., 185
Lydic, R., 89

McEwen, B. S., 135
McFarlane, A. C., 241, 258
MacLean, P. D., 155, 158, 217
Maestripieri, D., 196
Mahler, M., 11, 149, 158
Mahler, M. S., 198
Main, M., 27–28, 46, 63, 70, 120, 138, 150,
      187, 192, 193–95, 199, 223, 225–26,
      231, 239–40, 249, 250–51, 285
Malatesta-Magai, C., 31
mania, 35
Manning, J. T., 156–57
Manoach, D. S., 125
Marchbanks, R. M., 113
Marder, E. E., 106
Markowitsch, H. J., 219
Marks, G. A., 148

Martin, J. H., 51
maturation states, 102–3
Meares, R., 214, 227, 249
medulla oblongata, 34, 163, 213–14
memory
  amnesia, 219, 258
  of attachment relationship, 65, 79, 280, 285
  autobiographical, 83, 175
  brain sites, 62, 164–65
  and dissociation, 219
  and dopamine, 162–63
  of faces, 15–16, 225–26
  of maternal interactions, 22–23, 24
      negative, 194–95
  and PTSD, 258–59
  of reactions, 107–8
  and self-soothing, 24, 108
  short term, 278
Mender, D. M., 106
mental health, 138–44, 169–77, 184–87
Mesulam, M. M., 161
metabolism
  of brain, 90–91, 98–103
  in limbic system, 290
  and murderers, 211
  and trauma, 203–4, 205, 253–54
  see also energy
Michel, G. F., 90
Miller, L., 228
mirroring
  and dyadic relationship, 7–8, 38–42
  and limbic system, 34
  and state transitions, 7–8, 96
  of traumatic events, 185
mitochondria
  and apoptosis, 289
  and brain metabolism, 91, 101
  gene expression, 113–14
  and neurons, 99–103
  and psychopathology, 113, 117
  and trauma, 205
Moleman, N., 196
Mollon, P., 287
monoamine oxidase, 99
Morgan, C. A. , III, 234–35
mothers, 275, 286
  see also caregiver; caregiver–infant dyad
motivation
  brain sites, 162, 165, 280
  driving force, 61, 85, 169–70
  and limbic system, 105
  storage sites, 107–8
mouth, 156
murderers, 211
music, 60

Nauta, W. J. H., 49
negative affect
  and corticosteroids, 116

negative affect (*continued*)
  brain sites, 28, 163, 280–81
  calming, 163
  in caregiver, 142
  regulation of, 78, 165
  termination of, 124, 224
  in toddlers, 17–20, 24
  valence tagging, 61
neglect
  and affect, 268, 297, 300–301
  and cortisol, 254
  and facial expressions, 119
  neurophysiology, 254
  and parcellation, 204–5
  paternal, 287
  and personality disorders, 211, 299–
      300
  and socioemotional learning, 186
neonates
  and apoptosis, 254
  brain growth, 112–13, 183
  and dissociation, 217, 218
  early evaluation, 304–5
  energy demands, 101
  and pain, 218, 264
  preattachment phase, 157
  sensory modalities, 156
  stress in, 115
  and trauma, 183, 254
neo-toddlers, 11–13, 44–46, 250
neurons
  and adenosine triphosphate, 99–100
  circuits, 102
  energy demands, 101
  see also apoptosis; dendrites; parcellation;
      synapses
neurotransmitters
  and gaze, 81
  and psychopathology, 123
  and trauma, 191
  see also specific neurotransmitters
Nijenhuis, E. R. S., 192, 259, 260
N-methyl-D-aspartate (NMDA) glutamate
  and apoptosis, 290
  and brain development, 102–3
  and maternal care, 148
  and stress, 114, 117
  and trauma, 190–91
nonlinearity
  description, 89–91, 94–95
  and dopamine, 106–7
  and dyadic relationship, 96
  and right brain, 108–11
noradrenaline
  and aggression, 290
  caregiver effect, 41–42
  and early social experience, 33–34
  and frontal areas, 163–64
  and gaze, 81
  and infant distress, 115, 247, 282

from medulla, 21
  rate-limiting enzyme, 113
  role of, 21
  and trauma, 191, 205
  and Type D, 230
nucleic acid, 112–13
nucleus accumbens, 162
nucleus ambiguus, 214–15, 249, 301–2
nutrition, 183

objects, feelings about, 45–46
occipitoparietal association cortex, 52
Ohman, A., 51
olfaction, 7, 60, 155–56
opiates
  and caregiver-infant dyad, 148
  and early social experience, 33–34
  and mother's face, 81
  and trauma, 189, 191
orbitofrontal cortex
  and adaptivity, 60
  and affect, 25, 272
  and aggression, 278–81, 291–95
  and amygdala functions, 165
  anatomical properties, 60–61
  and biases, 25, 63
  and brain stem, 50(fig.)
  and chaos theory, 107
  chronology, 14–16, 20–25, 169
  and danger, 297
  defined, 14
  and dissociation, 218–21
  and evaluative system, 46–54
  and hypothalamus, 212
  impairment of, 35
  and learning, 69, 170, 208
  and limbic system, 105, 279
  and maltreatment, 194
  maturation, 14, 105, 161–66
  and mental health, 169–77
  and pain, 218–19
  and perinatal complications, 68
  and physical abuse, 298
  and psychopathology, 32–35
  and psychsomatic disease, 34–35
  and PTSD, 207–12, 255, 256
  right side
    and arousal, 111, 162, 224
    and earned security, 69
    functions, 50, 61, 84, 110, 111
    and relational trauma, 222–29
    see also right brain
  and self, 280
  and social bonding, 202
  in toddlers, 20–25, 199
  and trauma, 111, 199–207
    relational, 208–9
  vagal stimulation, 109
  ventromedial (*see* ventromedial cortex)
ornithine decarboxylase, 112–13

Ornstein, R., 74
Osofsky, J. D., 231
oxidative damage, 103, 191, 205–6
oxygen, and gene expression, 114
oxytocin, 81, 157–58

pain
    brain sites, 159–60
    in neonates, 218, 264
    and PTSD, 264
    tolerance of, 24
Pandya, D. N., 172–73
panic states, 119
Panksepp, J., 148, 172
Papousek, H., 274
paralimbic circuit, 152–53
parasympathetic nervous system (PNS)
    and arousal, 21
    and attachment transactions, 81–82
    bias toward, 25, 28
    coping mechanisms, 18, 109–10
    and dissociation, 118–19, 213–15
    and trauma, 189, 198
    vagal systems, 118–19, 249
parcellation
    and adolescence, 173, 230, 297–98
    and dissociation, 213
    in early years, 103–4, 115–21, 124–25,
        132
    and hyperarousal, 34, 255–56
    and personality disorders, 299
    and PTSD, 208
    and rage, 211, 291–93
    and trauma, 204–7, 208, 228, 255–59
    and Type D, 230
parenting, 44, 195–96, 305
paresthesia, 228
parietotemporal association cortex, 52
Paris, J., 211
peer teasing, 297
peptides, 106
periaqueductal gray, 218, 294
perinatal complications, 68, 202–3
Perry, B. D., 118–19, 188, 198, 199, 213, 215,
        247, 249
personality
    of caregiver, 27
    emotion biases, 25, 28, 52
    and PTSD, 261–62
    sympathetic bias, 29
    and systems theory, 120
personality disorders
    antisocial, 267, 268, 273, 302
    BPD, 35, 211, 267, 298–303
Petrovich, S. B., 64
phobic states, 35
physical contact, 27, 60
pituitary gland, 15
    see also hypothalamo-pituitary-adrenocortical
        (HPA) axis

play
    and attachment, 78
    and brain development, 104, 148, 158
    and learning, 13
    symbolic, 227
pleasure, 8–9, 27
Polan, H. J., 150
Porges, S. W., 21, 109, 136, 215, 249, 284
positive affect
    and attachment, 78, 143–44
    in infancy, 8–11
    regulation of, 78, 143, 165, 280–81
    and right posterior brain, 110–11
    in toddlers, 13, 17, 19–20
    tolerance levels, 34
    valence tagging, 61
Post, R., 205, 255
post traumatic stress disorders (PTSD)
    acute *versus* chronic, 263–64
    after infancy, 259–62
    and decompensation, 262–63
    and identity, 261
    in infancy, 191–92, 202, 207, 237, 251–
        55
    and limbic system, 259, 262–65
    and memory, 258–59
    and pain, 264
    and parcellation, 208
    pathogenesis, 240–41
    and personality disorders, 299
    predictors, 219, 234–36
    predisposing factors, 119, 187, 207–12
    and right brain, 123, 224–25, 239–43, 256,
        261–65
    and seizures, 291
pre-adolescents, 261, 296
preattentive stimulus analysis, 51–52
predators, 211–12
predictability, 28–29, 78, 160
pregnancy, 68
preschoolers, 296
Pribram, K. H., 38, 53
Pryce, C. R., 195
psychopathology
    and attachment, 30, 66, 85, 207
    of dissociation, 216–22
    functional deficits, 30–32
    genetic defect, 113
    intergenerational, 254
    and orbital prefrontal cortex, 32–35
    predisposing factors, 112–15, 121–26
    vulnerability causes, 115–21, 237–38
    see also personality disorders; posttraumatic
        stress disorders
psychosomatic disease, 34–35
psychotherapy
    for attachment disorders, 231–32, 304
    and attachment patterns, 69
    and critical periods, 232–33, 265, 304
    and relational trauma, 305

PTSD, *see* post traumatic stress disorders
Purves, D., 101, 102
Putnam, F. W., 214

rage, 211–12, 267–68, 291–95
Raine, A., 272, 273, 296, 301
Rapoport, S., 241
reality, perception of, 65
regulation
  orbitofrontal, 161–66
  and PTSD, 240–41
  and right brain, 166–69
  and self-esteem, 31
  see also affect regulation; self-regulation
regulation theory, xiv–xv, 129
Reid, S., 226–27
Reite, M., 12–13, 57
rejection, 31
relational trauma
  and aggression, 267–68, 284
  and brain development, 289–90
  chronic, 269
  defined, 181–82
  diagnosis, 229–30
  enduring effects, 264, 271–72
  and infants, 184–87
  interventions, 305
  in later childhood, 261
  and periaqueductal gray, 294
  physical effects, 199, 205–7, 218–20,
    246–47
  and PTSD, 207–12
  and resilience, 268–69
  and right brain, 222–29, 237–38, 252–59,
    270–73
  timing of, 199
representational capacity, 226–27
resonance, 76, 141, 146
resource allocation, xvi–xvii
responsivity, contingent, 39, 75–76, 96, 140
Rett syndrome, 113
reunion behavior
  and attachment quality, 12–13
  of insecure-avoidant toddler, 27
  and insecure-resistant child, 29
  of intrusive caregiver, 29
  and psychopathology, 30–32
  and stress, 17
ribonucleic acid (RNA), 112–13
right brain, 48(fig.), 201(fig.)
  and abuse, 186
  and aggression, 224, 272–73, 279–80
  and arousal, 111, 162, 224
  and attachment, 44, 61–62, 74, 108, 168,
    243–46
  and autonomic nervous system, 82–83, 168,
    243–46
  and autonomic response, 51
  of caregiver, 122, 276

and coping, 74, 83, 172, 235–36, 280
and culture, 83–84
and dissociation, 239–40
and dyadic relationship, 9, 43–44, 80–81,
  122, 144–50, 276
and empathy, 35
and faces, 15, 61, 79, 108–10, 147
fetal, 304
functions, 15, 23–24
growth phases, 69, 89–90, 126, 172–73, 229
imaging studies, 80, 125–26, 166–67,
  231–32
and intelligence, 176–77
and language, 171
and learning, 170
limbic structures, 152(fig.), 154(fig.),
  200(fig.)
and mental health, 169–77
and negative affect, 224, 280–81
as nonlinear system, 108–11
occipitoparietal association cortex, 52
and pain response, 264
parcellation, 255–59
parietotemporal association cortex, 52
and psychiatric disorders, 35, 123, 124
  PTSD, 123, 224–25, 239–43, 256,
    261–65
and regulation, 82–86, 166–69, 272
and self-esteem, 125, 224
and stress, 172–73, 236–39
structural pathology, 121–26
and trauma, 222–29, 252–59, 270–73
ventral *versus* dorsal, 168
and violence, 280–81, 303–4
see also limbic system
right cortical-limbic circuits, 154(fig.)
right hemisphere syndrome, 124–25, 227–28
right insula, 159–60
Rinaman, L., 136–37
Rogeness, G. A., 115
Rolls, E. T., 208
rostral limbic system
  and autonomic nervous sytem, 243
  components, 61, 105–6, 152
  decompensation of, 263
  and Hughlings Jackson model, 155
  and rage, 291–95
  and trauma, 255–56
Rotenberg, V. S., 229
Ruch, T. C., 213
Rutter, M., 32, 62, 120
Ryan, R. M., 62, 80, 169

sadness, 60, 163
safety, sense of, xvii, 13, 78
Salovey, P., 176
SAM axis, *see* sympathetic-adrenomedullary
  axis
Sander, L., 131–32, 141, 142, 169

Sapolsky, 203
Scaer, R. C., 260
Scherer, K. R., 147, 171–72
schizophrenia, 113, 118, 123, 124
Schoenbaum, G., 293
Schwalbe, M. L., 94–95, 96
security
    and adolescents, 174
    causes, xvii
    earned, 69
    and expectations, 83, 245
    and infancy, 6
    lack of, 115–21
    neurobiology, 241–43, 276–78
    origins of, 26, 169
    and toddlers, 19–20
seizures, 290–91
self
    and attachment, 287–88
    brain site, 280
    emergence of, 24, 169, 170–71
    and socialization, 170
self-awareness, 261
self-destructive behavior, 219
self-esteem, 31, 125, 224
self image, 23, 261
self-organization, 90–97, 95
self-organization theory, 80
self-regulation
    in adolescence, 173–74
    autoregulation *versus* interactive regulation,
        143–50
    brain site, 14–16, 60–64, 83–84, 169–70,
        278–79
    and human interaction, 5–6, 18, 84–85
    and memory, 24
    in toddlers, 84
self-related information, 243–44
self-soothing, 24, 108, 210
Semrud-Clikeman, M., 108
sensory modalities, 7–9, 60, 155–56
sensory stimuli, 81, 100
    tactile, 60, 156–57, 304
separation anxiety, 158–60
separation behaviors, 104, 158
separation stress, 29, 65
serotonin, 15, 33–34, 290
shame
    brain activity, 18
    and early attachment, 31
    and intrusive caregiver, 29
    and rage, 297
    and socialization, 17–20, 116–17
Shinbrot, T., 94
Shoffner, J. Slat M., 114
Silverman, R. C., 195
Singer, W., 102
skin, 156
Slade, A., 227

sleep, 148
social bonding, 202
social deficits, 33, 113
social interactions, 161–62
socialization experiences, 17–20
    and intrusive caregiver, 29
    stressful, 33–34, 116–17
social referencing, 44–46
social success, 24
somatic markers, 49–50
Spangler, G., 192
Spear, L. P., 173
spontaneous gut feelings, 164–65
Sroufe, L. A., 24, 199, 260
stalkers, 211–12
startle mechanism, 256–57, 282
state changes, 89–90
state sharing, 96
Stern, D. N., 76, 96, 140, 141–42, 143, 159,
        161, 170–71, 242, 274–75
stranger anxiety, 159
stress
    and adaptive ability, 22, 30–32
    and amygdala, 256–57
    and asynchrony, 143
    and brain growth, 21
    brain sites, 165–66
    and caregiver–infant dyad, 31
    and catecholamines, 114–15, 117, 118–19,
        247–48
    chronic, 34
    deprivational, 28
    and genes, 114
    and interpersonal contact, 31
    of life cycle events, 172–75
    in neonates, 115
    and oxidative damage, 103, 191, 205–6
    perinatal, 291
    and physical contact, 27
    physical effects, 205–6
    prenatal, 119, 123–24, 181–82, 190, 291
    prolonged, 110, 186
    proteins, 116–17
    recovery from, 19, 65
    and right brain, 236–39
    and sensory stimuli, 81
    of separation, 29, 65
    threshold, 183
    for toddler, 17–19, 21, 186
    see also coping; separation stress
Stuss, D. T., 254
Sullivan, R. M., 110
symbiosis, 149–50, 158
symbolic representations, 21
sympathetic-adrenomedullary (SAM) axis, 135
sympathetic nervous system (SNS)
    activation, 244
    and arousal, 18, 267
    bias toward, 29

sympathetic nervous system (SNS) (*continued*)
 coping mechanisms, 109–10
 dominance, 25
 hyperexcitation, 197
 and trauma, 188
synapses
 and adenosine triphosphate, 99–100
 and aggression, 288
 and dissociation, 253
 excess, 14
 and parenting, 44
 and stress, 117
 and Type D, 230
 see also parcellation
synchrony
 with caregiver, 75, 138–46, 158, 241–42,
 273–75
 with peers, 173
systems theory
 and attachment, 95–97
 basic principles, 89–91, 100, 122–23
 functional properties, 92–95
 and personality, 120

tactile stimulation, 156–57, 304
taste, 7, 60, 156
Taylor, G., 156
Taylor, G. J., 241
teasing, 297
Teicher, M. H., 199–200, 298
temperament
 brain sites, 25
 fearful, 213–14
 parasympathetic bias, 28
 sympathetic bias, 29
Terr, L. C., 185, 238
Thatcher, R. W., 173
Thelen, E., 94, 97
Thomas, A., 31
threat, 24
thyroid, 247–48
tickling, 158
Toates, F., 151
toddlers
 affect regulation in, 24
 aggressive, 296
 and arousal, 12, 18–20
 and corticosteroids, 116–17, 118–19
 and emotion biases, 52
 and excitation-inhibition balance, 25
 and fathers, 275–76
 insecure-avoidant, 27–28
 insecure-resistant, 29, 119–20
 limbic system, 52–53
 maltreated, 192–99, 228, 296
 neo-toddlers, 11–13, 44–46, 250
 orbitofrontal cortex, 20–25, 199
 and positive affect, 13, 17, 19–20

psychiatrically disturbed, 187
 self-regulation in, 84
 socialization, 17–20, 33–34, 116–17
 and stress, 17–19, 21
Tomkins, S., 19
tonic immobility, 208–9
touch, 60, 156–57, 304
transitions, between states, 23
trauma
 and affect development, 262
 and brain development, 180–84, 252–59
 in critical periods, 119, 199–207
 and limbic system, 189–91, 198, 199–202,
 206–7
 long term effect, 217
 in neonates, 183, 254
 neurobiology, 188–92, 246–49
 ongoing, 180, 183
 and parcellation, 204–7, 208, 228, 255–59
 physical, 202–3
 prenatal, 181, 182
 timing of, 260
 see also relational trauma
Trevarthen, C., 9, 42, 43, 78–79, 97, 139, 141,
 144, 146, 150, 158, 160, 182, 183, 271
Tronick, E. Z., 28, 30, 80, 142, 159, 188–89,
 247, 248, 283
Tucker, D. M., 23, 52, 83–84, 105, 170
Tustin, F., 221
Type D
 and adolescence, 202–3, 297–98
 and aggression, 284–91
 and cortisol, 254
 definition, 180
 diagnosis, 229–30
 freeze response, 210, 213
 interventions, 304
 neurobiology, 230, 281–84
 neuropsychology, 192–99, 249–52
 and parcellation, 230
 parental behavior, 195, 251, 285
 and PTSD, 239–40, 260
 and right brain, 187, 223–28
 and violence, 187, 224, 270
tyrosine hydroxylase, 113

uncertainty, 165–66
unpredictability
 in caregiving, 28–29, 78
 and orbitofrontal areas, 165–66, 245–
 46

vagal stimulation, 109
vagal tone
 and arousal states, 189, 284
 defined, 167
 maturation, 158, 167–68
 and personality disorders, 301

vagus nerve, 200(fig.)
  and arousal, 34
  and dissociation, 214–15
  and orbitofrontal cortex, 164, 208–9
  and parasympathetic system, 118–19, 211,
    249
  and PTSD, 263–64
  and relational trauma, 253–54
  ventral and dorsal systems, 249
Valent, P., 257
van der Kolk, B. A., 187, 224–25, 239, 257,
  261
vasopressin, 157, 248, 283
ventral striatum, 162
ventral tegmental limbic circuit, 34, 105, 162,
  205
ventromedial cortex
  and fear, 294
  role of, 165, 202, 278–79
  and sociopathy, 298
  trauma effect
    physical, 202
    relational, 209
Verny, T., 303
videotape, 67
violence
  and attachment theory, 270
  brain sites, 224, 269, 272, 280–81, 303–4
  definition, 267
  and early childhood, 269
  imaging studies, 211–12, 224
  predisposing factors, 273
  and psychopaths, 301

  risk markers, 296–97
  and Type D, 187, 224, 270
  types of, 299
vision
  and attachment, 42
  and gene-environment mechanisms, 112
  in infants, 7–9, 139
  and toddlers, 12, 44–46
vocalizations, 104, 158
voice, 43–44, 145, 300
Von Bertalanffy, L., 107
Vygotsky, L. S., 46

Wang, S., 262–63, 264
Weinfeld, N. S., 172
Weinstock, M., 135
Weintraub, S., 227
Werner, H., 151
Westen, D., 61, 169
Winnicott, D., 76, 145
Winnicott, D. W., 11, 18, 19, 80–81, 197,
  221
withdrawal, 28
  see also dissociation
Wittling, W., 109
Wong-Riley, M. T. T., 102

Yamada, H., 139, 145
Yehuda, R., 135–36, 253
Yeo, R. A., 204

Zajonc, R. B., 52
Zanarini, M. C., 211, 299